HUMANITARIAN ACTION

The laws governing humanitarian action stand at the intersection of several fields of international law, regional agreements, soft law and domestic law. Through in-depth case studies and analyses, expert scholars and practitioners come together to offer interdisciplinary approaches, which include contributions from legal policy, international relations and philosophical perspectives. Providing invaluable overviews and insights, this collection of essays sheds light on the subject and makes sense of the various elements involved, to elucidate the foundations of law and policy of humanitarian action.

ANDREJ ZWITTER is NGIZ Professor of International Relations at the University of Groningen and is also a co-chair of Research in Ethics and Globalization, a research section within the inter-faculty Institute of Globalisation Studies Groningen.

CHRISTOPHER K. LAMONT is an Assistant Professor of International Relations at the University of Groningen and a co-chair of Research in Ethics and Globalisation.

HANS-JOACHIM HEINTZE is Professor of International Law at the Institute of International Law of Peace and Armed Conflict at the University of Bochum.

JOOST HERMAN is Professor of Globalisation Studies and Humanitarian Action and Director of the Institute for Globalisation Studies Groningen, University of Groningen.

HUMANITARIAN ACTION: GLOBAL, REGIONAL AND DOMESTIC LEGAL RESPONSES

Edited by

ANDREJ ZWITTER, CHRISTOPHER K. LAMONT, HANS-JOACHIM HEINTZE, JOOST HERMAN

CAMBRIDGE
UNIVERSITY PRESS

CAMBRIDGE
UNIVERSITY PRESS

University Printing House, Cambridge CB2 8BS, United Kingdom

Cambridge University Press is part of the University of Cambridge.

It furthers the University's mission by disseminating knowledge in the pursuit of education, learning and research at the highest international levels of excellence.

www.cambridge.org
Information on this title: www.cambridge.org/9781107053533

First published 2015

by Clays, St Ives plc

A catalogue record for this publication is available from the British Library

Library of Congress Cataloguing in Publication data
Humanitarian action : global, regional and domestic legal responses / edited by Andrej Zwitter, Christopher K. Lamont, Hans-Joachim Heintze, Joost Herman
pages cm
ISBN 978-1-107-05353-3 (Hardback)
1. Humanitarian intervention. 2. Humanitarian law. 3. Humanitarian assistance.
I. Lamont, Christopher K., editor of compilation. II. Zwitter, Andrej, editor of compilation.
III. Heintze, Hans-Joachim, 1949– editor of compilation. IV. Herman, Joost, 1963– editor of compilation.
KZ6369.H855 2014
341.5′84–dc23 2014008068

ISBN 978-1-107-05353-3 Hardback

Additional resources for this publication at www.cambridge.org/9781107053533

CONTENTS

FOREWORD BY PROFESSOR DR DR H.C. MULT. KNUT IPSEN

Former President of the German Red Cross and former member of the Permanent Court of Arbitration

The decades after the termination of the east-west Confrontation have not brought the expected epoch of peace. The world has witnessed, on the contrary, an increasing number of serious armed conflicts. Consequently proposals have been put forward again within the international community to ensure that in such disputes a minimal level of humanity is maintained. There are voices in legal literature, however, arguing that it is obvious to an observer of the world scene since 1949 that the rules of international law which seek to protect the victims from the effects of armed conflicts have more frequently proved their weakness than the compliance of the parties to the conflicts. Acts of brutality and violations of fundamental rules of humanity clearly call for political reactions by the international community and in particular for a reaffirmation of and, in some fields, a progressive development of international humanitarian law.

Although a comprehensive approach is required to avoid the recourse to armed force, the suppression of its intolerable effects should not be neglected. Humanitarian action – ranging from short-term relief to rehabilitation and reconstruction activities and to development cooperation, including measures of disaster preparedness, prevention and risk reduction – constitutes an important field of international activity to reduce human suffering in disasters, man-made as well as natural. The international community must be encouraged again and again to provide assistance to share the burden of those in distress. Solidarity as a mutual commitment and a fundamental value, which is indispensable for every human entity, must be acknowledged and realised. International law as a law of cooperation is not conceivable without the principle of mutual assistance in distress. However, the concrete legal realisation of this principle leads to many complicated problems, which are still under discussion. International law of humanitarian assistance consists nowadays of regulations to be found in different fields. This book is therefore, an urgently needed publication to discuss the different aspects of humanitarian action, and will doubtless be of considerable practical utility to all those involved in the application of the law of humanitarian assistance.

LIST OF CASES

International Court of Justice (ICJ)

Belgium v. *Spain*. 'Barcelona Traction, Light and Power Company Limited.' *ICJ Reports* 1970.

Democratic Republic of the Congo v. *Uganda*. 'Armed Activities on the Territory of the Congo'. *ICJ. Reports* 2005.

Libya v. *United Kingdom*. Lockerbie case (Request for the Indication of Provisional Measures). *ICJ Reports* 1992.

Nicaragua v. *United States of America*. Military and Paramilitary Activities in and against Nicaragua Merits. Judgment. *ICJ Reports* 1986.

European Court of Human Rights (ECtHR)

Al-Skeini and Others v. *United Kingdom*. Application No. 55721/07. 7 July 2011.

Bankovic et al. v. *Belgium*. Application no. 52207/99. 12 December 2001.

Budayeva and others v. *Turkey*. No. 15339/02. 20 March 2008.

Burdov v. *Russia*. No. 59498/00. Reports 2002–III.

Hadzhiyska v. *Bulgaria*. No 20701/09. 15 May 2012. *Inadmissible*.

Ilascu and others v. *Moldova and Russia*. Case No. 48787/99. 8 July 2004.

Isayeva v. *Russia*. (Isayeva II) Case No. 57950/00. 24 February 2005.

Kolyadenko and others v. *Russia*. No. 17423/05. 28 February 2012.

Loisidou v. *Turkey*. Preliminary Objections, Judgment. 23 March 1995.

Öcalan v. *Turkey*. No. 46221/99. Grand Chamber Judgment. 12 May 2005.

Öneryildiz v. *Turkey*. No. 48939/99. Reports 2004–XII [GC].

Tyrer v. *United Kingdom*. No 5856/72. 1978, Series A no 26.

Yusupova and Bazayeva v. *Russia*. Nos. 57947/00, 57948/00 and 57949/00. 24 February 2005.

Inter-American Court of Human Rights (IACHR)

Bamaca Velásquez v *Guatamala*. Judgment, 25 November 2000.

Case of the Ituango Massacres v. *Colombia*. 1 July 2006. www.corteidh.or.cr/docs/casos/articulos/seriec_148_ing.pdf.

Coard et al. v. *USA*. Report No. 109/99. Case No. 10.951. 29 September 1999.

Juan Carlos Abella v. *Argentina.* ('Tablada Case'.) Case No. 11.137 *IACHR.* 18 November 1997.

Las Palmeras v. *Colombia* (Preliminary Objections) Case No. 67, Series C. Judgment, 4 February 2000,

Morales v. *Guatemala.* Street Children Case. Judgment of 19 November 1999. (Ser. C) No. 63, 139. www.corteidh.or.cr/seriecpdf_ing/seriec_63_ing.pdf.

International Criminal Tribunal for the former Yugoslavia (ICTY)

Delalić et al. (Čelebići – Case.) (Appeals Chamber), No. IT-96-21-A. 20 February 2001.

Furundžija. (Trial Judgment.) No. IT-95-17/1-T. 10 December 1998.

Kordić and Čerkez. (Trial Chamber.) IT-95-14/2. 26 February 2001.

Tadić. (Jurisdiction Appeal.) IT-94-1-AR72. 2 October 1995.

Tadić (Appeal Judgement.) IT-94-1-A. 15 July 1999.

International Criminal Tribunal for Rwanda (ICTR)

Akayesu. (ICTR Trial Chamber.) 2 September 1998. ICTR-96-4-T.

Bagilishema. (ICTR Trial Chamber.) 7 June 2001. ICTR-95-1A-T.

Kayishema and Ruzindana. (ICTR Trial Chamber.) 21 May 1999. ICTR-95-1-T.

Musema. (ICTR Trial Chamber.) 27 January 2000. ICTR-96-13-T.

Rutaganda. (ICTR Trial Chamber.) 6 December 1999. ICTR-96-3-T.

Semanza. (ICTR Trial Chamber.) 15 May 2003. ICTR-97-20-T.

Permanent Court of International Justice (PCIJ)

The Case Relative to the Exchange of Greek and Turkish Populations under the Lausanne Convention VI, (1925) Series B, No. 10, 20.

Other

African Commission on Human and Peoples' Rights, *Social and Economic Rights Action Center (SERAC) and Center for Economic and Social Rights (CESR)* v. *the Federal Republic of Nigeria,* Communication 155/96. Merits. (2001).

African Commission on Human and Peoples' Rights. *Socio-Economic Rights and Accountability Project (SERAP)* v. *Federal Republic of Nigeria.* Communication 338/07 (2010).

ILLUSTRATIONS

ABBREVIATIONS

AADMER	ASEAN Agreement on Disaster Management and Emergency Response
ACF	Action Contre la Faim
ACFDA	*Inter-American Convention to Facilitate Disaster Assistance*
ACHR	*American Convention on Human Rights*
AHA Centre	ASEAN Coordinating Centre for Humanitarian Assistance on Disaster Management
AHRD	ASEAN Human Rights Declaration
AICHR	ASEAN Intergovernmental Commission on Human Rights
ALNAP	Active Learning Network for Accountability and Performance in Humanitarian Action
AMIS	AU Mission in the Sudan
ARSIWA	Articles on the Responsibility of States for Internationally Wrongful Acts (formerly Draft Articles)
ASEAN	Association of East Asian Nations
ASIL	American Society of International Law
AU	African Union
AUC	Autodefensas Unidas de Colombia (United Self-Defense Forces of Colombia)
BNPB	*Badan Nasional Penanggulangan Bencana* (National Board of Disaster Response)
BPBD	*Badan Penanggulangan Bencana Daerah* (Local Board of Disaster Response)
BRICS	Brazil, Russia, India, China and South Africa
BSEC	Black Sea Economic Cooperation
CAAM	Comprehensive Action against Antipersonnel Mines
CARICOM	Caribbean Community
Case W. Res. J Int'l L	*Case Western Reserve Journal of International Law*
CBDRM	community-based disaster response management
CCAI	Center for Integral Action Coordination
CCoFDHA	Coordinating Committee on Forced Displacement and Humanitarian Action

CDEMA	Caribbean Disaster Emergency Management Agency
CDERA	Caribbean Disaster Emergency Response Agency
CEDAW	*Convention on the Elimination of all Forms of Discrimination against Women*
CESCR	Committee on Economic, Social and Cultural Rights
CIFTA	*(Inter-American) Convention against Illicit Manufacturing of and Trafficking in Firearms, Ammunition, Explosives and Other Related Materials*
COMESA	Common Market for Eastern and Southern Africa
CRC	*Convention on Rights of the Child*
DRC	Democratic Republic of Congo OR Danish Refugee Council
ECCHA	ECOWAS Code of Conduct for Humanitarian Action
ECHO	European Community Humanitarian Office
ECHR	*European Convention on Human Rights*
ECOSOC	Economic and Social Council
ECOWAS	Economic Community of West African States
ECSR	European Committee on Social Rights
ECtHR	European Court of Human Rights
EJIL	*European Journal of International Law*
ELN	National Liberation Army (Colombia)
ERC	Emergency Relief Coordinator (of OCHA/UN)
ESC	European Social Charter
EUFOR Libya	European Union Force in Libya
EWS	early warning system
FAO	Food and Agriculture Organisation
FARC-EP	*Fuerzas Armadas Revolucionarias de Colombia – Ejército del Pueblo* Revolutionary Armed Forces of Colombia – Peoples' Army
FPA	Framework Partnership Agreement
FSNAU	Food Security and Nutrition Analysis Unit (of the FAO)
GA	General Assembly (UN)
GFDRR	Global Facility for Disaster Risk Reduction
HAP	Humanitarian Accountability Partnership
HPG	Humanitarian Policy Group
HPN	Humanitarian Policy Network
HRC	Human Rights Committee
IAC	international armed conflict
IAP	Inter-American Plan for Disaster Prevention and Response and the Coordination of Humanitarian Assistance
IAPF	Inter-American Peace Force
IASC	Inter-Agency Standing Committee
ICC	International Criminal Court

ICDO	International Civil Defence Organisation
ICCPR	*International Covenant of Civil and Political Rights*
ICESCR	*International Covenant of Economic, Social and Cultural Rights*
ICISS	International Commission on Intervention and State Sovereignty
ICJ	International Court of Justice
ICMH	International Civilian Mission in Haiti
ICNL	International Center for Not-for-profit Law
ICRC	International Committee of the Red Cross
ICSV	International Commission for Support and Verification
ICTR	International Criminal Tribunal for Rwanda
ICTY	International Criminal Tribunal for the former Yugoslavia
IDI	Institut de Droit International/International Law Institute
IDP	Internally Displaced Person
IDRL	International Disaster Relief Laws
IFHV	Institute for International Law of Peace and Armed Conflict (Bochum)
IFRC	International Federation of Red Cross and Red Crescent Societies
ILC	International Law Commission
INTERFET	International Force for East Timor
IOM	International Organisation for Migration
IPU	Inter-Parliamentary Union
IRC	International Rescue Committee
IRIN	Integrated Regional Information Networks
IRRC	*International Review of the Red Cross*
ISDR	International Strategy for Disaster Reduction
IWMI	International Water Management Institute
JICA	Japan International Cooperation Agency
KUHAP	*Kitab Undang-Undang Hukum Acara Pidana* (Indonesian Criminal Procedural Code)
LAS	League of Arab States
MILF	Moro Islamic Liberation Front
MINUSTAH	United Nations Stabilisation Mission in Haiti
MIPONUH	United Nations Civilian Police Mission in Haiti
MPEPIL	*Max Planck Encyclopedia of Public International Law*
MRC	Mekong River Commission
MSF	Médecins Sans Frontières
NATO	North Atlantic Treaty Organisation
NIAC	non-international armed conflict
NPR	National Press Radio

NRC	Norwegian Refugee Council
NTC	National Transitional Council of Libya
OAS	Organisation of American States
OCHA	Office for the Coordination of Humanitarian Affairs
OECD–DAC	Development Assistance Criteria of the Organisation for Economic Co-operation and Development
OHCHR	Office of the High Commissioner for Human Rights
OIC	Organisation of Islamic Cooperation
OLAF	European Anti-Fraud Office
OSAFA	Office for Supervising the Affairs of Foreign Agencies
OSCE	Organisation for Security and Cooperation
PCIJ	Permanent Court of International Justice
PONJA	Post-Nargis Joint Assessment Report (ASEAN)
PSPR UGM	Universitas Gadjah Mada
REC	Regional Economic Communities
RUSI Journal	*Royal United Services Institute Journal*
SADC	Southern African Development Community
SALW	small arms and light weapons
SC	Security Council
SCDRR	Safer Communities for Disaster Risk Reduction
SFDFA	Swiss Federal Department of Foreign Affairs
STRATFOR	Strategic Forecasting, Inc.
TCG	Tripartite Core Group
UCDP	Uppsala Conflict Data Programme
UCLA J. Int'l L. & Foreign Aff	*University of California at Los Angeles Journal of International Law and Foreign Affairs*
UNAMID	African Union/United Nations Hybrid Operation in Darfur
UNCESR	United Nations Committee on Economic, Social and Cultural Rights
UNCLOS	*United Nations Convention on the Law of the Sea*
UDHR	Universal Declaration of Human Rights
UNDP	United Nations Development Programme
UNEP	United Nations Environment Programme
UN ESCAP	United Nations Economic and Social Commission for Asia and the Pacific
UNFPA	United Nations Population Fund
UN-HABITAT	United Nations Human Settlements Programme
UNHCR	United Nations High Commissioner for Refugees
UNICEF	United Nations Children's Fund
UN ISDR	United Nations International Strategy for Disaster Reduction
UNITAF	Unified Task Force
UNMIS	United Nations Mission in Sudan

UNOPS	United Nations Office for Project Services
UNOSOM	United Nations Mission in Somalia
UNSMIL	United Nations Support Mission in Libya
UNTAET	United Nations Transitional Administration in East Timor
VCLT	*Vienna Convention on the Law of Treaties*
WCHS	World Conference of Humanitarian Studies
WFP	World Food Programme
WHO	World Health Organisation

INTERNATIONAL CONVENTIONS, DECLARATIONS, STATUES, AND TREATIES

Title	Short Title	Adoption	Entry into Force	Place	Document Number or Source
Additional Protocol to the ACHR in the Area of Economic, Social and Cultural Rights	Protocol of San Salvador	17/11/1988	16/11/1999	San Salvador, El Salvador	A-52
African Charter on Human and Peoples' Rights	Banjul Charter	27/06/1981	21/10/1986	Nairobi, Kenya	OAU Doc. CAB/LEG/67/3 rev. 5, 21 I.L.M. 58 (1982)
African Charter on the Rights and Welfare of the Child	ACRWC / Children's Charter	11/07/1990	29/11/1999	Addis Ababa, Ethiopia	OAU Doc. CAB/LEG/24.9/49 (1990)
African Union Convention For The Protection And Assistance Of Internally Displaced Persons In Africa	Kampala Convention	22/10/2009	06/12/2012	Kampala, Uganda	http://www.au.int/en/sites/default/files/AFRICAN_UNION_CONVENTION_FOR_THE_PROTECTION_AND_ASSISTANCE_OF_INTERNALLY_DISPLACED_PERSONS_IN_AFRICA_%28KAMPALA_CONVENTION%29.pdf
American Convention on Human Rights	ACHR	22/11/1969	18/07/1978	San Jose, Costa Rica	OAS, Treaty series, No. 36
Arab Charter on Human Rights		24/05/2004	15/03/2008	Tunis, Tunisia	https://www1.umn.edu/humanrts/instree/loas2005.html
Charter of the Association of Southeast Asian Nations	ASEAN Charter	20/11/2007	15/12/2008	Singapore	http://www.asean.org/archive/publications/ASEAN-Charter.pdf
Charter of the United Nations	UN Charter	26/06/1945	24/10/1945	San Francisco, USA	1 UNTS XVI

Title	Short Title	Adoption	Entry into Force	Place	Document Number or Source
Convention (II) with Respect to the Laws and Customs of War on Land	The Hague Convention II	29 July 1899	04/09/1900	The Hague, the Netherlands	http://www.icrc.org/applic/ihl/ihl.nsf/Treaty.xsp?documentId=CD0F6C83F96FB459C12563CD002D66A1&action=openDocument
Convention (IV) respecting the Laws and Customs of War on Land	The Hague Convention IV	18/10/1907	26/01/1910	The Hague, the Netherlands	http://www.icrc.org/ihl/INTRO/195?OpenDocument
Convention against Torture and Other Cruel, Inhuman or Degrading Treatment or Punishment	CAT / Torture Convention	10/12/1984	26/06/1987	New York, USA	UN Treaties Chapter IV No. 24841 (United Nations, Treaty Series, vol. 1465, p. 85)
Convention concerning International Carriage by Rail, as amended by the Vilnius Protocol of 3 June 1999	COTIF	09/05/1980	01/07/2006	Berne, Switzerland	http://www.otif.org/fileadmin/user_upload/otif_verlinkte_files/07_veroeff/01_COTIF_80/cotif-1980-e.PDF
Convention of the Rights of the Child	CRC	20/11/1989	02/09/1990	New York, USA	UN Treaties Chapter IV No. 27531 (United Nations, Treaty Series, vol. 1577, p. 3)
Convention on Assistance in the Case of a Nuclear Accident or Radiological Emergency	Chernobyl Convention	26/09/1986	26/02/1987	Vienna, Austria	INFCIRC/336
Convention on Early Notification of a Nuclear Accident		26/09/1986	27/10/1986	Vienna, Austria	INFCIRC/335

Convention on Facilitation of International Maritime Traffic	FAL	09/04/1965	05/03/1967	London, UK	http://www.admiraltylawguide.com/conven/facilitation1965.html
Convention on International Civil Aviation	Chicago Convention	07/12/1944	04/04/1947	Chicago, USA	Doc 7300
Convention on Temporary Admission	Istanbul Convention	26/06/1990	27/11/1993	Istanbul, Turkey	PG0232E1
Convention on the Elimination of Discrimination Against Women	CEDAW	18/12/1979	03/09/1981	New York, USA	Resolution 34/180 UNGA (18 December 1979), United Nations, Treaty Series, vol. 1249, p. 13
Convention on the Prevention and Punishment of the Crime of Genocide	Genocide Convention	09/12/1984	12/01/1951	Paris, France	UN Treaties Chapter IV No. 1021 (United Nations, Treaty Series, vol. 78, p. 277)
Convention on the Privileges and Immunities of the United Nations		13/02/1946	17/09/1946	New York, USA	UN Treaties Chapter III No. 4 (United Nations, Treaty Series, vol. 1, p. 15, and vol. 90, p. 327)
Convention on the Rights of Persons with Disabilities	CRPD	24/01/2007	03/05/2008	New York, USA	Resolution 106 UNGA (24 January 2007), UNDocs A/RES/61/106)
Convention Relating to the Status of Refugees	Refugee Convention	28/07/1951	22/04/1954	Geneva, Switzerland	UN Treaties Chapter V No. 2545 (United Nations, Treaty Series, vol. 189, p. 137)
Convention to Combat Desertification in those Countries Experiencing Serious Drought and/or Desertification	UNCCD	14/10/1994	26/12/1996	Paris, France	UN Treaties Chapter XXVII No. 33480 (United Nations, Treaty Series, vol. 1954, p. 3)

Title	Short Title	Adoption	Entry into Force	Place	Document Number or Source
Customs Convention on the ATA Carnet for the Temporary Admission of Goods	ATA Convention	06/12/1961	30/07/1963	Brussels, Belgium	http://www.vi.is/files/Text%20of%20the%20ATA%20Convention_325520992.pdf
Customs Convention on the Temporary Importation of Private Road Vehicles	Private Road Vehicles Convention	04/06/1954	15/12/1957	New York, USA	UN Treaties Chapter XI No. 4101 (United Nations, Treaty Series, vol. 282, p. 249)
Draft Additional Protocols to the Geneva Conventions		01/10/1973		Geneva, Switzerland	http://www.loc.gov/rr/frd/Military_Law/pdf/RC-Draft-additional-protocols.pdf
Draft Convention on Expediting the Delivery of Emergency Assistance		18/06/1984		Geneva, Switzerland	Resolution 39/267 UNGA (18 June 1984) UNDocs A/39/267/Add.2 - E/1984/96/Add. 2 pp. 5–18
European Convention on Human Rights	ECHR	04/11/1950	03/09/1953	Rome, Italy	CETS No. 005
European Social Charter	ESC	18/10/1961	26/02/1965	Turin, Italy	CETS No. 035
Food Assistance Convention	FAC	25/04/2012	01/01/2013	London, UK	UN Treaties Chapter XIX No. 32022 (United Nations, Treaty Series, vol. 2073, p. 135)
Framework Convention on Civil Defence Assistance		22/05/2000	23/09/2001	Geneva, Switzerland	United Nations Treaty Series, vol. 2172, p. 213

Geneva Convention (I) for the Amelioration of the Condition of the Wounded and Sick in Armed Forces in the Field	GC I	12/08/1949	21/10/1950	Geneva, Switzerland	Final Record of the Diplomatic Conference of Geneva of 1949, Vol. I, Federal Political Department, Bern, pp. 205–224
Geneva Convention (II) for the Amelioration of the Condition of Wounded, Sick and Shipwrecked Members of Armed Forces at Sea	GC II	12/08/1949	21/10/1950	Geneva, Switzerland	Final Record of the Diplomatic Conference of Geneva of 1949, Vol. I, Federal Political Department, Bern, pp. 225–242
Geneva Convention (III) relative to the Treatment of Prisoners of War	GC III	12/08/1949	21/10/1950	Geneva, Switzerland	Final Record of the Diplomatic Conference of Geneva of 1949, Vol. I, Federal Political Department, Bern, pp. 243–296
Geneva Convention (IV) relative to the Protection and of Civilian Persons in Time of War	GC IV	12/08/1949	21/10/1950	Geneva, Switzerland	The Geneva Conventions of August 12, 1949, International Committee of the Red Cross, Geneva, pp. 153–221
Hyogo Framework of Action 2005-2015: Building the Resilience of Nations and Communities to Disasters	HFA	22/01/2005		Kobe, Hyogo, Japan	World Conference on Disaster Reduction A/CONF.206/6
International Convention on Oil Pollution Preparedness, Response and Co-operation	OPRC	30/11/1990	13/05/1995	London, UK	UN Treaties No. 32194 (United Nations, Treaty Series, vol. 1891, p. 77)

Title	Short Title	Adoption	Entry into Force	Place	Document Number or Source
International Convention on the Elimination of All Forms of Racial Discrimination	CERD	21/12/1965	04/01/1969	New York, USA	UN Treaties Chapter IV No. 9464 (United Nations, Treaty Series, vol. 660, p. 195)
International Convention on the Simplification and Harmonization of Customs procedures	Kyoto Convention	18/05/1973	25/09/1974	Kyoto, Japan	PG0229E1
International Convention on the Suppression and Punishment of the Crime of Apartheid	Apartheid Convention	30/11/1973	18/07/1976	New York, USA	Resolution 3068 (XXVIII) UNGA (30 November 1973) UNDocs A/RES/3068(XXVIII)
International Covenant on Civil and Political Rights	ICCPR	16/12/1966	23/03/1976	New York, USA	UN Treaties Chapter IV No. 14668 (United Nations, Treaty Series, vol. 999, p. 171 and vol. 1057, p. 407)
International Covenant on Economic Social and Cultural Rights	ICESCR	16/12/1966	03/01/1976	New York, USA	UN Treaties Chapter IV No. 14531 (United Nations, Treaty Series, vol. 993, p. 3)
Lausanne Peace Treaty VI. Convention Concerning the Exchange of Greek and Turkish Populations	Lausanne Peace Treaty	30/01/1923	06/08/1924	Lausanne, Switzerland	http://www.mfa.gov.tr/lausanne-peace-treaty-vi_-convention-concerning-the-exchange-of-greek-and-turkish-populations-signed-at-lausanne_.en.mfa

Optional Protocol to CEDAW	CEDAW Optional Protocol	06/10/1999	22/12/2000	New York, USA	Resolution 54/4 UNGA (6 October 1999), United Nations, Treaty Series, vol. 2131, p. 83
Protocol Additional to the Geneva Conventions of 12 August 1949, and relating to the Protection of Victims of International Armed Conflicts (Protocol I)	Additional Protocol I / AP I	08/06/1977	07/12/1978	Geneva, Switzerland	Protocols additional to the Geneva Conventions of 12 August 1949, International Committee of the Red Cross, Geneva, 1977, pp. 3–87
Protocol Additional to the Geneva Conventions of 12 August 1949, and relating to the Protection of Victims of Non-International Armed Conflicts (Protocol II)	Additional Protocol II / AP II	08/06/1977	07/12/1978	Geneva, Switzerland	Protocols additional to the Geneva Conventions of 12 August 1949, International Committee of the Red Cross, Geneva, 1977, pp. 89–101
Protocol Relating to the Status of Refugees	New York Protocol	13/01/1967	04/10/1967	New York, USA	UN Treaties Chapter V No. 8791 (United Nations, Treaty Series, vol. 606, p. 267)
Protocol to the African Charter on Human and Peoples' Rights on the Rights of Women in Africa		11/07/2003	25/11/2005	Maputo, Mozambique	http://www.au.int/en/sites/default/files/Protocol%20on%20the%20Rights%20of%20Women.pdf
Recommendation of the Customs Co-Operation Council to Expedite the Forwarding of Relief Consignments in the Event of Disasters		08/06/1970			T2-423 (http://www.ifrc.org/Docs/idrl/I237EN.pdf)

Title	Short Title	Adoption	Entry into Force	Place	Document Number or Source
Rome Statute of the International Criminal Court	Rome Statute	17/07/1998	01/07/2002	Rome, Italy	U.N. Doc. A/CONF.183/9
Statute of the International Court of Justice	ICJ Statute	26/06/1945	24/10/1945	San Francisco, USA	1 UNTS XVI (Chapter XIV)
Statute of the International Criminal Tribunal for Rwanda	ICTR Statute	08/11/1994		New York, USA	UNDocs S/RES/955 (1994)
Statute of the International Criminal Tribunal for the former Yugoslavia	ICTY Statute	25/05/1993		New York, USA	UNDocs S/RES/827 (1993)
Statute of the Office of the United Nations High Commissioner for Refugees	Statute of the UNHCR	14/12/1950		New York, USA	UNDocs A/RES/428(V)
Statute of the OIC Independent Permanent Human Rights Commission	Statute of the OIC IPHRC	17/02/2010		Jeddah, Saudi Arabia	OIC/IPCHR/2010/STATUTE
Statutes of the International Committee of the Red Cross	Statute of the ICRC	03/10/2013		Geneva, Switzerland	http://www.icrc.org/eng/resources/documents/misc/icrc-statutes-080503.htm

Statutes of the International Red Cross and Red Crescent Movement		08/06/1905		Geneva, Switzerland	http://www.icrc.org/eng/assets/files/other/statutes-en-a5.pdf
Tampere Convention on the Provision of Telecommunication Resources for Disaster Mitigation and Relief Operations	Tampere Convention	18/06/1998	08/01/2005	Tampere, Finland	UN Treaties Chapter XXV No. 40906 (United Nations, Treaty Series, vol. 2296, p. 5)
Treaty of Amsterdam amending the Treaty of the European Union, the Treaties establishing the European Communities and certain related acts	EC Treaty	02/10/1997	01/05/1999	Amsterdam, the Netherlands	1997/C 340/01
Treaty on European Union	Maastricht Treaty / TEU	07/02/1992	01/11/1993	Maastricht, the Netherlands	1992/C 191/01
Treaty on the Functioning of the European Union	Lisbon Treaty / TFEU	13/12/2007	01/12/2009	Lisbon, Portugal	Official Journal C 326 , 26/10/2012 P. 0001 - 0390
United Nations Convention on the Laws of the Sea	UNCLOS	10/12/1982	16/11/1994	Montego Bay, Jamaica	UN Treaties Chapter XXI No. 31363 (United Nations, Treaty Series, vol. 1833, p. 3)
Universal Declaration of Human Rights	UDHR	10/12/1948		Paris, France	Resolution 217 A (III) UNGA (10 December 1948), UNDocs A/RES/217(III) [A-E]
Vienna Convention on the Law of Treaties	VCT	23/05/1969	27/01/1980	Vienna, Austria	UN Treaties Chapter I No. 18232 (United Nations, Treaty Series, vol. 1155, p. 331)

UN GENERAL ASSEMBLY RESOLUTIONS AND DOCUMENTS

A/49/38	Report of the Committee on the Elimination of Discrimination Against Women, Concluding Observations: Ecuador	12 April 1994
A/53/951	Question of East Timor – Report of the Secretary-General	05 May 1999
A/55/305–S/2000/809	Report of the Panel on United Nations Peace Operations (Brahimi Report)	21 August 2000
A/56/10	Report of the International Law Commission	23 April 2001–1 June 2001 and 2 July–10 August 2001
A/63/10	Report of the International Law Commission	5 May–6 June and 7 July–8 August 2008
A/63/677	Secretary-General Report on the Implementation of the Responsibility to Protect	12 January 2009
A/64/10	Report of the International Law Commission	4 May to 5 June and 6 July to 7 August 2009
A/65/10	Report of the International Law Commission	3 May to 4 June and 5 July to 6 August 2010
A/66/551–S/2011/701	Letter from the Permanent Representative of Brazil to the United Nations Addressed to the Secretary-General	09 November 2011
A/66/594–S/2011/758	Letter from the Permanent Representative of the Russian Federation to the United Nations Addressed to the Secretary-General	07 December 2011
A/66/81–E/2011/117	Strengthening of the Coordination of Emergency Humanitarian Assistance of the United Nations	16 May 2011

A/67/L.39	Strengthening of the Coordination of Humanitarian and Disaster Relief Assistance of the United Nations, Including Special Economic Assistance: Strengthening of the Coordination of Emergency Humanitarian Assistance of the United Nations	07 December 2012
A/8052	UN Secretary-General Report 'Respect for Human Rights in Armed Conflict'	18 September 1970
A/CN.4/590	Protection of Persons in the Event of Disasters: Memorandum by the Secretariat	11 December 2007
A/CN.4/598	Preliminary Report on the Protection of Persons in the Event of Disasters, by Mr Eduardo Valencia-Ospina, Special Rapporteur	05 May 2008
A/CN.4/615	Second Report on the Protection of Persons in the Event of Disasters	07 May 2009
A/CN.4/629	Third report on the Protection of Persons in the Event of Disasters	31 March 2010
A/CN.4/643	Third Report on the Protection of Persons in the Event of Disasters	11 May 2011
A/CN.4/652	Third Report on the Protection of Persons in the Event of Disasters	09 April 2012
A/CN.4/L.758	Protection of Persons in the Event of Disasters. Text and Title of Draft Articles 1, 2, 3, 4 and 5 as Provisionally Adopted by the Drafting Committee	24 July 2009
A/CN.4/L.776	Protection of Persons in the Event of Disasters: Texts and Titles of Draft Articles 6, 7, 8 and 9 Provisionally Adopted by the Drafting Committee on 6, 7 and 8 July 2010	14 July 2010
A/CN.4/L.794	Protection of Persons in the Event of Disasters: Text and Titles of Draft Articles 10 and 11 Provisionally Adopted by the Drafting Committee on 19 July 2011	20 July 2011

A/CN.4/L.812	Protection of Persons in the Event of Disasters: Texts and Titles of Draft Articles 5 bis, 12, 13, 14 and 15, Provisionally Adopted by the Drafting Committee from 5 to 11 July 2012	12 July 2012
A/CONF. 32/ 41, XXIII, 18	Final Act of the International Conference of Human Rights, Teheran	12 May 1968
A/HRC/4/8	Report of the Independent Expert on Human Rights and International Solidarity, Rudi Muhammad Rizki	7 February 2008
A/HRC/4/20/ Add.1	Report of the Special Rapporteur on Extrajudicial, Summary or Arbitrary Executions. Philip Alston – Addendum – Summary of Cases Transmitted to Government and Replies Received	12 March 2007
A/HRC/12/27	Report of the Independent Expert on Human Rights and International Solidarity, Rudi Muhammad Rizki	22 July 2009
A/HRC/15/32	Report of the Independent Expert on Human Rights and International Solidarity, Rudi Muhammad Rizki	27 September 2010
A/HRC/15/L.14	Human Rights and Access to Safe Drinking Water and Sanitation	24 September 2010
A/HRC/17/44	Report of the International Commission of Inquiry to Investigate All Alleged Violations of International Human Rights Law in the Libyan Arab Jamahiriya	12 January 2014
A/HRC/19/68	Report of the International Commission of Inquiry on Libya	02 March 2012
A/RES/2029 XX	Consolidation of the Special Fund and the Expanded Programme of Technical Assistance in a United Nations Development Programme	22 November 1965
A/RES/2444 XXIII	Respect for Human Rights in Armed Conflicts	09 December 1968
A/RES/2597 XXIV	Respect for Human Rights in Armed Conflicts	09 December 1970

A/RES/2673 XXV	Protection of Journalists Engaged in Dangerous Missions in Areas of Armed Conflicts	09 December 1970
A/RES/2675 XXV	Basic Principles for the Protection of Civilian Populations in Armed Conflicts	09 December 1970
A/RES/2676 XXV	Respect for Human Rights in Armed Conflicts	09 December 1970
A/RES/2677 XXV	Respect for Human Rights in Armed Conflicts	09 December 1970
A/RES/2717 XXV	Assistance in Cases of Natural Disaster	15 December 1970
A/RES/2852 XXVI	Respect for Human Rights in Armed Conflicts	20 December 1971
A/RES/2853 XXVI	Respect for Human Rights in Armed Conflicts	20 December 1971
A/RES/3032 XXVII	Respect for Human Rights in Armed Conflicts	18 December 1972
A/RES/3102 XXVIII	Respect for Human Rights in Armed Conflicts	12 December 1973
A/RES/3500 XXX	Respect for Human Rights in Armed Conflicts	15 December 1975
A/RES/31/19	Respect for Human Rights in Armed Conflicts	24 November 1976
A/RES/32/44	Respect for Human Rights in Armed Conflicts	08 December 1977
A/RES/34/51	State of Signatures and Ratifications of the Protocols Additional to the Geneva Conventions of 1949 Concerning the Respect for Human Rights in Armed Conflicts	23 November 1979
A/RES/37/116	State of Signatures and Ratifications of the Protocols Additional to the Geneva Conventions of 1949 and Relating to the Protection of Victims of International Armed Conflicts (Protocol I) and the Protection of Victims of Non-international Armed Conflicts (Protocol II)	16 December 1982

A/RES/39/77	Status of the Protocols Additional to the Geneva Conventions of 1949 and Relating to the Protection of Victims of Armed Conflicts	13 December 1984
A/RES/41/120	Setting International Standards in the Field of Human Rights	04 December 1986
A/RES/41/72	Status of the Protocols Additional to the Geneva Conventions of 1949 and Relating to the Protection of Victims of Armed Conflicts	03 December 1986
A/RES/43/131	Humanitarian Assistance to Victims of Natural Disasters and Similar Emergency Situations	08 December 1988
A/RES/43/161	Status of the Protocols Additional to the Geneva Conventions of 1949 and Relating to the Protection of Victims of Armed Conflicts	09 December 1988
A/RES/45/100	Humanitarian Assistance to Victims of Natural Disasters and Similar Emergency Situations	17 December 1990
A/RES/45/38	Status of the Protocols Additional to the Geneva Conventions of 1949 and Relating to the Protection of Victims of Armed Conflicts	28 November 1990
A/RES/46/182	Strengthening of the Coordination of Emergency Humanitarian Assistance of the United Nations	19 December 1991
A/RES/47/30	Status of the Protocols Additional to the Geneva Conventions of 1949 and Relating to the Protection of Victims of Armed Conflicts	25 November 1992
A/RES/49/48	Status of the Protocols Additional to the Geneva Conventions of 1949 and Relating to the Protection of Victims of Armed Conflicts	17 February 1995
A/RES/51/155	Status of the Protocols Additional to the Geneva Conventions of 1949 and Relating to the Protection of Victims of Armed Conflicts	30 January 1997

A/RES/51/194	Strengthening of the Coordination of Emergency Humanitarian Assistance of the United Nations	10 February 1997
A/RES/53/96	Status of the Protocols Additional to the Geneva Conventions of 1949	20 January 1999
A/RES/55/148	Status of the Protocols Additional to the Geneva Conventions of 1949 and Relating to the Protection of Victims of Armed Conflicts	19 January 2001
A/RES/56/83	Annex to 'Responsibility of States for Internationally Wrongful Acts' (ARSIWA), 28 January 2002 (corrected by document A/56/49 (vol. I)/Corr.4).	28 January 2002
A/RES/57/14	Status of the Protocols Additional to the Geneva Conventions of 1949 and Relating to the Protection of Victims of Armed Conflicts	20 January 2003
A/RES/58/114	Strengthening of the Coordination of Emergency Humanitarian Assistance of the United Nations	17 December 2003
A/RES/59/36	Status of the Protocols Additional to the Geneva Conventions of 1949 and Relating to the Protection of Victims of Armed Conflicts	16 December 2004
A/RES/60/1	2005 World Summit Outcome	16 September 2005
A/RES/60/124	Strengthening of the Coordination of Emergency Humanitarian Assistance of the United Nations	15 December 2005
A/RES/61/134	Strengthening of the Coordination of Emergency Humanitarian Assistance of the United Nations	14 December 2006
A/RES/61/30	Status of the Protocols Additional to the Geneva Conventions of 1949 and Relating to the Protection of Victims of Armed Conflicts	18 December 2006
A/RES/62/94	Strengthening of the Coordination of Emergency Humanitarian Assistance of the United Nations	17 December 2007

A/RES/63/125	Status of the Protocols Additional to the Geneva Conventions of 1949 and Relating to the Protection of Victims of Armed Conflicts	15 January 2009
A/RES/63/139	Strengthening of the Coordination of Emergency Humanitarian Assistance of the United Nations	05 March 2009
A/RES/65/29	Status of the Protocols Additional to the Geneva Conventions of 1949 and Relating to the Protection of Victims of Armed Conflicts	10 January 2011
A/RES/66/119	Strengthening of the Coordination of Emergency Humanitarian Assistance of the United Nations	15 December 2011

UN SECURITY COUNCIL RESOLUTIONS AND DOCUMENTS

S/1999/1003	Eighth Report of the Secretary-General on the United Nations Observers Mission in Sierra Leone	28 September 1999
S/1999/1024	Report of the Secretary-General on the Situation in East Timor	04 October 1999
S/1999/513	Report of the Secretary-General on the Situation in East Timor	05 May 1999
S/1999/836	Eight Report of the Secretary-General on the United Nations Observers Mission in Sierra Leone	30 July 1999
S/2000/53	Report of the Secretary-General on the United Nations Transitional Administration in East Timor	26 January 2000
S/2009/277	Report of the Secretary-General on the Protection of Civilians in Armed Conflict	29 May 2009
S/2009/439	Report of the Secretary-General on the United Nations Stabilization Mission in Haiti	01 September 2009
S/2010/579	Report of the Secretary-General on the Protection of Civilians in Armed Conflict	11 November 2010
S/2012/376	Report of the Secretary-General on the Protection of Civilians in Armed Conflict	22 May 2012
S/22366	Report to the Secretary General on Humanitarian Needs in Kuwait and Iraq in the Immediate Post-crisis Environment by a Mission to the Area led by Mr Martti Ahtisaari, Under-Secretary-General for Administration and Management	20 March 1991
S/PRST/1997/34	Statement by the President of the Security Council on Protection for Humanitarian Assistance to Refugees and Others in Conflict Situations	19 June 1997

S/PRST/1998/36	Statement by the President of the Security Council on the Democratic Republic of the Congo	11 December 1998
S/PRST/2002/6	Statement by the President of the Security Council on the Protection of Civilians in Armed Conflict	15 March 2002
S/PRST/2004/46	Statement by the President of the Security Council Protection of Civilians in Armed Conflict	14 December 2004
S/PRST/2008/18	Statement by the President of the Security Council Protection of Civilians in Armed Conflict	27 May 2008
S/PRST/2010/25	Statement by the President of the Security Council Protection of Civilians in Armed Conflict	22 November 2010
S/PV.6498	The Situation in Libya	17 March 2011
S/PV.6509	The Situation in Libya	04 April 2011
S/PV.6527	Thc Situation in Libya	03 May 2011
S/PV.6541	The Situation in Libya	31 May 2011
S/PV.6566	The Situation in Libya	27 June 2011
S/PV.6595	The Situation in Libya	28 July 2011
S/PV.6606	The Situation in Libya	30 August 2011
S/RES/276	Namibia	30 January 1970
S/RES/688	Iraq	05 April 1991
S/RES/706	Escrow Account; Financial Arrangements	15 August 1999
S/RES/712	Release of Funds; Rights and Duties of UNSCOM staff	19 September 1991
S/RES/733	Somalia	23 January 1992
S/RES/748	Libyan Arab Jamahiriya	31 March, 1992
S/RES/751	Somalia	24 April 1992
S/RES/757	Bosnia and Herzegovina	30 May 2014
S/RES/778	Oil Monies to be put in Escrow Account	02 October 1992
S/RES/794	Somalia	03 December 1992
S/RES/814	Somalia	26 March 1993
S/RES/883	Libyan Arab Jamahiriya	11 November 1993
S/RES/912	Adjustment of the Mandate of the UN Assistance Mission for Rwanda due to the Current Situation in Rwanda and Settlement of the Rwandan Conflict	21 April 1994

S/RES/925	Extension of the Mandate and Deployment of the two Additional Battalions of the UN Assistance Mission for Rwanda and Settlement of the conflict in Rwanda	08 June 1994
S/RES/929	Establishment of a Temporary Multinational Operation for Humanitarian Purposes in Rwanda until the Deployment of the Expanded UN Assistance Mission for Rwanda	22 June 1994
S/RES/940	Authorisation to Form a Multinational Force Under Unified Command and Control to Restore the Legitimately Elected President and Authorities of the Government of Haiti and Extension of the Mandate of the UN Mission in Haiti	31 July 1994
S/RES/986	Authorisation to Permit the Import of Petroleum and Petroleum Products Originating in Iraq, as a Temporary Measure to Provide for Humanitarian Needs of the Iraqi People	14 April 1995
S/RES/1199	Kosovo	23 September 1998
S/RES/1260	Sierra Leone	20 August 1999
S/RES/1261	Children and Armed Conflict	25 August 1999
S/RES/1264	East Timor	15 September 1999
S/RES/1265	Protection of Civilians in Armed Conflict	17 September 1999
S/RES/1270	Sierra Leone	22 October 1999
S/RES/1272	East Timor	25 October 1999
S/RES/1279	Democratic Republic of the Congo	30 November 1999
S/RES/1289	Sierra Leone	07 February 2000
S/RES/1291	Democratic Republic of the Congo	24 February 2000
S/RES/1296	Protection of Civilians in Armed Conflict	19 April 2000
S/RES/1314	Children and Armed Conflict	11 August 2000
S/RES/1325	Women and Peace and Security	31 October 2000
S/RES/1355	Democratic Republic of the Congo	15 June 2001
S/RES/1379	Children and Armed Conflict	20 November 2001
S/RES/1410	East Timor	17 May 2002
S/RES/1417	Democratic Republic of the Congo	14 June 2002

S/RES/1460	Children and Armed Conflict	30 January 2003
S/RES/1493	Democratic Republic of the Congo	28 July 2003
S/RES/1502	Protection of United Nations Personnel, Associated Personnel and Humanitarian Personnel in Conflict Zones	26 August 2003
S/RES/1506	Letters dated 20 and 23 December 1991, from France, the United Kingdom of Great Britain and Northern Ireland and the United States of America (S/23306, S/23307, S/23308, S/23309 and S/23317); Letter dated 15 August 2003 from the Chargé d'affaires a.i. of the Permanent Mission of the Libyan Arab Jama	12 September 2003
S/RES/1539	Children and Armed Conflict	22 April 2004
S/RES/1556	Report of the Secretary-General on the Sudan	30 July 2004
S/RES/1565	Democratic Republic of the Congo	01 October 2004
S/RES/1590	Reports of the Secretary-General on the Sudan	24 March 2005
S/RES/1612	Children and Armed Conflict	26 July 2005
S/RES/1674	Protection of Civilians in Armed Conflict	28 April 2006
S/RES/1706	Darfur	31 August 2006
S/RES/1738	Protection of Civilians in Armed Conflict	23 December 2006
S/RES/1769	Reports of the Secretary-General on the Sudan	31 July 2007
S/RES/1820	Women and Peace and Security	19 June 2008
S/RES/1828	Reports of the Secretary-General on the Sudan	31 July 2008
S/RES/1856	Democratic Republic of the Congo	22 December 2008
S/RES/1861	Chad, the Central African Republic and the Sub-region	14 January 2009
S/RES/1881	Reports of the Secretary-General on the Sudan	06 August 2009
S/RES/1882	Children and Armed Conflict	04 August 2009
S/RES/1889	Women and Peace and Security	05 October 2009
S/RES/1894	Protection of Civilians in Armed Conflict	11 November 2009
S/RES/1935	Reports of the Secretary-General on the Sudan	30 July 2010
S/RES/1960	Women and Peace and Security	16 December 2010
S/RES/1970	Peace and Security in Africa	26 February 2011

S/RES/1973	Libya	17 March 2011
S/RES/1975	Côte d'Ivoire	30 March 2011
S/RES/1996	Reports of the Secretary-General on the Sudan	08 July 2011
S/RES/1998	Children and Armed Conflict	12 July 2011
S/RES/2009	Libya	16 September 2011
S/RES/2014	Middle East	21 October 2011
S/RES/2063	Reports of the Secretary-General on the Sudan	31 July 2012
S/RES/2068	Children and Armed Conflict	19 September 2012
S/RES/2076	Democratic Republic of the Congo	20 November 2012

CONTRIBUTORS

SANDRA BORDA is Associate Professor at the Department of Political Science, Universidad de Los Andes, Bogota, Colombia. She was a visiting fellow at the University of Groningen, The Netherlands.

SANNE BOSWIJK currently works as roaming legal adviser and humanitarian consultant in Africa. Before that she worked for the International Federation of Red Cross and Red Crescent Societies (IFRC) as Disaster Law Coordinator for Africa and legal adviser in International Humanitarian Law for The Netherlands Red Cross.

MORTEN BROBERG is Professor in International Development Law, Jean Monnet Chair holder, and member of the interdisciplinary research project 'Changing Disasters' at the University of Copenhagen, Denmark.

DABIRU SRIDHAR PATNAIK is Associate Professor of International Law and Director, Center for Postgraduate Legal Studies; Executive Director, Center for South Asian Legal Studies, Jindal Global Law School, O. P. Jindal Global University, NCR of Delhi, India and Fellow, International Law Seminar of the International Law Commission, United Nations, Geneva (2010).

ROTEM GILADI is a teaching fellow at the Hebrew University of Jerusalem.

HANS-JOACHIM HEINTZE is Professor of International Law at the Institute of International Law of Peace and Armed Conflict (IFHV) at the University of Bochum.

JOOST HERMAN is Professor of Globalisation Studies and Humanitarian Action and Director of the Institute for Globalisation Studies Groningen (GSG), University of Groningen.

MARLIES HESSELMAN is currently a lecturer and PhD candidate at the department of international and constitutional law at the University of Groningen.

STEFANIE JANSEN-WILHELM is a PhD candidate at Tilburg University, The Netherlands. She is the co-founder and owner of De Volder & Jansen International Law Consultancy and works for the Statelessness Programme at Tilburg University.

ABEL S. KNOTTNERUS LLM MA (Res) has completed a Research Master's degree in Modern History and International Relations (2012 – *cum laude)* as well as a LLM in International and European Law (2012 – *cum laude)* at the University of Groningen in the Netherlands. He is currently working there on his PhD dissertation concerning the sociological legitimacy of international law and international institutions.

JORIS KOCKEN is Associate Professor of Legal Theory at the Faculty of Law at the University of Amsterdam and Assistant Professor at the University of Groningen, Department of International Relations and International Organisation, the Netherlands.

EMILIE E. KUIJT is a lecturer and PhD Fellow at the University of Leiden, department of Public International Law / Grotius Centre for International Legal Studies.

CHRISTOPHER K. LAMONT is an Assistant Professor of International Relations at the University of Groningen and Co-Chair of Research in Ethics and Globalisation.

KUBO MAČÁK is Lecturer in Law at the University of Exeter and DPhil Candidate in International Law at the University of Oxford.

HEIKE MONTAG is a doctoral candidate at the Faculty of Law, University of Bochum.

DIANA PHILIP is a Research Analyst at Strategic Foresight Group, India. She holds an LLM from Harvard Law School with a concentration in human rights.

DIRK SALOMONS is the Director of the Humanitarian Affairs Track at the School of International and Public Affairs, Columbia University, where he also heads the International Organisations specialisation. He is a Non-resident Fellow at New York University's Center on International Cooperation.

HEIKE SPIEKER is Deputy Director of the International Services and National Relief Division at German Red Cross Headquarters in Berlin.

She is Adjunct Lecturer at University College Dublin, Ireland, and Lecturer at the Università della Svizzera Italiana, Lugano, Switzerland.

HERIBERTUS JAKA TRIYANA is a Senior Lecturer of International Law at the Department of Legal Studies, Universitas Gadjah Mada, Yogyakarta.

ANDREJ ZWITTER is NGIZ Professor in International Relations at the Faculty of Law, University of Groningen and Co-Chair of Research in Ethics and Globalisation, a research section within the inter-faculty Institute of Globalisation Studies, Groningen.

Introduction

ANDREJ ZWITTER, CHRISTOPHER K. LAMONT,
HANS-JOACHIM HEINTZE, JOOST HERMAN

Humanitarian assistance occurs when local or regional crises prompt international action to alleviate human suffering. In contrast to development aid, humanitarian aid is defined by its short-term focus and the immediacy of intervention. Given its crisis management character, humanitarian assistance presents a pressing challenge for international law because the provision of assistance operates under circumstances which depart from common state-centric understandings of how international politics and international law usually work.[1]

To be sure, in the context of humanitarian emergencies processes of inter-state negotiation and consensus-building are dramatically limited by the urgency of the need to assist populations vulnerable to the consequences of natural disaster or armed conflict.[2] *Humanitarian Action: Global, Regional and Domestic Legal Responses* directly responds to this pressing challenge by providing the first in-depth exploration of legal problems posed by contemporary humanitarian practice. Through two points of departure – one which explores the law and politics of humanitarian action, and the second which explores normative frameworks – this book provides legal professionals, scholars and policy-makers with a unique multidisciplinary resource that will help inform the theory and practice of humanitarian assistance. However, before embarking on a legal and political analysis of humanitarian assistance, this introductory chapter will set the stage for the following chapters. It will do this by presenting legal and political approaches through which humanitarian assistance can be

[1] These common understandings often focus on inter-state bargaining to resolve shared problems with a transnational character.

[2] Although international humanitarian assistance started within the realm of international conflicts, due to the decline in international conflicts and the increase of local conflicts after the end of the cold war, today the majority of humanitarian aid goes to people affected by local conflicts and natural disasters.

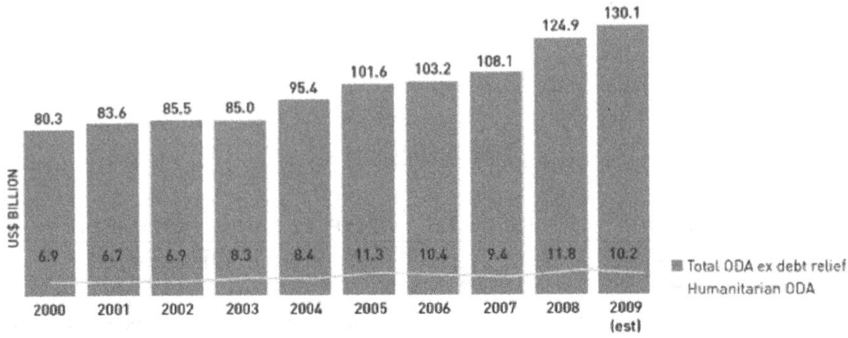

Figure 1: Humanitarian aid: share of official development assistance (ODA), 2000–2009.

approached to guide the reader through the complex issues raised by the contributors to this book.

The field of humanitarian aid continues to experience an unprecedented expansion. In 2010, donors provided approximately 127 billion US dollars for humanitarian and developmental activities in dozens of countries around the world, which is about 90 billion more than in 1960 and 66 billion more than in 1980 (see Figure 1).[3]

Furthermore, states and the International Federation of the Red Cross are by far no longer the main actors in the field as non-governmental organisations (NGOs) have increasingly assumed a key role in large areas of humanitarian aid. Indeed, this expansion has also found resonance within the halls of academia with a growing number of Masters programmes being offered in the field, and practitioners and scholars coming together to establish the International Humanitarian Studies Association to facilitate the development of further research and dialogue in the burgeoning field of humanitarian aid. In addition, the second World Conference on Humanitarian Studies was held in 2011 in Boston and attracted more than 300 participants, both scholars and practitioners, from all over the world. Equal numbers were attracted to the third World Conference in Istanbul, autumn 2013.

[3] The prices are USD in 2009 exchange rates, accessed 18 December 2011, http://webnet.oecd.org/dcdgraphs/ODAhistory/.

Nevertheless, despite a rapidly growing interest in humanitarian studies, the field is marked by a considerable degree of interdisciplinary fragmentation. Unlike many other fields of study, which emerged as sub-fields within a single discipline such as democratisation studies and comparative politics, most of the legal and political analyses in the area of humanitarian studies are dispersed over a broad range of disciplinary journals including *International Politics*, *Law and Development*, *Disasters*. Only recently the edited volume *International Law and Humanitarian Assistance* (2011), compiled by Heintze and Zwitter, shed first light on international and European legal regulations and the myriad legal intricacies confronted by humanitarian actors. Given the limited scope of Heintze's and Zwitter's volume, the editors felt the need to extend this perspective by combining legal and political analysis. Its goal has been to deepen our understanding of this complex and growing humanitarian policy area and to contribute to shaping the emergent field of humanitarian studies.

Humanitarian Action: Global, Regional and Domestic Legal Responses contributes to the nascent area of humanitarian studies by providing a coherent framework for understanding recent developments in international law and politics relevant to the conduct of humanitarian aid. It is unique in its approach as it is on the one hand a timely follow-up to Heintze's and Zwitter's earlier volume, while on the other hand it takes a broader perspective on the development of the regulatory frameworks of humanitarianism that are relevant to a broad range of debates concerning legal policy, international relations and philosophy. Indeed, it includes contributions on multiculturalism, humanitarian diplomacy, human security and the responsibility to protect. The interaction between these perspectives on humanitarian studies is particularly fruitful as it explains how local problems lead to the emergence of new international norms, as well as how international political and legal norms influence domestic and regional disaster response.

The causes and consequences of global, regional and local approaches to humanitarian action and the mutual influence they have upon each other became more tangible and visible since the end of the cold war. To be sure, this mutual influence is increasingly visible in the complex legal and political frameworks at various levels of analysis – local, regional and global – which makes humanitarian studies one of the most intricate fields of international law and international relations. Local problems such as man-made, natural and complex emergencies are met with a variety of responses by policy-makers and scholars. Approaches such as human security, 'Responsibility to Protect' and human rights have been elevated on the agenda of humanitarian action. At the same time, the international community tries to mitigate these developments by endorsing unifying frameworks such as the United Nations Office for the Coordination of Humanitarian Affairs (OCHA), a focal point for all disaster management, the European Union's humanitarian response centre, or by creating a framework of state obligations concerning the delivery of aid, as seen in the work of the International Law Commission. Regional organisations also play their own part in assuming humanitarian obligations, as with the Association of East Asian Nations (ASEAN) in the case of Myanmar (Chapter 15), or by facilitating domestic implementation such as in Indonesia (Chapter 14). Thereby, the focus on humanitarian assistance serves as a marvellous test case for the constitutionalisation/fragmentation debate in international law, which – as will be demonstrated in the next section – nicely captures the tension within regulatory frameworks governing humanitarian action. It is through a reflection on the constitutionalisation/fragmentation debate that the overall aim of this book will be achieved: to give the reader an understanding of the workings of this intricate field of interaction between local, regional and global norms, enabling the reader to trace possible developments in the future of humanitarianism.

1. Constitutionalisation or fragmentation of humanitarian norms?

The International Law Commission (ILC)'s work concerning the duty to protect persons affected by natural disasters is but one of the new steps towards international norms governing local disasters and humanitarian aid. According to its work, a state has the duty to accept the bona fide offer of aid by another state if it is not able to provide for the people on its territory. This approach, which is particularly visible in laws governing humanitarian aid, humanitarian law, or human rights, for example, shifts the criteria of applicability of the law from conditions among states to conditions within states. To some degree (at least from a bird's eye perspective on state obligations) these norms supersede and/or replace national legislation to the extent that national laws do not comply with international norms. Such legal frameworks attach their applicability to criteria within the usually sovereign sphere of states and attach international legal obligations to them.

This book offers practical, legal, political and philosophical insight into a highly controversial topic, which from a theoretical perspective can be best approached from the debate between constitutionalisation and fragmentation of international law. While far from being a new debate, it helps us to understand the consequences of the increasing complexity of international law of humanitarian action, its codification by the ILC, and regional special arrangements for the field.

The question of the unity of international law is as old as the question of what constitutes modern international law. As early as the end of the nineteenth[4] and the early twentieth century, authors raised the question of whether an international constitutional law, or world law, would or could exist.[5] The Viennese school of international law, particularly Verdross,[6] picked up this question and argued for the unity of the international legal order based on certain principles and structures such as Kelsen's Grundnorm *pacta sunt servanda.*[7]

Ever since, the interest of legal scholars in question has not declined but rather gained new interest via the question of fragmentation, or diversification, of international law. Simma, for example, sees two realms of debate concerning fragmentation, one regarding the increasing number of international judicial organs along with the International Court of Justice (ICJ), the other concerning the substance of law itself.[8] In its session in 2000, the ILC also raised questions about the consequences of fragmentation in international law. Hafner, a member of the ILC who wrote the report concerning this question, sees several factors that contribute to fragmentation:

- The proliferation of international regulations;
- Increasing political fragmentation (juxtaposed with growing regional and global interdependence in such areas as economics, the environment, energy, resources, health, and the proliferation of weapons of mass destruction);
- The regionalisation of international law due to a rise in the number of regional fora engaged in the formulation of international regulations;

4 Franz von Holtzendorff, *Handbuch des Völkerrechts* (Berlin, C. Habel, 1887), e.g. the title of vol. II ('Die völkerrechtliche Verfassung und Grundordnung der auswärtigen Staatsbeiehungen') and elsewhere.

5 See also: Raymond L. Bridgman, *The First Book of World Law: A Compilation of the International Conventions to Which the Principal Nations Are Signatory, with a Survey of Their Significance* (Ginn and Company Publishers, 1911), www.archive.org/details/firstbookworldl01foungoog.

6 Alfred Verdross, *Die Verfassung der Völkerrechtsgemeinschaft* (Wien: J. Springer, 1926).

7 Hans Kelsen, *Reine Rechtslehre* (Wien: Deuticke, 2nd ed., 1960), 221 et seq.

8 Bruno Simma, 'Fragmentation in a Positive Light', *Michigan Journal of International Law* 25 (2003–2004): 845–847.

- The emancipation of individuals from states; and
- The specialisation of international regulations.[9]

According to Hafner, fragmentation poses both a risk to international law through the loss of credibility and reliability due to sectionalism and regionalism, as well as a possible benefit of tailored laws to regional specificities and thematic requirements. This approach allows us to better match institutions and legal frameworks with the necessities of given disputes or issue areas.[10]

At the same time de Wet argues for an 'intensification of the shift of power and control over decision-making away from the nation State towards international actors' in which 'there is a co-existence of national, regional and sectoral (functional) constitutional orders that complement one another in order to constitute an embryonic international constitutional order'.[11]

In humanitarian action both issues converge. Regional legal arrangements, respect for local norms, and a variety of international norms applicable to a given crisis (for example human rights, international humanitarian law, refugee law, decisions of the Security Council and/or the General Assembly) need to be dealt with by practitioners. Furthermore, this area of issues opens the door to rather new political arguments that are deployed with increasing frequency, such as the concept of sovereignty as responsibility, the responsibility to protect, human security, and several others. This indicates cross-fertilisation between different norms and standards on various levels of analysis, for example the human rights obligation of states other than the one directly concerned towards its citizens. Whereas it is not the intention of the book to confirm or dispute either of the conceptions, the constitutionalisation/fragmentation debate is nevertheless useful to give flesh to the bones of the global–local interaction in the field of humanitarianism which the chapters tackle. In the concluding chapter, the following elements of the debate will be taken as focal points of analysis:

- Shift of decision-making power away from the national order,
- Complementarity of national, regional and international (sectoral – i.e. humanitarian) normative orders,

[9] Gerhard Hafner, 'Pros and Cons Ensuing from Fragmentation of International Law', *Michigan Journal of International Law* 25 (2003–2004): 849–850.

[10] Ibid., 859.

[11] Erika De Wet, 'The International Constitutional Order', *ICLQ* 55 (2006): 75.

- Proliferation of international norms of humanitarian action to lower levels of normative orders,
- Political fragmentation of sectors of international law and cross-fertilisation of sectoral norms with the humanitarian sector,
- De-internationalisation (regionalisation/localisation) of institutions and norms concerning humanitarian action,
- Emancipation of the individual as subject of international law in the field of humanitarian action,
- Specialisation of international/regional/local regulations on humanitarian action and crises.

2. Structure of the book

In order to shed light on the global/local interaction that is a defining feature of this field, this book will focus on two major areas of relevance for the humanitarian system: Part I deals with the laws about, and politics of, contemporary challenges to humanitarian action and will provide the basis for further inquiry into global–regional–local interaction; herein, authors introduce the challenge of global responses to local crisis, critically revisit common approaches, and explore new paradigms of international law and politics that try to breach the global/local divide in legal policy-making. It deals with the norms and practices that have emerged at the international level and keeps in mind the question of the appropriateness of a top-down approach to local problems. This part discusses norms that have emerged and are currently emerging at the global level, such as sovereignty, Security Council obligations to humanitarian action, and the duty to protect people affected by disasters. In addition it focuses on international norms regarding the individual divided into needs-based versus rights-based perspectives, and raises the pertinent question of the place of the individual human being in all these international developments.

Part II focuses on the interaction between international, regional and national conduct and calls for attention to regional and cultural specificities that need to be taken into account in these kinds of interactions. It puts emphasis on the interaction between international and regional responses to local problems, and raises the question of how these norms interact. It furthermore explores how local crises give rise to new legal and political approaches concerning humanitarian aid. Case studies include the roles, strategies and changing approaches of the international community in the Colombian conflict, the Haiti earthquake and the cyclone in Myanmar. Thus Part I provides the legal and philosophical ground for Part II, which investigates local/global interaction from legal and political perspectives in the form of case studies; these include European Union anti-corruption mechanisms for humanitarian funding (Chapter 11), national compliance with international norms (Chapters 12, 14), international humanitarian organisations as local peace-builders (Chapter 17), humanitarian aid coordination in Haiti (Chapter 18), Responsibility to Protect (R2P) and humanitarian diplomacy in Myanmar (Chapter 15).

Together both parts provide for a view of the intricate bottom-up and top-down interaction of norms that gives rise to a high degree of complexity within the international system of humanitarian action. Eventually, the conclusion will come back to the focal points of analysis for fragmentation and constitutionalisation mentioned above.

PART I

Law and politics of humanitarian action

1

International law and humanitarian space in the twenty-first century: challenged relationships

JOOST HERMAN

1. Introduction

Assessing the ongoing humanitarian crisis in Syria, which started in 2011, and looking back at the 2011 Libyan conflict, one has to agree that international humanitarian response patterns are not functioning *optima forma*, to say the least. Despite 150 years since the onset of modern humanitarianism with Henri Dunant of building up a humanitarian framework of action – unified, codified, globalised – the international community finds itself in a quagmire of half-hearted positions, issues of sovereignty, and blatant politically inspired inertia based on self-interest. Both (inter-)governmental as well as non-governmental agencies and organisations find empowerment in a variety of international (quasi-) legal codices – international humanitarian law (IHL), the humanitarian principles, international human rights law (IHRL) and, *in statu nascendi*, the Responsibility to Protect (R2P) – to enter Syrian humanitarian space, the physical area delineated by IHL and the humanitarian principles in which humanitarian needs can be met by humanitarian actors. In reality, however, most of these agencies find themselves outside the borders of Syria, which claims its sovereign right to determine who and what gets access to its territory. Restoring, defending and upholding the human dignity of the Syrian civilian victims to the conflict thus has become an ineffective operation.

The present general outcry of moral indignation is of a rather hypocritical nature. Over the past fifteen years many humanitarian crises have been characterised by elements such as deliberately blocking access to victims, disguising political goals in humanitarian terminology, making humanitarian space an insecure environment for aid-workers and aid recipients alike, abusing aid and exploiting aid agencies for political goals. Sudan, Somalia, Democratic Republic of Congo, Myanmar, China, Afghanistan are just a few examples in kind. Unashamed disrespect for

IHL, let alone IHRL, has been in evidence in these cases. Also concerning these conflict areas, the humanitarian community has been confronted with apparently ineffective humanitarian response patterns, admittedly firmly embedded in international law but in fact not adapted to the changing reality of the contemporary humanitarian space. A hundred and fifty years of a steady creation of principles and norms for the benefit of a secure space exclusively for humanitarian agencies have seemingly led to a degree of inflexibility and rigidity in dealing with contemporary challenges to humanitarianism and humanitarian space with the aim of providing effective aid to those who are in need.

In this chapter the twenty-first century's major challenges to humanitarianism and humanitarian space will be listed and scrutinised. Humanitarian principles and the growing corpus of applicable international law will be examined for their ongoing relevance for delineating, securing and accessing humanitarian space. It will be argued that the classical definition of humanitarian space – the physical area secured by IHL in which humanitarian actors are at liberty to perform needs assessments, to distribute aid and oversee its proper use, and to directly contact and interact with people in need, based on the humanitarian principles – is in need of reconceptualisation[1]. It will be stated that humanitarian history impedes an adaptation to modernity. A hundred and fifty years of linear humanitarian codification hampers growth towards a more metaphorical definition, which is needed. Such a definition would entail reconceptualising humanitarian space into a continuously fluctuating area, still delineated by the humanitarian principles and international law, but allowing for – necessitating even – much more negotiated access and pragmatic decision-making to maximise humanitarian effectiveness per given situation. Only through such a thoughtful reconceptualisation aimed at renewed long-term applicability can international humanitarianism remain relevant and efficient, to a degree.

2. Contemporary challenges to international humanitarianism

As stated, international humanitarianism in the twenty-first century faces many challenges. One can distinguish global trends of a mutually reinforcing nature. In a demonstrable way, the following are discernible:

[1] Johanna Grombach Wagner, 'An IHL/ICRC Perspective on Humanitarian Space', *Humanitarian Exchange Magazine* 23 (2005): 2; Daniel Thürer, 'Dunant's Pyramid: thoughts on Humanitarian Space', *International Review of the Red Cross* 89 (2007): 54.

- a growing need for humanitarian aid worldwide as a result of a higher frequency of natural disasters and persistent man-made conflicts;
- a steady increase of ever growing disrespect for IHL specifically and IHRL in general;
- heightened levels of insecurity for donors and recipients alike in humanitarian space;
- nevertheless, mushrooming numbers of (self-proclaimed) humanitarian actors and agencies, especially from the non-governmental corner, with agendas labelled humanitarian, but in fact being much wider-focused;
- unstable financial parameters as a result of volatile global economic developments;
- nevertheless, increasing levels of political and military interference with humanitarian action worldwide.

All of these challenges have fundamentally altered the space in which humanitarian action is conducted. However, due to a lack of international consensus, but above all a proclaimed unswerving belief in the classical principled (quasi-)legal framework of humanitarianism, the larger part of the humanitarian community is very slowly progressing towards a reconceptualisation of its work field.[2] In the remainder of this section four overarching challenges will be dealt with: the dominance of the classical approach, the changed nature of humanitarian crises, politicisation and militarisation of aid, and the increase in the number of actors in a changing scope of humanitarianism. Hence, the fluctuating nature of contemporary humanitarian space will be dealt with.

2.1 Classical IHL and humanitarian principles

The history and importance of classical IHL coincides with the dominance of the International Committee of the Red Cross (ICRC). Since 1864 IHL and its principal defender and promoter, the ICRC, have become the cornerstones of the system to assist and protect the victims of disaster

[2] For various discussions on the concepts of humanitarianism and the need for their adaptation, see for example: Sarah Collinson and Samir Elhawary, 'Humanitarian Space: a Review of Trends and Issues', *HPG report* 32 (2012): 2; Madalina E. Nan, 'New Humanitarianism with Old Problems: the Forgotten Lessons of Rwanda', *The Journal of Humanitarian Assistance* (2010); Peter J. Hoffman and Thomas G. Weiss, *Sword and Salve: Confronting New Wars and Humanitarian Crises* (Lanham: Rowman and Littlefield, 2006).

and conflict. Whilst IHL has stood and stands for an elaborate system of codified norms in the shape of the Geneva Treaties and Additional Protocols, the ICRC and its like-minded friends have created quasi-legal humanitarian principles – humanity, neutrality, impartiality and independence – that have become more and more codified. This continuous nurturing for over one and a half centuries explains the dominant position of IHL and the humanitarian principles.[3]

Indeed, from the creation of the ICRC in 1863 to the Geneva Conventions of 1949 and to the Additional Protocols to the Geneva Conventions (1977 and 2005), a steady growth is discernible in volume and importance when it comes to applicable international law in times of war and conflict. As such, 'legal humanitarianism' has positioned itself as a counterbalance to politically driven 'humanitarian' action such as states had exercised in the late nineteenth century, basically representing great power politics in disguise.[4]

Concerning the role of IHL one should state explicitly that from its inception up until now, the guiding characteristics were those of *jus in bello*. This indicates that IHL and its 'personification' (ICRC) always accepted the general features of international law, especially respect for state sovereignty, exclusive applicability to state parties locked in international armed conflict and the necessity of consent of warring parties to allow for humanitarian assistance. The fact that the Fourth Geneva Convention (1949), Common Article 3 of the 1949 Geneva Conventions and *Additional Protocols I* and *II* (1977) widened the concepts of protection and assistance to include civilians caught up in both international and non-international conflicts, did not alter the fundamental rules of the game referred to above. Any party (state as well as non-state) to a conflict should allow IHL to regulate its behaviour and should allow for humanitarian aid and protection by humanitarian actors, provided these actors ask for the consent of the authorities involved and deliver their aid according to the humanitarian principles, most importantly neutral and impartial in nature.[5] One may label this balance a 'quid pro quo' deal. Warring parties in principle cannot

[3] Jonathan Moore, *Hard Choices: Moral Dilemmas in Humanitarian Intervention* (Lanham: Rowman and Littlefield, 1998), 287–288; Michael N. Barnett and Thomas G. Weiss, *Humanitarianism in Question: Politics, Power, Ethics* (Ithaca: Cornell University Press, 2008), 73–79.

[4] Gelijn Molier, *De (on)rechtmatigheid van humanitaire interventie* (The (Il)legality of Humanitarian Intervention) (Boom: Meppel, 2003), chapters 2 and 3.

[5] Maurizio Geremia, 'Neutrality, Impartiality and Independence in Colombia: an ICRC Perspective', *Humanitarian Exchange Magazine* 45 (2010): 4–6; he describes this state of affairs as such: 'access has to be earned through acceptance',.

prevent humanitarian actors from gaining access to victims, combatants and non-combatants alike – by such acts admitting their existing obligation under general international law to protect and uphold the human dignity of the population under their effective control – but do have possibilities of blocking access for military reasons or the suspicion that humanitarian aid would favour the opposing side. In other words, IHL provides for the compelling possibility of humanitarian aid, provided that this aid is delivered according to the humanitarian principles and is given consent by the warring parties out of recognition for their sovereignty.[6] ICRC's legalised approach to humanitarian aid has been presented as simple and universally valid, being based on humanitarian values, and thus being able to strictly separate the humanitarian domain from the political arena.[7]

Solidly creating and upholding the legal edifice of universal humanitarianism well into the present age, the ICRC has seen a steady stream of followers, both of the intergovernmental – United Nations Children's Fund (UNICEF), United Nations High Commissioner for Refugees (UNHCR), United Nations Office for the Coordination of Humanitarian Affairs (OCHA), Humanitarian Aid and Civil Protection department of the European Commission (ECHO) – as well as the non-governmental persuasion – Oxford Committee for Famine Relief (Oxfam), Save the Children Fund (SCF), Concern Worldwide, Action contre la Faim (ACF). They have all cultivated the appearance of being non-political organisations, driven by universally valid humanitarian principles, carefully staying away from 'political poison', as one prominent ICRC theorist once phrased it.[8] For these followers, IHL and the humanitarian principles are safeguarding the purity of humanitarian action and protecting it from subjective politics.[9]

The legal approach broadened and deepened considerably when the newly created intergovernmental United Nations (and regional organisations like the Organisation of American States and the Council of Europe) started to build an extensive framework of IHRL and connected

[6] Joost Herman, 'Humanitaire bewegingsruimte in de 21^{e} eeuw: de rol van het recht' (Humanitarian Space for Manoeuvre in the 21st century: the Role of Law) in *Humanitaire Ruimte: Tussen onpartijdigheid en politiek* (Humanitarian Space: In between Impartiality and Politics), ed. Dennis Dijkzeul and Joost Herman (Gent: Academia Press, 2009/2010), 68–70; Collinson and Elhawary, 'Humanitarian Space', 1–27.

[7] David Chandler, 'The Road to Military Humanitarianism: How the Human Rights NGOs Shaped a New Humanitarian Agenda', *Human Rights Quarterly* 23 (2001): 679–682.

[8] Jean Pictet, 2, quoted in Chandler, 'The Road to Military Humanitarianism', 679.

[9] Ibid., 3.

this framework to existing IHL. Codices specifically devoted to protection of specific groups (refugees, women, children, IDPs) and general human rights declarations and treaties (*Universal Declaration of Human Rights*, *Civil and Political Rights Covenant*, the *Convention against Torture*) were from 1967 connected to IHL through United Nations Security Council Resolution 237 by stressing that human rights in general must be respected by all parties to a conflict, next to the obligations under IHL.[10] Together with the direct reference in the Additional Protocols of 1977 to general stipulations concerning anti-discrimination, a solid partnership in law was thus created with far-reaching consequences, especially as of the 1990s.[11]

The consequences of IHL and IHRL teaming up – or, in the words of the ICRC, representing a complementary approach to humanitarian action[12] – are to be discerned in the genesis of the so-called human rights-based approach to humanitarianism. Through this concept, humanitarian organisations have embraced a holistic approach to norms and laws applicable to humanitarian crises, thereby lessening the importance of the sovereignty of conflict parties involved, and the issue of necessary consent that for so long had been deemed of crucial importance to humanitarianism.[13]

At the core of the human rights-based approach to humanitarianism is the conviction that human beings both in circumstances of peace and of conflict are in need of having, and are entitled to have, their human dignity protected. Next to primary necessities such as water, food, shelter and medication, all human beings under all circumstances are also entitled to fundamental human rights like the right to life, the right not to be tortured, the right of religious freedom: in short, the full international human rights corpus. Whilst in 'ordinary' developed societies, effective governance and independent judiciaries guarantee these rights, in weakened or failed states submerged in chaos and conflict, such guarantees do not exist. As a consequence, populations in these crisis areas are dependent on external actors to offer protection of their human

[10] OCHA Fact Sheet no.13, 'International Humanitarian Law and Human Rights', www.ohchr.org/Documents/Publications/FactSheet13en.pdf.

[11] Ulrike von Pilar, *Humanitarian Space under Siege* (Bad Neuenahr: Background Paper Symposium Europe and Humanitarian Aid, 1999), 5.

[12] Angelo Gnaediger, 'Humanitarian Principles – The Importance of their Preservation during Humanitarian Crises' (Speech, Lisbon Conference, 'Humanitarian Aid', October 2007), 2–3.

[13] Herman, 'Humanitaire bewegingsruimte' (Humanitarian Space for Manoeuvre), 74–75.

dignity. However dependent they may be, they are considered to be entitled to this protection. No longer are human beings receiving aid and protection to be seen as distressed and powerless recipients. They are to be considered as rights-endowed clients whose rights are temporarily being violated, and whose rights should be restored – through humanitarian organisations for example – because of their entitlement.[14]

A second fundamental characteristic of the human rights-based approach, against the compelling background of peoples' entitlement to have human dignity restored and protected in all circumstances, is the necessity for humanitarian organisations to take a holistic approach to IHL and IHRL. Humanitarian actors in their work need to understand the linkages between the specific stipulations from IHL and the more widely conceived and massive amount of human rights provisions. Knowledge of all these relevant legal instruments, the ability to comprehend their cohesion and consistency, and the skill to analyse the effects when they are implemented in a complementary way, are obligatory instruments in the toolbox of humanitarian organisations under this rights-based approach. Needless to say, it puts great demands on operational planning, and on implementing and properly concluding humanitarian action, as Bosnia, Sudan, Iraq and Afghanistan have shown over the past decades.

The legal challenges to a human rights-based approach are tremendous. The duty to protect and/or restore human dignity in whatever kind of circumstances imposes on organisations the necessity to include in every humanitarian operation elements geared not only to the direct needs of victims – as was the case with classical humanitarianism – but also to their inalienable human rights. Supplying food and water needs to coincide with addressing the underlying causes for their absence in the first place; treating traumatised rape victims needs to go hand in hand with addressing endemic gender imbalance in certain societies. Put differently, in the rights-based approach every type of short-term emergency aid measure needs to be embedded in a long-term strategy for restoring human dignity and establishing a situation of respect for everyone's human rights. Besides being a formidable task, this approach has also influenced humanitarian organisations' stance vis-à-vis the issue of sovereignty.

14 This and following paragraphs on the human rights-based approach and R2P are based on ibid., 73–84.

In ordinary situations, with properly functioning states, humanitarian organisations evidently do not need to act. In conflict zones, however, their actions are needed. Since the late 1980s and beginning of the 1990s, fuelled by the emerging concept of the rights-based approach, humanitarian action has stealthily altered its stance towards the concept of sovereignty. More and more active in weak or failed states (see the sections on the changing nature of conflict and on humanitarian organisations and their fieldwork below), confronted with chaotic situations of various warring parties, humanitarian organisations in these circumstances have depicted sovereignty or authority over territory as obsolete or irrelevant. In their opinion they have taken up the duty to provide for humanitarian assistance in the context of IHL and IHRL, being convinced that no one else can protect and restore human dignity. Humanitarian organisations have, as it were, taken over the erstwhile sovereign right of the state to be responsible for the protection of its people. Justification for this position has also come inadvertently from the 150-year-old 'quasi-sovereign' locus humanitarian organisations had created for themselves in IHL and through the humanitarian principles, claiming exclusive and unhampered access to victims of conflict and disaster. The apparent friction between exactly these principles – particularly neutrality – and disavowing the importance of states'/authorities' consent to allow humanitarian action has been lost on the majority of humanitarian organisations. In the words of Larry Minear, humanitarian aid organisations have thus become 'fundamentalist' in justifying their human rights-based courses of action in which the principles of neutrality and impartiality in return for access are reinterpreted to the organisations' advantage.[15] In effect politicising their involvement in humanitarian crisis areas, most of the humanitarian organisations have kept reiterating their true conviction to the pure humanitarian principles through a shroud 'of morality and ethics'.[16]

The 1990s and the first decade of the twenty-first century have given ample evidence that taking over sovereignty, as it were, by humanitarian organisations to protect human dignity and thereby negating the importance of consent of the authorities involved in conflict, whilst declining to operate in a politicised way, has not become the *deus ex machina* one could have hoped for. In a multitude of cases – Somalia, Sudan, Kosovo,

[15] Larry Minear, *The Humanitarian Enterprise: Dilemmas and Discoveries* (Bloomfield: Kumarian Press, 2002), 54.

[16] Chandler, 'The Road to Military Humanitarianism', 683.

Mozambique, East Timor, Afghanistan, Iraq – humanitarian aid in its newest shape has led to, or has become part and parcel of, uncontrollable interventions with unforeseen consequences, including inefficient use of humanitarian means and materials, and sometimes even prolongation of conflict. The dominant application of IHL and IHRL and the ensuing consequences in any kind of humanitarian disaster situation – the apparent disregard for the soverighty of authorities involved in conflict – can be considered to be unrealistic and unconstructive.[17] An acknowledgement of this consideration can be found in the work of the International Commission on Intervention and State Sovereignty (ICISS) as of the year 2000. This commission, through its 2001 report and the acceptance of the main concept in 2005 at the United Nations World Summit, has launched the concept of 'The Responsibility to Protect', subdivided into the responsibility to prevent, to protect and to reconstruct. In the context of this chapter, the most important outcome of this concept is the reaffirmation of the sovereignty of states/authorities as a key asset in preventing human dignity from becoming threatened; in reconstructing human dignity after conflict settlements; and even in reacting to human dignity being assaulted. In all three cases sovereignty means states carrying the primary responsibility to ensure respect for and protection of the human dignity of their populations, with other states and organisations in a role of encouraging and assisting these states in fulfilling these responsibilities. Only in cases where states manifestly violate this responsibility to protect can states act collectively to protect victimised populations, but always in accordance with the *United Nations Charter* (i.e. collective action mandated by the Security Council). Thus the ambitions of humanitarian organisations – based on an expanded legal framework – to disregard sovereignty as a continuously important aspect of international life have been redressed. States and state organisations have prime responsibility for the protection of human dignity, in which process humanitarian organisations are auxiliary.[18]

The necessity to bring politics – sovereignty – back into a mechanism for the protection of human dignity in humanitarian emergencies, has not been shared by the ICRC and its followers. The ICRC President Jacob Kellenberger in 2003 stated that despite the numerous setbacks in humanitarian operations over the past fifteeen years – which were partially due to the diminished importance of sovereignty in combination

[17] Ibid., 53–54.

[18] Herman, 'Humanitaire bewegingsruimte' (Humanitarian Space for Manoeuvre), 79–84.

with a rather political interpretation of neutrality – the IHL approach including the humanitarian principles, complemented by IHRL, is the only way forward. Legal perseverance and purity remains the only option to secure access to victims in humanitarian space, in his opinion.[19] The further codification and regulation of international humanitarianism – the Code of Conduct, the Oslo Guidelines on civil–military co-operation in humanitarian action, the Sphere Project, Good Humanitarian Donorship, the Humanitarian Accountability Partnership, to mention a few – also point in this direction.[20] What the effects of this whole development of clinging on to IHL and IHRL, and even expanding it, have been on the concept of humanitarian space will be dealt with in greater detail in section 3 of this chapter.

2.2 *The changed nature of conflict and its effects on humanitarianism*

Despite numerous infractions of IHL and blocked access to victims of disasters and violence, based on the previous section one can argue that in the time frame 1863–1991 legalised humanitarianism was still perceived to be congruent to the nature of conflict up until then. The quid pro quo, of respect for the dominance of sovereign states/authorities engaged in armed conflict in return for unhindered access to a secure humanitarian space to care for wounded combatants (1899, 1907, 1949) and cornered non-combatants (1949, 1977), remained accepted. Sovereign states respecting IHL and imposing norms of behaviour on their combatants and officials went hand in hand with the ICRC and its like-minded followers seemingly rigorously sticking to their adjudicated position under IHL and closely observing, nurturing and fostering the humanitarian principles through dissemination. The implosion of the Soviet Union and the resulting end to the cold war changed this situation dramatically, though. The main aim of IHL has become threatened: regulating the behaviour of warring parties as a result of which the humanitarian principles could be applied unhindered in a physically delineated humanitarian space has not been evident any more.[21]

[19] Jakob Kellenberger, *Striving to Improve Respect for International Humanitarian Law* (San Remo: Key Note Speech, XXVIIIth Round Table, 2004).

[20] Herman, 'Humanitaire bewegingsruimte' (Humanitarian Space for Manoeuvre), 72.

[21] Collinson and Elhawary, 'Humanitarian Space', 5–7; Dennis Dijkzeul, 'Inleiding: Internationaal management van menslievendheid' (Introduction: International Management of Humanity) in Dijkzeul and Herman, *Humanitaire Ruimte* (Humanitarian Space), 7–12.

The post-1991 era can be characterised as the age in which crises have become ever more complex, chaotic and chronic, especially in so-called weak or failed states. Especially the latter characteristic has been of great importance: the prevalence of intra-state over inter-state conflict has proven to be a game-changer for humanitarianism. Four major effects are to be mentioned here for their effects on IHL and the humanitarian principles.

Firstly, the role of ideology and state power has diminished in importance in the case of intra-state conflict. Not so much complete control over the state and a takeover of complete political power have been goals, but more so access to specific areas, economical instruments, natural resources and possessions of targeted groups of a population. Afghanistan, Sierra Leone and Liberia are just a few examples. Most of these types of conflicts have occurred in weakened states, where the state and its organs are not capable of maintaining legal order any more; indeed, such states are just one of the warring factions making use of the same tricks of the trade as the opposing forces. As a result, these conflicts have become chronic, self-propelled through economic gains. The ordinary population has been caught up in a lawless environment, only left to rely on external help for their needs.[22]

Secondly, due to the nature of internal conflict the distinction between civilians and warring parties has faded considerably. Unlike standing armies – organised, disciplined, distinguishable and knowledgeable in IHL – rebel forces, criminal gangs and groups of the population forced to aid and abet local warlords in control of the territory are notoriously ill-disciplined, prone to breaking down into factions, hungry for their part of the spoils, wary of hierarchy and unfamiliar with, or outright hostile to, rules and regulations, including IHL.

Thirdly, and as a consequence of the foregoing, the fading distinction between combatants and non-combatants has seriously eroded the very concepts upon which IHL and the humanitarian principles were based. Originally, only soldiers *hors de combat* and civilians not participating in the hostilities were entitled to receive humanitarian aid. As with concepts of sovereignty and its ensuing obligations for the state, the concept of armed conflict, the understanding of armistice and labels like 'refugee' or 'internally displaced person', the principle of distinction has always been

[22] This and the following four paragraphs are based on Dennis Dijkzeul and Dirk Salomons, 'De politieke economie van humanitaire ruimte' (The Political Economy of Humanitarian Space), in Ibid., 29–64.

based on the presupposition of well-organised, properly functioning states and/or authorities. Now, these concepts at the localised level of complex internal conflict seem to fall hopelessly short of being functional.

Fourthly and finally, the differentiation between a situation of conflict and a situation of peace seems to have disappeared. The erstwhile essential goal of conflict – achieving victory and a return to normalcy, regulated by (existing, internationally recognised) norms and laws – has fundamentally altered. In present-day complex conflicts, too many parties abhor the perspective of a return to regularised normalcy, peaceful reconstruction and stability, since it will block their access to economic wealth. Even if rebelling forces negotiate a settlement in which they get partial responsibility for the governance of a territory, the result is seldom good governance. Such parties simply go about their illegal, lawless business but now under the guise of representing the state. As such, in many a situation there is neither war nor peace, and the fittest survives at the expense of the defenceless.

In all, the changing nature of conflict cannot but force the humanitarian organisations to critically evaluate the relevance and impact of IHL and the humanitarian principles, with immediate effects on the understanding of humanitarian space and its delineation. The possible effects of such an evaluation will be dealt with in section three of this chapter.

2.3 *Politicisation and militarisation of aid*

A second major change after 1991, with direct effects on IHL, the humanitarian principles and humanitarian space, is the so-called politicisation and militarisation of aid. For two reasons – either using humanitarianism to disguise inertia and unwillingness to address conflict and violence, or exerting political influence under the guise of humanitarianism – governments and their military apparatus have increasingly invaded the domain of humanitarian action.[23] For different reasons, however, intergovernmental organisations like the United Nations, upholding the classical principles of respect for sovereignty, neutrality and impartiality, can also be said to have politicised and militarised humanitarianism.[24]

[23] *Humanitarian Response Index* 2010 (Madrid: DARA, 2010); Collinson and Elhawary, 'Humanitarian Space', 8.

[24] Ibid. In this case, one can say that the UN for honourable reasons have been sucked into a process of expanding the traditional concept of peacekeeping into the concept of broad

In the late 1980s and the 1990s governments have increasingly become the main donors to humanitarian non-governmental organisations. As humanitarian organisations evolved from narrowly defined humanitarianism to the broader concept of human rights-based approaches to humanitarianism (see sections above on IHL and below on humanitarian organisations), they almost automatically entered the realm of long(er)-term projects addressing root causes of conflict and endemic humanitarian crises. Reconstruction processes, development projects, stabilisation programmes, these are all issue areas in which political choices and goals are evident. Given the broader scope of their activities and the deeper level of involvement, the major part of necessary funding was to be found only through governments.[25]

Being in possession of funds, governments (like the United States, Canada, the United Kingdom, The Netherlands, France, Japan) have created dependency amongst these humanitarian organisations, for example:

- using it as leverage for either buying off the necessity to officially act and being confronted with dissatisfied voters at home (Chad);
- or trying to contain the effects of conflicts *in situ*, making sure that refugee spill-over would be prevented by well-supported refugee camps in the conflict zones itself (Sudan);
- or, in return for financial support, imposing strategic choices on organisations (high-profile disasters like Haiti 2010 rather than forgotten crises such as in Uganda) and making demands on the receiving organisations for political goals in conflict areas in which states had intervened (Afghanistan).

The latter phenomenon has been accompanied by active participation of the military in presupposed humanitarian operations – governments using their military machinery for winning the hearts and minds of victimised populations in the war on terror, for example; for trying to recreate stability and order; and for polishing up their image in hostile

peace support operations in which the UN, with the full codex of international law in all its dimensions as a guiding framework, has been mandated to recreate decent societies, whilst these societies are hopelessly and often violently divided on the political choices to be made.

25 Joost Herman and Dennis Dijkzeul, 'Current Challenges to Humanitarianism', *The Broker* 24 (2010): 5.

environments.[26] The Provincial Reconstruction Teams in Afghanistan (the Dutch, German and British for example) serve as a specimen, having been criticised for blurring the lines between political action and impartial aid completely.[27]

For one of the biggest organisations this also holds true: the United Nations and its agencies like UNHCR, OCHA and UNICEF have also politicised during the 1990's. Coming from a one-dimensional concept of peacekeeping in which consent of the warring parties, impartiality and minimalist interference were paramount, the great geopolitical changes of the early 1990s have encouraged United Nations member states to allow for much more robust United Nations operations; such as operations carried out in Yugoslavia, Somalia and the Democratic Republic of Congo. In these operations, strongly aided and abetted by military force, politically motivated interference in deeply divided societies with conflict still raging has been increasingly the rule rather than the exception.[28] Like many of the other (non-)governmental organisations nevertheless, the humanitarian principles have been stressed as leading in any action taken.[29]

Once more, this development of blurring the lines of distinction between actors and their principled (or less so) motivation to be present in humanitarian space, also necessitates fundamental thinking on its present-day nature, legal delineation, rules for access, and the level of purity of claimed humanitarian principles. Section 3 will address this development in greater detail.

2.4 Humanitarian organisations and their field of work: extended scope

The moral imperative to help fellow brethren in need is of all times and figures and in all major religions and ethical treatises on the organisation

[26] Chandler, 'The Road to Military Humanitarianism', 4–5; Dennis Dijkzeul and Joost Herman, 'Hooggestemde beginselen en het kleinste kwaad' (Lofty Principles and the Smallest Evil), in Dijkzeul and Herman, *Humanitaire ruimte* (Humanitarian Space), 328–330.

[27] Kess Homan, 'Civiel-militaire relaties in complexe noodsituaties' (Civil-Military Relations in Complex Emergencies), in Dijkzeul and Herman, *Humanitaire ruimte* (Humanitarian Space), 257–279.

[28] Hugo Slim (1995) and James Mayall (2008), both quoted in Collinson and Elhawary, 'Humanitarian Space', 8.

[29] See for example *Statute of the Office of the United Nations High Commissioner for Refugees*, www.unhcr.org/3b66c39e1.html; OCHA's stance www.unocha.org/what-we-do/policy/overview; UNICEF's position, www.unicef.org/emerg/index_32032.html, all accessed 13 August 2013.

of society. Being of a charitable, individual and irregular nature based on the virtue of doing good, a more institutionalised approach originated in the second half of the nineteenth century.[30] The creation of the ICRC in 1863 once more serves as a pivotal moment in time. It has been argued that Henri Dunant acted from a position of individual virtue ethics, but its very creation set out the path to institutionalised duty ethics. Opposed to consequentialist ethics – the imperative to tackle the causes of the endangerment of human dignity and ensuing needs – classic humanitarianism for a hundred and fifty years delineated its activities according to the duty felt to humanise the consequence of conflict, and conflict itself, while not addressing the causes of conflict (as consequential ethics would dictate). Hence, *jus ad bellum* was accepted and for the narrow purpose of mitigation a limited framework of norms and values (IHL and the humanitarian principles) was supported, refined and nurtured. Up to the present day, the ICRC is the staunchest proponent of this humanitarianism driven by duty ethics, explained and justified in the adherence to the principles of humanity, neutrality, impartiality and independence.[31]

After those formative years, many new organisations took emerging norms under IHL and the principles of the ICRC for guidance. Spurred on by moments of great human suffering as a result of conflict, organisations like SCF in 1919, International Rescue Committee (IRC, in 1933), Oxfam (in 1942), Cooperative for Assistance and Relief Everywhere (CARE, in 1945), Médecins Sans Frontiers (MSF, in 1971) and Relief International (in 1991) have been created. The by-now massive commitment (more than 500 organisations)[32] to the 1994 ICRC Code of

[30] Michael Barnett and Thomas G. Weiss, 'Humanitarianism: A Brief History of the Present', in *Humanitarianism in Question: Politics, Power, Ethics*, ed. Michael Barnett and Thomas Weiss (Ithaca: Cornell University Press, 2008), 15–24.

[31] Ibid., 29; Th.A. van Baarda, 'Moral Ambiguities underlying the Laws of Armed Conflict', *Yearbook of International Humanitarian Law* 11 (2010), 3–49; for ICRC's continuous emphasis on its approach to humanitarian work, ICRC, 'The neutral intermediary role of the ICRC: at the heart of humanitarian action', accessed 25 May 2013, www.icrc.org/eng/resources/documents/interview/neutral-intermediary-interview-070708.htm; also MSF could be labelled a duty-ethics-driven organisation; MSF, 'MSF Charter and principles', accessed 25 May 2013, www.msf.org/msf-charter-and-principles; although its policy of témoignage could be labelled consequential ethics.

[32] OCHA, 'OCHA on Message: Humanitarian Principles', accessed 13 June 2013, https://ochanet.unocha.org/p/Documents/OOM-humanitarianprinciples_eng_June12.pdf; ICRC 'Code of Conduct for the International Red Cross and Red Crescent Movement and NGOs in Disaster Relief', *International Federation of Red Cross and Red Crescent Societies*, accessed 13 June 2013, www.ifrc.org/Global/Publications/disasters/code-of-conduct/codeconduct_signatories.pdf.

Conduct in which the classical humanitarian principles are proclaimed to be at the forefront, thus seems indicative of the level of observance of the traditional framework of legal and quasi-legal humanitarian norms.

The number of 500 humanitarian organisations committed to the Code of Conduct is a modest representation of the estimated total figure for 2012: 4,400 humanitarian organisations are listed in ALNAP's humanitarian review of 2012.[33] Evidently, the real change brought about by the post-1991 period is thus not so much continuous adherence to the classical humanitarian norms and principles, but the consequences of increasing numbers of actors in humanitarian space. Two major effects can be discerned.

Firstly, growing numbers of humanitarian NGOs have unwillingly facilitated the politicisation of aid. With rising numbers of organisations competing for funding and governments earmarking increasing amounts of monies for humanitarian window-dressing or active engagement in conflict areas based on political interest, many organisations have ended up being financially and strategically encapsulated by governmental donors.[34] Moreover, financial and strategic closeness to politically motivated actors in humanitarian emergencies has coincided with co-operating with, and the acceptance of, the military as 'just one of the other actors' in humanitarian space, turning a blind eye to the, by definition, non-neutral character of the military. Finally, the urge amidst a sea of competitors to gain first access to victims and generate media attention has led many of the smaller organisations into high-profile activities in conflict areas hitting the spotlights of media attention – and thus of politics – while these organisations' capacities do not match the requirements, and their actions hardly deserve the qualification 'principled', ' professional' and 'effective'.[35]

Secondly, the increase in organisations active in the field of humanitarianism, the competition for visible projects in conflict zones hitting the spotlights of international media attention, access to government funding and the rights-based approach to humanitarianism have resulted in widening the very scope and nature of humanitarian action and its

[33] Active Learning Network for Accountability and Performance in Humanitarian Action (ALNAP), *The State of the Humanitarian System* 2012 (London: ODI, 2012), 28.

[34] Collinson and Elhawary, '*Humanitarian Space*', 8–10.

[35] Abby Stoddard, 'Humanitarian NGOs: Challenges and Trends', *HPG Policy Briefs* 12 (2003), 1–4; Dijkzeul and Herman, 'Hooggestemde beginselen' (Lofty Principles), 331–332.

organisations. A few characterisations of these new roads taken may serve as an example. Even by the 1980s, though more in the 1990s, humanitarian organisations have widened their scope of activities from narrowly defined short-term humanitarian aid to projects of a long-term nature. The distinction between humanitarian and reconstruction/developmental aid has been waning or disappearing completely. While attending to dire human needs, becoming involved also in the redistribution of land, the recreation of livelihoods and contributing to post-conflict transitional justice has not been rare. The rights-based approach has dictated this wider involvement as the proper course to follow, but more often than not humanitarian organisations have been caught up in a situation of being willing to leave after administering emergency aid, but feeling unable to do so since no successor organisation in the field of reconstruction or development had the willingness or the means to show up.[36] Be that as it may, the extended version of humanitarianism has brought along with it the sense of justifiably taking over tasks and responsibilities that normally pertain to the state and/or authorities.[37] The humanitarian organisations have thus engaged in political and social reconstruction, a formidable task that has overstretched the capacity of the long-standing members of the humanitarian community and has attracted many newcomers who cannot always be labelled professional and knowledgeable.[38]

3. Humanitarian space: delineated by law, permeated by reality

Having taken in the dominance of the classical approach in international humanitarianism over the past 150 years, versus the many challenges humanitarianism faces in the twenty-first century as a result of major political changes at the international, national and local level, humanitarian space now becomes the focus of attention. In the following, the compelling impact the classical approach has on the concept of humanitarian space will be outlined. Then, briefly recalling the major changes and challenges occurring in 1991 and after, humanitarian space will be depicted based on the contemporary reality on the ground. A believable argument will be made that we need more mind-sets to delineate humanitarian space next to IHL, IHRL and the humanitarian principles.

[36] Herman and Dijkzeul, 'Current Challenges', 8.
[37] Chandler, 'The Road to Military Humanitarianism', 8.
[38] Herman, 'Humanitaire bewegingsruimte' (Humanitarian Space for Maneuvre), 71.

It was Daniel Thürer, professor in law, and long-standing member of the ICRC, who has created the metaphor of a pyramid to lucidly explain the law-based, classical point of view of the space in which humanitarian action takes place. As recently as 2007, graciously referring to Rony Brauman (one of the founders of MSF) who was first in coining the phrase 'humanitarian space/espace humanitaire', Thürer has soundly depicted humanitarian space as it was over the past 150 years and needs to be in forthcoming times.[39]

Thürer has outlined a geometrical abstract figure (a triangle) whose sides are able to enclose physical humanitarian space according to the ICRC's point of view. Thürer observes that the triangle contains hierarchically distinguished goals (furthering the cause of humanity), normative frameworks (laws) and operational principles (the humanitarian principles and the international law mechanisms to enforce compliance with the norms). He stresses that as in ordinary constitutional law systems the component parts are interconnected, from the general (the goals and norms) to the specific (the operational principles). As a consequence, it is not surprising that the three sides are synonymous with the main goals and tools of classical humanitarianism: humanity, IHL, general international law and customary law, and humanitarian principles. This strictly legal set-up is the only framework that makes humanitarian endeavour possible.[40]

Through his metaphor Thürer builds the case that the inside surface of the pyramid – humanitarian space – is only to be entered by humanitarian organisations such as the ICRC, because objectively these are the only ones meeting the criteria and adhering to them. As important, however, is ICRC's and other like-minded humanitarian organisations' continuous and ostentatious practice of adherence to the legal framework for all involved parties to see and believe.[41] Consequently, only actors unremittingly seen to respect the goals of humanitarian action through abiding by the directives creating the pyramid are – based upon consent by the warring parties – allowed to enter humanitarian space and restore human dignity for those affected by conflict. The legal approach to humanitarianism in the twenty-first century also supports ICRC's continued practice; ICRC's continued practice and results – despite setbacks and failures through infractions of the rules by warring parties – supports the unrelenting validity of the legal approach.[42]

[39] Thürer, 'Dunant's Pyramid', 47–61. [40] Ibid., 55. [41] Ibid., 59–60.
[42] Collinson and Elhawary, 'Humanitarian Space', 2.

Finally, and in continuation of the previous, it is important to note that Thürer tries to pre-empt criticism of ICRC's seeming outdatedness given the many challenges and changes in the twenty-first century. In his view, the pyramidal depiction and concrete delineation of humanitarian space is capable of supplanting the axiom that

> modern international humanitarian law is restricted to the basic tenet of the old law of war ... and to fit better with the panoply of international law, dominated as it is today by human rights. The aim of modern international humanitarian law is not simply to prevent excess in time of war . . . The key issue is that of human dignity.[43]

This lengthy quotation – a very impressive key passage in the article – serves the purpose showing that the ICRC according to Thürer adheres to its classical approach, with additions similar to the nature of IHL and the humanitarian principles, because applying the rules of relevant law and the principles remains pertinent also in the twenty-first century. The reference to IHRL especially serves the purpose of underlining the ICRC's adhering to the principle of respect of sovereignty, while allowing for new interpretations of the scope and solidity of sovereignty according to developments in IHRL (treaty-based supervision mechanisms) and other areas of (nascent) law like R2P. Equally interesting is Thürer's argument that humanitarian organisations like those from the United Nations family and MSF share ICRC's 'prototype' of humanitarian space, even though they use different formulas to describe the perimeters of the pyramid.[44]

Juxtaposed to the previous is a perception of humanitarian space that could be seen to be more fitting to the changing political landscape and the many challenges described in section 2 of this chapter. Not brushing aside the relevance of IHL, IHRL and the humanitarian principles, this approach depicts humanitarian space as a more metaphorical area, a fluctuating relatively open space in which the classical parameters of humanitarianism are just one of the influences on the shape this space takes.

In its twenty-first-century shape, challenged by and changed through the many developments since 1991, humanitarian space is to be seen as a complex, relatively open arena in which politics, the military and other armed parties to a conflict, the population and international law all meet and interact, as a result of which humanitarian space is delineated. Each

[43] Thürer, 'Dunant's Pyramid', 59. [44] Ibid., 60.

situation in which humanitarian space is created represents a different shape for these interactions, as a result of which each humanitarian space will fluctuate in content, size and location.[45]

Thea Hilhorst especially, in numerous publications based on empirical research, has convincingly argued why the metaphorical definition of humanitarian space as a complex arena best fits the changed circumstances in the twenty-first century.[46] The complex arena metaphor can meet many challenges: of many new actors in the humanitarian world, as a result of which the principles and motives to justify and delineate humanitarian action continuously differ and depart from the narrow justification under the classical legal approach; of the increased level of influence of politics and the military in humanitarian operations, as a result of which neutrality does not exist objectively, but is mainly in the eye of the beholder; of the fundamentally changed nature of conflict, characterised by localisation, fragmentation, complexity, by quickly (sometimes daily) shifting centres of gravity, and the deliberate targeting of populations and abusing aid and aid organisations, as a result of which humanitarian space materialises there where the opportunity may arise; and of the growing wide variety of operational principles and norms outside the classical framework of IHL and IHRL, being used to justify humanitarian action but challenging the erstwhile hegemony of IHL and IHRL, or interpreting its characteristics differently.

Taking the previous points into consideration, humanitarian space in the twenty-first century should be considered as an arena around and in which a multitude of actors continuously negotiate for the delineation of this space, the conditions for access to it, and the nature and size of the activities in it. The arena is a collection of political and social processes that cannot be defined by law only, but through a much broader spectrum of political, institutional, economical and social norms and values.

[45] Collinson and Elhawary, 'Humanitarian Space', 1–3; Dorothea Hilhorst and Bram J. Jansen, 'Humanitaire ruimte als arena: een perspectief op de alledaags praktijk' (Humanitarian Space as Arena: a Perspective on Everyday Practice) in Dijkzeul and Herman, *Humanitaire Ruimte* (Humanitarian Space), 124–156.

[46] Dorothea Hilhorst and Nadja Schmiemann, 'Humanitarian Principles and Organisational Culture: Everyday Practice in MSF-Holland', *Development in Practice* 12 (2002): 490–500; Dorothea Hilhorst, *Saving Lives or Saving Societies? Realities of Relief and Reconstruction* (Wageningen University Press, 2007); Hilhorst and Jansen, 'Humanitaire ruimte als arena' (Humanitarian Space as Arena), 125–156; Dorothea Hilhorst and Bram J. Jansen, 'Constructing Rights and Wrongs in Humanitarian Action: Contributions from a Sociology of Praxis', *Sociology: The Journal of the British Sociological Association* 46 (2012): 891–905. The remaining paragraphs in this section are based on her findings.

From the original concept of humanitarian space being a mere legal 'product', the modern times demand a perception of it as essentially political in nature, a dynamic relationship of norms (legal but also political), principles (the expanding framework of the various modi operandi of a wide variety of humanitarian organisations) and pragmatic considerations (strategic choice, trading principles for access) that each time shape anew different triangles that can be labelled humanitarian space. The once impregnable legal framework of classical humanitarianism has thus been permeated by developments in twenty-first-century reality.[47]

4. Conclusion

International humanitarian law has a 150-year relationship with humanitarian action, and has been complemented by international human rights law in the latter part of the previous century. Based on legal treaties (the Geneva Conventions, the Additional Protocols and later on the international human rights corpus) and quasi-legal arrangements (the humanitarian principles, codes of conduct, principles of operation), 'legal humanitarianism' has dominated the humanitarian scene. For many organisations, not least the ICRC, clinging on to legal perseverance and purity is the only option to pursue in order to reach out to people in need. For them, despite infractions and setbacks – like the ones most recently witnessed in Libya and Syria – international law and the humanitarian principles are the tool with which humanitarian space is delineated. Humanitarian space is, and remains, a physical area to which humanitarian organisations exclusively have access to address the needs of the victims of conflict and violence, in exchange for a strict adherence to two especially of the humanitarian principles: neutrality and impartiality. Both in IHL and IHRL as well as in the many documents on humanitarian principles created amongst the major humanitarian organisations, reference is made to this quid pro quo, guaranteeing access to people in need based on the consent of the warring parties, who can rest assured that humanitarian action will be non-political in motivation and will not interfere with the military situation. Dunant's pyramid, so aptly framed by Daniel Thürer, remains valid, also in the twenty-first century.

[47] Ibid.; Collinson and Elhawary, 'Humanitarian Space', 3–4.

Numerous developments, especially since the 1990s, have given rise to questions on the lasting validity of classical legal humanitarianism. Both external geopolitical developments and internal changes within the evolution of humanitarianism have permeated humanitarian space, as a result of which the classical approach to humanitarianism seems to have become partially inapplicable and unrealistic. IHL now being accompanied by new international legal instruments as IHRL and R2P, changing the concepts of respect for sovereignty and the essence of neutrality; the changing nature of conflict creating massive complexity and rapidly changing situations; the growing influence of governments and their military apparatus, politicising humanitarianism to the utmost degree; and the rapid rise in numbers of (self-proclaimed) humanitarian organisations with interpretations of goals, norms and principles that differ from the original ICRC one: all these developments seemed to necessitate a different conceptualisation of humanitarian space.

The reconceptualisation of humanitarian space has indeed been created, both by academics and by more operationally oriented organisations. In the twenty-first century, a metaphorical definition of humanitarian space as a complex permeable arena is most appropriate in their eyes. The complex arena approach takes in all the challenges and changes outlined and acknowledges that humanitarian space nowadays is inhabited by a multitude of actors with a variety of motivations and principles who continuously interact and negotiate with one another to shape humanitarian space and to arrange for access and activities. In this depiction influences from politics, socio-economics and law each play their role, supplanting the monopoly of IHL and, later on, IHRL. No less importantly, the arena metaphor helps us to understand the fluctuating present-day nature of humanitarian space, both in content as well as location.

The dominance of the classical – legal – approach over the past 150 years has made it difficult for a sizeable part of the community of humanitarian organisations to embrace the new concept of humanitarian space. Unlike the ICRC, many in practice have already incorporated principles and practices fitting the complex arena depiction of humanitarian space. However, for most of these organisations, ostentatiously clinging on to the legal framework of humanitarianism in order to claim incessant neutrality and impartiality as proof of being free from political poison, in the words of the late ICRC icon Jean Pictet, has been too appealing. It remains to be seen whether the current crisis in Syria will finally take away this appeal.

2

The perils of Dunantism: the need for a rights-based approach to humanitarianism

DIRK SALOMONS

1. Introduction

The Dunantist values of impartiality, neutrality and independence have held the humanitarian community in their spell for over 150 years. This chapter will argue that this spell needs to be broken, in order to remove the imaginary and even destructive roadblocks that now bar the way to effective and compassionate humanitarian aid.

These Dunantist values are based on specific assumptions that were valid on the battlefield in Solferino: wars were between states, combatants were clearly identifiable, and war was an interruption of an otherwise stable societal framework. When these values were further defined and formalised in the 1949 Geneva conventions, they included a commitment to protect civilians, based on the assumption that states behave in a civilised manner, that non-state actors are only marginally relevant, and that states can be trusted to provide security, allowing humanitarians to focus on relief. This normative framework has since lost all relevance.

This chapter will argue that these assumptions and values, now broadly applied and embedded in international normative frameworks such as the 'Sphere Project', are ill-matched with today's reality, and that their Dunantist roots stand in the way of an effective response to the displacement of vulnerable people.

The definition of a 'humanitarian crisis' itself is suspect: an argument will be made that humanitarian action glorifies the victims of sudden-onset crises, while neglecting the victims of chronic global poverty, and that the borders between relief and development need to be demolished – institutionally, financially, and conceptually. Dunantist values stand in the way: they are in fact strategies that may or may not be effective. Against this backdrop, this chapter will examine the potentially negative impact of blind adherence to impartiality, neutrality and independence in complex emergencies, and propose the introduction of an alternative 'colour coding' approach that identifies the divergent true value systems of humanitarian actors: a typology of a multifaceted cast.

It will conclude by advocating a different common normative framework for humanitarian actors, which will allow them, each coming from a different angle, to do what they do best: use the rich toolkit of human rights conventions. It will briefly describe the potential practical implications of such a rights-based approach – responding 'contextually' to the needs of those whose rights have been most blatantly violated, or who have been most visibly deprived of such rights. This will also reinforce programmes that bridge relief and development.

2. The unique context of Dunantist values

In the struggle for Italian unification, the battle of Solferino (24 June 1859) was the decisive episode: the French, headed by emperor Napoleon III, faced the Austrians in a sudden confrontation, which neither party had planned. Early in the morning, 300,000 men began slaughtering each other, and by late afternoon, there were 6,000 dead and 40,000 wounded. Medical services on both sides were overwhelmed, and only the wounded who were still able to walk made it to the nearest village in search of food, water and basic care. The rest were left behind in agony.

'I was a mere tourist with no part whatsoever in this great conflict; but it was my rare privilege, through an unusual train of circumstances, to witness the moving scenes that I have resolved to describe.'[1] Thus the Swiss businessman and charitable activist Henri Dunant begins his narrative of the horrendous suffering inflicted on the conflict's wounded survivors, and of the heroic measures he took to mobilise the entire village in support of those victims, for three days and three nights, in the Chiesa Maggiore and the narrow streets of Castiglione. 'Straw had been spread in the streets, courtyards and squares, and here and there, wooden shelters had been thrown up.'[2] One may wonder about Dunant's choice of itinerary as a tourist, but his arrival in Castiglione at the height of the conflict had long-lasting repercussions. In his memoirs of these traumatic events, which were published in 1862, Dunant appealed for the creation of relief societies with nurses to care for the wounded, and an

[1] Henri Dunant, *A Memory of Solferino* (Geneva: ICRC, 1986; original French edition 1862), 4.

[2] Ibid., 14.

international agreement to protect the volunteer helpers. This appeal found a broad audience.

In 1863, a private Committee of Five, chaired by Dunant, organised a conference in Geneva to which sixteen countries sent representatives. The conference recommended that in wartime the belligerent parties declare their lazarets and hospitals neutral, inviolate ground, and that the same inviolate status be given to medical personnel, as well as to the wounded themselves. This resulted in the creation of an International Committee for the Wounded, and when the Swiss Federal Council convened a diplomatic conference in the following year, it drew up a *Geneva Convention for the Amelioration of the Condition of the Wounded in Armies in the Field*, reflecting the principles set out by Dunant's committee, and adopting as its emblem the Swiss flag with colours reversed. The Committee then evolved into the International Committee of the Red Cross (ICRC). In 1929, prisoners of war were added to the persons of concern under the Convention.

It was only after the massive civilian casualties of the Second World War, and particularly the bombing of Rotterdam, London, Dresden, and ultimately Hiroshima and Nagasaki, that the protection of civilians as well was enshrined in a new set of Geneva Conventions, adopted in 1949, and that provisions were added addressing armed conflict not of an international character, in other words, civil war.[3]

These legal provisions all had as their common ground a set of principles advocated by Henri Dunant and his Committee: neutrality, humane conduct, impartiality in the execution of humanitarian operations, and independence of external influences on the part of those rendering humanitarian services.[4]

In order to ensure that the ICRC would benefit from such an independent status, the Geneva Conventions have given it a uniquely hybrid form: it is structured under Swiss law like a non-governmental organisation (NGO), with an independent Board, but it benefits from privileges and immunities usually only given to international intergovernmental organisations, with both staff (in their official functions) and premises

[3] See the *Geneva Convention Relative to the Protection of Civilian Persons in Time of War*, as well as the two protocols added in 1977, and particularly Protocol II, which deals with non-international armed conflicts.

[4] See, for these normative criteria, the 1864 *Convention for the Amelioration of the Condition of the Wounded in Armies in the Field*, ICRC, accessed 8 November 2011, www.icrc.org/eng/resources/documents/misc/57jnvr.htm.

inviolate to national authorities. While it receives funds from governments, a 'firewall' ensures that they have no say when it comes to ICRC policy or operations.[5]

It is noteworthy that these criteria of humanity, neutrality, impartiality and independence were all developed under highly specific conditions: armed conflict waged by established states, among clearly identifiable uniformed combatants acting under a clear chain of command, in a political setting where war was a temporary aberration from an otherwise stable and well-regulated society, subject to the rule of law.

How is it that these highly specific norms, created for very specific conditions, regulated by a specialised and unique humanitarian organisation, over time became the generic values for the entire aid industry, even when conflict is waged by unruly and lawless militias, fomenting civil wars, in societies where rule of law is at best a paper fiction or a long-term aspiration?

3. Emerging normative frameworks after the cold war

During the cold war, the ICRC played a major role in alleviating the suffering of the many civilians caught between the anvils and hammers of the proxy wars that ravaged much of South East Asia and Africa. In the areas under the control or influence of the western powers, a number of other NGOs provided disaster relief, and even worked on local development and early recovery programmes. When, at the end of the cold war, the Soviets and their allies withdrew from their zones of influence (pulling Cuban militias out of Angola, withholding funding from the Marxist government in Mozambique, agreeing to a peace accord in Cambodia), and when the western powers thus also lost interest in these battlefields (dropping Jonas Savimbi's UNITA movement in Angola, cutting all shipments of weapons and money to Renamo's insurgents in Mozambique), many of these conflicts were localised, and carried on with funding from the exploitation of natural resources – oil and timber for established governments, 'portable lootables' such as diamonds and coltan for rebel movements.[6]

[5] *Statutes of the International Committee of the Red Cross*, ICRC, accessed 8 November 2011, www.icrc.org/eng/resources/documents/misc/icrc-statutes-080503.htm.

[6] For a thoughtful discussion of this transformation, see Mats R. Berdal and David M. Malone, *Greed and Grievance: Economic Agendas in Civil Wars* (Boulder: Lynne Rienner Publishers, 2000).

At the end of the cold war also, as regional conflicts flared up, the United Nations General Assembly decided to strengthen the organisation's capacity to respond to complex emergencies and natural disasters by revisiting its decision, taken in 1971 under resolution 2816, to create a Disaster Relief Coordinator position. It elevated this function to the level of Under-Secretary-General, created an Inter-Agency Standing Committee to bring in non-United Nations partners, and established a Department of Humanitarian Affairs to provide institutional support.[7] It is interesting to note that the resolution delineating these decisions invokes the need to provide humanitarian assistance 'in accordance with the principles of humanity, neutrality and impartiality' (Article 2), while at the same time stressing the need to respect the 'sovereignty, territorial integrity and national unity of States', and emphasising that 'humanitarian assistance should be provided with the consent of the affected country and in principle on the basis of an appeal by the affected country' (Article 3). This approach in fact politicised the entire aid process, and has had negative repercussions across the years, most recently described by David Kirkpatrick of the *New York Times* in an article, dated early 2013, about the lack of assistance in some parts of Syria during the violent civil war there: 'The biggest obstacle blocking aid from rebel-held areas is the United Nations requirement that its relief agencies follow Mr Assad's rules – which limit access to opposition territory – as long as the international assembly recognises his government'.[8]

In the early nineties, as the United Nations speculated on a post-cold war 'peace dividend', the then Secretary-General, Boutros Boutros-Ghali, presented an analysis of the challenges to development based on the premise that absence of peace was at the root of global poverty, and that 'most people must strive to achieve their development against a background of past, present or threatened conflict'. He therefore saw a direct connection between conflict management and peace-building: 'Because the United Nations is active at the forefront of humanitarian aid, refugee assistance, and the range of peace operations, it is deeply and inextricably involved in peace as a fundamental dimension of development'.[9] From this perspective, humanitarian aid becomes part of a continuum,

[7] See General Assembly resolution (A/RES/46/182) 19 December 1991.

[8] David D. Kirkpatrick, 'In Parts of Syria, Lack of Assistance "Is a Catastrophe"', *New York Times*, 8 March 2013.

[9] Boutros Boutros-Ghali, *An Agenda for Development* (New York: United Nations, 1995), 20.

embedded in broader development strategies, no longer truly neutral or independent – and this is not necessarily a bad thing.

By the last decade of the twentieth century, therefore, non-governmental humanitarian and development actors suddenly found themselves in a rapidly changing ideological and political environment, and thus they flocked to the ICRC for guidance. This led, in 1994, to the establishment of the 'Code of Conduct for the International Red Cross Movement and NGOs in Disaster Relief', setting out standards of behaviour not only for the ICRC and the many national Red Cross and Red Crescent organisations, but also for a group of signatory NGOs.[10] Most of these sponsoring NGOs had a religious background, with the exception of Oxfam, and they were actually not that many, given the plethora of NGOs emerging like mushrooms in the fertile ground of post-cold war optimism.[11]

The Code of Conduct stressed the primacy of the humanitarian imperative, the right to humanitarian assistance and the obligation to provide it. Aid should be given based on needs alone, impartially, without adverse distinction of any kind. Aid should not be used to further a particular political or religious standpoint. The signatories agreed not to act as instruments of government foreign policy. Accountability would reach out in two directions: to those who received assistance and to those who provided the resources. This was very much in line with the specific ICRC mandate.

During the year that these norms were codified, genocide occurred in Rwanda, and subsequently, a massive aid operation brought relief and sustenance to the perpetrators of genocide and their dependents, two million in all, who had fled from Rwanda into eastern Zaire, once they were brought to heel by an army of Rwandan exiles. Tens of thousands of these refugees died as waterborne diseases ravaged the camps, and in the absence of an international military force to contain the murderous elements among the refugees, the aid provided in fact enabled the perpetrators of genocide to regroup and create a military structure that plagues the eastern Congo to this day. The operational and moral failures of this experience haunted the international community, and an

[10] 'Code of Conduct for the International Red Cross and Red Crescent Movement and NGOs in Disaster Relief', ICRC, 31 December 1994, www.icrc.org/eng/resources/documents/publication/p1067.htm.

[11] The NGO signatories were Caritas Internationalis, Catholic Relief Services, Lutheran World Federation, The World Council of Churches, and Oxfam.

evaluation was carried out to identify lessons learned, and to make recommendations.[12] Its findings, which came out in 1997, were devastating, and pointed at an uncoordinated and unprofessional group of humanitarian actors, lacking both professional standards and a clear moral compass.

This, in turn, brought the humanitarian aid agencies together, and led to a massive effort to come to common norms and standards, culminating in the 'Sphere Project', initiated in 1997, and leading to the publication in 2000 of the Humanitarian Charter as well as a set of technical norms in the fields of water and sanitation, food security and nutrition, shelter, and health services. The Humanitarian Charter was largely based on the Red Cross Code of Conduct, and all of a sudden there were hundreds of signatories, represented by umbrella organisations such as the United States-based InterAction, the European Voluntary Organisations in Cooperation in Emergencies (VOICE), and the Action by Churches Together (ACT).[13] All of a sudden, also, the Dunantist values embedded in the Red Cross Code of Conduct had become an international normative framework, universally adopted by the (western) humanitarian community, and supported by all the major donors (who had funded the Sphere Project). There was little discussion whether these concepts of humanity, independence, impartiality and neutrality were compatible with the structure and roots of the international aid industry.

4. Don't ask, don't tell: the erosion of 'humanity'

The Dunantist value of humanity conjures up images of the compassion and gallantry shown by the aid-workers in Castiglione in the days after the slaughter of Solferino, as described by Dunant:

> 'I don't want to die, I don't want to die!' shouted a Grenadier of the Guard fiercely. This man who, three days earlier, had been a picture of health and strength, was now wounded to death. He fully realised that his hours were inexorably counted, and strove and struggled against that grim certainty. I spoke to him, and he listened. He allowed himself to be

[12] DANIDA, *The Joint Evaluation of Emergency Assistance to Rwanda* (JEEAR), accessed 8 November 2011, www.um.dk/danida/evalueringsrapporter/1997-=_rwanda.

[13] For a detailed account, see Margaret Buchanan-Smith, *How the Sphere Project Came Into Being: A Case Study of Policy Making in the Humanitarian Aid Sector and the Relative Influence of Research* (London: Overseas Development Institute, 2003), Working Paper 215.

> soothed, comforted and consoled, to die at last with the straightforward simplicity of a child.[14]

This demonstration of deep humanity, of compassion, of face-to-face communication between the giver of aid and its recipient, this display of solidarity, provides an example and a norm that is hard to emulate these days. Aid organisations largely work to deliver volume, trying to meet the needs of large refugee populations or displaced victims of conflict, managing camps where tens of thousands, if not hundreds of thousands, are crowded together, and where aid-workers rarely interact with their beneficiaries. Frequently also, the actual contact with the beneficiaries is maintained by subcontractors, often local NGOs, while the international staff remain in their offices. More and more, we are confronted with aid delivery by 'remote control', such as the aid programmes for Somalia, managed out of Nairobi, that were meant to address the major famine in the Horn of Africa during the second half of 2011, or most of the aid programmes in Afghanistan and Iraq since the escalation of violence against aid-workers there, now a decade ago.[15] The question then arises: does it actually make any difference whether food is distributed by a commercial firm, such as Dyncorp, or by an NGO? Are we morally responsible for the security risks we pass on to the local staff whom we hire in order to stay safe ourselves?

For the staff working in aid organisations, this creates a moral dilemma: should they still see themselves as 'humanitarians', and thus constantly feel that they are falling short of enacting the ideal humanity, that is, the ability to express compassion as one human being to another? Or should they just accept that they are public servants, delivering services, and thus contributing to the global common good? This dilemma is particularly challenging for the staff of religious NGOs, who make an effort to express the essence of their faith through charitable actions, but who frequently find themselves reduced to cogs in a complex international bureaucracy.[16]

Beyond this, there is a larger concern when we flaunt humanitarian solidarity and compassion. What is so special about people who draw the attention of the media and the international community because they

[14] Dunant, *A Memory of Solferino,* 16.

[15] Abby Stoddard, Adele Harmer and Katherine Haver, 'Providing Aid in Insecure Environments: Trends in Policy and Operations', *HPG Briefing Paper* 24 (2006): 1–4.

[16] For a discussion of the religious humanitarian imperative, see Cardinal Avery Dulles SJ, 'Christianity and Humanitarian Action', in *Traditions, Values and Humanitarian Action,* ed. Kevin M. Cahill MD (New York: Fordham University Press, 2003), 5–20.

happen to be caught in the limelight as earthquakes and floods upended their homes, as outbursts of violence forced them to flee, or as protracted droughts affected their livelihoods? We measure their mortality and morbidity rates, we rush to revive their malnourished babies, and mobilise resources for their well-being through media campaigns and globally broadcast celebrity benefits. But what about the chronic poor, the 'bottom billion' so convincingly described by Paul Collier, who lead equally miserable lives, growing up stunted and intellectually maimed because of malnutrition, dying in childbirth, suffering from endemic diseases, constantly worrying where their next meal will come from, living in horrendous slums, without clean water or sanitation, without decent schools, without physical security or the rule of law?[17] Are they not of 'humanitarian' concern? What are the limits of our 'humanity'?

5. The illusion of impartiality

Picking through the wounded on a battlefield, as in the days of Solferino, it is possible to carry out a triage, ranking those most likely to benefit from medical assistance, and it is possible to do so without bias in terms of nationality, race, gender, political convictions – looking beyond the colour of the uniforms at the wounded individual, now *hors de combat*, no longer a belligerent. Can this principle of impartiality be carried over into the practice of humanitarian aid? It would, first of all, to be absolutely fair, require a methodology whereby we could compare relative needs on a global scale, assessing the relative value of helping flood victims in Pakistan versus providing food aid for the victims of famine in East Africa, so that we can judiciously allocate our resources accordingly. Such a methodology does not exist, and even if it did, political considerations would trump any efforts at equity.[18]

It is obvious, to illustrate this gap, that impartiality was not a consideration in deciding the levels of aid to be given to the refugees who fled Kosovo at a time that the needs in Sierra Leone and the Democratic Republic of Congo might have been equally pressing. In Kosovo, in 1999, the United Nations spent 207 dollars for each affected person; in Sierra

[17] For a vivid description of inhumane global poverty, see Paul Collier, *The Bottom Billion* (New York: Oxford University Press, 2007).

[18] For a thorough discussion of the weaknesses of the current needs-assessment methodologies in humanitarian crises, see James Darcy and Charles-Antoine Hoffmann, 'According to Need? Needs Assessment and Decision-making in the Humanitarian Sector', *HPG Report* 15 (2003): 1–71.

Leone's civil war, 16 dollars for each person; in the upheavals destroying the Democratic Republic of Congo, 8 dollars.[19] This was not an anomaly. The best yardstick for global humanitarian needs is probably the Consolidated Appeals Process introduced by the United Nations in 1992, at the time that it created its Department for Humanitarian Affairs, later transformed into the Office for the Coordination of Humanitarian Affairs (OCHA). The Consolidated Appeals Process (CAP) is much more than an appeal for money. It is a tool used by aid organisations to plan, implement and monitor their activities jointly. Working together in the world's crisis regions, they produce joint needs assessments, which they present to the international community and donors. Speaking with a common voice, United Nations agencies and NGOs have been able to raise funds for immediate action, demand greater protection, get better access to vulnerable populations, and work more effectively with governments and other actors. Since 1992, well over one hundred donor countries have provided more than 30 billion dollars for 244 appeals to address the needs of people in more than 50 countries and regions.[20]

OCHA's Financial Tracking Service gives an accurate overview of the outcome of these appeals. The table below provides an overview of some of the major consolidated appeals and flash appeals conducted in 2012, showing the wide discrepancy in the levels of coverage:[21]

Country	*Requirement*	*Funding*	*% Covered*
Afghanistan	$ 558,551,322	$ 222,451,177	40%
DR of the Congo	$ 791,331,026	$ 569,139,020	72%
Haiti	$ 151,080,810	$ 69,876,546	46%
Liberia	$ 97,912,181	$ 37,229,017	38%
Rep. of South Sudan	$ 1,176,892,213	$ 796,697,606	68%
Sudan	$ 1,051,018,271	$ 581,507,297	55%
Zimbabwe	$ 238,444,169	$ 203,938,526	86%

[19] Larry Thompson, Director of Advocacy for Refugees International, 'Humanitarian Emergencies: Why Does Kosovo Get More Aid Than the Congo?', Paper for the International Council of Voluntary Agencies Conference on NGOs in a Changing World Order, Geneva, 14–15 February 2003.

[20] 'Consolidated Appeal Process', OCHA, accessed 8 November 2011, www.unocha.org/cap/about-the-cap/faqs.

[21] OCHA Financial Tracking Service, Consolidated and Flash Appeals 2012, Summary of Requirements and Pledges/Contributions by affected country/region, accessed 13 April 2013, http://fts.unocha.org, table ref. 21.

It is hard to explain the donors' varied response to these appeals. The percentage of needs covered varies from 38 per cent for the victims of the continuing instability in Liberia to 86 per cent for the people affected by the food scarcity in Zimbabwe – what is the rationale for such a discrepancy? The level of media coverage is certainly a consideration, as is the political weight given by the donors to the need to create stability in the affected area. The image of the country in crisis may also play a role, or the level of empathy it can generate. There are also many 'forgotten crises' that have just disappeared from the radar screen of fund-raising efforts – who still worries about the many Burmese refugees trapped on the border of Thailand? The two million Iraqi refugees hiding all over the Middle East? They do not appear in the United Nations' overview of 2012 appeals.

At the country level, impartiality has also to give way for more practical factors – ease of access being one of them, the donors' habit of 'earmarking' their contributions another one. Far too often, donors specify that their money may only be used for one specific type of beneficiaries – be it in a region such as Darfur (at the expense of the needs registered in Blue Nile), be it for a specific activity such as water and sanitation (while leaving huge funding gaps for shelter), be it for a certain group such as women and children (at the expense of programmes to demobilise former combatants, for whom assistance is rare). None of these preferences are needs-based, but they do reflect the political choices made by donors, reflecting their national interests and priorities.[22] Impartiality is definitely not a criterion that carries much clout – stinginess in the levels of aid may be the most common denominator.

Subject: Full text of the Al-Shabaab ban notice to aid agencies

28 November 2011

In the Name of Allah the Most Beneficent, the Most Merciful:

OSAFA Fact-finding Committee Conducts Organisation Performance Appraisal. After a meticulous year-long review and investigation into the operations of the organisations currently working in Somalia, a fact-finding committee assigned by the Office for Supervising the Affairs of Foreign Agencies (OSAFA) has documented a fully comprehensive report, through highly credible internal as well as external sources, detailing the illicit activities and misconducts of some of the organisations.

[22] Once more, for a detailed discussion of these anomalies, see Darcy and Hoffmann, 'According to need?', 1–71.

(*cont.*)

In response to the findings of the committee, OSAFA has decided to permanently revoke the permissions of the following organisations to operate inside Somalia: Office of the United Nations High Commissioner for Refugees (UNHCR), World Health Organisation (WHO), United Nations Children's Fund (UNICEF), United Nations Population Fund (UNFPA), United Nations Office for Project Services (UNOPS), Food Security and Nutrition Analysis Unit (FSNAU), Norwegian Refugee Council (NRC), Danish Refugee Council (DRC), Concern, Norwegian Church Aid (NCA), Cooperazione Internazionale (COOPI), Swedish African Welfare Alliance (SAWA), German Agency For Technical Cooperation (GTZ), Action Contre la Faim (ACF), Solidarity, Saacid.

Apart from the collective misappropriation of funds and public trust in their operations, the following organisations were found to be:

- Generating and collecting data through dubious programmes under the guise of demographic surveys, vaccinations reports, demining surveys, nutrition analyses and population censuses.
- Using field data and analyses for dishonest policies and programmes other than poverty reduction, humanitarian aid, provision of life opportunities and development of sustainable living conditions.
- Working with international bodies to foster secularism, immorality and the degrading values of democracy in an Islamic country.
- Some organisations were found to be collaborating with trans-national ecumenical churches and acting as platforms for proselytising young, susceptible and often impoverished Muslim children.
- Conveying communications and disseminating information regarding the activities of the Muslims and particularly the Mujahideen.
- Financing, aiding and abetting subversive groups seeking to destroy the basic tenets of Islamic penal system.
- Persistently galvanising the local population against the full establishment of Islamic Shari′ah system.
- Lacking complete political detachment and neutrality with regard to the conflicting parties in Somalia, thereby intensifying the instability and insecurity gripping the nation as a whole.
- Undermining the livelihoods and cultural values of the population through the pervasive practice of corruption and bribery as means of operation.
- Working vigorously in partnership with several organisations in order to exploit the country of its natural resources.
- Acting as an impediment to the people's ability to reach long-term sustainability through the preservation and management of their natural resources in a self-determined manner.

(*cont.*)

- Amplifying the refugee crisis in the country and failing to implement durable solutions that satisfactorily resolve the suffering of internally displaced refugees.
- Promoting the fragmentation of the local population through the pursuance of tribal associations in their social interactions and partnerships.

In the light of these findings, OSAFA shall henceforth continue to dispatch a yearly fact-finding committee to evaluate and appraise the performance of all the organisations operating inside Somalia. Any organisation found to be supporting or actively engaged in activities deemed detrimental to the attainment of an Islamic State or performing duties other than that which it formally proclaims will be banned immediately without prior warning.

Source: Office for Supervising the Affairs of Foreign Agencies (OSAFA) 'Safeguarding the welfare of the Muslim Ummah'

6. The pitfalls of neutrality

The concept of 'neutrality' as a prerequisite for humanitarian action may be the most toxic obstacle to the effective delivery of assistance to people emerging from a humanitarian crisis. While it serves the ICRC well, given its unique mandate under the Geneva conventions, it defies the reality that most humanitarian actors can be clearly identified with an interest group or a less than universal value system.

The very sophisticated analysis presented by an Al-Shabaab 'fact-finding committee', reproduced in the text-box above, illustrates (in an extreme form) the high level of distrust that many aid recipients in the Global South harbour when confronted with western aid organisations. Particularly striking is their description of aid programmes as efforts to destroy livelihoods, spy on communities, proselytise, and spread immorality. Clearly, to these 'beneficiaries', the Dunantist mantra of independence, neutrality and impartiality rings hollow.

Thus the recipients' ability to assess the political and ideological forces behind the aid programmes being offered to them should not be underestimated.[23] They may be poor and displaced, but they are also critical,

[23] See Ian Buruma and Avishai Margalit, *Occidentalism: The West in the Eyes of Its Enemies* (New York: Penguin Press, 2004). They describe the deep cultural and religious divides that have fuelled an 'anti-western virus' and explain the fear shared by many in the global

often connected to a range of social media, and even able to manipulate the media from their perspective. It would therefore be much more effective if the various humanitarian actors working in crisis zones were to make it very clear where they are coming from (literally and figuratively), who funds them, what they believe, and what their intentions are.

One could actually, for reasons of transparency when dealing with 'populations of concern', or 'beneficiaries', introduce a system of colour coding:

- *White.* The ICRC, truly detached from governmental influence, and endowed with a unique mandate to work in conflict zones under the provisions of the Geneva conventions. Its neutrality is rarely questioned.
- *Green.* The tapestry of organisations working within the United Nations system: those with a 'pure' humanitarian mandate, such as OCHA, World Food Programme (WFP) and UNHCR, those with a broader mandate that includes humanitarian action – e.g., UNICEF, UNFPA, International Organisation for Migration (IOM), even the United Nations Environmental Programme (UNEP) – and those who work on the fringe of humanitarian operations, often emphasising early warning or early recovery – e.g. the Food and Agriculture Organisation (FAO). These are not neutral, but they derive their positions from decisions taken by the United Nations Security Council. In peace operations, this usually implies that these positions are determined by the Council's definition of which groups represent a threat to international peace and security, or which government it recognises.[24] The introduction of so-called Integrated Missions has further diminished the space between the political and the humanitarian arms of the United Nations: humanitarian action is fully embedded in a 'coherent

south that the aid organisations are merely a 'fifth column' of a western onslaught, meant to destroy their culture and their values.

[24] For a detailed discussion of heightened aid instrumentalisation, see Antonio Donini and Ian Smillie, *The Golden Fleece* (Boulder: Kumarian Press, 2012). Examples of the UN's lack of neutrality in humanitarian crises abound. One may recall the UN's reluctance to provide humanitarian assistance to the adherents of the Revolutionary United Front during the civil war in Sierra Leone, or, quite recently, as David Kirkpatrick noted in a *New York Times* article on 8 March 2013, the inability of the UN to provide aid in rebel-held areas during the civil war in Syria without the permission of the government, resulting in a very uneven allocation of aid resources. 'The government, whether you like it or not, is still the government', said the OCHA spokesman cited in the article (see also Kirkpatrick, 'In Parts of Syria').

support strategy', linking the 'different dimensions of peace-building (political, development, humanitarian, human rights, rule of law, social and security aspects)'.[25]

- *Blue.* The wide range of humanitarian programmes associated with regional organisations, first of all the European Union's ECHO, but also the increasingly active humanitarian operations of the African Union, the Arab League, and the Association of East Asian Nations (ASEAN). While these tend to focus on the devastation caused by natural disasters, they often find that such disasters occur in conflict zones, requiring them to take a political stand (e.g., ASEAN's soothing role in responding to cyclone Nargis in Myanmar, when the United Nations were denied access,[26] and when the foreign minister of France, Bernard Kouchner, pleaded for an armed humanitarian intervention[27]). These regional humanitarian actors all reflect the political stance and priorities of their framing organisation.
- *Orange.* The wide range of humanitarian/development entities operating as part of a government's foreign aid programmes: the United States' Office of Foreign Disaster Assistance, part of USAID; the United Kingdom's Department for International Development (DfID); Ireland's Irish Aid; the Canadian International Development Agency, and so on and so forth. Their allegiances and priorities are clear and unambiguous. Recently, non-western donors have entered the humanitarian scene, such as Saudi Arabia, China, Brazil, and Turkey. They also each have their own normative framework, quite distinct from the Dunantist principles.[28]

[25] UN Secretary-General, 'Guidance on Integrated Missions' (9 February 2006), illuminating a previous directive of 11 December 2002 on the relations among senior officials at the country level (United Nations internal document). On the one hand, this guidance note, in § 10, requires the Special Representative of the Secretary-General (SRSG) to 'uphold humanitarian principles (as outlined in GA resolution 46/182)'; at the same time, humanitarian independence is severely constrained by the provisions of §14, where the SRSG 'may request a given agency to re-orient its planned interventions in line with the broad strategic objectives of the mission'.

[26] 'ASEAN's role in the Cyclone Nargis response: implications, lessons and opportunities', HPN, accessed 8 November 2011, www.odihpn.org/humanitarian-exchange-magazine/issue-41/aseans-role-in-the-cyclone-nargis-response-implications-lessons-and-opportunities.

[27] Bernard Kouchner, 'Burma', *Le Monde,* 20 May 2008.

[28] See, inter alia, Andrea Binder and Claudia Meier, 'Opportunity knocks: why non-western donors enter humanitarianism and how to make the best of it', *International Review of the Red Cross* 93 (2011): 1135–1149.

- *Red*. Those secular non-governmental organisations that keep their distance from intergovernmental bodies such as the United Nations, and from national governments, no matter what their politics are: Médicins sans Frontieres (MSF) is prominent, with its national chapters raising money from the public at large to fund their operations; the Oxfam movement also immediately comes to mind. Their independence from governmental funding allows them to speak truth to power, and to operate in areas where less trusted agencies are barred.[29]
- *Yellow*. Non-governmental organisations that are largely funded by national governments. These tend to be a major presence among the humanitarian actors. Some of them are financed by the Gulf States, others by members of the Organisation for Economic Cooperation and Development (OECD). Some of them, like the United Kingdom's Save the Children, receive funding from more than a dozen governmental and intergovernmental sources, adding up to some 49 per cent of annual income (2011 data).[30] This gives them relative room for independent programming. Others are less fortunate. A quick look at the financial reports of some large NGOs based in the United States, for example, shows how in 2012 the International Rescue Committee received 247 million dollars in government grants out of a total 388 million dollars income (63 per cent),[31] while CARE International, in 2011, received 390 million dollars from the United States government, out of a total income that year amounting to 592 million dollars (66 per cent).[32] One could argue that a democratically elected government should not be seen as a 'partisan' donor – that is the 'Wilsonian' perspective going back to the days when the League of Nations was created, when states still could be seen as moral actors. The reality today, however, is less benign. NGOs are now asked to support military 'hearts and minds' operations with all last pretence of neutrality dropped. In a very thoughtful article, Peter Dula, a member of the

[29] To get a sense of the challenges of acting morally while trying to save lives, read Claire Magone, Michael Neuman and Fabrice Weissman, *Humanitarian Negotiations Revealed: The MSF Experience* (New York: Columbia University Press, 2011).

[30] 'A chance for every child: our Trustees' report and Financial Statementes 2011', Save the Children, accessed 13 April 2013, www.savethechildren.org.uk/resources/online-library/chance-every-child-our-trustees-report-and-financial-statements-2011.

[31] 'Financial information and Annual Report', IRC, accessed 13 April 2013, www.rescue.org/about/financial-information.

[32] 'CARE International Annual Report 2011', CARE International, accessed 13 April 2013, www.care-international.org/Annual-Report/annual-report.html.

Mennonite Central Committee, reflects on the dilemmas caused by this level of dependence on governmental largesse:

> Some of you will recall a couple of quotes that are now infamous in the aid industry. Firstly, Colin Powell in October 2001: 'I am serious about making sure we have the best relationship with NGOs who are such a force multiplier for us and such an important part of our combat team.' Later, in June 2003, Andrew Natsios, USAID boss and former World Vision director said that 'NGOs are an arm of the US government.' Natsios also threatened to 'personally tear up their contracts and find new partners' if they didn't get in line. Some NGOs complied with little resistance. Others were horrified at what they were being asked to do. Even so, the simple fact that Powell and Natsios have that impression is very revealing. The few conscientious NGOs were horrified not just by what they were being asked to do, but by the awareness that Powell and Natsios' 'misconceptions' were rooted in something real. They understood that they bore some responsibility for the very fact that NGOs were so perceived. Such comments threw an overdue spotlight on the soft underbelly of the humanitarian enterprise.[33]

- *Purple.* This might be the best colour to identify the wide array of religious NGOs, covering virtually all denominations, and originating in both western and non-western societies. They are all driven by a vision of humanitarian action shaped by the imperatives of their faith, some of them inclusive, others less so, but in setting their programme priorities, they will often seek out like-minded communities, areas where their aid might win souls, or opportunities to demonstrate the practical implications of their vision to a broader public. Here one encounters NGOs such as Islamic Relief (United Kingdom), American Jewish World Service, Catholic Relief Services, or the large Christian conglomerate World Vision International (with an annual budget of well over three billion US dollars, and a mission statement that emphasises its goal of 'working with the poor and oppressed to promote human transformation, seek justice, and bear witness to the good news of the Kingdom of God').[34]

[33] Peter Dula, Iraq Program Coordinator, 'Constantine, Colonialism and the NGOs', *Mennonite Central Committee,* 2007, accessed 8 November 2011, www.gordon.edu/ccs/usaspeakers/peterdula.

[34] World Vision, 'Financial Accountability', accessed 13 April 2013, www.worldvision.org/content.nsf/about/why-donate.

It may be a while before this system of colour coding has been accepted by all humanitarian aid organisations, until it has affected the design of their t-shirts and their vehicles, and has been explained to all potential beneficiaries in a series of multicultural PowerPoints, but it may not be beyond reason to expect all actors in humanitarian crises to show their true colours in communicating with the communities whose suffering they try to alleviate.

7. Beyond neutrality: early recovery makes it impossible to stay above the fray

In 2003 the government of Sweden convened a meeting to discuss good humanitarian donorship, during which a set of Principles and Good Practice of Humanitarian Donorship were agreed upon. The meeting was attended by representatives from sixteen donor governments as well as the European Commission, the OECD, the International Red Cross and Red Crescent Movement, NGOs, and academics. The twenty-three Principles and Good Practices defined by the group provide both a framework to guide official humanitarian aid and a mechanism for encouraging greater donor accountability. These principles, for the first time in donor history, firmly acknowledge that humanitarian action is not just about saving lives and alleviating suffering, but that it '*includes the protection of civilians* and those no longer taking part in hostilities, and the provision of food, water and sanitation, shelter, health services and other terms of assistance, undertaken for the benefit of affected people and *to facilitate the return to normal lives and livelihoods*' (author's emphasis).

The elements of 'protection' and of 'early recovery' both represent a level and a kind of engagement that require a choice of partners at the local, regional and even state level, an involvement in the strategies that bridge relief and development, and a type of programming that, from day one, connects relief operations in acute crises with planning for long-term recovery. In the United Nations' 'cluster system', whereby governmental and non-governmental aid agencies coordinate their humanitarian programmes around a range of thematic areas (such as the 'water-and-sanitation' cluster), there has been an effort to include 'early recovery' as an essential component – for this very reason: the point is to give people their lives back in a secure environment, not just to keep them alive. Neutrality, then, is not the answer, but developing relationships with national entities is, at all levels. Indirectly, our choice of local partners then shows who *we* are, which values *we* bring to the table.

8. Protection: where shame meets impotence

The responsibility to protect has always been the third rail of the humanitarian enterprise. Under the provisions of humanitarian law, non-combatants deserve to be shielded from violence, but in reality, those who have the capacity to protect rarely do so, and those who have a mandate to protect, the humanitarian actors, do not have the capacity. Fiona Terry, in her wonderfully angry book on the international community's ability to look the other way as civilians are being murdered, coined the phrase the 'well-fed dead' – describing the carnage in the Balkans, in Afghanistan, and in post-Rwanda Congo, where the aid community distributed its commodities while violent militias were able to massacre civilians without constraints.[35] Now, more than ten years later, as this is written, nothing has changed. At the beginning of 2013, the body count of civilians killed in Syria's civil war exceeded 60,000. Many more were wounded, millions fled, within the country or across borders. Discussions to create a no-fly zone, in order to cripple the government's capacity to bomb civilian settlements, floundered on 'realistic' objections. The United Nations Security Council provided a comfortable cover for passivity. Relief workers were asked to work without protection, in order to protect the victims of violent conflict.

The United Nations General Assembly's resolution 60/1, affirming that sovereignty is not absolute, and that the international community has an obligation to step in when governments can't (or won't) protect their own, has not had any impact thus far.[36] Countries with the capacity to protect are hiding behind their humanitarian operations, arguing that they are doing all they can, and this raises the question whether humanitarian organisations should time and again accept their role in serving as the fig-leaf covering their donors' pudenda – those parts of the body politic that they should be most ashamed of. Impartiality and neutrality then become embarrassing slogans, making the failure to protect even more obvious.

9. The way forward: towards norms that work universally

There is a growing consensus among the many agencies and institutions working in the field of 'emergency relief' that a different common

[35] Fiona Terry, *Condemned to Repeat? The Paradox of Humanitarian Action* (Ithaca: Cornell University Press 2002).

[36] See General Assembly resolution (A/RES/60/1), 16 September 2005.

platform of values is called for, setting the Dunantist norms aside in favour of a more universal framework. Increasingly, placing humanitarian action squarely within the normative context of human rights is seen as the answer. This in itself is not new. The argument has been made in the past by scholars such as Michael Barnett and Jack Snyder, who have mapped out a matrix of 'humanitarianisms' with variables such as acceptance or defiance of constraints, and of a political or apolitical stance.[37] In taking this approach, programming a humanitarian response then becomes an answer to the question: which human rights have been curtailed or violated as a result of this crisis, and what needs to be done in order to restore access to these rights? Thus programming aid is no longer a matter of charity, but of fairness.

In practice, this requires multidimensional needs assessments, covering political and civil rights as much as economic and social rights – much has been codified in a wide range of instruments, from the *Universal Declaration of Human Rights* and the related covenants to the *Convention on the Rights of the Child*, conventions against discrimination or torture, and even United Nations General Assembly resolutions reaffirming the right to water or to food. Rights established specifically for people affected by conflict, under the provisions of international humanitarian law or refugee conventions, are also part of this normative canon. Once needs have been determined in this way, rights-based programming and implementation follow, with the objective of giving people their lives back, not just warehousing them in perpetual camps. Thus a link is created with early recovery and development efforts, while retaining the unique nature of humanitarian action.

There is much in the Sphere Project's Humanitarian Charter that recalls treaties and customary law on human rights, protection and vulnerability: its annex contains an exhaustive annotated list of all the key documents that inform and support the Charter. Stripped of its Dunantist illusions, much of it remains valid. The next step, however, still needs to be taken: guidelines on how to apply these universal norms and standards against the backdrop of an organisation's individual profile. United Nations agencies cannot do what the ICRC does; World Vision International is not Médecins sans Frontières. But each can shape its own programmes by prioritising those

[37] Michael Barnett and Thomas G. Weiss, *Humanitarianism in Question: Politics, Power, Ethics* (Ithaca: Cornell University Press, 2008).

common values that most closely match their mandates and their operational strengths.

10. The aid worker's poor options

Meanwhile, humanitarian aid-workers can grow old waiting for the international community to truly accept its global responsibilities. What are the alternatives? First of all, acceptance:

- Accept that they work in a dysfunctional context, in the absence of rule of law, and in the absence of a credible capacity to protect;
- Accept that they may be serving as placeholders in the absence of political will or political action;
- Accept that the advocates of global solidarity are a minority in every member state of the United Nations;
- Accept that their opportunities to be useful are shaped by political or economic drivers, not by analysis of prioritised necessity;
- Accept that saving lives does not necessarily mean improving lives.

What else? Secondly, rights-based opportunism:

- Seek opportunities to build a constituency for global solidarity among our own communities;
- Seek opportunities to advocate the plight of people affected by specific crises or living blighted lives;
- Seek opportunities to demonstrate accountability to these people, rather than primarily to donors;
- Seek opportunities to work even in an environment where it becomes impossible to remain neutral or impartial – a life saved or improved is an absolute value, and choosing sides is a moral choice;
- Seek opportunities to hold states accountable for tolerating impunity or extreme poverty;
- Seek opportunities to respond to crises with action designed to support human rights, economic and social as well as individual, restoring livelihoods as much as saving lives.

Humanitarians are contrarians, acting where reason tells them not to.

3

A humanitarian crisis: reframing the legal framework on humanitarian assistance

EMILIE E. KUIJT

1. Introduction

The past years have shown a wide array of situations calling for the provision of humanitarian assistance. A few examples spring to mind, such as the devastating tsunami in the South Pacific Ocean in 2004, the earthquake in Pakistan in 2005 in the conflict area of Kashmir, and the earthquakes in l'Aquila (Italy) and Haiti in 2009 and 2010. More recently the world has seen the disastrous effects of the earthquake and ensuing tsunami in Japan in March 2011 and severe and ongoing droughts in east Africa, especially in Somalia. Indeed, droughts, tsunamis, earthquakes and other natural phenomena all fall within the umbrella term of 'natural disasters', often warranting the provision of humanitarian assistance. Yet such assistance has also been seen to be necessary in the more violent situations in the recent Arab Spring, such as in Libya and Syria for example, as well as in the complex situation in Sudan. Although the affected states are often considered to have the primary responsibility to fulfil such an instant need for humanitarian assistance of their population, authorities are often overwhelmed or sometimes unwilling to deliver.[1] Often, an overlap can be seen between situations of natural disaster and conflict, and the applicable legal regimes interact, raising various legal questions pertaining to the delivery of humanitarian assistance.

2. Humanitarian assistance and scope of application

If the notion of humanitarian assistance is examined, it becomes apparent that a single legal definition is lacking. Although various institutions

[1] See amongst others *UN Charter* Article 2(1) and UNGA Res. 46/182, 19 December 1991, Annex §4 (Guiding Principles on Humanitarian Assistance).

and resolutions (provided as soft law or secondary sources of international law) hold a rather broad definition of humanitarian assistance, common ground can at least be found in a more narrow definition of humanitarian assistance.[2] Such a definition also takes into consideration the attempts at definitions made through the United Nations (UN), renewed recently through its International Law Commission (ILC); and the International Committee of the Red Cross (ICRC).[3] This narrow definition of humanitarian assistance I would put forward as: *assistance consisting of food, medicine, shelter and logistics for its provision; for urgent purposes and which is indispensable to the survival of the people at which it is aimed.* According to the definition suggested here, the provision of assistance is restricted to urgent purposes. The qualification that it is to be indispensable to the survival of people during and in the aftermath of a humanitarian crisis suggests particular boundaries to the timeframe in which humanitarian assistance may be delivered.[4] Such assistance must at least be in conformity with the principles of humanity, neutrality and impartiality. The question then arises, whether a right to receive humanitarian assistance could exist for the people in need of food, water, medicine and shelter. And furthermore, whether the receipt of such assistance should be dependent on the particular crisis that such people find themselves in. Such emergency situations have often been qualified as 'natural disasters', 'conflict' or 'occupation'. Qualifying these circumstances provides for a large variety of legal rights and duties to become applicable with regard to the provision of assistance, specifically tailored to such individual occasions. As such, international humanitarian law (IHL) is applicable in time of armed conflict, yet not in the aftermath of a hurricane. However, dividing the protection a person may receive through humanitarian assistance into various rights and duties

[2] The International Institute of Humanitarian Law in San Remo, 'Guiding Principles on the Right to Humanitarian Assistance', April 1993, Principle 9; Institute of International Law, Sixteenth Commission, Resolution 'Humanitarian Assistance', Bruges Session 2 September 2003, §1.

[3] Article 59, *Geneva Convention IV Relative to the Protection of Civilian Persons in Time of War*, (GC IV), 12 August 1949; UN Doc. (A/2717) (XXV), General Assembly Resolution 'Assistance in Cases of Natural Disaster', 15 December 1970, §5(c); UN Doc. (A/CN.4/598), International Law Commission, 'Preliminary Report on the Protection of Persons in the Event of Disasters', 5 May 2008, §51.

[4] See for a more broad perspective on the timeframe: Budislav Vukas, 'Humanitarian Assistance in Cases of Emergency', in *Max Planck Encyclopedia of Public International Law* (Oxford Publication International Law, 2007), §7. For the purpose of restriction, it will here be applied to emergency situations only.

according to a specific circumstance appears artificial and inadequate. A person in need of food, water and shelter remains in need of such matters regardless of whether a conflict is ongoing, or whether a natural disaster has taken place. The common denominator in an emergency continues to be the specific 'need for assistance'. It is therefore relevant to establish that humanitarian assistance may be necessary in the event of a *humanitarian crisis*. To ensure equal protection for those in need of assistance, the provision thereof should be equally protected and regulated from a rather all-encompassing perspective, regardless of the particular circumstance in which it is needed.

This circumstance requiring the delivery of emergency assistance may then vary, such as a situation of occupation, conflict or natural disaster. But not all such individual situations warrant the provision of assistance.[5] Only if and when such a circumstance leads to an actual *humanitarian crisis* or emergency, does humanitarian assistance become a relevant factor, which will be addressed further on in this chapter. Taking an overarching approach to the provision of humanitarian assistance is valid from a variety of viewpoints. As such, it is not only logical from the perspective of the needy recipient, a human being with certain legal rights, but is also logical from the perspective of the providers of humanitarian assistance: commonly the affected state, third states or international organisations. Making the provision of such assistance dependent on specific legal criteria with regard to a situation of conflict, occupation or natural disaster appears rather artificial and is also not in line with the principle of humanity. This principle, focusing on humanitarian considerations, has long had a strong influence on the development of (international humanitarian) law, with early mentions in well-known legal documents such as the Lieber Code.[6] Moreover, as will be explored further in this chapter, international law in fact allows for an overarching approach to the provision of humanitarian assistance. This chapter puts forward this notion of a humanitarian crisis, as well as addressing how such an overarching approach to the provision of humanitarian assistance may be translated into legal rights and obligations, thereby practically assisting those in need of food, water and

[5] Edward Tsui, 'Analysis of Normative Development in Humanitarian Resolutions since the Adoption of 46/182', *Independent Review to OCHA* (2009): 11.

[6] See, for a further discussion of the principle of humanity and its legal value, Kjetil M. Larson, Camilla G. Cooper and Gro Nystuen, *Searching for a 'Principle of Humanity' in International Humanitarian Law* (Cambridge University Press, 2013).

shelter. In doing so, this chapter will firstly address the current legal framework pertaining to the potential right to receive humanitarian assistance. Lastly, the relationship between human rights law and IHL is discussed, given the relevance of both *corpora juris* in the provision of humanitarian assistance.[7]

3. The current legal framework concerning humanitarian assistance

3.1 State sovereignty

As stated above, humanitarian assistance is provided in various (legally qualifiable) circumstances, invoking a wide range of legal regimes, rights and duties. From a general perspective, state sovereignty is a continuous thread in the discussion and determination of the legal rights and duties in the provision of assistance. State sovereignty, as a legal concept, is a continued interchangeable standard throughout international law, regardless of whether a natural disaster takes place, or a conflict.[8] The premise taken here is that in international law today, sovereignty can and in fact must be seen to include responsibilities and obligations towards citizens.[9] Thus an overall and general responsibility for the affected state to provide assistance for one's people when a humanitarian crisis arises can be found in the current notion of sovereignty. Furthermore, as the concept of state sovereignty, including its legal responsibilities towards citizens, remains one and the same throughout all aspects of international law, the notion places the same obligation in that regard upon

[7] It is acknowledged that international refugee law can also be of relevance to the provision of humanitarian assistance. However, as the application of this body of law warrants the determination of a 'refugee status', it remains outside the scope of this chapter.

[8] Article 2(1) *UN Charter*. It is noted that concerning the acceptance of assistance from third parties, sovereigns have different obligations in situations of natural disaster or conflict. This 'external' aspect will however not be addressed in this chapter.

[9] Providing an in-depth discussion of the notion of sovereignty falls outside the scope of this chapter. However, the author would like to refer to the notion as argued by Anne-Marie Slaughter, that it is necessary to: 'understand sovereignty as at once a government's control of a defined territory and population and as a particular relationship between a government and its citizens. International law still upholds and safeguards a government's power and control over its citizens, including its right to invoke states of emergency and use force to maintain domestic order. But it also now protects the citizens of a particular state when their government fails grossly in its obligations toward them.' Anne-Marie Slaughter, 'Intervention, Libya, and the Future of Sovereignty', *The Atlantic*, 4 September 2011.

affected states throughout the various circumstances in which humanitarian assistance must be provided to their populations. As such, the concept of state sovereignty and the legal obligations flowing therefrom support the overarching manner in which the provision of humanitarian assistance can be approached. This notion is also supported by the work of the ILC in its development of 'Draft Articles on Protection of Persons in the Event of Disasters'. In particular Draft Article 9 declares a duty of the affected state to ensure that those persons on its territory receive assistance, and confirms the affected state's primary role in the fulfilment of this duty.[10]

3.2 *State responsibility*

In other aspects of international law such an overarching approach to possible obligations in the provision of humanitarian assistance may also be found. Today, the law on state responsibility, codified in the ILC's Articles on the Responsibility of States for Internationally Wrongful Acts (ARSIWA) allows for a responsibility not merely towards another state, but also towards other actors in the international field.[11] The purely bilateral view on state responsibility was progressively departed from, by incorporating a responsibility towards the international community in general.[12] In particular with a view to the provision of humanitarian assistance, state responsibility might therefore be invoked in the circumstance that a state does not fulfil its sovereign duty to provide assistance to its population, as a humanitarian crisis can affect the larger international community rather than solely one state. This approach by the ILC, diverging from the strict bilateral perspective, follows the International Court of Justice (ICJ) in its judgment in the Barcelona Traction, Light and Power Company Limited (*Belgium* v. *Spain*) case.[13]

[10] UN Doc. (A/CN.4/L.776) International Law Commission, 'Protection of Persons in the Event of Disasters'. Texts and titles of draft articles 6, 7, 8 and 9 provisionally adopted by the Drafting Committee, 14 July 2010, Article 9. It is indeed noted that the work of the ILC excludes the circumstance of applicability of IHL.

[11] UN Doc. (A/RES/56/83) Annex 'Responsibility of States for internationally wrongful acts' (ARSIWA), 28 January 2002 (corrected by document A/56/49(vol. I)/Corr.4).

[12] Articles 42 and 48 ARSIWA. See UN Doc. (A/56/10) Report of the International Law Commission Fifty-third session (23 April–1 June and 2 July–10 August 2001), 62, 66, 293 and 319–320. It is noted that Article 48 includes 'progressive development' aspects of international law.

[13] 'Barcelona Traction, Light and Power Company Limited' (*Belgium* v. *Spain*) case *ICJ Reports 1970*, 3 at 32, §33.

Furthermore, aside from obligations towards the international community, a state may also be held responsible for obligations towards its citizens. Articles 2 and 3 ARSIWA do not prevent the invocation of the law of state responsibility in the event of an attributable breach of international law following from such an obligation.[14] Such a form of state responsibility may also be invoked through attribution of certain acts to the state.[15] Naturally, the enforceability of these obligations remains currently to be seen. The violations amounting to state responsibility through attribution are often related to human rights law and humanitarian law, and will be discussed in more detail below.

3.3 *Human rights law*

Unlike the law of state responsibility or the concept of state sovereignty, human rights law as related to the provision of humanitarian assistance approaches the matter from the potential right of the recipient of such assistance, rather than the obligation of the state. An in-depth discussion of all relevant human rights provisions unfortunately remains outside the scope of this chapter. However, from the definition of humanitarian assistance it may be derived that the most relevant human rights to consider are the right to life, food, health (and water).[16]

3.3.1. An independent human right

Given the continuing developments in human rights law, and their continued applicability in all circumstances in which humanitarian assistance may be needed, a potential independent human right to humanitarian assistance must also be considered. Such a right could be considered part of so-called collective or solidarity rights.[17] Currently,

[14] See UN Doc. (A/56/10) at 62. See also Anne-Laure Vaurs-Chaumette, 'Peoples and Minorities', in *The Law of International Responsibility*, ed. James Crawford et al. (Oxford University Press, 2010), 994.

[15] See A/RES/56/83, Articles 4–11 ARSIWA.

[16] The right to water is not recognised in internationally legally binding treaties and is therefore considered of a different standing. See UN Doc. (A/HRC/15/32), 'Report of the independent expert on human rights and international solidarity Rudi Muhammad Rizki', 27 September 2010, §54.

[17] It remains outside the scope of this chapter to address the issues relating to the fairly novel status of these rights, as well as their premise on the collective rather than the individual and the enforcement issues this entails. For further reading see Zehra F. Kabasakal Arat, *Human Rights Worldwide: A Reference Handbook* (ABC Contemporary World Issues Series, 2006), 37 and Richard P. Claude and Burns H. Weston, *Human*

although none of the major international or regional human rights treaties directly refer to humanitarian assistance as a human right, the *Convention on the Rights of the Child* (CRC) and the *African Charter on the Rights and Welfare of the Child* (ACRWC) do refer to humanitarian assistance with regard to refugees or internally displaced persons (IDPs), and in connection with the enjoyment of that child's human rights.[18] Furthermore, the *Kampala Convention* which recently entered into force explicitly references the right of IDPs to the receipt of such assistance.[19] From the perspective of customary international law state practice remains lacking somewhat, as no clear state-driven initiatives have taken place outside the African Union. *Opinio juris* does appear to exist within the United Nations framework and other international and regional initiatives. Indeed, the commitment to recognise responsibility towards the victims of disasters is found in many soft law documents.[20] States have been hesitant to acknowledge the existence of a right to receive humanitarian assistance, as can also be derived from the absence of General Assembly or Security Council resolutions proclaiming the existence of such an independent right and states' lack of interpretative comments regarding potential relevant provisions in the human rights treaties they are party to. Yet efforts are being made to establish a right to receive humanitarian assistance, despite its current absence from international law and practice. Indeed, such a right in relation to refugee and IDP children has been claimed not only internationally, but also regionally in Africa. These attempts, next to the efforts of various soft law documents, have placed the concept of humanitarian assistance within

Rights in the World Community: Issues And Action (Philadelphia: University of Pennsylvania Press, 2006), 22; UN Doc. (A/HRC/4/8), Implementation of General Assembly Resolution (60/251) of 15 March 2006, 'Human Rights Council' – 'Human rights and international solidarity', Note by the United Nations High Commissioner for Human Rights, Section I. The Development of International Solidarity, C. Third-generation rights, §41–42; UN Doc. (A/HRC/4/87) February 2007, Report of the independent expert on human rights and international solidarity, Rudi Muhammad Riki, §42–45; Naomi Roht-Arriaza and Sara C. Aminadeh, 'Solidarity Rights: Development, Peace, Environment, Humanitarian Assistance', in *Max Planck Encyclopedia of Public International Law* (2007), §19.

18 UN Doc. (A/44/25), Convention on the Rights of the Child (CRC), Article 22; African Union, *African Charter on the Rights and Welfare of the Child*, Article 23.

19 Article 5(9) of the *African Union Convention For The Protection And Assistance Of Internally Displaced Persons In Africa* (*Kampala Convention*).

20 UN Doc. (A/HRC/12/27), 'Report of the Independent Expert on Human Rights and International Solidarity', 22 July 2009, §35.

the human rights discourse, which is relevant for the overarching manner in which such assistance may be approached.

3.3.2. The current status of human rights law

Given that the content of humanitarian assistance can be found in the rights to life, food, health (and water), its fundamental necessity for the survival of persons in the aftermath of a humanitarian crisis, its clear and identifiable content and scope, the possibility to identify implementation mechanisms as well as the support in the international community, it may indeed be justifiably developed into an independent human right within the United Nations context.[21] Whether this development occurs through the possible incorporation in an international human rights treaty or through the further development of state practice in international customary law, however, remains to be seen. Although arguments exist against the development of such an independent human right, such as the viewpoint that humanitarian assistance, given its basis in principles of humanity, neutrality and impartiality, should not be placed in a human rights discourse, such a development may however also contribute to the progressive development of human rights law and at the same time prevention of fragmentation of the law, in order to establish equal protection to all persons regardless of the disaster they have endured.[22] At this point in legal development however, the *provision* of humanitarian assistance can certainly be sought within the existing rights to life, food, health (and water), as expressed in the various international and regional treaties.[23] The provision of

[21] See the UN General Assembly's viewpoints on the requirements proposed for the development of new human rights: UN Doc. (A/RES/41/120), General Assembly Resolution 'Setting international standards in the field of human rights', 4 December 1986, §4.

[22] See UN Doc. (A/HRC/15/32), 'Report of Rudi Muhammad Rizki', §54.

[23] Regarding the right to life, see Article 6 of *International Covenant on Civil and Political Rights*, Article 2 of *European Convention on Human Rights*, Article 4 of *American Convention on Human Rights* and Article 4 *African Charter on Human and Peoples' Rights*. See also Article 3 of the *Universal Declaration of Human Rights*. Regarding the right to food, see Articles 2 and 11 of *International Covenant on Economic Social and Cultural Rights*, Article 24(2)(c) CRC, Article 12 of *Convention on the Elimination of All Forms of Discrimination Against Women*, Article 28 of the *Convention on the Rights of Persons with Disabilities*, Article 15 of the *Additional Protocol on the Rights of Women in Africa*, Article 12 of the *Additional Protocol to the ACHR in the Area of Economic, Social and Cultural Rights*. For the right to health, see Articles 2 and 12 ICESCR, Article 5(e) (iv) *International Convention on the Elimination of all forms of Racial Discrimination*, Article 24 CRC, Article 11 of the *Revised European Social Charter*, Article 10 of the *Additional Protocol to the ACHR in the area of Economic, Social and Cultural Rights*, Article 16

such assistance can be seen as a vehicle in the fulfilment of a state's obligations under human rights law.

3.4 *Humanitarian law*

Within the legal framework pertaining to the delivery of humanitarian assistance, IHL contains a variety of provisions that can be applicable in time of occupation or of conflict. With universal application and acceptance, clearly the most widely recognised provisions are those enshrined in the four Geneva Conventions of 1949.[24] Furthermore, the 1977 Additional Protocols to the four Conventions contain more explicit determinations regarding the provision of humanitarian assistance in time of international and non-international armed conflicts.[25] Together with the 'Hague law', these provisions form the core of existing law regarding the provision and receipt of humanitarian assistance as determined within IHL.[26] The relationship between IHL and human rights law will be addressed at a later stage, yet it is relevant to note that currently, unlike in human rights law, developments are lacking in treaty law with regard to IHL and the provision of humanitarian assistance. However, as these treaties are somewhat dated, most recent developments in IHL concerning humanitarian assistance have not been incorporated, such as possible

ACHPR, Article 14 of *African Charter on the Rights and Welfare of the Child*, Article 14 of *Protocol to the ACHPR on the Rights of Women in Africa*. See also Article 25 UDHR. Regarding the right to water, see Article 24(1)(c) CRC, Article 14(2)(h) CEDAW, Article 15(a) *Additional Protocol to the ACHPR on the Rights of Women in Africa*, 14(2)(c) *African Charter on the Rights and Welfare of the Child*.

[24] See in this regard Common Article 3 to the four Geneva Conventions: *Geneva Convention I for the Amelioration of the Condition of the Wounded and Sick in Armed Forces in the Field; Geneva Convention II for the Amelioration of the Condition of Wounded, Sick and Shipwrecked Members of Armed Forces at Sea; Geneva Convention III Relative to the Treatment of Prisoners of War; Geneva Convention IV Relative to the Protection and of Civilian Persons in Time of War*, 12 August 1949; Articles 23, 38, 55, 60, 61 and 59 GC IV. See also related Articles, although not strictly concerning direct provision of humanitarian assistance: Articles 12 and 32 GC I; Article 12 GC II; Articles 26, 28, 30–31 GC III; Articles 54, 56, 76, 81, 87, 89 and 91–92 GC IV.

[25] See *Additional Protocol I of 1977 to the Geneva Conventions of 1949*, Articles 54, 69, 70 and 71; *Additional Protocol II of 1977 to the Geneva Conventions of 1949*, Articles 14 and 18. See also related Articles, although not strictly concerning direct provision of humanitarian assistance: Articles 10–11 AP I; Articles 5 and 7 AP II.

[26] See in this regard in particular *Hague Convention (II) on the Laws and Customs of War on Land*, 1899 and *Convention (IV) respecting the Laws and Customs of War on Land* and its annex: *Regulations concerning the Laws and Customs of War on Land*. The Hague, 18 October 1907.

obligations regarding the provision of humanitarian assistance by non-state actors. Furthermore, as has been seen recently with the 'Arab Spring', more and more situations arise that are difficult to qualify as a (non-international) conflict, thereby perhaps preventing the invocation of IHL and its protective provisions.

Next to the Geneva Conventions and Protocols therefore, the United Nations Security Council is a source to consider in terms of the obligations of the affected state in the provision of humanitarian assistance in time of conflict. The Security Council has addressed the receipt of humanitarian assistance and its provision on numerous occasions, calling upon states to comply with their obligations under international law.[27] The Security Council issued a thematic resolution concerning the protection of civilians in armed conflict in 1999, urging all parties involved to 'comply strictly with their obligations under international humanitarian, human rights and refugee law, in particular those contained in the Hague Conventions of 1899 and 1907 and in the Geneva Conventions of 1949 and their Additional Protocols of 1977, as well as with the decisions of the Security Council'.[28] With time, the Security Council has reiterated its position that a primary responsibility to provide assistance lies with the affected state.[29] Indeed, as the Security Council also responds to factual circumstances, it has had the opportunity to address those topical issues not touched upon by the Geneva Conventions. With Security Council resolutions providing gap-filling statements to supplement the various provisions of the Geneva Conventions, the legal framework concerning humanitarian assistance often reaches detailed regulation in time of occupation and armed conflict. Yet the fact that these detailed provisions are only considered part of IHL, and therefore only applicable in certain instances of occupation or of international armed conflict, raises questions relating to the fragmentation of the law. The need for

[27] It falls outside the scope of this chapter to provide an exhaustive list of resolutions. But see, for example, amongst others UN Doc. (S/RES/794) 3 December 1992, §1; UN Doc. (S/RES/1199) 23 September 1998, §2; UN Doc. (S/RES/1265) 17 September 1999, §2, 7–8; UN Doc. (S/RES/1296) 19 April 2000, §8, 12, 15; UN Doc. (S/RES/1325) 31 October 2000, §12; UN Doc. (S/RES/1674) 28 April 2006, §21–23; UN Doc. (S/RES/1889) 5 October 2009, §12; UN Doc. (S/RES/1973) 17 March 2011, §3 and UN Doc. (S/RES/2076) 20 November 2012, §11.

[28] (S/RES/1265) 'Protection of Civilians in Armed Conflict', 1999, §4.

[29] (S/RES/1674) 'Protection of Civilians in Armed Conflict', 2006, §13; (S/RES/1674) 'Protection of Civilians in Armed Conflict', 2006, preamble; (S/RES/1894) 2009, preamble and §15.

humanitarian assistance, in practice, does not follow the legal divisions created by IHL. Indeed, this perspective can also be found within the approach of the Security Council as it views the responsibilities of the affected state to 'respect and ensure human rights of all individuals within their territory and subject to their jurisdiction' while reaffirming that primary responsibility is borne by parties to an armed conflict to 'take all feasible steps to ensure the protection of affected civilians'.[30]

3.5 *Determining a right to receive assistance?*

It remains essential that a people in need of assistance in the aftermath of a natural disaster, during conflict, occupation or other crisis, gains access to humanitarian aid. The fact that an individual human right to receive assistance from a sovereign or other authority exercising control is still under development does not imply that no rights or duties with regard to the receipt and provision of humanitarian assistance exist.[31] Enforcement of such rights and duties can on the one hand be sought through the existing human rights to life, food, health (and water). On the other hand, such rights and obligations may be found in humanitarian law and other provisions of general international law as seen above in the discussion of state responsibility and state sovereignty and even in the approach of the Security Council. Such rights and duties indeed follow from human rights obligations and through other obligations in international law, granting a rather umbrella-like protection to those in need of assistance.[32]

Even though consensus with regard to the existence of an independent established human right to receive humanitarian assistance from a

[30] UN Doc. (S/PRST/2010/25) 'Aide Memoire Protection of Civilians in Armed Conflict', 22 November 2010, preamble. This Aide Memoire follows the previous one of 15 March 2002 (S/PRST/2002/6), as well as the thematic resolutions 1265 (1999), 1296 (2000), 1674 (2006), 1738 (2006) and 1894 (2009) relating to the protection of civilians in armed conflict.

[31] This chapter considers the potential right to receive assistance from a sovereign or other authority exercising control. The often related 'right to offer assistance' of third parties through an external source is not addressed.

[32] For a succinct overview of various rights and duties, see SFDA, 'Humanitarian Access in Situations of Armed Conflict Handbook on the Normative Framework', *the Swiss Federal Department of Foreign Affairs* 1 (2011): 44–56. Support can also be sought in soft law documents; see in this regard the International Institute of Humanitarian Law in San Remo, 'Guiding Principles', and the Institute of International Law 'Humanitarian Assistance', Bruges Resolution.

sovereign or national authority may still be developing, the provision itself can be seen as a *vehicle* or a *means* to fulfil existing human rights and other obligations under international law. Though an independent human right to receive assistance may currently be developing, indeed, providing humanitarian assistance may already be the substantial fulfilment of a state's obligation to ensure a person's right to life, food, health (and water). Furthermore, such provision may be the fulfilment of a state's obligation under IHL and general international law. Yet basing the provision of humanitarian assistance strongly in existing human rights law falls in line with the aim of the provision of humanitarian assistance itself: aiding people in need of food, water and shelter, regardless of the situation they may find themselves in, namely a natural disaster, conflict or occupation. Thus it supports an approach to humanitarian assistance that is rather overarching. In fact, the culmination of the law of state responsibility, IHL, human rights law and the notion of sovereignty supports the suggestion that a right to receive humanitarian assistance may exist, although the exact determination of *when* such a right may be invoked remains disputed and will therefore be addressed in the subsequent section.

4. Humanitarian Crisis: an overarching approach

Humanitarian assistance is often necessary in complex situations such as a natural disaster occurring in time of conflict. In these circumstances an overlap of various legal regimes takes place. Given the fact that humanitarian assistance has been researched mostly from the perspective of the various (legally qualifiable) circumstances in which it occurs, an all-encompassing (legal) definition of such a crisis or emergency has not often been provided.

4.1 Attempts at defining a complex situation

Some attempts to bridge the distinction have been made, as the United Nations previously referred to 'natural disasters and other emergency situations'.[33] Various actors in the field adhere to a variety of terms such

[33] See for example UN Doc. (A/RES/46/182), General Assembly Resolution 'Strengthening the coordination of humanitarian emergency assistance of the United Nations', 19 December 1991, §33; as well as UN Doc. (A/RES/43/131), General Assembly Resolution, 'Humanitarian Assistance to victims of natural disasters and similar emergency situations', 8 December 1988, §1.

as 'crisis', 'emergency' and 'disaster'; further distinguished for example as 'slow-onset emergencies', 'man-made disasters', or 'complex emergencies'.[34] It thus becomes important to determine a working definition of a humanitarian crisis[35] that may serve as a common notion for the circumstances in which the provision of humanitarian assistance is relevant, namely in the above-defined situations of occupation, conflict and natural disaster. Such an all-encompassing definition may eventually also be of use to and applicable in such situations that lead to a call for humanitarian assistance, for instance internal disturbances, but that cannot be qualified as armed conflicts, and thereby not yet invoking IHL. Furthermore, the international community is often reserved or hesitant in its determination of an armed conflict, resulting in the fact that the protection offered by IHL is not always provided in practice. Should humanitarian assistance be provided each time a humanitarian crisis arises, this would ensure more equal protection under international law. Finding recourse in rights and obligations that have a more general character will offer greater protection on the ground.

4.2 *Material scope of application*

So, with the notion of a humanitarian crisis coined, what is this concept based on? How do we know whether and when it is applicable, and how must it be defined? In situations of occupation or conflict, support for the determination of circumstances when humanitarian assistance may be required can be sought in treaty provisions, whereas this is not the case in situations of natural disaster.

[34] For the terminology used by the IFRC see 'Types of Disasters: Definitions of Hazards', *IFRC*, accessed 21 October 2011, www.ifrc.org/en/what-we-do/disaster-management/about-disasters/definition-of-haard/; for OCHA see the 'Glossary of Humanitarian Terms in relation to the Protection of Civilians in Armed Conflict', 2004 as well as ReliefWeb's 'Glossary for Humanitarian Terms', 2008; for the World Health Organisation, see 'Definitions: Emergency', *WHO*, accessed 21 October 2011, www.who.int/hac/about/definitions/en/index.html.

[35] Although both 'humanitarian *crisis*' and 'humanitarian *emergency*' can be, and are used, here the phrase 'humanitarian crisis' is chosen. Both the Oxford and Merriam-Webster dictionaries consider unforeseeability to be an element of an emergency. As not all situations in which humanitarian assistance is necessary are unforeseen a choice has been made to use 'crisis' when referring to a situation in which a need may exist for humanitarian assistance.

4.2.1. Conflict and occupation

Article 59 of the Fourth Geneva Convention succinctly declares that relief schemes are necessary if a population of an occupied territory is 'inadequately supplied'. Yet the determination of this inadequacy is left entirely open-ended and Article 59 does not mention what level of 'inadequacy' must be reached for relief schemes to commence, which leads to uncertainty as to who will be making such a determination. Determining whether or not a territory is adequately supplied will then have to be determined on a case-by-case situation. From the *Commentary* to the corresponding Article 70 of *Additional Protocol I*, a similar 'case-by-case' observance can be deduced in times of international armed conflict, in relation to the urgency of the provision of assistance and the lack of specific legal qualification of the term 'inadequacy'.[36] Likewise, pertaining to non-international armed conflicts, Article 18 of *Additional Protocol II* provides for humanitarian assistance in the event that 'the civilian population is suffering undue hardship owing to a lack of the supplies essential to its survival'. Here too, the *Commentary* argues the impossibility of providing exact criteria for the determination of 'undue hardship', and relates this to a comparison with a more generally accepted standard of living.[37] Obviously, this may lead to problematic circumstances in which an occupying force may consider territory adequately supplied, whilst (parts of) the international community may not agree.[38]

It should however be possible to establish a minimum degree for which common ground can be found. The nature of 'relief schemes', as seen above in the discussion on the definition of humanitarian assistance, is related to the delivery of those supplies urgently needed for immediate survival. Thus it must be assumed that the level of 'inadequacy' should therefore be comparable to such a level of urgency that one can speak of amounting to a 'humanitarian crisis'.[39] Equally, such difficulties may exist in relation to natural disaster, where a state may claim that although the international community might think otherwise, it is in fact not overwhelmed by the disaster, and local capacity is equipped for an appropriate response. Such difficulties in the determination of the

36 See Yves Sandoz, Cristophe Swinarski and Bruno Zimmermann, *Commentary to the Additional Protocols, 1987 Protocol I* (Article 70), 817.

37 Sandoz, Swinarksi and Zimmermann., *Commentary, Protocol II* at 1479 (Article 18).

38 See, likewise (Article 55) GC IV. Some possibilities lie with the Protecting Power to safeguard the access to emergency supplies of the population.

39 The exact definition of a 'crisis' will be addressed further in this section.

adequacy of supply to a civilian population in times of occupation or conflict stress the importance of research into the various rights and obligations currently existing under international law in relation to humanitarian assistance. Furthermore, in relation to armed conflict, the provisions concerning the rendering and delivery of humanitarian assistance are quite dispersed and particular, and may not be enough to build on with the current changing nature of conflicts, as discussed above.[40] Aside from matters of occupation, IHL as such does not state at which level of severity an (international or non-international) armed conflict can be considered a humanitarian crisis. Such a threshold would ensure that the provisions with regard to humanitarian assistance become operable.[41] Clearly, with certain provisions specifically geared towards the provision of humanitarian assistance enshrined in the Geneva Conventions and Protocols, it is indeed the intention of IHL to protect the people in need of assistance. Yet determining which instances may result in the delivery of humanitarian assistance would provide more legal certainty. Thus in the absence of a clear statement concerning the moment at which the provision of 'relief' becomes applicable under international humanitarian law, its application must be derived from the fact that relief is directly related to the event of its necessity as seen above in regard to the definition of humanitarian assistance: it only entails the essential elements for a person's survival.[42] The Guiding Principles on the Right to Humanitarian Assistance (San Remo 1993) – although as soft law of a different standing – also acknowledge that not every situation of occupation or conflict may lead to the involvement of humanitarian assistance because, although not defining the concept of 'emergency', the Principles do apply that specific term in addressing humanitarian assistance.[43] From the discussion of the application of humanitarian assistance to situations of occupation and conflict, it is

[40] See Section 2.4.

[41] Jean Pictet, 'Commentary on the Geneva Conventions of 12 August 1949, *Convention IV Relative to the Protection of Civilian Persons in Time of War*, International Committee of the Red Cross (Article 10)', Geneva (1948): 98–99. Pictet argues that given the unforeseeability of future warfare, choices have been made to leave certain situations open, as at the time of the drafting of the Convention it was unclear what needs may be given rise to in future times. Furthermore Article 23 of GC IV only mentions 'essential foodstuffs' that are to be distributed as rapidly as possible without a corresponding clarification at which point in time such foodstuffs do indeed become 'essential'.

[42] Pictet, 'Commentary', (Article 23), 180–81

[43] See San Remo Principles, at Principle 2 and 3.

apparent that lack of legal clarity may lead to attempts to deter the deliverance of assistance in such times. Thus aspects of *willingness* to cope with the inadequacy of supply become a relevant criterion in the consideration of the determination of a humanitarian crisis.

4.2.2. Natural disaster

As the provisions concerning this issue are rather limited, an analogous view of natural disaster must be considered in order to distinguish more clearly at which point one can speak of a situation warranting the (external) provision of humanitarian assistance. Outside the scope of occupation or conflict, the United Nations General Assembly recognised that many emergencies' dimensions and durations are often beyond the capacity of the affected state, making international assistance of cardinal importance.[44] Thus the General Assembly connected the existence of an 'emergency' to the *capacity* of the affected state to deal with the occurring event. A few years prior, the United Nations 1984 'Draft Convention on expediting the delivery of emergency assistance' had already formulated that '"Disaster" means any natural, accidental or deliberate event (not being an ongoing situation of armed conflict) as a result of which assistance is needed from outside the State upon whose territory the event occurred or which has been affected by the consequences of the event'.[45] Following the Draft Convention and the United Nations General Assembly, the United Nations Department of Humanitarian Affairs defined an emergency to be a 'sudden and usually unforeseen event that calls for immediate measures to minimise its adverse consequences'.[46] Given the fact that the phrase 'emergency' is often linked to a certain degree of unexpectedness,[47] other terms are used too. Within the United Nations framework, it has also been suggested that the affected society's inability to cope with the disruption is a relevant element.[48]

[44] See UN Doc. (A/RES/46/182), Annex I §5: 'The magnitude and duration of many emergencies may be beyond the response capacity of many affected countries. International cooperation to address emergency situations and to strengthen the response capacity of affected countries is thus of great importance.'

[45] 1984 'Draft Convention on Expediting the Delivery of Emergency Assistance', Article 1(b).

[46] ReliefWeb's 'Glossary for Humanitarian Terms of 2008', 24.

[47] See note 35 on definitions of emergency.

[48] See the UN International Strategy for Disaster Reduction definition in ReliefWeb's 'Glossary', *supra* note 46, 22.

A clear link can thus be established between the (unexpected) unfolding of an event and the (local) capacity to deal with it, for the determination of the existence of a humanitarian crisis. This may be added to the above-mentioned 'willingness' to provide assistance. Similarly, also with regard to the notion of a disaster the International Federation of the Red Cross (IFRC) also considers the relationship between a state's own capacity and the extent of its vulnerability when a 'hazard' occurs.[49] Most of these analyses pertain to the notion of 'emergency' or 'disaster' within a non-conflict or -occupation setting. Yet a humanitarian crisis may not only unfold due to a lack of a state's *capacity* to handle a certain situation, since a state itself may be at the root cause of the crisis, as previously discussed. Thus *local* capacity may be unable to cope with a certain crisis situation, due to conflict or occupation. In fact, several organisations, amongst them the European Union, recognise this possibility in their definition of the notion of a 'disaster'.[50]

4.2.3. An overarching approach

The various definitions above consider that a humanitarian crisis may unfold itself not only in a situation of natural disaster, but also in conflict or occupation providing an overlap of various fields of law. Such considerations also support the argument made in this chapter that the approach to the legal framework of humanitarian assistance must occur through an overarching perspective. Indeed, such situations in which assistance is necessary are not always separate and a 'complex emergency' is a notion of particular relevance in the discussion of humanitarian assistance. Interestingly, the notion of a 'complex emergency', touching upon both conflicts and natural disasters, has been subject to various definitions in soft law instruments, perhaps connected to the fact that it is a situation in practice in which various fields of law come together. As a common denominator, from these definitions provided by soft law instruments it can indeed be seen that such a complex emergency is a

[49] See 'What is a Disaster?', IFRC, accessed 12 March 2013, www.ifrc.org/en/what-we-do/disaster-management/about-disasters/what-is-a-disaster/.

[50] See Joint Statement by the Council and Representatives of the Governments of the Member States Meeting within the Council, the European Parliament and the European Commission (2008/C25/01), 'The European Consensus on Humanitarian Aid', *Official Journal of the European Union*, 30.1.2008, C25/1–C25/12. See also amongst others, CRED, 'the EM-DAT Glossary', *the CRED*, accessed 12 March 2013, www.emdat.be/glossary/9#term81.

crisis which flows from both natural and man-made causes.[51] Furthermore, sometimes the need for 'international response' is considered an element.[52] Indeed, although the approach to the legal provisions pertaining to the delivery of assistance has occurred through separate regimes, the organisations involved in its actual provision do all recognise the factual circumstance that a crisis can occur in a more overarching and coinciding manner. Therefore, it becomes necessary to also approach the legal framework of the provision of assistance in such a manner.

4.3 *Defining a humanitarian crisis*

From the above, in the determination of a situation in which humanitarian assistance is needed, several criteria or common factors can be considered in relation to the definition of a humanitarian crisis.[53] Clearly, the legal value of these criteria must be seen in light of the fact that most of the above-mentioned sources attempting to explicitly define elements of a crisis are considered secondary sources in international law. Yet common factors can be deduced in determining the definition of a humanitarian crisis. As seen, these criteria can be, and indeed are, applied to the general notion of a humanitarian crisis, not distinguishing this into separate circumstances of application such as occupation, conflict and natural disaster. It is clearly relevant to establish a definition of a humanitarian crisis which can be applicable to these situations, in order to assess the current legal regime for the provision of humanitarian assistance. Furthermore, and most importantly, it would contribute to the needs of those people actually depending on humanitarian assistance. Based upon the analysis of the statements above, it is suggested by the author that a humanitarian crisis can be defined as *a situation deriving from a variety of origins, including natural and man-made disaster,*

51 See for example IFRC, 'Complex/manmade hazards: complex emergencies', which provides examples of possible complex emergencies, *IFRC*, accessed 12 March 2013, www.ifrc.org/en/what-we-do/disaster-management/about-disasters/definition-of-hard/complex-emergencies/. See also Institute of International Law, Bruges Resolution, §2; and Jon M. Ebersole, 'The Mohonk Criteria for Humanitarian Assistance in Complex Emergencies: Task Force on Ethical and Legal Issues in Humanitarian Assistance', *Human Rights Quarterly* 17 (1995): 192–208, at n. 7.

52 IASC, 10th meeting, December 1994. The IASC was established in June 1992, following the call thereto in the UN GA Resolution (46/182).

53 For further reading on definitions of disaster, see for example UN Doc. (A/CN.4/590/Add.1), 'Protection of Persons in the Event of Disasters', Memorandum by the Secretariat, Addendum, 26 February 2008.

occupation and armed conflict, causing grave damage of a personal or material nature to persons, where (external) assistance is needed as the local capacity is either overwhelmed, unable or sometimes unwilling to manage the circumstances. Ascertaining which qualifications of this definition exist for the various circumstances and situations will allow for the re-assessment and determination of the applicable rules relating to the provision of humanitarian assistance. Therefore, having established that the current legal regimes containing provisions related to humanitarian assistance allow for an overarching approach, as well as exploring the concept of a 'humanitarian crisis', it becomes relevant to briefly address the inter-relationship of the two main fields of law that are applicable in times of occupation, conflict and natural disaster if and when such situations amount to a humanitarian crisis.

5. The law applicable in a humanitarian crisis

As stated, the premise taken is that all people in need of assistance should be entitled to the utmost available protection under international law. Notions of human dignity and human rights, and the concept of humanitarian assistance itself, do not allow for a classification of the level of protection offered based on the determination of a natural disaster or conflict. Therefore, the applicable law in time of a humanitarian crisis must be addressed.

5.1 General international law

Depending on a legal qualification for the provision of assistance – such as the determination of an armed conflict in order to apply IHL rules – may also be dangerous as it may give reason to providers of humanitarian assistance not to fulfil certain obligations if they can argue that a situation does not amount to an armed conflict. Thus one must therefore look into which fields of law best protect humans in need of assistance, regardless of their circumstances.

In fact the Security Council, often calling upon states to either provide humanitarian assistance themselves, or allow access to international organisations for such provision, does so too. For example, the Security Council, when considering the situation in Libya in 2011, demanded 'that the Libyan authorities comply with their obligations under international law, including international humanitarian law, human rights and refugee law and take all measures to protect civilians and meet their basic needs, and to ensure the rapid and unimpeded passage of humanitarian assistance'.[54] Thus the Security Council calls upon the provision of humanitarian assistance based on international law as a whole, whilst including IHL and human rights law. In earlier instances, the Security Council has indeed also called upon parties and states to comply with their 'obligations under international law', without necessarily specifying it any further.[55] Equally, the General Assembly has often called upon the relevant parties to observe 'international law' obligations in allowing humanitarian access, rather than specific provisions.[56]

5.2 *IHL and human rights law*

Indeed, provisions protecting and ensuring the delivery of humanitarian assistance can mainly be found in IHL and human rights law. Therefore the relationship between these two fields of law needs to be addressed. Both human rights law and IHL have a shared goal and common denominator in their aspirations to protect persons. Yet this does not determine whether both *corpora juris* can be simultaneously applicable and thus whether they do indeed interact in the provision of humanitarian assistance. The continued applicability of human rights law in time of armed conflict will be taken as a premise.[57] The developments regarding

[54] UN Doc. (S/RES/1973) 'Libya', 17 March 2011, §3.

[55] See in this regard for example UN Doc. (S/RES/1674), 'Protection of Civilians in Armed Conflict', 28 April 2006, §5; UN Doc. (S/RES/1296), 'Protection of Civilians in Armed Conflict', 19 April 2000, §8. See also *supra* Section 2.4, Humanitarian Law.

[56] For a (non-exhaustive) compilation, see OCHA 'Compilation of United Nations Resolutions On Humanitarian Assistance. Selected resolutions of the General Assembly, Economic and Social Council and Security Council Resolutions and Decisions', July 2009: available at: www.refworld.org/docid/4a8e5b072.html.

[57] See amongst others UN Doc. (A/8052), UN Secretary General Report 'Respect for Human Rights in Armed Conflict', 18 September 1970, §16; UNGA Res. 2675 (XXV), 'Basic Principles for the Protection of Civilian Populations in Armed Conflict', 1970, §1; ICJ (Advisory Opinion), 'Legality of the Threat or Use of Nuclear Weapons', 8 July 1996, §25. See also UN Doc. (CCPR/C/21/Rev.1/Add.11) General Comment 29 pursuant to Article 4 'States of Emergency', 2001, §3, 9 and 11; and UN Doc. (CCPR/C/21/Rev.1/Add.13) Human Rights Committee, General Comment No. 31, 26 May 2004, §11. In particular in relation to humanitarian assistance, the relevant human rights treaty provisions are non-derogable. See also ICJ, 'Legal Consequences of the Construction of a Wall in the Occupied Palestinian Territory', *ICJ*, 9 July 2004, §106; and ICJ, 'Armed Activities on the Territory of the Congo' (*Democratic Republic of the Congo* v. *Uganda*), *I.C.J. Reports* (2005), Judgment, 19 December 2005, ICJ Rep., 2005, 1, §216. Lastly, see 'European Court of Human Rights Case of Isayeva', *Yusupova and Bazayeva* v. *Russia* (Applications nos. 57947/00, 57948/00 and 57949/00), Judgment, 24 February 2005;

the potential extraterritorial scope of application of human rights treaties, based upon a concept of 'effective control' or 'exercise of jurisdiction' by a state, are also noted, although the extent of such application and the notion of 'effective control', jurisdiction or authority remain a matter of continued debate.[58] As a result of the evolution in international practice, legal discussion is currently shifting from the matter of *whether* human rights law is indeed directly applicable in times of armed conflict, to *how* this law is applicable in relation to international humanitarian law.[59]

5.3 *Hierarchy or convergence of international legal norms?*

Having taken the premise that human rights law finds continued applicability in time of armed conflict and occupation and that humanitarian

'Inter-American Court of Human Rights', *Bamaca Velásquez* v *Guatamala* Judgment, 25 November 2000, §207.

[58] See in regard to this discussion the various viewpoints as provided by: ICJ, 'Armed Activities on the Territory of the Congo', §216; ICJ, 'Legal Consequences of the Construction of a Wall in the Occupied Palestinian Territory', §106–112; ECtHR (*Loisidou* v. *Turkey*), Preliminary Objections, Judgment, 23 March 1995, §62; European Court of Human Rights (ECtHR) (*Bankovic et al.* v. *Belgium*) Application no. 52207/99, 12 December 2001 §67–73; ECtHR (*Ilascu and others* v. *Moldova and Russia*) Case No. 48787/99, 8 July 2004, §317–318; ECtHR (*Öcalan* v. *Turkey*) Case no. 46221/99, Grand Chamber Judgment, 12 May 2005, §91; ECtHR (*Al-Skeini and Others* v. *United Kingdom*) Application No. 55721/07, judgment, 7 July 2011, §137–139; Inter-American Court of Human Rights (*Coard et al.* v. *United States of America*) Report No. 109/99 Case No. 10.951, September 29, 1999, §37; UN Doc. (CCPR/C/21/Rev.1/Add.13) Human Rights Committee, §10; Committee on Economic, Social and Cultural Rights, UN Doc. (E/C.12/1/Add.90) 'Concluding Observations of the Committee on Economic, Social and Cultural Rights – Israel', 23 May 2003, §31; the 'Maastricht Principles on Extra-Territorial Obligations (ETOs) of States in the Area of Economic, Social and Cultural Rights', 28 September 2011 (final version adopted 29 February 2012). It must be noted that multiple states have continued to reiterate their objection to possible extraterritorial application of the various human rights covenants. For a variety of viewpoints see Noam Lubell, 'Challenges in applying human rights law to armed conflict', *International Review of the Red Cross* 87 (2005): 740; Jean-Marie Henckaerts and Louise Doswald Beck, 'Customary International Humanitarian Law vol. I: Rules' (Fundamental Guarantees), *International Committee of the Red Cross* (2005): 305–306; Michael J. Dennis, 'Application of Human Rights Treaties Extraterritorially in Times of Armed Conflict and Military Occupation', *American Journal of International Law* 99 (2005): 119–141; Fons Coomans, 'Application of the International Covenant on Economic Social and Cultural Rights in the Framework of International Organisations', *Max Planck Yearbook of United Nations law* 11 (2007): 359–390; and Fons Coomans, 'The Extraterritorial Scope of the International Covenant on Economic, Social and Cultural Rights in the Work of the United Nations Committee on Economic, Social and Cultural Rights', *Human Rights Law Review* 11 (2011): 1–35.

[59] See Lubell, 'Challenges', 738.

law and human rights law can therefore apply simultaneously, their reciprocal relationship must be assessed. Such an assessment may determine which provisions that may invoke a right or duty relating to humanitarian assistance would perhaps receive precedence over another provision relating to humanitarian assistance. This is relevant to the notion of an overarching approach to the provision of humanitarian assistance. As human rights law has a general application, whereas IHL is tailored specifically to circumstances of armed conflict, the doctrine of *lex specialis derogat lex generalis*, which is generally accepted in national law, immediately springs to mind. Yet given the decentralised structure of the international legal body, applying this domestic regime to the international field does not necessarily immediately resolve the relationship between human rights law and humanitarian law.[60]

5.3.1. The '*lex specialis* principle'

How to balance the possible conflicting norms must however be addressed for the provision of humanitarian assistance.[61] Indeed, where the ICJ has declared affirmatively that human rights remain applicable in time of armed conflict, it has also addressed the particular relationship between both fields of law. Doing so firstly in its 1996 'Nuclear Weapons' Advisory Opinion,[62] and more elaborately in its 'Legal Consequences of the Construction of a Wall in the Occupied Palestinian Territory' Advisory Opinion, the ICJ stated:

> As regards the relationship between international humanitarian law and human rights law, there are thus three possible situations: some rights may be exclusively matters of international humanitarian law; others may be exclusively matters of human rights law; yet others may be matters of both these branches of international law. In order to answer the question put to it, the Court will have to take into consideration both these

60 Heike Krieger, 'A Conflict of Norms: The Relationship Between Humanitarian Law and Human Rights Law in the ICRC Customary Law Study', *Journal of Conflict and Security Law* 11 (2006): 269, 265–291.

61 A discussion of conflicting norms in general international law remains outside the scope of this chapter. See however amongst others Articles 53 and 64 of the *Vienna Convention on the Law of Treaties*; Article 103 UN Charter; ICJ, 'Case Concerning Military and Paramilitary Activities in and Against Nicaragua' (*Nicaragua* v. *United States of America*) (Merits), 27 June 1986, §177–179, 186; and UN Doc. (A/CN.4/L.682) 'ILC Fragmentation of International Law: Difficulties Arising from the Diversification and Expansion of International Law', 13 April 2006.

62 See ICJ, 'Legality of the Threat or Use of Nuclear Weapons', §25.

> branches of international law, namely human rights law and, as *lex specialis*, international humanitarian law.[63]

Thus the ICJ provides three possible scenarios to which the *lex specialis* doctrine may be applicable. These scenarios then depend on the content of the rights involved. The ICJ confirmed this approach in its subsequent ruling in the 'Armed Activities on the Territory of the Congo' case and thereby appears – at least for the time being – to have taken the above-mentioned approach towards the relationship between human rights law and humanitarian law.[64] The approach in which IHL functions as *lex specialis* is found equally in the work of the Inter-American Commission.[65] An alternative approach can be seen in the practice of the Human Rights Committee (HRC):

> the Covenant applies also in situations of armed conflict to which the rules of international humanitarian law are applicable. While in respect of certain Covenant rights, more specific rules of international humanitarian law may be especially relevant for the purpose of the interpretation of the Covenant rights, both spheres of law are complementary, not mutually exclusive.[66]

The HRC is hereby taking an approach of complementarity, as is also embraced amongst others by Philip Alston in his role as United Nations Special Rapporteur on extrajudicial, summary or arbitrary executions, declaring that humanitarian law must be examined for the interpretation of human rights law in time of armed conflict.[67] Such an approach

[63] See ICJ, 'Legal Consequences of the Construction of a Wall in the Occupied Palestinian Territory', §106.

[64] See ICJ, 'Armed Activities on the Territory of the Congo', §216. For a different reading see Krieger, 'A Conflict of Norms', 271, who argues in reference to the nuclear weapons case that the ICJ restricts itself to specific instances, and does not consider international humanitarian law to override human rights law 'en bloc'.

[65] See Inter-American Court of Human Rights (*Coard et al.* v. *United States of America*), §42.

[66] UN Doc. (CCPR/C/21/Rev.1/Add.13) Human Rights Committee, 'General Comment No. 31, on the Nature of the General Legal Obligation Imposed on States Parties to the Covenant (Article 2)', 26 May 2004, §11.

[67] UN Doc. (A/HRC/4/20/Add.1) 'Report of the Special Rapporteur on Extrajudicial, Summary or Arbitrary Executions, Philip Alston – Addendum - Summary of Cases Transmitted to Government and Replies Received', 12 March 2007, 348. See furthermore for a discussion of various authors Noëlle Quénevet, 'The History of the Relationship Between International Humanitarian Law and Human Rights law', in *International Humanitarian Law and Human Rights Law: Towards a New Merger in International Law*, eds. Roberta Arnold and Noëlle Quénevet (The Netherlands: Martinus Nijhoff Publishers, 2008), 8–10.

appears to suggest humanitarian law as a *lex specialis*, as it is argued that this body of law must be examined for the interpretation of a human rights principle in time of armed conflict. While indeed human rights law and humanitarian law continue to complement each other, such a haphazard interplay will result in a rather non-homogenous development of norms, which is not helpful to the progressive development of the legal framework on humanitarian assistance. This approach furthermore deviates somewhat from the ICJ's approach, as it does not necessarily view humanitarian law firmly as the *lex specialis* obtaining preference over human rights law in time of armed conflict, but rather would see human rights law interpreted in light of humanitarian law.

Yet another method is taken by Marco Sassòli and Laura M. Olson, who argue that it remains somewhat unclear which body of law is the *lex specialis* in situations where both are applicable.[68] As Sassòli puts forward, the relationship between human rights law and humanitarian law must be examined according to the *lex specialis* doctrine, but humanitarian law is not necessarily the more specialised law in each particular circumstance: 'The principle does not indicate an inherent quality in one branch of law, such as humanitarian law, or of one of its rules. Rather, it determines which rule prevails over another in a particular situation. Each case must be analysed individually.'[69] How then such a determination must be made, should according to Sassòli and Olson be done through a formal observation of which law in the particular circumstance has the most interfaces with the situation; the norm which has a more precise content, and/or with a more 'personal scope of application'.[70] Thus depending on the particular circumstances, either human rights law, or humanitarian law, may be the *lex specialis* at a particular time. Yet the *lex generalis* always remains present in the background.[71] This practice has indeed also been established in the ILC's Report of the 'Study Group on the Fragmentation of International Law', that argues the relational character of the special and the general rule.[72] Such an approach could also be read into the HRC's above comment with regard to 'specific' humanitarian rules. Concurring with Sassòli and Olson, Krieger notes that especially in circumstances such as non-international

[68] Marco Sassòli and Laura M. Olson, 'The Relationship Between International Humanitarian and Human Rights Law Where it Matters: Admissible Killing and Internment of Fighters in Non-international Armed Conflicts', *IRRC* 90 (2008): 600, 599–627.

[69] Ibid., 603–604. [70] Ibid., 604. [71] Ibid., 605.

[72] See ILC, ' Fragmentation of the Law', §104 and §112.

armed conflicts, where human rights law is often more specific, the general prevalence of humanitarian law would not seem fitting, despite it being a situation of armed conflict.[73] Such a gap-filling method by human rights law has also been the approach of the European Court of Human Rights (ECtHR) in the situation of non-international armed conflicts.[74] Certainly, considering the circumstances in which humanitarian assistance takes place, such an approach would be in line with the overarching perspective of a humanitarian crisis.

5.3.2. The common goal of both *corpora juris*

Such a more converging, harmonious approach would indeed be more fitting to the developments that have taken place in the evolution of the relationship between international human rights and humanitarian law over the past few decades. Where IHL began as strictly addressing states, and human rights law did not apply in time of armed conflict, it is now clear that both *corpora juris* pursue the same goal: the greater protection of persons. In fact, perhaps the time has come to affirmatively declare that both are cast along the same lines and share a common denominator, of which the notion of humanitarian assistance itself is proof. As such, Krieger suggests the 'most favourable principle' as an interpretative method, through which the norm that grants the greatest protection to the individual would be applied.[75] In relation to the provision of humanitarian assistance, aimed precisely at the protection of persons in a humanitarian crisis, such an interpretative method would indeed be relevant. In this regard, human rights law can indeed play a vital role, as individuals are often provided with more direct means of redress in case of violations than with humanitarian law.[76] Also importantly, as humanitarian assistance takes place in time of peace *and* in time of war,

[73] Krieger, 'A Conflict of Norms', 273.

[74] See ECtHR, Isayeva (*Yusupova and Bazayeva* v. *Russia*), §167 and §169; ECtHR (*Isayeva* v. *Russia*) (Isayeva II) Case No. 57950/00, *ECtHR* 128, 24 February 2005, §173; and ECtHR (*Ilascu and others* v. *Moldova and Russia*) Case No. 48787/99, *ECHR* 318, 8 July 2004. The debate whether or not (regional) human rights courts or other bodies should be applying humanitarian law remains outside the scope of this research. However, it is noted that the ECtHR restricted itself in *Bankovic and others* v. *Belgium* and 16 Other Contracting States, §75, whereas the Inter-American Court of Human Rights applied a more forward approach (*Juan Carlos Abella* v. *Argentina*) ('Tablada Case'), Case No. 11.137 *IACHR*, 18 November 1997, §161. However, this decision has been subsequently overturned by the IACtHR Las Palmeras (Preliminary Objections) Case No. 67, Series C. Judgment, 4 February 2000, §33 and (*Bámaca Velásquez* v. *Guatemala*), §209.

[75] Krieger, 'A Conflict of Norms', 274. [76] Ibid., 289.

such a converging approach is necessary and must be supported to ensure that the same rights and duties in relation to the receipt and provision of humanitarian assistance exist in *all* circumstances that amount to a humanitarian crisis. As IHL is invested in the protection of persons – given its specific provisions relating to humanitarian assistance – such a converging approach would be geared towards the very essence of the body of law. Equally, the United Nations Special Rapporteur on the protection of persons in the event of disasters has argued that several regimes are applicable to the protection of persons, and that such regimes are necessarily dependent upon each other:

> the regimes of protection of persons are international humanitarian law, international human rights law and international law relating to refugees and internally displaced persons. These regimes may apply simultaneously to the same situation because they essentially complement each other. In addition, they are guided by a basic identity of purpose: the protection of the human person in all and any circumstances. The three areas of law underscore the essential universality of humanitarian principles.[77]

Such an approach is precisely the premise put forward in this chapter: the protection of persons should be provided for to the greatest extent possible, regardless of the legally qualifiable situation these persons may be situated in. Thus the provision of humanitarian assistance must be sought in the basis of those provisions of humanitarian law and human rights law that provide the utmost protection in a given circumstance. It is precisely this approach to the *lex specialis* rule that will provide for the greatest protection of persons in need of food, water and shelter. This interdependence and growing realisation that a common minimum standard should exist that is applicable at all times has been asserted earlier.[78] Indeed, such a common standard could assist in countering the fragmentation of the law on humanitarian assistance, but could also assist in the joint interpretation of human rights law and

[77] Eduardo Valencia-Ospina, UN Doc. (A/CN.4/598) ILC 'Preliminary Report on the Protection of Persons in the Event of Disasters', 5 May 2008, §52.

[78] See the Turku/Åbo Declaration Of Minimum Humanitarian Standards (1990); *Furundzija* (Trial Judgment), No. IT-95-17/1-T, *ICTY*, 1998 and *Delalić et al.* (Celebici – Case) (Appeals Chamber), No. IT-96-21-A, *ICTY*, 2001; see also regarding the fact that such a convergence is welcome: Hans-Joachim Heintze 'Convergence Between Human Rights Law and International Humanitarian Law', in *International Law and Humanitarian Assistance*, eds. Hans-Joachim Heintze et al. (Heidelberg: Springer-Verlag, 2011), 85.

humanitarian law, especially in the event of doubt as to the preferred application of either.

6. Conclusion

From the above, it is clear that the provision of humanitarian assistance must be viewed with an all-encompassing and overarching perspective. Indeed, the current definition of humanitarian assistance itself, as well as the definition of state sovereignty as we know it today, do not allow for an artificial division of rights and obligations according to legally qualifiable circumstances. The developments in human rights law directly place the provision of humanitarian assistance within that discourse. The current development towards a potential human right to receive assistance furthermore supports that position, which is also underlined by the legal framework in the law of state responsibility. In fact, in practice the Security Council and General Assembly call upon the compliance with general obligations under international law in relation to humanitarian assistance, indicating that humanitarian assistance finds its basis at that more abstract level. The gaps in the law failing to protect persons in circumstances falling short of application of IHL furthermore warrant such an approach. Applying the legal framework regarding humanitarian assistance must therefore only be considered if and when the criteria of a humanitarian crisis are met, regardless of whether such a crisis can be categorised as a natural disaster, conflict or situation of occupation.

When considering the more specific fields of law, it has been shown that the relationship between human rights law and humanitarian law must be seen as one of mutual reinforcement. Thus with all legal ingredients related to the provision of assistance distinctly pointing towards such an overarching perspective on the rights and obligations related to the provision of humanitarian assistance, that viewpoint must be held. The persons in need of assistance *must* be able to depend on a single concept: the existence of a humanitarian crisis, through the fulfilment of the elements thereof. Developing a single view of the provision of humanitarian assistance will not only provide legal clarity, it will furthermore strengthen the existing rights and obligations relating to the provision of humanitarian assistance. Perhaps most importantly, it will factually aid people on the ground needing assistance, as well as those wanting to provide it, which is of course paramount.

4

The utility and limits of legal mandate: humanitarian assistance, the International Committee of the Red Cross and mandate ambiguity

ROTEM GILADI

1. Introduction

How does a legal mandate affect humanitarian assistance? Is it essential for conducting successful assistance operations, or merely a convenient or helpful asset in the toolbox of organisations undertaking them? Can it be an impediment to the provision of effective assistance? What, in other words, are the utility and limits of legal mandate?

Anecdotal evidence suggests that answers to these questions are both diverse and complex. The variety of organisations engaged today in humanitarian assistance is vast. Players on the relief scene include international organisations and religious bodies, national and international NGOs, government agencies and private corporations, militaries and others. Some come equipped with legal mandate, others not. The former invoke their respective mandates in varying forms, arenas, and frequency, and for a variety of purposes. The latter deliver assistance without grounding their work in any particular or general international legal right or obligation to do so. Some openly eschew legal mandate.[1] Their record suggests that the lack of legal mandate is not necessarily a

[1] Fiona Terry, 'Myanmar: Golfing with the Generals', in *Humanitarian Negotiations Revealed: The MSF Experience*, ed. Claire Magone, Michael Neuman, and Fabrice Weissman (New York: Columbia University Press, 2011), 109, 111. ('Having no official mandate to determine the types of situations to which it ought to respond, MSF freely chooses where it will and will not offer its humanitarian medical assistance'). MSF was founded as an 'independent association specialising in providing medical emergency assistance free from the administrative and legal constraints facing the ICRC': Rony Brauman and Joelle Tanguy, 'The MSF Experience' (1998), *MSF*, accessed on 31 March 2013, www.doctorswithoutborders.org/work/field/msfexperience.cfm.

bar to success. By contrast, those claiming some legal mandate to engage in assistance cannot always point to a record of unremitting success. Intuitively, legal mandate and effectiveness in humanitarian assistance operations are not *necessarily* positively linked. By itself, legal mandate is not the sole determinant of efficacy: factors other than the existence of and reliance on legal mandate are also at play. Yet the creation, invocation, and avoidance of mandate still require an inquiry of its utility, limits, and downsides.

Identifying all such factors and their undoubtedly intricate relationships may not, however, be indispensable for attaining a preliminary understanding of the utility and limits of legal mandate. This paper neither attempts to identify all factors affecting the success of assistance nor strives to isolate the legal mandate variable. Rather, it examines but one case study. The International Committee of the Red Cross (ICRC) openly invokes a legal mandate grounded in the Geneva Conventions to carry out humanitarian assistance in conflict situations. Interestingly, the arguments above provide the answers to the questions posited at the start of this chapter. In the ICRC's experience and perspective, legal mandate is crucial, helpful, *and* dangerous.

To demonstrate this claim and reflect on its significance, I start by analysing the pertinence and shortcomings, analytical and methodological, of using the ICRC as a case study for unravelling the utility and limits of legal mandate (Section 2). Section 3 firstly presents the assistance mandate *asserted* by the ICRC, its legal grounding and its reception; it then proceeds to *revisit* this assertion. Contrary to common perception, the ICRC legal assistance mandate is not a straightforward proposition; it is far more ambiguous than commonly noted. I demonstrate different sources and manifestations of the ambiguity surrounding the ICRC assistance mandate.

Section 4 examines the ICRC's stance on its 'relief' mandate in the legislative process of drawing up the 1949 Geneva Conventions. Legislative practice suggests that for the ICRC, a conventional mandate was both an imperative and a risk. These findings allow for a more nuanced assessment of the ICRC's broad assertion of mandate. Section 5 examines the assistance mandate *practised* by the ICRC. It illustrates that notwithstanding open, sweeping assertions about legal mandate to undertake assistance activities, the ICRC's operational practice reveals that it only invokes and relies on assistance mandate in a very limited, and flexible, fashion. Contemporary practice underscores, mainly, the limited utility of mandate.

Section 6 assesses these insights. Relating past and present practice, it offers a single, yet complex, answer to the question of utility, limits, and dangers of the ICRC's assistance mandate. It underscores ambiguity as a key concept characterising and explaining the ICRC experience. This chapter concludes by discussing the instruction of these findings for other actors engaged in humanitarian assistance and identifying possible avenues for future research.

2. The ICRC: a case study on assistance mandate

What makes the ICRC a pertinent case study is, firstly, that it openly invokes a legally grounded mandate to undertake assistance operations: 'A key characteristic of the ICRC is that it was given a mandate ... by the States party (*sic*) to the Geneva Conventions to help victims of armed conflict. Its work is therefore firmly rooted in public international law.'[2] Secondly, the ICRC has been engaged in assistance operations for the last hundred and fifty years or so.[3] Its vast experience, today practised on a global scale,[4] promises some lessons on legal mandate. But legal mandate and long experience also combine to render the ICRC a problematic case study.

Two factors make the ICRC a less-than-ideal model. Analytically, in the first place, the ICRC, as humanitarian assistance organisations go, is atypical. Commentators, indeed, are wont to note its idiosyncrasies: in legal status, mandate, modes of operation, approach, etc.[5] ICRC mandate, moreover, is not limited to assistance (and, for that matter, protection): it has long invoked and practised, alongside its operational role in the field, also a *legal* role. In its own parlance, it is both the 'promoter and guardian' of the Geneva Conventions.[6]

[2] ICRC, 'The International Committee of the Red Cross: Its Missions and Work', *IRRC* 874 (2009): 399, 401–2 (notes omitted).

[3] Pierre Boissier, *History of the ICRC: From Solferino to Tsushima* (Henry Dunant Institute, 1985); Francois Bugnion, *The International Committee of the Red Cross and the Protection of War Victims* (Oxford: Macmillan, 2003).

[4] ICRC, *Annual Report 2011* (Geneva: ICRC, 2012).

[5] David P. Forsythe, 'The ICRC: A Unique Humanitarian Protagonist', *IRRC* 865 (2007): 63; Tarcisio Gazzini, 'A Unique Non-State Actor: the International Committee of the Red Cross', *Human Rights and International Legal Discourse* 4 (2010): 32; Geoffrey Best, *War and Law Since1945* (Oxford University Press, 1994), 90 ('anomalous and unique').

[6] Yves Sandoz, 'The International Committee of the Red Cross as Guardian of International Humanitarian Law' (1998), ICRC, accessed on 31 March 2013, www.icrc.org/eng/resources/documents/misc/about-the-icrc-311298.htm; ICRC, *International Humanitarian Law: Answers to Your Questions* (Geneva: ICRC, 2002), 31, 33.

In its legal role, the ICRC plays a unique and crucial role in humanitarian lawmaking, promulgates its own interpretation of international humanitarian law (IHL), strives to clarify the status and content of legal norms, and encourages and assists state ratification of IHL treaties. It disseminates knowledge of IHL norms to states and other parties to armed conflicts, monitors IHL implementation, and reminds them of their obligations.[7]

Yet the ICRC also fulfils a victim-centred *operational* role in the field. The ICRC describes itself as 'an impartial, neutral and independent organisation'[8] and asserts an 'exclusively humanitarian mission ... to protect the lives and dignity of victims of armed conflict and other situations of violence *and to provide them with assistance*'.[9] Protection and assistance lie at the core of the ICRC's operations on behalf of victims.[10] Though 'intrinsically linked',[11] and often mutually reinforcing, protection and assistance may compete or clash. Thus the provision of material relief may reveal that beneficiaries are vulnerable to targeted violence from armed forces, and addressing such vulnerability may expose, in turn, material needs. Limited resources, however, may prioritise one type of operation at the expense of the other. In other cases, the

[7] See Steven R. Ratner and Rotem Giladi, 'The Role of the ICRC', in *The Geneva Conventions in Context: A Commentary*, eds. Andrew Clapham, Marco Sassòli and Paola Gaeta (OUP, forthcoming).

[8] Ibid. These are three of the movement's 'Fundamental Principles': Jean S. Pictet, *The Fundamental Principles of the Red Cross: Commentary* (Geneva: Henry Dunant Institute, 1979). For the ICRC, impartiality rejects 'any form of discrimination' and 'calls for equal treatment ... according to ... needs'. Neutrality requires abstention from 'taking sides in hostilities or controversies of a political, racial, religious or ideological nature', enabling the ICRC to 'keep everyone's trust ... to make more contacts and gain access to those affected'. Independence means detachment from 'national and international politics', which gives it the 'autonomy ... to accomplish the exclusively humanitarian task entrusted to it with complete impartiality and neutrality'. It allows the ICRC to position itself as distinct 'from political decision-making processes', espousing no 'ulterior political motives': ICRC, 'Missions and Work', 404. Larry Minear, 'The Theory and Practice of Neutrality: Some Thoughts on the Tensions', *IRRC* 81 (1999): 63; Pierre Krähenbühl, 'The ICRC's Approach to Contemporary Security Challenges: A Future for Independent and Neutral Humanitarian Action', *IRRC* 855 (2004): 505.

[9] Emphasis added: ICRC, 'The ICRC's Mission Statement' (19 June 2008), *ICRC*, accessed on 31 March 2013, www.icrc.org/eng/resources/documents/misc/icrc-mission-190608.htm.

[10] ICRC, 'Protection Policy', *IRRC* 871 (2008): 751; ICRC, 'Assistance Policy', *IRRC* 855 (2004): 677; ICRC, *Assistance for People Affected by Armed Conflict and Other Situations of Violence* (Geneva: ICRC, 2nd ed., 2012), 2.

[11] ICRC, 'Protection Policy', 752; Bugnion, *Protection*, xxxiii.

provision of assistance may expose beneficiaries to novel threats (for example by tying them to locations where they are vulnerable, or simply by alleviating the consequences of harmful policy, thereby minimising its costs, relieving the author of its responsibilities, and effectively perpetuating the harm). The choices inherent in a dual operational role, then, somewhat limit the instruction of the ICRC mandate experience.[12]

Having a *legal* alongside an operational role compounds this problem. It undoubtedly places the ICRC in a unique position of expertise, allowing it to harness law to operational requirements and use operational lessons to shape new law or promote legal interpretation.[13] Yet its legal and operational roles can also clash. The requirements of real-world operations may well vary from the letter or even the spirit of the law. Often they do: legal norms are not always the best avenue to assist the victims of violence or ensure that their legal protections are respected. When this happens, law often takes a role secondary to humanitarian operations: in ICRC praxis, law (and law-talk) 'is a tool calibrated to match operational needs'.[14] And if law, notwithstanding its centrality in the ICRC world,[15] can be subordinate to operational exigencies, so can legal mandate.

Such tensions, perhaps, are not unique to the ICRC. Yet these and other tensions – David Forsythe aptly speaks of characteristic 'paradoxes'[16] – appear typical of the ICRC and its institutional culture.[17] Equally unique to the ICRC is the manner in which it negotiates, mediates, or reconciles such tensions. As a result, the particular ICRC blend of assistance and protection mandates and, more so, of operational and legal roles, limits whatever instruction we may find in this example.

[12] Not that all other humanitarian organisations always engage in 'pure' assistance: David Rieff, *A Bed for the Night: Humanitarianism in Crisis* (New York: Simon and Schuster, 2002).

[13] ICRC, 'Missions and Work', 401; Jean-Philippe Lavoyer and Louis Maresca, 'The Role of the ICRC in the Development of International Humanitarian Law', *International Negotiation* 4 (1999): 501, 506.

[14] Steven R. Ratner, 'Law Promotion Beyond Law Talk: The Red Cross, Persuasion, and the Laws of War', *EJIL* 22 (2011): 459, 473.

[15] Ibid., 477 ('historic centrality of IHL to the institution').

[16] David P. Forsythe, *The Humanitarians: The International Committee of the Red Cross* (Cambridge University Press, 2005), 2, 281 (ICRC 'replete with paradoxes' and 'since 1863 present a complex picture, full of paradoxes'); Dominique D. Junod, *The Imperiled Red Cross and the Palestine Eret-Yisrael Conflict 1945–1952* (London: Kegan Paul, 1996), 46 ('contradictory character').

[17] ICRC, 'Missions and Work', 401 ('This dual nature thus reinforces the very identity of the ICRC and distinguishes it from other international humanitarian organisations'.)

The class of like cases is bound to be small, comprising institutions that combine legal mandate, assistance and protection activities, and law promotion: the UNHCR comes to mind.[18]

Yet ICRC atypicality offers certain analytical advantages. Its variety of roles produces not one but several answers to the question of utility and limits of legal mandate. While few other, if any, assistance agencies may be compared to the ICRC, the spectrum of answers offered by the ICRC example is broad enough to contain generally valid insights.

A second difficulty besetting the ICRC example is methodological. Its principal compliance-inducing strategy is the persuasion of parties to a conflict to abide by their IHL obligations. This usually takes place in confidential dialogue.[19] ICRC operational practice, therefore, is not on public record. This secrecy makes it hard to gauge where, when, and how the ICRC uses its legal mandate.

Yet the plurality of ICRC roles, and the different strategies it employs under these different roles, also means that ICRC praxis takes place in multiple arenas. The ICRC may address or rely on its assistance mandate, in other words, also in the context of law development (for example the 1949 Diplomatic Conference), law clarification (for example the Geneva Conventions' Commentaries), or law dissemination, or vis-à-vis donors. Unlike persuasion, these arenas are to some extent public. While one cannot assume that ICRC praxis on legal mandate is the same across roles or arenas – or, indeed, over time – this plurality of roles and arenas enables critical comparison of ICRC praxis.

These considerations inform the design of what follows. I examine ICRC practice on assistance mandate in three different arenas: the mandate it publicly asserts; the mandate it promoted during the enactment of the 1949 Geneva Conventions; and the mandate it practises in its operations.

3. Mandate asserted

The ICRC asserts legal assistance mandate publicly, broadly,[20] and frequently. A typical document notes

[18] Gil Loescher, *The UNHCR and World Politics: A Perilous Path* (Oxford University Press, 2001); David P. Forsythe, 'UNHCR's Mandate: The Politics of Being Non-Political', *New Issues in Refugee Research Series, Working Paper* 33 (2001): 1–34; Michael Barutciski, 'A Critical View on UNHCR's Mandate Dilemmas', *Int'l J. of Refugees L.* 14 (2002): 365.

[19] Ratner, 'Law Promotion', 465 *et seq.*

[20] 'Under [the Geneva Conventions and their Additional Protocols], the ICRC is authorised to undertake a wide variety of activities', Lavoyer and Maresca, 'Role of the ICRC', 503.

> it was given a mandate (or rather mandates) by the States party (*sic*) to the Geneva Conventions to help victims of armed conflict. Its work is therefore firmly rooted in public international law...
>
> The main legal basis for the ICRC's work is to be found in international humanitarian law.
>
> States gave the ICRC the responsibility of monitoring the faithful application of international humanitarian law.[21]

Similar allusions to formal, conventional assistance mandate are common in contemporary ICRC materials and in scholarship.[22] The ICRC's own Statutes provides that its role includes:

> c) to undertake the tasks incumbent upon it under the Geneva Conventions...
>
> d) to endeavour at all times – as a neutral institution whose humanitarian work is carried out particularly in time of international and other armed conflicts or internal strife – to ensure the *protection of and assistance* to military and civilian victims of such events and of their direct results.[23]

Nonetheless, the ICRC conventional assistance mandate is not a straightforward proposition. It is far more ambiguous than statutory or other public assertions suggest. Anchoring such assertions in actual treaty text proves elusive: a wide gap separates broad asserted mandate from the meagre language of provisions mandating ICRC assistance (and protection) activities. These read, rather, like 'a series of disconnected obligations which, together, do not make up a coherent whole'.[24]

21 Notes omitted; ICRC, 'Missions and Work', 401–2. ICRC, 'Assistance: General Introduction' (2000), ICRC, accessed on 31 March 2013, www.icrc.org/eng/assets/files/other/assistance-general-report-intro-2000.pdf. ('The ICRC acts on the basis of a specific mandate conferred upon it by the States party [*sic*] to the Geneva Conventions and its Additional Protocols. The mandate outlines ... protection and assistance of victims of armed conflict and internal violence').

22 Rüdiger Wolfrum and Dieter Fleck, 'Enforcement of International Humanitarian Law', in *Handbook of International Humanitarian Law*, ed. Dieter Fleck (Oxford University Press, 2008), 675, 713–4. ('The Geneva Conventions and their Additional Protocols recognise the special status of the ICRC and assign specific tasks to it, including ... providing relief to the population of occupied territories'.) Rieff, *Bed*, 19 ('oldest of the humanitarian organisations ... its mandate is the clearest').

23 Emphasis added; Article 4(1), *Statutes of the International Committee of the Red Cross*, 8 May 2003, *ICRC*, accessed on 31 March 2013, www.icrc.org/web/eng/siteeng0.nsf/html/icrc-statutes-080503; see also Article 5, *Statutes of the International Red Cross and Red Crescent Movement*, 1986 (amend. 1995), *ICRC*, accessed on 31 March 2013, www.icrc.org/eng/assets/files/other/statutes-en-a5.pdf.

24 Bugnion, *Protection*, 350.

Provisions on 'relief' in the Conventions do allude to the ICRC. Their terms, however, are not consonant with broad assertions of mandate. They do not grant the ICRC a general right to provide assistance in armed conflicts. They imply much more than they express: the roles they foresee for the ICRC in assistance are limited to specific sets of beneficiaries, types of relief, circumstances – and, often, the consent of the belligerents. They rarely accord the ICRC any preference over others, and hardly assign it a robust assistance role.

Thus its entitlement to propose limits on shipment of relief to PoWs only 'in respect of [ICRC's] own shipments' does not amount to an explicit right to provide assistance. The focus in Article 72, at any rate, is on the entitlement of PoWs to receive 'individual parcels or collective shipments'.[25] Nor can such a right be firmly grounded in Article 75, under which the ICRC and others 'may undertake to ensure the conveyance' of relief shipments where 'military operations' prevent the parties from meeting their obligation to assure transport. Even its right 'to supervise' distribution of relief to POWs is implied – in the rule that special agreements cannot restrict such supervision (Article 73).[26]

Similarly, no explicit, general right to provide relief to civilians can be found in the Civilians Convention. Article 30 entitles civilians to have 'every facility' 'for making application' to the ICRC and other organisations. It obliges the authorities to grant such organisations 'all facilities for that purpose'. The reference to 'spiritual aid or material relief' defines 'other organisations', but gives them no right to assistance – and does not, apparently, cover the ICRC.[27]

It is true that in occupied territories, the ICRC and others may undertake 'relief schemes' on behalf of civilians. Yet this entitlement is heavily qualified, even if the occupant is obliged to 'agree to relief schemes' and 'to facilitate them' (Article 59). It applies only if 'the whole or part of the population of an occupied territory is inadequately supplied'. Likewise, prior agreement is required for the ICRC to play a role in

[25] *Convention Relative to the Treatment of Prisoners of War* 12 August 1949, 75 UNTS 135 (1950).

[26] For similar provisions on civilian internees, Arts.108, 109, 111, *Convention Relative to the Protection of Civilian Persons in Time of War*, 12 August 1949, 75 UNTS 287 (1950).

[27] *Cf.* however Article 81, UNTS, '*Additional Protocol to the Geneva Conventions of 12 August 1949, and Relating to the Protection of Victims of International Armed Conflicts (Additional Protocol I)*', 1125 UNTS 3 ('the humanitarian functions assigned to it by the Conventions and this Protocol in order to ensure protection and assistance to the victims of conflicts').

the distribution of relief consignments (Article 61). And all this is limited to international armed conflicts: in non-international armed conflict, the only conventional basis for relief activities is the Common Article 3 under which any 'impartial humanitarian body, such as the [ICRC], may offer its services to the Parties'.[28] This is not tantamount to an assistance mandate.

Two provisions may better anchor assertions of mandate. But even the ICRC's 'special position ... in this field', 'to be recognised and respected at all times', does not quite amount to an explicit grant of mandate. Articles 125, GC III and 142 GC IV mention it only concerning the right of the detaining power to limit the number and supervise the activities of other organisations 'distributing relief supplies'.[29] They give no detail on what the ICRC's special position entails and where its limits lie. Rather, they point at empowerment outside of, and predating, the Conventions.[30] Similarly, the 'saving clause' in Common Article 9/9/9/10 vests no right in the ICRC. It only stipulates that the Conventions 'constitute no obstacle to the humanitarian activities which the [ICRC] or any other impartial humanitarian organisation may, subject to the consent of the Parties to the conflict concerned, undertake for the protection of prisoners of war and for their relief'. The article does not mandate humanitarian activities; it subordinates them to state consent but, at the same time, insinuates that relief activities exist outside the conventional framework.[31]

Textual ambiguity is reinforced by ambiguity of multiple sources. IHL is but the 'main legal basis' of ICRC work.[32] It also asserts an assistance mandate based in its own Statutes, or in the Statutes of the Red Cross Movement.[33] Both, in turn, reference the 'tasks incumbent upon' the

[28] Articles 5, 18, '*Additional Protocol to the Geneva Conventions of 12 August 1949, and relating to the Protection of Victims of Non-International Armed Conflicts* (Protocol II)', 1125 UNTS 609 do not mention the ICRC. *Cf.* Article 6, 'Seville Agreement', repr. *IRRC* 322 (1998): 159–76.

[29] Jean S. Pictet, *Commentary: The Geneva Convention Relative to the Treatment of Prisoners of War* (Geneva: ICRC, 1960), 600–1.

[30] Ibid., 601. Indeed, the ICRC argues that IHL 'like the Statutes of the Movement, confirms a historical tradition of ICRC action which predates its successive codifications': ICRC, 'Missions and Work', 402. Bugnion, *Protection*, 29, suggests that 'providing assistance to war victims' itself first 'went beyond the self-imposed confines of its original role' forced on the ICRC 'by the pressure of circumstances'.

[31] Pictet, *Commentary*, 103.

[32] ICRC, 'Missions and Work', 401–2. ICRC, 'Assistance: General Introduction' (2000).

[33] ICRC, 'Missions and Work', 402.

ICRC 'under the Geneva Conventions'.[34] And the ICRC also draws its mandate from 'resolutions of the International Conference of the Red Cross ... and the Council of Delegates'.[35]

Compounding this ambiguity of sources is the ICRC's invocation of a 'right of initiative' whose expression is at times conventional and at others statutory. This amorphous right entitles it to 'take any humanitarian initiative which comes within its role as a specifically neutral and independent institution and intermediary, and [to] consider any question requiring examination by such an institution'.[36] The right of initiative suggests that the ICRC's mandate is always subject to state consent.[37] At the same time, it also implies mandate that is, in principle, limitless; and whose scope depends, ultimately, on the ICRC itself and its unbound discretion: who is to say which 'humanitarian initiative' does not come 'within its role as a specifically neutral and independent institution and intermediary' or deny that any question does not require 'examination by such an institution'?

Ambiguity inheres in the variety of legal bases for ICRC assistance mandate: conventional and statutory, express or implied in the 'right of initiative'. Invoking a multiple of bases for legal mandate necessarily blurs the precise contours and actual contents of this mandate. Unless the ICRC scrupulously references precise legal bases in practice – and, at least publicly, it does not – it is near impossible to tell which treaty or statutory provision any of its relief activities falls under or, having regard to the 'right of initiative', what humanitarian activities can even fall outside its mandate.

Ambiguity, lastly, is also fostered by the diverse vocabulary ICRC and ICRC writers have used to describe its mandate. The ICRC speaks, as we just saw, of 'mandate' and 'tasks incumbent upon', but also of 'task

[34] Article 4(1), Red Cross Statute; Article 5.1(c), Red Cross Statute.

[35] ICRC, 'Missions and Work', 402.

[36] Article 5, ICRC Statutes. See also Common Article 3 and Article 9/10/10/10, GCs; Yves Sandoz, 'Le droit d'initiative du Comité international de la Croix-Rouge', *German Yearbook of International Law* 22 (1979): 352; Jean-Marie Henckaerts and Louise Doswald-Beck, *Customary International Humanitarian Law* (Cambridge University Press, 2005), 442 (Rule 124); cf. Raphael van Steenberghe, 'Non-State Actors from the Perspective of the International Committee of the Red Cross', in *Participants in the International Legal System*, ed. Jean D'Aspremont (Oxford: Routledge, 2011), 204, 205 *et seq.*

[37] The relevant preparatory document is ICRC, *Report on the Preliminary Conference of National Red Cross Societies for the Study of the Conventions and of Various Problems Relative to the Red Cross, Geneva, 26 July to 3 August 1946: Documents Furnished by the ICRC, Vol. IV: Specific Red Cross Problems* (transl., n.d.) ['*Documents IV*'].

entrusted',[38] legal basis,[39] rights,[40] prerogatives,[41] responsibility,[42] duties,[43] obligations,[44] function,[45] mission,[46] 'special role',[47] *etc.* If multiple sources make the limits of asserted mandate undetectable, sundry vocabulary obfuscates its very nature: who does it exactly bind, and is it binding at all?

The terms of mandate asserted by the ICRC suggest that, for this institution, legal mandate is important indeed. It is important enough for the ICRC to connect what seems like few random points into a picture portraying a broad conventional mandate. It is important enough for the ICRC to supplement a rather thin conventional mandate by additional sources. Yet at the same time, the ICRC surrounds its asserted assistance mandate by ambiguity as to its source, boundaries, and nature. This ambiguity has a history.

4. Mandate enacted

The role played by the ICRC in the IHL legislative arena provides another vantage point on the utility and limits of legal mandate. The making of the Geneva Convention of 1949 – the mainstay of the ICRC treaty-based mandate – was a long-drawn-out process. Initiated in 1945,[48] it unfolded in a 1946 Preliminary Conference of National Red Cross Societies;[49] a 1947 Conference of Government Experts;[50] the 1948

[38] ICRC, 'Missions and Work', 404. Sandoz, *Guardian* ('function . . . formally entrusted to it by the international community').

[39] ICRC, 'Missions and Work', 401–2. ICRC, 'Assistance: General Introduction' (2000).

[40] IHL 'expressly confers certain rights on the ICRC, such as that of visiting prisoners of war or civilian internees and providing them with relief supplies': ICRC, 'Missions and Work', 401, n.9.

[41] Yves Sandoz et al., *Commentary on the Additional Protocols of 8 June 1977 to the Geneva Conventions of 12 August 1949* (Geneva: ICRC, 1987), 936 ('Diplomatic Conference of 1949 confirmed the prerogatives entrusted to the ICRC and extended them to the four Conventions'); ICRC, 'Protection Policy', 756.

[42] ICRC, 'Missions and Work', 402; ICRC, 'Protection Policy', 755.

[43] ICRC, 'Missions and Work', 9.

[44] Bugnion, *Protection*, 350; *Documents IV*, 12–13.

[45] ICRC, 'Missions and Work', 399.

[46] ICRC, 'Mission Statement'.

[47] ICRC, 'Missions and Work', 399.

[48] Best, *War*, 81.

[49] *Documents IV*. See also ICRC, *Report on the Work of the Preliminary Conference of National Red Cross Societies for the Study of the Conventions and of Various Problems Relative to the Red Cross, Geneva, 26 July–3 August* 1946 (1947) ['*Preliminary Conference*'].

[50] ICRC, 'Report on the Work of the Conference of Government Experts for the Study of the Conventions for the Protection of War Victims' (Geneva, 14–26 April 1947), ['*Government Experts*'].

Stockholm International Red Cross Conference;[51] culminating in the 1949 Geneva Diplomatic Conference.[52] It produced thousands of pages of reports, minutes, and drafts revealing the ICRC perspective on assistance mandate.

Of this vast record, two insights appear particularly pertinent.[53] One is that, at different phases of the process, the ICRC attitude to legal mandate manifested different, sometimes contradictory, perspectives on its utility. Another is that, throughout this process, the ICRC was driven by the imperative of promoting an *ambiguous* 'relief' mandate.

4.1 *The first phase: A framework for arguing mandate*

The first phase of the process saw the ICRC preparing for and participating in the 1946 Preliminary Conference. It first elaborated, then presented, a framework for arguing its own mandate on relief and otherwise. Its key position here was open aversion, if not outright hostility, to express legal mandate vesting in the ICRC or other Red Cross organs.[54] This was a principled position. The ICRC emphasised that the Red Cross institution 'rests on a relatively weak foundation as regards codified International Law'.[55] The Geneva Conventions, it noted, 'are concerned far more with the red cross emblem by which the persons, buildings, and objects to be protected are marked, than with the 'Red Cross' as a relief-giving institution'.[56] It interpreted references to the ICRC in the 1929 PoWs Convention not as grants of mandate, but only as 'official recognition' of its humanitarian work.[57] It readily conceded that 'up to the present day, no adequate provision has been made in treaty law for its particular form of organisation and its manifold activities'.[58]

This was not a problem to solve but, rather, an achievement to preserve. The ICRC was averse to legal basis, but it did hail past

[51] '17th International Red Cross Conference: Stockholm, August 1948: Report' (1948) [*Stockholm Report*].

[52] Federal Political Dept., 'Final Record of the Diplomatic Conference of Geneva 1949' (Berne, 1951) ['*Final Record*'].

[53] This section summarises some of the main findings of a study of the ICRC's behaviour in the legislative setting: Rotem Giladi, 'An Ambiguous Mandate: The Making of the ICRC Conventional Relief Mandate, 1946–1960' (in progress).

[54] Consider its apprehensive stance on 'new tasks' by national societies carried out 'over and beyond their original purpose' under 'the Red Cross emblem': *Documents IV*, 1–2; for background: Best, *War*, 92.

[55] *Documents IV*, 9. [56] Ibid., 9. [57] Ibid., 9–10. [58] Ibid., 10.

expansion of Red Cross activities.[59] Having no firm legal basis, for the ICRC, meant also that law contained 'nothing which would hinder [Red Cross] development. Up to the present, such support as is given to it therein has sufficed to give it a place in international relations which many other private associations might envy.'[60] Lack of conventional mandate was precisely what allowed ICRC operations to expand; this entailed the denial of mandate. For the ICRC,

> whose widespread activities during the war grew up outside the framework of codified international law, this disadvantage turned out to be an advantage, since the Committee was bound by no mandate, nor, – as its action is not governed by any treaty, – was its work dependent upon the putting into effect of such treaties or conventions by the different States.[61]

The ICRC thus put a premium not on legal mandate but on independence resting on private character and tradition.[62] This aversion to regulation of mandate translated to a prescription of circumspection:

> the greatest caution must be observed when making proposals tending to strengthen the basis of the Red Cross under international law, and account must always be taken of the double effect of any such changes, in contrast to the present position, which has the advantage of being an extremely elastic arrangement.[63]

Programmatically, the ICRC did indicate a few points that 'might be more precisely defined' in the emerging Conventions. These, at first, included scant reference to relief, but also 'mention of the role of the delegates' of the ICRC – without specifying what such a role may be.[64] Later, it was willing to expand or augment the shortlist of 'the chief cases where the Red Cross might be mentioned more specifically'.[65] In time, it would also change its tone. At the Preliminary Conference it invoked a 'right' in the 1929 PoWs Convention 'to pursue . . . humanitarian task in behalf of prisoners of war, subject to the consent of the belligerent concerned'.[66] It also seemed to accept that 'future Red Cross activities must rest on a firmer basis than agreements concluded for each particular

[59] Ibid., 1. ('Since its inception, the Red Cross has constantly widened its scope, including gradually more and more activities, till it reached its present immense development, which touches upon practically all forms of human suffering . . . during the second World War the Red Cross extended its concern to all *victims* of the war, no matter who they were'; emphasis in the original.)

[60] Ibid., 10. [61] Ibid., 10; see also *Preliminary Conference*, 124–5.

[62] *Documents IV*, 3–4. [63] Ibid., 10. [64] Ibid., 10–11.

[65] *Preliminary Conference*, 126. [66] Ibid., 73.

case. International law must be brought into line with actual facts'.[67] Specifically, it promoted 'a broader juridical basis' for the work of its delegates.[68] It did not, however, seek to reconcile this ambivalence.

These shifts underscore the ambiguity in the argumentative framework deployed by the ICRC at this preliminary phase. On the one hand, it was averse to regulation of Red Cross and ICRC mandate, and even denied having legal mandate. On the other, it was somehow open to some codification of some existing activities. Like its very mandate, this framework for arguing legal mandate afforded the ICRC extreme elasticity.

4.2 *Second phase: promoting, not arguing, mandate*

The next phase of the process signified, in one sense, complete departure on the ICRC's part from the arguments it elaborated for and presented at the Preliminary Conference. Between 1947 and 1949, the ICRC did not use that argumentative framework at all. It altogether abstained from denying or confirming that it had legal mandate or arguing about whether or not it ought to have one. Indeed, the word 'mandate' (or 'legal basis') is patently missing from ICRC statements and reports pertaining to the proceedings of this phase. The ICRC no longer *argued* mandate.

Instead, it would now *promote* its relief mandate. In this sense, what started at the Preliminary Conference was a sign of things to come. From the Conference of Government Experts to the Diplomatic Conference, the ICRC would engage in a more-or-less sustained effort to entrench, albeit selectively, its own mandate, including on relief, in the emerging new Conventions.

The ICRC now worked to expand and solidify certain aspects of its mandate. It would now embody the role of a technical expert – but one that also had a legitimate stake in the outcome of revision – availing its vast experience to government experts, thus combining its operational and legal roles. In doing so, the ICRC would not reference its earlier arguments, especially its aversion to mandate, even when these were reproduced by states seeking to undermine its position under the emerging texts.[69]

[67] Ibid., 107. [68] Ibid., 73–4.

[69] Discussed *infra*; nor did it respond to the Holy See's allusion to a mistaken belief that the 1929 Convention gave 'the Red Cross the monopoly of relief work': *Stockholm Report*, 48–9.

Mandate promotion was affected by means other than argument. At times, the ICRC was content with not being named in specific proposals, if only the formula used was broad enough to somehow include it.[70] At others, it found ways to include explicit references to itself.[71] At times, it openly declined proposed mandate.[72] It heavily recalled its past activities and expertise in relief,[73] but where established practice went well beyond existing language, it did not always seek express recognition of the former.[74] Frequently, its expertise and experience were called on; at times it offered these on its own initiative.[75] Where favourable, it recalled the debates or recommendations of previous stages of the legislative process. But it also 'tinkered with ... drafts that issued from' one conference en route to the next.[76] It let others sing its praise (regardless of their true motives)[77] and, often, it would let others promote the positions or language it favoured.[78]

The record suggests that securing an explicit, broad mandate concerning 'supervision', or 'control' of the Conventions' application, i.e. visits by its delegates, was of paramount priority for the ICRC.[79] But ensuring it had *some* relief mandate also must have ranked high. This had three aspects: firstly, the ICRC did not seek a positive, explicit treaty right for itself to engage in relief. Rather, it consistently promoted, in the context of the right of relief agencies to deliver relief supplies, the preservation of its own 'special position'.[80] Secondly, it laboured not only to preserve the

[70] *Government Experts*, 194–5.

[71] Ibid., 189, 196, 200, 227, 233, 234–8, 249–53; ICRC, 'Draft Revised or New Conventions for the Protection of War Victims Established by the International Committee of the Red Cross with the Assistance of Government Experts, National Red Cross Societies and Other Humanitarian Associations – XVIIth International Red Cross Conference' (Stockholm, August 1948) (May 1948) ['*May Draft*'] 9, 36, 157, 175, 177, and 224.

[72] *Government Experts*, 67 (resisted role in appointing commissions of enquiry into violations).

[73] *Final Record II.A*, 666, 750; it submitted its three-volume, *Report of the International Committee of the Red Cross on its activities during the Second World War*, 1 September 1939–30 June 1947 (Geneva: ICRC, 1948) to the Stockholm Conference: *Junod, Imperiled*, at 234.

[74] *Government Experts*, 256–7.

[75] E.g. *Final Record II.A*, 262, 750, 751, 755, 766, etc.

[76] Best, *War*, 3.

[77] E.g. *Final Record II.A*, 10–12, 16, 260, 409, 730 etc.; *Final Record II.B*, 371, 515–17, etc.

[78] *Government Experts*, 254, 270–1.

[79] Ibid., 200, 227 262 *et seq.*, 296–7, 137–8, 148, 180; *Final Record II.A*, 302–3, 687, 773.

[80] *Government Experts*, 254–5 (PoWs), 290–1 (civilians); *May Draft*, 131; *Stockholm Report*, 98.

saving clause, inserting it in all four drafts,[81] but also to ensure that it now would refer also to 'relief' in addition to 'protection'[82] (in both matters, unnamed state delegations made the proposals). Thirdly, it strove to defend the text of different draft provisions dealing with relief (including its mandate) against undue restriction,[83] ensure they contained some reference to the ICRC, and infuse these with a broad measure of discretion.[84]

In sharp contrast to what it expressed at the preliminary phase, now the ICRC would not elaborate on whether mandate was an impediment to or a necessary tool for its relief operations. Yet there were many occasions where arguing mandate, its merits and pitfalls, would have appeared warranted. Most arose during the Diplomatic Conference, which saw several challenges to the ICRC's relief tasks.

One such case occurred early, when its special expertise on relief came under challenge.[85] It maintained its silence. Another concerned a British proposal, somewhat supported by the Holy See, to delete an explicit reference to the ICRC's 'special position' in the field of relief. The grounds cited were that this position was 'already recognised' elsewhere in the text; that 'another reference' may weaken the position of 'other relief societies'; but also that – echoing the ICRC's own preliminary arguments – another mention of the ICRC 'would only tend to weaken [its] . . . position'.[86] The ICRC representative only agreed to other aspects of the Holy See's proposal: he let the Venezuelan delegate justify 'the special reference to the [ICRC] in view of the activity and efficiency of that organisation'.[87] On the British proposal, the ICRC 'thought the reference was valuable and helpful as far as its own activities were concerned'; but rather than demur on principle, he merely invoked the pedigree of the text in question.[88] What objections it had, the ICRC raised privately.[89]

81 *May Draft*, esp. 56, 8, 36, and 156–7.
82 *Government Experts*, 268, 280–1, 293, 298; *Stockholm Report*, 11, 33, 54 and 116.
83 *Final Record II.A*, 286–7, 300, 498–9, 644, 751, etc.
84 *Government Experts*, 187–9, 192–3; *May Draft*, 147, 175; *Stockholm Text*, 77, 112.
85 *Final Record II.A*, 15–17, 24–8 (French proposal to give the League of Red Cross Societies equal recognition at the conference, due to expertise in e.g. 'distributing relief').
86 Ibid., 301, 458.
87 Ibid., 301.
88 Recounting that the text 'had not been made at the request of the ICRC, but had been introduced in 1947, at the Conference of Government Experts, at the suggestion of the delegation': *Final Record II.A*, 302; see also 286–7 (limits on ICRC's role on individual relief to PoWs); 667 (whether Occupying Power's right to refuse relief consignments refers also to the ICRC).
89 Later, the UK withdrew its proposal: *Final Record II.A*, 341, 458.

Negotiating the saving clause provided governments with another occasion for limiting ICRC mandate and reversing its earlier aversions against it. The United Kingdom 'feared' that too many mentions of the ICRC would not safeguard its position but 'would have the opposite effect as, the more precisely the duties of the Committee were defined, the more risk there was of governments opposing all activities which had not been expressly foreseen'. It proposed to delete, in 'the interest of the humanitarian work' of the ICRC, 'the mention of certain detailed functions of the Committee'.[90] In 1946, the ICRC itself might have argued this. But now, to retain the text, the ICRC admitted that the 1929 provision proved 'extremely useful' in light of the need 'to exercise considerable activity' during the Second World War. It even emphasised 'the importance attached by the I.C.R.C. to this'.[91] But it also played down the innovative nature of the language, belittled the extent of obligations it imposed on governments,[92] and noted that it was 'introduced at previous Conferences and at the request of different countries'.[93] Here and on similar occasions,[94] it would not rectify such representations on the nature of its own mandate as were made by others.

4.3 *Fostering mandate ambiguity*

At different stages of the process of producing the Geneva Conventions, the ICRC presented, by statements and behaviour, conflicting positions on the utility of assistance mandate.[95] From initial aversion to, even open denial of, having a treaty-drawn legal mandate, the ICRC shifted to promoting legal mandate in the emerging texts of the new treaties. Mandate was an impediment but, at the same time, *some type* of mandate was also 'extremely useful'. What really mattered for the ICRC,

[90] *Final Record II.B*, 20. [91] Ibid., 20–1.

[92] Ibid., 20 (text 'involved no commitment for the governments and merely restated the freedom of action of the [ICRC]').

[93] Ibid., 21.

[94] In another context, the French and others would take the 1946 ICRC arguments even further: the ICRC 'does not act by virtue of a mandate but according to moral laws which go far beyond all mandates': *Final Record II.B*, 22; see also 23, 27, 34, 98–9, 101.

[95] It also contradicted itself on its own character in relief. When asked 'Can the International Committee of the Red Cross be called a relief society?' it replied 'No! Strictly speaking it is not a relief society. In ... the late war [the ICRC] transported ... relief supplies, but only in the capacity of a neutral intermediary': *Final Record II.B*, 350. On other occasions it argued that its 'chief duty, in time of war, is to be an agency for relief': *Documents IV*, 23.

it appears, was to have the ability to rely on legal mandate but, at the same time, to deny it. And the mandate it did promote was quite ambiguous: on the one hand, it gave the ICRC a very few, very limited, and hardly exclusive roles in matters of assistance. On the other, it contained two provisions that hinted at a much broader role in assistance, one that predated the Conventions and existed, somehow, outside their proper framework. The Diplomatic Conference and the Conventions it produced, in one sense, gave the ICRC assistance mandate;[96] in another, they only sanctioned it.

Rather than mandate, what the ICRC promoted by word and deed between 1946 and 1949 was mandate ambiguity. It fostered ambiguity by expressing different positions on its mandate; by departing from declared aversion to active promotion of mandate; by remaining silent when others had relied on its own arguments on the nature, utility and pitfalls of its mandate; and by its consistent effort to secure mandate that was, itself, ambiguous. After 1949, notwithstanding its legislative achievements, the ICRC would retain this ambiguity. Parallel to formulating and presenting the broad assertion of conventional mandate with which we are familiar today, it also reverted to some mandate aversion.[97] In 1962 it would argue that it had a conventional 'mandate to fulfil' but also that, unlike protecting powers, the 'ICRC is not the mandatory of anyone, but acts on its own initiative with complete independence'.[98]

5. Mandate practised

Finally, the utility and limits of assistance mandate are demonstrated by how the ICRC uses that mandate in its operational practice.[99] The starting point here must be that what assistance operations the ICRC

[96] Resolution 11, *Final Record I*, 362 ('the Geneva Conventions require the [ICRC] to be ready at all times and in all circumstances to fulfil the humanitarian tasks entrusted to it by these Conventions'); see *Junod, Imperiled*, at 276–7.

[97] Pictet, *Commentary*, 103–6 (saving clause), 600 *et seq.* (ICRC's 'special position').

[98] ICRC, *Course of Five Lessons on the Geneva Conventions* (Geneva: ICRC, 1962), 18–19, 30.

[99] Between January and March 2013, I conducted semi-structured interviews with seven ICRC delegates in management, assistance, and other professional positions. Combined, this group had a vast operational experience in terms of years, geographical coverage, and types of situations. The interviews were conducted under a guarantee of anonymity, and sought no country- or actor-specific information; they are on file with the author. This section relies heavily on these interviews, while some of what follows is loosely based on Ratner, 'Law Promotion'.

undertakes today bear very little relation to its conventional mandate. Indeed, more ICRC activities today take place in internal armed conflict than in international armed conflict, and more in 'other situations of violence' than in any type of armed conflict. Its operational profile, in other words, necessarily takes the ICRC beyond the 'core' situations dealt with by the Conventions into areas where activities cannot be related to any conventional text.

Speaking to ICRC delegates, one encounters a recurring answer to questions about the actual use of assistance mandate: 'it depends'. The variety of today's assistance operations, the violent situations where they take place, the actors involved and the beneficiaries they target makes it so. Clearly, there are no uniform answers. One non-state armed group may itself inquire as to the ICRC's legal basis of, or precedent for, operating relief programmes. Another may be hostile to law-based arguments. In one setting – for example vis-à-vis a state with developed bureaucracy and legal services – basing a proposed assistance project on conventional mandate may facilitate its acceptance by the authorities; or, as I will show below, be superfluous.

Yet certain trends appear. One is that flexibility is an operational necessity. It is also clear that broad public assertions of mandate do not quite reflect how the ICRC in fact approaches concrete assistance operations. In assistance operations, legal mandate is an instrument: as one delegate put it, it will be used when, and only when, relying on mandate would promote the assistance mission.

Beyond assessed utility, some factors may support the invocation of mandate while others militate against it. Such invocations will be more likely to be made at the initial stages of ICRC involvement in specific situations. Operating, without exception, with the consent of the parties to conflict, the ICRC will tend to invoke legal mandate when reminding them of their obligations or offering its services. Even then, where the qualification of the situation (for example as an armed conflict or occupation) is controverted, or the parties uninterested in ICRC involvement or in acknowledging its entitlement to be involved, the ICRC may avoid citing its mandate altogether.

Within the ICRC, assistance mandate tends to be used at higher levels (within delegations) or from its Geneva headquarters (only a few delegations have legal advisers). Correspondingly, mandate is more likely to be invoked vis-à-vis higher levels of authorities and interlocutors, i.e. decision-makers at strategic or political levels. Interviewees in managerial positions displayed more knowledge and nuanced understanding of the

ICRC's assistance mandate and its use in practice than those engaged in operating assistance programmes. Both groups generally shared the perception that the latter's involvement in the assessment, design, and implementation of specific assistance programmes, including dialogue with authorities, requires technical or professional expertise rather than mandate (or legal) erudition.

Another variable concerns acceptability. At times, invoking mandate will be superfluous. Assistance programmes, a few delegates noted, are 'less controversial' than protection activities involving monitoring the parties' compliance (i.e. violation) record. Whether aimed at support for or substitution of capacities or action, assistance usually offers parties concrete economic, political, even moral benefits. There is no need to invoke mandate to addressees willing to receive assistance. Likewise, there may be more receptiveness to, but less use for, dialogue on the ICRC mandate where a working relationship with the authorities on an institutional or personal level has already established knowledge and trust of the ICRC. Conversely, mandate reliance will often be avoided where actors are simply uninterested in allowing ICRC assistance on grounds of security, sovereignty and so on. To an extent, the operational utility of mandate appears limited by paradox: at the core of ICRC activities, where mandate is firm, it is accepted but less needed. At the periphery, outside armed conflict, it is thinnest, least accepted, but most needed.

Variety characterises also the ways in which the ICRC alludes to its legal mandate. It can invoke mandate by very loose reference to the Geneva Conventions (or other sources) or reference specific treaty provisions at its own initiative or upon request. But it can also volunteer or respond to a challenge by mere reference to similar practice elsewhere, to precedent, or even to a very broad analogy. Likely effects determine not just whether mandate will be used but also how it will be used.

The limited, if unforeseeable, role of mandate reliance in assistance is underscored through comparison to protection. To varying degrees, all interviewees have noted that mandate (and legal) arguments play a relatively minor role in assistance, as compared to protection operations (even if assistance needs may at times be dealt with under 'protection', and vice versa). Beyond interests and acceptability, the reasons offered for this difference are the different *nature* of these activities. Protection is rights-based, and thus more amenable to legal and mandate arguments. Need-based assistance, however, is more technical. Assistance delegates turn to ICRC lawyers much less than their protection counterparts, and ICRC lawyers are occupied with protection much more than with assistance. It is no accident that no single reference to legal mandate (or law) can be found in the public version of the ICRC's 'Assistance Policy'; the counterpart 'Protection Policy' is rife with references to legal bases.[100]

6. Mandate assessed

The three arenas discussed here – public position, legislative process, and operational practice – offer different perspectives on assistance mandate. For the ICRC as an organisation engaged in assistance operations, legal mandate is crucial, helpful, and dangerous all at the same time. To an extent, this answer is a product of the ICRC's idiosyncratic combination of legal and operational roles and other aspects of its institutional culture; but it is often also grounded in the challenges of assistance operations. If so, then underscoring the differences, even contradictions, in what the ICRC says and does in different arenas cannot be enough. The question really is whether some coherence and instruction can be found in such diverse, or divergent, practice. What is it about assistance, legal mandate, and the ICRC itself that make it display divergent perspectives on assistance mandate? To answer these questions, we need first to consider what makes legal mandate hazardous, helpful, and crucial.

The dangers of codified, detailed mandate were noted by the ICRC in the preliminary phase of the legislative process producing the Geneva Conventions of 1949. In the argumentative framework it presented in 1946, mandate aversion underscored that, parallel to empowerment, mandate also imposes political, operational, and legal constraints. Legal mandate makes ICRC work 'dependent' on states; lack of mandate makes the ICRC independent from whether states ratify and abide by the treaties containing such mandate.[101] Legal mandate spells rigidity; its absence, elasticity and independence.[102] Worse, mandate hinders future institutional and operational development; this is anathema to the ICRC's very identity, as is patent in the view of its own history – or for that matter, of IHL – as a tale of progressive yet cautious incrementalism.[103] And worst yet, too broad a mandate for assistance organisations

[100] *Supra* note 10, I am told that this difference exists also in the internal versions.
[101] *Documents IV*, 10; see also *Preliminary Conference*, 124–5.
[102] *Documents IV*, 3–4.
[103] See text cited n. 59; Bugnion, *Protection*, 351; ('every activity . . . by the ICRC can be traced back to an initiative taken by it on some occasion'); Forsythe, *Humanitarians*, 2, 281; J. D. Armstrong, 'The International Red Cross Committee and Political Prisoners', *International Organisation* 39 (1985): 615, 621; Marco Sassòli, Antoin Bouvier, and

may entail complete exemption of the authors of needs and wants: 'had specific duties been entrusted to the [ICRC] and its activities imposed upon the belligerent parties, the latter might have been tempted to shift to the Committee the responsibility for carrying out their own obligations'.[104]

These concerns all combine to explain the ICRC's insistence that private character and tradition underscore the expansion of its work, and that its mandate really is to be found somewhere preceding or outside the conventional framework.[105] Such markers of independence from the fetters of mandate were explicit in 1946. They also underscored the limited mandate sought by the ICRC later in the legislative process. Consequently, today they are implicit in the multiplicity of sources for the ICRC's asserted mandate and, in particular, in its right of initiative. The flexibility required by the variety of assistance exigencies today appears to vindicate the ICRC's apprehensions. And broad assertions of mandate by the ICRC have not curtailed its independence: that much of its assistance activities take place beyond the core of its mission attests to that.

Yet for the ICRC, mandate is also crucial. For all the aversion it expressed, it had also consistently worked to ensure that the 1949 Conventions contain language that can be construed as legal mandate to undertake assistance and other activities. The depth of the ICRC's commitment to mandate is underscored by the measure of the obstacles it had to surmount in those post-war years in order to secure it. The ICRC was beset, on the one hand, with acute moral and financial crisis; on the other it faced, during the legislative process, a series of challenges – within the Red Cross Movement and by states – to internationalise, subordinate, weaken, even depose it.[106]

Anne Quintin, *How Does Law Protect in War?* (Cambridge University Press, 3rd ed., 2011), 465.

[104] Pictet, *Commentary*, 104; emphases added. Note also the assertion that 'Article 9 is of great value from the point of view of principle, since it provides a corner for something which no legal text can prescribe': ibid., 109. Cf. *infra* note 111.

[105] *Documents IV*, 3–4, 10.

[106] For background: Best, *War*, 80–179; *Junod, Imperiled, passim*, who suggests that revising the conventions helped the ICRC deflect threats to dismantle or replace it and reinforced its position within the movement, 23 *et seq.*, esp. 30–3; she implies, similarly, that expansion of mandate was designed to aid the ICRC in overcoming its financial crisis: 'the Committee's financial recovery was closely linked to the continuation of its activities and their possible extension'. She goes too far, however, in stating that 'the ICRC wanted future conventions to expand its own legal grounds for intervention by assigning to it

The import of legal mandate stems in no small measure from the ICRC's own culture and identity: how can it be otherwise for the 'guardian and promoter' of IHL? In part, it stems from how the ICRC views the function of mandate: no less an entitlement for future activities than approbation of activities past.[107] Indeed, the ICRC reads such approbation, express or implied, not only in treaties but also in the Movement Statutes and its resolutions. Likewise, in the lack of state protest it reads approbation by acquiescence.[108] In this sense, mandate expresses not the consent of this or that state, but legitimisation of the ICRC and its work by the international community as a whole. Yet the significance of mandate is rooted also in operational considerations.

For the ICRC, working with the consent of the parties is a *sine qua non* for the imperative of gaining access to victims.[109] Mandate can be a formal right to provide assistance; sometimes, the ICRC invokes mandate as a claim of source legitimacy. But for the ICRC, greater merit resides in the social legitimacy of the demand to have access to those in need of assistance. In this sense, mandate is not about normative right, but about social acceptability and operational access. It is small wonder that, in 1949, the ICRC objected to a proposal to make acceptance of its offer of services mandatory on parties to non-international armed conflict. It worked to weaken, not strengthen, the legal force of its offer of service.[110]

This interpretation of mandate explains why the ICRC promoted treaty texts envisaging a 'soft' role in assistance rather than a general, positive, explicit right to provide relief. If access to victims requires the consent of the authorities anyway, there is little to be gained by insisting on 'hard' mandate. Subordinating ICRC mandate to such consent comes with little, if any, cost. 'Soft' mandate, comprised of the right to offer, advise, recommend, etc., has the advantage of increasing the likelihood that the ICRC can engage in a conversation about assistance needs and

every foreseeable task'; 36 *et seq.* Mandate expansion had its contemporary uses, but tradition and other imperatives, as I show, militated against an unbridled expansion of mandate.

107 See pp. 92, 95, 101.

108 *Government Experts*, 255 ('ICRC's qualification as a recognised Aid Society has never been questioned').

109 Jakob Kellenberger, 'Speaking out or Remaining Silent in Humanitarian Work', *IRRC* 855 (2004): 593, esp. 600 *et seq.*; Jean-Luc Blondel, 'Getting Access to the Victims: Role and Activities of the ICRC', *Journal of Peace Research* 24 (1987): 307.

110 *Final Record II.B*, 95 (ICRC 'strength ... was its independence, which would be jeopardised if the ICRC were mentioned in any mandatory clause').

the ways to solve them. If soft mandate is more acceptable than hard mandate, it also tends to promote the acceptability of ICRC engagement in assistance. It also helps manage responsibility.[111] From this perspective, securing a *legitimate* role matters more than its precise contours and shape. This view of mandate also explains the ends to which the ICRC asserts broad legal mandate notwithstanding its expression in 'a series of disconnected obligations which, together, do not make up a coherent whole'.[112] Like invoking multiple sources for mandate,[113] assertions of broad mandate seek to denote its acceptance while, at the same time, avoid the rigidity and constraints it entails. This view of mandate, equally, informs the conflation, in ICRC mandate vocabulary, of 'right', 'duty', 'prerogative', etc.[114]

This suggests that the utility of mandate is somewhat less limited than that suggested by the infrequent use of mandate in actual assistance operations. Diverse variables may make, in most cases, direct reliance on assistance mandate neither necessary nor beneficial. But being able to demonstrate, and not in legal terms, the social acceptability of its involvement in assistance may be precisely what gives the ICRC just enough acceptability to initiate a dialogue about assistance. Together with impartiality, neutrality and independence, ICRC mandate – explicit, implicit, even imputed – may create openings even where belligerents find assistance suspect or objectionable. Mandate is one of the factors making the ICRC predictable and, as such, more acceptable.

Finally, mandate may present other advantages. Externally, mandate sometimes gives an ICRC a 'comparative advantage', as one ICRC delegate put it, over other assistance actors lacking it.[115] It is in part the reason why the ICRC can demonstrate, more readily than some other humanitarian actors, its impartiality, neutrality, and independence to suspecting authorities and armed actors: its very claim of mandate encapsulates these traits. And, internally, mandate equips the ICRC with

111 Having mandate conditioned on state consent offers a shielding advantage: as much justification for action as for inaction, it furnished the ICRC with a useful argument to cleanse its tarnished WWII record: per *Junod, Imperiled*, 45–6, the 1929 'Conventions relieved it of much of the responsibility for its failures or successes, since these always depended ultimately on the consent of the belligerents'.

112 Bugnion, *Protection, 350.*

113 See *supra* notes 31–35.

114 See *supra* notes 36–45.

115 That edge over others is implicit in the 'special position' clause. Pictet, *Commentary*, 601 makes the implication explicit: 'restrictions on the activities of relief societies could not, in principle, be applied to the [ICRC] or at least that the Committee was the last body to which they should be applied'.

tools to both facilitate and monitor the development of its own operations. It helps preserve institutional identity and ensure that operational independence does not stray too far from core missions.

7. Conclusion

The ICRC example suggests that legal mandate offers actors engaged in assistance both risks and advantages. But even if these insights are deeply rooted in ICRC idiosyncrasies, these idiosyncrasies in turn reflect dilemmas to which other assistance organisations are no strangers: independence, access, acceptance, substitution, and so forth. And while different agencies cope with these dilemmas in different ways, the ICRC example – perhaps because of its complexities – holds insights that may often be true for others.

The key insight is that legal mandate is not, and perhaps should not be, a straightforward proposition. Assertion, invocation, and reliance on legal mandate are not necessarily tantamount to excessive doctrinal legalism, hyper-formalism, or operational rigidity. The ICRC's experience illustrates that mandate does not preclude ambiguity, and that ambiguity has its merits. Mandate ambiguity – in text, source, or vocabulary – is precisely what enables the ICRC to mediate between the different imperatives of its many roles across different arenas. And it is precisely what enables the ICRC to operate with predictable consistency in the vast diversity of conditions and variables characterising today's assistance operations. Ambiguity also helps the ICRC to avoid some of the pitfalls of mandate while drawing on some of its advantages: not always, not everywhere, but significantly enough.

That the ICRC has managed, for all its assertions of broad legal mandate grounded in positive international law, to hold onto its operational independence is the best defence of ambiguity. If the last few decades saw, as David Rieff argues, an unparalleled growth in the dependence of humanitarian assistance on governments, their agenda and their funding, this only makes mandate ambiguity all the more imperative. Evidently, the ICRC example shows that having legal mandate does not necessarily entail loss of independence; it appears that the converse is equally true: being entirely free from legal mandate is no guarantee against dependence.

This leads to a host of new questions about mandate and about ambiguity: how does each operate in the minds of those who author it or those to whom it is addressed? How can the ICRC get away with displaying, in the same arena, open hostility to mandate while promoting it? How does it come to terms with saying and doing different things in different arenas? Does ambivalence to mandate inhere in this peculiar institution, or did it emerge only with the expansion of its operational profile in the Second World War? And, not the least important, what costs attach to mandate ambiguity – costs to normative clarity, to the ICRC, to others engaged in assistance, to intended beneficiaries? These and other questions cannot be answered here; but they offer, surely, exciting avenues for future inquiries into interactions of law, humanitarian action, and institutional cultures.

5

Issues of state consent and international humanitarian assistance in disasters: the work of the International Law Commission

DABIRU SRIDHAR PATNAIK

1. Introduction

This chapter is drawn from the study that has been undertaken by the United Nations International Law Commission (ILC or Commission) on the 'Protection of Individuals in the Event of Disasters'. Presently there is no comprehensive multilateral treaty existing at the international level that inculcates principles of law governing disasters albeit there are certain rules that have been codified in some multilateral treaties,[1] at the global and regional levels, and in bilateral treaties and memoranda of understanding. The international law governing disaster response has developed into a complex set of rules governing the initiation of relief, issues of status, and the provision of relief itself, and questions of access. After the study was commissioned in 2007, the Special Rapporteur submitted five reports as of August 2012 adopting draft articles. Significant issues that were the subject matter of these reports pertain to the question

[1] For instance, the *Convention on Assistance in the case of a Nuclear Accident or a Radiological Emergency* (1986), the *Tampere Convention on the Provision of Telecommunications Resources for Disaster Mitigation and Relief Operations* (1998). Other multilateral treaties of relevance with specific disaster relief activities in the context of land, air, maritime transportation and customs proceedures are the *Convention on the Privileges and Immunities of the United Nations* (1946), the *Convention concerning International Carriage by Rail* (1980), the *Convention on International Civil Aviation* (1944), the *Convention on Facilitation of International Maritime Traffic* (1965), *International Convention for the Simplification and Harmonisation of Customs Procedures* ('Kyoto' Convention of 1973), *Customs Convention on the ATA Carnet for the Temporary Admission of Goods* (1961), *Convention on Temporary Admission* ('Istanbul' Convention 1990), all for addressing relief consignments. See for a survey of multilateral treaties in areas of disaster relief and coordination with a thematic scope, David Fisher, 'Overview of Current Legal Frameworks Applicable to International Disaster Response Law', in IFRC, *Law and Legal Issues in International Disaster Response Law: a Desk Study* (Geneva: IFRC, 2007), 33–82.

of the primary responsibility of the affected state for protecting persons under its territorial jurisdiction and the affected state's consent for providing international assistance, which also raised issues concerning the fundamental principles of sovereignty and non-intervention. The introduction of these provisions has undoubtedly given a fresh impetus to the debate on state consent versus obligation to receive international humanitarian assistance. It necessitates reflection on some of the core questions to be answered. They are: whether there is an obligation on the affected state not to reject humanitarian assistance in situations of human suffering, and if so, what the role of people living in the affected state in response to such a situation should be; how and when authority shifts to the international capacity for protection of people in the event of disasters, without that power being misused; and when humanitarian concerns should surpass sovereignty. International law, through the work of the Commission, should answer these questions in order to have a clear formulation for predictability and coherence to reconcile the tension between humanitarian access, humanitarian perspectives and sovereignty. It is envisioned that understanding of these complexities will bring out subject matter of norms of duty to cooperate and duty to seek aid. While addressing issues mentioned in the foregoing, the aim of this paper is to reflect and evaluate the work of the ILC and the implications of its draft legal rules on humanitarian access concerning disasters, particularly viewed from the perspective of developing countries.

The paper is divided into three parts. Section 1 of the paper deals with setting of the work of the International Law Commission. Section 2 will address the analytical concerns relating to role of states vis à vis international humanitarian assistance. Section 3 of the paper will deal with possible approaches to the dilemmas of international humanitarian assistance within the sources of a theoretical framework. Some concluding observations are offered in the later part of the paper.

2. The background and work of the International Law Commission

During the first World Conference of Humanitarian Studies (WCHS) hosted by the University of Groningen in 2009, the author had the privilege of presenting a paper entitled 'Towards an International Legal Regime for Protection of Persons in the Event of Disasters'.[2] This paper is

[2] Dabiru Sridhar Patnaik, 'Towards an International Legal Framework for the Protection of Individuals in the Event of Disasters: An Initial Inquiry', in *International Law and*

based on the work of the International Law Commission (ILC or Commission) that had on its agenda the topic 'Protection of Individuals in the Event of Disasters'. At the time of the first WCHS, the ILC had just commenced its work. By this time, to speak of further developments, the Commission had before it draft articles proposed by the Special Rapporteur. So, for future formulation, while assessing issues of international humanitarian assistance, the author advocated the need for states to understand the functional interdependence between human rights, human dignity and international responsibility. Yet this having been said, for now Draft Article 8[3] is relevant, and particularly the phrasing of the Draft Article relating to humanitarian assistance for the normative aspects relating to the international legal framework in situations of disasters. It lays emphasis on the primary responsibility factor of states in providing humanitarian assistance in situations of disasters. With all its labyrinthine developments, it is important to examine the implications of Draft Article 8, as it entails the willingness or consent of states to receive assistance of such a nature. In the process, it is also relevant to inquire if there is a right for intervention to offer humanitarian assistance. This is a touchy issue given its historical and current contexts.

In 2007, the International Law Commission (ILC or Commission) at the 59th session included the topic 'Protection of Persons in the Event of Disasters' on its agenda. At the 60th session in 2008, the Commission considered the Preliminary Report of the Special Rapporteur. It studied the evolution of protection of persons in disasters, identifying the sources of law on the topic and the earlier efforts towards codification and progressive development of law in the area. The Commission also

Humanitarian Assistance: A Crosscut through Legal Issues pertaining to Humanitarianism, eds. Hans-Joachim Heintze and Andrej Zwitter (Heidelberg: Springer-Verlag Berlin, 2011), 129–141. It is a revised version of the paper presented to the first World Conference of Humanitarian Studies, University of Groningen, The Netherlands. The conference was organised by the Universities of Groningen, Wageningen and Ruhr-Bochum, 4–7 February 2009.

3 Draft article 8: Primary responsibility of the affected state:

'1. The affected State has the primary responsibility for the protection of persons and provision of humanitarian assistance on its territory. The State retains the right, under its national law, to direct, control, coordinate and supervise such assistance within its territory.
2. External assistance may be provided only with the consent of the affected State.'

See 'Third report of the Special Rapporteur, 62nd Session of the International Law Commission' (A/CN.4/629), 31 March 2010, 34.

considered the Memorandum by the Secretariat that focused primarily on natural disasters providing an overview of current legal instruments and texts applicable to aspects of disaster prevention and relief assistance.

The second report of the Special Rapporteur was considered by the Commission at its 61st session in 2009. It analysed the scope of the topic – material, personal and temporal – and issues relating to definition of disasters, as well as emphasising the basic duty to cooperate.

The Commission at its 62nd session, in 2010, considered the third report of the Special Rapporteur. It provided for views of states on the work of the Commission apart from dealing with consideration of principles that inspired the protection of persons in disasters. Most importantly the Commission considered the issue relating to the responsibility of the affected state. There were proposals for three draft articles in the report. They are: Draft Article 6 ('Humanitarian principles in disaster response'); Draft Article 7 ('Human dignity') and Draft Article 8 ('Primary responsibility of the affected State').[4] The third report of the Special Rapporteur was based on the debate held on the second report and the Special Rapporteur was asked to focus on two issues of paramount importance. These are, in the first place, the issue of state consent and humanitarian principles of humanity, neutrality and impartiality and, secondly, the issue of the primary responsibility of the affected state for the protection of persons under its territorial jurisdiction. These aspects, as we are aware, also raise issues relating to fundamental international law principles of sovereignty and non-intervention.[5] In the subsequent reports in 2011 and 2012, the International Law Commission considered issues relating to responsibility of the affected state to seek assistance where its national response capacity has been exceeded, and the duty of the affected state not to arbitrarily withhold consent to external assistance, followed by the consideration of conditions of provision of assistance that were discussed in the Commission respectively.

3. Analytical concerns: issues of responsibility of states and humanitarian assistance

If the present project on international legal aspects for protection of victims of disasters should succeed, then as a point of departure, the

[4] Report of the International Law Commission (3 May–4 June and 5 July–6 August 2010), General Assembly Official Records, 65th Session, Supplement No. 10 (A/65/10), §294, 313.

[5] Ibid., §300, 314.

International Law Commission should make certain fundamental issues clear. Obviously a reasoned choice had to be made on those questions whose answers depend upon a careful assessment of normative and institutional inadequacies. Questions relevant and necessary for the purpose of analysis are, what if states took a hard-line position to refuse or deny international humanitarian assistance; and and what the elements of consideration should be to address such a scenario. In order to answer these aspects, further insights are needed as to what obligations states owe to their subjects; while simultaneously asking what obligation states or the international community owe to fellow human beings abroad in target states that deny or refuse international humanitarian assistance. These issues merit considerable study.

According to the Commission commentary, several members proposed to restate the principles of sovereignty and non-intervention in the domestic affairs of a state and suggested that they should constitute the primary principles on the basis of which the legal regime for the protection of persons in the event of disasters was to be developed. Such an approach would reflect the rights of the affected state vis à vis humanitarian assistance. The other view expressed was that the reference to principles of sovereignty and non-intervention in Draft Article 8(2) requiring state consent was inadequate and that there should be greater understanding of the current nuances of state sovereignty.[6] According to the Commentary, some members were of the view that primary responsibility did not mean exclusive responsibility and that states are responsible for the refusal to accept external humanitarian assistance that could lead to the existence of an international wrongful act if such refusal undermined the rights of affected individuals under international law.[7] It was also suggested that there should be reference to secondary responsibility of the international community.[8] But there was a further view that rightly suggests that under contemporary international law, the international community did not enjoy a secondary responsibility for the protection of victims of disasters. In the debate about the nature of secondary duties in international law, Stephen Vasciannie[9] notes that the words 'primary responsibility' imply that there are secondary duties and exhort states

[6] Ibid., §316, 318. [7] Ibid., §318, 318. [8] Ibid., §318, 319.

[9] Stephen Vasciannie, 'International Law and disasters', *Jamaica Observer*, 27 June 2010, accessed 3 May 2011, www.jamaicaobserver.com/columns/International-law-and-disasters_7744354.

to undertake secondary responsibilities. This might set a stage for the possibility of intervention against the will of the affected state.

Therefore, there were views expressed that reference to 'primary' responsibility should be deleted as it implied the existence of secondary duties, which might lead to unwarranted interference. A reading of the draft article could indeed be done in diverse ways, and it is subject to interpretation. Difficulties do arise in grasping the intentions of the drafters. Even though the Special Rapporteur is right to mention the practical significance of aspects relating to primary responsibility and consent by referring to various sources of law on the topic, the structure of the draft article still could give rise to many legal implications. To give an example, the import of such observations could be traced back to the UNGA Resolution 46/182 of 17 December 1991. Even advocates of humanitarian imperatives against the will of sovereign states had concerns for the wording of the General Assembly resolution. One such commentator, Nancy Arnison, notes that: 'the significance of state consent goes beyond what is provided for in the resolution. While the resolution affirms sovereignty and states that consent of the "target country" should be obtained before providing humanitarian assistance, the carefully worded language avoids requiring the government's consent, thus opening the door to non-consensual humanitarian intervention'.[10] This analogy is valid in the current situation. These dilemmas have to be dispersed by the Commission. The wording of the draft article could have been tighter and more appropriate. On this issue, at the 63rd session in 2011, the Commission considered the fourth report and the Special Rapporteur, considering the significant relevance of the principles of sovereignty and non-interference, was of the opinion that the contents of the principle of consent of the affected state should be developed.[11] This was an important development considering the underlying tensions between 'protection and principles of respect for territorial sovereignty and non-interference in the internal affairs of the State'.[12] The Special Rapporteur suggests that

[10] Nancy D. Arnison, 'International Law and Non-Intervention: When do Humanitarian Concerns Supersede Sovereignity?', *Fletcher Forum of World Affairs* 17 (1993): 199–211, 204.

[11] 'Report of the International Law Commission' (26 April–3 June and 4 July–12 August 2011), General Assembly Official Records, 63rd Session, Supplement No. 10 (A/66/10), §275, 250.

[12] Ibid.

> principles of sovereignty and non-interference were not to be considered in isolation but rather in the light of the responsibilities of the State in exercising its sovereignty. Such obligations could be seen horizontally in the relationship of the State with the international community, as well as vertically in relation to the people in the State which has suffered the disaster and under its jurisdiction.[13]

As a consequence to this development, there was discussion in the Commission on Draft Article 12 on the right to offer assistance. There was support expressed to the general assertion made in Draft Article 12 that 'offers of assistance were not, *ipso facto*, illegitimate, nor could they be construed as unlawful interference in the internal affairs of the State'.[14] However, it is subject to the condition that the assistance offered did not affect the sovereignty of the affected state. The Special Rapporteur points out that offering assistance in the international community is the practical manifestation of solidarity.[15] Although there was support expressed for this viewpoint, still it was suggested that provisions dealing with the 'right to offer assistance' should clearly lay down circumstances that allow the freedom for the affected state to reject offers of external assistance. In terms of a supplementary view in the Commission, the Draft Article 12 was superfluous, as in the absence of a specific rule of prohibition to the offer of external assistance, then all persons, both natural and legal, had the right to offer assistance to an affected state.[16] It was further suggested, and rightly so, that the provision should avoid reference to 'legal rights' as offers of international assistance from the international actors 'were typically extended as part of international cooperation as opposed to an assertion of rights'.[17] Another salient feature in the development of the work of the International Law Commission on legal rules pertaining to international assistance was the emphasis on 'Conditions on the Provision of External Assistance' (Draft Article 13), discussed at the 64th session of the Commission in 2012. According to this, the affected state may place conditions on the provision of external assistance, in accordance with the applicable rules of international law, and the national law of the affected state. It further builds on the relevance of the needs of the persons affected by disasters and the quality of assistance while formulating the scope and type of assistance sought.[18] It was also suggested that it

[13] Ibid., §276, 250. [14] Ibid., §277, 251. [15] Ibid., §279, 252.
[16] Ibid., §282, 252. [17] Ibid., §281, 252.
[18] Report of the International Law Commission (7 May–1 June and 2 July–3 August 2012), General Assembly Official Records, 64th Session, Supplement No. 10 (A/67/10), 85.

had to be clarified that the conditions imposed by the affected state for the provision of assistance should comply with the national and international human rights norms.[19] It seems possible to affirm that discussions in the Commission should consider the international political arguments relating to concepts of sovereignty and non-interference. Alongside the political arguments, the Commission should consider the key positions of developing countries on the legal evaluations of international law doctrines for subsequent approval of the Commission's work at the Sixth Committee of the United Nations. To a perceptive observer, a thorough examination of contemporary analyses of global events involving situations of disasters and other calamities reveals a compassionate approach towards maintaining positions of international humanitarian assistance. But such benevolent approaches should clearly be influenced by legal considerations put forward by states instead of providing superficial or explicit approval to principles enunciating offers of international assistance in situations of disasters. Any solutions that are offered in the context of international humanitarian assistance in the event of disasters should be congruent with municipal or domestic legal and political choices. It is important to discern and develop legal content for principles of solidarity so as to avoid any unintended consequences to political events.

4. Dichotomy of humanitarian norms

4.1 Operative and substantive norms

These dilemmas of accumulation and legitimacy of international legal norms of disaster relief and humanitarian assistance reappear in one way or another, resulting in a dichotomy of standards. It is an outcome of lack of clarity on issues of state consent and international humanitarian assistance. There cannot be a dichotomy of evolution of international legal standards on one hand, and continued inadequacies of international law in addressing issues of international humanitarian assistance on the other. There has been growth in the discipline ever since the establishment of the United Nations, addressing issues of human rights, nature and flow of investments as they affect trade and economic areas, scientific evolution in the field of genomics, drug inventions, the evolving role of information and communication technology in development leading to

[19] Ibid., §70, 89.

debates concerning the digital divide, protection of cultural diversity, etc. If such was the maturity of thought displayed by the international community, a similar understanding is imperative to clarify certain standards pertaining to humanitarian aid that have remained unresolved for years. In all major aspects, if it is not addressed, the functional utility of the international legal framework would be at stake, which states explicitly or implicitly would not want to happen. The other dichotomy that deserves attention in the given context is that we have operational coordination with the United Nations Office for the Coordination of Humanitarian Affairs as the focal point, but normative coordination is still an issue. Operational and normative procedures that occur in good faith may provide the desired results: otherwise operational goals, however well coordinated, will only compound the crises and leave many more issues unsettled. In this context, one may cite the example of the many international conventions on disaster relief (Tampere, Hyogo et al.) that only provide for operational goals.[20] In a curious sense, if international conventions on disaster relief are alluded to as standard-setting instruments, then the whole exercise of the ILC is uncalled-for. There is a greater need than ever before for a synergy between operational and substantive aspects. A solution is being sought in the elaboration of clear standards in law on aspects of international humanitarian assistance. Any efforts of progressive development and codification of law on the subject should reflect normative transparency/harmonisation, both on substantive and procedural aspects. This endeavour could be achieved if all those agencies, intergovernmental and non-governmental, dealing with human rights and development are involved in the process of creating new international humanitarian norms. If these norms are to have some real meaning and to instil confidence among states and non-states about measures relating to international humanitarian assistance, then other reforms within the United Nations should also take place.

[20] To cap it all, please read the introduction to the IFRC's '*Law and Legal Issues.*' It states that despite the number of international instruments known as 'International Disaster Response Laws, Rules and Principles' (IDRL) there are a number of gaps that are obstructive to international disaster relief operations. Some of the impending issues with respect to disaster relief are initiation and termination of relief operations, facilities for entry and for operations and transport etc. IFRC study, accessed 4 May 2011, www.ifrc.org/PageFiles/41194/113600-idrl-deskstudy-low-en.pdf.

4.2 Humanitarian imperatives and sovereignty

Confronted with the need to provide humanitarian assistance in the absence of state consent, the announcement of humanitarian concerns over sovereign imperatives gathered ground in recent years. Nancy Arnison notes, while referring to A/Res/46/182, that although the resolution does not recognise an explicit right to intervene for humanitarian purposes, it leaves room for the United Nations to decide in particular cases that massive suffering requires humanitarian assistance despite a government's refusal to consent to such aid.[21] In situations of states denying humanitarian access, Nancy Arnison argues for the role of the Security Council to authorise non-forcible or forcible humanitarian intervention, if there is a threat to maintenance of peace and security, and even to include disasters under its ambit.[22] But this argument needs to be embedded with logic at the outset, as we are talking about such measures in peacetime circumstances. Even though the ILC excluded the applicability of the concept of responsibility to protect from the scope of application of draft articles in 2009, nonetheless reference to secondary duties, even if implicit, again warrants the application of the 'Responsibility to Protect' (R2P). The context of the application of R2P *ab initio* is different and cannot even be considered. For a body of the United Nations endowed with the task of progressive development and codification of international law, as has been suggested by this author earlier, the Commission should clearly have made a definitive study of the processes and norms of R2P, and could have ruled out liberating viewpoints of its application to situations of disasters. This could have resulted in creating and sustaining the ethos of legality and fair play in the application of doctrines that still need to be established within legal consciousness. We should understand that international law is not an absolute truth and a veritable framework, even though it should propel optimism in ensuring protection networks. The impact of this feature cannot be overemphasised, and any expansion to the concept of R2P[23] will only lead to further scepticism in the application of international humanitarian assistance.

21 Arnison, 'International Law', 204. 22 Ibid., 208.

23 The appropriateness of extending the concept of the 'Responsibility to Protect' (R2P) and its relevance to the present topic both require careful consideration. Even if R2P were to be recognised in the context of protection and assistance of persons in the event of disasters, its implications would be unclear. This position was subsequently separately taken by the Secretary-General, who, in his 2008 report on implementing the R2P (A/63/677), had indicated that R2P applies, until member states decide otherwise, only to four

5. Approaches: the weighing of the 'publicness' factor

5.1 *Whither multilateralism?*

Any excursions for role of the Security Council to authorise humanitarian assistance in disasters intensifies the need to have a system of United Nations that epitomises multilateralism but not diverse multiple interests.[24] Since the establishment of the United Nations has become a reality and the process of decolonisation had started, all nations have become sovereign and equal recipients of rights and duties in international law. Of relevance here is an observation made by Yogesh Tyagi, about the problems of multiple decision-making with member states of the General Assembly and the Security Council having their respective self-interests, and because of which countries might be unwilling to join expensive humanitarian missions.[25] For a collectivity so large and ideologically diverse, it is important to find out views of developing countries on the nature of international humanitarian assistance that could well serve as a guiding factor in order to ascertain political, normative and operational dilemmas. It is imperative to situate the work of the International Law Commission within old and new paradigms of sovereignty, and to ask how far it travels in the direction of purposes that should be achieved. Therefore, the norm of non-interference becomes important because imbalances in power situations lead to elements of suspicion as intervention to assist enhances the power situation of countries. If we are seeking to postulate this as the purpose of international law, then one can deduce some formidable questions, as viewed from the perspective of developing

specified crimes and violations: genocide, war crimes, ethnic cleansing and crimes against humanity. To try to extend it to cover other calamities such as HIV/AIDS, climate change or response to natural disasters would undermine the 2005 consensus and stretch the concept beyond recognition or operational utility. See 'Fourth Report of the Special Rapporteur', 63rd Session of the International Law Commission (A/66/10), 26 April to 3 June and 4 July to 12 August 2011, §286, 253. For a developing-countries perspective, with reference to South Asia, on the responsibility, see Dabiru Sridhar Patnaik, 'International Law and Responsibility to Protect: South Asian Perspective', *Journal of Global Studies, An Occasional Supplement* (2013): 173–189.

24 This thought of 'public character of international law to address matters that concern international society as a whole' remains crucial to the work of Jean d'Aspremont, 'Contemporary International Rule-making and the Public Character of International Law', *International Law and Justice Working Paper*, December 2006, NYU Law School, accessed 27 December 2010, www.iilj.org. Insights for reflections on mutual interests and responsibilities in solving global problems are drawn from this work.

25 Yogesh Tyagi, 'The Concept of Humanitarian Intervention Revisited', *Michigan Journal of International Law* 16 (1995): 883–910, 901.

countries. Let us assume then, if the purpose of public international law is regulation of conduct of states through multilateral institutions, that the questions that need to be raised are, who are the international law makers, and whether, in the making of international law, concerns of cultural relativism and moral pluralism are accommodated. International law is supposed to be universally applicable among all states in equal measure.[26] As Yasuaki Onuma observes, 'we must grasp international law from a transcivilisational perspective to understand, appreciate and assess international law'.[27] Underlying the significance of universality of international law, and with a strong plea for Asian and African countries' contribution to development of international law, R. P. Anand, a foremost international lawyer who has worked on the historical traditions of international law, aptly writes:

> As we study and look at international law from historical perspective, especially in the context of the role of Asian and even African countries in its origin and development, there are several questions which have been raised but not satisfactorily answered. After the fifteenth century, Europeans went to Asian countries for their own needs and developed not only active trade and commercial relations, but intimate political relations as well with these independent Asian communities, especially in India and the East Indies. What rules of inter-state conduct applied between these European countries and Asian states? Without some common rules of international law, Europeans could not have survived in Asian countries. [28]

It is important to consider both negative and positive influences in the process of creating new concepts or interpreting existing principles that can stand the test of time within the framework of providing international humanitarian assistance.

5.2 *Towards a notion of solidarity for human dignity*

A key approach or strategy to address this issue is to understand the functional interdependence between human rights, human dignity and international responsibility. This continuum of functional relationship

[26] R. P. Anand, 'Universality of International Law: An Asian Perspective', accessed 15 May 2012, www.profrpanand.org/sites/default/files/articles/UniversalityofIL.pdf.

[27] See generally Yasuaki Onuma, *A Transcivilisational Perspective on International Law* (New Delhi: Martinus Nijhoff, 2010).

[28] R. P. Anand, *Studies in International Law and History: Asian Perspective* (New Delhi: Martinus Nijhoff, The Hague and Lancer Books, 2004), xii.

throws light on the concept of 'Solidarity' that is an emerging structural principle in contemporary international law. The structural principle of solidarity has become relevant for humanitarian assistance. One of the aspects of the principle of solidarity, as outlined by Rüdiger Wolfrum, is 'the achievement of common objectives through differentiated obligations of States [so that those] actions could benefit particular States'.[29] And states should consider 'respective legal regimes and work towards amelioration of deficits [that] certain States may have in pursuing objectives of the Community of States'.[30] As David Caron states, solidarity might be a complicated notion in the practicum of international law, but nevertheless, there should be a figment of thought as to how states should think about solidarity globally.[31] An evolution of the concept of solidarity may lead to balancing interests of duty to cooperate in accordance with the provisions enshrined in the Charter of the United Nations and also to acquire a certain moral objectivity in the provision of humanitarian assistance. It might also lead to a situation for states to analyse and assess the merits and demerits of the role of the international community in providing humanitarian assistance. The goal would be to safeguard the target state from not losing its political legitimacy amongst the comity of nations and to further outline the humanitarian responsibilities of the international community. It is notionally possible to deduce lessons from the principle of solidarity and to evaluate reasons for state consent not forthcoming in issues relating to humanitarian assistance. Some scholars have endeavoured to do so, primarily to elicit reasons for non-consent. While talking about political legitimacy, Yogesh Tyagi notes, 'one has to address this situation in a realistic manner and if a situation of refusal of consent arises, then the question that begs to be asked is, why consent is not forthcoming?'[32] In a seminal article, he gives an example of the United Nations Human Rights Committee that addressed the issue of lack of compliance with reporting obligations by states that are parties to the *International Covenant on Civil and Political Rights*. The conclusion arrived at was that 'non-compliance was not due to bad faith of states and

[29] Rüdiger Wolfrum, 'Solidarity amongst States: An Emerging Structural Principle of International Law', *Indian Journal of International Law* 49 (2009): 1, 1–19.

[30] Ibid., 19.

[31] David D. Caron, 'Addressing Catastrophes: Conflicting Images of Solidarity and Self interest', in *The International Aspects of Natural and Industrial Catastrophes*, eds. David D. Caron and Charles Leben (Martinus Nijhoff, Hague Academy of International Law, 2001), 28.

[32] Tyagi, 'Concept of Humanitarian Intervention', 895.

that a variety of factors were responsible for [such] cases of non-compliance'.[33] Let us not ignore the fact that any humanitarian assistance which is forthcoming without consent is contentious and, as noted by a commentator, 'there is scope for greater clarity, and indeed an advance in thinking, on the legal aspects relating to the rights and responsibilities of the [international community] in providing humanitarian relief in circumstances where a sovereign request is not, for a number of reasons, forthcoming'.[34] Analysis of lack of consent may be an enabler in finding viable legal solutions for responses to humanitarian crises and thereby mobilising support for humanitarian missions. This further necessitates the need for objective criteria for humanitarian assistance, without which there will be continuation of a lack of clarity in the practice of states, the United Nations and the international community at large in the provision of humanitarian assistance, and the mission will become more controversial than before. A relevant example is the view of the Sixth Committee of the United Nations on the concept of 'duty to offer external assistance'. The Special Rapporteur observed that many states in the Sixth Committee had, in their statements, answered the Commission's question in the negative, arguing that such 'a duty had no basis in existing international law'.[35]

6. Conclusions

In this process, the International Law Commission should further make clear, if individuals have particular rights against their own governments to obtain external aid; if individuals have the right to obtain assistance from the international community; and a corresponding duty of the international community to provide aid.[36] In this wrinkle of issues concerning state consent and humanitarian assistance, the trajectory of developing humanitarian norms should not be constrained and conditioned; and there is a need for a comprehensive mechanism within the United Nations architecture. The emergent situation that contributes to the appraisal of the United Nations architecture for developing humanitarian norms is well captured by Antonio Donini. Donini posits the cardinal idea of 'structures and mechanisms dealing with humanitarian assistance'. He notes:

[33] Ibid. [34] As cited by Tyagi, 'Concept of Humanitarian Intervention', 894.
[35] (A/67/10) §57, 86. [36] As cited by Arnison, 'International Law', 207.

> The structures and mechanisms for dealing with humanitarian assistance largely developed incrementally, responding on an ad-hoc basis to emerging needs rather than in a coherent manner. Given the deep roots of the United Nations system in functionalist theory, the state of North-South and East-West relations, and the prevalence of rhetoric and ideology in the mainstream United Nations political fora, this was perhaps inevitable. The result has been a separate development of the clusters of United Nations activity dealing with political and peacekeeping affairs from those dealing with human rights and humanitarian activities on the one side, and with various facets of economic and social development on the other.[37]

If the purpose of states is mutual sharing of ways and wisdom, then the subsequent development should be a human rights model to be adopted for issues of humanitarian assistance in disasters within the framework of the United Nations. It is possible to construct this model by appointing a working group within the Office of the High Commission for Human Rights and a Special Rapporteur for disasters. There is a need for human rights treaty bodies to issue a General Comment focusing on meaningful humanitarian assistance and determining scope, oversight and scrutiny. And the lack of clarity, consistency and credibility on issues of state consent and international humanitarian assistance within the framework of international law may be augmented by the efforts of humanitarian diplomacy to better serve the purpose of protection of individuals in disasters. The overarching aim should be to provide a comprehensive legal framework for protection of victims in disasters, which in turn means the promotion and protection of human rights. Such an endeavour befits appreciation for its sanguine goals. However, if fundamental realities that hamper the project are not addressed then it will not yield the desired results. Therefore the question that should be answered is: how can there be international responsibility for humanitarian assistance that is effective and appropriate in terms of international legal norms? As of today, it is not timely to offer a coherent account of the success and form that the project of 'Protection of Individuals in the Event of Disasters' might take, considering the inevitable political ramifications, and any solutions, based on the principles of international law, has to be clearly examined and implemented amidst the broad contours of international politics. However, for the moment states can devote their interest to the

[37] Antonio Donini, 'Beyond Neutrality: On the Compatibility of Military Intervention and Humanitarian Assistance', *Fletcher Forum of World Affairs* 19 (1995): 31–45, 32.

soft law materials available to deal with situations of disasters, and the importance of such materials can be guiding factors to look beyond the formal package of international legal rules of humanitarian assistance for the protection of individuals in situations of disasters. In moving towards a far-reaching effort of developing an international legal framework for assistance to individuals in situations of disasters, it is important not to disengage from theoretical analysis of factors, as noted above, that could be enablers in developing a comprehensive law on the subject under consideration.

6

United Nations involvement in humanitarian assistance: competences of the Security Council to face today's obstructions

HEIKE MONTAG

1. Introduction

On the battlefield in Solferino in 1859 when Henri Dunant provided humanitarian aid to wounded soldiers, he did not face the dangers, obstacles or dilemmas of contemporary humanitarian assistance activities. Not only are some states not willing to accept humanitarian assistance in case of need, sometimes states do not have the means to stop perpetrators from counteracting humanitarian aid. The involvement of the United Nations (UN) in humanitarian assistance as such, and the potential of the United Nations Security Council (SC) to resist obstructions thereof, will be the core of this chapter.

In this chapter the terms 'humanitarian aid' or 'assistance' are used synonymously. They are to be understood as 'all acts, activities and the human and material resources for the provision of goods and services of an exclusively humanitarian character, indispensable for the survival and the fulfilment of the essential needs of the victims of disasters', while disasters in the sense of this definition encompasses those of natural origin, man-made disasters of technological origin, and disasters caused by armed conflicts or violence.[1]

In principle, 'the affected State has the duty to take care of the victims in its territory'. This 'State or the territorial entity where humanitarian assistance is needed' carries primary responsibility in organising,

[1] IDI, Bruges Session, 'Humanitarian Assistance', 2 February 2003, Article I §1. The 2003 Bruges Resolution is a resolution of the non-governmental IDI dedicated to humanitarian assistance, which predominantly serves as a guideline for existing law and makes only occasional contributions to the development of international law; IDI, 'History', www.idi-iil.org/idiE/navig_history.html.

providing and distributing humanitarian aid.[2] However, often there is a need for additional assistance provided by external actors. Due to the principle of state sovereignty, humanitarian actions and also competent international organisations involved in humanitarian assistance, like the United Nations, are generally subject to the consent of the affected state. The minimum standard of humanitarian assistance consists of the duty of states not to arbitrarily disagree to the provision of bona fide humanitarian assistance from the outside. Once accepted, humanitarian objects and personnel have to be protected.[3]

United Nations humanitarian assistance deployments have the purpose to quickly relieve urgent needs of the population for humanitarian reasons and are rather short-term matters, both in contrast to post-conflict peace-building.[4] The latter aims to resolve the root causes of

[2] IDI, 'Humanitarian Assistance', Article I §4, III §1. It may be states, *de facto* authorities, occupying powers, or parties to the conflict exercising control over a part of a territory or in control of the civilian population of any territory except occupied territory.

[3] For armed conflicts, international: occupation: Article 55 I *et seq.*, 59 GC IV (*Geneva Convention (IV) Relative to the Protection of Civilian Persons in Time of War*. Geneva, 12 August 1949, 75 UNTS 287), 68 *et seq.* AP I (*Additional Protocol I to the Geneva Conventions of 12 August 1949, and relating to the Protection of Victims of International Armed Conflicts)*, 8 June 1977, 1125 UNTS 3); other than occupied territories: Article 23 GC IV, 70 *et seq.* AP I; non-international: Article 18 II AP II (*Additional Protocol II to the Geneva Conventions of 12 August 1949, and relating to the Protection of Victims of Non-International Armed Conflicts – Additional Protocol II*), 8 June 1977, 1125 UNTS 609); see, for one or several of these, Heike Spieker, 'Humanitarian Assistance, Access in Armed Conflict and Occupation', in *Max Planck Encyclopedia of Public International Law (MPEPIL) online*, ed. Rüdiger Wolfrum, www.mpepil.com/, §9 *et seq.*, 15 *et seq.*, 19 *et seq.*, 27 *et seq.*; Yves Sandoz, 'Article 69', in *Commentary on the Additional Protocols*, eds. Yves Sandoz, Christophe Swinarski and Bruno Zimmermann (Dordrecht: Kluwer, 1987), 811, §2783; Jean-Marie Henckearts and Louise Doswald-Beck, *Customary International Humanitarian Law*, vol. I: *Rules* (Cambridge University Press, 2005), Rule 31 *et seq.*, 55 *et seq.*; Annette Simon, *UN-Schutzzonen – Ein Schutzinstrument für verfolgte Personen?: Eine Analyse anhand der internationalen Schutzzone im Irak, in Ruanda und Bosnien-Herzegowina mit besonderem Blick auf die schweren Menschenrechtsverletzungen in der* safe area *Srebrenica* (Berlin, Heidelberg, New York: Springer, 2005), 182 *et seq.*; Joakim Dungel, 'A Right to Humanitarian Assistance in Internal Armed Conflicts Respecting Sovereignty, Neutrality and Legitimacy: Practical Proposals to Practical Problems', *Journal of Humanitarian Assistance* (2004): 2.3.

For peacetime: see for tasks arising from human rights or the discussion that the need has to be covered by external assistance: Budislav Vukas, 'Humanitarian Assistance in Cases of Emergency', www.mpepil.com/, §9, 20 *et seq.*, 23; Simon, *UN-Schutzzonen*, 184 *et seq* (*cf.* fn. 235 inter alia referring to UN Human Rights Committee, General Comment No. 6, §5).

[4] Christian Drews, *Post-Conflict Peace-Building* (Baden-Baden: Nomos, 2001), 95 *et seq.*

conflict in a longer-term perspective.[5] On the other hand, humanitarian assistance tackles the symptoms of conflict but not the root causes of it. It aims to ease the situation rather than to achieve the purpose of peace, which is of mere secondary importance.[6] However, this is not to say that humanitarian assistance is not a means for the maintenance of international peace and security.

The Security Council bears primary responsibility for the maintenance of peace and security. On a quite regular basis, the United Nations organ recommends, urges, demands or mandates humanitarian assistance.[7] Moreover, there are situations in which the Security Council takes an even stronger stance on humanitarian assistance in ensuring its facilitation: it mandates enforcement measures. In its resolution dedicated to humanitarian assistance the Institute of International Law (IDI) refers to these actions and their regulation.[8] It provides that 'if a refusal to accept a bona fide offer of humanitarian assistance or to allow access to the victims leads to a threat to international peace and security, the Security Council *may take the necessary measures* under Chapter VII of the Charter of the United Nations'.[9] But what precisely are the remits of the SC? What are the competences of the United Nations and especially of the Security Council, in regard to humanitarian assistance, in particular in situations that concern the maintenance of international peace and security and that necessitate enforcement action?

Starting with a discussion of the United Nations' involvement in humanitarian assistance and notably the problems in the field (Section 2), this article turns to the United Nations' – and especially the Security Council's – competences towards humanitarian assistance (Section 3) to counter these problems.

The scope of this chapter is limited to existing law and will not cover any new trends, soft law, or emerging law. It will not delve into the delegation of power by the Security Council or other aspects of the effective exercise of Council competence. This also applies to control of compliance and enforcement of law limiting the Security Council's conduct. Furthermore, this chapter will not focus on the question

5 UN Doc. (A/47/277-S/24111) 17 June 1992, §13, 15; *cf.* Drews, *Peace-Building*, 53 *et seq.*

6 For the latter: Drews, *Peace-Building*, 95.

7 For instance UN Doc. (S/RES/1970) 26 February 2011, §26 or UN Doc. (S/RES/733), 23 January 1992, §2.

8 I.e. IDI, 'Humanitarian Assistance', Articles III §3, IV, V §3, 4, VI, §1, VII, VIII, §2, 3.

9 Article VIII §3, emphasis added.

whether enforcement of humanitarian assistance might be unsuccessful or even counterproductive to strengthen humanitarian assistance, as it cannot be neutral.[10]

2. United Nations involvement in humanitarian assistance

This part provides a short overview of the factual involvement of the United Nations in humanitarian assistance (Section 2.1) and how it faces obstructions to this (Section 2.2).

2.1. United Nations practice

The United Nations itself has established a significant amount of programmes and funds, subsidiary organs as well as specialised agencies mandated with humanitarian assistance functions, like the United Nations Development Programme (UNDP),[11] Office for the Coordination of Humanitarian Affairs (OCHA),[12] and the World Health organisation (WHO),[13] to name but a few.[14] Furthermore, the United Nations has created a coordinating unit to combine and strengthen United Nations involvement, the Emergency Relief Coordinator (ERC).[15] The ERC chairs, for example, the Inter-Agency Standing Committee through which OCHA primarily carries out its functions, like the coordination of humanitarian response and humanitarian advocacy.[16] Aside from the United Nations programmes and funds, organs and agencies, other humanitarian partners, like the International Red Cross and Red Crescent Movement[17] and other non-governmental organisations (NGOs)[18]

[10] Cf. Dungel, 'Right', 5.2.

[11] UN Development Programme, UN Doc. GA resolution (2029) (XX), 22 November 1965.

[12] OCHA, 'A Brief History of OCHA', *Office for the Coordination of Humanitarian Affairs,* http://ochaonline.un.org/AboutUs/tabid/3939/language/en-US/Default.aspx.

[13] World Health Organisation, for more information, *cf.* www.who.int/en/.

[14] See Lance Bartholomeus, 'The Legal Framework of Humanitarian Assistance in the UN System' (Presentation at the 7th AIDA IHL Forum, Al-Ram, 10 May 2006), www.diakonia.se/documents/public/ihl/ihlfoum/th7/lance_legal_framework_of_humanitarian_assistance_in_the_un_system_final.pdf.

[15] UN Doc. (A/RES/46/182) 19 December 1991; OCHA, 'A Brief History of OCHA'.

[16] OCHA, 'A Brief History of OCHA.'

[17] 'International Red Cross and Red Crescent Movement', ICRC, www.icrc.org/eng/who-we-are/movement/index.jsp.

[18] For a great overview, see Global Humanitarian Assistance, 'Public Support for Humanitarian Crises Through NGOs', *Development Initiatives,* 2009, www.globalhumanitarianassistance.

participate in the field as well. They are mostly members of the above-mentioned Committee; thus OCHA aims to ensure inter-agency decision-making.[19]

More and more, human rights systems foresee juridical procedures at international or regional courts, committees of treaties or procedures of responsibility before organs of international organisations or states that cover violations of humanitarian law as well.[20] In particular, the United Nations Human Rights Council is active in investigating violations of humanitarian as well as human rights law.[21]

The United Nations plays an important role in promoting of and ensuring compliance with international humanitarian law,[22] in determining, reaffirming, enforcing the law etc. This development and the increased importance of the protection of the human being in armed conflict were influenced inter alia by the General Assembly's (GA) engagement in this area of international law. In addition, several other United Nations organs deal with the implementation of humanitarian law in armed conflict, such as the Secretary-General, the International Court of Justice and the Economic and Social Council.[23] The General Assembly has been actively and continuously engaged in humanitarian law aspects since 1968:[24] with regard to protection of victims in armed conflict it urges progress and compliance of states with existing humanitarian law and thus reiterates it.[25]

org/wp-content/uploads/2010/07/2009-Focus-report-Public-support-for-humanitarian-crises-through-NGOs.pdf.

[19] OCHA, 'A Brief History of OCHA'; in detail Inter-Agency Standing Committee, 'Inter-agency Contingency Planning Guidelines for Humanitarian assistance', IASC, www.who.int/hac/network/interagency/news/contingency_guidelines/en/.

[20] Hans-Peter Gasser and Nils Melzer, *Humanitäres Völkerrecht: Eine Einführung*, 2nd ed. (Urich, Basel, Geneva: Nomos, Schulthess, 2012), 12.

[21] UN Human Rights Council (HRC), resolution (5/1) 19 June 2007, annex A; resolution (9/9) 18 September 2008; UN OHCHR, *International Legal Protection of Human Rights in Armed Conflict* (New York, Geneva: United Nations, 2011), 102 *et seq.*; cf. Marten Zwanenburg, 'United Nations and International Humanitarian Law', in *MPEPIL online*, ed. Rüdiger Wolfrum, www.mpepil.com/, §48 *et seq.*

[22] See Zwanenburg, 'United Nations', §28.

[23] Michaela Schneider-Enk, *Der völkerrechtliche Schutz humanitärer Helfer in bewaffneten Konflikten: Die Sicherheit des Hilfspersonals und die 'neuen' Konflikte* (Hamburg: Verlag Dr Kovac, 2008), 122.

[24] Zwanenburg, 'United Nations', §28.

[25] The process started in 1968 with the Final Act of the International Conference on Human Rights, UN Doc. (A/CONF. 32/41), XXIII, 18, 12 May 1968. See for instance UN Doc. resolution 2444 (XXIII), 2597 (XXIV), 2673 (XXV), 2675 (XXV), 2676 (XXV), 2677 (XXV) all 9 December 1970; 2852 (XXVI), 2853 (XXVI) both 20 December 1971; 3032

For the responsibility of states in natural disasters, the General Assembly is furthermore actively involved in the developing and concretisation process of humanitarian assistance.[26] In each session the organ adopts a resolution summing up actual problems and conclusions regarding this topic.[27]

These first impressions underscore extensive United Nations involvement in the complex patched-up regime of humanitarian assistance in both peace and wartime.[28] Organs of the United Nations are often involved in situations of armed conflict assigned to stop human rights violations.[29] Human rights and humanitarian law are sized in the same breath.[30] The connections of humanitarian law and human rights law are manifold and complementary.[31] This is particularly apparent for humanitarian aspects in the law of war – regarding the human being in armed conflict.[32] Humanitarian assistance is part of these humanitarian

(XXVII) 18 December 1972; 3102 (XXVIII) 12 December 1973; 3500 (XXX) 15 December 1975; 31/19 24 November 1976; 32/44 8 December 1977; 34/51 23 November 1979; (A/RES/37/116) 16 December 1982; (A/RES/39/77) 13 December 1984; (A/RES/41/72) 3 December 1986; (A/RES/43/161) 9 December 1988; (A/RES/45/38) 28 November 1990; (A/RES/47/30) 25 November 1992; 49/48, 17 February 1995; (A/RES/51/155) 30 January 1997; (A/RES/53/96) 20 January 1999; (A/RES/55/148) 19 January 2001; (A/RES/57/14) 20 January 2003; (A/RES/59/36) 16 December 2004; (A/RES/61/30) 18 December 2006; (A/RES/63/125) 15 January 2009; (A/RES/65/29) 10 January 2011. For the efforts of the UN in regard to humanitarian assistance, see Andrej Zwitter, 'United Nations' Legal Framework of Humanitarian Assistance', in *International Law and Humanitarian Assistance: Legal Issues Pertaining to Humanitarianism*, eds. Hans-Joachim Heintze and Andrej Zwitter (Berlin: Springer, 2011), 52 *et seq.*

26 For instance UN Doc. (A/RES/43/131) 8 December 1988; (A/RES/45/100) 17 December 1990; (A/RES/46/182); cf. Vukas, 'Humanitarian Assistance', §12. For the beginning of this process see Martin Lailach, *Die Wahrung des Weltfriedens und der internationalen Sicherheit als Aufgabe des Sicherheitsrates der Vereinten Nationen* (Berlin: Duncker und Humblot, 1998), 229 *et seq.*

27 Vukas, 'Humanitarian Assistance', §12.

28 Drews, *Peace-Building*, 95.

29 Gasser and Melzer, *Völkerrecht*, 32.

30 For the SC: Gasser and Melzer, *Völkerrecht*, 32, 209 *et seq.* referring to UN Doc. (S/RES/1591) 29 March 2005, preambular §9; (S/RES/1974) 22 March 2011, preambular §22; see also for the Responsibility to Protect (R2P), UN Doc. (A/RES/60/1) 24 October 2005, §138 *et seq.*, which applies in case of gross violations of fundamental human rights, and war crimes, i.e. violations of international humanitarian law.

31 Gasser and Melzer, *Völkerrecht*, 32 *et seq.*

32 *Cf.* Sylvia Maus, 'Human Rights in UN Peacekeeping Missions: A Framework for Humanitarian Obligations?', in *International Law and Humanitarian Assistance: Legal Issues Pertaining to Humanitarianism*, eds. Hans-Joachim Heintze and Andrej Zwitter (Berlin: Springer, 2011), 106 *et seq.*, with further references; with regard to the law of occupation, *cf.* Hans F. Kiderlen, *Von Triest nach Osttimor: Der völkerrechtliche Rahmen*

aspects as it aims to help 'groups of human beings whose fundamental human rights or whose essential needs are endangered'.[33] United Nations organs thus reaffirmed the importance of and influenced the development and approximation of human rights and humanitarian law aspects in and outside armed conflicts.

2.2. *Factual problems*

There are a considerable number of dangers, obstacles, and troubles in present-day humanitarian assistance activities. Since 2009, for instance, in reports on the protection of civilians in armed conflict at the request of the Security Council, the Secretary-General analyses the most common constraints on humanitarian access with the most severe consequences for the affected.[34] They name inter alia bureaucratic constraints imposed by governments and other authorities and further restrictions on the movement of humanitarian workers or goods; active hostilities and their intensity; interference in humanitarian activities; and violence against humanitarian workers.[35]

In addition to the General Assembly, which is the principal United Nations organ mainly concerned with humanitarian assistance, the Security Council – primarily responsible for maintaining peace and security – gets involved as well. Since 1999 the Security Council has adopted a series of resolutions on the protection of civilians, women and children in armed conflict as well as on the protection of United Nations personnel, associated personnel and humanitarian personnel in conflict zones.[36]

für die Verwaltung von Krisengebieten durch die Vereinten Nationen (Berlin, Heidelberg: Springer, 2008), 342 *et seq.*, with further references.

33 IDI, 'Humanitarian Assistance', Article I 3; *cf.* also Spieker, 'Humanitarian Assistance', §1 *et seq.*

34 UN Doc. (S/PRST/2008/18) 27 May 2008, 2; (S/2009/277) 29 May 2009, §58 *et seq.*, annex; (S/RES/1894) 11 November 2009, §17; (S/2010/579) 11 November 2010, §73 *et seq.*, annex; (S/PRST/2010/25) 22 November 2010, 3; (S/2012/376) 22 May 2012, §57 *et seq.*, annex.

35 UN Doc. (S/2012/376) annex, §2; (S/2010/579) §2; (S/2009/277) annex, §6.

36 Civilians: UN Doc. (S/RES/1265) 17 September 1999; (S/RES/1296) 19 April 2000; (S/RES/1674) 28 April 2006; (S/RES/1738) 23 December 2006; (S/RES/1894). Women: (S/RES/1325) 31 October 2000; (S/RES/1820) 19 June 2008; (S/RES/1889) 5 October 2009; (S/RES/1960) 16 December 2010. Children: UN Doc. (S/RES/1261) 25 August 1999 (S/RES/1314) 11 August 2000; (S/RES/1379) 20 November 2001; (S/RES/1460) 30 January 2003; (S/RES/1539) 22 April 2004; (S/RES/1612) 26 July 2005; (S/RES/1882) 4 August 2009; (S/RES/1998) 12 July 2011; (S/RES/2068) 19 September 2012. Personnel: (S/RES/1502) 26 August 2003; (S/RES/1738).

Thereby did the Security Council not only reaffirm and recommend but also clarify this particular topic.[37] In many of these thematic resolutions (i.e. resolutions not focusing on a special situation) the Security Council referred to compliance and implementation of remits with regard to humanitarian assistance.[38] For the latter, inter alia the full unimpeded access and the protection and freedom of movement of humanitarian personnel were of relevance, as well as the facilitation of their operations.[39]

However, not only in abstract thematic resolutions, but also with regard to concrete situations, the Security Council refers to humanitarian law:[40] Gasser and Melzer point out that the Security Council regularly calls upon the parties to comply with humanitarian law whenever it passes a resolution on a specific conflict.[41] Thus the Security Council often calls 'upon all parties to ensure the safe and unhindered access of humanitarian assistance' and to 'guarantee the safety and security of humanitarian personnel'.[42] Furthermore, the Security Council's subsidiary organs are frequently mandated to humanitarian assistance remits, such as to 'assist in the resumption of humanitarian relief operations',[43] or to ensure their access to those in need.[44]

In these cases, in which the Security Council recommends certain behaviour to address these concerns, or mandates humanitarian tasks of a United Nations operation with the consent of the concerned, it uses merely hortatory terms.[45] But its appeals very often remain unheeded.[46] However, the Security Council is vested with enforcement power to face obstructions (under Chapter VII of the *United Nations Charter*[47]). In case of unheard recommendations in that regard the Security Council occasionally tends to move gradually to assert them by binding decisions. Also it intensifies binding decisions. It does so by means of a

[37] Zwanenburg, 'United Nations', §29.

[38] Inter alia: Gasser and Melzer, *Völkerrecht*, 223; cf. Schneider-Enk, *Schutz*, 125; UN Doc. (S/RES/1296) §3, 5, 8, 13, 15; (S/RES/1502) §3.

[39] Zwanenburg, 'United Nations', §29; UN Doc. (S/RES/1502) §4.

[40] Schneider-Enk, *Schutz*, 125 *et seq.*

[41] Gasser and Melzer, *Völkerrecht*, 222 *et seq.*

[42] Exemplary UN Doc. (S/RES/1260) 20 August 1999, §14.

[43] UN Doc. (S/RES/912) 21 April 1994, §8 (b).

[44] UN Doc. (S/RES/1260) §4 and (S/1999/836) 30 July 1999, §38 (f). These missions (cf. previous fn.) did not provide an authorisation under Chapter VII UNC.

[45] Yoram Dinstein, 'The Right to Humanitarian Assistance', *Naval War College Review* 4 (2000): 86.

[46] Dinstein, 'Humanitarian Assistance', 86.

[47] Charter of the United Nations, 24 October 1945, 1 UNTS XVI.

binding determination that parties have to behave in a certain way, by imposing non-military sanctions, and authorising the use of force to ensure assistance,[48] as in the Democratic Republic of Congo (DRC) and Libya.

Democratic Republic of Congo At the end of the 1990s, rebellions under the influence of Laurent Kabila took place in the Democratic Republic of Congo.[49] The situation 'threatened peace, security and stability in the region, and ... [caused] grave humanitarian consequences', for example a 'worsening of tension', 'resulting in a deterioration of the food situation for the civilian population'.[50] The Security Council decided to concentrate United Nations liaison personnel and to establish a mission (MONUC), initially without enforcement power, inter alia to facilitate humanitarian assistance.[51] In the preamble of this resolution the Security Council noted with concern the humanitarian situation and called on member states in that regard.[52] But access of humanitarian personnel remained problematic and the security situation deteriorated.[53]

The following expanded mandate of MONUC allowed the use of force to protect personnel.[54] But it was still limited with regard to the authorisation of the necessary action, since only the protection and assurance of security and movement of United Nations personnel was expressed in the robust element of the mandate.[55] 'Robust' means the ability to engage against those who undermine their commitments to peace by violence (see Section 3.2.2.2).[56]

In 2003, acting under Chapter VII UNC, the Security Council finally enlarged the mandate. The organ substantiated it inter alia by its profound preoccupation with 'the humanitarian situation' and its demand

48 Dinstein, 'Humanitarian Assistance', 86.
49 UN, 'MONUC Background', *United Nations*, www.un.org/en/peacekeeping/missions/monuc/background.shtml.
50 UN Doc. (S/PRST/1998/36) 11 December 1998, 1, 2.
51 UN Doc. (S/RES/1279) 30 November 1999, §5 (e).
52 UN Doc. (S/RES/1279) preambular §8.
53 UN Doc. (S/RES/1291) 24 February 2000, preambular §19; (S/2009/30) 17 January 2000, §9.
54 UN Doc. (S/RES/1291) preambular §8.
55 See UN Doc. (S/RES/1291) §7 (g); (S/RES/1355) 15 June 2001, §19, 33; (S/RES/1417) 14 June 2002, §7.
56 For the term 'robust mandate', see Brahimi Report, UN Doc. (A/55/305–S/2000/809) 21 August 2000, §55.

'that all the parties guarantee the security of the civilian population thereby enabling MONUC and humanitarian organisations to have total, unrestricted and immediate access'.[57] Firstly, it decided upon an arms embargo and the prohibition on any assistance with regard to military activities.[58] At the same time, MONUC was authorised 'to take the necessary measures in the areas of deployment of its armed units, and as it deems it within its capabilities... to protect civilians and humanitarian workers under imminent threat of physical violence; and to contribute to the improvement of the security conditions in which humanitarian assistance is provided'.[59] A more recent example of the increasing use of Security Council enforcement power to face obstruction of humanitarian assistance is the 2011 situation in Libya.

Libya A wide protest movement in the Middle East – the so-called Arab Spring – spread to Libya in the middle of February 2011. There – as in other places – it aimed at removing the dictatorial government. Despite United Nations reactions due to protester deaths, violence against the protesters continued.[60]

In resolution 1970 of 26 February 2011, acting under Chapter VII UNC, and taking measures under its Article 41 UNC, the Security Council urged 'the Libyan authorities to: ... [e]nsure the safe passage of humanitarian and medical supplies, and humanitarian agencies and workers, into the country' and accordingly called upon 'all member states, working together and acting in cooperation with the Secretary General, to facilitate and support the return of humanitarian agencies and make available humanitarian and related assistance in the Libyan Arab Jamahiriya ... and expresses its readiness to consider taking additional appropriate measures, as necessary, to achieve this'.[61] It furthermore decided, among other measures, on an arms embargo on the

[57] UN Doc. (S/RES/1493) 28 July 2003, §12. [58] UN Doc. (S/RES/1493) §20.

[59] UN Doc. (S/RES/1493) §25, indents 3, 4; see also (S/RES/1565) 1 October 2004, §4 (b), 5 (b).

[60] For this background information, see Jordan Paust, 'The Libya Conflict', www.law.uh.edu/news/faculty-news/summer2011/0630Paust.pdf.

[61] UN Doc. (S/RES/1970) §2 (c), 26. Former sanctions concerning the Libyan Arab Jamahiriya, beginning in March 1992 (UN Doc. (S/RES/748) 31 March 1992 and UN Doc. (S/RES/883) 11 November 1993) were terminated in 2003, UN Doc. (S/RES/1506) 12 September 2003, §1, 2), *cf.* UN Security Council Sanctions Committees, www.un.org/Security Council/committees/.

Libyan Arab Jamahiriya, and travel bans and asset freezes on specified individuals.[62] Thus it used forcible means to convince the Libyan authorities to ensure passage of humanitarian relief.

Less than a month later the Security Council deplored the failure to comply with resolution 1970. By '[e]xpressing its determination to ensure ... the rapid and unimpeded passage of humanitarian assistance and the safety of humanitarian personnel' and by '[c]onsidering that the establishment of a ban on all flights in the airspace of the Libyan Arab Jamahiriya constitutes an important element for ... the safety of the delivery of humanitarian assistance', the Security Council – acting under Chapter VII UNC – among other things demanded 'that the Libyan authorities comply with their obligations under international law ... and take all measures to ... ensure the rapid and unimpeded passage of humanitarian assistance', authorised the member states 'to take all necessary measures ... to protect civilians and civilian populated areas under threat of attack ... while excluding a foreign occupation force of any form on any part of Libyan territory,' and decided to establish a no-fly zone.[63]

Thus resolution 1973 provides an authorisation to use armed force to protect civilians. Nevertheless, it does not explicitly authorise the use of armed force to ensure humanitarian assistance. However, the resolution is loosely formulated and leaves room for interpretation. Enabling passage of humanitarian assistance and protection of its personnel could be subsumed as part of the protection of civilians and civilian-populated areas under threat of attack.[64]

This interpretation is reflected in practice: North Atlantic Treaty Organisation (NATO) allies and partners, who implemented the mandate, took respective humanitarian assistance for granted.[65] They agreed to continue the operation until 'the regime permitted immediate,

[62] UN Doc. (S/RES/1970) §9 *et seq.*, 15 *et seq.*, 17 *et seq.*

[63] UN Doc. (S/RES/1973) 17 March 2011, preambular §9, 26, §3, 4, 6 *et seq.* The euphemism 'all necessary means/measures' is commonly employed to express the use of force; Dinstein, 'Humanitarian Assistance', 87.

[64] For the broad authorisation of the use of force in resolution 1973, Mehrdad Payandeh, 'The United Nations, Military Intervention, and Regime Change in Libya', *Virginia Journal of International Law* 52 (2012): 355, 383 *et seq.*; *cf.* Zwanenburg, 'United Nations', §55.

[65] NATO, 'NATO and Libya', www.nato.int/cps/en/natolive/topics_71652.htm; 'Press Briefing on Libya', 5 April 2011, www.nato.int/cps/en/natolive/opinions_72027.htm?selectedLocale=en; 'Joint Press Briefing on Events Concerning Libya', 12 April 2011, www.nato.int/cps/en/natolive/opinions_72290.htm?selectedLocale=en.

full, safe and unhindered access to humanitarian aid for the Libyan people'.[66]

With regard to humanitarian assistance, the Security Council frequently argues, in the preambles to its resolutions, for using its enforcement power to face obstruction of humanitarian assistance:[67] for instance, 'effective and unhindered delivery of humanitarian assistance, including safe and secure access',[68] 'security to humanitarian relief operations',[69] 'violations and abuses of human rights and international humanitarian law',[70] 'deterioration of the humanitarian situation',[71] 'need for continued humanitarian relief assistance'[72] and 'condemning all attacks against . . . humanitarian personnel'.[73]

2.3. *Interim results*

The United Nations is involved in the promotion of and ensuring compliance with humanitarian assistance remits in peace and wartime. The Security Council calls upon compliance with this, but it furthermore uses enforcement power to face obstructions to it, and to maintain peace and security. The above-mentioned IDI resolution echoes the ability of the Council to take the necessary binding enforcement measures. Whether or not the behaviour complies with the legal competences will be discussed in the following part.

3. United Nations and Security Council specific competence concerning humanitarian assistance

As the founding treaty of the organisation that created the organs of the United Nations, the *United Nations Charter* is the primary source for the competences of the organisation as well as its organ's powers. In light of the facts presented above we firstly need to analyse whether the United

[66] NATO, 'NATO and Libya'; 'Unified Protector', NATO Operation, Ministry of Defence Republic of Latvia, www.mod.gov.lv/en/Par_aisardibas_noari/Politikas_istenosana/Latvijas_%20daliba_starpt_oper/NATO_operac/Libija_Unified_Protector.aspx.
[67] See Zwanenburg, 'United Nations', §55.
[68] UN Doc. (S/RES/757) 30 May 1992, preambular §6.
[69] UN Doc. (S/RES/925) 8 June 1994, preambular §10.
[70] UN Doc. (S/RES/1291) preambular §10.
[71] UN Doc. (S/RES/794) 3 December 1992, preambular §4.
[72] UN Doc. (S/RES/814) 26 March 1993, preambular §10.
[73] UN Doc. (S/RES/1856) 22 December 2008, preambular §15.

Nations (Section 3.1) is a competent international organisation and the Security Council (Section 3.2) a competent organ for humanitarian assistance. It needs to be determined whether the Council is the competent organ not only to make recommendations but to decide upon enforcement measures.

3.1. United Nations competence

The *raison d'être* and main purpose of the United Nations is, as previously mentioned, international peace and security.[74] It is given as a reason for the United Nations' competence not only to deal with compliance with humanitarian law in special cases, as one aspect of re-establishing peace amongst states, but also to deal with humanitarian law in general.[75] This can be applied with regard to fundamental human rights as well, which today are accepted as being of direct relevance for world peace and security.[76]

Humanitarian assistance issues are particularly mentioned in the Charter. The achievement of 'international co-operation in solving international problems of . . . humanitarian character, and in promoting and encouraging respect for human rights', as stated in Article 1 III UNC, is one of the purposes of the United Nations. Article 55 UNC is considered the implementing provision of Article 1 III UNC, which specifies the latter. It explicitly commits the United Nations itself to 'promot[ing] . . . b. solutions of international . . . health, and related problems' which include solutions of humanitarian problems and 'c. universal respect for, and observance of, human rights'.[77] It entitles the United Nations to endorse and develop, as well as to support, its implementation (for some of the results, see above Section 2.1). The international organisation of the United Nations was endowed with competence for humanitarian assistance.

[74] Eckart Klein and Stefanie Schmahl, 'Die Internationalen und die Supranationalen Organisationen', in *Völkerrecht*, ed. Wolfgang Graf Vitzthum (Berlin, New York: Walter de Gruyter, 2010), 359, §205.

[75] Schneider-Enk, *Schutz*, 121 *et seq.*; Gasser and Melzer, *Völkerrecht*, 222 *et seq.*, 239.

[76] See Michael Bothe, 'Friedenssicherung und Kriegsrecht', in *Völkerrecht*, ed. Wolfgang Graf Vitzthum (Berlin, New York: Walter de Gruyter, 2010), 680 *et seq.*, §44.

[77] Wolfrum, 'Article 1', §6, 23 and 'Article 55 (a) and (b)', §1 *et seq.*, 63 both in *The Charter of the United Nations: A Commentary*, 2nd ed., ed. Bruno Simma (Munich: C. H. Beck, 2002).

3.2. *Security Council competence*

The primary responsibility for the main purpose of the United Nations – the maintenance of peace and security – was conferred on the Security Council by United Nations member states, Article 24 I UNC. Article 24 II, second sentence UNC, specifies that the 'specific powers granted to the Security Council for the discharge of these duties are laid down in Chapters VI, VII, VIII, and XII', of which the first two are of relevance here.

In case of an endangerment of the maintenance of or a threat to peace, Chapter VI and VII UNC provide the Council with options to react, considering the severity of the endangerment: with regard to non-military action it may call upon states and non-state parties to comply with humanitarian law, condemn violations of it, reiterate that humanitarian law must be respected, and that there will be no impunity for violators of the law, demand reports, appoint a special representative, commit non-robust peacekeepers to monitor the implementation of Security Council decisions, decide upon sanctions, and so on. Furthermore, Article 42 UNC provides for military action.[78]

3.2.1. Measures outwith Chapter VII UNC

Whenever the Council considers a situation to be likely to endanger the maintenance of international peace and security (Chapter VI UNC), i.e. an indirect threat to peace, it already falls under its primary responsibility and thus it can recommend measures.[79]

However, Article 25 UNC states that '[t]he Members of the United Nations agree to accept and carry out the decisions of the Security Council in accordance with the present Charter'. Pursuant to this provision only decisions are binding for United Nations members.[80] This is not to say that the Council cannot take a binding decision outside of Chapter VII UNC. In fact, it depends on the expression of the intention of the SC.[81] However, Article 25 UNC meanwhile provides that as long as the Security Council does not make a decision but merely a

[78] Gasser and Melzer, *Völkerrecht*, 239. [79] Bothe, 'Friedenssicherung', 679, §41.

[80] Dinstein, 'Humanitarian Assistance', 86.

[81] ICJ, Advisory Opinion, 'Legal Consequences for States of the Continued Presence of South Africa in Namibia (South West Africa) Notwithstanding Security Council Resolution 276 (1970), *ICJ Reports* 1971, 15, 52 *et seq.*, §113; Sydney Bailey and Sam Saws, *The Procedure of the UN Security Council*, 3rd ed. (Oxford: Clarendon Press, 1998), 268.

recommendation, a call, a demand, or the like, the *effect* of the resolution largely depends on the consent of the concerned state(s).

3.2.2. Measures under Chapter VII UNC

Chapter VII UNC allows the Council to apply enforcement measures and thus it is the only way the United Nations can 'intervene in matters which are essentially within the domestic jurisdiction of any State' (Article 2 VII UNC) and mandate divergence from the basic stipulations of the prohibition of the use of force (Article 2 IV UNC).[82]

The precondition for such an authorisation is that the Security Council 'determine[s] the existence of any threat to the peace' (Article 39 UNC).[83] Although the Security Council does not act independently from or above the law, the UNC grants it a considerable prerogative for the actions under Chapter VII UNC.[84]

Article 1 I UNC provides the United Nations purpose 'to take effective collective measures for the prevention and removal of threats to the peace'.[85] However, the above-mentioned United Nations purposes regarding the endorsement and development of humanitarian assistance as well as the support of its implementation find mentions in Article 1 III UNC. Obstructions thereof as such are in general not necessarily sufficient to qualify as a threat to the peace. However, situations counteracting humanitarian assistance might arise to a threat to the peace.

Regarding the precondition for measures under Chapter VII UNC the definition of peace is of central importance for which there is still no approved fixed contour.[86] The Charter provision and its interpretation imply a definition of peace with a negative meaning, which cannot be

[82] See Joakim Dungel, 'Humanitarian Use of Force? The Right to Afford Humanitarian Assistance in Internal Armed Conflicts' (MA thesis, University of Gothenburg, 2004), https://gupea.ub.gu.se/bitstream/2077/2013/1/200422.pdf, 71.

[83] Bothe, 'Friedenssicherung', 679, §42.

[84] Anne Rausch, *Responsibility to Protect: Eine juristische Betrachtung* (Frankfurt/M: Peter Lang Verlag, 2011), 93, with further references; with reference to Article 39 UNC, see for a detailed analysis, Kiderlen, *Triest*, 137 *et seq.* Cf. also 233 *et seq.*, 310 *et seq.*; particularly for the former: ICJ, Advisory Opinion, 28 May 1948, Conditions of Admission of a state to membership in the United Nations (Article 4 of the Charter), *ICJ Reports* 1948, 57, 64; ICTY, Case No. IT-94-1-AR72, *Prosecutor* v. *DuskoTadic*, *ILM* (1996), 35, §28.

[85] See Dungel, 'Use of Force?', 72.

[86] Horst Fischer, 'Kollektive Sicherheit und Verteidigungsbündnisse', in *Völkerrecht*, ed. Knut Ipsen (5th ed. Munich: Verlag C. H. Beck, 2004), § 60, §8; see also elaborations by Stephan Hobe, *Einführung in das Völkerrecht*, 9th ed. (Tübingen: Narr Francke Attempto Verlag, 2008), 346 *et seq.*

exclusively based on the humanitarian situation inside a state.[87] In line with that, the Security Council did not directly consider serious humanitarian situations as threats to the peace.[88] However, the Charter provision has undergone significant informal change to a more positive definition of peace, which states peace to be more than the mere absence of military use of force between states.[89] The positive definition includes non-military, state-internal causes of conflict like economic, social, ecological, and humanitarian reasons.[90] Today, the Security Council may determine a situation of severe humanitarian issues inside a state as a case under Chapter VII UNC.[91] Recently, the Council takes or authorises measures to sanction violations and ensure implementation of humanitarian and fundamental human rights law.[92] In general, the international community is said to be more willing to qualify serious humanitarian situations as matters of international concern for peace and security, and not merely domestic affairs within a *domaine réservé*.[93]

Only in the last decade of the twentieth century did this development become apparent: for the first time, the Security Council determined a *threat to the peace* by solely referring to the severe humanitarian situation inside a state.[94] The Security Council even went one step further and for the first time it authorised the use of force for 'exclusively humanitarian internal reasons', as pronounced by Boutros-Boutros Ghali, the then United Nations Secretary-General.[95] The Security Council referred to the establishment of 'a secure environment for humanitarian relief operations' when authorising the use of enforcement measures in Somalia.[96]

[87] Rausch, *Responsibility*, 95 *et seq.*, with further references; dissenting with regard to interpretation, but with equal consequence, Tania Bolaños Enrique, *Anwendung des humanitären Völkerrechts auf militärische Interventionen der Vereinten Nationen in internen bewaffneten Konflikten unter besonderer Beachtung der bewaffneten Konflikte in Afrika* (Konstanz: Hartung-Gorre Verlag, 2011), 9 *et seq.*

[88] Bothe, 'Friedenssicherung', 680 *et seq.*, §44; for most gross violations of human rights, *cf.* Clemens Feinäugle, *Hoheitsgewalt im Völkerrecht: Das 1267-Sanktionsregime der UN und seine rechtliche Fassung* (Heidelberg et al.: Springer, 2011), 77.

[89] Rausch, *Responsibility*, 102 *et seq.*

[90] Hobe, *Völkerrecht*, 346.

[91] Rausch, *Responsibility*, 121; Bolaños Enrique, *Anwendung*, 9 *et seq.*

[92] See for humanitarian law, Schneider-Enk, *Schutz*, 127; for fundamental human rights, Bothe, 'Friedenssicherung', 680 *et seq.*, §44.

[93] See Spieker, 'Humanitarian Assistance', §4, listing cases.

[94] Rausch, *Responsibility*, 105 *et seq.*; see also Hobe, *Völkerrecht*, 354; Schneider-Enk, *Schutz*, 128 with further references, saw it already in UN Doc. resolution 688, 5 April 1991, §1.

[95] Dungel, 'Right', n. 1 quoting Mary Ellen O'Connell.

[96] UN Doc. (S/RES/794) §10.

Somalia In the beginning of the 1990s the 'country as a whole was without any form of central government. Banditry was rife'. The Somalis were trapped by civil war and famine.[97] In the beginning of 1992, the Security Council urged the parties 'to ensure the safety of personnel sent to provide humanitarian assistance'. With reference to the 'peace in the region' it decided under Chapter VII UNC on a general and complete weapons and military equipment embargo on Somalia.[98] Three months later, and parallel to the embargo, the mission in Somalia (UNOSOM I) was established to provide 'urgent humanitarian assistance',[99] but it was not authorised under Chapter VII UNC. Only eight months later, the Security Council determined 'that the magnitude of the human tragedy caused by the conflict in Somalia, further exacerbated by the obstacles being created to the distribution of humanitarian assistance, constitute a threat to international peace and security'.[100]

'Gravely alarmed by the deterioration of the humanitarian situation in Somalia and underlining the urgent need for the quick delivery of humanitarian assistance in the whole country', the Security Council welcomed the additional establishment of the unified tasked force (UNITAF) operation and authorised it under Chapter VII UNC – as abovementioned – 'to use all necessary means to establish as soon as possible a secure environment for humanitarian relief operations'.[101] In 1993, both operations were replaced by UNOSOM II.[102]

A humanitarian state-internal reason was of international concern and thus a threat to international peace and security. This procedure was followed in corresponding situations,[103] in which the Security Council considered gross violations of human rights and humanitarian law as threats to the peace. Furthermore, enforcement action was established for humanitarian assistance (see Sections 3.2.2.1 and 3.2.2.2).[104]

[97] UN Department of Public Information, 'Somalia – UNOSOM I', *UN*, www.un.org/Depts/DPKO/Missions/unosomi.htm.

[98] For an overview see UN, Dept of Public Information, 'Somalia – UNOSOM I'; UN Doc. S/RES/733, §5, 8.

[99] UN Doc. (S/RES/751), §2, 7, preambular §2.

[100] UN Doc. (S/RES/794) preambular §3.

[101] UN Doc. (S/RES/794) §8, 10.

[102] UN Doc. (S/RES/814) §5 *et seq.*, 14.

[103] See inter alia, UN Doc. (S/RES/929) 22 June 1994, preambular §10, cf. Rausch, *Responsibility*, 106; UN Doc. (S/RES/1264) 15 September 1999, §3; (S/1999/1003) 28 September 1999, §61 in conjunction with (S/RES/1270) 22 October 1999, preambular §4; (S/RES/1769) 31 July 2007, preambular §6.

[104] Dungel, 'Right', 1, 3; Dinstein, 'Humanitarian Assistance', 87.

Because of the involvement and concern of the Security Council in cases of deprived humanitarian assistance, United Nations member states established and consolidated a direct link between a violation of the norms concerning humanitarian assistance and a threat to the peace.[105] Human rights and humanitarian law then formed part of the drive to securing peace in Article 1 I UNC.

Once the Security Council has determined a threat to the peace, it 'shall make recommendations, or decide what measures shall be taken in accordance with Articles 41 and 42, to maintain or restore international peace and security' (Article 39 UNC). Following that, although it has determined a threat to the peace the Council can choose to merely make recommendations[106] or deem provisional measures and demand compliance therewith (Article 40 UNC).[107] Provisional measures constitute either a pre-stage or a backing of Articles 41 *et seq.* UNC, and can either constitute recommendations or binding measures.[108] Of course, the implementation of recommendations also depends on the consent of the affected state.[109] However, even recommendations and provisional measures can indirectly have a forceful effect.[110]

It follows that although the scope to apply binding enforcement measures was affected by determining a threat to the peace, the Security Council can ignore the opportunity to use these means. If the Council decides to go beyond recommendations or provisional measures, it can choose between non-military and military measures.

3.2.2.1 Non-military force With regard to Article 41 1st sentence UNC '[t]he Security Council may decide what measures not involving the use of armed force are to be employed to give effect to its decisions, and it may call upon the Members of the United Nations to apply such measures'. It thus uses non-military measures to increase the pressure on an actor that does not comply with its duties to peace and security. Non-military measures are, inter alia, the establishment of criminal courts,

[105] Cf. with regard to the SC, Ruth A. Stoffels, 'Legal Regulation of Humanitarian Assistance in Armed Conflict: Achievements and Gaps', *IRRC* 86 (2004): 532.

[106] Bothe, 'Friedenssicherung', 679, 681 *et seq.*, §42, 46; Michael Wood, 'United Nations, Security Council', in *MPEPIL online*, www.mpepil.com/, §23.

[107] Julia-Pia Schütze, *Die Zurechenbarkeit von Völkerrechtsverstößen im Rahmen mandatierter Friedensmissionen der Vereinten Nationen* (Berlin: Duncker & Humblot, 2011), 23.

[108] Schütze, *Zurechenbarkeit*, 23 *et seq* with further elaborations.

[109] Bothe, 'Friedenssicherung', 681 *et seq.*, §46.

[110] See Schütze, *Zurechenbarkeit*, 23.

disarmament and arms control mechanisms, and – of significance here – embargos and boycotts.[111] These sanctions force out – for example – an acceptance that the bona fide aid is delivered. In contrast, an armed operation on the ground physically pushes the relief in.[112]

The non-exhaustive list in Article 41 2nd sentence UNC includes complete interruptions of economic relations, i.e. comprehensive embargos on the state.[113] However, not only the actor that is in power to decide upon compliance with the duties of the state, but the entire population is affected by such comprehensive sanctions.[114] Probably the best-known and most widely criticised situation of comprehensive sanctions is the situation in Iraq.

Iraq Comprehensive sanctions and means to implement them have been imposed on Iraq since 1990 – exempting medicine, in humanitarian circumstances, food and, since April 1991, further humanitarian needs as approved by the established Sanctions Committee.[115] However, they 'caused great suffering to the most vulnerable section of Iraqi society', i.e. children, the elderly, the sick and the poor.[116] This is why the United Nations initiated the 'Oil for Food' programme, which was supposed to mitigate the citizens' suffering from the pressure of the sanctions.[117]

Already in 1991 a mission was dispatched by the Secretary-General in order to assess the humanitarian needs. It observed that 'the Iraqi people may soon face a further imminent catastrophe, which could include epidemic and famine, if massive life-supporting needs are not rapidly met'.[118] With growing concern over the humanitarian situation, the United Nations insisted that Iraq allow 'immediate access by international humanitarian organisations', and proposed measures under Chapter VII UNC to enable the sale of limited quantities of oil to relieve the people's distress. But the offers, of course, depended on Iraq's cooperation, and were declined.[119] In 1995, the Security Council was 'convinced

[111] Bothe, 'Friedenssicherung', 682 *et seq.*, §48.
[112] Dungel, 'Right', 5.1.1.
[113] Bothe, 'Friedenssicherung', 682 *et seq.*, §48.
[114] Ibid.; Hobe, *Völkerrecht*, 349.
[115] UN Doc. resolution 661, 6 August 1990, §3 *et seq.*; resolution 678, 29 November 1990, §2; resolution 687, 3 April 1991, §20.
[116] Sarah Denne, 'Re-thinking Humanitarian Aid in the Post-Gulf War Era: the International Committee of the Red Cross Takes the Lead', *Case W. Res. J. Int'l L.* 39 (2007–8): 868, 871.
[117] See. Zwitter, 'Legal Framework', 59; cf. Denne, 'Re-thinking', 868 *et seq.*, 871.
[118] UN Doc. (S/22366) 20 March 1991, §1, 37.
[119] For the quote: UN Doc. resolution 688, §3, UN Office of the Iraq Programme Oil-for-Food, 'Fact Sheet', www.un.org/Depts/oip/background/fact-sheet.html. UN Doc.

of the need as a temporary measure to provide for the humanitarian needs of the Iraqi people' and 'of the need for equitable distribution of humanitarian relief to all segments of the Iraqi population throughout the country'. Again – with concessions – it authorised states to permit notwithstanding the economic sanctions 'the import of petroleum and petroleum products originating in Iraq'.[120] The programme made the condition that the payment for the oil was directly deposited in an escrow account, and decided 'that the funds in the escrow account shall be used to meet the humanitarian needs of the Iraqi population'.[121] The programme provided Iraq with another opportunity to improve its population's humanitarian situation, and finally, Iraq agreed to cooperate at the end of 1996.[122]

The United Nations has estimated that the sanction regime has caused more than 500,000 deaths.[123] A decrease in the life expectancy and an increase of child mortality was proven.[124]

To avoid such severe situations, tailored/targeted sanctions have been applied in recent practice.[125] They are targeted on relevant areas and/or persons that are pertinent to bring the desired change. These sanctions are seen to be the most appealing alternative to forcible means, to convince a responsible authority to accept humanitarian assistance:[126] not only does it make sanctions more effective by 'hitting a regime where

resolution 706, 15 August 1999, preambular §3, §1, 2; resolution 712, 19 September 1991, preambular §3, §1, 5; resolution 778, 2 October 1992, preambular §4, 6, §1, 2.

120 UN Doc. (S/RES/986) 14 April 1995, preambular §3, 4, §1; see James Cockayne and David Malone, 'The Security Council and the 1991 and 2003 Wars in Iraq', in *The United Nations Security Council and War – The Evolution of Thought and Practice since 1945*, eds. Vaughan Lowe, Adam Roberts, Jennifer Welsh, Dominik Zaum (Oxford University Press, 2008), 391.

121 UN Doc. (S/RES/986) §1 (b), 8.

122 'Fact Sheet', UN Office of the Iraq Oil-for-Food programme.

123 Robin Geiss, 'Humanitarian Safeguards in Economic Sanctions Regimes: A Call for Automatic Suspension Clauses, Periodic Monitoring, and Follow-Up Assessments of Long-Term Effects', *Harvard Human Rights Journal* 18 (2005): 168, fn. 5 with further reference.

124 WHO, UN Doc. (WHO/EHA/96.1), 1996; (S/1999/356), 30 March 1999, Annex II, §17–27; Amnesty International, 'Iraq: UN Security Council Considers the Humanitarian Panel's Report on Sanctions', AI Index: MDE 14 June 1999; cf. Larry Minear et al., 'Toward More Humane and Effective Sanctions Management: Enhancing the Capacity of the United Nations System', *Occasional Paper* 31 (1998): xx *et seq.*, Institute for International Studies, Brown University.

125 Dungel, 'Right', 5.1; cf. Feinäugle, *Hoheitsgewalt*, 78 ('individual sanctions').

126 Dungel, 'Right', 5.1.1.

it hurts', but it also renders them less harsh on a civilian population since the latter in principle is exempt from their effects.[127]

The humanitarian impact caused by tailored/targeted sanctions on the civilian population is most likely to be less than the use of military force. But non-military sanctions do not always bring the desired success; not only in these cases the Council has recourse to armed force.

3.2.2.2 Armed force Military enforcement measures allow divergence from the basic stipulation of the prohibition of the use of force.[128]

Ideally, there is a stepping-up from Article 41 UNC to Article 42 UNC measures, but that is no precondition for the applicability of the latter. It is merely sufficient that the Security Council *considers* 'that measures provided for in Article 41 would be inadequate or have proved to be inadequate' (Article 42 UNC).[129]

The system of the UNC provides that the United Nations itself takes such action by conducting forces (United Nations-led) and that the member states make these forces available to the Council (Articles 42 1st sentence, 43 I UNC).[130] Article 43 UNC contains provisions that members and the United Nations shall conclude agreements on the availability of forces, their number, types, etc. However, these agreements have not been concluded so far and member states are free to make forces available.[131]

In addition to these United Nations-led missions, the Security Council can authorise states, groups of states or regional organisations (Chapter VIII, in particular Article 53 I UNC) to use all necessary means/measures, i.e. armed force. Thus the United Nations merely mandates but does not lead the forces. However, the concentration of authority to decide upon enforcement measures by states is contrary to the concept of the UNC. It is deemed legally and politically doubtful,[132] as it 'would be naïve and dangerous to expect that states would use such a power altruistically on their own initiative and not abuse it for their own interests'.[133] Nevertheless, an implied authorisation of the Council for state authorisation can be deduced from the sum of the competences in Articles 39, 40, 42, 48 UNC.[134] Armed measures depend on the support

[127] Dungel, 'Right', 5.1. [128] Bothe, 'Friedenssicherung', 664 *et seq.*, §24.
[129] Hobe, *Völkerrecht*, 349. [130] Bothe, 'Friedenssicherung', 683 *et seq.*, §49.
[131] Ibid. [132] Bothe, 'Friedenssicherung', 684, §50. [133] Dungel, 'Use of Force?', 77.
[134] Bothe, 'Friedenssicherung', 684, §50; for further suggestions and their limits, see Schütze, *Zurechenbarkeit*, 39 *et seq.*

of states (and/or regional organisations) as member states are not obliged by the UNC.[135] Therefore, the gain of power by troop-contributing states has to be considered an unpleasant but natural by-product. Although states are not bound to provide troops, at least they should refrain from contradicting decisions of the Council (Article 2 V UNC).[136]

The following example on the severe humanitarian situation in the Sudanese region Darfur shows the Council's dependency on reluctant member states and thus the systematic problem in the implementation of Chapter VII UNC.

Darfur In 2003 a civil war erupted in Darfur, which caused 'tens if not hundreds of thousands' of deaths and 1.8 million internally displaced people.[137] With the consent of the conflicting parties, the African Union (AU) established the AU Mission in the Sudan (AMIS).[138] Although the Council – by calling on the government of Sudan to fulfil immediately all commitments, 'including particularly by facilitating international relief for the humanitarian disaster by means of a moratorium on all restrictions that might hinder the provision of humanitarian assistance and access to the affected populations' – advocated the overstrained AMIS, the United Nations was not able to militarily engage itself until 2006.[139] However, the Security Council decided upon an arms embargo.[140]

In 2006, the mandate of the United Nations Mission in Sudan (UNMIS) was expanded to include deployment to Darfur.[141] The mandate included the facilitation and coordination of humanitarian assistance.[142] With a view to giving the mission a 'robust mandate' it was authorised under Chapter VII UNC to actively intervene in favour of humanitarian personnel to 'ensure the security and freedom of movement of . . . humanitarian workers'.[143] Hence the use of force was limited

[135] Hobe, *Völkerrecht*, 607.
[136] Bruno Simma, 'Article 2 (V)', in *The Charter of the United Nations: A Commentary*, 2nd ed., B. Simma vol. I (Munich: C. H. Beck, 2002), §6 *et seq.*
[137] UN, 'UNAMID Background', www.un.org/en/peacekeeping/missions/unamid/background.shtml.
[138] Schütze, *Zurechenbarkeit*, 70 *et seq.*; UN, 'UNMIS Background', www.un.org/en/peacekeeping/missions/unmis/background.shtml.
[139] UN Doc. (S/RES/1556) 30 July 2004, §1, 2; Schütze, *Zurechenbarkeit*, 71.
[140] UN Doc. (S/RES/1556) §7 *et seq.*
[141] UN Doc. (S/RES/1706) 31 August 2006, §1; 'UNMIS Background'.
[142] UN Doc. (S/RES/1590) 24 March 2005, preambular §10, §4 (b).
[143] UN Doc. (S/RES/1590) §16 (i); *cf.* Maus, 'Framework?', 122.

to the protection of relief personnel and their mobility. But due to the government of the Sudan's opposition to a peacekeeping operation undertaken solely by the United Nations, UNMIS was not able to deploy in Darfur and the United Nations embarked on an alternative, innovative approach.[144]

In the resolution that then established the African Union/United Nations Hybrid Operation in Darfur (UNAMID), the Security Council – deeply concerned for the security and access of humanitarian workers – even condemned 'those parties to the conflict who have failed to ensure the full, safe and unhindered access of relief personnel to all those in need in Darfur as well as the delivery of humanitarian assistance'.[145] With a robust mandate, United Nations-mandated UNAMID was – as UNMIS – authorised under Chapter VII to take the necessary action, 'to ensure the security and freedom of movement of its own personnel and humanitarian workers'.[146] The previously emphasised call to 'full, safe and unhindered access of relief personnel to all those in need and delivery of humanitarian assistance' was repeated.[147] But the international community still falls short of its potential: in resolutions extending the mandate, the Security Council had to underline the 'need for UNAMID to make full use of its mandate' to ensure (safe, timely and unhindered) humanitarian access.[148] The mission had problems regarding implementation of operational strength and equipment.[149]

In addition to the implementation problem, the situation in Darfur is an ostensible example of robust peacekeeping. Peacekeeping measures – depending on the consent of the host state – are combined with coercive measures to enforce a limited number of measures.[150] Legally they are based on Chapter VI and Chapter VII UNC[151] (or Article 40 UNC or Chapter VI UNC or the system of maintaining peace and security in total).[152] If the peacekeeping mandate contains a reference to Chapter VII UNC and authorises the use of necessary measures, this action is

[144] UN, 'UNMIS Background.' [145] UN Doc. (S/RES/1769) preambular §13, §1.

[146] UN Doc. (S/RES/1769) §15 (a) (i); see for UN-mandated, Schütze, *Zurechenbarkeit*, 71.

[147] UN Doc. (S/RES/1590) §6; (S/RES/1769) §19.

[148] For example: UN Doc. (S/RES/1828) 31 July 2008, §7; (S/RES/1881) 6 August 2009, §2; (S/RES/1935) 30 July 2010, §2 (b); (S/RES/2063) 31 July 2012, §3 (b); for the latter see UN Doc. (S/RES/1828) §18.

[149] Schütze, *Zurechenbarkeit*, 71.

[150] Yvonne Dorf, *Völkerrecht* (Munich: C. H. Beck, 2011), 135 *et seq.*; Bothe, 'Friedenssicherung', 674 *et seq.*, §36.

[151] Dorf, *Völkerrecht*, 136. [152] Hobe, *Völkerrecht*, 359.

independent from a consensus of the state's authority, i.e. robust.[153] Therefore, it is included in this section regarding the authorisation of military means for humanitarian assistance measures.

One further example with regard to enforcement action for humanitarian aid is the situation in East Timor in 1999. The Council decided upon a very far-reaching mandate.

East Timor The security situation in East Timor deteriorated after the popular consultation for the purpose of ascertaining whether the East Timorese people accepted or rejected special autonomy within Indonesia. The great majority of the East Timorese people rejected the proposed autonomy and thus voted in favour of a transition towards the independence of East Timor.[154]

The Council, 'appalled by the worsening humanitarian situation' emphasised – while acting under Chapter VII UNC – the 'urgent need for coordinated humanitarian assistance and the importance of allowing full, safe and unimpeded access by humanitarian organisations and called upon all parties to cooperate . . . so as to ensure . . . the effective delivery of humanitarian aid'.[155] To implement this need among others, the Security Council authorised the establishment of a multinational force and states participating in the force to take all necessary measures with the task 'to facilitate humanitarian assistance operations'.[156] Shortly after, the United Nations-mandated multinational force was followed by the Transitional Administration in East Timor (UNTAET).[157] It was empowered to exercise all legislative and executive authority. This United Nations-led mission was mandated under Chapter VII UNC to 'take all necessary measures' to 'ensure the coordination and delivery of humanitarian assistance'. Furthermore 'a humanitarian assistance and emergency rehabilitation component' was one of the three main components of the Transitional Administration.[158] UNTAET was endued 'to ensure the comprehensive delivery of multisectoral humanitarian assistance'.[159] The Secretary-General considered the humanitarian disaster as the most pressing crisis facing UNTAET.[160]

[153] See Bolaños Enrique, *Anwendung*, 28.
[154] UN Doc. (A/53/951) (S/1999/513), 5 May 1999, §1, 2, annex 1, Article 6.
[155] UN Doc. (S/RES/1264) preambular §7, §2. [156] UN Doc. (S/RES/1264) §3.
[157] UN Doc. (S/RES/1272) 25 October 1999, §1; see for UN mandated (INTERFET), Schütze, *Zurechenbarkeit*, 54.
[158] UN Doc. (S/RES/1272) §2 (d), 3 (b), 4; *cf.* for UN-led, Schütze, *Zurechenbarkeit*, 32.
[159] UN Doc. (S/1999/1024) 4 October 1999, §71.
[160] UN Doc. (S/2000/53) 26 January 2000, §29.

In 2002 East Timor declared independence. It thus ended more than 450 years of colonisation. UNTAET was removed by a United Nations support mission[161] 'until all operational responsibilities were fully devolved to the East Timorese authorities'.[162]

It follows from this that the Security Council mandates missions not only to facilitate humanitarian assistance but also to provide for aid.

3.3. *Interim results*

Competence for humanitarian assistance was conferred on the United Nations. The Security Council is the competent organ for the maintenance of international peace and security. Therefore, it is the competent organ to recommend and also to enforce humanitarian assistance. For the latter, it can decide on either non-military measures to force out an acceptance of humanitarian assistance or on armed measures which (additionally) push humanitarian assistance physically in. Implementation of military means completely depends on the support of the member states. They either provide forces for an United Nations-led mission or the Council authorises states, groups of states or regional organisations. Furthermore, the Security Council may determine that serious humanitarian situations inside a state constitute or continue to constitute a threat to the peace by themselves.

In line with this finding, the IDI's resolution dedicated to humanitarian assistance provides that the Security Council may take the necessary measures under Chapter VII UNC if 'a refusal to accept a bona fide offer of humanitarian assistance or to allow access to the victims, leads to a threat to international peace and security'.

4. Closing remarks

The aim of this chapter was to show the factual involvement and the corresponding competences of the United Nations with respect to the Security Council to humanitarian assistance, in particular in situations that concern the maintenance of international peace and security that necessitate enforcement action.

[161] UN Doc. (S/RES/1410) 17 May 2002.

[162] UN, 'UNMISET', www.un.org/en/peacekeeping/missions/past/unmiset/index.html.

It has underlined United Nations involvement and competence in the promotion of, and ensuring compliance with, humanitarian assistance remits in general and in special cases in both peace and wartime.

Since the main focus of this chapter is on situations that concern the maintenance of international peace and security for which the Security Council holds primary responsibility, this United Nations organ was at the core. As the competent organ, the Security Council calls for compliance, but it furthermore uses enforcement power when faced with obstructions of humanitarian assistance and to maintain peace and security, not only by facilitating humanitarian assistance in manifold facets but also by providing aid.

As a precondition for the use of enforcement powers, the determination of an existence of any threat to the peace, the Security Council even may, and does, refer to serious humanitarian situations inside a state. Enforcement measures can be non-military - such as embargos and boycotts - or armed measures. In the case that non-military sanctions do not bring the desired success regarding humanitarian assistance, the Security Council also has recourse to military force.

However, this chapter simply refers to the competence of the Security Council to face today's obstruction of humanitarian assistance. By taking a look at Myanmar and the humanitarian catastrophe caused by cyclone Nargis, the decisive difference between a competence and an obligation to act can be easily demonstrated: since the government had refused to accept or even impeded an offer of humanitarian assistance or to allow access to the victims after the cyclone,[163] action by the Security Council was called for by many voices. But the Security Council did not fulfil these demands.[164] However, thoughts about whether the Security Council has an obligation to take action are a different kettle of fish.

[163] 'Uno-Generalsekretär zornig über schleppende Hilfe', *Spiegel Online*, 12 May 2008, www.spiegel.de/panorama/0,1518,552830,00.html; N. Luhmann, 'Humanitäre Hilfe in Burma: Das Geheimnis des Deltas', *Jungle World*, 5 June 2008. http://jungle-world.com/artikel/2008/23/21929.html.

[164] *Bundesregierung*, 'Merkel: UN-Sicherheitsrat mit Myanmar befassen', *Die Bundesregierung*, 9 May 2008, www.bundesregierung.de/Content/DE/Archiv16/Artikel/2008/05/2008-05-09-bk-birma.html; for lack of action in the Security Council, see Richard K. Radtke, 'Bomben auf Rangun?: Maynmar und die "Responsibility to Protect"', *Welthungerhilfe, Brennpunkt* 3 (2008): 4.

7

International norms informing domestic disaster response schemes

HEIKE SPIEKER

1. Introduction

Although international law provides for a certain regulation of natural or technological disasters,[1] the practical responsibility to grant protection lies first and foremost with national governments and local authorities. Domestic authorities implement this responsibility quite often in the form of domestic disaster response schemes and mechanisms.[2] Such schemes and mechanisms reflect decisions on the identification of needs, on the recognition of potential beneficiaries, on the determination of adequate means and instruments, as well as on the identification of appropriate actors. In other words decision-makers on a domestic level need to decide which needs are to be met in which form for whom and by whom. This chapter gives an overview of existing and proposed international legal rules which have the potential to inspire domestic legislators when designing disaster response schemes and taking a protective approach in regard to people affected by natural disasters.

The international legal framework for humanitarian assistance in the broader sense distinguishes categorically between assistance being provided in situations of armed conflict on the one hand and in non-conflict situations on the other hand.[3] Domestic legal regimes, in particular in the context of disaster response schemes and mechanisms, either distinguish

[1] Carlo Focarelli, 'Duty to Protect in Cases of Natural Disasters', *The Max Planck Encyclopedia of Public International Law* (2010), www.mpepil.com; Heike Spieker, 'Humanitarian Assistance, Access in Armed Conflict and Occupation', *The Max Planck Enyclopedia of Public International Law* (2009), www.mpepil.com; Heike Spieker, 'The Right to Give and Receive Humanitarian Assistance', in *International Law and Humanitarian Assistance*, eds. Hans-Joachim Heintze and Andrej Zwitter (Berlin Heidelberg: Springer-Verlag, 2011), 7–31.

[2] IFRC Disaster Law Database, accessed 29 April 2014, www.ifrc.org/en/publications-and-reports/idrl-database/.publication.asp.

[3] Spieker 'Right', 7, 8.

categorically, too, or cover both types of situations in one approach. This chapter focuses on international law applying to non-conflict situations, i.e. mainly natural disasters, and thus excluding regulation under international humanitarian law. Historically, organised domestic disaster response in non-conflict situations started to develop generally in the eighteenth century. Rural populations broadly used to be referred to their own support systems, while disaster response in urban settings became a matter for local authorities who often had recourse to auxiliary institutions and units such as fire-fighters or forms of militia.

2. Framework conditions for domestic disaster response schemes

Today, a broad majority of states avail themselves of domestic disaster response schemes and mechanisms of various legal character, different legally binding force, and in varying effectiveness and adequacy. Persons affected by natural disasters encounter a broad range of issues and problems. Very often the most urgent comprise, for example, (in)equality of access to assistance, negative discrimination and adverse distinction in the provision of assistance, enforced relocation of populations, sexual and gender-based violence, internal displacement as a consequence of natural disasters, individuals' loss of legal documentation, unsafe or involuntary return or settlement, and issues of property restitution.

2.1 The 'primary role' of the affected state

'To take care of the victims of natural disasters and other emergencies' is 'first and foremost' the responsibility of the state on whose territory the disaster occurs. This proposition has emanated from Resolution 46/182 on the Strengthening of the Coordination of Humanitarian Emergency Assistance of the United Nations of 19 December 1991.[4] In its annex, the Resolution contains Guiding Principles on humanitarian assistance provided by the United Nations. Besides qualifying the principles of humanity, neutrality and impartiality as mandatory for humanitarian assistance of the United Nations,[5] the Guiding Principles explicitly refer to humanitarian assistance being provided in non-conflict disaster situations for 'victims of natural disasters and other emergencies'. Based on this 'first

[4] (A/RES/46/182), accessed 1 June 2013, www.un.org/documents/ga/res/46/a46r182.htm.

[5] Ibid., '2. Humanitarian assistance must be provided in accordance with the principles of humanity, neutrality and impartiality.'

and foremost' responsibility of the state concerned, the resolution confirms the requirement of consent of the state on whose territory humanitarian assistance is to be provided for both armed conflicts and non-conflict disaster situations. It reiterates the sovereignty of states and determines that 'humanitarian assistance should be provided with the consent of the affected country and in principle on the basis of an appeal by the affected country'. In consequence, it is the state who has the 'primary role in the initiation, organisation, coordination, and implementation of humanitarian assistance within its territory',[6] as a result of its national sovereignty.[7]

2.2 *Legal frameworks*

In order to facilitate domestic disaster response operations, governmental authorities often adopt legal frameworks for such operations. Notwithstanding manifold country-specific and even region-specific[8] differences, disaster response laws and contingency plans generally regulate responsibilities, procedures and competences of different actors in coping with the effects of disasters. Such regulation is necessitated by experience and recognition of the fact that disasters disrupt the usual functioning of a society, seriously affecting both the civilian population as well as civilian or military governmental authorities. Very often, such laws and plans extend to the areas of disaster preparedness and disaster mitigation in addition to disaster management in its strict sense. Modern approaches include, for example, disaster risk reduction, possibly climate change adaptation, disaster prevention and rehabilitation in domestic disaster laws and plans.

Domestic disaster laws and plans generally envisage assisting governmental and non-governmental actors and the affected population. Laws and plans have to decide whether, and in which priority, life, health, the natural environment, private or public properties are to be protected, and

[6] Ibid., §3 and 4.

[7] The question whether this sovereignty may be set aside in certain circumstances is discussed in Spieker, 'Right', 11–12 and 28–30.

[8] For example, in Germany it is not the federal state which is responsible for domestic disaster response, but the Länder states who are responsible. As a rule, the federal state only has a supporting responsibility, in particular in situations where the disaster has cross-border effects among Länder states and several Länder states are affected by the same disaster. In consequence, there are sixteen different disaster management acts and, in addition, one framework act at federal level.

to what extent. The different roles, responsibilities and competences need to be identified, distinguished from each other and defined. Institutions have to be identified and possibly created; monitoring and obligations with a view to precautionary measures have to be designated. Operating procedures are to be identified and agreed to and the different actors have to exercise their practical application. Actors further have to be equipped in terms of logistics, technology and human resources, and all equipment needs to be maintained and updated, both in terms of technological and scientific standards and in terms of education and training. With a view to individuals, their rights and duties in different phases of a disaster are to be determined.

A decision on whose, and which, needs are to be met, and in which form, encompasses – but is not satisfied by – activities such as identification of disaster risks and risk assessment as well as monitoring of, for example, vulnerabilities, risk development and management capacities. In a situation where a government considers putting a domestic disaster response plan in place, different types of regulation have to be enacted on different levels, depending on, respectively, the issue to be tackled, the actor to be authorised and the behaviour to be regulated. This is particularly relevant in contexts where governments decide to take a protective approach, explicitly striving to protect individuals and communities affected by natural disasters.

International law applicable in situations other than armed conflict is able to inspire law- and decision-makers with a view to drafting domestic disaster response schemes. Although international law does not provide norms specifically addressing this issue, it contains norms which are able to give a broader guidance in this context.

In identifying certain rights and obligations, universal human rights law indicates decisions on rights, freedoms and liberties being endowed with protection, and indicates a certain prioritisation. Such universal human rights are not necessarily specifically intended to cover the issue of domestic disaster response schemes, but they are generally applicable to this issue. The same goes for specialised human rights treaties, as for example legal regulation on the protection of refugees,[9] on the protection of children[10] and

[9] *Convention and Protocol Relating to the Status of Refugees*, 1951 and 1967, www.unhcr.org/3b66c2aa10.html.

[10] *Convention on the Rights of the Child*, 1990; General Assembly Resolution 44/25, UN Doc. (A/44/25) 20 November 1989.

of women,[11] as well as the prohibition of racial discrimination[12] and prohibition of torture.[13] Such instruments cover specific issues and at the same time have a certain impact on the situation of people affected by natural disasters under certain framework conditions. Therefore regional and sectoral international treaties have a similar impact on domestic disaster response laws and plans.

2.3 *Nature and effect of human rights law and guidance Documents*

The following overview focuses on the more general and comprehensive international law instruments and documents which nevertheless have a direct impact on the design and scope of national disaster response schemes and plans.

In a nutshell, human rights law comprises regulations which oblige states and governmental authorities to guarantee the fundamental rights and freedoms of individuals – as well as groups of individuals, as the case may be – under their jurisdiction.[14] They feature three major characteristics: Firstly, human rights laws per se are open to restrictions. The mere notions of 'human right', 'fundamental freedom', 'guarantee' or 'entitlement' imply that – as a rule – the right, liberty, freedom, guarantee or entitlement does not exclude limitation and restriction. As such, not one human right is absolute, not even the right to life: although the majority of domestic legal systems protect the individuals' right to life, most of these legal systems legally require at the same time that policemen or firefighters or soldiers, for example, potentially sacrifice their individual lives under specific circumstances. This is a concept which is not only tolerated by human rights law, but which is an integral part of the philosophy of human rights law. Secondly, this question of restrictions is to be distinguished from the question whether a governmental

[11] *Convention on the Elimination of All Forms of Discrimination against Women*, 1981; General Assembly, Resolution 34/180, UN Doc. (A/34/180) 18 December 1979.

[12] *Convention on the Elimination of All Forms of Racial Discrimination*, 1969; General Assembly, Resolution 2106 (XX), UN Doc. (A/2106 (XX)) 21 December 1965.

[13] *Convention against Torture and Other Cruel, Inhuman or Degrading Treatment or Punishment*, 1987; General Assembly, Resolution 39/46, UN Doc. (A/39/46) 10 December 1984.

[14] Thomas Buergenthal, 'Human Rights', MN 1, *The Max Planck Encyclopedia of Public International Law*, www.mpeil.de: Human rights are defined as the rights of individuals and groups that are recognised as such in international treaties and declarations as well as by customary international law. They include civil and political rights; economic rights; social and cultural rights; the rights of minorities and peoples.

authority may temporarily or permanently lift its human rights obligations. Human rights law implements the concept of derogation and distinguishes between derogable and non-derogable human rights. The rule is that human rights are derogable, i.e. a state bound by a human rights obligation is able to lift this obligation under certain conditions.[15] By way of exception, certain human rights are enhanced by being exempted from such derogability and cannot be derogated from, not even on a temporary basis.[16] As a result, non-derogable rights cannot be derogated from, but they may be restricted in specific contexts.[17] Lastly, the different types of human rights – often referred to as 'human rights generations'[18] – require different types of governmental activity. Civil and political – first-generation – rights require a specific act or omission: authorities have to respect and, as the case may be, protect a certain right or, in the case of prohibitions, are prevented from a specific behaviour. In contrast to civil and political rights and freedoms, economic, social and cultural – second-generation – rights have a more programmatic character. Article 2 paragraph 1 explicitly determines that states parties are obliged to 'undertake[s] to take steps ... to the maximum of [their] available resources, with a view to achieving progressively the full realisation of the rights'.[19] Required action in this context is a furthering and enhancement of such rights with the view to their full realisation.

[15] E.g. ICCPR, Article 4 §1: 'In time of public emergency which threatens the life of the nation and the existence of which is officially proclaimed, the states Parties to the present Covenant may take measures derogating from their obligations under the present Covenant to the extent strictly required by the exigencies of the situation, provided that such measures are not inconsistent with their other obligations under international law and to not involve discrimination solely on the ground of race, colour, sex, language, religion or social origin.'

[16] E.g. ICCPR, Article 4 §2.

[17] ICCPR, Article 4 §2, lists the following human rights as non-derogable rights: right to life, Article 6; right not to be subjected to torture or to cruel, inhuman or degrading punishment or treatment, Article 7; prohibition of slavery, Article 8; prohibition of imprisonment for failure to comply with a contractual obligation, Article 11; prohibition on the retroactive application of penal laws, Article 15; right to recognition of the legal personality of the person, Article 16; and freedom of thought, conscience and religion, Article 18.

[18] F. Ouguergouz, 'African Charter on Human and Peoples' Rights', MN 14f, *The Max Planck Encyclopedia of Public International Law* (1981), www.mpepil.com; Stein von Buttlar, *Völkerrecht* (Köln, München: Carl Heymanns Verlag, 2009), 361, §1002.

[19] For 'developing countries' and in the area of economic rights, Article 2 §3 lifts the extent of obligation even more: 'Developing countries, with due regard to human rights and their national economy, may determine to what extent they would guarantee the economic rights recognised in the present Covenant to non-nationals.'

In contrast to international human rights law, guidance documents – regardless of their specific coverage and scope – do not have legally binding force. Initiated and adopted by different authors and addressed to different audiences, they cover different topics and may be named differently. Their common feature is that they do not legally bind either authors or addressees, but have the quality of recommendations or encouragements instead. Disregarding their content or not acting according to their recommendations does not constitute a violation of international law and thus does not bear any legal consequences. Therefore guidance documents carry psychological as well as political value, hoping to inform and possibly direct governmental behaviour. Beyond such behavioural effect, guidance documents have the potential to influence the development of international law in that they may trigger the conclusion of international treaties[20] or may initiate the development of international customary law.[21] In contexts where guidance documents initiate or support the evolution of international custom, as evidence of a general practice accepted as law, such acts or omissions by states and, in addition, a coinciding legal conviction of states that such act or omission is required by international law – the so-called *opinio iuris* – may become legally binding as international customary law. In such cases it is not the guidance document itself, but the behaviour of states accompanied by respective legal conviction, which may become legally binding.

3. International treaty law informing domestic disaster response schemes

3.1 Universal human rights law

Together with the *International Covenant on Economic, Social and Cultural Rights* (ICESCR),[22] the *International Covenant of Civil and Political*

[20] Article 38 §1 lit. a., *Statute of the International Court of Justice*: '1. The Court, whose function is to decide in accordance with international law such disputes as are submitted to it, shall apply: a. international conventions, whether general or particular, establishing rules expressly recognised by the contesting states'; acccessed 8 June 2013, www.icj-cij.org/documents/?p1=4&p2=2&p3=0#CHAPTER_II.

[21] Article 38 §1 lit. b., *Statute of the International Court of Justice*: '1. The Court, whose function is to decide in accordance with international law such disputes as are submitted to it, shall apply: b. international custom, as evidence of a general practice accepted as law'.

[22] OHCHR, *International Covenant on Economic, Social and Cultural Rights*, accessed 1 June 2013, www.ohchr.org/EN/ProfessionalInterest/Pages/CESCR.aspx.

Rights (ICCPR)[23] forms the universal and comprehensive international human rights regime.[24]

3.1.1 The *International Covenant of Civil and Political Rights*

The ICCPR contains so-called 'first-generation' human rights, in particular the right to life, Article 6; the right to liberty and security of person, Articles 9, 10 and 11; the prohibition of slavery, torture and inhuman or degrading punishment or treatment, Articles 7 and 8; the right to liberty of movement and freedom to choose residence, Article 12; the protection from arbitrary or unlawful interference with privacy, family, home or correspondence, Article 17; the right to freedom of thought, conscience and religion, Articles 18 and 19; the right of peaceful assembly and the right to freedom of association, Articles 21 and 22; the right to recognition as a person before the law, Article 16; as well as procedural rights and guarantees, Articles 14 and 15.

Articles 6 paragraph 1, 9 paragraph 1 and 2 paragraph 1 ICCPR are of general relevance to domestic disaster response. Article 6 paragraph 1 ICCPR protects the right to life in that it formulates that '[e]very human being has the inherent right to life. This right shall be protected by law. No one shall be arbitrarily deprived of his life.'[25] The right to life is a non-derogable right according to Article 4 paragraph 2 ICCPR. Article 2 paragraph 1 ICCPR contains the principle of non-discrimination, obliging states parties to the Covenant to 'undertake to respect and to ensure to all individuals within its territory and subject to its jurisdiction the rights recognised in the present Covenant, without distinction of any kind, such as race, colour, sex, language, religion, political or other opinion, national or social origin, property, birth or other status'.[26] Article 3 obliges governments to 'ensure the equal right of men and women to the enjoyment of all civil and political rights set forth in the

[23] OHCHR, *International Convenant on Civil and Political Rights*, accessed 1 June 2013, www.ohchr.org/EN/ProfessionalInterest/Pages/CCPR.aspx.

[24] Regional human rights regimes are, in alphabetical order, *The African Charter on Human and Peoples' Rights* (ACHPR), 1981, www.achpr.org/files/instruments/achpr/banjul_charter.pdf; *The American Convention on Human Rights* (ACHR), 1969, www.oas.org/dil/treaties_B-32_American_Convention_on_Human_Rights.pdf; and *The European Convention for the Protection of Human Rights and Fundamental Freedoms* (ECHR), 1950, http://conventions.coe.int/Treaty/en/Treaties/Html/005.htm.

[25] Similar protection is provided by ACHPR, Article 4; ACHR, Article 4; and ECHR, Article 2.

[26] Cf. ACHPR, Article 2; ACHR, Article 1 §1; and ECHR, Article 14.

present Covenant'. The guarantee is one of the bases for governmental responsibilities with a view to access of persons affected by a disaster to humanitarian goods and services and standards of such goods and services.

More specifically, Article 12 paragraph 1 ICCPR touches upon the question of housing and shelter: 'Everyone lawfully within the territory of a state shall, within that territory, have the right to liberty of movement and freedom to choose his residence.' Paragraph 2 provides for the right to leave any country, including his or her own. The general possibility to restrict human rights – including the right to liberty of movement and the freedom to choose residence according to Article 12 ICCPR – is further specified and limited in paragraph 3: the rule is that the freedom to choose may not be restricted. Only by way of exception may the guarantee be limited, i.e. in case provided by law and on the basis of necessity for the protection of national security, public order (*ordre public*), public health or morals or of the rights and freedoms of others, and if consistent with the other rights recognised in the Covenant.[27]

Article 13 ICCPR further provides protection against being expelled from a foreign country for 'aliens lawfully in the territory' of a state party to the Covenant, except 'in pursuance of a decision reached in accordance with law'. In case of lawful expulsion, the individual concerned has a right to submit reasons against the expulsion and to have the case reviewed by the competent authority or its representative, except where compelling reasons of national security require otherwise. Both human rights have specific relevance for issues of displacement and dislocation in the context of natural disasters.

Article 9 para 1 ICCPR contains the right to security of person: 'Everyone has the right to liberty and security of person. No one shall be subjected to arbitrary arrest or detention. No one shall be deprived of his liberty except on such grounds and in accordance with such procedure as are established by law'.[28] Article 16 ICCPR provides procedural guidance in that it determines everyone to 'have the right to recognition everywhere as a person before the law'. This right is non-derogable according to Article 4 paragraph 2 ICCPR. Article 14 guarantees fair trial procedures: 'All persons shall be equal before the courts and tribunals', Article 14 paragraph 1.[29] Additional guarantees apply in case of criminal charges, proceedings and convictions. All these human rights

[27] Cf. ACHPR, Article 12 §1; ACHR, Article 22; and ECHR, Article 2 Protocol 4.
[28] See also ACHPR, Articles 4 and 6; ACHR, Article 7; and ECHR, Article 5.
[29] Similar protection is provided by ACHPR, Article 7; ACHR, Article 8; and ECHR, Article 6.

are relevant with a view to legislative and administrative schemes and mechanisms for domestic responses to disasters.

3.1.2 The *International Covenant of Economic, Social and Cultural Rights*

The ICESCR contains so-called 'second-generation' human rights which have a more programmatic character. This emanates not only from the design of the Covenant and its provisions, but also from the mere wording of its rules. These are in particular the right to work (Article 6); the right to fair pay and rest time (Article 7); the right to social security (Article 9); the right to protection of and assistance to the family (Article 10); the right to an adequate standard of living including adequate food, clothing and housing, and to the continuous improvement of living conditions (Article 11); the right to the enjoyment of the highest attainable standard of physical and mental health (Article 12); as well as the right to education (Article 13).

The prohibition of adverse discrimination of Article 2 paragraph 1 ICCPR is reiterated in Article 2 paragraph 2 ICESCR: states parties 'undertake to guarantee that the rights enunciated in the present Covenant will be exercised without discrimination of any kind as to race, colour, sex, language, religion, political or other opinion, national or social origin, property, birth or other status'. According to Article 11 paragraph 1, states 'recognise the right of everyone to an adequate standard of living for himself and his family, including adequate food, clothing and housing, and to the continuous improvement of living conditions'. Paragraph 2 recognises a fundamental right of everyone to be free from hunger and, consequently, a responsibility to take measures for example which are needed to improve methods of distribution of food.

The ICESCR further formulates a 'right of everyone to the enjoyment of the highest attainable standard of physical and mental health' (Article 12 paragraph 1), and lists by way of example the following measures to be taken: steps with a view to the reduction of the stillbirth rate and of infant mortality, and for the healthy development of the child, to the improvement of all aspects of environmental and industrial hygiene, and to the prevention, treatment and control of epidemic, endemic, occupational and other diseases (paragraph 2).

Article 13 paragraph 1 provides for a right of everyone to education.[30] Families 'should be' accorded the 'widest possible protection and

[30] Similar protection is provided by ACHPR, Article 17; and ECHR, Article 2 Protocol (1952), accessed 5 June 2013, http://conventions.coe.int/Treaty/en/Treaties/Html/009.htm.

assistance' (Article 10 paragraph 1), and special protection should be accorded to mothers during a reasonable period before and after childbirth (Article 10 paragraph 2). According to Article 10 paragraph 3, special measures of protection and assistance should be taken on behalf of all children and young persons without any discrimination for reasons of parentage or other conditions.[31]

This cursory inventory of universal human rights treaty and customary law shows a rather diverse and inconsistent picture of indicated issues to be covered by domestic disaster response schemes, mechanisms, plans and instruments. The principle of non-discrimination is contained in both covenants (Article 2 paragraph 1 ICCPR and Article 2 paragraph 2 ICESCR). The ICCPR embodies constitutive regulations on the protection of life, security of the person and freedom of movement (Articles 6, 9 and 12). It further contains certain hints with regard to the issues of residence, housing and shelter (Articles 12 and 13), and due processes (Article 16). The ICESCR comprises standards on living (Article 11), health and medical care (Article 12), education (Article 13), and on special protection for the family, mothers and children (Article 10). Issues such as protection of property,[32] guarantees of effective remedy and compensation[33] or judicial protection and fair trial guarantees[34] are not tackled in substance.

3.2 *Sectoral and regional international treaties*

The question is whether regional or sectoral international law is more informative on these questions.

3.2.1 Sectoral approaches

There is neither a general and comprehensive international treaty nor customary law providing a legal framework for disaster response in non-conflict situations. The so-called Chernobyl Convention,[35] the so-called *Tampere Convention*[36] and the *Civil Defence Framework*

[31] See also ACHPR, Article 17; and ACHR, Article 17.

[32] Cf. ECHR, Article 1 Protocol (1952). [33] E.g. ECHR, Article 13.

[34] See ACHR, Article 8; and ECHR, Article 6.

[35] International Atomic Energy Agency, *Convention on Assistance in the Case of a Nuclear Accicent or Radiological Emergency*, entry into force 26 February 1987, accessed 6 June 2013, www.iaea.org/Publications/Documents/Infcircs/Others/infcirc336.shtml.

[36] Intergovernmental Conference on Emergency Telecommunications, *Tampere Convention on the Provision of Telecommunication Resources for Disaster Mitigation and Relief Operations*, entry into force 8 January 2005, accessed 1 June 2013, www.itu.int/ITU-D/emergencytelecoms/Tampere_convention.pdf.

Convention[37] as the most comprehensive multilateral treaties in this area do not provide for extensive regulation. On the basis of a preservation of the affected state's sovereignty,[38] all three treaties focus on the issue of mutual assistance, starting with an invitation to call for assistance in case of need.[39] The duty to provide facilities and services[40] 'to the extent of its capabilities'[41] is complemented by an obligation to 'ensure protection of personnel, equipment and materials'.[42] States parties are further obliged to 'afford ... the necessary privileges, immunities and facilities' for the functioning of personnel[43] and to facilitate,[44] and in particular to determine[45] entry, staying in and departure from the respective territory of personnel. Other states parties are committed to 'seek to facilitate the transit ... of duly notified personnel, equipment and property'.[46]

A reference to the concept of domestic disaster response schemes and mechanisms is not contained in any of the more comprehensive, sectoral multilateral international treaties.

3.2.2 Regional approaches

3.2.2.1 The League of Arab States and the Black Sea Economic Cooperation Details and modalities of mutual assistance are also the focus of the Arab Cooperation Agreement Regulating and Facilitating Relief Operations[47] (1987, Arab League Relief Operations Agreement) and the Agreement among the Governments of the Participating states of the Black Sea Economic Cooperation (BSEC) on collaboration in Emergency Assistance and Emergency Response to Natural and Man-Made Disasters (BSEC Emergency Agreement).[48] The Arab Cooperation Agreement covers 'organising and facilitating relief actions between

[37] ICDO, *Framework Convention on Civil Defence Assistance*, 22 May 2000, accessed 6 June 2013, www.icdo.org/files/framework-convention.pdf.

[38] Article 3 lit. a., 'Chernobyl Convention'; Article 4, *Tampere Convention*; Article 3, *Civil Defence Framework Convention.*

[39] Article 2, 'Chernobyl Convention'. [40] Articles 6, 7, 8, 'Chernobyl Convention'.

[41] Article 3 lit. b., 'Chernobyl Convention'.

[42] Article 3 lit. b., 'Chernobyl Convention'; Article 4, 'Civil Defence Framework Convention'.

[43] Article 8 §1 and 2, 'Chernobyl Convention'; Article 5, *Tampere Convention*; Article 4, *Civil Defence Framework Convention.*

[44] Article 8 §5, 'Chernobyl Convention'.

[45] Article 6, *Tampere Convention*; Article 4 §6 *Civil Defence Framework Convention.*

[46] Article 9, 'Chernobyl Convention'.

[47] The unofficial English translation, accessed 4 June 2013, www.ifrc.org/Docs/idrl/N644EN.pdf.

[48] English Translation, accessed 4 June 2013, www.ifrc.org/Docs/idrl/I260EN.pdf.

member states' (Articles 2),[49] and the coordination of their efforts in disaster and emergency situations (Article 3). Although they commit themselves to 'speeding up and facilitating measures' in order to facilitate 'rapid access' (Article 3), this is not addressed as an element of domestic disaster response schemes. The BSEC Emergency Agreement 'establishes principles and frameworks of the co-ordinated activities of the parties in case of natural and man-made disasters' (Article 1 paragraph 1). On the basis of the expectation that states parties 'cooperate ... in order to provide prompt relevant information and assistance' (Article 3 paragraph 1), further details of mutual assistance are agreed; for example, request for assistance (Article 3 paragraph 2); provision of assistance (Article 3 paragraphs 3 and 12); support of passage (Article 5); coordination of assistance (Articles 6 and 8); and involvement of external actors (Article 16). Neither of these two regional treaties incorporates the concept of domestic disaster-response schemes and mechanisms.

3.2.2.2 The ASEAN Agreement on Disaster Management and Emergency Response The Association of South East Asian Nations (ASEAN) Agreement on Disaster Management and Emergency Response (AADMER)[50] is a result of an initiative taken by the Special ASEAN Leaders' Meeting on Aftermath of Earthquake and Tsunami. The Special Meeting adopted the 'Declaration on Action to Strengthen Emergency Relief, Rehabilitation, Reconstruction and Prevention on the Aftermath of Earthquake and Tsunami Disaster'. The 2005 Agreement is the result of such action and constitutes a framework for the development of operational procedures to respond collectively and quickly to disasters. It contains provisions on disaster risk identification, monitoring and early warning, preparedness and response, and it establishes the ASEAN Coordinating Centre for Humanitarian Assistance on disaster management (AHA Centre, Article 20). States parties to the agreement intend to provide 'effective mechanisms to achieve substantial reduction of disaster losses in lives and in [their] social, economic and environmental assets' (Article 2). The explicit aim is to 'respond to disaster emergencies

[49] Article 7 covers 'shipment or transit of food relief items', Article 8 'facilities needed for the travel of relief teams and delegates of Member States', and Article 9 'facilities possible to accredited national relief organisations and committees, and telecommunications'.

[50] ASEAN, accessed 1 June 2013, www.asean.org/news/item/asean-agreement-on-disaster-management-and-emergency-response-vientiane-26-july-2005–2. All ten ASEAN member states are parties to the agreement.

through concerted *national efforts* and intensified regional and international cooperation' (emphasis added).

The ASEAN Agreement emphasises the principle of sovereignty and reiterates the primary responsibility of states parties to respond to disasters.[51] Interestingly, the agreement does not satisfy its approach by way of listing the obligations to 'immediately respond to a disaster occurring within [member states'] territory'.[52] It details the incumbent responsibility both in terms of type of governance measures and of areas to be covered. Article 4 lit. d obliges member states to 'take legislative, administrative and other measures as necessary to implement their obligations under this Agreement'. States parties are further obliged to 'take appropriate measures to identify disaster risks ... covering, among others ... natural and human-induced hazards; risk assessment; monitoring of vulnerabilities; and disaster management capacities'.[53] Article 6 formulates the obligation of states parties to 'develop strategies to identify, prevent and reduce risks from hazards' and to 'undertake measures to reduce losses from disasters'. Domestic disaster response plans are explicitly referred to in the context of early warning, Article 7 paragraph 1: 'The Parties shall, as appropriate, establish, maintain and periodically *review national disaster early warning arrangements*' (emphasis added). Parties are further expected to 'develop strategies and contingency/ response plans' and 'as appropriate, prepare Standard Operating Procedures for ... national action' (Article 8). Finally, under the heading 'national emergency response', Article 10 requires states parties to 'ensure according to their national legislation that the necessary measures are taken to mobilise equipment, facilities, materials, human and financial resources'. The AHA Centre, according to Article 20, is endowed with the task to facilitate cooperation and coordination among states parties, with the United Nations and with international organisations. States parties are expected to establish national focal points in addition to one or more 'Competent Authorities' in the implementation of the agreement (Article 22).

[51] Article 3 §1; Article 3 §6 indicates stakeholders to be involved in the exercise of sovereign rights in emergency response: 'The parties, in addressing disaster risks, shall involve, as appropriate, all stakeholders including local communities, non-governmental organisations and private enterprises, utilising, among others, community-based disaster preparedness and early response approaches.'

[52] Article 4 lit. a.7 [53] Article 5 §1.

3.2.2.3 The Caribbean Disaster Emergency Management Agency

The 2008 Agreement Establishing the Caribbean Disaster Emergency Management Agency (CDEMA)[54] tackles both mutual assistance in natural disasters and domestic response schemes. Article V defines particularly the objectives of 'mobilising and coordinating disaster relief' and 'mitigating or eliminating ... the immediate consequences of disasters'. At the same time it encourages states parties to adopt 'disaster loss reduction and mitigation policies and practices at the national and regional level' and to adopt 'cooperative arrangements and mechanisms to facilitate the development of a culture of disaster loss reduction'. The Agency aims at 'coordinating the establishment, enhancement and maintenance of adequate emergency disaster response capabilities among the Participating States', (Article V lit. f). The so-called Technical Advisory Committee as an organ of the Agency consists of the national disaster coordinators of the Participating States (Article X), and has the tasks, among others, to 'recommend standards and procedures for the fair and equitable deployment of resources for disaster management' and to 'recommend the standards and procedure for triggering the disaster response mechanism' (Article XI). Functions of the so-called Coordinating Unit as another organ of the Agency comprise, for instance, to 'establish, equip and maintain a coordinated emergency operations system capable of responding to emergency situations' and to 'establish and maintain a reliable system of communications with the heads of national disaster management Agencies and ensure that their disaster response capabilities are maintained at agreed levels of operational efficiency' (Article XIII). In consequence, Participating States undertake, in particular, to:

> establish and maintain ... national relief organisations capable of responding swiftly, effectively and in a coordinated manner ... establish emergency disaster planning groups and define national policies and priorities ... ensure that national disaster management agencies and their coordinators have specific functions and responsibilities to ensure the development of an adequate response capability ... review and rationalise legal arrangements for disaster mitigation and emergency action ... [and] develop ... an emergency shelter policy and programme involving the full participation of local officials from community-based organisations.
>
> (Article XIX)

[54] CDEMA, accessed 4 June 2013, www.caricom.org/jsp/secretariat/legal_instruments/agreement_cdema.pdf.

Both the 2005 ASEAN Agreement and the 2008 CDEMA Agreement focus on, among other things, domestic disaster response schemes and mechanisms as an asset to achieve and to enhance. They do so in a general and broader manner, leaving space, flexibility and discretion to states. The Agreements leave issues such as beneficiaries' access to assistance, relocation and displacement of individuals, return and resettlement as well as property restitution up to the responsibility and authority of governments.

4. Legally non-binding guidance documents

Guidance documents as such do not possess legally binding force – see above Section 2.3. As encouragements and recommendations they are intended to impact on an actor's behaviour without creating legal expectations and obligations. Guidance documents on domestic disaster response mainly focus on the 1998 Guiding Principles on Internal Displacement, the 2005 Principles on Housing and Property Restitution for Refugees and Displaced Persons and the 2006 IASC Guidelines on Human Rights and Natural Disasters. All three documents are partly derived from existing law and partly designed for filling in gaps remaining from these legally binding rules. It remains to be seen whether they are able to address issues being left open by existing law, and able to inspire domestic disaster response schemes and mechanisms.

4.1 The Guiding Principles on Internal Displacement

Both the United Nations Human Rights Commission and the United Nations General Assembly endorsed the Guiding Principles on Internal Displacement (1998, IDP Guidelines).[55] They took note of the Principles, welcomed their use as an important tool and standard, and encouraged United Nations agencies, regional organisations, governments and non-governmental organisations to disseminate and apply them. Their purpose is to protect internally displaced persons (IDPs)[56] in 'conflict and

[55] ECOSOC, 'Guiding Principles on Internal Displacement', (E/CN.4/1998/53/Add.2), 11 February 1998.

[56] Internally displaced persons (IDPs) are defined in this context as persons or groups of persons who have been forced or obliged to flee or to leave their homes or places of habitual residence, in particular as a result of, or in order to avoid the effects of, armed conflict, situations of generalised violence, violations of human rights or natural or human-made disasters, and who have not crossed an internationally recognised state

crisis situations'.[57] Broadly based in existing law – in particular existing human rights law – the Principles identify rights and guarantees relevant to the protection of IDPs in all phases of displacement. They incorporate principles relating to protection from displacement and during displacement, as well as principles relating to humanitarian assistance in general and principles to return, resettlement and reintegration.

4.2 The so-called 'Pinheiro Principles'

The so-called 'Pinheiro Principles' (2005) are annexed to the Final Report of the United Nations Special Rapporteur on Housing and Property Restitution for Refugees and Displaced Persons.[58] The Principles focus on housing, land and property restitution under international law with regard to refugees, IDPs and persons in similar situations where displacement has led to the fact that persons are arbitrarily or unlawfully deprived of their former homes, lands, properties or places of habitual residence. They are based on lessons learnt by experts in the field, 'best practices', particularly in post-conflict situations, and on pre-existing national restitution policies and programmes. As a rule, they are not based on existing international law, but take a forward-looking and holistic approach. Their aim is to formulate legal standards *de lege ferenda* for the protection of the rights of refugees and displaced persons to return to their original home or, if this is not possible, to receive an adequate compensation for the loss of their housing, land and property. Thus they provide guidance on the implementation of restitution programmes and mechanisms.

4.3 The IASC Operational Guidelines on the Protection of Persons in Situations of Natural Disasters

The Inter-Agency Standing Committee (IASC) Operational Guidelines on the Protection of Persons in Situations of Natural Disasters (2006,

border. Being displaced by the effects of natural disasters is thus explicitly referred to and covered by the Principles on Internal Displacement, Introduction, §2.

57 Sergio Vieira de Mello, UN USG for Humanitarian Affairs, *OCHA*, accessed 5 June 2013, www.internal-displacement.org/8025708F004CFA06/(httpKeyDocumentsByCategory)/37BEFA013DA18845802570A000467AA1/$file/GPsEnglish.pdf.

58 OHCHR, accessed 6 June 2013, www.ohchr.org/Documents/Publications/pinheiro_principles.pdf.

IASC Guidelines)[59] take a human rights-based approach to protecting persons affected by natural disasters. The Guidelines cover disaster response, recovery from disasters and disaster preparedness[60] in situations of natural disasters. They are based on the proposition that the longer an emergency phase and/or a displacement situation last, the greater the risk of human rights violations. They primarily aim at helping international and non-governmental humanitarian organisations and members of the IASC to ensure that disaster relief and recovery efforts are conducted within a framework that protects and further develops human rights of affected persons. In addition, they are explicitly aiming at governmental actors, 'in particular disaster management institutions, who are primarily responsible for providing protection and humanitarian assistance to affected persons. Furthermore, they may also inform national laws and policies'.[61] The Guidelines identify the following key principles for a rights-based approach in natural disasters: preventing and stopping harm; securing access to relevant goods, services and opportunities for affected persons; ensuring that affected persons are in a position to claim their rights; and preventing discrimination.

4.4 The IDRL Guidelines

The Guidelines on the Domestic Facilitation and Regulation on International Disaster Relief Law and Initial Recovery Assistance[62] (IDRL Guidelines, 2007) are intended for the use of states to strengthen their laws, policies and/or procedures related to international disaster response. Their purpose is to 'contribute to national legal preparedness by providing guidance to states interested in improving their domestic legal, policy and institutional frameworks' (point 1.3). However, their focus is not the protection of individuals who are affected by a disaster. Their main focus is the provision of legal facilities to be granted to governmental or non-governmental humanitarian actors (point 1.3),

59 'IASC Operational Guidelines', accessed 6 June 2013, https://ochanet.unocha.org/p/Documents/Operational%20Guidelines.pdf.

60 Disaster preparedness is one of the issues being introduced into the 2011 revised version, accessed 3 June 2013, http://ochanet.unocha.org/p/Documents/Operational%20Guidelines.pdf.

61 Under point I.4.

62 Adopted by the 30th International Conference of the Red Cross and Red Crescent in 2007, Resolution 4 and Annex, accessed 4 June 2013, www.icrc.org/eng/assets/files/other/icrc_002_1108.pdf.

although their recommendation is to 'adopt comprehensive legal, policy, and institutional frameworks and planning for disaster prevention, mitigation, preparedness, relief and recovery' (point 8.1). The IDRL Guidelines do not provide any details on issues to be addressed in domestic disaster response schemes and mechanisms beyond the encouragement of the 'international community' to 'support . . . to build . . . capacities to prevent, mitigate, prepare for and respond to disasters domestically' as well as to 'adequately implement legal, policy and institutional frameworks to facilitate international relief' (points 9.1 and 2).

5. Protection issues

5.1 General protection issues

All four guidance documents reiterate the primary role of the affected state in case of natural disasters occurring on their territory and responsibilities resulting there from. Both the IDP Guidelines and the IDRL Guidelines explicitly refer to a 'primary duty and responsibility to provide protection' (Principle 3.1 IDP Guidelines), and humanitarian assistance (Principle 25), and the 'primary responsibility to ensure' assistance (point 3.1 IDRL Guidelines). In line with their focus on IDPs and human rights, the IDP Guidelines further develop such 'responsibility to provide protection' as resulting in a 'right to request and to receive protection and humanitarian assistance' from domestic authorities (Principle 3.2 IDP Guidelines), and a duty to 'respect and ensure respect for their obligations under international law . . . to prevent and avoid conditions that might lead to displacement of persons' (Principle 5). They state a 'prohibition of arbitrary displacement' and a 'right to be protected against being arbitrarily displaced from his or her home or place of habitual residence' (Principle 6). The prohibition of arbitrary displacement explicitly includes situations of disasters, but exempts cases where safety and health of affected persons requires evacuation. The IASC Guidelines rather generally pronounce a right of individuals and groups of individuals affected by natural disasters to 'request and receive . . . protection and assistance from their governments' (Introduction), and advocate for 'all appropriate measures necessary to protect' affected individuals and communities (A.1.1 and A.2.1). The Pinheiro Principles join the IDP Guidelines in recognising a 'right of everyone' 'to be protected against being arbitrarily displaced from his or her home, land or place of habitual residence' (Principle 5.1). This right's reflection on governmental responsibilities is yet softer, stating that 'States should incorporate protections against displacement into domestic legislation . . . and should extend these protections to everyone within their legal jurisdiction or effective control' (Principle 5.2).

The IDRL Guidelines require that assistance is provided in accordance with the principle of impartiality and without any adverse distinction 'such as in regards to nationality, race, ethnicity, religious beliefs, class, gender, disability, age and political opinions' (point 4.2). The IASC Guidelines satisfy themselves with stating that 'persons affected by natural disasters should enjoy the same rights and freedoms under human rights law as other in their country and not be discriminated against' (I.I). The Pinheiro Principles directly address national legislators in building on the 'right to be protected from discrimination on the basis of [certain grounds]'[63] and requiring from states to 'ensure that *de facto* and *de jure* discrimination' on the grounds listed 'is prohibited and that all persons, including refugees and IDPs, are considered equal before the law' (Principles 3.1 and 3.2). The IDP Guidelines incorporate the prohibition of adverse distinction several times and directly address national legislators in requiring them to apply the IDP Guidelines 'without discrimination of any kind'[64] (Principles 1, 2 and 4.1). However, they explicitly mention an entitlement to special protection and assistance of persons with specific conditions or special needs,[65] Principle 4.2.

The right of 'every human being . . . to recognition everywhere as a person before the law' is confirmed by both the IDP Guidelines, Principle 20, and the Pinheiro Principles, Principle 20.1 This recognition of legal personality of affected persons is further specified in the requirement that governmental authorities shall issue 'all documents necessary for the enjoyment and exercise of their legal rights, such as passports, personal identification documents, birth certificates and marriage certificates' (IDP Principle 20.2 and Pinheiro Principle 20.2), equally to women

[63] As potential grounds of discrimination are listed race, colour, sex, language, religion, political or other opinion, national or social origin, property, disability, birth or other status.

[64] As potential grounds of discrimination are listed race, colour, sex, language, religion or belief, political or other opinion, national, ethnic or social origin, legal or social status, age, disability, property, birth, or on any other similar criteria. The fact of being displaced is expressly excluded from eventual grounds of distinction (Principle 1).

[65] By way of example, the Guidelines refer to children, especially unaccompanied minors, expectant mothers, mothers with young children, female heads of households, persons with disabilities and elderly persons.

and men and in their own names (IDP Principle 20.3 and Pinheiro Principle 20.3). Authorities are also expected to issue new documents or replace documents which are lost in the course of displacement, 'without imposing unreasonable conditions' (IDP Principle 20.2 and Pinheiro Principle 20.2).[66] The issue of documentation is taken up by the IASC Guidelines as well. They require states to take measures 'as early as possible, including the emergency phase' to restore personal documentation being lost or destroyed in a natural disaster (Principle D.1.2). In addition to equal documentation of men and women in their respective own names (Principle D.1.3), the same is required with regard to unaccompanied or orphaned children (Principle D.1.4).

On national procedures, institutions and mechanisms the IASC Guidelines require to entitle all communities affected by natural disasters to 'easy accessible information' concerning, in particular, nature and level of the disaster, possible risk-mitigation measures, early-warning information and information on humanitarian assistance being provided, recovery efforts and respective individual entitlements. In the specific context addressed by the Pinheiro Principles these recommend taking all appropriate administrative, legislative and judicial measures to 'support and facilitate the housing, land and property restitution process' (Principle 12.3). More specifically, they call for 'equitable, timely, independent, transparent and non-discriminatory procedures, institutions and mechanisms to assess and enforce housing, land and property restitution claims' (Principle 12.1).[67]

5.2 *Specific protection issues*

Based on the right to life of people affected by natural disasters, the IASC Guidelines explicitly recognise an entitlement to 'unimpeded . . . access to goods and services necessary to address their basic needs' (B.1.1), and require states to take measures in order to grant such access, including priority access for vulnerable groups (B.1.3).[68] They additionally demand a meaningful consultation of those affected and granting the opportunity

[66] The latter gives the example of requiring the return to one's area of habitual residence in order to obtain documents.

[67] Even in more detail the Principles advocate for ensuring that the rights of 'tenants, social-occupancy rights holders and other legitimate occupants or users of housing, land and property' are recognised within restitution programmes (Principle 16).

[68] The IDP Guidelines reiterate this demand with regard to the specific case of internally displaced persons (Principle 18).

to take charge of their own affairs 'to the maximum extent possible' (I.3). In this, they are seconded by the Pinheiro Principles, requiring 'adequate consultation and participation' (Principle 14).

The protection approach is enhanced by requirements of providing people affected by a natural disaster with the minimum assets for an adequate standard of living (Principle 18 IDP Guidelines), including in particular adequate food, water and sanitation, shelter,[69] clothing, and essential health services as well as psycho-social assistance and social services (B.2.1 and B.2.5 IASC Guidelines). Principle 19 IDP Guidelines extend governmental responsibilities to medical care for the wounded and sick, including prevention of contagious and infectious diseases. In natural disasters generally, persons displaced by the disaster should 'to the maximum extent possible, be provided with the means to recover as quickly as possible and become self-sustainable' (IASC Guidelines A.4.1). 'Camps are a last resort'; in the case that they are established, they must be installed in places with a low natural hazard risk (A.4.2 IASC Guidelines). Authorities have to envisage a speedy transition from temporary or intermediate shelter to temporary or permanent housing (C.3.1). With a view to the rights to liberty and freedom of movement the Guidelines on IDPs reiterate the freedom to choose residence (Principle 14), and foresee that internment or confinement, if in exceptional circumstances absolutely necessary, does 'not last longer than required by the circumstances' (Principle 12).

Camps should be managed by civilians as soon as possible (A.4.6 IASC Guidelines). Security should be provided in camps (A.4.1 and A.4.3). To ensure the security of affected persons is a general responsibility of governments, throughout all phases of the disaster, including the avoidance of violence and other violations of human rights (A.3.1 and A.3.2 IASC Guidelines). Prior to taking decisions on displacement, states are required to ensure that 'all feasible alternatives are explored in order to avoid displacement altogether' (Principle 7 IDP Guidelines). In case of organised displacement, authorities need to ensure that 'displacements are effected in satisfactory conditions of safety, nutrition, health and hygiene, and that members of the same family are not separated'. Finally, appropriate measures are to be taken in order to enable persons displaced by a disaster to return to their homes or places of habitual residence,

[69] The term 'shelter' being defined as, the right to live somewhere in security, peace and dignity' (B.2.4 IASC Guidelines).

or to remain or to resettle voluntarily in another part of the country (D.2.3 IASC Guidelines).

Principle 16 IDP Guidelines pronounces the right of all IDPs 'to know the fate and whereabouts of missing relatives'. Authorities concerned are therefore to strive to establish the fate and whereabouts of missing relatives and to inform the next of kin on the progress of the investigation and results obtained (D.3.4 IASC Guidelines).[70] Moreover, appropriate measures should be taken to collect and identify the mortal remains of deceased persons (D.3.5 IASC Guidelines).[71] Cremation of unidentified bodies should be avoided (D.3.6 IASC Guidelines), and burials should be conducted respecting the dignity and privacy of both the dead and their family members (D.3.7). Measures should be taken to protect funerary sites (D.3.8), and family members should be fully informed about the location of grave sites and have full access to them; authorities should give the opportunity to erect memorials and conduct religious ceremonies as needed (D.3.9). Based on the right to respect for family life, Principle 17 IDP Guidelines calls on authorities to allow family members who wish to remain together to do so during displacement and to strive to reunite them as quickly as possible should they so wish.[72] D.3.2 IASC Guidelines specifies that appropriate measures should be taken 'as early and as quickly as possible' to re-establish contacts between members of families having been separated.

On the basis of the right not to be 'arbitrarily deprived of property and possessions' and to the 'peaceful enjoyment of his or her possession' as reiterated by Principle 21 IDP Guidelines and Principle 7 Pinheiro Principles, the IASC Guidelines request authorities to protect 'to the maximum extent possible, against looting, destruction, and arbitrary or illegal appropriation, occupation or use of property and possessions left behind by persons or communities displaced by the natural disaster' (C.2.1). Authorities are further required to take appropriate measures to protect against 'undue or illegal attempts by landlords, speculators, local authorities and other actors' to deprive persons of their property and possessions (C.2.8). At the same time, the Guidelines open the option to allocate unused private property and possessions temporarily

[70] See also Principle 16.2 IDP Guidelines: 'The authorities concerned shall endeavour to establish the fate and whereabouts of internally displaced persons reported missing'.

[71] Similarly Principle 16.3 IDP Guidelines: 'The authorities concerned shall endeavour to collect and identify the mortal remains of those deceased'.

[72] See also D.3.1 IASC Guidelines.

to persons displaced by the natural disaster, 'but no longer than absolutely necessary' (C.2.2). Owners whose land deeds or property documents have been lost or damaged due to the disaster should be provided with 'accessible procedures' to reclaim ownership of their original land and property without undue delay (C.2.5).

Prohibitions on remaining in or returning to certain areas and prohibitions on rebuilding, respectively, should not be supported 'unless they are based on law and, in the individual case, necessary for reasons of safety, health, disaster prevention, or the implementation of reconstruction and development schemes' (C.2.9 IASC Guidelines). On the specific situation of IDPs, Principle 28 IDP Guidelines specifies the 'duty and responsibility to establish conditions, as well as provide the means, which allow internally displaced persons to return voluntarily ... to their homes or places of habitual residence, or to resettle voluntarily in another part of the country'.[73]

Finally, the Pinheiro Principles explicitly pronounce a right of 'all refugees and displaced persons' 'to have restored to them any housing, land and/or property of which they were arbitrarily or unlawfully deprived, or to be compensated for any housing, land and/or property that is factually impossible to restore as determined by an independent, impartial tribunal' (Principle 2.1). Moreover, states shall 'demonstrably prioritise the right to restitution as the preferred remedy for displacement and as a key element of restorative justice' (Principle 2.2). States are requested to ensure 'as a rule, that restitution is only deemed factually impossible in exceptional circumstances, namely when housing, land and/or property is destroyed or when it not longer exists... even under such circumstances the holder of the housing, land and/or property right should have the option to repair or rebuild whenever possible' (Principle 21.2). The Principles reiterate a right to full and effective compensation as an integral component of the restitution process (Principle 21.1).

6. Concluding remarks

The responsibility to respond to natural disasters first and foremost lies with the affected state. This responsibility comprises the responsibility of

[73] Cf. also Pinheiro Principle 10, which specifies that 'voluntary return ... must be based on a free, informed, individual choice', as well as A.1.6 and A.1.7 IASC Guidelines. Principle 19 IDP Guidelines adds the duty and responsibility to assist returned and/or resettled internally displaced persons to recover, to the extent possible, their property and possessions which they left behind or were dispossessed of upon their displacement.

national governments and local authorities to provide protection for individuals and groups of individuals affected by the disaster. International norms by and large are only partially able to inform and inspire national governments and local authorities when these implement their responsibility to protect.

Universal human rights law contains norms relevant for domestic approaches to protect those prone to be affected or being affected. Due to their universal and general character, they do not specifically relate to natural disasters and do not provide any more specific guidance. Sectoral international treaties like the so-called Chernobyl Convention, the *Tampere Convention* and the *Civil Defence Framework Convention* do not address domestic disaster response schemes and mechanisms. Regional treaties applying to issues of disaster response either do not mention the concept of domestic protection from the effects of natural disasters (the Arab League Relief Operations Agreement and the BSEC Emergency Agreement), or focus on domestic schemes and mechanisms in a general and broad manner and as an asset to achieve and enhance. Issues like beneficiaries' access to assistance, relocation and displacement of individuals, return, resettlement or restitution of property are not covered.

All or several of these issues are addressed by a number of legally non-binding guidance documents. These documents endeavour to assist states in implementing their responsibility to protect in the context of natural disasters. They do not create legal obligations for governmental authorities, but have the potential of informing and inspiring governmental domestic disaster response planning and legislation.

8

A duty to accept humanitarian assistance under the ICESCR?

STEFANIE JANSEN-WILHELM

1. Introduction

Within the current legal framework of international disaster response, there is no explicit obligation for states to accept international humanitarian assistance.[1] Some recent cases illustrate, however, that states at times refuse international aid while also being unable or unwilling to adequately respond to a natural disaster themselves. Probably the best-known example is Myanmar's inaction after cyclone Nargis struck in 2008, but also incidents such as the response of the United States to hurricane Katrina, Italy's response to the l'Aquila earthquake, Japan's response to the tsunami and nuclear disaster, and the Chinese response to the earthquakes in recent years can be mentioned as examples of situations where a civilian population is suffering unnecessarily due to an ineffective response by its government. In these cases, the existence of a duty to accept humanitarian assistance offered by other states, international organisations and non-governmental organisations (NGOs) would be helpful to protect disaster victims from further harm.

Even though such a duty to accept is not explicitly laid down in the legal framework, public international law dictates in various instruments that states have certain obligations towards their own populations. One example is the extensive body of international human rights law, where states take duties upon themselves to grant freedoms and entitlements to

[1] Even though a distinction is often made between man-made and natural disasters, in this chapter the distinction is irrelevant, since the focus lies on the consequences of disasters and not on the causes. With 'disaster', a situation is indicated with natural causes, man-made causes, or a combination of both, not being a situation in which international humanitarian law is applicable, which causes harm to the affected population to an extent that it is beyond only the affected state's capacity to address. This also includes the situation in which the affected state is not willing to address the consequences and refuses to accept international assistance.

their population. In this line, it can be argued that through the human rights to life, food, housing, and health, states have an obligation to take care of disaster victims who are on the state's territory or under the state's jurisdiction. Moreover, Article 2(1) of the *International Covenant on Economic, Social, and Cultural Rights* (ICESCR) dictates that states must realise the rights 'individually or through international assistance and cooperation'. The question can accordingly be posed, to what extent the ICESCR can be understood to contain a duty for states to accept international humanitarian assistance in the aftermath of a disaster.

In this chapter, the general legal framework of disaster response will be considered, to establish which rules and principles exist in the field of international humanitarian assistance and disaster response, excluding armed conflicts. From this analysis it will become clear that state sovereignty governs the rules and principles, making international humanitarian assistance subject to the consent of the receiving party (henceforth referred to as the 'affected state'), while at the same time stating that this consent may not be withheld 'arbitrarily'. After this, we will examine exactly what specific duties and rights the ICESCR provides for disaster situations, and to what extent there can be understood to be a duty to accept international humanitarian assistance. As such, we will test whether the ICESCR can be of use within the general legal framework as a way to work with the rules derived from state sovereignty, or in other words, whether it can explain what 'arbitrary' means. To this end, Article 2(1) will be interpreted to establish its meaning and scope. Moreover, Article 2(1) will be considered together with a few examples of substantive rights of the ICESCR to define possible obligations. This paper will end with the main conclusions, where it will be explained how the ICESCR can be used as an argument for a duty to accept aid and to substantiate the rule that consent may not be withheld arbitrarily. These conclusions may shed some light on the terms used by the ILC in the draft articles on the 'Protection of Persons in the Event of Disasters'.

2. Legal framework and gaps

The legal framework on international disaster response consists on the one hand of instruments of a general nature, which are nonetheless useful in times of disaster, like international humanitarian law, human rights law, and refugee and IDP law, and on the other hand of instruments which are especially designed for disaster response and the delivery of humanitarian assistance.[2] Both categories taken together provide a number of rules and principles that are relevant for the understanding of the issue of accepting international humanitarian assistance in response to a disaster, and will therefore be discussed briefly here.

International humanitarian law is only applicable in situations of armed conflict and is therefore only relevant for this chapter insofar as a natural disaster occurs in a context of war. Even so, international humanitarian law contains a number of provisions on the delivery of humanitarian assistance by others than by the state of the population in need. The Fourth Geneva Convention concerning the protection of civilians (GCIV) and the two Additional Protocols to the Geneva Conventions on the protection of victims of international and non-international armed conflict (API and APII) are especially relevant in this respect. The line taken in these instruments is that a civilian population in need 'shall' receive humanitarian assistance.[3] However, consent of the receiving state is at all times required before humanitarian aid can be delivered.[4] This means that there is, on the one hand, an indication that civilians are entitled to receive humanitarian assistance when they so need but, on the other hand, this 'entitlement' is immediately limited by the principle of sovereignty, giving states a right or freedom to give or withhold consent.

Indeed, the requirement of consent was included with due regard for state sovereignty, as explained in the commentary to the APs, yet was not meant as a wildcard: the requirement of consent 'did not imply that the parties concerned had absolute and unlimited freedom to refuse their agreement to relief actions. A Party refusing its agreement must do so for valid reasons, not for arbitrary or capricious ones.'[5] Consequently, the

[2] Besides the fields already mentioned, the first category of the legal framework includes rules and principles on numerous topics relevant in disasters, like customs, traffic by air or water, use of telecommunications, privileges and immunities and many more.

[3] See inter alia *Geneva Convention (IV) Relative to the Protection of Civilian Persons in Time of War*, Geneva, 12 August, 1949 GCIV, Articles 23, 38, 59.

[4] See inter alia Article 10 GCIV, Article 70(1) *Additional Protocol I* (API), Article 18(2) *Additional Protocol II* (APII). In some instances, the word 'consent' is explicitly used (e.g. in Article 10 GCIV, using 'subject to the consent of'). In other examples, the words 'shall allow' or 'shall agree' is used, indicating a limited freedom to give or withhold consent (e.g. Article 23 on protection of populations, Article 59 GCIV on occupied territories).

[5] ICRC, *Commentary on the Additional Protocols of 8 June 1977 to the Geneva Conventions of 12 August 1949*, International Committee of the Red Cross and Red Crescent (1987): §2805. See also Eduardo Valencia Ospina, 'Fifth Report on the Protection of Persons in the Event of Disasters' (UN Doc. (A/CN.4/652) 9 April 2012).

rule that consent is required before aid can be delivered has been interpreted in such a way that consent may not be withheld arbitrarily.[6] Also in the customary law study by the ICRC it is determined that it is 'self-evident that a humanitarian organisation cannot operate without the consent of the party concerned' and that 'such consent must not be refused on arbitrary grounds'.[7] What exactly falls under 'arbitrarily withholding consent' is, however, not entirely clear.[8] Whilst these rules are only applicable in armed conflicts, it will be seen that the same line can be found in other instruments as well.

Like international humanitarian law, human rights law provides some insight into the duties of states in the aftermath of a disaster as well. As already explained in the introduction, human rights law contains rights to life, food, shelter, health, and – indirectly – to water. These rights are all highly relevant in the aftermath of a natural disaster. Since the ICESCR will be considered in more detail below, only a few remarks will be made here on human rights law. Some argue that a right to humanitarian assistance exists in international law.[9] While this is not the question under scrutiny in this chapter, it must be noted here that the existence of such a right cannot be sufficiently proved at this stage, and consequently this paper will proceed on the assumption that such a right does not (yet) exist. Another point to be made with regard to human rights law is the existence of the state of emergency. Under the *International Covenant on Civil and Political Rights* (ICCPR) it is determined

[6] See, amongst others, Ruth A. Stoffels, 'Legal Regulation of Humanitarian Assistance in Armed Conflict: Achievements and Gaps', *International Review of the Red Cross* 86 (2004): 515–545, 534.

[7] Jean-Marie Henckaerts and Louise Doswald-Beck, *Customary International Humanitarian Law: vol. I: Rules* (Cambridge University Press, 2005), 196–197.

[8] Arguably the requirement of non-arbitrariness is related to the humanitarian principles. If humanitarian aid meets these principles (impartiality, neutrality, humanity, independence), there is less freedom for a state to withhold its consent. See ILC, 'Fourth Report', §66, where this is indicated with reference to ICRC, *Draft Additional Protocols to the Geneva Conventions of August 12, 1949* (1973), 78–79.

[9] See inter alia Joana Abrisketa, 'The Right to Humanitarian Aid: Basis and Limitations', in *Reflections on Humanitarian Action: Principles, Ethics and Contradictions*, ed. Humanitarian Studies Unit (London/Sterling: Pluto Press, 2001), 55; Rohan Hardcastle and Adrian Chua, 'Victims of Natural Disasters: The Right to Receive Humanitarian Assistance', *The International Journal of Human Rights* 4 (1997): 35; Joakim Dungel, 'A Right to Humanitarian Assistance in Internal Armed Conflicts Respecting Sovereignty, Neutrality and Legitimacy: Practical Proposals to Practical Problems', *Journal of Humanitarian Assistance* (2004): §2.2, accessed 31 May 2013, http://sites.tufts.edu/jha/archives/838.

that during the state of emergency a state may derogate from its obligations stemming from a number of rights of the ICCPR.[10] Such a derogation clause does not exist for the ICESCR, creating uncertainty as to whether it is possible to derogate from economic, social and cultural rights. This uncertainty will be taken into consideration when discussing the ICESCR in more detail below.

Closely related to human rights law, is the law on refugees and Internally Displaced Persons (IDPs). Refugee law, officially applicable to those who cross state borders when fleeing for fear of persecution, requires states to provide for a number of basic rights for refugees on their territory, such as equal treatment with nationals with regard to rationing, housing and public relief.[11] It is, however, the law on IDPs that is most explicit on disasters and humanitarian assistance. In the international context, there are the Guiding Principles on Internal Displacement,[12] a soft law instrument adopted in 1998. These principles acknowledge that internal displacement can be caused by the occurrence of a natural disaster.

IDPs are persons (or groups of persons) who had been forced to flee as a result of, amongst other causes, natural or human-made disasters.[13] As IDPs are citizens of the affected state, they are automatically entitled to general protection of the human rights instruments their state is a party to. Additionally, the Guiding Principles take into account the marginalised and vulnerable situation IDPs find themselves in. In this line, a right to request and receive protection and assistance from national authorities is laid down in the Guiding Principles along with the explicit recognition of the primary responsibility and duty of the affected state.[14] This primary duty is repeated in Principle 25(1), where a right to offer services is granted to 'international humanitarian organisations and other appropriate actors'.[15] In line with the International Court of Justice (ICJ)'s Nicaragua case, it is provided that such offers cannot be regarded as an

[10] For more information on derogation from human rights during the state of emergency, see Jaime Oraá, *Human Rights in States of Emergency in International Law* (Oxford: Clarendon Press, 1992).

[11] Articles 20, 21, and 23 of the 1951 *Convention Relating to the Status of Refugees* (Refugee Convention).

[12] Francis M. Deng, *Guiding Principles on Internal Displacement*, UN Doc. E/CN.4/1998/53/Add.2, 11 February 11 (New York, 1998). https://docs.unocha.org/sites/dms/Documents/GuidingPrinciplesDispl.pdf.

[13] See the introduction to the Guiding Principles under (2).

[14] Guiding Principles 3(1) and 3(2).

[15] Guiding Principle 25(2).

unfriendly act or interference in a state's internal affairs. Moreover, it is determined that 'consent thereto shall not be arbitrarily withheld, particularly when authorities concerned are unable or unwilling to provide the required humanitarian assistance'.[16] Consequently, the Guiding Principles take the same approach to humanitarian assistance as the one seen above in the field of international humanitarian law.

In the regional context, a convention exists on IDPs. In October 2009, the African Union adopted the *Convention for the Protection and Assistance of Internally Displaced Persons in Africa* (the *Kampala Convention*) which is currently the only international (although regional) legally binding instrument on IDPs.[17] The *Kampala Convention* urges its state parties to cooperate internationally,[18] yet a certain emphasis exists on the sovereignty of states. For example, the *Convention* provides that where available resources are inadequate to protect IDPs sufficiently, states shall cooperate in seeking assistance of international organisations and humanitarian agencies, yet at the same time it is said that 'nothing in this Article shall prejudice the principles of sovereignty and territorial integrity of states'.[19] Since the *Kampala Convention* only entered into force in December 2012, it remains to be seen which role the principles of sovereignty and territorial integrity will fulfil exactly in practice. Yet as the contracting parties have not waived their sovereign powers in this matter, it is very likely that the consent rule will be applied here.

Apart from these more general fields of international law, there is a wide variety of treaties that do not deal with disaster response as such, but are specifically focused on issues which could potentially hamper the effectiveness of humanitarian operations.[20] Barriers for assistance like

[16] Ibid.

[17] The *Kampala Convention* entered into force on 6 December 2012 after the fifteenth instrument of ratification was deposited by Swaziland. The other fourteen states are Benin, Burkina Faso, Central African Republic, Chad, Gabon, Gambia, Guinea-Bissau, Lesotho, Niger, Nigeria, Sierra Leone, Togo, Uganda and Zambia. Over thirty states signed the Convention: IRIN, 'IDPs: African IDP Convention Comes into Force', 6 December 2012, accessed 31 May 2013, www.irinnews.org.

[18] Article 5(2) and (3) *Kampala Convention*.

[19] Article 5(5) and (6) respectively 5(12) *Kampala Convention*.

[20] Examples of such instruments are the *Food Aid Convention* of 1999, Recommendation of the Customs Co-Operation Council to Expedite the Forwarding of Relief Consignments in the Event of Disasters of 1970, the *Tampere Convention on the Provision of Telecommunication Resources for Disaster Mitigation and Relief Operations* of 1998, the UN *Convention to Combat Desertification in those Countries Experiencing Serious Drought and/or Desertification* of 1994, the *Nuclear Accident Convention* or the *Oil Pollution Convention*, the *Customs Convention on the Temporary Importation of Private Road*

strict custom requirements, strict visa rules for humanitarian personnel and operational restrictions for humanitarian agencies can hinder relief operations.[21] The International Disaster Response Laws (IDRL) project of the International Federation of the Red Cross and Red Crescent Societies (IFRC) aims to make national legal systems susceptible to international humanitarian assistance, to which end it created the 'IDRL Guidelines'.[22]

In addition to the more universal legal framework discussed so far, many regional instruments have been created explicitly for the purpose of facilitating disaster relief, for example the 2005 Agreement on Disaster Management and Emergency Response by the Association of South East Asian Nations (ASEAN);[23] the Agreement Establishing the Caribbean Disaster Emergency Response Agency (CDERA) by the Caribbean Community (CARICOM); and the *Inter-American Convention to Facilitate Disaster Assistance* adopted by the Organisation of American States (OAS). Within the European Union there is the European Commission Humanitarian Aid Office (ECHO),[24] and the Economic Community of West-African States (ECOWAS) has established a 'Mechanism for Disaster Reduction'. The North Atlantic Treaty Organisation (NATO) and the African Union (AU) have included humanitarian assistance within their policies; the African Union may take decisions on common policies, which include humanitarian action and disaster response,[25] and NATO has included disaster assistance in its activities since 1953.[26]

Apart from the legal instruments discussed so far, NGOs and international organisations have created a vast body of resolutions, standards

Vehicles of 1954 and the *Convention on Facilitation of International Maritime Traffic* of 1965. For a full overview, see IFRC, '*Law and Legal Issues in International Disaster Response: A Desk Study*', *International Federation of the Red Cross and Red Crescent Societies* (Geneva, 2007).

21 It is possible that a state is willing to accept international humanitarian assistance on the surface, while using barriers like those mentioned here to hamper the international efforts, therefore refusing assistance *de facto* without too much risk of international criticism.

22 IFRC, 'Guidelines for the Domestic Facilitation and Regulation of International Disaster Relief and Initial Recovery Assistance' were adopted on 30 November 2007 at the Red Cross and Red Crescent Movement's 30th International Conference.

23 ASEAN has played an important role in negotiating disaster relief after cyclone Nargis.

24 IFRC, 'Desk Study', 71.

25 Article 13(1) under (e) of the AU Constitutive Act.

26 It must be noted that many bilateral agreements exist on mutual assistance in case of a disaster. These agreements will not be discussed in more detail here.

and guidelines to be used in humanitarian operations. It is beyond the scope of this chapter to mention all of these; only some relevant rules and principles will be discussed.[27] One important category is formed by United Nations General Assembly (GA) resolutions.[28] Currently, GA Resolution 46/182 is considered to be the basis for disaster response operations. In this resolution, the line is followed which can also be found in other General Assembly resolutions, namely that the sovereignty, territorial integrity and national unity of states must be fully respected, that assistance should only be provided with the consent of the affected state and in principle on the basis of an appeal by this state.[29] Also, the primary responsibility to provide for disaster victims lies with the affected state, which includes the initiation of humanitarian assistance.[30] The resolution further recognises that situations may occur in which the 'magnitude and duration of many emergencies may be beyond the response capacity' of the affected state, in which context the role of international cooperation is emphasised.[31] The resolution finally dictates that humanitarian assistance 'must be provided in accordance with the principles of humanity, neutrality and impartiality'.[32] Making sure that offers of assistance follow these principles would give the affected state less reason to refuse to accept it.

Also the aforementioned IDRL project follows the line taken in the General Assembly resolution. The IDRL Guidelines contain a number of recommendations for states.[33] According to IDRL, assistance cannot be given without a request.[34] Moreover, the Guidelines dictate that the affected state has the primary responsibility to ensure humanitarian assistance in its territory; that the affected state

[27] Other examples are the UNISDR 'Hyogo Framework for Action' of 2005; the Sphere Handbook with its 'Humanitarian Charter and Minimum Standards for Disaster Response' of 2004; and the 'Code of Conduct for the International Red Cross and Red Crescent Movement and NGOs in Disaster Relief' of 1994.

[28] The General Assembly has adopted a number of resolutions on disaster response, most notably GA Resolutions A/RES/43/131 of 1988, A/RES/45/100 of 1990, and A/RES/57/150 of 2002.

[29] UN General Assembly Resolution A/RES/46/182 of 19 December 1991, Annex, §3.

[30] UN GA, Res. A/RES/46/182, under 4.

[31] UN GA, Res. A/RES/46/182, Annex, §5.

[32] UN GA, Res. A/RES/46/182, Annex, §2.

[33] 'IDRL Programme: Plan 2010–2011', *IFRC* (Geneva: IFRC, 2010), 2.

[34] Horst Fischer, 'International Disaster Response Law Treaties: Trends, Patterns and Lacunae', *International Disaster Response Laws, Principles and Practice: Reflections, Prospects and Challenges* (Geneva: IFRC, 2003), 34.

is required to 'seek international and/or regional assistance in case the affected state determines that a disaster situation exceeds national coping capabilities';[35] and it confirms that international relief and assistance can only be delivered with the consent of the affected state.[36]

One project that must further be mentioned in the legal framework is the ongoing work of the United Nations International Law Commission (ILC) on the 'Protection of Persons in the Event of Disasters'. Starting his work in 2007, Special Rapporteur Eduardo Valencia-Ospina has been the driving force behind the adoption of fourteen draft articles to date.[37] In these draft articles, there is a clear emphasis on the rights of disaster victims. On the other hand, the draft articles provide rules for affected states, which were also seen in other sources of the legal framework, as discussed above. It is as such provided that the affected state has the 'duty to ensure the protection of persons and provisions of disaster relief and assistance on its territory' and that, 'by virtue of its sovereignty', it has the 'primary role in the direction, control, coordination and supervision of such relief and assistance'.[38] When the national capacity for response is overwhelmed, the affected state has a duty to seek international assistance.[39] Even so, international humanitarian assistance can only be provided with the consent of the affected state, which, however, may not be withheld arbitrarily.[40] There is a clear emphasis on the role of international cooperation within the draft articles, emphasised as a duty to international cooperation in Draft Articles 5 and 5bis. In Draft Article 5 it is provided that states shall cooperate among themselves and with the United Nations, IFRC, ICRC, other international organisations, and NGOs.[41] This article has been made more specific at a later stage where international cooperation is understood as 'humanitarian

[35] Heike Spieker, 'The Right to Give and Receive Humanitarian Assistance', in *International Law and Humanitarian Assistance: A Crosscut Through Legal Issues Pertaining to Humanitarianism*, eds. Hans-Joachim Heintze and Andrej Zwitter (Heidelberg: Springer, 2011), 24, deriving this from IDRL Guideline 3.2.

[36] Spieker, 'The Right to Give and Receive Humanitarian Assistance', 26; IDRL Guideline 10.1.

[37] Which is the status at the time of writing (May 2013).

[38] Draft article 9, UN ILC, UN Doc. (A/CN.4/L.776) 14 July 2010.

[39] Draft article 10, UN ILC, UN Doc. (A/CN.4/L.794) 20 July 2011.

[40] Draft article 11 (1) and (2), UN Doc. (A/CN.4/L.794).

[41] Draft article 5, UN ILC, UN Doc. (A/CN.4/L.758) 24 July 2009.

assistance, coordination of international relief actions and communications, and making available relief personnel, relief equipment and supplies, and scientific, medical and technical resources'.[42]

From this overview of the legal framework, a number of conclusions can be drawn. In the first place, it has become clear that there is a strong emphasis on the sovereignty and territorial integrity of states. As a consequence, the rule that the affected state has the primary responsibility in responding to a disaster is widely acknowledged. Another consequence is the requirement of consent from the affected state before assistance can be delivered from outside and the role of the affected state in coordinating all aid, which returns in most instruments. Due to this requirement, states have a 'right' to give or withhold their consent to international humanitarian assistance. A limitation to this right is mentioned in a number of instruments, namely that consent may not be withheld arbitrarily. It is, however, nowhere defined exactly what can be understood as 'arbitrary' reasons. Only in the context of the Additional Protocols to the Geneva Conventions is it determined that a state must have valid reasons, instead of arbitrary or capricious ones, without specifying further. Also, if offers of aid meet the humanitarian principles, there would be less ground for refusal. Another limitation of the right of affected states to withhold consent can also be found in most instruments: when the response capacity of the affected state is overwhelmed, the state must make use of international cooperation. As such, a state cannot withhold its consent to international humanitarian assistance when its individual response is insufficient.

Consequently, it appears that the freedom to withhold consent is subject to certain qualifications, yet these qualifications remain vague as to their meaning. What is therefore needed, is to create some understanding of what constitutes 'arbitrariness'. In that respect, it can be wondered whether refusing international assistance when the affected state's capacity is overwhelmed is a qualification in itself, or falls under 'arbitrary reasons' for refusal. In the following, the ICESCR will be used to assess whether this treaty can be understood as a way to give meaning to 'arbitrariness' and as such to a qualified freedom to withhold consent for those states that are a party to the Covenant. This approach remains respectful towards the reigning principle of sovereignty, since the basis of

[42] Draft article 5bis, UN ILC, UN Doc. (A/CN.4/L.812) 12 July 2012.

the qualified freedom to withhold consent would lie in a treaty to which states have become a party out of free will.

3. Article 2(1) ICESCR

3.1 Introducing the ICESCR and the VCLT

The ICESCR is based on the *Universal Declaration of Human Rights* (UDHR) and forms the counterpart of the ICCPR.[43] Where the UDHR contains civil and political rights as well as economic, social and cultural rights, these two categories were split up in the two Covenants. The reason for doing so is often explained with reference to negative and positive obligations, where the ICCPR contains freedoms, entailing abstention from the state, and the ICESCR contains rights that need an effort and investment by the state. While it is now recognised that this division is not tangible as the realisation of civil and political rights also require state action and (parts of) ESC-rights can also be realised through abstention, the traditional division of rights resulted in some interesting differences in the provisions of both Covenants. One of these is the provision on general obligations of state parties. Article 2(1) of the ICCPR provides: 'Each State Party to the present Covenant undertakes to respect and to ensure to all individuals within its territory and subject to its jurisdiction the rights recognised in the present Covenant, without distinction of any kind'. In the second and third paragraph of this article it is stated that, if not already done so, states must take measures and undertake to take the necessary steps to adopt such measures, and must ensure an effective remedy in case of violation of a right; that there is a judiciary to apply this effective remedy, and a competent authority to enforce the remedy.[44] This language clearly indicates that the rights established in the ICCPR must be respected and ensured by the state, giving the state party immediate obligations, and that the state is also capable of potentially violating the rights.

In contrast, Article 2(1) of the ICESCR paints a different picture. The text of this provision reads as follows:

> Each State Party to the present Covenant undertakes to take steps, individually and through international assistance and co-operation,

[43] Together these three instruments are referred to as the International Bill of Rights.

[44] Article 2(2) and (3) under a. to c., *International Covenant on Civil and Political Rights* (ICCPR).

> especially economic and technical, to the maximum of its available resources, with a view to achieving progressively the full realisation of the rights recognised in the present Covenant by all appropriate means, including particularly the adoption of legislative measures.

What immediately becomes clear is that the language used here does not necessarily refer to legal obligations. Instead, the provision speaks of having 'a view to achieving progressively the full realisation of the rights'. Even so, the Covenant does contain substantive rights in its third part, among which are the right to an adequate standard of living (including the rights to food and housing) in Article 11 and the right to the highest attainable standard of health in Article 12.[45] It is questionable to what extent these rights contain actual claims for those surviving a disaster if the ESC-rights cannot be seen as containing immediate obligations for states. Moreover, Article 2(1) speaks of 'taking steps' towards realisation, either individually or through international assistance and cooperation. Whether any elements of these words contain obligatory content (and if so, which content), remains to be seen.

That the ICESCR indeed contains concrete obligations for state parties follows from, inter alia, the adoption of the *Optional Protocol* establishing an individual complaint mechanism, as is already in place for the ICCPR. Moreover, states have not acted in good faith when they can be assumed to 'have gone through the formal motions of ratifying ... a treaty that, appearances on the contrary notwithstanding, gives rise to no obligation on their part to do anything whatsoever of any substance'.[46] It is true that for some provisions of the ICESCR the drafters did not intend to create any obligations, as they made explicitly clear.[47] For the majority of the articles such a statement has not been made, making the argument that these provisions constitute concrete obligations even stronger. The UN

[45] The right to water is often based on these rights since health cannot be maintained without clean water and food cannot be prepared without water.

[46] P. Alston and G. Quinn, 'The Nature and Scope of State Parties' Obligations under the International Covenant on Economic, Social and Cultural Rights', *Human Rights Quarterly* 9 (1987): 156–229, 160. Based on the ICJ Nuclear Test Case, Alston and Quinn cite Virally on the three roles he identifies of good faith. While very interesting, these three roles are not directly relevant in this research, as it has through other means become clear that the ICESCR contains 'real' legal obligations. Michel Virally, 'Review Essay: Good Faith in Public International Law', *American Journal of International Law* 77 (1983): 130 cited by Alston and Quinn, 161.

[47] The example mentioned by Alston and Quinn is article 15, of which it is noted in the preparatory work that no obligations were intended. Alston and Quinn, 'The Nature and Scope of State Parties' Obligations', 186.

Committee on Economic, Social and Cultural Rights (CESCR) has aided in this debate by identifying minimum core obligations for each right, that must at the very least be achieved by the state parties. The idea that its nature as a programmatic right and its reference to progressive realisation constitutes a provision so vague as to amount to an aspiration without creating obligations is therefore clearly outdated.[48] Moreover, understanding the ICESCR as not obligatory would completely undermine the treaty: 'the overall objective, indeed the *raison d'être*, of the Covenant . . . is to establish clear obligations for States Parties in respect of the full realisation of the rights in question'.[49] So if the phrases of Article 2(1) can be considered as obligations for state parties, there could be consequences for these parties in the aftermath of a disaster. In order to establish the exact scope and meaning of Article 2(1) ICESCR, the rules and theory of treaty interpretation will be applied in this chapter.

According to the *Vienna Convention on the Law of Treaties* (VCLT), the general rule of interpretation entails that '(a) treaty shall be interpreted in good faith in accordance with the ordinary meaning to be given to the terms of the treaty in their context and in the light of its object and purpose'.[50] Consequently, it must be considered what the ordinary meaning of the words as used in Article 2(1) ICESCR is. This meaning must be further specified in consideration of their context and must be seen in the light of the treaty's object and purpose. What exactly falls under 'context' is specified in Article 31(2) and (3) VCLT, which provide that the context at least consists of the text, preamble and annexes of the treaty and also of agreements made between the state parties with regard to the adoption of the treaty and of agreements made subsequently between the parties.[51] Finally, the object and purpose must be included in the interpretation. At first glance, 'object' and 'purpose' appear synonymous. When looking at the French version of the VCLT where 'object' is '*l'objet*' and 'purpose' is '*le but*', more becomes clear. A distinction must be made between '*objet ou effet direct et immédiat de l'acte*' and '*but ou résultat de l'effet juridique produit par l'acte*'.[52]

[48] Magdalena Sepúlveda, *The Nature of the Obligations under the International Covenant on Economic, Social and Cultural Rights* (Antwerp: Intersentia, 2003), 311.
[49] CESCR, General Comment 3 on 'The Nature of States Parties Obligations', 14 December 1990 (Fifth Session, 1990) §9, cited by Sepúlveda, *The Nature of the Obligations*, 312.
[50] *Vienna Convention on the Law of Treaties (VCLT)*, Article 31(1).
[51] See article 31(2) under a. and b. and (3) under a. to c. VCLT.
[52] Charles Rousseau, *Droit International Public* vol. I (Paris: 1970), 272 cited by Isabelle Buffard and Karl Zemanek, 'The "Object and Purpose" of a Treaty: An Enigma?', *Austrian Review of International and European Law* 3 (1998): 311, 325.

Put in other words: *'l'objet est un finalité, le but immédiat recherché par les parties ... la situation que l'auteur de l'acte a en vue ..., l'effet recherché par l'auteur de l'acte'*.[53] According to this understanding, the purpose of a treaty is the final situation or goal and the object is the means to achieve the purpose: *'(l)e but est la raison de l'objet, la situation en vue de laquelle l'objet est donné; l'objet est l'instrument du but'*.[54] The object is therefore the substantial content of a norm, i.e. the rights and obligations. The purpose is the result that must be achieved by the parties.[55]

Article 31 VCLT also dictates that the ordinary meaning of words according to context and in the light of object and purpose must be found in good faith. This element is crucial here, since the goal is to come to an objective reading of Article 2(1) ICESCR instead of describing *lex ferenda*. A result which is as objective as possible can only be achieved when including certain safeguards. Even though the VCLT speaks of the rule of interpretation in singular form, it is impossible to take all steps of Article 31(1) VCLT in one motion. To make the process of interpretation visible and therefore verifiable, the ordinary meaning of words, context, object and purpose must be defined step by step.[56] As such, it will become possible to check the interpretative choices made.[57] In the second place, it must be noted that the ICESCR is a human rights instrument. Human rights law has evolved strongly over time, and the view on human rights in the 1960s cannot be compared to the role of human rights today. Human rights instruments are often interpreted as 'living instruments' which must be 'interpreted in the light of present-day conditions', applicable also to the ICESCR.[58] These issues will be taken into account when establishing the meaning of Article 2(1) ICESCR.

[53] Philippe Weckel, *La Concurrence des Traités Internationaux* (Thèse Strasbourg III, 1986), 25–6, cited by Buffard and Zemanek, 'The "Object and Purpose" of a Treaty', 325.
[54] Ibid. [55] Ibid., 326.
[56] This idea is derived from Richard K. Gardiner, *Treaty Interpretation* (Oxford University Press, 2008), 30, who writes: 'Elements can only be taken up one at a time, but they are to be evaluated together. Thus interpretation may require going round the circle more than once if a factor presents itself under an element of the rules later in the list and which appears to outweigh one already taken up.'
[57] For a more extensive overview of the interpretative process of article 2(1) see the full dissertation; Stefanie Jansen-Wilhelm, *A Duty to Accept Aid in the Aftermath of a Disaster* (forthcoming, 2014).
[58] ECtHR (*Tyrer* v. *United Kingdom*) (App no 5856/72) (1978) Series A no 26; (1979–80), 2; EHRR 1, §31.

3.2 *Interpreting Article 2(1)*

Being the most authoritative body with regard to the ICESCR, the CESCR has given various interpretations of the provisions of the ICESCR in so-called General Comments. Besides having a General Comment specifically on Article 2(1), there are over twenty other Comments on other provisions.[59] Within the ICESCR, Article 2(1) is placed in Part II of the treaty where general provisions can be found, such as the one on non-discrimination. The articles of Part II are relevant for the understanding of all substantive articles that can be found in Part III of the treaty. This indicates that Article 2(1) is a general article that is applicable to all the rights laid down in Part III, just as for example the principle of non-discrimination is. In the General Comments, the CESCR is confirming this, not only by discussing Article 2(1) in General Comment 3 before going into the substantive rights in later Comments, but also by using the phrases of Article 2(1) continuously in all other Comments to indicate and define the obligations for each of the substantive articles.

To be able to define obligations more precisely, the CESCR started to make distinctions between immediate obligations and long-term obligations and also between obligations of conduct and obligations of result.[60] The phrase 'undertakes to take steps' is understood by the CESCR as constituting immediate obligations. During the drafting of the treaty, 'progressive realisation' through 'taking steps' was preferred over requiring to 'guarantee' the rights of the ICESCR.[61] Even so, 'undertakes to take steps' must be understood as an obligation for state parties that requires them 'to take the necessary action to execute the provisions of the Covenant'.[62] Even though no immediate result is expected necessarily, the phrase does indicate that immediate action is required and expected

[59] The General Comment that deals explicitly with article 2(1) ICESCR is CESCR, General Comment 3.

[60] Obligations of conduct refer to the steps that a state must make in order to reach a certain goal; obligations of result are those obligations that must be achieved in the end. CESCR, General Comment 3, §1. See CESCR, General Comment 12 on 'The Right to Adequate Food' (UN Doc. (E/C.12/1999/5) 12 May 1999) §16; see also CESCR, General Comment 13 on 'The Right to Education' (UN Doc. (E/C.12/1999/10) 8 December 1999) §43: 'While the Covenant provides for progressive realisation and acknowledges the constraints due to the limits of available resources, it also imposes on States Parties various obligations which are of immediate effect.'

[61] Alston and Quinn, 'The Nature and Scope of State Parties' Obligations', 165–173.

[62] Craven calls this 'a general rule of international law' which he bases on PCIJ, *The Case Relative to the Exchange of Greek and Turkish Populations under the Lausanne Convention VI* (1925) Series B, No. 10, 20; Matthew C. R. Craven, *The International Covenant on*

from states.[63] The CESCR has identified certain obligations that must be realised at all times, like non-discrimination and the core contents of each right (as identified in the General Comments for most rights). Consequently, 'undertakes to take steps' is an obligation of conduct 'to move as expeditiously and effectively' (i.e. progressively) as possible towards realising the final goal – indicated in Article 2(1) as 'full realisation'[64] – and an obligation of result, consisting of long-term obligations (progressive but full realisation) and immediate obligations (the obligation to take steps, realise the core obligations and non-discrimination).[65]

With regard to the phrase 'progressive realisation', it may still be wondered what is expected of state parties exactly when requiring them to realise the rights 'progressively'. This particular phrase has been referred to as the 'linchpin of the whole Covenant' as the meaning and nature of state obligations turns on this phrase.[66] Traditionally, 'progressive realisation' has been understood as subscribing the special nature of ESC-rights, a thought that is enforced by the absence of this phrase in the ICCPR. Yet it is now clear that 'progressive realisation' does not postpone obligations; states must immediately start working towards full realisation of the rights, as seen above with the phrase 'undertakes to take steps'. 'Progressive realisation' constitutes a certain level of flexibility, taking into account the various levels of development of each state party. It further means that no retrogressive measures may be taken, but two exceptions are foreseen by the CESCR; an economic crisis which makes progression impossible even if all available resources are used or when a 'retrogressive measure is taken for the purpose of improving the situation with regard to the "totality of the rights in

Economic, Social and Cultural Rights: A Perspective on its Development (Oxford: Clarendon Press, 1998), 114.

63 CESCR, General Comment 3, §2.

64 CESCR, General Comment 3, §2 and §9; CESCR, General Comment 13, §43, 44, and 52; CESCR, General Comment 14 on 'The Right to the Highest Attainable Standard of Health' (UN Doc. (E/C.12/2000/4) 11 August 2000) §30; CESCR, General Comment 15 on 'The Right to Water' (UN Doc. (E/C.12/2002/11) 20 January 2003) §17; CESCR, General Comment 17 on 'The Right of Everyone to Benefit from the Protection of the Moral and Material Interests Resulting from any Scientific, Literary or Artistic Production of which he or she is the Author' (UN Doc. (E/C.12/GC/17)12 January 2006) §26; CESCR, General Comment 18 on 'The Right to Work' (UN Doc. (E/C.12/GC/18) 6 February 2006) §19 and 20; CESCR, General Comment 19 on 'The Right to Social Security' (UN Doc. (E/C.12/GC/19) 4 February 2008) §40.

65 CESCR, General Comment 14, §30, which is repeated in CESCR, General Comment 15, §17 and in CESCR, General Comment 17, §25.

66 Alston and Quinn, 'The Nature and Scope of State Parties' Obligations', 172.

the Covenant"'.[67] Whether retrogressive measures can be justly used in cases of disaster remains to be seen. In general, when a state is recovering from armed conflict or natural disasters, the Committee has adopted a more flexible approach on retrogressive measures.[68] Still, in order to justify a retrogressive measure, a state must adhere to a number of conditions, including that of proving that it has unsuccessfully sought international assistance.[69]

The phrase 'international assistance and cooperation' as understood by the CESCR is rather ambiguous. On the one hand, the CESCR appears to understand it as a means to achieve obligations stemming from the ICESCR, while at other times the phrase is considered as an obligation in its own right.[70] According to the preparatory work, 'assistance' was added to the phrase at a later stage, upon which states argued that providing assistance could never be seen as an obligation.[71] However, '(i)n the context of a given right it may, according to the circumstances, be possible to identify obligations to cooperate internationally that would appear to be mandatory on the basis of the undertaking contained in Article 2(1) of the Covenant'.[72] In other words, to determine whether an obligation exists, it must be considered what the circumstances are in individual cases for separate rights.[73] As such, there is room for any future developments unforeseen at the time of drafting: 'it might be possible in the future to attribute specific implications to the undertaking contained in Article 2(1)'.[74] This is in line with the idea of interpreting

[67] Craven, *The International Covenant on Economic, Social and Cultural Rights*, 132.

[68] For example in the Concluding Observations on the report by Honduras, as the country was recovering from hurricane Mitch (CESCR, 'Consideration of Reports Submitted by States Parties under Articles 16 and 17 of the Covenant – Concluding Observations' (E/C.12/1/Add.57, 21 May 2001) §11); Sepúlveda, *The Nature of the Obligations*, 329.

[69] As is in line with the Maastricht Guidelines, Guideline no 13, cited by Sepúlveda, *The Nature of the Obligations*, 331.

[70] In the first and second General Comment, international assistance and cooperation is not considered to be an obligation. This changed with General Comment 3, where 'harder' language is used; CESCR, General Comment 3, §14, repeated in CESCR, General Comment 21 on 'The Right of Everyone to Take Part in Cultural Life' (UN Doc. (E/C.12/GC/21) 21 December 2009) §58. At the time of General Comment 15, the CESCR returns to seeing international assistance and cooperation as a means to realise other rights; CESCR, General Comment 15, §18.

[71] Alston and Quinn, 'The Nature and Scope of State Parties' Obligations', 190–1.

[72] Ibid.

[73] While perhaps not completely satisfactory from a certainty-of-law point of view, this is the approach that will be taken in the following.

[74] Alston and Quinn, 'The Nature and Scope of State Parties' Obligations', 191.

the ICESCR as a living instrument, yet it remains to be seen how the phrase about international assistance and cooperation has developed. According to Paul Hunt, (former) Special Rapporteur on the right to health, the meaning of Article 2(1) must have certainly evolved: '(i)f there is no legal obligation underpinning the human rights responsibility of international assistance and cooperation, inescapably all international assistance and cooperation fundamentally rests upon charity. While such a position might have been tenable in years gone by, it is unacceptable in the twenty-first century'.[75] Although it can be argued that there are certain obligatory elements stemming from this phrase, a certain context is needed to define in more detail what the obligations are: '(i)n the context of the human rights responsibility of international assistance and cooperation, the devil is *not* in the detail, but in sweeping generalisations of an entirely abstract nature'.[76]

Even so, one other phrase of Article 2(1) gives some detail with regard to obligations of international assistance and cooperation. In relation to the use of 'maximum available resources', the CESCR has made it clear that these resources include those acquired internationally, transforming 'international assistance and cooperation' into an obligation of conduct which comes into force when a state party does not have sufficient resources to realise its obligation of result.[77] Only when discussing the obligation to make use of resources available internationally is there an indication of a duty to seek and possibly to request international assistance. This duty is in line with what has been seen in the legal framework above: where the national capacity to respond to a disaster is overwhelmed, the affected state must seek humanitarian assistance. Not having sufficient resources for realising human rights can therefore only be used as a justification for non-compliance when a state can show that it has sought international assistance. Even then, claiming that there are

[75] Paul Hunt (2008), §133, cited by Judith Bueno de Mesquita, Paul Hunt and Rajat Khosla, 'The Human Rights Responsibility of International Assistance and Cooperation in Health', in *Universal Human Rights and Extraterritorial Obligations*, eds. Mark Gibney and Sigrun I. Skogly (Philadelphia: University of Pennsylvania Press, 2010), 112.

[76] Bueno de Mesquita, Hunt and Khosla, 'The Human Rights Responsibility', 128–9 (emphasis in original).

[77] CESCR, General Comment 3, §13. This was repeated in General Comment 4: 'To the extent that any such steps are considered to be beyond the maximum resources available to a State Party, it is appropriate that a request be made as soon as possible for international cooperation'; CESCR, General Comment 4 on 'The Right to Adequate Housing', 13 December 1991, §10.

insufficient resources available will not always be successful since certain obligations must be fulfilled at all times.[78] In this respect it must be noted that 'real' resources should be taken into account instead of only considering allocations made by the government.[79] Furthermore, 'resources' were meant 'to include whatever international as well as national resources were available', so that states were not free to 'arbitrarily and artificially determine for themselves the level of commitment required by the Covenant'.[80] Using the maximum of available resources is therefore an immediate obligation of conduct, aiming to fulfil both long-term and immediate obligations of result. Nonetheless, we must consider what exactly can be expected in times of disasters, where resources are especially strained.

The phrase 'by all appropriate means', finally, must be understood as an open-ended indication of obligations of conduct, where the purpose is the full realisation of rights, and consequently the object is not precisely defined besides arguing that they must be 'reasonable' and 'effective', and they must produce results compatible with the obligations under the Covenant.[81] The 'appropriate means' can be considered as meaning the requirement to take steps; the obligation dictates that steps must be taken immediately; which steps these are remains undecided. Also in the ICCPR, the phrase 'by all appropriate means' can be found, in which context it has been described as imposing a 'conditional obligation of conduct'.[82]

So far, it has become clear that the CESCR defined certain obligations stemming from Article 2(1) ICESCR. These obligations are mostly part of the 'object' (*l'objet*) of the treaty (i.e. the obligations of conduct) and are to a lesser extent part of the 'purpose' (*le but*) (i.e. obligations of result). What has not been determined explicitly at this point is what exactly this 'purpose' of the ICESCR is, although the obligations of result indicate that it is the 'full realisation' of the ICESCR's rights. It is important to confirm the purpose, since otherwise it remains unclear what the 'object' seeks to achieve. The CESCR, however, pays little attention to the purpose of the treaty and does not confirm that full realisation of the

[78] CESCR, General Comment 13, §31.
[79] Alston and Quinn, 'The Nature and Scope of State Parties' Obligations', 178.
[80] Ibid., 179. [81] Sepúlveda, *The Nature of the Obligations*, 337.
[82] For example article 23(4) ICCPR, providing 'States Parties to the present Covenant shall take appropriate steps'. Craven, *The International Covenant on Economic, Social and Cultural Rights*, 117.

rights is indeed the purpose. When looking at the preamble of the ICESCR, where the purpose can be found most often, it must be concluded that the preamble of the ICESCR cannot be considered separately from those of the ICCPR and the UDHR, yet these instruments appear to have a collective purpose which is the full realisation of the rights of the International Bill of Rights. Indeed, taking the right to life as an example illustrates that this right cannot be achieved without realising the rights to food, water and health. Through the preamble, this purpose is immediately linked to the *United Nations Charter*: 'in accordance with the principles proclaimed in the Charter of the United Nations'.

In its Articles 1 and 2, the *United Nations Charter* provides the purposes and principles of the United Nations. While the principles of Article 2 refer to peaceful co-existence of states, one of the purposes of Article 1 is to 'develop friendly relations among nations based on respect for the principle of equal rights and self-determination of peoples' and another purpose is 'to achieve international co-operation in solving international problems of an economic, social, cultural, or humanitarian character, and in promoting and encouraging respect for human rights'.[83] The principles of the *United Nations Charter* do link to the question of international cooperation in humanitarian emergencies (and consequently disasters), yet they are not very explicit and detailed. Cooperation is stressed, but what this entails in practice does not become very clear.

International cooperation is further emphasised in Articles 55 and 56 *United Nations Charter*. Article 55 explains that certain conditions are required for international stability and peace, like higher standards of living, international cultural and educational cooperation, and universal respect for human rights. These purposes must be achieved, according to Article 56, through joint and separate action of states in cooperation with the United Nations. Again, international cooperation is emphasised, and in these articles it is clear that certain goals must be achieved through such cooperation. Universal respect for human rights is mentioned here.

Taking the preamble of the ICESCR and the aforementioned provisions of the *United Nations Charter* together, it appears that full realisation of (all) human rights, or at least universal respect for human rights, is indeed the purpose of the ICESCR. This is confirmed by others and it also follows from Article 2(1): 'the objective of the State obligations is

[83] Article 1(2) and (3) UN Charter.

clearly stated in Article 2(1), namely the "full realisation of the rights recognised" in the Covenant'.[84] Article 2(1), consequently, is a rather ambiguous provision. It contains the formulation of the purpose of the treaty, it contains certain indications of the object, and it is not a substantive article. Rather, Article 2(1) is a programmatic article, making it not uncommon to contain both the purpose and the object of the treaty. Indeed, '(a)lthough emphasis is placed on the result, namely "the full realisation of the rights", there are plenty of indications within Article 2(1) and the substantive articles themselves as to what steps are to be taken'.[85]

From the foregoing it follows that the CESCR has identified concrete obligations stemming from Article 2(1). State parties to the ICESCR must eventually achieve the full realisation of rights. While this is a long-term obligation of result, the CESCR has also identified immediate obligations of conduct. These are to immediately take steps towards the full realisation, to at least realise the core contents of the rights, and not to discriminate when working on realisation of the rights. Even when the state has insufficient resources for the realisation of rights, it must still adhere to these immediate obligations and it moreover has a duty to seek international assistance and cooperation. Understanding Article 2(1) in this way is to a large extent in line with the intentions of the drafters, yet some elements, like the obligatory nature of international assistance and cooperation, are twenty-first-century interpretations following the idea that the ICESCR is a living instrument.

Even so, despite the fact that these obligations have been identified, it does not become clear what is exactly expected from states when a disaster occurs. In the first place, this is caused by the ambiguity following the lack of a state of emergency clause, making it questionable whether derogation during emergencies is possible under the ICESCR. In the second place, the obligations stemming from Article 2(1) are of such a general nature that no concrete duties can be based on it. To define more concrete duties in times of disasters, the obligations of Article 2(1) must be considered in the light of the substantive rights of the ICESCR. In the following section, these two issues will be discussed.

[84] Craven, *The International Covenant on Economic, Social and Cultural Rights*, 109.
[85] Craven, *The International Covenant on Economic, Social and Cultural Rights*, 107.

4. Obligations of state parties to the ICESCR in disaster situations

4.1 The state of emergency

In the ICCPR, a provision is included making it possible to derogate from certain obligations during the state of emergency.[86] Such a provision is not present within the ICESCR. The lack of a derogation-clause in the ICESCR can have two implications. On the one hand, it could mean that derogation from the rights of the ICESCR during the state of emergency is not possible. On the other hand, it could mean that derogation during disasters is possible but that no clause is required for doing so. In the first scenario, two arguments can be made. Firstly, it can be argued that due to the nature of ESC-rights a derogation clause is not required, as these rights cannot be violated during an emergency. This argument is not very plausible considering the conclusion that (at least the core contents of) economic, social and cultural rights contain concrete and immediate obligations and, moreover, when taking into account that the *European Social Charter*, consisting of economic, social and cultural rights, also contains a state-of-emergency clause. The other argument that can be made for the first scenario is that the progressive realisation formulation used in Article 2(1) indicates that during an emergency no progression can be expected as there is usually a strong retrogression of standards which cannot be easily mended due to resource constraints. Derogation would therefore not be required as a justification for non-compliance. However, as seen in the foregoing, this cannot be accepted too easily. When resources are strained, a state must seek international assistance and cooperation. Moreover, even in times of emergency some progression can be made. How much progression can be expected from states remains to be seen.

For the second scenario (derogation is possible but no clause is required), two arguments can be made as well. In the first place, it is possible to argue that the derogation clause of Article 4 ICCPR contains elements of customary law which can therefore be applied to situations outside the ICCPR.[87] Derogation during emergencies would therefore be possible by relying on and following these customary law elements,

[86] This is Article 4, ICCPR.

[87] See the reasoning of Jaime Oráa; Jaime Oraá, 'The Protection of Human Rights in Emergency Situations under Customary International Law', in *The Reality of International Law: Essays in Honour of Ian Brownlie*, eds. Guy S. Goodwin-Gill and Stefan Talmon (Oxford: Clarendon Press, 1999), 423ff.

without needing a derogation clause within the ICESCR. Another argument is that derogation is automatically possible through the words used in Article 2(1) ICESCR. Basically, this argument comes very close to the second argument of the first scenario; due to the requirement of progressive realisation and the maximum available resources rule, a derogation clause is implied in Article 2(1). Somehow, we must assess what is expected of states in terms of progression made after a disaster to see to what extent a lack of progression is deemed acceptable or whether certain standards are expected even in disasters.

4.2 *Obligations in disaster situations*

Besides referring to the core obligations that must be realised at all times, the CESCR has referred explicitly to duties in the event of disasters, both in General Comments and in Concluding Observations.[88] In this section, it will be assessed which obligations can be defined when looking at the interpretation of Article 2(1) in relation to four substantive rights. The rights that have been selected are those that are highly relevant in disaster situations, namely the rights to housing, food, water and health. In this chapter, the focus will lie on the General Comments; the Concluding Observations by the CESCR in relation to disasters are discussed elsewhere.[89]

With regard to the right to adequate housing, the CESCR has identified a number of aspects that determine 'adequate'. Some of these aspects are directly linked to disasters and other emergency situations. The legal security of tenure, for example, must also apply to emergency housing.[90] Another aspect, availability of services, materials, facilities and infrastructure, determines that for a house to be adequate, it must contain facilities essential for 'health, security, comfort and nutrition'.[91] The aspect 'habitability' indicates that a house must protect its inhabitants from 'cold, damp, heat, rain, wind or other threats to health, structural hazards, and disease vectors', indicating protection in disaster-prone areas,[92] and under the requirement of 'accessibility' special attention is required for 'victims of natural disasters' and 'people living in disaster-prone areas',

[88] See for example: CESCR, General Comment 3, 'The Nature of States Parties' Obligations'.

[89] Marlies Hesselman, 'Towards a Full "Cycle of Protection" for Victims of Disaster: Contributions from the Regional and International Human Rights Supervisory Bodies', *Tilburg Law Review* 13 (forthcoming, 2013).

[90] CESCR, General Comment 4, §8(a). [91] Ibid., §8(b). [92] Ibid., §8(d).

for whom some degree of priority consideration must be ensured as they can be considered to be a 'disadvantaged group'.[93]

As an immediate obligation, the CESCR mentions 'facilitating "self-help" by affected groups'.[94] If realising this immediate obligation is beyond the maximum available resources of the affected state, 'it is appropriate that a request be made as soon as possible for international cooperation'.[95] Moreover, the CESCR determined that 'external factors can affect the right to a continuous improvement of living conditions' yet that 'despite externally caused problems, the obligations under the Covenant continue to apply'.[96] As minimum core content, it can be argued that 'a state party in which any significant number of individuals is deprived of ... basic shelter and housing' is violating its obligations under the ICESCR.[97] As such, in a disaster situation, a state must at the very least provide basic shelter and housing, where resource constraints due to the disaster may not count as a justification for non-compliance: '(t)he minimum state obligations approach affirms that even in highly strained circumstances, a state has irreducible obligations that it is assumed to be able to meet'.[98]

With regard to the right to food, the CESCR has also explicitly referred to duties in disaster situations, as there is a strong link between the right to food and disasters: 'millions of people are suffering from famine as the result of natural disasters'.[99] States therefore 'have a core obligation to take the necessary action to mitigate and alleviate hunger as provided for in paragraph 2 of Article 11, even in times of natural or other disasters'.[100] In this same paragraph, there is also the requirement of physical and economic access at all times to adequate food or means for its procurement. The phrase 'at all times' is not indicating an exception for disaster situations.

General Comment 12 further provides that 'whenever an individual or group is unable, for reasons beyond their control, to enjoy the right to

[93] Ibid., §8(e); Charles W. Gould, 'The Right to Housing Recovery After Natural Disasters', *Harvard Human Rights Journal* 22 (2009): 169, 175.

[94] CESCR, General Comment 4, §10. [95] Ibid., §10. [96] Ibid., §11.

[97] CESCR, General Comment 3, §10 cited by Rebecca Barber, 'Protecting the Right to Housing in the Aftermath of Natural Disasters: Standard in International Human Rights Law', *International Journal of Refugee Law* 20 (2008): 432–68, 458.

[98] A. Chapman and Sage Russell, *Core Obligations: Building a Framework for Economic, Social and Cultural Rights* (Antwerp: Intersentia, 2002), 10 cited by Barber, 'Protecting the Right to Housing', 459.

[99] CESCR, General Comment 12, §5. [100] Ibid., §6.

adequate food by the means at their disposal, States have the obligation to *fulfil (provide)* that right directly. This obligation also applies for persons who are victims of natural or other disasters'.[101] Moreover, a 'violation of the right to food can occur through the direct action of states or other entities insufficiently regulated by States. These include . . . the prevention of access to humanitarian food aid in internal conflicts or other emergency situations'.[102] Therefore states have a joint responsibility to provide disaster relief and humanitarian assistance in case of an emergency.[103] A state would violate its obligations under the right to food 'if it let people starve when they were in desperate need and had no way of helping themselves'.[104] Again, asking for international humanitarian assistance turns into an obligation 'if [the state] is itself unable to provide assistance'.[105]

The right to water is not mentioned explicitly in the ICESCR, but it is considered to be essential for realisation of the rights to food – as much food aid consists of dried food, like dried noodles and sacks of rice – and health.[106] In its General Comment on the right to water, the CESCR argues that '(r)efugees, asylum-seekers, internally displaced persons and returnees have access to adequate water whether they stay in camps or in urban and rural areas';[107] moreover, that 'groups facing difficulties with physical access to water, such as . . . victims of natural disasters . . . are provided with safe and sufficient water'.[108] It is further provided that 'States parties are also obliged to fulfil (provide) the right when individuals or a group are unable, for reasons beyond their control, to realise that right themselves by the means at their disposal'.[109] 'States parties should adopt comprehensive and integrated strategies and programmes to ensure that there is sufficient and safe water . . . Such strategies and programmes may include . . . response mechanisms for emergency

[101] Ibid., §15, italics in original. [102] Ibid., §19.

[103] Ibid., §38, where requirements for food aid are laid down in §39.

[104] Federica Donati and Margret Vidar, 'International Legal Dimensions of the Right to Food', in *Global Obligations for the Right to Food*, ed. George Kent (Lanham: Rowman & Littlefield Publishers Inc., 2008), 58.

[105] Donati and Vidar, 'International Legal Dimensions of the Right to Food', 58. In the same paragraph, Donati and Vidar also note that 'States that, through neglect or misplaced national pride, make no such appeals or deliberately delay such appeals are violating their obligation.'

[106] David Fisher, 'Fast Food: Regulating Emergency Food Aid in Sudden-Impact Disasters', *Vanderbilt Journal of Transnational Law* 40 (2007): 1127–52, 1137.

[107] CESCR, General Comment 15, §16(f). [108] Ibid., §16(h). [109] Ibid., §25.

situations'.[110] The 'failure to adopt mechanisms for emergency relief' is considered to be a violation of the right to water.[111]

The right to the highest attainable standard of health is not only relevant in disasters because of injuries sustained during the disaster and having access to medical support accordingly, but in most cases it relates to the prevention, treatment and control of diseases, as laid down in paragraph 2(c) of Article 12 ICESCR. According to the General Comment, this includes 'the creation of a system of urgent medical care in cases of accidents, epidemics and similar health hazards, and the provision of disaster relief and humanitarian assistance in emergency situations'.[112] The obligation to respect the right to health includes, inter alia, 'refraining from denying or limiting equal access for all persons'.[113] The obligation to fulfil (provide) means that states are obliged to fulfil a right 'contained in the Covenant when individuals or a group are unable, for reasons beyond their control, to realise that right themselves by the means at their disposal'.[114]

To realise the right to health, General Comment 14 emphasises the role of international cooperation by also referring to the *United Nations Charter*: 'to cooperate in providing disaster relief and humanitarian assistance in times of emergency, including assistance to refugees and internally displaced persons'.[115] It is further determined that '(p)riority in the provision of international medical aid, distribution and management of resources, such as safe and potable water, food and medical supplies, and financial aid should be given to the most vulnerable or marginalised groups of the population'.[116]

One of the core obligations of the right to health is to ensure the right of access to health facilities, goods, and services; access to the minimum essential food; to ensure access to basic shelter, housing and sanitation, and an adequate supply of safe and potable water; to provide essential drugs; to ensure equitable distribution of all health facilities, goods and services.[117] Moreover, one of the obligations of comparable priority is that to take measures to prevent, treat, and control epidemic and endemic diseases.[118] An example of a violation of the obligation to

[110] Ibid., §28(h). [111] Ibid., §44(v).
[112] CESCR, General Comment 14, §16. [113] Ibid., §34.
[114] Ibid., §37. According to the General Comment, this goes for all ICESCR-rights.
[115] Ibid., §40. [116] Ibid. This is repeated in para 65 of the same General Comment.
[117] Ibid., §43(a)–(e). [118] Ibid., §44(c).

respect this as such includes the 'denial of access to health facilities, goods, and services' (mentioned here as an effect of discrimination).[119]

5. Conclusions

The current legal framework on international disaster response and humanitarian assistance provides that international aid can only be delivered with the consent of the affected state, yet the affected state may not withhold this consent 'arbitrarily'. This approach has also been taken by the ILC: 'Consent to external assistance shall not be withheld arbitrarily'.[120] Besides the indication that a state must have 'valid' reasons for withholding its consent, it is not entirely clear what 'arbitrary reasons' entail. Even so, states are not entirely free to withhold their consent to offers of international assistance. A 'qualified right' to withhold consent means that in some cases a state cannot withhold its consent to offers of international assistance.

In this chapter, we have analysed what is expected of states in times of disaster under the ICESCR. It has become clear that as a long-term obligation, state parties are expected to realise human rights and must immediately start taking certain steps to this end. Some obligations must be realised at all times, which include the core contents of rights. If states do not have sufficient resources to do this, they have a duty to seek international assistance and cooperation. That these duties remain applicable in disaster situations follows from the General Comments on the rights to housing, food, water and health, where many references are made to disasters and emergencies. The CESCR has identified obligations explicitly for disaster situations, which must be realised even in times of resource constraints. As such, the lack of a derogation clause in the ICESCR can be more easily explained: derogation from the core obligations is not possible nor allowed, and derogation from duties that do not belong to the core obligations automatically falls under the 'progressive realisation' formulation. Even if the derogation clause of Article 4 ICCPR would be customary law (something which is not established here), it would not apply to the ICESCR.

Especially during disasters and emergencies, state parties to the ICESCR are expected to facilitate access to shelter, food, clean water and health services. If the affected state is not able to do this, it must

[119] Ibid., §50. [120] Draft article 11(2), UN Doc (A/CN.4/L.794) 20 July 2011.

seek international assistance and cooperation. The special circumstance of the occurrence of a disaster does clearly not stand in the way of these obligations. Consequently, when a state party must fulfil its obligations under the ICESCR, it cannot refuse offers of international assistance when this refusal would result in violations of the core obligations of the ICESCR. A refusal of international assistance in such a situation could be called 'arbitrary'.

What has been assessed here, in the context of the ICESCR, can also be assessed with regard to other (human rights) treaties. Where a state would violate rules of international law by refusing offers of assistance, there is a strong argument that such refusal would be 'arbitrary' and therefore not allowed. However, what has not been discussed here is that states could also have valid reasons for refusing assistance, when this assistance is, for example, conditional or does not meet humanitarian principles otherwise. As it is difficult to establish what would take precedence – the duty to accept when refusal would lead to human rights violations or the right to refuse conditional offers – there is a clear appeal in getting parties to adhere to the standards that exist on humanitarian aid.

9

Regional human rights regimes and humanitarian obligations of states in the event of disaster

MARLIES HESSELMAN

1. Introduction

The adequate protection of persons in the event of disasters has received ample attention over the past decades. The occurrence of major natural disasters, including hurricanes Katrina, Mitch and Sandy, cyclone Nargis in Myanmar, the 2004 Indian Ocean tsunami, or the devastating earthquakes in Haiti, China and Japan have all contributed to the international, regional and national contemplation of stronger protective frameworks, including on the basis of human rights. A prime example of a regional instrument that is very innovative is the African Union (AU) *Convention for the Protection and Assistance of Internally Displaced Persons* (*Kampala Convention*), which entered into force in December 2011.[1] This Convention is the first legally binding framework that provides groundbreaking provisions on the protection of internally displaced persons (IDPs), on the basis of human rights, for both victims of natural disaster and armed conflict.[2]

The purpose of this chapter will be to examine regionally available human rights protection for victims of disaster. In particular, it will analyse the work of regional human rights treaty supervisory bodies in interpreting human rights instruments, considering that human rights treaties generally do not pertain to disaster situations explicitly, whether at the international or regional level – although with some notable

[1] AU, *African Union Convention for the Protection and Assistance of Internally Displaced Persons*, adopted by the Special Summit of the Union held in Kampala, Uganda, 23 October 2009, http://au.int/en/content/african-union-convention-protection-and-assistance-internally-displaced-persons-africa.

[2] See e.g. Articles 1(k), 3.1(d), 4.1., 4.4(d) and (h), and 13(d) of the *Kampala Convention*; See also generally on the *Kampala Convention*: Won Kindane, 'Managing Forced Displacement by Law in Africa: The Role of the New African Union IDPs Convention', *Vanderbilt Journal of Transnational Law* 44 (2011): 1–85.

exceptions.[3] The work of supervisory bodies in interpreting human rights instruments in the context of disaster situations is paramount to understanding whether and which humanitarian obligations currently might be incumbent on states under regional human rights law. However, even in cases of explicit reference to disasters it is important to understand the implications of human rights provisions in concrete disaster settings. Through application and interpretation of humanitarian obligations arising from abstract treaty provisions, protection can be brought down to the national level in concrete settings, ultimately also allowing victims to claim redress.

Before embarking on the discussion of the various human rights regimes in the following sections, it is briefly noted there that while the *Kampala Convention* is unique in referencing both victims of disaster and armed conflict, this chapter will solely concern humanitarian obligations under human rights law in disaster settings. The definition of 'disaster' as used in this article will be outlined in more detail in a later section.

2. Some observations on fledgling regional human rights systems: ASEAN and the Arab/Islamic world

The oldest and most established regional human rights systems, with the strongest codes of binding human rights and the most independent and comprehensive monitoring systems, are found on the European, African and Inter-American continents. However, there are also a number of budding other regional human rights regimes that deserve brief attention here; notably, the Asian region, the Arab world and the Islamic world all have seen recent developments in the field of human rights. Since some of these regions are exceptionally prone and vulnerable to natural disasters, for example South East Asia, it is worthwhile to include a few comments before addressing the other regions.

2.1 ASEAN

Firstly, over the past years progress on human rights has been made in the context of the so-called Association of South East Asian Nations

[3] E.g. the *Kampala Convention*; the *African Charter on the Rights and Welfare of the Child*, to be discussed in more detail in section 3.1.; or the *UN Convention on the Rights of Persons with Disabilities*, adopted 13 December 2006, entered into force 3 May 2008, 2515 UNTS 3, Article 11.

(ASEAN), which currently includes ten South East Asian member states.[4] Recently, ASEAN has seen a process of institutionalisation, including, most notably, in the field of human rights.[5] In 2007, the ASEAN adopted the ASEAN Charter, which sets out in greater detail than ever before what the purposes and nature of ASEAN are. In Article 1(7) it states that one of the purposes is to promote and protect human rights and fundamental freedoms, with due regard to the rights and responsibilities of the member states of ASEAN.[6] On the basis of this new Charter, the ASEAN Intergovernmental Commission on Human Rights (AICHR) was established in 2009, which has the function of promoting human rights protection in the region, but which also was involved in the drafting of the first ASEAN Declaration on Human Rights as adopted in November 2012.[7] This Declaration, although not binding in nature, includes a rather comprehensive list of human rights, as also relevant to humanitarian action in disaster situations, such as the right to life, the right to food, housing, clothing, water and sanitation and the right to health.[8] Only time will tell how the ASEAN human rights system develops further, especially since there are also some criticisms towards it.[9] However, most noteworthy for present purposes is the fact that the

[4] ASEAN member states include, at the time of writing: Brunei Darussalam, Cambodia, Indonesia, Lao PDR, Malaysia, Myanmar, the Philippines, Singapore, Thailand and Viet Nam.

[5] See e.g. Irene I. Hadiprayitno, 'The Institutionalisation of Human Rights in ASEAN', in *Defending Human Rights: Tools for Social Justice*, eds. Ida Lintel, Antoine Buyse and Brianne McGonigle Leyh, Volume in Honour of Fried van Hoof at the Occasion of his Valedictory Lecture and the 30th Anniversary of the Netherlands Institute of Human Rights (Cambridge: Intersentia, 2012), 54–58, 49.

[6] Also see Article 2(2)(i) of the ASEAN *Charter of the Association of South East Asian Nations*, adopted at the 13th ASEAN Summit, Singapore, 2007, www.asean.org/archive/publications/ASEAN-Charter.pdf.

[7] ASEAN, Article 14 *ASEAN Charter*; *Terms of Reference of the ASEAN Intergovernmental Commission on Human Rights*, adopted in 2009, and the *ASEAN Human Rights Declaration*, adopted at the 21st ASEAN Summit in Phnom Phen, Cambodia on 18 November 2012, both available at: http://aichr.org/documents/.

[8] ASEAN, Articles 11 and 28–9 of the *ASEAN Human Rights Declaration*.

[9] See general opinions on the success of the human rights developments in ASEAN, including more negative stances, e.g. Hadiprayitno, 'Institutionalisation of Human Rights in ASEAN', 49–5; Yuval Ginbar, 'Human Rights in ASEAN – Setting Sail or Treading Water', *Human Rights Law Review* 10 (2010): 516–18, presenting mixed feelings on certain developments and prospects; Mitsue Inaumi, 'Towards the Establishment of a Regional Human Rights Mechanism in Asia', in Lintel et al., *Defending Human Rights*, generally and at 83 in particular; Shaun Narine, 'Human Rights Norms and the Evolution of ASEAN: Moving without Moving in a Changing Regional Environment',

AICHR will specifically take up the issue of human rights protection in disaster situations in the near future: its work plan for 2010–2015 indicates a study on 'women and children in conflict and disaster'.[10] This will surely shed some light on the AICHR's considerations on the matter.

Finally, it is worthwhile to mention that ASEAN has also developed a few other human rights instruments over the past years, which actually could feed into the work of the AICHR, such as the ASEAN Declaration on the Protection and Promotion of the Rights of Migrant Workers and its supplementary Commission on Migrant Workers (2007), or the ASEAN Commission for the Promotion of Women and Children's Rights (2010).[11] The latter commission especially has as its main purpose to promote and assist ASEAN member states in their implementation of internationally recognised women's and children's rights, and it has already concerned itself with promoting these rights in the sphere of disaster response.[12] Moreover, it is noted that the United Nations Committee on Women's Rights has already concerned itself with some aspects of disaster response in ASEAN countries, for instance expressing concerns over access to housing and food aid for Indonesian female disaster victims and female-headed households as a result of the 2004 tsunami,

Contemporary Southeast Asia 34 (2012), 365–388, who is generally more pessimistic about developments; See also: 'UN Official Welcomes ASEAN Commitment to Human Rights, But Concerned Over Declaration Wording', *UN News Centre*, 19 November 2012, accessed 1 April 2013, www.un.org/apps/news/story.asp?NewsID=43536#.UUNOvay1LSg; HRW, 'Civil Society Denounces Adoption of Flawed ASEAN Human Rights Declaration', *Human Rights Watch*, 19 November 2012, accessed 1 April 2013, www.hrw.org/news/2012/11/19/civil-society-denounces-adoption-flawed-asean-human-rights-declaration.

10 'Five-year Work Plan of the ASEAN Intergovernmental Commission on Human Rights', 2010–2015, accessed 1 April 2013, via http://aichr.org/documents/.

11 See for some comments on the instruments and developments: Hadiprayitno, 'Institutionalisation of Human Rights in ASEAN', 61–2; or Ginbar, 'Human Rights In ASEAN', 515–16; 'ASEAN Declaration on the Protection and Promotion of the Rights of Migrant Workers', accessed 1 April 2013, www.asean.org/communities/asean-political-security-community/item/asean-declaration-on-the-protection-and-promotion-of-the-rights-of-migrant-workers-3.

12 See e.g., the Press Release on the 'Joint commemoration of the ASEAN Day for Disaster Management and the International Day for Disaster Reduction': ASEAN, *Women and Girls: The Visible Force of Resilience Children and Women of ASEAN, Step Up for Disaster Risk Reduction!*, 12 October 2012, accessed 1 April 2013, www.asean.org/news/asean-secretariat-news/item/women-and-girls-the-visible-force-of-resilience-children-and-women-of-asean-step-up-for-disaster-risk-reduction-a-joint-commemoration-of-the-asean-day-for-disaster-management-and-the-international-day-for-disaster-reduction?category_id=27.

i.e. aid being distributed to men, or in respect of access to (reproductive) health, clothing, housing and safety.[13] Here, a synergy in the identification of obligations under international and regional human rights could take place, inter alia, in the context of the AICHR's study.

2.2 *Arab/Islamic world*

Apart from Asia, also in other parts of the world some significant developments in human rights instruments have taken place, notably in the context of the League of Arab States (LAS) and the Organisation of Islamic Cooperation (earlier also known as the Organisation of the Islamic Conference, both abbreviated 'OIC').

2.2.1. League of Arab States

Firstly, in the LAS, comprising at present twenty-two Arab member states across Africa and the Middle East,[14] there has been a major regional human rights development in 2004 when, after decades of relative inaction on human rights issues, the LAS adopted the new *Arab Charter on Human Rights.*[15] This legally binding bill of rights, which came into force in 2008, contains a long list of human rights, including as relevant to disaster situations, i.e. the 'right to life', the 'right to health', or the 'right to an adequate standard of living', including 'food', 'clothing', 'housing' and a 'healthy environment'.[16] Like the ASEAN Human Rights Declaration, the document has remained somewhat controversial, primarily for its Islamic/Shari'ah interpretations of already established international human rights standards; however, the

[13] UN CEDAW, Concluding Observations Indonesia, 2007, UN Doc. (CEDAW/C/IDN/CO/5) §38–39.

[14] The current member states of the LAS are: Algeria, Bahrain, Comoros, Djibouti, Egypt, Iraq, Jordan, Kuwait, Lebanon, Libya, Mauritania, Morocco, Oman, Palestine (as represented by the Palestine Liberation Organisation), Qatar, Saudi Arabia, Somalia, Sudan, Syria, Tunisia, United Arab Emirates, Yemen.

[15] Frans Viljoen, *International Human Rights Law in Africa*, Second Edition (Oxford University Press, 2011), 13–14; Javaid Rehman, *International Human Rights Law* (Londen: Longman, 2010), 378–384.

[16] Arab Human Rights Committee, Articles 5, 38–9 of the 2004 *Arab Charter on Human Rights*, adopted by the League of Arab States on 22 May 2004, reprinted in 12 *International Human Rights Reports* 893 (2005), accessed 1 April 2013, www1.umn.edu/humanrts/instree/loas2005.html.

document is generally considered a good step for increased human rights protection in the region.[17]

Most interesting for present purposes, the *Arab Charter on Human Rights* also established the Arab Human Rights Committee, which is a human rights monitoring body, consisting of seven independent experts, with a main task to scrutinise states' periodic reports on the implementation of the *Charter*.[18] Unfortunately, however, the work of the Arab Human Rights Committee has seemingly taken a while to take shape, while at the same time information on its work seems to remain somewhat shrouded, leaving it difficult to obtain any insights.[19] As an indication, presently there are only four state reports published on the website of the committee – although periodic state reports are due one year after entry into force – while the reports are available in Arabic only. In addition, any other information on the committee's work is also only available in Arabic, and some have already critiqued the sparse availability of public information on the work of the committee generally, presumably both in Arabic and non-Arabic.[20] Nevertheless, it seems obvious that LAS may include interesting avenues for further research in the future.

2.1.2. Organisation of Islamic Cooperation (OIC)

Finally, in respect of the OIC, a relatively unknown organisation established in 1969, but embracing fifty-seven self-proclaimed Islamic states in various parts of the world, there have been a number of developments in the field of human rights.

Developments specific to the OIC include the early adoption of the non-binding 1990 Cairo Declaration on Human Rights in Islam or the more recent adoption of the binding 2004 *Covenant on the Rights of the Child in Islam* – which has not entered into force yet for lack of the

[17] See e.g. Mervat Rishmawi, 'The Arab Charter on Human Rights and the League of Arab States: An Update', *Human Rights Law Review* 10 (2010): 170–72; Viljoen, *International Human Rights Law in Africa*, 14; Rehman, *International Human Rights Law*, 383–84.

[18] Arab Human Rights Committee, Articles 45 and 48 *Arab Charter on Human Rights*, for the elaborate provisions on the establishment and mandate of the Arab Human Rights Committee.

[19] Rishmawi, 'The Arab Charter on Human Rights', 169, 172.

[20] The limited availability of information and documents, including documents not made public, has led to some critique, see e.g. Mervat Rishmawi, 'The League of Arab States; Recent Developments on Human Rights and Social Justice', in Lintel et al., *Defending Human Rights*, 45; Rishmawi, 'The Arab Charter on Human Rights', 169–175.

prerequisite twenty ratifications.[21] Both documents include rights such as 'the right to life',[22] the 'right to medical and social care'[23] and the right to a 'decent living', 'including food, clothing, housing, education, medical care and all other basic needs',[24] and the right of a child especially to survival,[25] although often the rights are tailored to a specific Islamic setting.[26] In addition, when the 2004 Covenant enters into force, a special intergovernmental supervisory committee should be established, which will monitor implementation of the Covenant by a two-yearly conference.[27] However, in terms of presently relevant developments, a final note must especially be made on the recent establishment of the Independent Permanent Human Rights Commission, in 2011, on the basis of the new 2008 OIC Charter, which, like the new ASEAN Charter, references human rights more broadly.[28] The Statute of the Commission includes a number of promotional tasks, and even refers to 'monitoring' of the human rights of Islamic communities; however, at present it seems too early to tell what the exact functions of this commission will be and how its work will take shape. Again, as with the other regional developments, the work of this committee may turn out interesting results in the future, and as such deserves further attention.

[21] OIC, 'Cairo Declaration on Human Rights in Islam', as adopted by the member states of the Organisation of the Islamic Conference, accessed 1 April 2013, www.oic-oci.org/english/article/human.htm; *Covenant of the Rights of the Child in Islam*, adopted by the Organisation of the Islamic Conference at OIC Doc. (OIC/9-IGGE/HRI/2004/Rep.Final), accessed 1 April 2013, www.oic-oci.org/english/convenion/Rights of the Child In Islam E.pdf (*sic*); Rehman, *International Human Rights Law*, 367–373; Viljoen, *International Human Rights Law in Africa*, 15–16.

[22] OIC, Article 2 of the 'Cairo Declaration on Human Rights in Islam'; Article 6 on the Right to Life of the 'Covenant of the Rights of the Child in Islam'.

[23] OIC, Article 17(b) of the 'Cairo Declaration on Human Rights in Islam'; Articles 14 and 15 of the 'Covenant of the Rights of the Child in Islam.'

[24] OIC, Article 17(c) of the 'Cairo Declaration on Human Rights in Islam'; Articles 14 and 15 of the 'Covenant of the Rights of the Child in Islam'.

[25] OIC, Article 6(2) on the Right to Life of the 'Covenant of the Rights of the Child in Islam.'

[26] Viljoen, *International Human Rights Law in Africa*, 16; Rehman, *International Human Rights Law*, 367–73.

[27] Article 24 of the *Covenant of the Rights of the Child in Islam.*

[28] See on the mandate of the Commission: OIC Resolution (2/38-LEG), *On the Establishment of the OIC Independent Permanent Human Rights Commission*, adopted at the Thirty-eighth Session of the Council of Foreign Ministers, Astana, Republic of Kazakhstan, 28–30 June 2011; OIC, The Statute of the *OIC Independent Permanent Human Rights Commission* is included in OIC Doc. (OIC/IPCHR/2010/STATUTE) appended to the Resolution, accessed 1 April 2013, http://oic-info.org/sites/default/files/user_upload/ResolutiononOICIPHRCandStatute.pdf. (*sic*), see Articles 8–11 of the Statute especially; Rehman, *International Human Rights Law*, 366.

3. Analysis of regional jurisprudence on human rights and humanitarian action in disaster situations in Africa, the Americas and Europe.

As already mentioned above, the European, African and Inter-American human rights systems can be considered the most established regional human rights systems. While the functions of the supervisory bodies may vary, most bodies have at least as main functions the scrutiny of general periodic State Reports and the examination of complaints by victims, but also other functions – such as the award of precautionary measures or issuing of advisory opinions and interpretative statements – may be included amongst their work.

The approach to the analysis of the work of supervisory feeding into this chapter has been rather empirical in nature, in that jurisprudence on the application of human rights in disaster settings – broadly understood as including the various work of bodies mentioned above – was searched on the basis of a set of search terms considered relevant to disaster situations. The terms used in (full-text searches in) the databases of work available from various bodies included therefore 'disaster', 'earthquake', 'hurricane', 'flood', 'cyclone', 'tsunami', 'explosion' and 'slide' (in terms of mudslide or landslide). In addition, the term 'humanitarian assistance' has also been used to find case law, or, when precedents were encountered, in databases or literature, the titles of such precedents were used, such as the *Budayeva* case in the European context, discussed below.

While the method may be critiqued for incompleteness, or, for example, as possibly referring to both 'natural' and 'man-made' disasters – a distinction sometimes maintained elsewhere – it is believed that the account below should be a relatively complete one. Again, as a reminder, situations of armed conflict are left out of the analysis, while disaster situations are generally understood here as calamitous events or series of events, presenting or causing a large-scale loss of life or threat of loss of life or suffering, while local capacities are overwhelmed.[29]

[29] Different definitions of disaster are possible, but they mostly presuppose the elements as stated; consider e.g. the discussions by the United Nations' International Law Commission and its Special Rapporteur on the 'Protection of Persons in the Event of Disaster' in the 'Second Report on the Protection of Persons in the Event of Disasters', Mr Eduardo Valencia-Ospina, Special Rapporteur of the International Law Commission, 7 May 2009, UN Doc. (A/CN.4/615), §39–49; 'Protection of Persons in the Event of Disaster': Texts of draft articles 1, 2, 3, 4 and 5 as provisionally adopted by the Drafting Committee, 24 July 2009, UN Doc. (A/CN.4/L.758) Draft Article 3 'Definition of Disaster'; or IFRC, *Law and Legal Issues in International Disaster Rresponse: A Desk Study*, International Federation of

3.1 The African human rights system

The first regime discussed here is the African human rights system, which has been elaborated under the auspices of the Organisation of African Unity (OAU), which has been the African Union (AU) since 2001.[30] All the African Union member states are currently states parties to the main human rights instrument in the African Union, the *African Charter on Human and Peoples' Rights*, which has been in force since 1986; in turn, all states on the African continent, except for Morocco, are Members of the African Union,[31] which means the coverage of regional human rights is near-universal in Africa.

The *African Charter on Human and Peoples' Rights* (hereinafter *Banjul Charter*) is a binding human rights instrument, containing both civil, political and some socio-economic and cultural rights, for instance the 'right to life', the 'right to health', the 'right to a healthy environment' and 'the right to social, economic and cultural development',[32] as also relevant to situations of disaster. The Charter has also been interpreted, over the years, as including or implying other socio-economic rights relevant to disaster situations, such as the rights to 'food', housing, 'water' and 'sanitation', although this practice has at the same time been contested.[33]

the Red Cross (2007), 22–23, accessed on 1 April 2013, www.ifrc.org/PageFiles/41194/113600-idrl-deskstudy-en.pdf.

[30] AU, 'Constitutive Act of the African Union', adopted by the 36th Ordinary Session of the Assembly of Heads of State and Government, 11 July 2000, Lome, Togo, accessed 1 April 2013, http://au.int/en/sites/default/files/Constitutive_Act_en_0.htm.

[31] Morocco withdrew from the OAU when Western Sahara was recognised as a state in 1984. Manisuli Ssenyonjo, 'An Introduction to the Development of the African Regional Human Rights System', in *The African Regional Human Rights System: 30 Years after the African Charter on Human and Peoples' Rights*, ed. Manisuli Ssenyonjo (Leiden: Martinus Nijhoff Publishers, 2012), 7.

[32] Articles 4, 16, 24 and 22 ACHPR, *African Charter on Human and Peoples' Rights*, adopted by the 18th Assembly of Heads of State and Government of the Organisation of African Unity on 27 June 1981 in Nairobi, Kenya (*Banjul Charter*).

[33] See on this interpretative practice, including some critical notes and questions, e.g. Manisuli Ssenyonjo, 'Economic, Social and Cultural Rights in the African Charter', in Ssenyonjo, *The African Regional Human Rights System*, 55–100; Anselm Chidi Odinkalu, 'Analysis of Paralysis or Paralysis by Analysis? Implementing Economic, Social, and Cultural Rights Under the African Charter on Human and Peoples' Rights', *Human Rights Quarterly*, 23/2 (2001), 327–369; Christopher Mbazira, 'Enforcing the Economic, Social and Cultural Rights in the African Charter on Human and Peoples' Rights: Twenty Years of Redundancy, Progression and Significant Strides', *African Human Rights Law Journal*, 6/2 (2006), 358 – 381; see also the new reporting guidelines for State Reports to the ACHPR, as launched by the Commission at its 50th session in 2011: AU, 'Principles and Guidelines on the implementation of economic, social and cultural rights in the

Apart from the *Banjul Charter*, other binding regional human rights instruments also exist in the context of the African Union, such as, the *African Charter on the Rights and Welfare of the Child*, or the earlier mentioned *Kampala Convention for the Protection and Assistance of Internally Displaced Persons*, both explicitly relevant to disaster situations.[34] For example, the *Kampala Convention*, which focuses on protection of persons displaced by disaster as well, requires states parties, inter alia, to devise early warning systems in areas of potential displacement to 'establish and implement disaster risk reduction strategies, emergency and disaster preparedness and management measures' and to provide, if necessary, 'immediate protection and assistance'.[35] Moreover, if protection and assistance is not provided ultimately, states can be held liable to repair any damages suffered per Article 12 of the *Kampala Convention*.[36] In turn, the *African Charter on the Rights and Welfare of the Child* explicitly confirms that states should ensure that children struck by disaster 'receive appropriate protection and humanitarian assistance in the enjoyment of the rights set out in this Charter and other international human rights and humanitarian instruments to which the States are Parties'.[37] Both treaties thus present clear affirmations of humanitarian obligations in disaster situations.

Below, the manner in which African monitoring bodies have applied provisions under the African human rights treaties will be further considered, discussing the African Commission on Human and Peoples Rights (operative since 1987), the African Court of Human and Peoples Rights (operative since 2006), and the African Committee of Experts on the Rights and Welfare of the Child (operative since 2001).[38]

African Charter on Human and Peoples' Rights' (Nairobi Principles), www.achpr.org/files/instruments/economic-social-cultural/achpr_instr_guide_draft_esc_rights_eng.pdf; and the AU 'State Party Reporting Guidelines for Economic, Social and Cultural Rights in the African Charter on Human and Peoples' Rights' (Tunis Reporting Guidelines), www.achpr.org/files/instruments/economic-social-cultural-guidelines/achpr_instr_tunis_reporting_guidelines_esc_rights_2012_eng.pdf.

[34] See more generally on other human rights documents in the AU, such as the *Protocol to the African Charter on Human and Peoples' Rights on the Rights of Women in Africa*, e.g. Ssenyonjo, 'An Introduction', 8.

[35] AU, Article 4(2) of the *Kampala Convention*.

[36] AU, Article 12 of the *Kampala Convention*.

[37] AU, Articles 23(1) and (4) of the *African Charter on the Rights and Welfare of the Child*.

[38] See for more info on either body: Rehman, *International Human Rights Law*, 328–334; or the contributions of Magnus Killander, Gina Bekker and Prof. Githu Muigai in Ssenyonjo, *The African Regional Human Rights System*: Viljoen, *International Human Rights Law in Africa*, 169 onwards.

3.1.1 African Commission on Human and Peoples' Rights

The African Commission on Human and Peoples' Rights (ACHPR) is arguably the main human rights supervisory body in the context of the African Union at present; it has most influence in terms of monitoring the human rights norms applicable to African Union member states, primarily as under the *Banjul Charter* and the Protocol to the African Charter on Human and Peoples' Rights on the Rights of Women in Africa.[39] It considers both state reporting and complaints. Very interestingly, the *Kampala Convention* also now requires states to periodically report to the ACHPR, as part of the regular scrutiny of state reports under the Banjul Charter.[40] Thus it should be worthwhile to see how the content of the *Kampala Convention* is further elaborated upon in the future, as (first) reports on its implementation come in.

It must be mentioned that none of the work of the ACHPR is legally binding; while at the same time the African regional human rights mechanisms remain relatively underutilised when compared to the Inter-American and European systems. Presently, fewer than 200 petitions have actually been dealt with by the ACHRP and the African Court of Human and Peoples' Rights has only received 25 cases at the time of writing (of which 13 have been concluded).[41] This contrasts starkly with the 128,100 cases pending before the European Court of Human Rights per 31 December 2012.[42] Of course, the limited engagement with the African human rights mechanisms, also impacts on the manner in which African supervisory bodies have been able, to date, to contribute to the clarification of obligations under the relevant instruments and enforce such obligations.

[39] For more information on the work of the ACHPR specifically, its competencies and some of the perceived deficiencies, e.g. Magnus Killander, 'The African Commission on Human and Peoples' Rights' in Ssenyonjo, *The African Regional Human Rights System*, 235–248; Frans Viljoen, 'The African Human Rights System and its Potential For Delivering or at Least Contributing to, Social Justice', in Lintel et al. *Defending Human Rights, 23–34*; or Ssenyonjo, 'An Introduction to the Development of the African Regional Human Rights System', 18.

[40] AU, Article 14(4) of the *Kampala Convention*.

[41] Information obtained from the websites of the ACHRP and ACtHRP, www.achpr.org/communications/ and www.african-court.org/en/index.php/2012-03-04-06-06-00/list-cases.

[42] ECtHR, 'European Court of Human Rights' Annual Report 2012', 149, accessed 1 April 2013, www.echr.coe.int/NR/rdonlyres/9A8CE219-E94F-47AE-983C-B4F6E4FCE03C/0/2012_Rapport_Annuel_EN.pdf.

However, all in all, the following worthwhile observations on protection in disaster situations, as per the work of the ACHRP, can be made. First of all, recently, disaster response has been explicitly incorporated into novel State Reporting Guidelines in the area of economic, social and cultural rights. Indeed, these Guidelines now include specific references to disaster response, for instance to the effect that states should indicate which steps were taken to ensure that 'the right of everyone to be free from hunger and to mitigate and alleviate hunger, including in times of natural or other disasters' has been guaranteed'.[43] Also, the Guidelines mention 'measures to ensure that surplus food protection is safely stored against famine, drought and other hardships' in the context of the right to food,[44] as well as 'adequate and functioning mechanisms of early warning to prevent or mitigate the effects of natural or human-made disasters' and the taking of 'appropriate emergency preparedness measures, such as keeping food stocks, and establishing adequate systems for distribution'.[45] Indirectly, in respect of the 'right to water', the Guidelines also consider that 'the right to water and sanitation imposes . . . obligations, amongst others', to 'adopt comprehensive and integrated strategies and programmes to ensure that there is sufficient and safe water for present and future generations', including through 'response mechanisms for emergency situations'.[46] How the implementation of the 2011 Guidelines turns out in practice seems too early to tell at present. Interestingly, the latest report of Côte d'Ívoire, as submitted in July 2012 and discussed in October 2012, included some references to positive action taken in the area of disaster prevention under Article 24 *Banjul Charter*, the right to a satisfactory environment.[47] Unfortunately, no response of the ACHPR to this report is available as yet.

Finally, in terms of the petitions received by the ACHPR, it can be noted that no valuable references to disaster response were found. There has been one case which involved a large explosion of an oil pipeline in Nigeria, causing the alleged loss of life of 700 persons, including women and children, and ill-treatment of injured persons in the wake of the explosion, but the case was declared inadmissible for a procedural reason

43 AU, Tunis Reporting Guidelines, 7; AU, Nairobi Guidelines, 42, §69.

44 AU, Nairobi Guidelines, 45, §70.

45 Ibid., 45, §70 (xxiv).

46 Ibid., 45, §75 (ii).

47 ACHPR, Initial and Combined Report of the Republic of Côte D'Ivoire to the African Commission on Human Rights Peoples' Rights, 46, accessed 1 April 2013, www.achpr.org/files/sessions/52nd/state-reports/1-1994-2012/initial_combined_periodic_report_194_2012_eng.pdf.

and thus not further contemplated.[48] Another famous case on gradual environmental pollution in Nigeria and the serious local consequences of that, relating to Shell's oil extraction in Ogoniland, can also be considered, but arguably the complaints and ultimate decision in that do not relate or amount to obligations of 'humanitarian action' as such, in terms of emergency action.[49]

3.1.2 African Court on Human and Peoples' Rights and African Committee of Experts on the Rights and Welfare of the Child

As already mentioned, the African Court on Human and Peoples' Rights (ACtHRP) has only dealt with thirteen cases at present. No reference to humanitarian action in disaster situations was found amongst the cases; and the same can be noted for the Advisory Opinions of the ACtHRP, as another prime judicial function.[50]

Finally, the African Committee of Experts on the Rights and Welfare of the Child, despite the promising references to the rights of children in disaster settings in the *African Charter on the Rights and Welfare of the Child*, has also not pronounced itself on the issue of disaster response. Neither of the two petitions dealt with to date relate to disaster response, and no reference has been made to disaster response in the currently available set of nine 'Observations' on State Reports.[51] In fact, generally the work of the Committee has been somewhat subject to

[48] 'African Commission on Human and Peoples' Rights', *Communication* 338/07 (2010), *Socio-Economic Rights and Accountability Project (SERAP)* v. *the Federal Republic of Nigeria, inadmissible*, §1–9.

[49] 'African Commission on Human and Peoples' Rights', *Communication* 155/96 (2001), *Social and Economic Rights Action Center (SERAC) and Center for Economic and Social Rights (CESR)* v. *the Federal Republic of Nigeria, merits*; See on the consideration that 'disasters' can both be defined as 'sudden-onset' and 'slow-onset', i.e. as related to climate change, crop failure and drought, e.g. Eduardo Valencia-Ospina, Special Rapporteur of the International Law Commission, 'Preliminary Report on the Protection of Persons in the Event of Disasters', 5 May 2008, UN Doc. (A/CN.4/598) §48.

[50] Find the petitions of the ACtHRP at the following webpage, accessed 1 April 2013, www.african-court.org/en/index.php/2012-03-04-06-06-00/list-cases; and the Advisory Opinions here, accessed 1 April 2013, www.african-court.org/en/index.php/2012-03-04-06-06-00/advisory-opinion.

[51] See the work of the Committee, in terms of the communications and State Reports it has received, at the following webpages, accessed 1 April 2013, http://acerwc.org/communications/; and http://acerwc.org/state-reports.

critique for its slow operation, deference to states parties, and the limited engagement of states parties with the body.[52]

3.2 *The Inter-American Human Rights System*

The Inter-American Human Rights System, which embraces all the present independent states of the Americas, thus including the Latin-American countries but also the United States and Canada, has been developed in the context of the Organisation of American States (OAS).[53] It seems somewhat stronger than the African system, and at least has been more utilised.

The main human rights instruments within OAS are the early non-binding *American Declaration of the Rights and Duties of Man* (1948),[54] the binding *American Convention on Human Rights* (1969),[55] and the *Additional Protocol to the American Convention on Human Rights in the Area of Economic, Social and Cultural Rights* (Protocol of San Salvador).[56] The constitutive document of the OAS, the OAS Charter, also provides for human rights protection, which is important, since a number of states have not formally subscribed to the relevant binding human rights documents and their supervisory mechanisms, i.e. the Inter-American Commission on Human Rights (IACHR) and the Inter-American Court of Human Rights (IACtHR).[57] That means that for those states, human rights supervision occurs on the basis of the OAS Charter, as further given shape through the *American Declaration of the Rights and Duties of Man*.[58]

[52] Gina Bekker, 'The African Committee of Experts on the Rights and Welfare of the Child', in Ssenyonjo, *The African Regional Human Rights System*, 250–259.

[53] See for an overview of membership of OAS, OAS, accessed 1 April 2013, www.oas.org/en/about/member_states.asp. There are a number of territories in the Americas which do not fall under the OAS, as they still belong with overseas territories.

[54] OAS, *American Declaration of the Rights and Duties of Man*, adopted by the Ninth International Conference of American States, Bogotá, Colombia, 1948, available at: www.oas.org/en/iachr/mandate/Basics/2.AMERICAN%20DECLARATION.pdf.

[55] OAS, *American Convention on Human Rights*, signed at the Inter–American Specialied Conference on Human Rights, San José, Costa Rica, 22 November 1969, available at: www.oas.org/en/iachr/mandate/Basics/3.AMERICAN%20CONVENTION.pdf.

[56] OAS, *Additional Protocol to the American Convention on Human Rights in the Area of Economic, Social and Cultural Rights*, San Salvador Protocol, adopted at the Eighteenth Regular Session of the General Assembly of OAS, 17 November 1988, accessed 1 April 2013, www.oas.org/juridico/english/treaties/a-52.html.

[57] See, for more information on the Inter-American human rights structure, Rehman, *International Human Rights Law*, 271–286.

[58] Rehman, *International Human Rights Law*, 271–272.

While the instruments jointly secure a score of human rights relevant to humanitarian action in disaster situations, not unlike the instruments and rights already mentioned in previous sections, this chapter will not dwell too long on the development of humanitarian obligations in the Inter-American human rights system; they are covered elsewhere in this book, by Knottnerus and Heintze.[59]

However, for sake of reference and completeness, it is worthwhile to briefly mention the following results of the search for jurisprudential developments.

First of all, it is clear that disaster situations have been a topic of concern in the Inter-American system, which might be expected, considering the region's proneness and vulnerability to disasters. Basic evidence is found in a number of special 'hearings' that were convened by the IACHR on the matter especially, such as the 2006 general hearing on 'Human Rights and Disasters',[60] or the 2000 hearing on the 'Human Rights Situation during the Natural Disaster in Venezuela'.[61] Interestingly, in the 2006 hearing, the adequate protection of human rights by the United States of America in the aftermath of hurricane Katrina has seemingly featured strongly. For example presenters at the hearing had alleged that 'following hurricanes Katrina and Mitch, the migrant population was deprived for six months of assistance from the United States government including food, water, clothing, shelter, and medical attention'.[62] But other criticism has also been levelled against the United States, for example regarding the poor evacuation and provision of shelter or other assistance to poorer, predominantly Afro-American parts of the population in New Orleans.[63] This has also led to condemnation

[59] Cf. Chapters 16 and 18.

[60] OAS, Inter-American Commission on Human Rights, Hearing on 'Protection of Human Rights in Natural Disasters', 124th Period of Sessions, 3 March 2006, *AICHR*, www.oas.org/es/cidh/audiencias/Hearings.aspx?Lang=en&Session=19; and as shortly referenced in the Annual Report of the IACHR of 2006, §XX.

[61] Hearing on OAS, Inter-American Commission on Human Rights, 'Human Rights Situation during the Natural Disaster in Venezuela', 106th Period of Sessions, 3 March 2000, *AICHR*, www.oas.org/es/cidh/audiencias/Hearings.aspx?Lang=en&Session=43.

[62] 'Evaluation of Human Rights in the Americas during IACHR Regular Sessions', *IACHR Press Release* No. 07/06, 17 March 2006, accessed 1 April 2013, www.cidh.oas.org/Comunicados/English/2006/7.06eng.htm.

[63] International Human Rights Law Clinic, Boalt Hall School of Law, 'When Disaster Strikes: A Human Rights Analysis of the 2005 Gulf Coast Hurricanes', The Inter-American Commission of Human Rights General Situation Hearing on Natural Disaster and Human Rights, 3 March 2006, 3–4, 17–46, accessed 1 April 2013, www.law.berkeley.edu/files/IHRLC/Briefing_Paper_Report_When_Disaster_Strikes_2_Mar_06.pdf.

by various international human rights supervisory bodies, such as the United Nations Human Rights Committee and the United Nations Committee against Racial Discrimination.[64]

Of course, the destructive earthquake striking Haiti in 2010 has also been cause to consider the protection of human rights in disaster situations more closely. Two remarkable awards of precautionary measures in 2010 can be especially mentioned in this regard, requiring the protection of persons in IDP camps and the position of women and children in particular.[65] Also, there were hearings and a report issued on the protection of rights in Haiti after the earthquake.[66]

Finally, another set of precautionary measures, dating from 2010, also deserves brief mention here, related to the planned construction of a liquid petroleum gas storage facility on a geological fault line, thus very vulnerable to natural disasters. The construction allegedly would pose danger of a chain explosion in the gas tanks, leading to the death of between 103 and 1,400 people, a risk which was described as 'unacceptable'. The AICHR asked the responding state, Honduras, 'to take the steps necessary to ensure the company's effective observance of the environmental regulations and laws in place in Honduras, and to adopt the measures needed to reduce the danger to the lives and persons of the inhabitants of the community of Omoa to an acceptable level'.[67] We will see below that the considerations of prevention of disasters, for example

[64] See CCPR, Concluding Observations on the United States, 2006, UN Doc. (CCPR/C/USA/CO/3/Rev.1) §26; CERD, Concluding Observations on the United States of America, 2008, UN Doc. (CERD/C/USA/CO/6) §31.

[65] OAS, Inter-American Commission on Human Rights, 'Women and Girls Residing in 22 Camps for Internally Displaced Persons in Port-au-Prince, Haiti' (2010); OAS, Inter-American Commission on Human Rights, Forced Evictions from Five Camps for Displaced Persons, Haiti, accessed 1 April 2013, www.oas.org/en/iachr/decisions/precautionary.asp.

[66] See e.g. OAS, Inter-American Commission on Human Rights, 'Chapter V of the Annual Report of the Inter-American Commission on Human Rights', 2010, e.g. §19–23, accessed 1 April 2013, www.cidh.org/annualrep/2010eng/Chap.V.HAITI.doc; or consider the audio recording of the 2010 hearing on OAS, 'Economic and Social Rights in Haiti following the Earthquake', 138th Period of Sessions, 28 March 2010, www.oas.org/es/cidh/audiencias/Hearings.aspx?Lang=en&Session=118.

[67] OAS, Inter-American Commission on Human Rights., Inhabitants of the community of Omoa, Honduras , PM 17/10, November 8, 2011, http://www.oas.org/en/iachr/decisions/precautionary.asp. See on the ability of the AICHR to provide precautionary measures generally, e.g. Eva Rieter, *Preventing Irreparable Harm: Provisional Measures in International Human Rights Adjudication* (Antwerp: Intersentia, 2010), 158–169.

in the context of the 'right to life', very much resemble the pronouncements of the European Court of Human Rights, as discussed below.

3.3 *The European human rights System*

Indeed, the final regional human rights system to be discussed is the European human rights system, which has been established in the context of the Council of Europe Organisation. It is duly noted that there are multiple European organisations involved in human rights issues now, for example the European Union or the Organisation for Security and Cooperation in Europe (OSCE), but the Council of Europe has currently the largest membership and the strongest human rights mechanisms, and is the only Organisation that will be discussed here.[68]

The main human rights instrument in the Council of Europe Organisation, which currently embraces forty-seven member states across the European continent, including Russia and Turkey, is the *European Convention on Human Rights and Fundamental Freedoms* (1950), as supervised by the strong European Court of Human Rights (ECtHR).[69] In 1961, a new instrument was drafted to remedy the omission of socio-economic human rights in the *European Convention on Human Rights* (ECHR), i.e. the *European Social Charter* (ESC), as revised in 1996.[70] The ESC is supervised by a separate body, the European Committee on Social Rights (ECSR), with less strong monitoring capacities than the ECtHR. Whereas the main monitoring task of the ECtHR is the scrutiny of individual complaints in a binding manner for parties to the case, none of the work of the ECSR is formally binding,[71] and its work generally includes recommendations on state reporting and entertainment of 'collective complaints', as mostly brought by non-governmental organisations on behalf of victims.[72] On another note, it is often said that the

[68] Also, note that the work of the European Union in the field of humanitarian action will be discussed elsewhere in this volume.

[69] See generally on the European human rights system, Rehman, *International Human Rights Law*, 182 onwards.

[70] *Revised European Social Charter*, adopted by the Council of Europe Organisation, Strasbourg, 3.V.1996, accessed 1 April 2013, http://conventions.coe.int/Treaty/en/Treaties/Html/163.htm; see generally on the *European Social Charter*: Rehman, *International Human Rights Law*, 232–237.

[71] See generally on the work of the ECSR: Rehman, *International Human Rights Law*, 237–242.

[72] Rehman, *International Human Rights Law*, 237.

ECtHR has fallen prey to its own success; the number of cases that the ECtHR is presented with each year ranges towards the thousands, and the number of cases currently still pending (including as a backlog) is more than 100,000; this has of course consequences for effectiveness.[73] At the same time, the output of the ECtHR is high, and as such its crystallisation of norms is advanced, including in the sphere of disaster relief.

It is noted at the outset that the ECHR and ESC jointly include a substantial number of rights that are possibly relevant to disaster situations, such as the 'right to life', the 'right to protection of private life, family life and the home', the 'right to property' (all ECHR), or the 'right to health', 'the right to social security', the right to 'social and medical assistance' ('for every person in need'), the rights to 'social, legal and economic protection' or the 'right to housing' and 'protection against poverty and social exclusion' (all ESC). Below, the developments in respect of the application of such rights to disaster situations will be discussed for both bodies.

3.3.1 European Committee on Social Rights

Firstly, as to the non-binding work of the ECSR, it demonstrates that disaster response has been an issue, but perhaps not something that is systematically brought up. In the ECSR's collective complaints system there were no references found at all, but in the searches of 'Conclusions' on state reports there were a few observations of interest, which are briefly noted below.

First of all, generally, the ECSR's observations on disasters have related to 'the right to social and medical assistance' in Article 13 ESC and 'the right of the family to social, legal and economic protection' in Article 16 ESC. Most observations pertain to issues of social security and benefits for victims of disaster, however, rather than to 'humanitarian action' per se. To illustrate, the ECSR noted in respect of Moldova, for example, the existence of special benefits for 'victims of the Chernobyl disaster and for the veterans of the Second World War,[74] or in respect of the former Yugoslav Republic of Macedonia the existence of 'one-off financial assistance', in the form of a lump sum payment, 'to any person or family

[73] Rehman, *International Human Rights Law*, 230–231; European Court of Human Rights' Annual Report 2012, 149, accessed 1 April 2013, www.echr.coe.int/NR/rdonlyres/9A8CE219-E94F-47AE-983C-B4F6E4FCE03C/0/2012_Rapport_Annuel_EN.pdf.

[74] ECSR Conclusions Moldova, 2009, accessed 1 April 2013, www.coe.int/t/dghl/monitoring/socialcharter/Conclusions/State/Moldova2009_en.pdf.

who find themselves in a position of social risk due to a natural disaster or an epidemic'.[75] Alternatively, the ECSR has held in respect of Greece, on housing and construction of housing, that 'specific programmes have ... been implemented according to the needs of regions, especially in those areas hit by natural disaster. The Committee requested further information on the continuation of housing policies, in particular on the effectiveness of the implementation of these programmes.'[76] Unfortunately, generally, it is not always clear from the pronouncements of the ECSR in state reporting what it considers concrete appropriate action in the implementation of particular provisions of the ESC. An exception seems to be the report from Turkey in 2003. In this case the ESCR noted explicitly that the reporting period had been 'marked by natural disaster (the 1999 earthquake) and economic crisis, leaving many families in a situation of want. The Committee is aware of the efforts of the Turkish authorities to respond to pressing social problems with the assistance of the World Bank', while it also considered 'that institutional and legislative reform in the field of social protection should make the economic protection of the family a priority if Turkey's obligations under Article 16 of the Charter are to be honoured'.[77]

Thus it is clear that the ECSR has concerned itself with the consequences of disaster situations, although generally this is in the sphere of social (financial) benefits, rather than, perhaps, concrete 'humanitarian action' of an emergency nature. In addition, it is not always fully clear which particular concrete action is warranted by a certain provision or not.

3.3.2 The European Court of Human Rights

However, if we turn to the ECtHR, there is a different picture painted; the ECtHR in fact has pronounced relative clearly on humanitarian obligations in the sphere of disaster relief in a number of cases – which is a worthwhile observation since the ECtHR can also be considered the strongest human rights body of all regions. Below, the main cases are discussed. Other cases could also be mentioned, predominantly as related

[75] ECSR Conclusions Former Yugoslav Republic of Macedonia, 2009, accessed 1 April 2013, www.coe.int/t/dghl/monitoring/socialcharter/Conclusions/State/MKDXIX2_en.pdf.

[76] ECSR Conclusions Greece, 1998, accessed 1 April 2013, www.coe.int/t/dghl/monitoring/socialcharter/Conclusions/Year/XIV1Vol1_en.pdf.

[77] ECSR Conclusions Turkey, 2003, accessed 1 April 2013, www.coe.int/t/dghl/monitoring/socialcharter/Conclusions/State/TurkeyXVI2_en.pdf.

to the Chernobyl disaster; however, these cases, like the discussions in the ECSR, mostly relate to issues of payment of benefits to victims, rather than humanitarian action of a more emergency nature per se.[78] They will thus not be further discussed here.

In discussing the main cases before the ECtHR, first of all it is important to observe that the cases all relate to somewhat different circumstances. For example, in the first case of *Öneryildiz* v. *Turkey* (2004),[79] the complaint concerned the loss of life, in total thirty-nine persons living in slum dwellings, who were killed by a methane explosion at a nearby rubbish tip, resulting in a flood of refuse engulfing the slums. Thus the disaster is a relatively specific one, and distinctly man-made. In *Budayeva and others* v. *Turkey* (2008),[80] on the other hand, the ECtHR was asked to rule on a situation pertaining to loss of life due to seasonal mudslides, of which the authorities were aware of, but ill-prepared for. Eight persons died due to the neglect of the authorities. Subsequently, in *Kolyadenko and others* v. *Russia* (2012),[81] the situation concerned one of damage and threat to life (but not loss of life) due to the flooding of dwellings after a large-scale emergency evacuation of water from a poorly maintained river reservoir, which in turn was necessitated by exceptionally heavy rainfall, in an area known as being prone to typhoons and heavy rain. Finally, in *Hadzhiyska* v. *Bulgaria* (2012)[82] an applicant complained about flooding of her house and in particular her basement, resulting in violation of her right to property, due to heavy rainfall and the breaking of river banks, which the authorities had not prevented. Thus the scale of the 'disaster' situations differs, as does the nature of the situation. This will be discussed in more detail below, as it seems important in the determination of particular burdens and obligations of humanitarian action on the part of the state.

Starting the analysis, firstly, in the case of *Öneryildiz* v. *Turkey* the ECtHR started to lay out the basis for obligations of protection in respect of the right to life in disaster situations. Particularly, it held that states parties to the ECHR have a positive obligation for the protection of the right to life, i.e. in ensuring 'all appropriate steps to safeguard life' and including 'above all a primary duty on the state to put in place a

[78] E.g. (*Burdov* v. *Russia*), No. 59498/00, Reports 2002-III.
[79] ECHR (*Öneryildiz* v. *Turkey*), No. 48939/99, Reports -XII [GC].
[80] ECHR (*Budayeva and others* v. *Turkey*), No. 15339/02, 20 March 2008 §137.
[81] ECHR (*Kolyadenko and others* v. *Russia*), No. 17423/05, 28 February 2012.
[82] ECHR (*Hadzhiyska* v. *Bulgaria*), No. 20701/09, 15 May 2012, *inadmissible*.

legislative and administrative framework designed to provide effective deterrence against threats to the right to life'. In the context of man-made, industrial disasters, this primarily includes a system of regulation and standard-setting, and the monitoring of industrial hazards.[83]

However, then, in *Budayeva, Kolyadenko* and *Hadzhiyska*, the ECtHR was evidently asked to expand on *Öneryildiz* v. *Turkey* in situations more akin to 'natural disaster' – albeit, again, of varying nature and kind.

A first matter to take away from the line of reasoning developed by the ECtHR in this series of cases is the observation that the scale of a disaster, and the possible impact on the 'right to life' versus other rights, is very much relevant for the scope and type of obligations. In fact, the ECtHR confirmed that 'the right to life', 'the right to protection of home and private life', and 'the right to property' all apply in disaster situations and deserve protection; however, in particular, a distinction should be made between 'the right to life', which is a right that deserves absolute protection, and the 'right to property', which does not. In *Hadzhiyska* the ECtHR held on this matter that:

> Because of the fundamental importance of the right to life, the positive obligations under [that norm] include a duty to do everything within the authorities' power in the sphere of disaster relief for the protection of that right. By contrast, the obligation to protect the right to the peaceful enjoyment of possessions is not absolute, and cannot extend further than what is reasonable in the circumstances. Accordingly, in deciding what measures to take in order to protect private possessions from weather hazards the authorities enjoy a wider margin of appreciation than in deciding on the measures needed to protect lives. Furthermore, natural disasters, which are as such beyond human control, do not call for the same extent of State involvement as dangerous activities of a man-made nature. Accordingly, the State's positive obligations to protect property against the former do not necessarily extend as far as those in the sphere of the latter. [84]

Thus first of all, obligations in respect of protection of the 'right to life' seem broader than, for example, in respect of the 'right to property'. In *Budayeva* and *Kolyadenko* this was also already confirmed by the ECtHR, as it found a broad range of obligations to emanate from the 'right to life',

[83] See also for a discussion of these cases earlier, Marlies Hesselman, 'Establishing a Full "Cycle of Protection" for Disaster Victims: Preparedness, Response and Recovery according to International and Regional Supervisory Bodies', *Tilburg Law Review* 18 (2013, forthcoming).

[84] ECHR (*Hadzhiyska* v. *Bulgaria*).

including the taking of 'regulatory measures', the putting in place of 'early warning systems' and a proper 'defense infrastructure',[85] or the existence of 'advance arrangements for emergency evacuation', 'catastrophic flood hazard zones', or appropriate 'town planning restrictions'.[86] It is interesting to note at this point that the provisions of the *Kampala Convention*, as mentioned in the introduction, are rather similar in this respect; the *Kampala Convention* also includes provisions on early warning systems or the establishment and implementation of disaster risk reduction strategies, emergency and disaster preparedness and management measures or the provision of 'immediate protection and assistance'.[87]

Secondly, however, a rather difficult and challenging issue is also arising in the case law of the ECtHR, as stemming from the second part of the quote from the *Hadzhiyska* case mentioned above, i.e. this relates to the nature of the disaster situation and any obligations of a state deriving thereof. Indeed the ECtHR clearly considered that the nature and origin of a disaster, man-made or natural weather hazard, bears on the type and extent of obligations to be involved. This is also the case in the protection the right to life. For example, it held in *Budayeva* that in 'the sphere of emergency relief, when States are directly involved in the protection of lives through mitigation of disasters', obligations should 'apply in so far as the circumstances of a particular case point to the imminence of a natural hazard that had been clearly identifiable, and especially where it concerned a recurring calamity affecting a distinct area developed for human habitation or use'.[88] Moreover, 'the scope of the positive obligations imputable to the State in the particular circumstances depend on the origin of the threat and the extent to which one or the other risk is susceptible to mitigation'.[89] The ECtHR considers in this respect that a purely 'meteorological event' might include lesser standards of protection than a 'man-made disaster', especially in the preparedness and prevention stage, since such events are 'as such beyond human control'.[90]

[85] ECHR (*Budayeva and others* v. *Turkey*), § 149, 155, including on the failure to set up temporary observation posts at the start of the mudslide season.

[86] ECHR (*Kolyadenko and others* v. *Russia*), § 173, 182, 185; ECHR (*Budayeva and others* v. *Turkey*), § 150, 152.

[87] Article 4(2) of the *Kampala Convention for the Protection and Assistance of Internally Displaced Persons*.

[88] ECHR (*Budayeva and others* v. *Turkey*), §137. [89] Ibid.

[90] Consider ECHR (*Budayeva and others* v. *Turkey*), §135.

In addition, it seems that the ECtHR attaches great consequence to the fact that a state has been 'negligent', i.e. in terms of acts or omission towards a situation of which the danger was known to the state and could have prevented.[91] This caused the ECtHR to rule in *Budayeva* that there was a violation of the right to life, considering that there had been poor management of recurring and foreseeable seasonal mudslides, at mortal risk, while the flooding of river banks due to heavy rainfall in *Hadzhiyska* and the damage to her basement under the right to property were considered inadmissible, considering that the state had no indication of its possible occurrence. Arguably due to differences in circumstances, the application of the ECHR by the ECtHR to disaster situations has not fully crystallised.

However, at the same time, the reasoning of the Court opens up a number of very interesting questions related to humanitarian action in disaster situations, primarily as it relates to adequate preparedness and prevention in disasters. Since nowadays we have a much greater understanding of the predictability of events, but also the pre-existing local vulnerabilities that can exacerbate consequences, or the factors of disaster mitigation and risk reduction that can play a role in protecting lives, a question arises as to how these insights should impact on the application of human rights in situations.[92] Does the 'human right to life' require indeed the action of human rights protection in the face of seasonal hurricanes or in earthquake-prone areas as well, for example as so often occur on the American continent? Moreover, an interesting question arises – which is not further covered here, because there were no references to it by regional bodies – in trying to clarify whether there is a role and responsibility for the international community as well, especially if it is accepted that disaster situations are exacerbated by climate change, or that the consequences of disasters could be worsened by international policies towards a developing country, such as has been alleged in the case of Haiti?[93]

[91] ECHR (*Kolyadenko and others* v. *Russia*), § 215.

[92] E.g. Charles W. Gould, 'The Right to Housing Recovery After Natural Disasters', *Harvard Human Rights Journal* 22 (2009): 180–181; or generally, Hesselman, 'Establishing a Full "Cycle of Protection"'.

[93] See e.g. the analysis of heightened vulnerability of Haitian victims, Brian Concannon and Beatrice Lindstrom, 'Cheaper, Better, Longer-Lasting: a Right-Based Approach to Disaster Response in Haiti', *Emory International Law Review* 25 (2011): 1159–1167.

4. Conclusions

This paper has presented an overview of the humanitarian obligations currently to be considered incumbent on states parties to regional human rights treaties, as per the instruments directly, or as per the elaborations of regional human rights supervisory bodies in the application and interpretation of treaty provisions. It seems confirmed that regional instruments have a role to play in disaster situations, since all regional human rights bodies, except perhaps for the fledgling human rights regimes in Asia and in the Arab and Islamic world, which were also briefly addressed for their potential future contributions, have pronounced themselves on disaster response on multiple occasions already, although perhaps not necessarily always in a systematic manner.

Jointly, the regional bodies have referenced a number of obligations in respect of the delivery of assistance, such as related to food, water and medical assistance for survival and subsistence in response phases; or the protection of health and safety generally; in addition, very importantly, the need to adequately prepare for disasters so as to effectively protect the right to life or other rights has also been affirmed by bodies, and in treaties. Indeed, the African, Inter-American and European human rights regimes all include references in respect of obligations of preparation and response to disasters, thereby reflecting concerns that effective disaster response includes a full 'cycle of protection' for victims in disaster settings, encompassing all three phases of 'preparedness', 'response' and 'recovery'.[94] The purpose of such an approach is to make sure that vulnerabilities of victims are not heightened as 'a result of inadequate planning and disaster preparedness, inappropriate policies and measures to respond to the disasters, or simple neglect', as is often the case, while at the same time recovery phases can lend themselves to improved humanitarian action for the next event.[95]

Of course, another question, only partly answered by the analysis above, is whether ultimately effective claims for protection by actual disaster victims are made in the preparation and recovery phases, i.e.

[94] Walter Kälin, 'Report of the Representative of the Secretary-General on the Human Rights of Internally Displaced Persons', Addendum on 'Protection of Internally Displaced Persons in Situations of Natural Disasters', 2009, UN Doc. (A/HRC/10/13/Add.1) §21; Hesselman, 'A Full "Cycle of Protection"'.

[95] IASC Operational Guidelines on the Protection of Persons in Situations of Natural Disasters, revised January 2011, The Brookings–Bern Project on Internal Displacement, 2.

considering the often overwhelmed local infrastructures in the actual disaster phase itself. In this sense, adequate preparedness may be the key to effective humanitarian action, as evacuation plans etc. are executed in the actual disaster phases. However, at the same time, individual complaints on humanitarian action in disaster settings, given the noted exceptions discussed above, seem to be lacking generally. It is suggested here that this might be due to both a lack of appropriate avenues and possibilities at the regional level – or the international level for that matter[96] – and the lack of understanding still, across the board, of concrete human rights obligations in disaster settings.

All in all, the application of regional human rights regimes to disaster situations may be subject to further elaboration in the future, based on the first clarification of obligations as discussed above. A full understanding of humanitarian obligations in disaster settings under regional human rights treaties is likely to evolve with the sustained monitoring of specific disaster settings. At the same time, efforts are taking place elsewhere, such as on the international plane in the context of supervision of international human rights law, or the work of the International Law Commission (ILC) in elaborating Draft Articles on the 'Protection of Persons in the Event of Disasters', which can also usefully inform developments at the regional level.[97] In this sense, the full appreciation of human rights implications might benefit from the different systems looking at each other in grasping and consolidating particular developments, especially when there is overlap in supervision at the international and regional level, but also amongst regional systems, as is the case with the development of other case law. Finally, it is hoped that the work of the ILC Special Rapporteur especially can provide impetus in bringing approaches together; his work can act as a platform to systemically bring together currently overlapping developments and concerns at the international, regional and national level, while, at the same time, it may provide inspiration for further development at such various levels, as appropriate.[98] Ultimately, effective humanitarian action, at the right

[96] Individual complaints on humanitarian action in disaster settings are even more scant at the international level. See Hesselman, 'A Full "Cycle of Protection"'.

[97] See Hesselman, 'A Full "Cycle of Protection"', for a further discussion of especially the international developments as well.

[98] Note that the ILC Special Rapporteur, in his various reports, refers to and draws from both international and regional human rights instruments, such as the European, African and Inter-American human rights conventions, or the *Kampala Convention* specifically, as well as including international and regional (non-human-rights related) agreements

level, within a framework of possibly various applicable systems might only come about if approaches are sufficiently aligned and obligations under the scope of each of the applicable instruments fully clarified to all involved in the action.

and instruments on disaster management specifically. Examples of the latter instruments would be the 'ASEAN Agreement on Disaster Management and Emergency Response' (2005) or the OAS *Inter-American Convention to Facilitate Disaster Assistance* (1991). All in all, the Rapporteur thus takes a very broad, systemic approach to his inquiry, which should help consolidate the broad range of current initiatives and frameworks on disaster response. All the reports of the ILC Special Rapporteur, the discussions in the International Law Commission and the current Draft Articles can be accessed via the ILC website, accessed 17 June 2013, http://untreaty.un.org/ilc/guide/6_3.htm.

10

Assessing the complex normative pluralism in humanitarian crises: do local norms matter?

JORIS KOCKEN

1. Introduction

Most western humanitarian actors base their intervention in humanitarian crises on a rights-based approach. In this approach the victims of humanitarian crises are seen as bearers of rights. In that approach rights have two functions. They have a moral value in the sense that the ascribed rights can be seen as moral entitlements of the bearer of rights. Secondly, they have a practical value in the sense that rights are seen as practical tools for persons to improve their actual position. The rights-based approaches are not introduced into normative vacuums. In humanitarian crises different actors (local and non-local) bring in their different normative orientations. The actors promoting a rights-based approach have to compete or cooperate with actors supporting other normative regimes to be successful in establishing their preferred normative regime.

My claim in this paper is that the different normative regimes 'active' in humanitarian crises are not compatible and cannot cooperate, and that victims of humanitarian crises are not helped by introducing the current rights-based approaches. In my view the ineffectiveness of the rights-based approach cannot be explained by the popular notion that there is a lack of enforcement and therefore these people cannot enjoy their rights. It is true that norms for their effectiveness also rest on their enforcement. But I will argue that it is not (only) an enforcement issue but that there is another issue: it is unclear which rights victims have.

My claim is that the different normative, mostly legal, regimes that try to influence the position of victims, compete with each other for dominance but fail to establish a coherent set of rights for the victims. So the problem is not enforcement, although that is a huge problem in itself. It is the problem, preceding the enforcement issue, that there is no clear and coherent set of norms that can be used to improve the situation of these victims.

Some argue that the human rights approach can solve this problem by functioning as the only relevant normative regime. There have been some attempts to make the human rights approach the dominant regime. I will show later that a lack of consensus on the validity of human rights and the weakness of this regime itself will make those attempts unsuccessful. So the problem is not only the lack of a clear hierarchy in regimes but also the unclear limits and content of these regimes themselves that makes it hard to determine what the legal position of victims of humanitarian crises is.

To rephrase it, the problem I want to discuss is that international legal regimes do not do what they intend to do (regulate behaviour according to their norms) because in real situations, these regimes are not clear and coherent themselves and are, on top of that, competing with other normative regimes for influence over the actors on the ground. They intend to establish a coherent set of rights for people caught up in humanitarian crises, but they fail to do so.

In this chapter I will discuss eight normative regimes that play an important role in the lives of victims of man-made humanitarian crises. The eight regimes are six different international legal or quasi-legal regimes and two national and local normative regimes. The international regimes I will discuss are (a) public international law in general, (b) humanitarian law, (c) human rights law, (d) rule of law projects, (e) legal empowerment projects and (f) the sets of rules brought in by the organisations (humanitarian actors like the United Nations High Commissioner for Refugees (UNHCR) and western non-governmental organisations (NGOs)) that intervene in humanitarian crises. I will not discuss the exact set of rules they contain but focus on their clarity and main thrust as far as establishing subjective rights is concerned. The two remaining regimes are national and local: (g) national legal systems and (h) local or customary law systems.

Before giving a short description of the eight normative regimes, I want to work out the point I just made about the vagueness and incoherence of legal regimes. Although normative regimes can in theory be constructed as clear sets of norms, in social reality they lack that clarity. There are two reasons that make sets of norms diffuse. Firstly there is the often overlooked problem of validity. Every norm system has to make a clear distinction between norms that are part of the regime and norms that do not belong to it. In my view there is often a profound disagreement over which norms are 'in' and which norms are 'out'. The second problem, familiar to legal experts, is the problem of interpretation. Because if one has overcome the problem of validity, in the sense that one has established which norms are part of the regime, there is the inescapable problem that rules get their meaning in their application to concrete real-life cases. In legal theory it is common sense that here again there is room for disagreement on what criteria we should use for interpretation. The problem of validity will be discussed before I try to describe the relevant regimes. The problem of interpretation is a more familiar problem and therefore will not be discussed extensively.

In this chapter I will start by discussing the concept of complex legal pluralism. Next I will explain my approach to legal validity. Then I discern the three basic ways in which validity is constructed in international law. I will then present six concrete legal and quasi-legal regimes that are to a large extent 'international'. After that I will discuss the construction of validity in national state law; then I will discuss two other important regimes: state law and local, often 'customary' legal regimes. I will conclude by stating that international legal regimes lack the coherence and the local legitimacy to function as a coherent framework for a rights-based approach in humanitarian crises. Looking these problems in the eye (and looking for ways to solve them) is one of the conditions for improving the rights of people in humanitarian crises.

2. Complex legal pluralism

A key concept to order my own perception of the situations studied here is the concept of complex legal pluralism. This concept helps to order social facts. Its aim is to highlight the multiplicity of legal and quasi-legal normative orders that are simultaneously active in a certain social situation. It is a quasi-descriptive term I use to make sense of the world I want to analyse. I add the adjective 'complex' to the concept of legal pluralism to relate to the concept of legal pluralism as developed in legal anthropology, while at the same time keeping a bit of a distance from it.

Legal pluralism was and still is a much-debated term in legal anthropology. Merry gives a basic definition: 'Legal Pluralism is generally defined as a situation in which two or more legal orders coexist in the same social field'.[1] The concept is used to make room for a view of law

[1] Sally E. Merry, 'Legal Pluralism', *Law & Society Review* 22 (1988): 870.

that is not exclusively focused on traditional notions of state-made national and international law. The traditional combination of state-made national law and state-ratified international law is an important legal regime but is very often not the only legal regime in a certain territory. Room had to be made for customary law or 'folk law'.

So on a certain territory we find a plurality of legal orders. That conclusion gave rise to the normative question: in a conflict between legal orders existing at the same time and in the same place, which order should prevail? And to another question: which systems of social control should be called law and which not? For example, can a social system with traditional leaders and unwritten rules and procedures for conflict resolution be called (a system of) law? The matter has obtained prominence because concepts matter.[2] Labelling customary systems of dispute resolution and behavioural regulation as law made these systems more visible and gave them more authority. The western traditional view that customs will sooner or later wither away due to the global force of modernisation, and thus can safely be ignored, was disputed and opposed by the view that customary law was relevant and, some claimed, in some ways superior to traditional state law.

In the concept of complex legal pluralism I attempt to include both the question of the multiplicity of legal orders and the questions about the limits and content of these regimes. The last questions will be addressed by introducing the concept of validity as crucial to understanding why legal regimes tend to have blurry borders and uncertain content.

3. The construction of legal validity and complex legal pluralism

Validity is a crucial element in tackling my first problem: how does one identify a legal regime? Which rules are part of a regime and which are not? The problem of validity is one of the key debates in current legal theory. The problem of validity is felt most keenly in the debate on international law, but can easily be recognised in other legal arenas as well. In this paragraph I will explain my approach to legal validity and explain its relevance for the description of the complex legal pluralism in humanitarian crises. The next paragraph will be focused

[2] Brian Z. Tamanaha, 'The Folly of the Societal Scientific Concept of Legal Pluralism', *The Journal of Law & Society* 20 (1993): 192–217. In his discussion of the concept for instance he points out that legal pluralist scholars do not share a clear concept of law.

on the different ways that are used in international law to claim validity of international legal norms.

The concept of legal validity I will use is the concept as introduced by legal theorist Herbert Hart in his book, *The Concept of Law*. His well-known concept of law states that law is a union of primary and secondary rules. His concept is a sociological concept of law and therefore useful in the discussion of legal orders. Under primary rules 'human beings are required to do or abstain from certain actions, whether they wish to or not'.[3] And, secondary rules 'provide that human beings may by doing or saying certain things introduce new rules of the primary type, extinguish or modify old ones, or in various ways determine their incidence or control their operations'.[4] Secondary rules thus construct the ways in which the primary rules can be changed.

Hart's concept of validity is tied to the idea that there are two ways to look at law: from an internal (participating in the social situation) perspective, and from an external (studying the social situation) one. The idea of validity is a notion which has meaning solely from the internal perspective. Validity of a primary rule is determined by using a fundamental secondary rule, the rule of recognition, for its identification. So looking for legal validity is looking for rules of recognition. Rules of recognition 'will specify some feature or features, possession of which by a suggested rule is taken as a conclusive affirmative indication that it is a rule of the group to be supported by the social pressure it exerts'.[5] Rules of recognition are for example 'the fact of their having been enacted by a certain body, their long customary practice or their relation to judicial decisions'.[6] Validity is thus constructed by the, often implicit, use of rules of recognition by the participants in a legal regime (internal perspective) to determine the status of primary rules. Validity discerns which rules are part or not part of a legal regime.[7]

In this paper I will accept Hart's idea that the internal perspective and the external perspective are different ways of looking at the world, but will not accept that validity of law is something delegated to the participants in the world of legal experts. Who determines the validity of law is a difficult discussion between, on the one hand, insiders who claim that

[3] Herbert L. A. Hart, *The Concept of Law* (Oxford: Clarendon Press, 1961), 78.

[4] Ibid., 79. [5] Ibid., 92. [6] Ibid., 92.

[7] Rules of recognition can also be identified from the external perspective by observation. According to Hart the external perspective cannot determine the validity of rules but can identify the existence of rules.

their special position and privileged knowledge should give them the power to determine what law is, and on the other hand, outsiders that dispute these claims for several reasons. The most basic critique boils down to the following: law is something that concerns all members of a certain society, all legal subjects are thus participants, although most of them will be laypersons. They are part of the internal perspective, or perhaps better, they have an internal perspective, and their use of rules of recognition has a role to play. In that sense determining legal validity can never be done without taking into account the legal consciousness of the (prospective) subjects of a legal regime. Legal elites are important in establishing legal validity but their use of rules of recognition can and often is (but are seldom seen to be) contested, both internally as well as externally.

There is another function of rules of recognition relevant to this paper. Rules of recognition are used in complex normative situations where on first inspection legal norms from different sources and standing are incompatible with each other. The rules of recognition will give a rule to order these competing rules in a more-or-less consistent whole. Typical are the rules of preference: statute over case law, new rules over old rules, state rules over more local rules and specific rules over more general rules. From the internal perspective the problem of incoherence and multiplicity is seen to be solved that way. There is a problem, however: these internal perspectives start with a choice for a certain legal order, and even a specific interpretation of that order, and from that point they order the world. The rules of recognition are thus bound to specific legal orders (national lawyers tend to see everything from the perspective of state law, international lawyers tend to start with international law as the preferred system). Rules of recognition reduce the normative complexity of a social situation to one legal order, and in a certain sense cannot take other legal orders seriously. This goes to the heart of the problem of understanding the complexity of legal pluralist situations: the internal perspectives of participants compete.

4. Validity in international law

In this section I will try to determine which rules of recognition are used in the different legal regimes to give a foundation to their validity. To make matters a little less complicated I will reduce and simplify the debate of validity in international law in this paper by assuming that there are three typical rules of recognition in international law: the legal positivist view, the natural law view and a view that can be seen as a mix of the first two.

The first rule of recognition I identify is the idea that primary rules are valid if they are established by the free act of the legislative body of a state. States make legal rules (national law) and sign treaties (international law) and make these legal rules valid on their territory or in their relation with other states. In the second form, the basic idea is thus taken from natural law theory stating that rights of citizens and states and some obligations of states exist, are valid, and are independent of any act of consent by the state and/or its citizens. The third form of claiming validity is a hybrid of the first two forms. The third form claims validity of international legal norms on the basis of internationally grown custom combined with a stronger or weaker claim of universality of that custom. A short explanation is called for.

The first rule of recognition builds on traditional notions of validity in international law, which are closely linked to popular notions of sovereignty of the nation state. This approach is often called legal positivism. The form the rule of recognition takes is often that of specific bodies for legislation and adjudication that are constructed and act within certain legal conditions, and are the 'sources' of law within a certain territory. The source of international law, in the sense that some primary rules of international law are seen as valid on the territory of this state and are binding on and constraining the acts of this state, is the active consent of a certain body or some officials of this state (again appointed and acting under certain conditions) to establish these rules. This traditional rule of recognition that uses the centrality of the nation state as an actor in international law has competition from other rules of recognition used by different legal elites.

A rule of recognition based in natural law in the strict sense is perhaps more of an academic endeavour but certainly not without influence in legal practice. The natural law position starts with the understanding that law and morality cannot, both logically and empirically, be separated. One pillar under the idea that human rights have a universal quality is the concept that rights are entitlements based on universal morality and cannot be given or discarded by states. The other pillar can be found in the hybrid rule of recognition that I will turn to in a moment. The natural law tradition starts with a widely felt intuition that all human beings have something in common and should have the same basic entitlements to a good life. The tradition is relatively weak in legal theory because of the difficulty of pinpointing which rights are part of this basic package of entitlements and which are not. This last problem makes it also hard to use as a rule of recognition in legal practice. Yet that does not mean that a natural law-like approach is not very influential in the social and political world. I will come to that in the next section.

The third rule of recognition regularly used in international legal practice I will simply call custom. It tries to overcome the limits of the first rule of recognition without getting dragged into the discussion on natural law. In a sense it is a hybrid version of the other two. It accepts another source of international law in either the great practicality of some rules or in the fact that the acts of most states are in accordance with the rule. So there seem to be two basic ideas in this rule of recognition. The first states that international common sense makes certain international legal rules logical and thus valid. It is a pragmatic and watered-down version of a natural law foundation. The second holds that the customs of large groups of states under certain conditions can be understood to be an expression of international legal norms. It deviates from the legal positivist rule of recognition because in its use it holds primary rules of international (public) law to be valid without the active and explicit consent of states.

The role of custom is contested. Especially powerful states see it as an encroachment on their power, weaker states will sometimes see it as rules stemming from an international practice they have difficulty being part of in the first place. International legal scholars recognise custom as a source of law, the judges of the International Court of Justice do, but as Koskenniemi states 'modern legal argument lacks a determinate, coherent concept of custom'.[8] Clear criteria for calling a custom a legal rule are lacking.

The conclusion of this section is that international law should be understood as an arena wherein competing notions of legal validity exist.[9] In the next section we take a closer look at some of these international legal regimes.

8 Martti Koskenniemi, *From Apology to Utopia: The Structure of International Legal Argument* (Cambridge University Press, 2005), 409.

9 An extra complication can be seen in the discussion of so-called 'soft' international law. It is not a real complication because the discussion of soft law is a discussion of the actual effects of certain rules on the behaviour of actors in international law arenas. Soft international law is a highly relevant phenomenon if you look for the existence of rules from an external perspective. Yet rules of recognition are not about the existence of rules but about the validity of rules.

5. Competing non-local (international) normative regimes

In this section I will try to give an answer to my next question: which non-local legal regimes claim validity in humanitarian crises?

The increasing internationalisation and politicisation of humanitarian crises is accompanied by a juridification of these crises. Many different and in some way competing international legal regimes claim to apply in the same situation. Traditionally human rights regimes have claimed influence in all humanitarian crises. New or renewed prominence is gained by the regime of international criminal law and by international humanitarian law.[10]

I will distinguish five different non-local (quasi-)legal regimes and discuss a sixth regime which is a non-local and non-legal normative regime. I discuss as legal regimes: (1) (general) public international law, (2) human rights regimes, (3) the humanitarian law regime, (4) rule of law projects and (5) legal empowerment projects. The sixth regime is (6) the sets of rules brought in by the international public and private organisations that intervene in humanitarian disasters.

5.1 *Public international law*

The legal regime containing the general rules of public international law cannot be discussed in detail here. I will discuss it shortly for the sake of completeness. The importance of this regime is the connection it has to both national legal regimes and the human rights regime. In the legal positivist view public international law validates the state as a bearer of rights and obligations (external sovereignty) and makes the state the undisputed lawmaker on a certain territory (internal sovereignty). In legal positivist views it reduces natural persons (and other legal persons) to subordinates of the state of their nationality and or the state they live/reside in. If we approach public international law from a natural law perspective, public international law is something completely different. In that perspective, present at least since Hugo Grotius, public international law is the regime of universal rules that have reason, and moral content, and are therefore rules we all should follow.

[10] Hans-Joachim Heintze and Andrej Zwitter, *International Law and Humanitarian Assistance. Legal Issues Pertaining to Humanitarianism* (Berlin: Springer, 2011) give a thorough overview of emerging legal regimes in humanitarian assistance situations.

5.2 *Human rights regime(s)*

Of the five non-local legal regimes the human rights regime is for (western) outsiders the most visible. Human rights claim to be universal and relevant in all situations. The regime is special in the sense that it tends to list abstract rights and does not always imply clearly who has to honour these rights (and has the legal obligation to honour them). Most human rights treaties have their own procedural rules, but in general it is not clear what a right-bearer can do if others do not honour the right.

The current power of the human rights discourse is such that all other legal discourses are in one way or another influenced by it. However, the human rights discourse is not as clear-cut as it seems. We can identify different human rights discourses that compete with each other. From a legal positivist perspective we can look at human rights treaties and conventions and simply check if they 'exist' in a certain area at a certain moment by finding out if the relevant state or states have signed and ratified the human rights treaty. The legal positivist perspective does not support the claim of the universality of human rights and reduces the validity of human rights to recognition of the rights as stated in a treaty by states. The rights that are not in ratified treaties are not valid.

Yet when it comes to human rights, non-positivist approaches seem to prevail. Politicians, NGOs and international lawyers routinely assume there is more to human rights than what is written in treaties and ratified by states. The human rights discourse is felt as a highly desirable discourse from a moral point of view. To state it in simple terms: most people involved in these discussions presume that no sane person can have objections to human rights. This 'feeling' has such a force that discussing human rights without automatically acknowledging this moral basis of human rights is very hard. Although understandable from a moral perspective, this emotional involvement obscures the complex discussion on human rights.

Both the routinely made claim of universality of human rights, as well as the lack of clarity about the selected rights, have given rise to useful and necessary objections. The cultural basis of the subjective individual rights selected as human rights should be considered. The content and logic of human rights have undeniable roots in western culture. Is that a problem? The compatibility of rights with each other is often lacking: which right has priority over others? Are lists of human rights logically coherent? Which people have, and in what way, access to these rights? Or in other words: who can benefit by enforcing human rights claims? The actors in humanitarian crises tend to ignore these questions and formulate their own priorities only loosely related to human rights.

In short, human rights are both powerful and highly problematic. In humanitarian practice some try to solve this problem in a pragmatic way. Human rights are boiled down to a shortlist of the most essential or most elementary (and seen as undisputed) rights. But the reduction of the list does not help to answer the fundamental questions asked about human rights.

5.3 Humanitarian law

Humanitarian law is important because it provides specific rules for humanitarian assistance. Spieker identifies rules for humanitarian assistance in armed conflict and the dispersed regime for non-violent conflict. The first regime (Geneva Convention 1949 and two additional protocols to the Geneva Convention of 1977) was constructed to create legal context for intervention by neutral actors in humanitarian assistance. It is traditional public international law because it focuses on creating rules through treaties and hoping states will act accordingly. It makes room for large international non-governmental organisations (INGOs) like the Red Cross and the Red Crescent to give humanitarian assistance in accordance with their notions of neutrality.

Spieker's discussion[11] of the humanitarian law regime makes clear that legal positivism and natural law approaches compete in answering the questions on what legal rules are valid. A good example is the interpretation of Article 70 paragraph 1 *Additional Protocol I*, as regards the right of a civilian population to receive humanitarian assistance in situations where it is not adequately provided with supplies essential to its survival. The natural law approach gives an extensive interpretation of these rules in the light of humanitarian morality and sees a 'right to receive humanitarian assistance'. The legal positivist approach connects to an interpretation where this right is only valid under the conditions of the receiving state's approval and the absence of refusal for non-arbitrary and practical reasons. The third regime – custom can create international law[12] – appears

[11] Heike Spieker, 'The Right to Give and Receive Humanitarian Assistance', in Heintze and Zwitter, *International Law and Humanitarian Assistance*, 14–15.

[12] Ibid. 16; Jean-Marie Henckaerts, 'Study on Customary International Humanitarian Law: A Contribution to the Understanding and Respect for the Rule of Law in Armed Conflict', *International Review of the Red Cross* 87, No. 857 (2005): 201.

for example in the legal obligation to protect the objects used in humanitarian assistance and to protect relief personnel.[13]

5.4 Rule of law projects

Perhaps 'rule of law projects' does not sound like a proper legal regime at all. Yet rule of law projects can be understood as consisting of meta-rules for proper legal regimes. Rule of law projects thus form quasi-legal regimes in the sense that besides setting out meta-rules for legal orders they are wide open to political steering by the funders and enactors of these projects.

The rule of law is the idea and practice that holds as a key idea that those having the political power can and should be controlled by known, clear, enforceable and enforced rules that outline what those in political power can and cannot do. The rule of law in this simple basic understanding is opposed to the rule of men, that is: the uncontrolled will of the powers that be. Rule of law is an evaluative idea: a certain legal order can be appraised by asking if the order meets the requirements necessary to earn the qualification of rule of law.

There is a lively debate about what should be included in the institutional and ideational set up before a rule of law can be established. Waldron discusses both the sceptical views and the constructive views.[14] Waldron discerns two sceptical views. The first is sceptical of the use the concept of rule of law can have after the content is hollowed out by the opportunistic use of the concept in daily politics. The second is sceptical in the Hobbesian tradition. Those holding this position claim that laws

[13] 'Operational Security Management in Violent Environments', *Good Practice Review* 8 (Revised Edition), Humanitarian Practice Network (London, 2010), 23, shows a good example of a mix of classic sources of international law and customary sources of international law. It states as key conventions, frameworks and resolutions on aid-worker security: *Convention on the Safety of United Nations and Associated Personnel* (1994), President of the Security Council, 'Protection of United Nations Personnel, Associated Personnel and Humanitarian Personnel in Conflict Zones', (S/PRST/2000/4, 9 February 2000); Security Council Resolution S/RES/1502, which condemns all forms of violence against those participating in humanitarian operations and urges states to ensure that crimes against such personnel do not go unpunished (2003), General Assembly Resolution A/RES/59/211 on the safety and security of humanitarian personnel and the protection of UN personnel (2004), and General Assembly *Optional Protocol* 60/123 (2006).

[14] Jeremy Waldron, 'Is the Rule of Law an Essentially Contested Concept (in Florida)?', *Law and Philosophy* 21 (2002): 153–159.

are made and applied by men and therefore the crucial idea of rule of law, that legal rules can rule over men, is untenable.

The constructive views discussed by Waldron try to give requirements for a legal order to count as a rule of law. The idea of formal equality ('equality before the law') is a starting point for a formal approach to the rule of law. This basic requirement is accompanied by requirements for the legal rules produced. Fuller's list of requirements is a good example: laws should be general, publicly promulgated, prospective, intelligible, consistent, practicable, not too frequently changeable and actually congruent with the behaviour of the officials of a regime.[15] The requirement of having an independent judiciary is based on the idea of separation of powers as introduced by Montesquieu.[16]

More substantive concepts of the rule of law include substantive principles. For instance, the idea that legal rules should only be given through democratic law-making. Or: the application of rules in adjudication should be in accordance with values of procedural justice. And: the rule of law cannot be realised without including founding political–legal principles.[17]

In the development debate and in the debate on peace-building rule of law is often presented as a universal good that cannot be missed in a society that wants to rise above strife, corruption and poverty. The message of the importance of rule of law is prominently send out by organisations like the United Nations, the Organisation for Security and Cooperation in Europe (OSCE) and the European Union. Establishing the rule of law is seen as a necessary part of an institutional package that holds a set of indispensable and interlinked institutions. It links representative democracy with an open-market economy and the rule of law, in a specific way. The main accent is put on necessary legal institutions. In that sense a 'formal' idea of what the rule of law is dominates the

[15] Lon L. Fuller, *The Morality of Law*, revised edition (New Haven: Yale University Press, 1969), 39.

[16] Charles de Montesquieu, *The Spirit of Laws*, Book XI, under 6 powerfully states: 'Again, there is no liberty, if the judiciary power be not separated from the legislative and executive. Were it joined with the legislative, the life and liberty of the subject would be exposed to arbitrary control; for the judge would be then the legislator. Were it joined to the executive power, the judge might behave with violence and oppression.' Complete text available at: www.constitution.org/cm/sol-02.htm.

[17] A basic scheme of options in the debate is provided by Brian Z. Tamanaha, 'The Folly of the Social Scientific Concept of Legal Pluralism', *Journal of Law & Society* 20 (1993): 192–217.

practical agenda. There must be a constitution, there must be 'modern' laws, for example a property and contract law that is instrumental for open-market economies, there should be a neutral judiciary, a non-corrupt police force, sufficient prison capacity and so on. Specific attention is given to the separation of powers, with emphasis on the reduction of influence of 'politicians' on public prosecutors, police and especially judges.

The idea that there is a universal set of best institutions (representative democracy, rule of law and a market economy) reflects mainstream liberal political theory, and has of course met with severe criticism. This institutional package can be seen as serving the agenda of the most powerful states pursuing their economic and security interests. There is a widespread dissatisfaction with the effects of these prescriptions on smaller and weaker states. The universal claims of the package do not sound too bad but they obscure the political goals that can be pursued through rule of law projects. These goals do not seem to serve the collective interests of the bulk of the people in the receiving countries.

Part of the problem is that the rule of law programmes in their universalist self-understanding tend to ignore local norms and institutions or treat them as inferior. The local practices are often simply seen as part of the problem and do not fit the one-size-fits-all ideas about the desirable institutional make-up. Rule of law programmes fail because of lack of legitimacy.[18] Yet overriding economic and security concerns seems to leave the western powers impervious to this lesson.

5.5 *Legal empowerment projects*

A more promising practice has gained some momentum: so-called legal empowerment. I understand this to be another quasi-legal regime. It can be seen as part of the reformed neo-liberal programme that has emerged in the last ten years. Yet legal empowerment projects have the potential to go beyond that. I will first describe the idea and practice of legal empowerment and some critiques. Subsequently, I will explain why the concept of legal empowerment can be attractive and in which way a more emancipatory practice of legal empowerment can be envisioned.

[18] A well-documented example of a quite unsuccessful rule of law project is the EULEX mission in Kosovo. See for a critical review of the results of the project: International Crisis Group, *The Rule of Law in Independent Kosovo*, Europe Report No. 204, 2010.

The basic idea of legal empowerment is that people have either an incomplete set of rights, or are not able to enforce their rights when others do not respect them. Legal empowerment can thus be the assignment of additional rights above the subjective (or individual) rights already acknowledged, and always concerns the strengthening of a certain actor to realise their subjective rights in confrontation with others.

A remarkable aspect of the current practices of legal empowerment is that it is focused on certain rights that are deemed important from a specific perspective.[19] A lot of effort and funding is funnelled into beefing up the *economic* rights of certain societal strata. For example the legal position of small businesspeople acting on local markets is enhanced. Or rights to land, often partly defined by local custom and without written registration of title, are modernised so that (small) landowners can use the land in a market-efficient way, for instance making it possible to get loans with the title to the land as security.

Legal empowerment is thus often focused on strengthening legal positions relevant in the economic sphere. They are often tailored to the idea that individuals need to have rights to function conforming to the *homo economicus* the market presumes. This focus is understandable given the fact that legal empowerment is part and parcel of policies of, for example, the United Nations Development Programme (UNDP) and the World Bank. These policies aim to reform the old neo-liberal economic agenda towards a more inclusive market approach.[20]

Yet their policies tend to steer clear of the legal empowerment citizens (could) want vis-à-vis the state. Subjective rights focused on protecting and enhancing the political participation of citizens, thereby giving

[19] The UNDP project Legal Empowerment of the Poor is a strong example of this approach. Madeleine Albright and Hernando De Soto holding the co-chairs of the Commission on the Legal Empowerment of the Poor state: 'The lesson is clear. When democratic rules are ignored and there is no law capable of providing shelter, the people who suffer most are those who can least afford to lose. Creating an infrastructure of laws, rights, enforcement, and adjudication is not an academic project, of interest to political scientists and social engineers. The establishment of such institutions can spell the difference between vulnerability and security, desperation and dignity for hundreds of millions of our fellow human beings.' Madeleine Albright and Hernando De Soto, Commission on the Legal Empowerment of the Poor, *Making the Law Work for Everyone*, vol. I, New York, Commission on Legal Empowerment of the Poor and United Nations Development Programme, 2008, ii, www.unrol.org/files/Making_the_Law_Work_for_Everyone.pdf.

[20] Especially the (new) attention given to access to means for building up a livelihood, for example by working towards secure access to tillable land for the many landless farming families, is heartening.

substance to the idea of democracy, are of essential importance. Legal empowerment should encompass both the economic and the political democratic rights. In addition, subjective rights should be connected to local normative orders. A bottom-up approach of legal empowerment does not start with a fixed package of rights but tries to form the package through the practice of empowerment itself.

5.6 *Non-local, non-legal normative regimes: the regime brought in by humanitarian actors*

There is a sixth regime that brings a separate set of norms to the humanitarian disaster situation. It is different from the regimes described above in the sense that it goes a step further and can be seen as a regime mainly constructed by the acts of the actors on the ground. It does not bring a legal regime in the sense of a more or less coherent set of norms, although many international NGOs will try to use neutrality as a central principle guiding their acts, but they bring in rules by executing power in the actual crisis situation. It consists of the set (or sets) of norms brought in by the concrete acts of the organisations and their employees who appear on the scene to organise the humanitarian aid for those struck by disaster.

Take, for instance, setting up a refugee camp. The humanitarian actors play a huge role in terms of how life will be for refugees. They have the power to do things as they see fit. Through their acts of setting up and running the camp, providing food, water and other goods, providing education, organising supply routes and trying to take care of security interests of different categories of actors, they establish how things will be done in the camp. Through the choices they make they establish a powerful normative regime that regulates for instance the arrangement and use of tents, the distribution of food, the content of the education provided, who will be on the camp council, who they will employ, and many other crucial matters.

Refugees live their lives in the camps in almost total dependence on their benefactors. Although their benefactors have a policy called a 'rights-based approach', it is unclear which rights are meant and how they can be enforced. Verdirame and Harrell-Bond point out that these situations lead to a permanent tension between benefactors and beneficiaries;[21] the

[21] Guglielmo Verdirame and Barbara Harrell-Bond, *Rights in Exile – Janus-faced Humanitarianism* (New York: Berghahn Books, 2005), Chapter 6.

benefactors becoming angry about ungrateful refugees and lack of praise for the difficulties of their work, the refugees often feeling insecure and totally dependent on people who clearly live in a world very different from theirs.

This section leads to the following interim conclusion. It is clear that many international normative regimes can be discerned during protracted crises. These regimes all suffer (but not all in the same way) from a certain inherent vagueness and lack of coherence. Earlier we have seen that these legal and quasi-legal regimes can be understood in different ways depending which criteria for validity are used. This interim conclusion leads to another one: there is no legal regime that is able in a more technical sense to function as a meta-regime. Even if there were a consensus about the moral superiority of one of the regimes – the human rights regime would be the obvious candidate – the regime is not able to coordinate the interplay of the different regimes.

6. Constructing validity of national law

The problem of validity is also an important debate in current legal theory on national law. I have already discussed the emergence of the notion of legal pluralism. The concept of legal pluralism contains a non-traditional notion of validity of legal norms on the national level. Legal pluralism has succeeded, in the academic debate, in seriously undermining the (legal positivist) notion that there is only one source of law on the national level, the state. But undermining this notion is just one step. The second step demands that an alternative notion of legal validity must be found. What can that notion entail?

The debate on legal validity on the national level is closely tied to the debate on legal validity on the international level, mentioned above. There is again, simply put, a legal positivist tradition, a natural law position and a hybrid position to take.

The legal positivist tradition dominates in most countries. The dominant perspective on the national level starts often with the idea that there must be a sovereign power and that its natural location is the state. The rules of recognition are thus based on the dominance of the state. The primary sources are state-related: legal rules are made by the national legislature, and legal precedent is formed by a national judiciary. The centrality of the state and, both in the west and in its former colonies, centuries of state-led legal unification policies, make it hard to take other sources of law seriously. Local custom or indigenous law cannot, or only in a very marginal sense, be(come) law. At best they can be rules that through adoption in the national legislative process can be transformed into 'normal' legal rules.

The natural law position is more open to sources outside the state. It states that important moral rules can be found by rational thought[22] and that these rules are the base of any legal system. Rules that have this inherent universal moral content are by definition part of (any) law. The problems as discussed on the international level reappear on the national level. It is crucial that there is no consensus which moral claims should be grounding the legal order. Thus competing moral claims make it hard to come to a clear view of what national law should look like. An additional problem I just want to mention, but cannot discuss at length, is that the modern natural law theory is rationalist, and rationalism tends to see local traditions as non-rational. On the basis of this assumption of backwardness, customary law is often given no attention at all.

The third hybrid position, which finds a rule of recognition in custom, is perhaps more promising for local and indigenous normative traditions. From the three approaches this one is the least fundamentalist in the sense that not all law is in the end stemming from one source. It does not start with centrality of state sovereignty or with the idea of an infallible ratio, and in that way can accommodate more diverse sources of law. However, in almost all national states custom does not have the prominent position that it has in international law. In most states a legal positivist approach held by the national political and legal elites excludes any notion of non-state sources of law.

7. Competing local normative regimes: national state law versus customary law

Local normative regimes are hard to discern under the extraordinary circumstances of humanitarian crises. I will examine, in a very general way, the legal validity and the practical role of local regimes in humanitarian crises to get an idea of the importance of local normative regimes to actors locally involved. Two regimes clash with each other: national state-made law competes with local customary legal regimes.

Given the importance attached by most politicians and lawyers to national law, the question often asked is often if there can be room for

[22] Natural law can of course also be based on religious convictions. I limit myself to the rationalist tradition in natural law thinking.

other legal regimes vis-à-vis the national legal regime. Most national law regimes in the non-western world are so-called 'legal transplants'. They are in their overall structure variations on the two most important western legal families: common law systems and civil law systems. Most of the national legal regimes worldwide had their basic structure and concepts imposed on them during colonial times and reworked colonial law to a national legal order, or imported whole or part of western legal regimes in periods of modernisation in an attempt to adapt to the emerging global economic order. Still, all national governments or lawmakers reserve the right to be the sovereign and give law as they see fit. In reality most national lawmakers, especially in weak states, struggle with their democratic legitimacy and their lack of resources to create and enforce laws.

Politics in a lot of countries shows that the national legal order is confronted by critique on suppressing or subduing other local (legal or quasi-legal) normative regimes. Political initiatives based for example on religious, cultural or regional identity claim more room for their own norms, either as a rewriting of national legal rules or as a separate sphere which the national legal rules have to condone.[23] If identity groups express their struggle for recognition of their normative systems in terms of the addition or rewriting of national legal rules, the dominant system stays intact because the claims take the form of regular political opposition within the confines of the established political institutions. If the protesting identity groups win, their identity is in some way written into national law. An obvious disadvantage of this strategy is not only that these political struggles can be long and can be lost, but that even if these struggles are won, the translation of custom, for example customary entitlements to land, can dramatically change the content of these entitlements. The local custom in that scenario is to a certain extent lost and modern legal concepts and forms take over. Another strategy can be to claim an autonomous legal space within national law to solve conflicts within one's own group with the help of group norms. This strategy is rarely successful because national majorities often oppose this 'preferential' treatment of certain minorities. When it is successful, often only a limited autonomy in conflicts of minor importance can be established.

Much more difficult is the claim for just keeping or re-establishing an alternative legal order that is *not* in some way submissive and dependent

[23] More radical claims, like claims for regional independence, are not discussed because they try to create a new national sphere wherein the discussed problems often reappear.

on the existing national legal order. The logic of the (sovereignty of the) modern state seems to exclude even the possibility of establishing a normative regime that competes with the national law. The state claims centrality and citizens can only voice their preferences through the power of the state. Traditionally religion is one of the few spheres where state power was, and in some ways is, reluctant to claim its might. Historically speaking this is not surprising, since the modern state appeared in Christian Europe. Religion is an identity that can be built upon for non-state, non-legal regimes, but only the major religions can count on this respect for religion. Non-typical religions (for example animist) and major religions without much local power tend to be ignored or get pushed aside.

Non-state-controlled sources of law seem to have little influence. In the national arena state-made law and precedent rule supreme. The political and legal elites tend to have state-centric world-views and do not easily allow competition by other local norm systems. There seems to be no higher principle that can appease the opposition between national law and local legal orders. They remain in competition.

International actors also recognise the existence of legal pluralism. Human rights approaches are recognised as being in contradiction to local customary law. There is no consensus on handling this problem. Depending on strategic and moral considerations, international actors choose to accept some customary rules to fight others, to fight all customary rules not in accordance with human rights, or to accept the local norms as an addition to the value of diversity and in that way forming part of a human rights approach.[24] Local actors do not seem to play an important role in the choice of policy in this matter.

8. Competing local and international regimes: is there room for both?

In humanitarian crisis situations we encounter cases of complex legal pluralism. A wide range of national and international legal and quasi-legal regimes compete for validity. In this chapter I have shown that there are many different regimes present at the same time and in the same place. They operate through the acts of those who are carriers of

[24] Daniel A. Bell and Joseph H. Carens, 'The Ethical Dilemmas of International Human Rights and Humanitarian NGOs: Reflections on a Dialogue Between Practitioners and Theorists', *Human Rights Quarterly* 26, No. 2 (2004): 303–309.

those regimes. It will be obvious that it is quite hard to discern these rules because of their vagueness and their dependency on the rules of validity that are used by their participants. Yet the regimes are clearly incompatible with each other and they compete because there is no meta-rule that could order the different regimes into one hierarchical and coherent system.

On the international level the diversity in the views on how to establish the validity of international legal rules is a bit disconcerting. There is no clear consensus on what must count as an international legal norm. The different international legal regimes put together do not form a coherent whole. The 'explosion' of international legal norms we have witnessed in the last three decades has only led to more incoherence.

On the national level, the traditional dominance of legal positivist perspectives on the validity of national law still persists. But the increasing interlocking of international and national legal systems, driven by global political and economic forces, and visible in the interventionist legal programmes of rule of law and legal empowerment, will weaken the legal positivist dominance in the validity issue.

Local norms are often disregarded and belittled both from the perspective of international legal discourses and from the perspective of national legal discourse. The first position is fed by the force of the biggest global players and by a preference for, at this moment, a clearly insufficiently elaborated and incoherent human rights discourse, that is intolerant towards other normative regimes. The national legal discourse is clinging to the old ideal of a sovereign state that is even more intolerant towards any competing source of law. Although in today's world even the strongest states have problems in realising this ideal, the idolisation of (the centrality of) the state seems to blind many to the possibility of establishing the validity of legal rules in different ways.

The dominance of the human rights approach over national and local regimes reflects to a great extent the power positions of the actors involved. Because of that we should be suspicious: power relations in complex humanitarian crises can easily be hidden behind big moral claims. Local regimes are present, they have validity for their participants and should be taken seriously. All international and national legal regimes should take into account the identities of the people on the ground and acknowledge the need to somehow accommodate the normative expectations that flow from the identities they have, with a realistic account of what global normative systems like human rights have in store for them.

Legal empowerment could be the banner under which we can proceed to try and integrate normative systems from the bottom up and not from the – international or national – top down. However, before we do that, we have to understand the multiplicity of legal and quasi-legal regimes that act upon us and the extra problems the different approaches to legal validity bring. We are a long way from forming a coherent set of norms that can unite all actors in humanitarian crises. As long as we are in that position we should be careful not to overstate the practical and moral importance of international (quasi-)legal regimes.

PART II

International, regional and domestic responses to contemporary challenges

11

Thou shall not . . . misappropriate humanitarian aid: on European Union humanitarian aid and the fight against corruption

MORTEN BROBERG

1. Introduction

In early 2009, on national Danish television, the then head of The United Nations Children's Fund (UNICEF)'s[1] programme in Somalia explained that whenever UNICEF wanted to bring a truck with food aid to the many starving children in the poverty-stricken country they would have to pay each time the truck was to pass one of the many roadblocks set up by the Somali militia. Typically the cost of bribing the militia to let one truck pass all the roadblocks would total more than €3,300.[2] The UNICEF head emphasised that this extortion by the militia constituted a very considerable problem, but he also made it clear that the alternative to paying the bribes was that thousands of Somali children would starve to death within a short time.

Not only UNICEF has been faced with this dilemma. Other emergency relief organisations, be they international, national or non-governmental organisations (NGOs), regularly have to choose between bribing local militia and custom officers etc. out of their limited funds and thereby being able to help some, or to refuse to bribe which may mean that they will help none.

How to minimise corruption while still being able to respond to the humanitarian imperative, i.e. the obligation of the international community 'to provide humanitarian assistance wherever it is needed', has long

[1] The United Nations Children's Fund (originally United Nations International Children's Emergency Fund).

[2] The information was first provided on Danmarks Radio (Danish Broadcasting Corporation) in February 2009; see 'Dansk FN-chef i Somalia: Vi bestikker de mange militser for at få maden frem: 25.000 kr. pr. lastbil', *U-landsnyt*, 10 February 2009, www.u-landsnyt.dk/nyhed/10-02-09/dansk-fn-chef-i-somalia-vi-bestikker-de-mange-mili.

been one of the fundamental dilemmas facing humanitarian aid practitioners. In the present chapter I consider this dilemma from a legal perspective and do so by examining the European Union's approach to inappropriate use of humanitarian aid funds provided by it. Before embarking on this examination it may be useful to make a few observations on the approach and the terminology I use.

Firstly, corruption may be both internal and external to the emergency relief organisation. Internal corruption is where employees of the organisation themselves seek to gain from the corruption – for example by 'fixing' procurement procedures. External corruption is where external parties, such as the militia in the above example, seek to exploit the emergency relief organisation. There are fundamental differences between the two situations and the way they should be handled. In this chapter the focus will primarily be upon external corruption.[3] Moreover, the examination will concentrate on those stages where the emergency relief organisation controls the emergency relief. This essentially means those situations that may arise up until the humanitarian aid-workers hand over the aid to the beneficiaries; for example where a container with urgently needed medical equipment is 'detained' in a local port . . . and will only be released if the responsible local authorities receive some 'facilitation payment',[4] or the situation where a truck loaded with food aid is not allowed to pass a police checkpoint unless a bribe is paid.

Secondly, the chapter's primary focus will be upon the European Union's regulation of its funding of emergency relief aid via NGOs. Funding via international organisations such as UNICEF will only be touched upon incidentally.

Thirdly, it is useful to establish what 'corruption' means. Whilst no universally accepted definition of 'corruption' exists, the international NGO Transparency International[5] has laid down a widely used one which goes as follows: 'the abuse of entrusted power for private gain'. This is a very wide definition where the corruption can include 'gain' that

[3] A good part of the findings in this chapter apply to both internal and external corruption, however.

[4] Facilitation payments have been defined as 'small payments made to public or other officials in order to expedite or secure activities and actions of a routine nature. Routine nature is here defined as activities and actions that are part of our staff's daily duties and functions', DanChurchAid, Anti-Corruption Policy, p. 4, note 2, www.danchurchaid.org/content/download/77278/642671/version/1/file/AntCorruptPol_Eng_Final_WEB.pdf.

[5] Transparency International is a global civil society organisation whose principal objective is the fight against corruption. See further www.transparency.org/whoweare.

is not limited to financial abuse, but may also include, for example, sexual exploitation. For the purposes of the present chapter the focus will however be upon misappropriation of funds (be it in the form of cash or tangible goods).

Fourthly, this chapter is concerned with humanitarian aid that is administered by the European Commission's Humanitarian Aid and Civil Protection Office (ECHO), whilst it does not (directly) concern aid administered by the individual member states. For ease of reference I will, nevertheless, use the term 'European Union' when referring to ECHO-administered aid; without thereby intending to include also member state-administered aid.

The examination which follows below is made up of four main sections. After this introduction I briefly set the context with regard to European Union humanitarian aid and the circumstances in which this aid is provided (Section 2). Thereafter I provide an outline of the workings of European Union humanitarian aid (Section 3). Next I consider how the European Union approaches corruption in the field of humanitarian aid (Section 4). Finally, I will put forward suggestions for improving the legal regulation of the apparently irreconcilable objectives of both fighting corruption and getting much-needed humanitarian aid to those in need – even where some kind of inappropriate payments are unavoidable – and I will make a comment on how the European Union may improve its fight against what may be termed 'avoidable corruption' (Section 5).

2. Setting the context

In 2011, ECHO[6] – the European Commission's Directorate-General for Humanitarian Aid and Civil Protection – provided assistance to third countries to the amount of approximately €1,154 million.[7] This has firmly placed ECHO amongst the world's largest humanitarian aid donors. As a donor, ECHO conspicuously pursues a principle of zero

[6] ECHO originally stood for European Community Humanitarian Aid Office. In 2004 it became the Directorate-General for Humanitarian Aid before integrating with Civil Protection in 2010. Formally speaking its present name is Directorate-General for Humanitarian Aid and Civil Protection, but in practice references are widely made to 'ECHO' or 'DG ECHO'.

[7] European Commission, 'Report from the Commission to the European Parliament and the Council – Annual Report on the European Union's Humanitarian Aid and Civil Protection Policies and their Implementation in 2011', COM (2012) 489 final, 5.

tolerance when it comes to corruption.[8] In combination these two factors make an examination of the question of corruption in connection with humanitarian aid funded by the European Union particularly relevant. Perhaps some would object that a large number of humanitarian-aid NGOs equally take a zero-tolerance approach to corruption. However, whereas the NGOs working in the field have to accept that they may not be able to prevent all bribes,[9] I would argue that the European Commission differs. Whilst the European Union (ECHO) has representatives (technical advisors) in countries with ECHO-funded projects who approve and monitor these projects, the European Union itself does not carry out the actual activities and for that reason it can sustain a more principled approach against the giving of bribes etc.

ECHO's humanitarian aid is provided in crisis situations, be they the outcome of natural disasters, of disasters caused by human activity, or of structural crises,[10] and the aid is primarily aimed at people in developing countries.[11] Hence humanitarian-aid practitioners working on ECHO-funded projects may have to distribute emergency relief as a matter of urgency in what may be a chaotic crisis situation in countries or regions where police, local government and other public institutions are frequently weak or even non-existent.[12] This means that the setting in

[8] See for example the commissioner for development and humanitarian aid, Louis Michel, 'Post-tsunami Relief Effort: the Commission's Humanitarian Response and the Need for Sound Aid Management', Speech/05/177, Brussels 15 March 2005, who refers to the 'policy of zero tolerance for fraud' – albeit he also acknowledges that zero risk, as such, does not exist. The speech is available, inter alia, at reliefweb.int/node/168620. See also ECHO's 'Humanitarian Aid: Frequently Asked Questions', MEMO/07/238, Brussels 13 June 2007 (question 7), available at europa.eu/rapid/press-release_MEMO-07-238_en.htm; and ECHO's finances available at ec.europa.eu/echo/funding/finances_en.htm.

[9] See Bond for International Development, 'Anti-Bribery Principles and Guidance for NGOs – June 2011', 15, www.mango.org.uk/Pool/NGO-Anti-bribery-Principles-and-Guidance-Final.pdf, where it is expressly observed that 'NGOs with a zero-tolerance approach may not be able to prevent all bribes'.

[10] See Council of the European Union, Council Regulation (EC) No. 1257/96 of 20 June 1996 concerning humanitarian aid, OJ L163/1, Article 1. The Regulation has undergone two subsequent amendments. A consolidated version of the Regulation is available at eur-lex.europa.eu/LexUriServ/LexUriServ.do?uri=CONSLEG:1996R1257:20090420:EN:PDF.

[11] Regulation 1257/96, Article 1.

[12] Or, as EU institutions and EU member states have put it: humanitarian aid is often provided in a 'complex political and security contexts', see Council of the European Union, 'Joint Statement by the Council, and the Representatives of the Governments of the Member States meeting within the Council, the European Parliament and the

which humanitarian aid is distributed frequently provides fertile ground for inappropriate use of the funds.[13] Indeed, a study on corruption in connection with the provision of humanitarian aid has found that '[c]orruption was generally perceived as an unavoidable part of the emergency environment and the prevention of corruption was often considered as just another routine part of doing business'.[14] Others have held that humanitarian aid in particular has been characterised by '[l]ax donor control and follow up' thereby in itself increasing opportunities for corruption.[15]

That corruption almost appears to be an integral part of humanitarian aid may also be linked to the fact that the provision of such aid lays open a considerable number of situations where corruption may arise. Thus in order to effectively combat corruption in connection with humanitarian aid, Pete Ewins et al. have carried out a study to map out those instances

European Commission' (European Consensus on Humanitarian Aid) 2008, OJ C25/1, §10. See also D. Maxwell, P. Walker, C. Church, P. Harvey, K. Savage, S. Bailey, R. Hees and M.-L. Ahlendorf, 'Preventing Corruption in Humanitarian Assistance – Final Research Report', *Transparency International* (Berlin 2008), 8–10, http://transparency.dk/wp-content/uploads/2011/06/Preventing_Corruption_in_Humanitarian_Assistance_Report_July_2008.pdf.

13 Cf. D. Maxwell et al., 'Preventing Corruption in Humanitarian Assistance', 7; and Transparency International, 'Preventing Corruption in Humanitarian Operations – Handbook of Good Practice', X. Indeed, sometimes widespread corruption in a country or region constitutes one of the root causes for a conflict which has necessitated the provision of humanitarian aid, cf. Philippe Le Billon, 'The Political Economy of War: What Relief Agencies Need to Know', *HPN Network Paper* 33 (2000): 11, Overseas Development Institute, available at www.odihpn.org/documents/networkpaper033.pdf; and with particular regard to the conflict in Liberia, Kevin Savage with Mulbah S. Jackollie, D. Maxim Kumeh and Edwin Dorbor, 'Corruption Perceptions and Risks in Humanitarian Assistance: a Liberia case study', *HPG Background Paper* (2007): 11, available at www.odi.org.uk/resources/download/287.pdf.

14 Cf. D. Maxwell et al., 'Preventing Corruption in Humanitarian Assistance', 7. These authors go on to note that '[t]here were also interesting exceptions to this general picture with some agencies at both headquarters and field level according to the issue greater priority'. See also Corinna Kreidler, 'Corruption as an internal problem for emergency operations', *The Journal of Humanitarian Assistance* (July 2006), http://sites.tufts.edu/jha/files/2011/04/a190.pdf, who observes that 'aid practitioners easily agree that [corruption] is a widespread phenomenon which is part and parcel of aid operations in a large number of countries, affecting a large number of organisations active in all the different sectors of aid'.

15 Ivar Kolstad, Verena Frit and Tam O'Neil, 'Corruption, Anti-corruption Efforts and Aid: Do Donors Have the Right Approach?', *Working Paper* 3 (January 2008): 62, available at www.odi.org.uk/resources/download/1525.pdf.

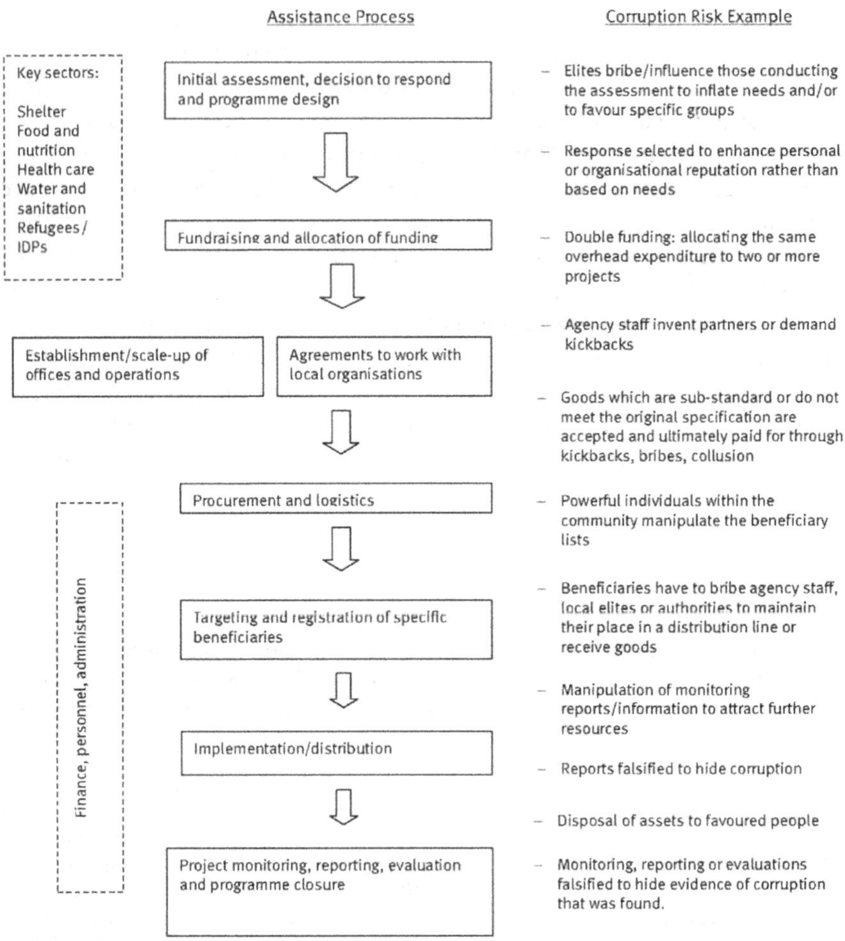

Figure 11.1: Map of corruption risk in humanitarian assistance (taken from Ewin et al. 2006.)

where the corruption may arise.[16] Their findings, which are summed up in Figure 11.1, convincingly illustrate the very considerable number of situations where corruption may occur as part of humanitarian aid provision.

16 Pete Ewins, Paul Harvey, Kevin Savage and Alex Jacobs, 'Mapping the Risks of Corruption in Humanitarian Action', *Overseas Development Institute* (July 2006), www.odi.org.uk/resources/download/607.pdf.

It may be noted that arguably, Figure 11.1 reflects a 'one-off' humanitarian situation. In practice humanitarian situations are often long-running or regularly recurring, however, which means that both the corruptee and the corruptor may change their 'strategy'. For instance, a local partner organisation may be trained in how to prevent corruption (for instance, in connection with procurement or with the logistics) and the European NGO (administering the aid) may be able to establish efficient monitoring systems (thereby for example minimising the risk of double funding). Moreover, not only is the likelihood of being caught in connection with corruption higher in cases of long-running or recurring humanitarian situations, but also the consequences for a local partner who is caught, such as being banned as a local partner, are much graver if otherwise they could have expected to receive renewed contracts in the years to come. In other words, Figure 11.1 may have to be adapted according to the type of humanitarian situation.

By definition, inappropriate use of humanitarian aid adversely affects the fulfilment of the objective which the humanitarian aid is intended to achieve,[17] and arguably infringes the basic humanitarian 'do no harm' principle[18] that must govern all humanitarian aid provision.[19] When considering humanitarian aid funded by the European Union, the EU's above-mentioned principle of zero tolerance when it comes to corruption must also be taken into account. A strict pursuance of a zero tolerance principle – i.e. where 'zero' really means 'zero' – would bar the European Union from providing humanitarian aid in some of the gravest emergency situations. Nevertheless, in these situations the European Union is also an important donor, thereby giving testimony to the fact that in one way or the other the European Union must necessarily take a more pragmatic approach to its zero-tolerance principle. In other words, there appears to be a discrepancy between, on the one hand, the European

[17] For a similar view, see Transparency International, 'Handbook of Good Practices: Preventing Corruption in Humanitarian Operations', 31 January 2010, www.transparency.org/whatwedo/pub/handbook_of_good_practices_preventing_corruption_in_humanitarian_operations, as well as Maxwell et al., 'Preventing Corruption in Humanitarian Assistance', who at pp. 9–10 rightly observe that '[t]he costs of corruption in humanitarian assistance can mean lives lost, not just loss of profits or lower growth'.

[18] Cf. Transparency International, 'In the Wake of Disaster: Preventing Corruption in Tsunami Relief and Reconstruction', *In Focus* 2005, available at http://archive.transparency.org/news_room/in_focus/2005/tsunami.

[19] See European Consensus on Humanitarian Aid, §42.

Union's hard-spoken legal discourse on corruption and on the other hand, the approach taken to what in practice happens 'on the ground'.

3. Workings of European Union humanitarian aid

We find the legal basis of the European Union's provision of humanitarian aid in Regulation 1257/96 of 20 June 1996 concerning humanitarian aid. The regulation lays down the objectives and general principles of humanitarian aid, and thereby establishes the framework within which all the European Union's humanitarian aid must be provided.

In practice the European Commission (DG ECHO) provides financing and is responsible for coordinating the action, whilst when it comes to the actual implementation of the aid, the Commission relies on the assistance from international agencies and organisations[20] as well as from about two hundred primarily European Union-based NGOs. Indeed, the European NGOs will frequently subcontract the actual work on the ground to local NGOs of the countries where the aid is to be provided.[21]

For a European NGO to become eligible to receive European Union financing, it must first pass an evaluation based on a number of criteria.[22] Several of these criteria will also have a bearing on the NGO's ability to prevent corruption from occurring – or on handling corruption if nevertheless it does occur. For instance, the European Union will consider the NGO's administrative and financial management capacities, its previous experience in the field of humanitarian aid, the results of previous operations carried out by the NGO, and in particular those financed by the European Union, the NGO's impartiality in the implementation of humanitarian aid, and the NGO's previous experience (if any) in the third country involved in the humanitarian operation concerned. Having a track record of inappropriate handling of cases of corruption, and/or

[20] Inter alia, the International Committee of the Red Cross and UN agencies like UNHCR and WFP.

[21] This has been explicitly recognised in the DG ECHO Framework Partnership Agreement (FPA), Annex III, Article 1.2. These local NGOs are referred to as 'implementing partners' and 'contractors'.

[22] The Humanitarian Aid Regulation does not require the UN and similar international agencies to undergo the same examination in order to be eligible for financing. Moreover, whilst the European Union's relationship with the NGOs in respect of humanitarian aid is governed by the FPA, the European Union's relationship with the UN and similar international agencies in the field of humanitarian aid is governed by the Financial and Administrative Framework Agreement (FAFA).

not having adequate resources to handle such cases, will not exactly be conducive for the Commission's admission of an NGO to the list of organisations which may be funded to carry out specific humanitarian aid tasks.[23]

If, following an examination of an NGO that has applied for being added to the list, the Commission finds the NGO to be eligible and capable, it will be offered the possibility of entering into a so-called 'Framework Partnership Agreement' or FPA.[24] The FPA establishes the role, rights and obligations of the Commission and the NGO (the partners) and the legal provisions that apply to European Union-funded humanitarian aid operations.[25] The FPA's great advantage is that it enables the Commission and the NGOs to speed up the procedure when an emergency situation arises, thereby ensuring quick, effective and efficient aid. The signing of an FPA is therefore, in principle, a precondition for making financial grants in support of specific humanitarian operations. However, as is apparent from the name, it is merely a framework agreement, not a financing agreement. The financing as such is regulated in separate agreements that are referred to as 'contribution agreements'.

The FPA enables the Commission to monitor and control the NGOs' activities. This is done, firstly, through monitoring of the implementation of actions, through in-depth checks of the final report and through *ex post* audits of actions.[26] Secondly, it is based on *ex ante* evaluation of internal control procedures, risk management and the award of contracts by the NGOs, as well as on *ex post* audits of the implementation of their rules and procedures.[27] In addition, the Commission periodically assesses the NGOs which are party to FPAs using a two-stage procedure. The first stage, which is carried out annually and is compulsory for all NGOs, aims to verify the eligibility and aptitude criteria. In this context, the

[23] In this regard, see also ECHO Commission paper, 'Control Mechanism Applicable to Partners', available at http://ec.europa.eu/echo/files/partners/humanitarian_aid/fpa/A_or_P_assessment_en.pdf.

[24] FPA with humanitarian organisations (2008–2012) – extended until 31 December 2013 (cf. Article 21 of the FPA) available at http://ec.europa.eu/echo/partners/humanitarian_aid/fpa_en.htm.

[25] The present presentation of the FPA draws on the Commission's summary of EU legislation with regard to these Agreements, accessible at http://europa.eu/legislation_summaries/humanitarian_aid/r10007_en.htm.

[26] Referred to as 'mechanism A', cf., 3 in Annex IV to the FPA.

[27] Referred to as 'mechanism P', cf., 2 in Annex IV to the FPA.

Commission is to receive a copy of the annual accounts, an external audit report and a copy of the annual activity report for the previous financial year, as well as any additional documentation considered relevant.[28] The second stage consists of an in-depth evaluation, which is to be performed at least once every three years.[29]

Following the annual evaluation, the Commission essentially has three options: Depending on the outcome of the evaluation the Commission can either *confirm* its partnership with the NGO in question, or *suspend* the FPA, or *terminate* the FPA by giving prior notice. In the event of non-compliance with the criteria, the Commission may suspend the partnership with 45 days' written notice. If the FPA is suspended, the NGO is no longer eligible for new financing during the suspension period. It may however see its active status restored if it can show once again that it meets the aptitude criteria. Where there are grounds for suspecting an infringement of the contractual obligations by the NGO, the Commission may suspend the FPA with immediate effect. After one year's suspension, the partnership agreement will be terminated. Other cases of termination result from non-compliance with the eligibility requirements set out above, breach of the values, principles or objectives of the FPA and cases of substantial irregularity which may cause (or have caused) loss to the European Union's budget. Here too, 45 days' written notice must be given.

4. The European Union's approach to corruption – in the field of humanitarian aid

As has been pointed out above, in many places where humanitarian aid is to be distributed it will often be practically impossible to completely avoid some corruption from taking place. At the same time the European Union pursues a principle of zero tolerance towards corruption. Therefore, as is observed in Section 2 above, it may seem somewhat surprising that the European Union is also a major donor of humanitarian aid in places where corruption in reality is unavoidable. We shall examine this situation of apparent incompatibility in what follows.

Under both European Union law and international humanitarian law, the European Union must ensure that its humanitarian aid is provided in a way that enhances recovery; and recovery is difficult to attain if the aid

[28] Cf. Article 12.1 of the FPA. [29] Cf. Article 12.1 of the FPA.

ends up in the wrong pockets.[30] The logical inference will seem to be that to some extent, the European Union is under a legal obligation to combat corruption relating to its humanitarian aid. In this respect the important question is, how far the European Union should go to achieve this end – and in particular whether it would go too far if the European Union were to firmly enforce its zero-tolerance principle with regard to corruption?[31]

The FPA, together with its annexes, lays down specific rules on the implementing parties' reporting to the European Commission. Moreover, specific rules are also laid down regarding European Commission (as well as the Court of Auditors and European Anti-Fraud Office, or OLAF) controls and audits of the implementing parties as well as possible reactions where irregularities are discovered.

By way of illustration, Annex II (General conditions 2013) to the FPA in Article 4.1 requires that typically three months 'before the end of the implementation period of the Action . . . the Humanitarian Organisation shall submit a[n] Intermediate report on the Action's implementation, covering the implementation up to one month before the reporting date'.[32] And in Article 4.2 the same Annex lays down that '[t]he Humanitarian Organisation shall submit the Final narrative and financial reports within three months after the end of the implementation period of the Action'.

In Annex III, Article 23 empowers the Commission – as well as the Court of Auditors and OLAF – to gain access 'to any location where the Action is implemented and to all documents and information, including information in electronic format, necessary to assess, or audit the implementation of the Action and the Grant Agreement'. The same provision empowers the Commission – or any other organisation mandated by the Commission – to 'audit the Humanitarian Organisation's use made of the European Union contribution. Such audits may be initiated during

30 Cf. European Consensus on Humanitarian Aid, §43 and 46 as well as §94.

31 In legal terms: whether the European Union enforces its zero-tolerance principle with regards to corruption to such extent that it 'disproportionately' harms those in need of humanitarian aid.

32 'Humanitarian Organisation' has been defined in Annex IV to the FPA in the following way: 'The term Humanitarian Organisation refers to non-profit-making autonomous organisations eligible for European Union financing for the implementation of Actions under the Humanitarian Aid Regulation. It refers to National Societies of the Red Cross and Non-Governmental Organisations signatories of the Framework Partnership Agreement, hereafter FPA' (emphasis in original has not been reproduced).

the implementation of the Grant Agreement until four years after Final payment of the Grant Agreement.'[33]

Annex III, Article 23 moreover obliges the Humanitarian Organisation to 'ensure that all the relevant information is available to ensure at all times a sufficiently detailed audit trail' and this provision also requires that the relevant documentation is kept for a period of five years after the end of the action.

Whilst the FPA fairly comprehensively regulates how to ensure that no misappropriation takes place, it is almost silent when it comes to the consequences of the Commission (or other European Union body) finding that there is a situation of misappropriation of Union funds. However, section 16.3, letter g, of Annex III to the FPA provides that the Commission may terminate a grant agreement with immediate effect 'if the Humanitarian Organisation has been the subject of a judgment or administrative decision which has the force of *res judicata* for fraud, corruption, involvement in a criminal organisation or any other illegal activity detrimental to the European Union's financial interests'. Article 16.3 goes on to state that '[t]he grounds for termination by the Commission with immediate effect . . . also apply, *mutatis mutandis*, to actions committed by the implementing partners, contractors or staff of the Humanitarian Organisation to the extent that they are related to the implementation of the Action'. Hence, the 'sanction' referred to in Article 16.3 is the immediate termination of a grant agreement; this does not appear to imply a penal element.

The above obviously merely provides a limited number of examples. Nevertheless, these few examples show that whilst the FPA identifies a number of situations as unacceptable misappropriation, the Commission only has the power to impose immediate sanctions with regard to a part of these situations. I would argue, firstly, that by drafting the FPA in this way it has rather clearly been laid down that, as a matter of principle, misappropriation of European Union funds for humanitarian aid is not accepted. But secondly, the Agreement equally makes it clear that immediate sanctions will only be imposed if such misappropriation has been made in the inappropriate interest of the implementing party – or of someone representing that party; for instance in the form of embezzlement to the benefit of the implementing party. It is submitted that hereby the FPA operates an important and well-founded distinction whereby

[33] Note that the provision only empowers the European Commission to audit the use made of 'the European Union contribution'.

the sanctioning depends on the party in whose interest the misappropriation is made.

Hence, where the misappropriation is made to the benefit of a humanitarian organisation (or an implementing partner or contractor) the European Union is prepared to react swiftly and firmly. In contrast, if the misappropriation is not made to the benefit of these parties, the reaction appears to be less categorical. Whilst this difference in approach does not mean that the European Union accepts the latter kind of misappropriation, it nevertheless seems safe to conclude that the European Union does not consider all types of misappropriation to be equally unacceptable. In this regard we may recall the statement by the then head of UNICEF's programme in Somalia, set out in the very beginning of the present chapter, where he explained that UNICEF was paying bribes since this was the only way of enabling their trucks to pass a large number of roadblocks so that the emergency relief could get to those in need. Where an implementing partner is faced with this kind of extortion the above approach does not seem to allow the European Commission to introduce immediate sanctions under the FPA.[34]

Still, formally speaking the European Union does not accept misappropriation, such as the payment of bribes. Where an NGO or other humanitarian organisation has found it necessary to pay such bribes in connection with the provision of European Union-funded humanitarian aid, the organisation will therefore have to find a way of 'getting round' this when preparing the accounting reports.

It seems that an obvious solution whereby an NGO providing humanitarian aid funded by the European Union can comply with the European Union's formality requirements, whilst not being completely barred from paying bribes where this is unavoidable, is to hire an intermediary to carry out the tasks that are most clearly associated with the bribing. For instance where some aid has arrived in a port and where the customs clearance will be unduly slow unless the NGO bribes the customs officers, the NGO may simply hire an intermediary to bring the aid through the customs clearance. The NGO may not know whether any bribe is being paid, and the NGO will be able to produce fully valid receipts for the work carried out by the intermediary.[35] Another obvious solution is to

[34] In order to avoid misunderstandings it may be noted that UNICEF is not covered by the FPA, but by the FAFA signed by ECHO and a number of UN bodies and agencies. See further http://ec.europa.eu/echo/partners/humanitarian_aid/fafa_en.htm.

pay 'a duty' and to receive a receipt for this payment. A third solution will be to pay the bribes out of funds that either do not come from the European Union or which are non-accountable to the European Union. Since the European Union is primarily concerned with the use of its own funds, and since the European Union's reporting requirements only concern Union funds, the NGO will not have to show that it has had to pay facilitation payments (i.e. to bribe)[36] when it submits its report to the European Commission. Moreover, 7 per cent of the financing provided by ECHO on any given project is dedicated to administration on the project in question (overhead costs). This means that it is not as such specifically accountable, meaning that the NGO is not required to produce documentation for this 7 per cent.[37] Hence, even if the NGO cannot draw on non-European Union funding when paying the bribes, it is still possible to pay these out of the European Union funding – within the 7 per cent dedicated to administration. However, every time one euro of 7 per cent non-accountable overhead funding is spent on corruption, the NGO will have one euro less to cover its administrative costs – thus creating a new problem.

The above 'solutions' do not mean that the NGOs can simply spend all the emergency funding as they please, but it does mean that it is possible to avoid having to account for more limited 'facilitation payments'.

Essentially the problem here is that whilst misappropriation is never good, in the case of humanitarian aid paying a bribe may be the 'lesser evil'. This means that some kinds of misappropriation may be deemed acceptable out of *jus necessitates* considerations.[38] It must be acknowledged, however, that from a legal point of view this creates a grey area between what is lawful and what is unlawful that may prove difficult to handle.

5. Suggestions for a better legal framework

Above I have argued that in practice it will frequently be impossible to provide humanitarian aid without accepting a certain level of corruption. At the same time the European Union applies a zero-tolerance principle

[35] Indeed, it appears that this 'solution' is frequently used by embassies representing governments pursuing a zero-tolerance approach to corruption.

[36] See DanChurchAid, Anti-Corruption Policy.

[37] This is not to say that the NGO shall not obtain the necessary documentation for all costs – including facilitation payments. But it means that the NGO will not have to produce this documentation to ECHO.

[38] At times the 'request' for bribes may be 'supported' by threats against the aid personnel – thereby underlining the *jus necessitates* aspect of the situation.

towards corruption – and, to a considerable extent, this is reflected in the legal regulation of the European Union's funding of humanitarian aid.

The consequence is that the NGOs and other humanitarian organisations working in the field to help those in need may find themselves trapped between the devil and the deep blue sea: on the one hand it may only prove to be possible to get the humanitarian aid to those in need through the use of bribes. On the other hand the humanitarian organisations may face sanctions by the European Union if they decide to use bribery. Today the solution is to find loopholes whereby it is possible to get the humanitarian aid to those in need without having to show this in the reports to the European Union. I believe that it would be better if the European Union established clear guidelines for how the humanitarian organisations may use bribes and required these organisations to be transparent about their use of funds to this end. Changing the European Union's approach in this way may not affect the way that humanitarian aid-workers act in the field – they are likely to continue to use bribes where this is the only solution or where the costs of not bribing will be disproportionate. But it will mean that what today may best be described as a 'legal void' will be replaced by a fair level of legal certainty. Requiring transparency with respect to the use of bribes entails the risk that support for humanitarian aid amongst the European public will wane.[39] On the other hand, the more transparency there is surrounding the matter, the easier it will be to map out when corruption occurs and the easier it may therefore be to find ways of countering this corruption.

To the extent that the European Union is going to 'accept' certain types of corruption, it is important to draw a fundamental distinction. Paying corruption money is only acceptable where it appreciably furthers the provision of humanitarian aid. In contrast, it will be completely unacceptable where for example the misappropriation benefits the humanitarian organisation itself or benefits one or more of those working

[39] Cf. Maxwell et al., 'Preventing Corruption in Humanitarian Assistance', 4, and Transparency International, 'Preventing Corruption in Humanitarian Operations – Handbook of Good Practice', XII. Of course there may also be a number of other reasons why humanitarian organisations may not want to openly address questions of possible corruption: see C. Kreidler, 'Risking embezzlement', *D+C – Magazine for Development and Cooperation*, December 2006, available at www3.gi.de/E+/content/archive-eng/12-2006/tribune_art2.html.

for that organisation (be it employees or representatives). In other words, I am of the view that whether the European Union should accept the payment of bribes (and so on) in certain cases must depend upon whether such payments genuinely are made in order to further the provision of humanitarian aid or not.

If the European Union were to formally accept the use of bribes in cases that qualify as *jus necessitates*, then clear guidelines would be needed so as to unequivocally delimit this category of situations from those situations where the use of bribes is unacceptable. Moreover, it would seem advisable that in order for the European Union to enter into an FPA with an NGO, the latter should not only have in place effective control and reporting systems,[40] but also an adequate and well-functioning anti-corruption programme so as to enable fieldworkers to competently handle cases of corruption.[41] In this regard it is important not merely to focus on the procedures as such, but also on the implementation thereof at field level.[42]

Today a number of standard procedures have been established at the international level, which may aid the NGOs in setting up their own procedures.[43] The primary objective of these procedures is to avoid any bribe being paid, and to provide guidance on how to follow up on the situation in order to avoid or prepare for new similar incidents. Situations may however arise where it is not possible to refuse to pay a bribe – this will particularly be the case where refusal to pay the bribe will mean that the humanitarian organisation is prevented from providing life-saving relief to people in acute need or where the refusal may lead to direct threats against the NGO staff. In these cases the NGO should be allowed to pay the bribe by following a predetermined procedure.

[40] The European Union already today requires the humanitarian organisations to establish effective control and reporting systems: see FPA Article 11 and Annex III (2013) Article 23.

[41] Such guidelines have already been established by various humanitarian organisations. Specific recommendations for how to combat corruption in humanitarian aid may inter alia be found in Maxwell et al., 27–31.

[42] See Maxwell et al., 'Preventing Corruption in Humanitarian Assistance', 27.

[43] See, for instance, Transparency International, 'Resist – Resisting Extortion and Solicitation in International Transactions', International Chamber of Commerce, United Nations Global Compact, *World Economic Forum*, 2011, available at www.transparency.org/content/download/43250/690884/file/RESIST_09-05-09.pdf.

Example

Some transnational corporations require that where their staff are required to pay a bribe as part of their activities they must follow the following basic steps. First they must attempt to refuse to pay and they must make it clear that if the other party insists the corporation's staff will be obligated to inform their superior, which will mean that 'our boss will bring this matter up with your boss'. If the other party still insists, the corporation's staff must balance the consequences of refusing to pay (and thus not receiving the service in question) against the negative consequences of paying the bribe (whilst receiving the service in question). If the staff find that they must accept paying a bribe, they should ask for a receipt as documentation for the payment. This request is likely to be turned down, however. If the staff find that they will have to pay the bribe and that no receipt will be provided, they must themselves, as far as possible, establish the necessary documentation. Moreover, the incident must be reported back to the corporation's management and must be evaluated so as to consider whether similar situations may be avoided in the future.[44]

Finally, turning to the question of how the European Union should react to cases of corruption which cannot be accepted, I must note that to my mind, the European Union's present contractual framework with regard to humanitarian aid does not appear to adequately address corruption by humanitarian organisations, where this corruption is made to the benefit of the organisation or of the employees or representatives thereof. Therefore, in my opinion more effective measures for preventing this kind of corruption should be considered.

Through a fairly simple 'decision tree' and an 'equation', Robert Klitgaard has attempted to identify the factors that are decisive for whether a person becomes corrupt or not (see Figure 11.2).

According to Robert Klitgaard's equation, amongst the various factors in the equation, the ones which the European Union have a real possibility of influencing in order to more effectively combat corruption are (1) the likelihood of the culprit being caught, meaning well-educated staff and efficient control systems, and (2) the sanction imposed on the culprit if so caught.[45]

[44] See also Transparency International, 'Handbook of Good Practices: Preventing Corruption in Humanitarian Operations', providing instructions for how to handle various situations of corruptions; for instance payment for access to aid resources or beneficiaries, 75–76.

[45] The importance of effective sanctions has also been pointed out by Kreidler, 'Corruption as an Internal Problem for Emergency Operations'.

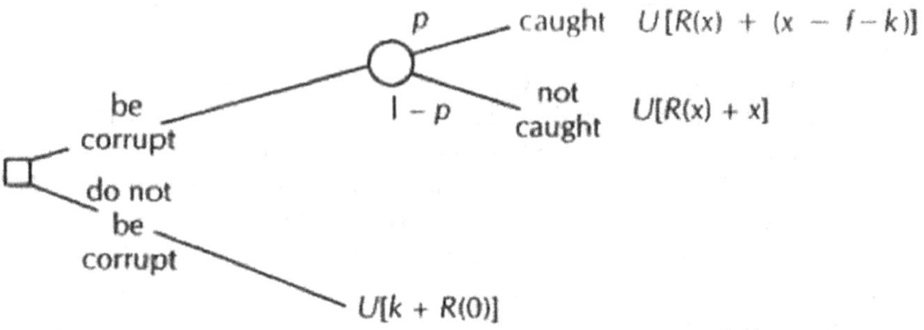

Figure 11.2: Decision tree for the potentially corrupt agent (identifying the factors that in practice can be influenced from the outside). Taken from Klitgaard (1988), 71.

It appears that today the European Union's principal sanctioning mechanism is to declare certain costs within a financial report as 'non-eligible' and (much less frequently) to discontinue the cooperation with a humanitarian organisation that has engaged in misappropriation of European Union funding. I believe that much firmer sanctions should be applied in cases of misappropriation of humanitarian aid. Of course, if the European Union were to follow the above recommendation of formally accepting that humanitarian organisations engage in bribing in cases of *jus necessitas*, these cases should not be sanctioned. On the other hand, where misappropriation goes beyond these limits it is submitted that effective and discouraging sanctions should be applicable. In practice this may mean that where the humanitarian organisation itself does not impose sanctions that are a sufficient deterrent, the European Union should have the power to impose such sanctions. This essentially means that the European Union will have to find ways of introducing what in practice will qualify as (obligatory) penal sanctions directly aimed at the persons who engage in such misappropriation (and who may benefit therefrom).[46] Perhaps one way of introducing such sanctions is through the FPA, so that by signing such an agreement the humanitarian organisations and the individuals working for them submit to a specific

[46] Note, however, that it must first be considered to what extent the European Union possesses the competence to do this.

contractual sanctioning system, which enables the European Union to impose such sanctions.[47]

Edelt er mennesket,
jorden er rik!
Finnes her nød og sult[48]
skyldes det svik.

[47] In this regard it may be observed that the FPA Contract in Annex IV, Article 5.3 explicitly refers to 'contractual and regulatory sanctions' (although it is difficult to see that the provision encompasses 'contractual sanctions'). It is also worthy of note that Transparency International has put forward a somewhat similar suggestion, albeit restricted to only cases of public procurement, where the organisation suggests that '[p]ublic contracts should contain an explicit anit-corruption clause embodying effective sanctions for breach'; see Transparency International, 'In the wake of disaster: Preventing corruption in tsunami relief and reconstruction', *In Focus*, 2005, available at http://archive.transparency.org/news_room/in_focus/2005/tsunami.

[48] Verse from Norwegian poem, 'Til Ungdommen' ('For the Youth'), by Nordahl Grieg. Essentially, the text states that the earth is so rich that if anyone is suffering or starving, this can only be due to deceit by others. In the English translation available on Wikipedia, the text goes as follows: 'Noble is everyone, earth, rich and sweet! Hunger and suffering, caused by deceit.'

12

Developments in African disaster law: a view from the field

SANNE BOSWIJK

1. Introduction

In the exceptional situation of a natural or man-made disaster, laws and regulations designed for day-to-day use do not always suffice. On 13 March 2011, two days after the Tōhoku earthquake and tsunami hit the east of Japan, the American Broadcasting Cooperation reported that Japan's customs regulations on importing animals inadvertently delayed a Swiss search-and-rescue team from getting their rescue dogs through customs.[1] While the death toll in Japan grew rapidly, these rescue dogs, trained in locating disaster victims lying under the rubble of collapsed buildings, remained waiting for hours in Japan's customs area. In normal circumstances, importing animals into a highly regulated country like Japan (or the United Kingdom, or Switzerland, for that matter) could take up to three months. From that perspective, the response of the Japanese authorities should be praised. In that same year, a stubborn drought persisted in the Horn of Africa, driving millions of people to the brink of famine. The international community soon responded, but Al Jazeera reported that the United Nations flights deployed to airlift food aid into Ethiopia, Kenya and Somalia had been delayed 'after a wait for clearance permission in Nairobi, Kenya, where the mission is being flown from, did not come on time'.[2]

These examples are a few of many that illustrate how laws and regulations can have a serious impact on emergency operations, and in extreme cases may even cost lives. They also demonstrate that a law or regulation that is designed for day-to-day implementation cannot simply

[1] 'Foreign Rescue Team Delayed By Japanese Bureaucracy', *ABC News*, accessed on 1 April 2013, http://abcnews.go.com/International/japanese-bureaucracy-delays-foreign-search-rescueteams/story?Id=13126904#.UWg2Sb9pu2w.

[2] 'Red tape delays Africa aid airlift', *Al Jazeera*, last modified on 27 July 2011, www.aljazeera.com/news/africa/2011/07/2011727161975756l.html.

be applied without negative consequences during a situation of emergency. Legal preparation for disasters that require international support is of the essence for an efficient and effective delivery of assistance to those affected. Especially in an age when we see more and larger-scale disasters, some of them televised in real time, with many different humanitarian responders, it is much more challenging for governments of affected states to efficiently facilitate and effectively regulate the influx of disaster response activities on their territory. Lack of legal and regulatory preparedness for international disaster response tends to result in barriers to said response. Delays and costs may emerge relating to questions of the authorisation of initiation of disaster response, visas for disaster personnel, customs clearance of relief items and equipment, taxation on the import of humanitarian items or operations, issuance of work permits and recognition of professional qualifications and matters relating to lack of legal personality of the responding entity.[3] On the other hand, lack of preparedness can leave the affected state with a lack of oversight and control over foreign entities operating on their territory and, consequently, over the quality of the relief items and type of support these entities are providing to the affected population. The net result of legal and regulatory barriers is that humanitarian assistance reaches the affected population more slowly, and is more expensive and less effective.

The phenomenon of legal and regulatory barriers to humanitarian response operations is universal, and in no way limited to less developed countries. In addition, legal and regulatory bottlenecks are just as prone to occur in highly regulated systems as in under-regulated ones. Delays in delivery of time-sensitive emergency assistance were experienced in disaster response operations in the United States, Haiti, Japan and Kenya alike.

However, while some global examples will be referred to in this chapter, the focus lies on the recent developments relating to the facilitation and regulation in the African continent, both in the inter- and intra-state realm. It mostly avoids the question of the legal justification of humanitarian intervention in natural or man-made disasters, but rather focuses on more practical issues relating to the entry and operations of humanitarian assistance, such as customs regulations and import taxation, visa and work permits for disaster relief personnel and quality

[3] IFRC, *Law and Legal Issues in International Disaster Response: A Desk Study* (International Federation of Red Cross and Red Crescent Societies, 2007).

standards in food aid and medicine.[4] As a whole, what follows should not be read as a comprehensive listing of all developments in the great African continent, but rather as key issues partly based on a desk study of relevant documents, and partly on involvement of the author in the developing field of disaster law in Africa.[5]

2. The legal framework pertaining to international disaster response

The importance of law and regulation vis–à–vis international disaster cooperation has gained significant momentum in the past decade. Many areas of the broad range of legal and regulatory issues that are encountered in the practice of international disaster cooperation are a result of under-regulation of the entry and operations of border crossing emergency response. Other issues relate to law and regulation tailored for day-to-day situations that frustrate the speed and efficiency needed in a situation of emergency. While there is a solid body of law that relates to situations of armed conflict, natural and man-made disasters are regulated by a much less coherent set of international treaties and a body of soft law in the international realm. When it comes to domestic laws, few states address this issue adequately. However, due to the work, amongst others, of the International Federation of Red Cross and Red Crescent Societies (IFRC), international governmental organisations and their individual member states in Africa are showing progressive developments towards the legal preparation for international disaster cooperation.

2.1 International treaties

The legal and regular bottlenecks of international disaster response have not as of yet prompted a general international treaty on the topic, but there are a great many international instruments that regulate elements of international disaster response. Firstly, some elements of disaster response are addressed in the bodies of humanitarian, human rights and refugee law. However, while the essential human rights norms

[4] Ibid.

[5] Although much of the material presented here was acquired during employment by the IFRC, views in this article do not necessarily represent those of the IFRC.

arguably apply during disasters,[6] they have little direct effect on the technical aspects of carrying out efficient and effective international disaster response operations. The United Nations International Law Commission has been developing activities that seemed like a promising step in that direction, but the Draft Articles on the Protection of Persons in the Event of Disasters[7] with their rights-based approach and focus on protection, however valuable and relevant, will not address the more technical issues of international disaster response operations.

Some international instruments do address the operational aspects of international disaster response.[8] Direct effect on international disaster response operations can be derived from treaties that regulate a general topic, but have special sections relating to humanitarian relief. For example, customs treaties like the *International Convention on the Simplification and Harmonisation of Customs Procedures*[9] and the Istanbul Convention on Temporary Import[10] have annexes that explicitly prescribe the facilitation of importation of humanitarian relief goods. In addition, some types of disasters or types of response are regulated by specific instruments, like for example the *Convention on Assistance in Case of a Nuclear Accident or Radiological Emergency*[11] and the *Tampere Convention*, which regulates the import and use of emergency telecommunication systems.[12] However, possibly with the exception of said *Tampere Convention*, which was signed and ratified by forty-six states as of June 2012, many of these treaties have little effect due to lack of ratification, or lack of implementation.[13]

6 For a complete overview of human rights norms applicable to the protection of persons in disasters see: Erica Harper, 'International Law and Standards Applicable in Natural Disaster Situations', *International Development Law Organisation* (2009).

7 UN Treaty, http://untreaty.un.org/ilc/guide/6_3.htm, accessed on 13 April 2013.

8 For a detailed overview of current legal frameworks applicable to international disaster response see: IFRC, *Law and Legal Issues in International Disaster Response: A Desk Study*, Part II.

9 World Customs Organisation, *International Convention on the Simplification and Harmonisation of Customs Procedures (Kyoto Convention)*, revised 2006.

10 World Customs Organisation, *Convention on Temporary Admission*, 26 June 1990.

11 International Atomic Energy Agency, *Convention on Assistance in the Case of a Nuclear Accident or Radiological Emergency*, 18 November 1986, accessed 1 April 2013, www.iaea.org/Publications/Documents/Infcircs/Others/infcirc336.shtml.

12 Intergovernmental Conference on Emergency Telecommunications, *Tampere Convention on the Provision of Telecommunication Resources for Disaster Mitigation and Relief Operations*, 18 June 1998, accessed 13 April 2013, www.itu.int/ITU-D/emergencytelecoms/tampere.html.

13 IFRC, *Law and Legal Issues*, 8.

2.2 Global and regional institutions

Global and regional organisations with legal mandates to work in disasters also have developed (soft) law on international disaster response and coordination.[14] This includes some significant United Nations General Assembly Resolutions (notably the famous Resolution 46/182 on Strengthening of the Coordination of Humanitarian Emergency Assistance of the United Nations)[15] and the humanitarian arm of the United Nations, such as the World Health Organisation (WHO) and the Office for the Coordination of Humanitarian Affairs (OCHA) who, as can be seen below, have developed guidelines for several aspects of international disaster response. In Africa, the African Union (AU) is stepping up its efforts in humanitarian action, as is detailed below. The African Regional Economic Communities such as the Common Market for Eastern and Southern Africa (COMESA), the Economic Community of West African States (ECOWAS) and the South African Development Community (SADC), commonly have frameworks and strategies in place for joint regional disaster-preparedness, although few have an operational framework to implement it. Some have come to realise that intra- and inter-regional disaster response is something that should be both facilitated and regulated in law and policy. On 12 September 2012, ECOWAS announced at a conference on disaster law in west Africa, which it co-hosted with the IFRC, that the lack of a legal framework in the ECOWAS region was causing difficulties in the preparation and response to the floods that many of its member states experience. For this reason, ECOWAS announced the development of their Code of Conduct for Humanitarian Action (ECCHA) for civilian humanitarian actors, to complement the Code of Conduct of Armed Forces and Security Services in west Africa.[16] SADC, in a similarly organised forum co-hosted with IFRC, reaffirmed its interest in developing an instrument to address border-crossing disaster assistance in the region.[17]

[14] IFRC, *Law and Legal Issues*, 62–79.

[15] United Nations General Assembly Resolution (A/RES/46/182), 'Strengthening of the Coordination of Humanitarian Emergency Assistance of the United Nations', December 1991, accessed on 30 March 2013, www.un.org/documents/ga/res/46/a46r182.htm.

[16] 'ECOWAS Code of Conduct on Humanitarian Action in The Pipeline', *ECOWAS Press Release* No. 257, 2012, accessed on 30 March 2013, http://news.ecowas.int/presseshow.php?nb=257&lang=en&annee=2012.

[17] Sanne Boswijk, 'SADC Members Convene to Enhance Legal Preparedness in the Region', *Disaster Law Newsletter*, October 2012, accessed on 13 April 2013, www.ifrc.org/en/what-we-do/idrl/latest-news/disaster-law-newsletter-october-2012/sadc-60169/.

2.3 *Soft law*

In addition, there is quite a bit of international soft law regarding the behaviour of humanitarian actors and quality of assistance, often developed by the humanitarian community itself.[18] Examples are the Code of Conduct for the International Red Cross and Red Crescent Movement and NGOs in Disaster Relief[19] and the Sphere Humanitarian Charter and Minimum Standards in Humanitarian Response,[20] as well as several guidelines developed by the Inter-Agency Standing Committee (IASC),[21] such as the IASC Guidelines on Mental Health and Psychosocial Support in Emergency Settings and IASC Operational Guidelines on Human Rights and Natural Disasters. These instruments of soft law are evidently hard to enforce in a court of law, but nevertheless are regarded as directive and have a strong impact in the international humanitarian community, which adapts its strategy, planning and implementation to these guidelines. Some of the basic principles adhered to in this context are those that derive from international humanitarian law (IHL), and are considered to be equally appropriate to humanitarian action during situations that do not amount to armed conflict, such as the principles of neutrality and impartiality. Other factors in the acceptance of guidelines that are more specific, such as the quality of guidelines and the nature of specific types of assistance or with regard to specific groups, are due to the process of development of said guidelines: many of the international guidelines regarding humanitarian response are drafted by representatives of the humanitarian community. The IASC, for example, is composed of delegates from the Food and Agriculture Organisation (FAO), the International Organisation for Migration (IOM), Oxfam, the Red Cross and Red Crescent Movement and United

[18] IFRC, *Law and Legal Issues*, 58–61.

[19] ICRC, 'Code of Conduct for The International Red Cross and Red Crescent Movement and NGOs in Disaster Relief', International Federation of Red Cross and Red Crescent Societies and the ICRC, Caritas Internationalis, Catholic Relief Services, the International Federation of Red Cross and Red Crescent Societies, International Save the Children Alliance, Lutheran World Federation, Oxfam and the World Council of Churches (members of the Steering Committee for Humanitarian Response), together with the International Committee of the Red Cross, accessed 30 March 2013, www.icrc.org/eng/assets/files/publications/icrc-002-1067.pdf.

[20] Sphere Project, 'Humanitarian Charter and Minimum Standards in Humanitarian Response', accessed on 30 March 2013, www.spherehandbook.org.

[21] Inter-Agency Standing Committee products, accessed on 14 April 2013, www.humanitarianinfo.org/iasc/pageloader.aspx?page=content-products-default.

Nations agencies with a humanitarian mandate such as the United Nations Development Programme (UNDP), the United Nations Human Settlements Programme (UN-Habitat), the United Nations High Commissioner for Refugees (UNHCR), etc. Many of the United Nations guidelines, such as the World Health Organisation (WHO) Guidelines, are drafted in collaboration with the United Nations member states. Of course, the adoption of guidelines in the General Assembly or another international forum can be a decisive factor in their acceptance and application. The WHO Guidelines on Drug Donations, for example, were developed at the request of the World Health Assembly.

2.4 Domestic law

As the international framework is seen as not being comprehensive, and due to the clear lack of an international treaty governing the practical, legal and regulatory barriers to international disaster response, the solution for legal preparedness hinges on the domestic legal framework of the affected state. Often, this involves not only its disaster-management law, but also the customs regulations, labour and taxation laws and so forth. Few states have laws in place that apply specifically to disasters that legislate the different powers and mandates during such a time and underpin the national disaster response mechanism. A growing number of laws are being designed to address the specific situation of international disaster cooperation, that is to say, border-crossing disaster response. In what follows, some examples of this progressive development from the African context are highlighted.

3. The IDRL Guidelines and the IDRL Model Act

The IFRC, the world's largest humanitarian and development network, has made considerable efforts in the promotion of legal preparedness of global institutions and individual states for disasters of a scale that requires international disaster response cooperation. The IFRC has developed the IDRL Guidelines to improve legal preparedness for international disaster response.[22] These Guidelines are based on the existing norms of the international instruments outlined above. They contain recommendations for states on how to legally prepare for international

[22] IFCR, 'Guidelines for the Domestic Facilitation and Regulation of International Disaster Relief and Initial Recovery Assistance', *IFRC*, 30 November 2007.

disaster response. The IDRL Guidelines are recognised and welcomed by the International Conference of the Red Cross and Red Crescent, but also in several United Nations resolutions, such as the UN Economic and Social Council (ECOSOC) resolution E/2012/L.11[23] and the United Nations General Assembly Resolutions 63/139[24] and A/67/L.39,[25] all on the coordination of humanitarian action. In 2011, the Model Act for the Facilitation and Regulation of International Disaster Relief and Initial Recovery Assistance (IDRL Model Act) was developed by the IFRC in collaboration with the Inter-Parliamentary Union (IPU) and OCHA. The instrument is designed to serve as a practical reference tool for governments as they develop domestic legislation to manage international disaster response operations on their territories.

The IDRL Guidelines and the IDRL Model Act focus on the practical aspects of entry and operations of an international disaster response operation. They provide guidance in the drafting of a legal framework that allows for the affected state to set the rules for entry and operations in return for certain legal faculties. This includes a model on how to regulate the initiation and termination of disaster assistance,[26] and how to prepare legally for international disaster cooperation by proposing a model for a focal point and reception teams at customs for international actors.[27] On the other hand, the Model Act provides model clauses setting out the basic responsibilities of humanitarian actors operating in a foreign territory.[28] A crucial chapter suggests clauses to implement legal facilities for certain humanitarian actors entering a state with the purpose of emergency response.[29] These clauses relate to immigration of personnel, import of goods and equipment, domestic legal status of foreign disaster response actors, taxation, transport and security. For example, when it comes to the importation of disaster relief goods and

[23] ECOSOC Resolution (E/2012/L.11) 'Strengthening of the coordination of emergency humanitarian assistance of the United Nations', 11 July 2012, §6.

[24] A/RES/63/139, www.iom.ch/jahia/webdav/shared/shared/mainsite/policy_and_research/un/63/A_RES_63_139_EN.pdf.

[25] UN GA Resolution (A/67/L.39) 'Strengthening of the coordination of humanitarian and disaster relief assistance of the United Nations, including special economic assistance: strengthening of the coordination of emergency humanitarian assistance of the United Nations', 7 December 2012, §17.

[26] IFRC, 'Model Act for the Facilitation and Regulation of International Disaster Relief and Initial Recovery Assistance', Chapter 2. March 2013, accessed on April 12, 2013, www.ifrc.org/en/what-we-do/idrl/model-act-on-idrl/.

[27] IFRC, 'Model Act', Chapter 3.

[28] IFRC, 'Model Act', Chapter 4.

[29] IFRC, 'Model Act', Chapter 5.

equipment exported or imported by a response actor deemed eligible, paragraph 17 of the IDRL Guidelines advises that originating, transit and affected states should:

- Exempt them from all customs duties, taxes, tariffs or governmental fees;
- Exempt them from all export, transit and import restrictions;
- Simplify and minimise documentation requirements for export, transit and import;
- Permit re-exportation of any equipment or unused goods which the assisting state or assisting humanitarian organisation owns and wishes to retain.

In Part 2 of Chapter 5 of the Model Act, Entry of International Disaster Goods and Equipment, several model clauses provide a model to implement the suggestions in paragraph 17 of the IDRL Guidelines. For example, a model clause on facilitation at customs is provided:

> **Article 29 Customs Facilitation and Priority Treatment**
>
> As further described in this Part, the [customs authority] shall facilitate the rapid importation of consignments of Goods and Equipment by Eligible Actors and shall accord them priority treatment in handling.

In addition, a model is suggested to implement the advised import tax exemptions:

> **Article 32 Exemption from Import Duties, Taxes and Restrictions**
>
> Consignments of Goods and Equipment by or on behalf of Eligible Actors shall benefit from:
>
> a. exemption from all duties and taxes;
> b. waiver of economic prohibitions and restrictions except for categories of special Goods and Equipment as provided in Part 3 of this Act; and
> c. clearance without regard to the country of origin or the country from which the Goods have arrived, subject to monitoring for reasons of public health and security.

Other model clauses relate to immigration of disaster response personnel:

> **Article 25 Disaster Visa**
>
> a. The International Personnel of Eligible Actors shall be entitled to a Disaster Visa, unless national security or public health and safety concerns related to the particular individual preclude it. Disaster Visas shall be issued without a fee for an initial period of [three months], and renewable without a fee for periods of up to [six months] from within

[country name], then as often as necessary throughout the International Disaster Relief and Initial Recovery Periods . . .

c. After the termination of the International Disaster Relief Period but during the International Initial Recovery Assistance Period, Disaster Visas shall be issued by prior application to the appropriate [country name] embassy, which shall adjudicate them within a [specified time].
d. Holders of the Disaster Visa shall be allowed to undertake Disaster Relief and Initial Recovery work for their sponsoring entities during the International Disaster Relief and Initial Recovery Assistance Periods without the requirement to seek a separate residence or work permit.

These types of clauses may be integrated into existing domestic legislation on customs or be adopted in a separate instrument specifically applicable to situations of disaster. Other examples of how the IDRL Guidelines and IDRL Model Act propose to draft legal facilities follow below.

The facilities proposed in the IDRL Guidelines and Model Act are not designed to be available for any actor wishing to provide emergency relief during a disaster, but instead should only apply to those humanitarian actors deemed eligible. Some actors may automatically be deemed eligible, such as assisting states, relevant intergovernmental organisations, including United Nations and actors from the Red Cross Red Crescent movement. Other actors, such as international NGOs and private entities, could be offered a procedure to apply for eligibility. This system of application for eligibility allows a state to keep track of actors wanting to operate on its territory and ties quality control to facilities granted in relation to disaster response. A procedure to attain eligibility for facilities as described above could be incorporated in domestic legislation as proposed in the IDRL Model Act:

Article 22 Application for Eligibility for Legal Facilities by Assisting Actors

a. With the exception of those deemed eligible pursuant to Article 21, Assisting Actors seeking eligibility shall apply in accordance with this Article. Assisting International Actors may apply only if they are recognised as a legal person in a foreign country or under international law.
b. The eligibility of private businesses for Legal Facilities shall be limited to assistance from which they make no profit or other commercial gain.
c. Applications for eligibility may be made in advance of any Disaster, or after the onset of a Disaster. In the event that eligibility for Legal Facilities is granted in advance of a Disaster, it will remain valid for [5 years], after which a new application is required. The Legal Facilities

will enter into legal effect only during an International Disaster Relief or Initial Recovery Period.

d. All Assisting Actors seeking eligibility shall submit:
    (i) certified copies of documents evidencing their legal personality in a foreign jurisdiction or under international law, in the case of Assisting International Actors, or under the laws of [country name], in the case of Assisting Domestic Actors;
    (ii) the name and full contact details of the authorised representative of the organisation and the address of its headquarters, if any, in [country name];
    (iii) documentation relating to their previous experience and current capacity in providing effective Disaster Relief or Initial Recovery Assistance;
    (iv) documentation of adequate liability insurance; and
    (v) an undertaking relating to their organisational commitment and practices concerning the responsibilities set out in Chapter IV.

As can be seen, especially from section d ((i)–9v)) in this model Article, elements of quality assurance are incorporated in a successful application for eligibility for legal facilities. In particular, paragraph (v) refers to responsibilities as set out in Chapter IV of the Model Act, which refers to responsibilities relating to adherence to international standards in quality and manner of delivery of international disaster response. These standards include adherence to the principles of humanity, neutrality and impartiality, as well as more particular standards deriving from these principles as set out in paragraph 4 of the IDRL Guidelines, such as calculation of aid priorities on the basis of need alone, provision of aid without distinction and without a political or religious agenda or to gain strategic information about the receiving state. Furthermore, both the IDRL Guidelines and the IDRL Model Act confirm the obligations of those who provide assistance to abide by local law and coordinate their activities with local authorities, something which applies to any natural or legal person entering a foreign territory but is sometimes overlooked by international humanitarian actors.

Since their adoption, there has been a significant increase in the developments in this field. The IDRL Guidelines and their annotations are being used in the efforts of governments and intergovernmental organisations alike to prepare for the initiation, entry and operations of international disaster response operations. Some African states have already made use of the IDRL Model Act,[30] as illustrated below.

[30] Ibid.

4. Key legal and regulatory issues in international disaster response in Africa

The examples from Africa illustrate the theory of legal and regulatory bottlenecks outlined above, and, in some cases, demonstrate how these can be minimised, or avoided altogether, by preparing legally for international actors entering an affected state. The outline below must not be understood as comprehensive, but rather as key issues encountered in the practice of disaster law in the African continent. It must be stressed again that these issues are not unique for Africa, but are a global phenomenon registered in disasters all over the world.

4.1 Initiation, assessment and definition of disaster

More often than not, disasters, especially when televised, will attract many actors volunteering to support the affected population. This type of unsolicited assistance may originate from other states or non-state humanitarian actors like NGOs, individuals or even private companies. Unsolicited aid may be inappropriate for the needs of the affected population and burden the existing coordination mechanism with quality assurance and delivery. Examples range from donations of expired medication, unnecessary and overwhelming amounts of used clothing, to foodstuffs containing genetically modified organisms and other relief items delivered without proper marking or a distribution plan.

As confirmed in the United Nations General Assembly's resolution 46/182 and the IDRL Guidelines, disaster response support should be initiated only with the consent of the affected state and, in principle, on the basis of an appeal by the affected state. Such an appeal may be substituted by a less formal message from a state to indicate that it welcomes international support.[31] This consideration is meant to imply that it is not appropriate or desirable for international disaster response actors to initiate operations without an explicit invitation or the acceptance of the affected state. It is important to note that this resolution has no bearing on the more essential question of whether there is an obligation for the affected state to accept offers of assistance. By way of example, in some cases, the international community may be of the opinion that international assistance is warranted, whereas the affected

[31] IFRC, 'Annotations to the Draft Guidelines for the Domestic Facilitation and Regulation of International Disaster Relief and Initial Recovery Assistance', October 2007, 24.

state itself feels it is capable of addressing the situation domestically. A recent example is Myanmar's initial refusal to allow foreign humanitarian actors into its territory after cyclone Nargis in 2008. In Africa, this has been the case for Zimbabwe, which in the past has denied facing an unmanageable food security situation and was pressurised by international actors to accept food aid. A notorious and more extreme case of a state unwilling to receive international support is that of the (former) Sudan, which expelled NGOs from its territory during the civil war with its southern region. For now, the international community has not established by custom or law an obligation to accept offers of assistance, but with Resolution 46/182 it has definitely indicated that initiation of international disaster assistance requires acceptance by the affected state.

This soft law rule as expressed in Resolution 46/182 echoes a consistent message of African governments, that international assistance is not invited in all cases and – in spite of OCHA's coordination mechanism – not always sufficiently coordinated with the national authorities. National authorities of disaster-prone countries like Mozambique, Ethiopia and Rwanda report an influx of foreign humanitarian actors arriving at their borders with relief consignments that are not requested – and sometimes not required.[32] After a televised drought leading to food insecurity, many actors will turn up at the border of Ethiopia with well-intended but unsolicited aid. This type of aid may cause problems for the affected state and the United Nations coordination mechanism with respect to the delivery and quality assurance of support. For example, the 2011 drought in the Horn of Africa happened to coincide with Ramadan, the Islamic month of fasting and self-restraint. This prompted a wealthy individual to donate several million dollars-worth of food aid to be delivered to the border of one of the affected countries. However, the consignment was unannounced and no transportation or distribution was organised, which left the already overburdened coordinating body OCHA in charge of quality assurance and distribution.[33] One way for states affected by disasters to avoid an

[32] As reported by the authorities of respective countries through consultations on disaster law during country-level or regional workshops on the topic, organised by the IFRC in 2012–2013. See, for example, IFRC, www.ifrc.org/en/what-we-do/idrl/meetings-and-events/past-events/workshop-on-disaster-law-and-the-drought-relief-operations-in-the-horn-of-africa-17-19-april-2012/ and www.ifrc.org/docs/IDRL/Workshop%20report%20SADC%20(final).pdf, accessed on 5 June 2013.

[33] As reported during individual consultations by the author with representatives of OCHA Eastern Africa.

influx of spontaneous assistance is to make a clear statement, as suggested in the resolution, on whether and what kind of assistance would be welcomed. Unfortunately, few African states have the capacity or system in place adequately to make such an announcement. The IDRL Model Act proposes such a system, which could entail a clause in domestic law authorising the relevant body to invite assisting actors, as well as a procedure for assisting actors to make a formal offer for assistance:

Article 6 Requests for International Disaster Assistance

a. Upon the advice of the [relevant disaster management authority], the [President/Prime Minister] may make a request for International Disaster Assistance. That request may be specifically directed to particular international actors, or it may be a general request directed to the international community as a whole. [In the latter case, the request shall be directed to the [relevant regional organisation and] the United Nations Emergency Relief Coordinator for assistance in dissemination to potential Assisting International Actors.]
b. The request shall be accompanied by:
   (i) information as to the extent and type of assistance required, based on the list prepared by the [relevant disaster management authority] pursuant to Article 5, unless this would lead to undue delay; and
   (ii) information on the procedures for Assisting International Actors to make offers or provide assistance pursuant to Article 7 . . .

Article 7 Offers and Acceptance of International Assistance

a. Except as otherwise provided in subsection (d), Assisting International Actors may provide International Disaster Assistance in [country name] only if they have made an offer that has been accepted pursuant to this Article.
b. Assisting states and intergovernmental organisations (including the United Nations) interested in providing International Disaster Assistance direct offers to [the Ministry of Foreign Affairs through the appropriate [country name] embassy]. Offers should indicate, in general terms, the type, amount and estimated duration of assistance to be provided. The Ministry of Foreign Affairs shall then consult with the [relevant disaster management authority] about such offers. Upon the direction of the [relevant disaster management authority], the Ministry of Foreign Affairs may accept such offers, in whole or in part.

Implementing domestic legislation in line with the model suggested by the IDRL Model Act, adapted where necessary to the domestic context, allows governments to formalise their relationship with incoming actors, minimise the risk of unsolicited aid and enhance coordination of disaster response activities on their territory.

4.2 *Domestic institutional frameworks for (international) disaster response*

While most African states have a national disaster management agency for the operational response to natural and man-made disasters, not all of those states have the legal and policy framework that allocates power to certain authorities to make and execute decisions in a disaster situation, let alone a mechanism that regulates and facilitates the entry and operations of international responders. A disaster often impacts the mandates of several governmental agencies. For example, a large-scale flooding in Botswana will trigger the involvement of the local District Disaster Management Committee and that of the National Disaster Management Committee, while the overall responsibility lies with the Office of the President. However, the role of the Ministry of Health may well come into play if cholera breaks out in the affected area, and perhaps that of the police or defence forces if the population is urged to evacuate and refuses. The situation becomes more complicated when international disaster response units get involved: then as a minimum, the Ministry of Foreign Affairs and the Department of Customs and Excise will want to have their say in the operations as well. Logically, an issue that tends to come up in the development of disaster-management frameworks is to convince the ministries involved to give up a little of their power in the case of an emergency, as was the case during the Cabinet discussion of Rwanda's draft Disaster Risk Management Act (at the time of writing the document is passing through parliament).[34]

Lack of a clear and comprehensive legal framework that allocates authority to make and execute decisions in a disaster scenario may impede domestic response efforts through competing mandates of the responsible government institutions and agencies. In addition, absence of such a legal framework will be likely to frustrate international disaster response operations; lack of a clear national focal point for disaster response will result in conflicting instructions and requirements. For example, different agencies will be involved in the transport of personnel into the country (for example Home Affairs or Foreign Affairs), importation of goods like food (for example Customs, Ministry of Public Health,

[34] Maren Schulte, 'Profile in Disaster Law Advocacy: Captain Jean Damascène Kayitana', *Disaster Law Newsletter*, February 2013, accessed on 14 April 2013, www.ifrc.org/fr/introduction/-droit-des-catastrophes/dernieres-nouvelles-et-derniers-rapports-sur-le-droit-des-catastrophes/disaster-law-newsletter-february-2013/profile-in-disaster-law-advocacy-captain-jean-damascene-kayitana-60800/.

Ministry of Agriculture) and medication (for example Customs, Ministry of Health), travel into disaster-struck areas (for example Home Affairs, National Police, National Disaster Management Agency), etc.

Several African governments recently initiated the development of national disaster management laws – in particular in east and southern Africa. For example, the IFRC has been involved in the development of legislation in Namibia, Malawi, Mozambique, Rwanda, the Seychelles and Tanzania, whilst a parliamentary platform in Uganda has announced its efforts to initiate the development of a disaster management law. While South Africa is famous for its excellent Disaster Management Act 2000,[35] it is currently under review to further encourage its implementation. Namibia has been the most recent African country to formally adopt a law that provides a good example of recently developed disaster risk management legislation with its Disaster Risk Management Act,[36] adopted in September 2012. This comprehensive instrument outlines in detail the roles and responsibilities of the multitude of government institutions involved in disaster risk management at the national and the decentralised level. The Act institutionalises decentralised disaster management committees down to local authorities and prescribes the adoption of disaster management plans for all decentralised levels. As for international assistance, it tasks the National Disaster Risk Management Committee with the periodical review of policy issues regarding appeals for and use of international assistance, including issues of international personnel.[37] It indicates that the prime minister may enter into an agreement concerning disaster risk management with any entity or person, including those outside of Namibia as long as this person or entity shall:

(a) respect the sovereignty of Namibia;
(b) obey local laws;
(c) cooperate with authorities;
(d) abstain from political or commercial activities; and
(e) ensure that the assistance given is both appropriate to the assessed needs and compliant with domestic quality, health and other standards.[38]

35 South Africa, Act No. 57, 2000, Disaster Management Act.
36 Namibia, Act No. 10, 2012. Disaster Risk Management Act.
37 Article 5 (q), Act No. 10, 2012 Disaster Risk Management Act, 2012, Namibia.
38 Article 54 (3), Act No. 10, 2012 Disaster Risk Management Act, 2012, Namibia.

Namibia's Act mentions the obligation for specific bodies to provide facilities for international disaster response, such as in Article 52 (3):

(a) immigration must facilitate the entry and operation of international relief personnel and experts, including the expeditious granting of visas and waiver of work permits for relief personnel and experts;
(b) finance must facilitate reduced and simplified customs procedures, exemption from duties, taxes and charges for donations of equipment and materials, including food, made during disaster situations including possessions of relief personnel.

Although a pioneering instrument in Africa when it comes to regulation and facilitation of international disaster assistance in domestic legislation, Namibia's law leaves the details to the development of regulations. Therefore it can be said Rwanda's draft Disaster Management Act, which is currently awaiting parliamentary approval, is the first African legal framework with an extensive section dedicated to the initiation, facilitation and regulation of international disaster response operations.

4.3 Customs clearance and import taxation

One of the first issues that springs to mind when evaluating the impact of law and regulation on disaster-response operations is that of customs clearance and import taxation. As outlined in the foregoing, there are two customs treaties that contain annexes on the facilitation of humanitarian relief, namely the Kyoto and Istanbul conventions. However, these annexes are very sparsely ratified and indeed most African countries have not ratified these annexes (at the time of writing, the Kyoto convention has fifteen African state parties, while the Istanbul Convention has only six African ratifications). It is often down to domestic law and regulation to decide how to deal with disaster relief consignments, both when it comes to customs clearance and import taxation. The baseline assumption here should be that if there is no law or regulation that explicitly applies to humanitarian relief goods, any consignment will be handled as regular importation of goods. Hence, clearance procedures will be standard and import taxation can be levied.

Within the Regional Economic Communities (RECs), taxation is not a problem since all of the communities are tax unions. However, these apply only to goods that are travelling within those regions, whereas most relief goods come from outside Africa. Furthermore, even if no taxation is applied within the region, this does not affect clearance requirements at the internal borders. Special regulations for relief are found in several African domestic legal systems, no doubt due to the large number of relief providers active in the continent as a whole. But more often than not, the process is lengthy and cumbersome. This inefficiency of the process for acquiring a tax waiver is often justified by the authorities through allegations of abuse of the privileges by persons or entities taking advantage of the system. In the case of South Sudan, a relatively new state, relief items from any provider, including those of the United Nations agencies and assisting states, are granted a tax exemption in a procedure that can take up to three weeks due to the several government agencies involved in authorising the waiver. In October 2012, the government of South Sudan issued a press release in which it announced its third reorganisation of this system, due to alleged abuse of the waiver.[39] Another example is Sierra Leone, which suffered abuse of its tax exemption structure by businessmen who imported used clothes (very common and often unnecessary relief goods) for commercial purposes, and so decided to suspend this.[40]

When discussing the delicate issue of tax exemptions for relief providers, the approach of Mozambique's national disaster management agency is illustrative of the issues surrounding this matter. The authorities in Mozambique pointed out that for a developing nation, the costs of receiving large numbers of humanitarian actors are significant. It may wear out infrastructure of airports and roads and requires a significant increase in overtime for government staff and equipment to process the importation and coordination of international staff and equipment. This is especially unfortunate in the case of unsolicited assistance. As a result, negotiating a waiver on import taxes will be perceived as loss of income by the central government, the compensation for which will be sought through the responsible agency, in this case the national disaster management agency. Whether this argument is perceived as reasonable by all parties or not, it does outline the very real limitations of an affected state's available resources as well as the burden of unsolicited aid.

39 *The Citizen*, 14 November 2012, South Sudan.

40 Reported by the Sierra Leonean authorities during a workshop on IDRL in Freetown, July 2009, accessed 5 June 2013; IFRC, 'International Disaster Response Laws, Rules and Principles (IDRL) Programme: Plan 2010–2011', accessed 5 June, 2013. www.ifrc.org/PageFiles/53419/MAA0000410p.pdf.

4.4 Immigration of personnel: visa, work permits, professional qualifications

In many African states, persons entering the country for disaster response work are required to obtain a visa. In most, if not all, African states, an additional work permit for any professional activity is required, although some states have waivers or expedited procedures in place for disaster response personnel. The procedure to obtain a visa and work permit may be (very) lengthy and even costly. For example, to obtain a regular work permit in Botswana formally takes thirty days,[41] although in practice the waiting period can be significantly longer. The applicant is required to submit a host of documents, including contract of employment, certified copies of certificates obtained and a medical report. Applying for a work permit costs approximately 180 US dollars. While there is no explicit exemption for disaster response personnel in emergency situations, the Commissioner of Labour is authorised to waive this requirement in cases where it is deemed fit and for as long as it is deemed necessary.[42] The flexibility provided in this national regulation is effective to solve the immediate problems of immigration of disaster relief personnel, but many other states do not have regulations that allow for such a waiver. In those circumstances, an ad hoc waiver is sometimes 'invented' on the spot to allow for quick entry, but that in turn leads to legal complications down the line – with normal rules being enforced once the emergency situation has passed its peak.[43] In the 2011 drought in the Horn of Africa, several staff members of the international organisation Save the Children, who had travelled into Ethiopia on a tourist visa, were apprehended and expelled for not abiding by the requirement of obtaining a business permit for professional activities. In some cases, immigration is restricted to personnel from certain states: in Africa this was the case when Kenya, which is a hub for humanitarian activity in the East African region, ceased to accept Somali passports due to alleged fraud.[44]

In addition to a work permit, certain personnel, especially those in the medical profession, need additional recognition of qualifications and

[41] Elisabeth Macharia-Mokobi, 'International Disaster Response Law (IDRL) in Botswana: An Audit on Legal Preparedness for Facilitating and Regulating International Disaster Assistance', *Botswana Red Cross Society*, draft of March 2013, 82–84.

[42] Botswana, Employment of Non-Citizens Act Chapter 47, 02, as amended by Act 19, 1992. www.ilo.org/wcmsp5/groups/public/—ed_protect/—protrav/—ilo_aids/documents/legal-document/wcms_125672.pdf.

[43] IFRC, *Law and Legal Issues*, 116.

[44] Ibid., 117.

registration with the relevant national authorities to be allowed to operate in the country. On the global level, there is no guidance in this particular and problematic area. The reason this issue is so pressing is the substantial risk of legal liability derived from unregistered medical practice.[45]

4.5 *Registration of foreign entities and domestic legal status*

For a disaster response actor to operate legally and enjoy the facilities necessary for successful operations, such as opening a bank account to fund its operation and enter into rental and employment contracts with local actors, some form of legal personality is required. In Africa, this often means that assisting actors should get registered as an organisation. In particular for organisations that are new to the country, this process may take unsuitably long in an emergency disaster response operation. For example, a report on IDRL in Sierra Leone[46] found that the registration process was too lengthy because it involves departments of several government institutions. In most African countries, such a registration procedure would be lengthy, involving authorities from the immigration department, foreign affairs and the agency responsible for national disaster management. Sometimes the process of registration for NGOs is deliberately restrictive, in particular where NGOs with activities of an advocacy or political nature are concerned. At one point in time, Ethiopia literally hosted thousands of NGOs working on its territory in both emergency and development work. Ethiopia's Proclamation to Provide for the Registration and Regulation of Charities and Societies prohibits NGOs that are funded by more than 10 per cent by external funders from engaging in activities relating to human rights and democracy promotion.[47] The alternative was perhaps illustrated by the ongoing controversy of Egypt's prosecution of some forty employees of NGOs engaged in advocacy for democracy for inciting protests against the nation's military rulers.[48]

[45] Ibid., 119.

[46] IDRL in Sierra Leone, 'Legal Preparedness Study for Strengthening the Legal and Policy Framework for Foreign Disaster Response', *IFRC*, 2011, 34.

[47] ICNL, 'NGO Law Monitor: Ethiopia', *The International Center for Not-for-Profit Law*, last modified on 20 February 2013, www.icnl.org/research/monitor/ethiopia.html.

[48] 'Egypt "lifts" travel ban on US NGO workers', *BBC News*, last updated on 1 March 2012, www.bbc.co.uk/news/world-us-canada-17210327.

4.6 *Appropriateness and quality of assistance*

The importance of tailored assistance that meets the needs and respects the dignity of the affected population is an issue that cannot be underestimated, and sadly there are a host of examples of aid that has gone wrong in Africa. For the purpose of this chapter, examples will be limited to those that may be solved by developing a legal framework to effectively and efficiently control the entry and distribution of relief goods.

One type of relief that leads to particular problems is that of emergency medicine. As everywhere else, most – if not all – African states regulate the import and distribution of medicines, often through the national drugs or medicine law. Such an instrument will provide for regulations of essential medicines allowed to be imported into the country – and ideally of substances that are deemed illegal to import – as well as detailed regulation on import licensing. In addition, there will be clear regulations on the authorisation to distribute medication to the general public. Just as anywhere else, of course, this is usually limited to licensed medical practitioners and pharmacists. In the practice of international disaster response, these rules are almost impossible to abide by, and, as a consequence, emergency medicine is difficult to import.

On the other hand, there are many reports of donated medication that was of inadequate quality, in some cases even harmful for the affected population. A common problem is donated medication that is so close to, or even past, the expiry date that it will pose a risk to affected populations. In other cases, like Mozambique, the Mozambique Red Cross reports that it experienced delays in customs to the extent that donated medicine reached the expiry date.[49] Another common issue is that donated medication is not accompanied by a prescription in a language that the affected population understands.[50] An example is the case of Namibia, where the national Disaster Management Agency received a large consignment of unidentifiable drugs which were labelled entirely in Russian. WHO, aware of these widespread issues, developed its Guidelines for Medicine Donations.[51] These Guidelines are directed at donating parties and cover issues of shelf-life, labelling and adherence to national laws of the recipient country. Guidance for governments wishing to control the quality of donated medicines imported into their

[49] IFRC, 'Disasters in Africa: the case for legal preparedness', 2011.
[50] IFRC, *Law and Legal Issues*, 112–113.
[51] WHO, 'Guidelines for Medicine Donations', *World Health Organisation*, 2010.

territory is found in the IDRL Guidelines and Model Act. For example, the Model Act suggests the following model clause for the import and distribution of medicines:

Article 38 Medications

a. Eligible Actors shall be permitted to import medications and medical Equipment for the purpose of Disaster Relief or Initial Recovery Assistance so long as they conform to the requirements of this Article.
b. Any such medications and medical Equipment shall be appropriate to the needs of the Disaster-affected persons, and shall be legal for use in the country of origin according to its laws as well as in [country name] according to [appropriate law on pharmaceuticals]. Pursuant to subsections (c) and (d) below, a distinction shall otherwise be made between medications intended to be donated for the use of others and those that Eligible Actors intend to use directly in providing medical Services.
c. Medications that Eligible Actors intend to use directly in providing medical services in Disaster Relief or Initial Recovery Assistance, shall be:
   (i) transported and maintained by the Eligible Actor in appropriate conditions at all times to ensure their quality and;
   (ii) guarded against misappropriation and abuse.
d. Medications intended for donation for the use of others shall be:
   (i) at least 12 months from their expiry date upon arrival, unless otherwise specifically agreed by the [relevant health authority];
   (ii) transported and maintained by the Eligible Actor in appropriate conditions to ensure their quality until they reach their intended domestic recipients; and
   (iii) appropriately labelled in a language understood in the affected state with the International Non-proprietary Name or generic name, batch number, dosage form, strength, name of manufacturer, quantity in the container, storage conditions and expiry date.[52]

Disaster response to food insecurity can also illustrate the need for appropriateness of relief goods. During a session on disasters and law in Ethiopia, one of the participants recounted an example of the delivery of large quantities of food aid containing corn. The standard diet of the majority of the Ethiopian population, which totals over 80 million people, consists of *injera*, a product of a grass called *teff*, which is native to Ethiopia. Upon reception of the much-needed food aid, the affected

[52] IFRC, 'Model Act'.

population was not aware of how to prepare the maize – a foreign product that was hard for their digestive systems to process in the first place. A controversial example has been the donation of food aid containing Genetically Modified Organisms (GMOs), in particular maize. In 2002, southern Africa experienced a situation of food insecurity that prompted the response of the international community, in particular the United States, who is the largest food donor worldwide. Zambia refused the donations, because it was likely to contain kernels of corn that were genetically modified and considerations of public health prohibited distribution of modified organisms to the population.[53] While a solution to the dilemmas of GMOs in food aid is not necessarily straightforward, these incidents do illustrate the need to consider carefully the nature of donated goods meant for humanitarian relief.

The nature of these problems may sometimes be found in conflicting laws and regulations. For example, according to a recent study, Namibia was found to have a scattered body of laws on food safety, which means that in the event of food imports, the importer would have to have regard to the Control of the Importation and Exportation of Dairy Products and Dairy Product Substitutes Act 5 of 1986, the Meat Industry Act 12 of 1981, and the Sugar Act 28 of 1936.[54] During the operations in the Horn of Africa in 2011, the Kenyan airport authorities refused the entry of some forty World Food Programme (WFP) shipments of grains containing GMOs, based on a newly adopted law restricting these. This rather impactful decision went against an earlier approval by customs to receive these shipments as transfer to other African countries suffering food insecurity.

4.7 *Transfer of humanitarian relief goods*

As we have seen above in the example of the United Nations' airlifts of food that were delayed by a clearance permit from the Kenyan authorities, the rules on transfer of goods may have an impact on emergency relief as much as on the affected state. It should be borne in mind that a clearance procedure of one day may be perfectly sufficient in a regular

[53] Abigail Hauslohner, 'Egypt's NGO Crisis: How Will US Aid Play in the Controversy?', *Time*, last modified on 9 February 2012, www.time.com/time/world/article/0,8599,2106420,00.html; 'Famine-hit Zambia rejects GM food aid', *BBC News*, last modified on 29 October 2002, http://news.bbc.co.uk/2/hi/africa/2371675.stm.

[54] IFRC, 'Strengthening Legal Preparedness for International Disaster Assistance in Namibia', *IFRC/Namibia Red Cross Society*, draft of December 2012.

situation, but for disaster response operations waiting for goods and equipment can have a serious impact. Moreover, when a disaster generates support from a large number of disaster response actors and organisations, it is likely that the relief shipments will be lining up to the extent that the regular clearance mechanism of the receiving or transferring state becomes overburdened, which in turn leads to even longer delays. On the qualitative side, transfer states may also have a great impact on the transfer of relief items, as can be seen above from Kenya's refusal to transfer foodstuffs that contained genetically modified grains through Mombasa harbour. This is all the more pressing in Africa, where much transport happens by road, with trucks passing multiple borders: for instance in the case of Namibia, where the National Disaster Risk Management Committee reports that the flood-relief goods sometimes come from as far away as Zimbabwe, the transport of these items will be delayed at every one of the border crossings involved.[55] In the absence of an instrument facilitating the transport, transfer is often managed on an ad hoc basis with friendly customs officers. An added dimension to delays and sometimes refusal to transfer humanitarian relief goods and equipment is animosity between or within African states. Just one example is that of Sudan, which is reluctant and sometimes plainly refuses to be a point of transfer to South Sudan.

5. The African Union's progress in the regulation and facilitation of international disaster response

The African Union (AU) is Africa's supreme political body, established in 1999 by African heads of state and the governments of the Organisation of African Unity (OAU). When it comes to the facilitation and regulation of disaster response in the continent, the African Union's efforts in the areas of peace and security have been complemented in the past years by a growing involvement in humanitarian affairs, in particular in the assistance and protection of refugees and internally displaced persons (IDPs). Originally, the OAU, which was established in 1963, had focused on supporting liberation movements in territories under colonialism and apartheid. The African Union has a much wider

[55] As reported by Namibia's disaster risk management authorities during a workshop on disaster law in Windhoek in November 2011, accessed 5 June 2013, www.ifrc.org/en/what-we-do/idrl/latest-news/idrl-newsletter-december-2011/windhoek-workshop-explores-namibias-legal-preparedness-for-disasters/.

set of objectives than the OAU. According to its Consitutive Act, the objectives of the African Union range from achieving greater African unity and solidarity, promoting peace and security on the continent, encouraging sustainable development and the application of (African) human rights in the continent, as well as representing Africa's voice in the global economy.[56] However, a role in disaster response activities is not explicitly mentioned. The African Union's role in disaster response would have to derive from the objectives '(k) promote co-operation in all fields of human [sic] activity to raise the living standards of African peoples' and '(n) work with relevant international partners in the eradication of preventable diseases and the promotion of good health on the continent'.[57] Both these objectives leave room for interpretation, even if one assumes that the term 'human activity' is meant to indicate humanitarian activities. A more evident legal underpinning of the African Union's activities in the realm of disaster management and response is the authority of the Executive Council, composed of the (foreign affairs) ministers designated by the African Union's member states,[58] to coordinate and take decisions on policies in areas of common interest to the member states, including environmental protection, humanitarian action and disaster response and relief.[59] From this context it is telling that the Department for Humanitarian Affairs, Refugees and IDPs (HARDP), the African Union's main focal point for all humanitarian activities, falls under the Political Affairs Department. Regardless of its organisational allocation, the HARDP is in the process of contributing significantly to the continental coordination of humanitarian action in Africa, in particular through the development of the draft African Humanitarian Policy Framework with its attached African Union Disaster Management Policy as well as the development and promotion of the *African Union Convention for the Protection and Assistance of IDPs in Africa* (the *Kampala Convention*).

5.1 *The African Union's draft African Humanitarian Policy Framework and DM Policy*

At the time of writing, the African Union was in the process of adopting a policy framework on humanitarian action on the African continent,

[56] Constitutive Act of the African Union, 11 July 2000, Article 3 outlines the objectives.

[57] AU, 'Constitutive Act of the African Union, 11 July 2000', available at: http://www.refworld.org/docid/4937e0142.html (accessed 30 April 2014).

[58] AU, 'Constitutive Act', Article 10(1).

[59] AU, 'Constitutive Act', Article 13.

including a disaster management policy for the African continent in its annex.[60] The aim of this document is to officially outline the coordinating role of the African Union in all humanitarian action on the continent, complementing the United Nation's coordinating mechanism (OCHA) as well as that of Africa's Regional Economic Communities (RECs). It establishes a strategic approach to the preservation, protection and saving of lives, as well as the alleviation of suffering caused by natural and man-made disasters in Africa. Whereas it applies to all humanitarian interventions in Africa, which arguably involves many non-African actors, it starts from the ambition that ideally Africa should be its own first responder, thus appealing to the OAU's original objective of promoting solidarity among African states.

In the document that the Executive Council will be reviewing, which is not yet publicly available,[61] the role of the African Union is proposed to be at the strategic level and to culminate in the development of common approaches and strategies in collaboration with the Coordinating Committee on Forced Displacement and Humanitarian Action (CCoFDHA – the main advisory body on humanitarian issues in the African Union), RECs and the humanitarian community including OCHA, the IASC and the Red Cross and Red Crescent Movement. In particular, the HARDP is to provide technical and material support to the African Union's member states through advocacy and capacity-building for emergency preparedness and response, the establishment of early warning systems, and the legal preparedness to overcome legal and regulatory barriers to disaster response.

The draft humanitarian framework policy sets out the framework on a range of topics, including protection of returnees, refugees and IDPs, the promotion of International Humanitarian Law (IHL), recovery and development, humanitarian resource mobilisation and early warning systems. The document also incorporates a section on disaster management, preparedness and response, focusing on natural and man-made disasters, but it excludes situations of armed conflict due to the application of IHL to that category of humanitarian action. The strategic focus in this area is determined as building the continental capacity for early warning, preparedness and response, coordinating resource

[60] Information in this paragraph is based on the author's personal involvement in the drafting procedure of the quoted instrument.

[61] The author has had extensive access to the document through involvement in the drafting process.

mobilisation for effective disaster management amongst member states, RECs, the African Union and partners, and building sustainable recovery, rehabilitation, reconstruction and resilience including promoting learning and good practice on disaster management. It goes on to implement the African Union Disaster Management Policy, which is annexed to the policy framework. Notably, this draft African Union disaster management policy promotes and assists the implementation of the IDRL Guidelines, and encourages and facilitates continental, regional and bilateral agreements relating to border-crossing relief and recovery assistance and the effective use of the Model Act.

5.2 The African Union *Convention for the Protection and Assistance of IDPs in Africa* (the *Kampala Convention)*

Globally, the instruments of international humanitarian law and human rights law address aspects of the situation of IDPs: notably, the (non-binding) Guidelines on Internal Displacement.[62] In Africa, the first legally binding instrument relating to IDPs was the Great Lakes Protocol on Internally Displaced Persons of 2006. To address the gap of a specific and binding legal instrument for the entire African continent, the African Union developed the *Convention for the Protection and Assistance of IDPs in Africa* (the *Kampala Convention*).[63] The African Union actively promoted ratification by its member states, leading to its coming into force on 6 December 2012.

Aside from its wider geographical application, the *Kampala Convention* also, as regards content, goes beyond the principles outlined in the Great Lakes Protocol. Just like the Great Lakes Protocol, the *Kampala Convention* binds state parties to provide protection to IDPs on their territory and gives them primary responsibility for assistance. Aside from the comprehensive articles on the prevention and protection of IDPs, the convention contains specific clauses on the facilitation and regulation of humanitarian assistance to IDPs. For example, in Article 5 the *Kampala Convention* gives primary responsibility to state parties to ensure assistance to IDPs by meeting their basic needs: 'States Parties shall bear the primary duty and responsibility for providing protection of and humanitarian assistance to internally displaced persons within their territory or

[62] OCHA, 'Guidelines on Internal Displacement', 2001.

[63] ECOSOC, 'Guiding Principles on Internal Displacement', (E/CN.4/1998/53/Add.2), 11 February 1998.

jurisdiction without discrimination of any kind'.[64] Furthermore, that same article obliges the state parties to allow and facilitate rapid and unimpeded access by humanitarian organisations and personnel:

> States Parties shall take necessary steps to effectively organise relief action that is humanitarian, and impartial in character, and guarantee security. States Parties shall allow rapid and unimpeded passage of all relief consignments, equipment and personnel to internally displaced persons. States Parties shall also enable and facilitate the role of local and international organisations and humanitarian agencies, civil society organisations and other relevant actors, to provide protection and assistance to internally displaced persons. States Parties shall have the right to prescribe the technical arrangements under which such passage is permitted.[65]

An innovative and important element of this obligation is the obligation on state parties to take all necessary measures to 'effectively organise relief action that is humanitarian, and impartial in character ... allow rapid and unimpeded passage of all relief consignments, equipment and personnel to internally displaced persons' – this legal obligation for the state parties to facilitate (amongst others) international assistance is new in situations outside those prescribed in the Geneva Conventions, which apply to situations of armed conflict exclusively.

Whilst the previous articles impose duties concerning the facilitation and regulation of disaster relief to IDPs, Article 6 sets out basic standards for assisting actors: 'International organisations and humanitarian agencies shall be bound by the principles of humanity, neutrality, impartiality and independence of humanitarian actors, and ensure respect for relevant international standards and codes of conduct.'[66] However, it is especially the obligation of state parties to organise humanitarian action and allow for rapid and unimpeded passage to IDPs, which, once implemented, may have an important effect on legislative and legal frameworks pertaining to disaster response, at least when it comes to situations in which IDPs are involved.

6. Concluding remarks

Without a legal framework for the reception of international disaster response, humanitarian action in natural and man-made disasters is

[64] AU, *Convention for the Protection and Assistance of IDPs in Africa* (the *Kampala Convention*), Article 5(1).

[65] AU, *Kampala Convention*, Article 5(7).

[66] AU, *Kampala Convention*, Article 6(3).

likely to suffer delays, unnecessary expenses and quality problems in the delivery of relief to the affected population. In the absence of a general international treaty on the regulation and facilitation of international disaster response, the solution to these problems hinges on domestic laws. In Africa, disasters are often of a scale that requires governments to rely on assistance from their neighbours, and coordinated action from their regional bodies or, and maybe most often, international actors from outside of Africa. Nevertheless, although mostly unintended, African domestic legal frameworks are in effect frustrating the rapid entry of humanitarian assistance starting at the border, and continuing to do so once the operations take off inside the country; as was illustrated by examples relating to transfer of food aid in Kenya, customs procedures in South Sudan and the registration of NGOs in Sierra Leone. Additionally, humanitarian actors responding to disasters do not always coordinate appropriately with local authorities, and, in the absence of a monitoring mechanism, do not always deliver services of appropriate quality or nature.

Without a legal or policy framework on the domestic level that facilitates and regulates international assistance, it is likely that humanitarian response is hindered to such an extent that it becomes much more costly and much less efficient than is required in an emergency. One way of achieving a more universal domestic legal preparedness for international disaster response is to oblige states to implement legislation by means of an international treaty, similar to the way in which the Geneva Conventions have achieved the implementation of IHL into domestic legal frameworks in many states. Moreover, some of the key issues mentioned in this chapter, such as matters relating to initiation of disaster assistance and recognition of foreign qualifications, would in fact be more easily addressed in an international treaty pertaining to international disaster response cooperation.

The developments in the drafting of legal instruments relating to international disaster response in Africa show that progress to address the above issues is being made. The African Union is taking up its role as coordinator of humanitarian action on the continent, through the development and promotion of the *Kampala Convention* and the draft African Humanitarian Policy Framework. Awareness of the issues is growing on the regional and domestic levels, and some states have commenced the drafting of legal frameworks that streamline the reception of disaster response from outside their borders. Front-runners in this respect are Namibia and Rwanda, who have adopted or are about to adopt laws that facilitate and regulate international disaster response operations in their respective territories.

These endeavours to strengthen the (cost-)effectiveness of international and domestic disaster response mechanisms, ultimately aimed at improving the situation of those affected by the disaster, are not yet universal and often in the preparatory phase. Hence, widespread improvement of the reception of international humanitarian operations has not yet been witnessed. This indicates that there is still a clear case for the up-scaling of legal preparedness for international disaster response in Africa. Important players in this are the RECs and the African Union, who are in a position to coordinate and develop treaties and other instruments at the regional and continental level respectively. However, individual states should also take responsibility in their growing awareness and endeavours to prepare their legal systems for disaster situations. One way of encouraging overall legal preparedness for international disaster response, and ensuring the facilitation and regulation between (amongst others) Africa and its supporters outside the continent, would be the development of a global treaty on international disaster cooperation that addresses the key issues outlined above, to ensure the efficient, economical and quality international cooperation in emergencies that people affected by disasters require.

13

Humanitarian assistance and the right to water: an ASEAN region perspective

DIANA PHILIP

1. Introduction

Water is a fundamental necessity synonymous with life, an idea captured beautifully in the oft-quoted words of the famous poet, W. H. Auden – 'Thousands have lived without love, not one without water.'[1] However, it is a vast and complex interdisciplinary subject of global relevance posing numerous challenges and involving multiple stakeholders. Issues can range from the straightforward, like availability (including qualitative aspects) and access, to the complex, like sustainability and legal rights under international law. Water also assumes significance because of the fact that since history water has been both the cause of armed conflict as well as the target of military action. Moreover, almost all natural disasters and conflicts tend to critically affect availability of water fit for human consumption. Because of its very nature, availability of water is considered to be amongst the top priorities in emergency situations. In these scenarios any issues with quantity, quality, access, cost, etc. could have deadly implications on the affected populace.

South East Asia is home to more than 600 million people.[2] Geographically, South East Asia has been blessed with adequate natural sources of fresh water. But it is getting increasingly threatened by rapid and unbalanced development and climate change. South East Asia is also extraordinarily prone to natural disasters and has in addition been affected by several conflicts. In such situations, affected persons are left without the very basics, including water. Due to a variety of reasons, which would include length of time, scale, inadequate infrastructure, availability of

[1] W. H. Auden, 'First Things First', 1956, accessed 7 April 2013, www.poets.org/viewmedia.php/prmMID/19467.

[2] 'Selected Basic ASEAN Indicators as of 14 January 2013', *ASEAN Stats*, accessed 1 April 2013, www.asean.org/images/2013/resources/statistics/Selected%20Key%20Indicators_/SummaryTable.pdf.

information, existing political dispensation, etc., mounting relief operations in this region has been a challenge. There have even been situations where relief agencies were outright denied access to the affected population.

'Relief operations do not take place in a legal vacuum.'[3] Therefore it is very important to understand the applicability of the right to water and what challenges exist in its full realisation during situations of emergencies. In the last decade there have been significant advancements in legal thinking resulting in the recognition of the right to water. This right acquired definite contours after the publication of General Comment No. 15 (hereinafter 'GC-15') by the United Nations Committee on Economic, Social and Cultural Rights in 2002.[4] It is now clearly established that every individual has a right to water which is inextricably interwoven with the right to life and an adequate standard of health and living. South East Asian states have now, through the ASEAN Human Rights Declaration of 2012, given recognition to the right to water at the regional level and have indicated their willingness to promote the same.

This paper seeks to examine the vulnerability of South East Asia to emergency situations wherein availability of water is affected, the right to water in the regional context, evolution of this right under international law, and lastly touches upon enforcement of this right regionally. This paper restricts itself to the states that are part of the Association of South East Asian Nations (ASEAN) and does not deal with the right to sanitation.

2. Water situation in South East Asia

Water resources in South East Asia are 'unequally distributed geographically and seasonally'.[5] Though, in the simple terms of access to water, the

[3] The Brookings-Bern Project, 'Synthesis Report of Regional Workshop on Protecting and Promoting Rights in Natural Disasters in South East Asia: Prevention and Response', May 14–15, 2010, 2, accessed 1 April 2013, www.brookings.edu/~/media/events/2010/5/14%20idp%20indonesia%20workshop/0514_idp_indonesia_workshop.pdf.

[4] CESCR, 'General Comment No. 15: The Right to Water' (Twenty-ninth session, 2003), UN Doc. E/C.12/2002/11 (2003), reprinted in Compilation of General Comments and General Recommendations Adopted by Human Rights Treaty Bodies, UN Doc. HRI/GEN/1/Rev.6 at 105 (2003).

[5] IWMI, 'IWMI research in South East Asia', *International Water Management Institute*, accessed 9 March 2013, http://sea.iwmi.org/Data/Sites/14/Documents/pdfs/iwmi_south_east_asia_brochure.pdf.

South East Asian Region is at present faring well and is close to meeting the states' respective Millennium Development Goals.[6] However, as pointed out in a report by Asian Development Bank entitled 'Asian Water Development Outlook 2013', the ground reality is that access to water sources varies greatly between urban and rural populations and between rich and poor.[7] Further, the vulnerable population (due to financial reasons or otherwise) still lacks access to safe water.[8] In the entire region only about 35 per cent of households have access to a tapped water source,[9] which is regarded as one of the improved drinking sources as opposed to unimproved drinking sources such as unprotected dug wells, spring water, or vendor-provided water.[10] Alarmingly, some researchers claim that the per capita availability of water in South East Asia has decreased by 55 per cent in the last fifty years.[11] Furthermore, for states like Indonesia, certain activists contest the official figures and claim that only 30 per cent of the population have access to drinking water in the cities, while for villages it is less than 10 per cent.[12] Similarly, for the Philippines it is claimed that around 86 per cent of the population has access to safe drinking water but around 31 per cent of the population suffers from water-related illnesses, indicating issues with quality.[13]

[6] Mukand S. Babel and Shahriar M. Wahid, 'Fresh Water Under Threat: South East Asia Vulnerability Assessment of Fresh Water Resources to Environmental Change, Mekong River', *UNEP*, 2009, 10, accessed 31 March 2013, www.unep.org/pdf/SEA_Water_report.pdf.

[7] Asian Development Bank, 'Asian Water Development Outlook 2013: Measuring Water Security in Asia and the Pacific', *Asia Pacific Water Forum*, 2013, 20, www.adb.org/sites/default/files/pub/2013/asian-water-development-outlook-2013.pdf; see also UNESCAP 'Statistical Yearbook for Asia and Pacific 2012', published on 6 November 2012, Poverty and Inequality, Access to Water and Sanitation, Table I.39, I.41, www.unescap.org/stat/data/syb2012/index.asp.

[8] Asian Development Bank, 'Asian Water Development Outlook 2013', 20.

[9] Asian Development Bank, 'Asian Water Development Outlook 2013', 19.

[10] CDC, 'Assessing Access to Water and Sanitation', *Centers for Disease Control and Prevention*, 31 October 2012, accessed 23 June 2013, www.cdc.gov/healthywater/global/assessing.html.

[11] Douglas L. Vermillion, 'Finding Solutions to Asia's Water Challenges through Integrated Water-Resources Management' (Background Note Issued Prior to the Meeting), 7, accessed 31 March 2013, http://publications.iwmi.org/pdf/h032971.pdf.

[12] 'Indonesia's Clean Drinking Water Crisis Worst in Southeast Asia: Expert', *Jakarta Globe*, 5 July 2012, accessed 22 February 2013, www.thejakartaglobe.com/health/indonesias-clean-drinking-water-crisis-worst-in-southeast-asia-expert/528758.

[13] Aaron Salzberg, 'Foreign Policy and International Water Development', accessed 25 March 2013, www.youtube.com/watch?v=s_CUt4wq4Xg.

The majority of the states in South East Asia face multiple challenges in the water sector, which range from lack of access to water, depletion of water sources, falling quality of water, and severe impact of natural disasters.[14] In fact, Cambodia, Indonesia, Laos, and the Philippines have been termed 'water hot-spots' by the United Nations Economic and Social Commission for Asia and the Pacific (UNESCAP), due to the presence of several of the challenges mentioned above.[15] Conflicts, displacement and refugee situations only add to these woes. Rapid urbanisation without due regard for environmental protection, diversions by upper riparian countries and population growth are also leading to water scarcity problems.[16] This in turn has an adverse impact on food production, health and environment.

There are about fifteen main river basins in the region,[17] of which Mekong is the longest, running over 4,900 km with its basin being 800,000 km^2 in size.[18] The Mekong originates in Tibet and flows through Myanmar, Thailand, Lao, Cambodia and Vietnam.[19] It is one of the most important sources of water in the region and is vital for its socio-economic development. The Mekong Basin is home to about 80 million people, which is expected to rise to over 100 million by 2025.[20] The river, however, has started to show signs of strain due to excessive use and pollution from industrial and municipal wastes. The Lower Mekong-region countries such as Laos, Vietnam, the Philippines and Cambodia are taking steps to address pollution, but enforcement mechanisms seem to be inadequate.[21] It is seen that about 38 per cent of the population in

[14] 'Statistical yearbook for Asia and Pacific 2011', accessed 30 March 2013, www.unescap.org/stat/data/syb2011/ii-environment/water-availability-and-use.asp; also see UNESCAP, 'Preview Green Growth Resources and Resilience Environmental Sustainability in Asia and Pacific', (ST/ESCAP/2582) 2010 (Box 2.2 Water Hot Spots2010.) 23, www.unescap.org/esd/environment/flagpubs/ggrap/documents/Green%20Growth-16Sept%20(Final).pdf.

[15] UNESCAP 'Green Growth Resources', 23.

[16] Eric T. Craswell, 'Water and Poverty in Southeast Asia – the Research Agenda from a Global Perspective', 3–6, accessed 19 March 2013, www.gwsp.org/fileadmin/downloads/Asian_Ag_Prod_Journal.pdf.

[17] Babel and Wahid, 'Fresh Water Under Threat', 10.

[18] Susanne Schmeier, *Governing of International Watercourses: The Contribution of River Basin Organisations to the Effective Governance of Internationally Shared Rivers and Lakes* (London: Routledge, 2013), 119.

[19] Ibid. [20] Ibid., 121.

[21] Joseph Yun, 'Challenges to Water and Security in Southeast Asia', 23 September 2010, accessed 18 March 2013, www.state.gov/p/eap/rls/rm/2010/09/147674.htm.

the Lower Mekong region do not have access to safe drinking water.[22] The quality of other rivers in the region is also said to be deteriorating.[23]

3. Emergencies in South East Asia and their impact on water

South East Asia is considered to be one 'of the largest disaster-prone areas in the world'[24] where about 176 million people were affected by natural disasters in 2011 alone.[25] Amongst the twenty-five worst disasters in the world in 2011, as many as twelve occurred in the South East Asian region, in countries such as Cambodia, the Philippines, Thailand, Vietnam and Myanmar.[26]

A diagrammatic representation of the breakup of natural disasters affecting South East Asia in recent years is given in Figure 13.1.

Some of the deadliest disasters in South East Asia in recent years would include the 2004 tsunami,[27] the 2008 cyclone Nargis in Myanmar[28] and the 2011 Thailand floods.[29] Climate change is only expected to lead to increased floods and droughts, as well as salt water intrusion.[30] It has already been observed that floods and storms hit the region with increased intensity and frequency.[31] Adding to this is the concern that

[22] Babel and Wahid, 'Fresh Water Under Threat', 19.

[23] Asian Development Bank, 'Asian Water Development Outlook 2013', 58.

[24] ECHO, 'Disaster Preparedness Regional Initiatives in SE Asia', 2007, 1, http://ec.europa.eu/echo/files/policies/dipecho/presentations/se_asia_11_07_en.pdf.

[25] OCHA, 'Humanitarian Chief Highlights Disaster Management in South East Asia', 23 March 2012, accessed 3 April 2013, www.unocha.org/top-stories/all-stories/humanitarian-chief-highlights-disaster-management-south-east-asia.

[26] Natural Disaster Data Book 2011 (An Analytical Overview), Asian Disaster Reduction Center, 2011, Table 6–1, 10, www.adrc.asia/publications/databook/ORG/databook_2011/pdf/DataBook2011_e.pdf.

[27] John Pickrell, 'The Worst Natural Disasters in Recent History', *ABC Environment*, last modified 2 May 2011, www.abc.net.au/environment/articles/2011/04/27/3197103.htm.

[28] Jijo Jacob, 'Factbox: Key Facts About Cyclone Nargis', *Reuters* (US Edn.), accessed 6 April 2013, www.reuters.com/article/2009/04/30/idUSSP420097.

[29] 'Top Five Worst Natural Disasters of 2011', 31 December 2011, accessed 25 March 2013, www.globalpost.com/dispatch/news/regions/asia-pacific/japan/111229/worst-natural-disasters-2011.

[30] Schmeier, *Governing of International Watercourses*, 124.

[31] EU, ECHO 'Fact Sheet East and South East Asia, and the Pacific', *European Commission*, 2012, 1, accessed 9 March 2013, http://ec.europa.eu/echo/files/aid/countries/factsheets/esea_en.pdf.

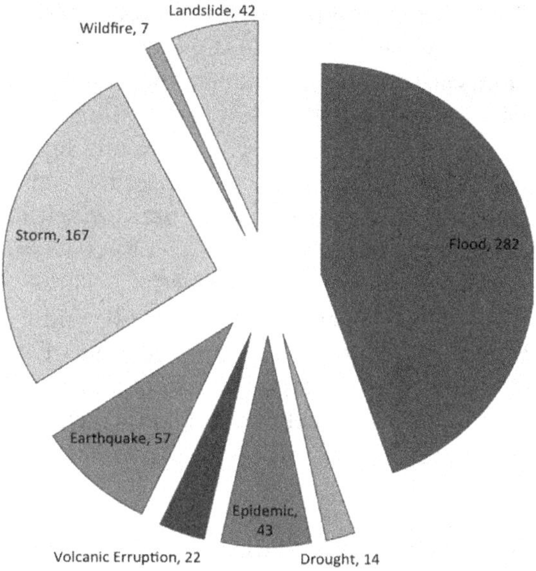

Figure 13.1: Number of natural disasters in South East Asia – 2001 to 2012. (Note: no data for landslide after 2009. Also, not all the natural disasters require international assistance, which is often given based on the scale, the extent of damages and the government's inability to address the situation in a timely and effective manner.)

the region's 'capacity to overcome such disasters' is lower than even the East Asian nations, which face the highest number of natural disasters.[32] Countries which are 'heavily exposed' to natural disasters are also left facing huge financial losses.[33]

To add to the above, South East Asia and the Pacific have faced the most number of conflicts in the world since the Second World War.[34] Some of the countries in the South East Asian region have faced long, protracted armed conflicts of varying intensities.[35] At present

[32] Asian Development Bank, 'Asian Water Development Outlook', 64, 65.

[33] Mark Kinver, 'Asian Nations "Face Greatest Natural Disaster Risk"', *BBC*, 15 August 2012, accessed 30 March 2013, www.bbc.co.uk/news/science-environment-19254685.

[34] Terry Gennet, 'Civil War in South East Asia and the Pacific: Conflict Resolution and the Problem of Recurrence', in *Unravelling Internal Conflicts in East Asia and Pacific: incidence, consequences and resolution*, ed. Jacob Berkovitch and Karl DeReuben Jr. (Maryland: Lexington Books, 2011), 96.

[35] Asian Research Center for Migration, 'Children Caught in Conflicts: The Impact of Armed Conflict on Children in South East Asia', Institute of Asian Studies, Chulalongkorn University, 2007, 12, www.crin.org/docs/CIDA_Caught_Conflict.pdf.

Myanmar, Thailand, the Philippines and Indonesia face internal conflicts.[36] Myanmar has faced internal conflict for the last sixty years, which is the longest-running conflict in the world.[37] Thailand faces border problems with Cambodia as well as militancy in its southern parts where there is a demand for greater autonomy or complete independence.[38] The Philippines on the other hand continue to experience clashes in Mindanao Island between ethnic Moros and the Philippine army. Indonesia faces a forty-year-old separatist struggle called the Free Papua Movement.[39] These conflicts have resulted in about 946,000 internally displaced people (IDPs) in the region in 2011 alone.[40] Thus we see that the South East Asian region faces a staggering overlap of natural disasters and conflicts leading to situations of emergencies, which have a direct effect on water and water resources.

3.1 *Impact of natural disasters and conflicts on water*

During conflicts and natural disasters there is contamination of water sources, deliberate obstruction of access to water[41] and widespread destruction of water infrastructure.[42] This in turn leads to either lack of distribution or distribution of water unsafe for consumption. Sometimes there is also a lack of resources, such as necessary chemicals to purify water, and theft or destruction of data necessary for the proper

[36] Elsina Wainwright, 'Conflict Prevention in Southeast Asia and the South Pacific', April 2010, 7–9, www.humansecuritygateway.com/documents/CIC_ConflictPreventionIn-SoutheastAsiaAndTheSouthPacific.pdf.

[37] Gennet, 'Civil War in South East Asia', 96.

[38] Uppsala Conflict Data Programme, 'Thailand', *UCPD Conflict Encyclopaedia*, accessed 30 March 2013, www.ucdp.uu.se/gpdatabase/gpcountry.php?id=154&regionSelect=7-Eastern_Asia.

[39] Wainwright, 'Conflict Prevention', 7, 8.

[40] Number of IDPs computed from IDMC, 'Internal Displacement in South and South East Asia', Internal Displacement Monitoring Center, 2011, 84, www.internal-displacement.org/8025708F004BE3B1/(httpInfoFiles)/0E27234251BE6E48C12579E400369AA9/$file/global-overview-asia-2011.pdf.

[41] OCHA, 'Water Scarcity and Humanitarian Action, Key Emerging Trends and Challenges', *OCHA Occasional Briefing Series*, September 2010, 8, accessed 19 March 2013, http://ochanet.unocha.org/p/Documents/OCHA%20OPB%20Water%20%2011Nov10%20fnl.pdf.

[42] UNOPS, 'Water Treatment', www.unops.org/english/whatwedo/services/physical-infrastructure/experience-capacity/Pages/water-treatment.aspx.

functioning of water systems.[43] In the first Gulf War in 1990 there was massive damage to water infrastructure such as water pumping stations, major dams, municipal water and sewage facilities and water purification units, leading to severe contamination of water sources.[44] The Second Gulf War in 2003 once again led to serious damage to the still-recovering water networks, and once again caused an acute shortage of water. As a result, even after so many years, in 2009 as many as 70 per cent of the population was living without an adequate water supply. The list does not end here. Angola, Liberia, Rwanda, Yemen, Bosnia-Herzegovina, Libya and Syria[45] are all recent examples where conflict had a damaging impact on water resources and in turn on the civilian population.[46]

A very good example from South East Asia would be Cambodia, where due to three decades of conflict under the Khmer Rouge regime, a majority of the water infrastructure was destroyed.[47] On the other hand, in Myanmar, cyclone Nargis caused contamination of the drinking-water sources by 'rotting animal carcasses, human corpses, salt water and debris'.[48] The 2011 tropical storm Washi caused flash floods in the southern Philippines leaving an estimated 1,000 dead while destroying water networks in the hardest-hit provinces in Mindanao and Visayas regions.[49]

[43] Kristina Donnelly et al. 'Water as a Casualty of Conflict: Threats to Business and Society in High-Risk Areas', June 2012, 7,9, accessed 18 March 2013, http://unglobalcompact.org/docs/issues_doc/Environment/Water_as_a_casuality.pdf.

[44] SFG, 'Cost of Conflict in the Middle East', Strategic Foresight Group, 2009, 48.

[45] 'NATO Bombs the Great Man-Made River', *Human Rights Investigations*, 27 July 2011, http://humanrightsinvestigations.org/2011/07/27/great-man-made-river-nato-bombs/. 'Syria: ICRC helps provide clean water for 10 million people', 17 December 2012, accessed 1 March 2013, www.icrc.org/eng/resources/documents/update/2012/12-17-syria-water.htm. See also OCHA, 'Draft Syria Humanitarian Assistance Plan', accessed 1 March 2013, www.unocha.org/cap/appeals/draft-syria-humanitarian-assistance-response-plan-2012.

[46] ICRC, 'Civilians in War', 1 October 1995, accessed 1 March 2013, www.icrc.org/eng/resources/documents/misc/57jmk.htm#a6.

[47] JICA, 'Water Problems at Angkor Wat', *Japan International Cooperation Agency*, March 2009, accessed 6 April 2013, www.jica.go.jp/english/news/focus_on/water/water_1.html.

[48] ICRC, 'Myanmar: Clean water reaches isolated residents in Dedaye', 28 May 2008. www.icrc.org/eng/resources/documents/feature/2008/myanmar-feature-280508.htm.

[49] ICRC, 'Philippines: Red Cross delivers vital aid', *ICRC Resource Centre*, 23 December 2011, accessed 6 April 2013, www.icrc.org/eng/resources/documents/update/2011/philippines-update-2011-12-23.htm.

3.2 *Multifarious character of water*

The very nature of water is such that it has 'multiple and conflicting demands on its use'.[50] Hence, as Peter Gleick has rightfully opined, 'water and water-supply systems are increasingly likely to be both objectives of military action and instruments of war'.[51] Many conflicts involving water have occurred in the past in different parts of the world.[52] In the 1990s, shrinking of Lake Chad caused border disputes between Nigeria, Chad, Cameroon and Niger and ultimately led to a full-scale war between Nigeria and Cameroon.[53] In 2009, North Korea unexpectedly released 40 million cubic metres of water from Hwanggang Dam, which caused flash floods and resulted in casualties in the South.[54] In the sixteen-year civil war in Mozambique which ended in 1992, landmines were used intentionally to block access to water for civilians.[55]

It is also seen that small-scale water riots or instability in many regions is increasingly felt in the present-day context, including in Thailand.[56] Homer-Dixon has observed that one of the reasons for this is that water scarcity leads to competition, which in turn leads to conflict amongst people.[57]

[50] Aaron T. Wolf, '"Water Wars" and Water Reality: Conflict and Cooperation Along International Waterways' in *Environmental Challenge, Adaptation and Security*, ed. Steve C. Lonergan (Netherlands: Kluwer Academic Publishers, 1997), 251.

[51] Peter H. Gleick, 'Water and Conflict: Fresh Water Resources and International Security', *International Security* 18, No. 1 (Summer, 1993): 79–112, 79, www.pacinst.org/reports/international_security_gleick_1993.pdf.

[52] Gabriel Eckstein, 'Water Scarcity, Conflict, and Security in a Climate Change World: Challenges and Opportunities for International Law and Policy', *Texas Wesleyan University School of Law*, 9 December 2009, 429, http://papers.ssrn.com/sol3/papers.cfm?abstract_id=1425796.

[53] Ernest Waititu, 'Diminishing Water Resources Threaten Peace', 26 May 2009, accessed 30 March 2013, http://pulitercenter.org/articles/diminishing-water-resources-threaten-peace.

[54] James Sturcke, 'South Korea Demands North Korea Apology for Flash Flood that Killed Six', *The Guardian*, 8 September 2009, accessed 30 March 2013, www.guardian.co.uk/world/2009/sep/08/south-korea-flood-kills-campers.

[55] Catarina de Albuquerque, *The Human Right to Water and Sanitation: The Legal Framework and a Guide to Advocacy, for Field Review* (France: ACF, 2009), 39, www.worldwatercouncil.org/fileadmin/wwc/Right_to_Water/Project_8_HRTWS_in_Emergencies_Handbook.pdf.

[56] 'Bloody Clashes in Indonesia's Maluku Claim Another Life', *Jakarta Globe*, 8 March 2012, accessed 7 April 2013, www.thejakartaglobe.com/news/bloody-clashes-in-indonesias-maluku-claim-another-life/503346.

[57] Thomas F. Homer-Dixon, 'Environmental Scarcities and Violent Conflict: Evidence from Cases', *International Security* 19, No. 1 (Summer, 1994): 5–40, http://graduateinstitute.ch/webdav/site/iheid/shared/summer/IA2009_readings/MD1.pdf.

Lack of water or its scarcity is predicted to have a major impact on the future stability of nations.[58] President Truong Tan Sang of Vietnam, stated on 7 September 2012 that 'it would not be over-exaggerating . . . to view the water resources of the twenty-first century as the oil of the nineteenth and twentieth centuries'.[59] This was in relation to the exploitation of Mekong River where burgeoning hydropower projects may lead to water security issues.[60] This poses as a contentious issue between Thailand, Cambodia, Laos, Myanmar and China,[61] though military conflict is not likely to be a possibility.

In this context it is also worthwhile bearing in mind that water may even be used as a tool in terrorism.[62] There are a number of terrorist attacks in recent times that have been directed at water infrastructure, including the dumping of chemicals into the Meuse River in France and the placing of a bomb in a water reservoir in South Africa.[63] The Philippines witnessed a threat by the Moro Islamic Liberation Front (MILF) that it would poison the water sources in the region.[64] It is said that water installations will become a target of terrorist attacks in the future.[65] It is not clear whether the state machinery in South East Asian nations has anticipated or is adequately equipped to deal with such situations.

[58] US Department of State, 'Global Water Security, Intelligence Community Assessment', February 2012, iv, www.dni.gov/files/documents/Special%20Report_ICA%20Global%20Water%20Security.pdf.

[59] 'Vietnam Warns of Water Conflicts', *AFP*, 7 September 2012, www.google.com/hosted-news/afp/article/ALeqM5grQeVwutLgCMASLtuccOtxjKGO9A?docId=CNG.ed18aee1f8d766ca66096e5c8b6c1e1a.b41.

[60] For definition of 'water security' see Brahma Chellaney, *Water: Asia's New Battleground* (India: Harper Collins, 2011), 10.

[61] Michael Richardson, 'Dams in China Turn the Mekong into a River of Discord', *Yale Global Online*, 16 July 2009, accessed 29 March 2013, http://yaleglobal.yale.edu/content/dams-china-turn-mekong-river-discord.

[62] Peter H. Gleick, 'Water and Terrorism', *Water Policy* 8 (2006): 481–503, 482, accessed on 6 April 2013, www.pacinst.org/reports/water_terrorism.pdf.

[63] Frederick M. Lorenz, 'The Protection of Water Facilities under International Law', UNESCO and World Water Assessment Programme, Norway, 2003, 28, accessed 6 April 2013, http://unesdoc.unesco.org/images/0013/001324/132464e.pdf.

[64] John Unson, 'Moro rebs to poison sources of water?', *PhilStar*, 26 March 2003, www.philstar.com/nation/200342/moro-rebs-poison-sources-water. See also Pacific Institute, 'Water Conflict Chronology Timeline', accessed 28 March 2013, www.worldwater.org/conflict/timeline/

[65] Lorenz, 'Protection of Water Facilities', 3.

3.3 *Water and humanitarian assistance*

Issues relating to water security have a direct bearing on humanitarian assistance. According to the Office of Humanitarian Affairs (OCHA), scarcity of water will lead to an increase in the 'Humanitarian case-loads' and 'depth of Humanitarian Assistance'.[66] It will also make it operationally difficult to deliver assistance. The challenge also stems from insufficient data in relation to the quality and quantity of water during emergencies. However, the biggest hurdle comes from the lack of political will in ensuring that the vulnerable population have basic necessities such as water during and after emergencies. In some cases there are deliberate attempts by the government to prevent humanitarian assistance from reaching the vulnerable people on the ground, including by the expulsion of humanitarian agencies. However, in the case of water a genuine inability on the part of states to provide the same cannot be denied. Also, while governments may allow humanitarian agencies to help during emergencies in bringing relief aid in terms of food and medical supplies, they usually take a defensive stance when it comes to humanitarian assistance relating to water. This is due to the fact that unlike other supplies, ensuring sufficient water is not a short-term measure but a sustained and coordinated one, which may range from a few months to years. This makes governments reluctant to admit or entertain aid agencies when it comes to water.

South East Asia presently confronts a gamut of water security issues. The region's vulnerability to natural disasters, as well as its long and sustained internal conflicts, which have a definite impact on the availability of water, make it necessary to think in the direction of the application of the right to water, recognised under international as well as regional instruments during situations of emergency.

4. Development of the right to water: regionally and internationally

4.1 *Public international law and water*

In 1977, during the United Nations Water Conference in Mar del Plata, Argentina, the nations for the first time declared that 'all peoples,

[66] OCHA, 'Water Scarcity and Humanitarian Action', 3.

whatever their stage of development and their social and economic conditions, have the right to have access to drinking water in quantities and of a quality equal to their basic needs'.[67] This was followed by the 1979 *Convention for the Elimination of all Forms of Discrimination against Women* (CEDAW), which was the first human rights treaty to explicitly recognise the 'right to water'.[68] The 1989 *Convention on the Rights of the Child* (CRC) under Article 24(2) made it obligatory for 'state parties to take appropriate measures to combat disease and malnutrition through the provision of adequate and nutritious foods and clean drinking water'.[69] Further, the 1990 *African Charter on the Rights and Welfare of the Child*,[70] as well as the 2006 *International Convention on the Rights of Persons with Disabilities*,[71] gave recognition to the right to water.

In the year 2002, the United Nations Committee on Economic, Social and Cultural Rights (UNCESR) in GC-15 considered that the right to water derived from the right to an adequate standard of living (Article 11) and the right to health (Article 12) under the *International Covenant for Economic, Social and Cultural Rights* (ICESCR). The General Comment of UNCESR is not binding per se; however, it provides 'a critical mechanism for developing a normative and contextualised understanding of the provisions of the ICESCR'.[72] While GC-15 did not create a new right to water, it recognises that this right is central to the enjoyment of certain fundamental rights enshrined in the Covenant. Thus GC-15 represents a turning point in the development of the right to water and its scope.

[67] United Nations Water Conference, 14–25 March 1977, Mar del Plata. Report of the United Nations Water Conference, UN Doc. (E/CONF.70/29) 1, www.ielrc.org/content/e7701.pdf.

[68] UN, *Convention for the Elimination of all Forms of Discrimination Against Women* (CEDAW) 1979, Article 14(h): www.un.org/womenwatch/daw/cedaw/text/econvention.htm#article14.

[69] UN Doc. (A/44/25) *Convention on the Rights of Child*, 1989 (CRC), Article 14(2)(c). www2.ohchr.org/english/law/pdf/crc.pdf.

[70] AU, *African Charter on the Rights and Welfare of the Child*, 1990, Article 14(c). www.au.int/en/sites/default/files/Charter_En_African_Charter_on_the_Rights_and_Welfare_of_the_Child_AddisAbaba_July1990.pdf.

[71] UN, *International Convention on the Rights of Persons with Disabilities*, 1999, Article 28: www.un.org/disabilities/convention/conventionfull.shtml.

[72] M. A. Salman and Siobhán McInerney-Lankford, 'Human Right to Water: Legal and Policy Dimensions', *World Bank*, 2004, Introduction, 5, accessed 23 June 2013, www-wds.worldbank.org.

Over the years, other treaty bodies such as the Committee on the Rights of the Child as well as the Committee on the Elimination of Discrimination against Women have emphasised the right to water in its general comments and in its examination of state reports. For example, the CRC in its General Comment No. 7 stated that 'states parties have a responsibility to ensure access to clean drinking water',[73] while the CEDAW committee in its general observation on Ecuador's state report that 'before enjoying legal rights, women need to be given basic human rights such as safe drinking water'.[74]

In 2010, the United Nations General Assembly Resolution (64/292) formally recognised the 'right to safe drinking water and sanitation as a human right that is essential for the full enjoyment of life and all human rights'. The UNGA resolution was adopted by 121 votes and 41 abstentions. It is a non-binding resolution, but it is indicative of the fact that the international community is now more conscious of the right to water as an enforceable right. [75]

In September 2010, the United Nations Human Rights Council also passed a resolution which in practice takes the General Assembly resolution forward and offers additional detail.[76] It makes the right to water a part of the right to life, thus making it legally binding upon nations. This resolution was passed by consensus.[77]

[73] Committee on the Rights of the Child, 'General Comment No. 4, Adolescent Health and Development in the Context of the Convention on the Rights of the Child' (Thirty-third session, 2003), UN Doc. CRC/GC/2003/4 (2003).

[74] Committee on the Elimination of Discrimination Against Women, 'Concluding Observations: Ecuador', UN Doc. (A/49/38) §499–545 (1994), §509, www1.umn.edu/humanrts/cedaw/cedaw-Ecuador.htm.

[75] UN, 'General Assembly Adopts Resolution Recognising Access to Clean Water, Sanitation as Human Right by Recorded Vote of 122 in Favour, None Against and 41 Abstentions', 28 July 2010, accessed 1 March 2013, www.un.org/News/Press/docs/2010/ga10967.doc.htm.

[76] UN, 'Human Rights and Access to Safe Drinking Water and Sanitation', *United Nations Human Rights Council*, 24 September 2010 (A/HRC/15/L.14), http://daccess-dds-ny.un.org/doc/RESOLUTION/LTD/G12/168/66/PDF/G1216866.pdf?OpenElement.

[77] Rachel Ordu Dan-Harry, 'UN Human Rights Council Affirms Safe Drinking Water and Sanitation as a Human Right', *Unitarian Universalist Service Committee*, 15 October 2010, accessed 25 March 2013, www.uusc.org/blog/entry/2404/un_human_rights_council_affirms_safe_drinking_water_and_sanitation_human_right.

See also OHCHR, 'A Landmark Decision to Make the Right to Water and Sanitation Legally Binding', *Office of the High Commissioner for Human Rights*, 6 October 2010, accessed 30 March 2013. www.ohchr.org/EN/NewsEvents/Pages/RightToWaterAndSanitation.aspx.

4.2 *Scope of the right to water*

The right to water as recognised under GC-15 of the UNCESCR requires 'that all persons have affordable access to a supply of safe water in quantities adequate for essential personal and domestic uses, which include drinking, sanitation, clothes washing, food preparation and personal use and household hygiene'.[78]

As per the GC-15, there are three main components to this right – 'accessibility, quality and availability'.[79] This is further clarified by the Special Rapporteur on Right to Water and Sanitation, Catarina de Albuquerque, in her 2009 report, 'Human Right to Water and Sanitation in Emergency Situations'.[80] Thus the realisation of this right entails that:[81]

a) Water resources must be within reach of the population without any discrimination and should be affordable by all.[82]
b) Water so accessible should be safe for human consumption and free from contaminants that lead to serious health problems. A certain quality of water is essential for people to survive and this means that the water should be free of chemical or microbial substances and radiological hazards.[83]
c) Water should be available in adequate quantity. 'The water supply for each person must be sufficient and continuous for personal and domestic uses.'[84] According to the Sphere Minimum Standards there must be at least 15 litres of water per person per household per day during Humanitarian Emergencies.[85]
d) Lastly, the state parties must ensure that all persons have a right to water, take measures to remove any form of discrimination and give 'special attention' to groups of people who cannot exercise their right for various reasons including humanitarian

[78] David R. Boyd, 'Right to Water: Moving from International Action to National Recognition', in *The Global Water Crisis: Addressing an Urgent Security Issue*, eds Harriet Bigas, Tim Morris, Bob Sandford and Safar Adeel (Thomas S. Axworthy, 2011–2012), 129: www.inweh.unu.edu/WaterSecurity/documents/WaterSecurity_FINAL_Aug2012.pdf.

[79] GC-15, para 12 (a)(b)(c).

[80] De Albuquerque, *The Human Right to Water*, 37–38.

[81] De Albuquerque, *The Human Right to Water*, 37–46.

[82] GC-15,§12(c).

[83] GC-15, §12(b).

[84] GC-15, §12(a).

[85] Sphere Handbook, 'Water Supply Standard 1: Access and Water Quantity', *The Sphere Handbook: Humanitarian Charter and Minimum Standards in Humanitarian Response*, accessed 30 March 2013, www.spherehandbook.org/en/water-supply-standard-1-access-and-water-quantity/.

emergencies.[86] This provision ensures that vulnerable groups of populations including women, children, refugees and IDPs are protected.

In addition, the right also provides for accountability, which is crucial to its realisation. Persons denied of their right to water should have access to effective judicial or appropriate remedies.[87] A judicial enforcement could ensure that this right is not denied or violated. Also, people should have the 'right to seek, receive and impart information concerning water issues'.[88]

GC-15 also lays down the duties of the governments which would lead to the full and effective realisation of this right. These duties include:

a) Refraining from arbitrary interference with the right to water. Governments cannot deny water services to people or indulge in practices that would limit the access to water or lead to the deterioration of the quality or quantity of water.[89] Furthermore, GC-15 makes it obligatory for states to refrain from causing any harm which may impede the enjoyment of this right by nationals of another state, thus preventing transboundary harm.[90]
b) Bringing in measures such as domestic legislation and policies for the protection of this right.[91] States are required to legislate and ensure that right to water becomes a part of their domestic law and policy.
c) Effectively implementing domestic legislations, regulation and policies relating to water. This will pave the way for measures to reduce and prevent depletion of water, improve quality of water, reduce water wastage through distribution, establish response mechanisms for emergency situations and establish competent monitoring and implementation bodies.[92]

The GC-15 also lays down certain specific duties for states to follow during emergencies such as the protection of vulnerable groups affected in emergency situations[93] and giving priority to the rights under the ICESCR, including the right to water during relief assistance.[94] States are also prohibited from violating principles of international humanitarian law (IHL)[95] or taking any measures such as 'attacking, destroying or limiting the access to water as a punitive measure in violation to

[86] GC-15, §13–16. [87] Ibid., §55. [88] Ibid., §12(c) (iv). [89] Ibid., §21.
[90] Ibid., §31. [91] Ibid., §26. [92] Ibid., §28. [93] Ibid., §16(h).
[94] Ibid., §34. [95] Ibid., §22.

International Humanitarian Law'.[96] A welcome development in this regard is the publication of the 'Technical Notes on Drinking Water, Sanitation and Hygiene During Emergencies' (2011) published by the World Health Organisation (WHO)[97] along with the Sphere Standards 2011, which can now be taken as an authoritative framework for emergency relief which will help the stakeholders in the enforcement of this right.

4.3 *International humanitarian law and water*

It is said that 'contaminated water and lack of water can be more deadly than a whole array of weapons'.[98] The provisions under the Geneva Conventions III[99] and IV[100] offer protection to prisoners of war and civilian internees. The Conventions state that the protected persons should not be deprived of water for drinking and personal use.[101] Geneva Convention III prohibits 'collective disciplinary measures affecting food'[102] and this provision has been interpreted to include water within its ambit. However, water is afforded better protection under their Additional Protocols, which are yet to be ratified by a majority of the states in the world.

Additional Protocols I[103] and *II*[104] of the Geneva Conventions give emphasis to the protection of water as a resource. Article 54(2) of Protocol I provides 'protection for objects indispensable to the survival

[96] GC-15, §21.

[97] WHO, 'Technical Notes on Drinking Water, Sanitation and Hygiene during Emergencies', 2011, accessed 30 March 2013, www.who.int/water_sanitation_health/publications/2011/tn9_how_much_water_en.pdf.

[98] ICRC, 'Civilians in War', 1 October 1995, www.icrc.org/eng/resources/documents/misc/57jmk.htm.

[99] *Geneva Convention III Relating to Treatment of Prisoners of War*, 1946, www.icrc.org/ihl.nsf/FULL/375.

[100] *Geneva Convention IV Relating to the Protection of Civilian Persons in Time of War*, 12 August 1949, www.icrc.org/ihl.nsf/full/380.

[101] Article 20, 26, 29 and 43 of *Geneva Convention III*. Article 85, 89, 127 of *Geneva Convention IV*.

[102] *Geneva Convention III*, Article 26.

[103] UNTS, *Additional Protocol to the Geneva Conventions of 12 August 1949, and relating to the Protection of Victims of International Armed Conflicts* (*Additional Protocol I*), 8 June 1977, www.icrc.org/ihl.nsf/FULL/470?OpenDocument.

[104] UNTS, *Additional Protocol to the Geneva Conventions of 12 August 1949, and relating to the Protection of Victims of Non-International Armed Conflicts* (*Additional Protocol II*), 8 June 1977, www.icrc.org/ihl.nsf/full/475?opendocument.

of the civilian population', which includes water. It also states that 'starvation of civilians as a method of warfare is prohibited' and that 'it is prohibited to attack, destroy, remove or render useless objects indispensable to the survival of the civilian population ... drinking water installations and supplies and irrigation works, for the specific purpose of denying them for their sustenance value to the civilian population or to the adverse Party'. Derogations from this rule (under Article 54 of *Additional Protocol I*) are possible only if the infrastructure or water source is used solely for the purpose of sustaining armed forces. However, if this would result in the starvation or migration of the civilian populations then the parties are to refrain from such acts despite the fact that doing so sustains the military. Derogation may also be justified out of military necessity, provided it is done by a party in the territory under its control. An important clause under the provision is that that water source/installation 'shall not be made the object of reprisals'.[105]

Article 55 of *Additional Protocol I* affords environmental protection. Article 56 provides for protection to dams and dykes in the event that their destruction would lead to 'severe losses among the civilian population'. Furthermore, 'the High Contracting Parties and the Parties to the conflict are urged to conclude further agreements among themselves to provide additional protection for objects containing dangerous forces'.[106]

Dams and dykes in any region are vulnerable, and often a target of military missions. This tactic was seen in raids carried out by the 'Dambusters' squadron of the British Royal Air Force in 1943 during the Second World War which attacked two key dams in the Ruhr Valley in Germany.[107] Also, during the Korean War, 'operations against dams and dykes were considered one of the most successful campaigns carried out by the United States Air Force'.[108] Vietnam was also a victim of such tactics being adopted by the United States forces in 1972.[109]

The *Additional Protocol II* on the Protection of Victims of Non-International Armed Conflict, under its Articles 14 and 15, affords protection to water sources and installations as *Additional Protocol I* does,

[105] Article 54(4) *Additional Protocol I.* [106] Article 56(6) *Additional Protocol I.*

[107] 'Fact File: Dambusters Raid', 16, 17 May 1943, *BBC*, accessed 30 March 2013, www.bbc.co.uk/history/ww2peopleswar/timeline/factfiles/nonflash/a1057402.shtml.

[108] Lorenz, 'The Protection of Water Facilities', 15.

[109] Pacific Institute, 'Water Conflict Chronology List', accessed 5 April 2013, www.worldwater.org/conflict/list/.

but it is pertinent to note that the derogations permitted in *Additional Protocol I* are not permitted in *Additional Protocol II*.

During the civil war in Sudan water sources like water wells were poisoned or bombed. In Darfur, it is said that there was intentional contamination of water in order to harass the displaced population.[110] These cases will certainly fall within the prohibitive standards of *Additional Protocol II*. Also, relief agencies were made to leave Sudan, as a result of which about a million people were left without water.[111] Millions in Vietnam have been directly or indirectly exposed to various harmful chemicals including Agent Orange and dioxin over forty years since herbicides were sprayed by the United States forces between 1967 and 1971. Such chemicals have remained in 'the soil and in the sediment of waterways of southern Vietnam'.[112]

Provisions related to the protection of basic needs of the detainees, protection of objects indispensable for civilian population, prohibition of starvation as well as protecting water resources and the environment in general as civilian objects, are a part of customary international law applicable to all parties to the conflict, whether national or international.[113]

Apart from the Geneva Conventions and its Protocols, the *Rome Statute* also has provisions which may be relevant during conflicts or humanitarian emergencies. Article 8(2)(b)(xxv) of the Statute states inter alia that subjecting civilians to starvation as a means of warfare by depriving them of those basic necessities essential for their survival, and also by wilfully obstructing relief supplies, is a war crime.[114] Also, Article 8(2)(b)(4) states that 'intentionally launching an attack in the

[110] Amnesty International, 'Sudan Darfur: "Too Many People Killed for No Reason"', 3 February 2004, accessed 25 March 2013, www.amnesty.org/en/library/asset/AFR54/008/2004/en/452c12ed-d640-11dd-ab95-a13b602c0642/afr540082004en.html.

[111] Rebecca Barber, 'Facilitating Humanitarian Assistance in International Humanitarian and Human Rights Law', *International Review of the Red Cross* 91, No. 874 (2009): 378, www.icrc.org/eng/assets/files/other/irrc-874-barber.pdf.

[112] Michael F. Martin, 'Vietnamese Victims of Agent Orange and US–Vietnam Relations', *Congressional Research Service*, 29 August 2012, 14, 15, accessed 5 March 2013, www.fas.org/sgp/crs/row/RL34761.pdf.

[113] Jean-Marie Henckaerts and Louise Doswald-Beck, *Customary International Humanitarian Law, vol. I, Rules* (Cambridge University Press, 2009), Rules 43, 53–54, 118, www.icrc.org/eng/assets/files/other/customary-international-humanitarian-law-i-icrc-eng.pdf, in De Albuquerque, *The Human Right to Water*, 62.

[114] Article 8(2) (b) (xxv), UN, *Rome Statute of the International Criminal Court*, UN Doc. (A/CONF.183/9), http://untreaty.un.org/cod/icc/statute/romefra.htm.

knowledge that such attack will cause incidental loss of life or injury to civilians or damage to civilian objects or widespread, long-term and severe damage to the natural environment which would be clearly excessive in relation to the concrete and direct overall military advantage anticipated' would be a war crime. This provision is also interpreted to include within its ambit water infrastructure. Though there has been no prosecution made for attacks against water installations as yet at the International Criminal Court (ICC), the option certainly exists.

4.4 *Right to water vis à vis humanitarian assistance in South East Asia*

In the context of South East Asia, the right to water as enumerated in the previous sections can be critical in situations like that in the Rakhine province in Myanmar, which has been engulfed in secessionist internal conflict and has also felt severe effects of natural disasters. About 45.8 per cent of the population lacks access to safe water while the figure for the rest of the country is only 20 per cent.[115] The situation is worsened by discrimination against the residents by local authorities and denial of even basic rights. In this region 'essential services such as healthcare, water, sanitation and education are woefully inadequate and in most cases non-existent'.[116]

Problems also exist in IDP camps and communal shelters where there is a lack of improved water and sanitation[117] as seen in the Myanmar's Kachin state.[118] The unregistered IDPs suffer further problems as they receive no governmental or international aid, and aid to them is impeded by threats from the local community groups.[119]

[115] UNICEF, 'Myanmar', *UNICEF* Humanitarian Action for Children, 2011, 2, accessed 19 March 2013, www.unicef.org/hac2011/files/HAC2011_4pager_Myanmar.pdf.

[116] UNHCR, 'Myanmar 2013 UNHCR country operations profile', accessed 18 March 2013, www.unhcr.org/pages/49e4877d6.html.

[117] IRIN, 'Wash Woes for Myanmar's Rakhine IDPs', *IRIN Humanitarian News Analysis*, 18 January 2013, accessed 20 March 2013, www.irinnews.org/Report/97279/WASH-woes-for-Myanmar-s-Rakhine-IDPs.

[118] UN News Centre, 'Myanmar: UN Aid Reaches People in Conflict-affected Kachin Area', *UN News Centre*, accessed 4 April 2013, www.un.org/apps/news/story.asp?NewsID=44257#.UUhsHjf7yQ.

[119] IRIN, 'Unregistered IDPs in Myanmar's Rakhine without aid', *IRIN*, 25 March 2013, accessed 25 March 2013, www.irinnews.org/Report/97729/Unregistered-IDPs-in-Myanmar-s-Rakhine-without-aid.

In the Philippines, the Committee on the Elimination of Discrimination against Women noted with concern that the indigenous as well as Muslim women in the conflict-prone Mindanao region lacked access to safe drinking water and called upon state parties to address the same.[120]

In this regard the recognition of the right to water in South East Asia's regional human rights instrument could be a significant step towards meeting the basic needs of people during humanitarian emergencies.

5. ASEAN Human Rights Declaration

On 18 November 2012, ASEAN adopted the Human Rights Declaration (AHRD),[121] during their annual summit held in Cambodia. The AHRD was drafted by the ASEAN Intergovernmental Commission on Human Rights (AICHR) in pursuance of its mandate given under its terms of reference.[122] The drafting and adoption process became a matter of concern to the international community as the draft declaration was not officially made available for public discussion and scrutiny.[123] Nevertheless, the adoption of the declaration is considered to be a landmark event, for it elevates ASEAN to the league of other regional blocs such as the African Union, the Organisation of American States and the European Union, all of which have a regional human rights instrument.[124]

The declaration contains provisions on civil and political rights as well as economic, social and cultural rights. It also gives recognition to the right to development and the right to peace which is a unique facet in a regional human rights instrument. The right to water also forms a part of the AHRD under its Article 28 which states that: 'Every person has the

[120] 'Compilation: General Recommendations and Concluding Observations Relevant to the Rights of Indigenous Women', *Forest Peoples Programmes*, September 2012, 54, accessed 23 June 2013, www.forestpeoples.org/sites/fpp/files/news/2011/06/Compilation%20CEDAW%20%20ENG%20(Update%20September%202012).pdf.

[121] ASEAN, 'ASEAN Human Rights Declaration', *Association of South East Asian Nations*, 19 November 2012, accessed 15 February 2013, www.unhcr.org/refworld/docid/50c9fea82.html.

[122] AICHR, 'Terms of Reference', *ASEAN Intergovernmental Commission on Human Rights*, 2009, §(1) (1.4), http://aichr.org/about/.

[123] OHCHR, 'UN Rights Chief Welcomes Focus on Human Rights and Democracy, Calls for Review of ASEAN Draft Human Rights Declaration', *Office of the High Commissioner for Human Rights*, 8 November 2012, www.ohchr.org/en/NewsEvents/Pages/DisplayNews.aspx?NewsID=12753&LangID=E.

[124] Paul Gerber, 'ASEAN Human Rights Declaration: a step forward or a slide backwards?', *MONASH University*, 21 November 2012, accessed 23 June 2013, http://theconversation.com/asean-human-rights-declaration-a-step-forward-or-a-slide-backwards-10895.

right to an adequate standard of living for himself or herself and his or her family including . . . e. The right to safe drinking water and sanitation'.[125] AHRD in its present form has been subject to harsh criticisms.[126] As Victoria Nuland of the State Department of the United States commented:

> many of the ASEAN Declaration's principles and articles could weaken and erode universal human rights and fundamental freedoms as contained in the UDHR. Concerning aspects include: the use of the concept of 'cultural relativism' to suggest that rights in the UDHR do not apply everywhere; stipulating that domestic laws can trump universal human rights; incomplete descriptions of rights that are memorialised elsewhere; introducing novel limits to rights; and language that could be read to suggest that individual rights are subject to group veto.[127]

Despite the problems, the AHRD is a step in the right direction.[128] Considering its recent adoption, it is hard to predict the kind of influence it will have on state action. Also, unlike the ASEAN Charter of 2007 which is legally binding upon parties, the AHRD being only a declaration has no such obligatory value. However, it does signify the will of the nations and 'indicates the member states' aspirations and commitments in relation to the rights of their people'.[129] Commenting on the significance of the ADHR, Surin Pitsuwan, the Secretary-General of ASEAN, stated that the declaration 'can be used to monitor the practice, the protection, the promotion of human rights here in the ASEAN countries'.[130] It can thus

[125] ASEAN, 'ASEAN Human Rights Declaration', Article 28,

[126] HRW, 'Civil Society Denounces Adoption of Flawed ASEAN Human Rights Declaration: AHRD Falls Far Below International Standards, *Human Rights Watch*, 19 November 2012, accessed 25 March 2013. www.hrw.org/news/2012/11/19/civil-society-denounces-adoption-flawed-asean-human-rights-declaration; ICJ, 'ICJ Condemns Fatally Flawed ASEAN Human Rights Declaration', *International Commission of Jurists*, 19 November 2012, accessed 25 March 2013, www.icj.org/icj-condemns-fatally-flawed-asean-human-rights-declaration/.

[127] Victoria Nuland, 'ASEAN Declaration on Human Rights', *Press Statement, US Department of State*, Washington DC, 20 November 2012, accessed 31 March 2013, www.state.gov/r/pa/prs/ps/2012/11/200915.htm.

[128] Katherine G. Southwick, 'Bumpy Road to the ASEAN Human Rights Declaration', *Asia Pacific Bulletin* 197 (22 January 2012), accessed March 27, 2013, www.eastwestcenter.org/sites/default/files/private/apb197_1.pdf.

[129] Rodolfo C. Severino, 'ASEAN's Declaration Advances Human Rights in Asia', *ASEAN Studies Centre*, 8 February 2013, East Asia Forum, accessed 18 June 2013, www.eastasiaforum.org/2013/02/08/aseans-declaration-advances-human-rights-in-asia/.

[130] Constance Johnson, 'ASEAN: Leaders Adopt Human Rights Declaration', Global Legal Monitor, *The Library of Congress*, 21 November 2012, accessed 23 June 2013, www.loc.gov/lawweb/servlet/lloc_news?disp3_l205403405_text.

be a tool to rally for measures for the protection and implementation of the right to water during emergencies.

According to the 2009 report by the Asian Development Bank, at present comprehensive legislation does not exist on water rights for 'basic human needs' in Cambodia, Indonesia, the Philippines, Thailand and Vietnam.[131] However, water-use priorities have been defined in some form under legislation in all of these countries.[132] Some of the South East Asian states have specific provisions relating to water during emergencies.[133] For example, in Cambodia and Laos areas could be declared protection zones during emergencies,[134] while in Vietnam it is mandated to prioritise the use of water for living purposes during emergencies.[135] There are also monitoring or coordinating bodies set up for mostly water-resource management purposes.

Domestic courts have also been involved. For example in Indonesia, the courts have held that the 'right to water is an implicit but enforceable constitutional right'.[136] The Constitutional Court stressed that the state has the obligation to respect, protect and fulfil the human right to water and held that the responsibilities of the government as laid down in the Law on Water Resources must be interpreted in light of the right to water.[137]

131 Jeremy Bird, Wouter Lincklaen Arriens and Dennis Von Custodio, 'Water Rights and Water Allocation: Issues and Challenges for Asia, Water for All, Series 17', *Asian Development Bank*, 2009, 42, 43, 49–50, 52–55, www.adb.org/sites/default/files/pub/2009/Water-Rights.pdf.

132 Ibid.

133 See WaterLex, Indonesia, legal basis, §3.12, 4.11, accessed 5 April 2013, http://faolex.fao.org/cgi-bin/waterlex.exe?rec_id=000040&database=waterlex&search_type=link&lang=eng&format_name=ERALL&table=wtl; WaterLex, Thailand, legal basis, §3.12, 4.11, accessed 5 April 2013, http://faolex.fao.org/cgi-bin/waterlex.exe?rec_id=000032&database=waterlex&search_type=link&lang=eng&format_name=ERALL&table=wtl. Please note there is no information regarding the Philippines.

134 WaterLex, Cambodia, legal basis, §3.12, 4.11, accessed 5 April 2013, http://faolex.fao.org/cgi-bin/waterlex.exe?rec_id=000060&database=waterlex&search_type=link&lang=eng&format_name=ERALL&table=wtl; See also WaterLex, Laos, Legal basis, §3.12, 4.11, accessed 5 April 2013, http://faolex.fao.org/cgi-bin/waterlex.exe?rec_id=000043&database=waterlex&search_type=link&lang=eng&format_name=ERALL&table=wtl.

135 Waterlex, Vietnam, legal basis, §3.12, accessed 5 April 2013, http://faolex.fao.org/cgi-bin/waterlex.exe?rec_id=000050&database=waterlex&search_type=link&lang=eng&format_name=ERALL&table=wtl].

136 Boyd, 'Right to Water', 132.

137 World Water Council, Judicial Review of the Law No. 7 of 2004 on Water Resources, Constitutional Court of the Republic of Indonesia, 058-059-060-063/PUUII/2004, 19 July 2005, in 'Legal Resources for the Right to Water and Sanitation, International and

ASEAN nations also have many noteworthy endeavours on disaster risk management and mitigation as well as on transboundary water resource management. The intraregional Mekong River Commission (MRC) was established by Laos, Vietnam, the Philippines, and Cambodia in 1995 to promote sustainable management and development of water and related resources in the Mekong Basin.[138] The MRC also has programmes on flood management and mitigation. It also has a mandate towards social development of the population dependent upon the river.[139] Myanmar and China, the other two riparian states are currently Dialogue Partners of the MRC.[140]

In 2005 ASEAN states signed the ASEAN Agreement on Disaster Management and Emergency Response (AADMER), which is among the world's first regional agreements to address disaster response in a binding manner. It lays down principles dealing with disaster risk identification, monitoring and early warning, prevention and mitigation, preparedness and response, rehabilitation, technical cooperation and research, mechanisms for coordination, etc. The agreement has led to the establishment of the ASEAN Co-ordinating Centre for Humanitarian Assistance on Disaster Management (AHA Centre) which facilitates 'co-operation and coordination among the Parties, and with relevant United Nations and other international organisations, in promoting regional collaboration'.[141]

Though AADMER is not applicable to conflicts and does not expressly speak of the right to water, it lays down certain key mechanisms relating to cooperation and disaster response. With the adoption of the AHRD, recognition of the right to water can be introduced into the region-wide policies and practices in disaster response and disaster management. Similarly, the MRC is tasked with developing the foremost source of water in the region and is also a stakeholder in flood management in the

National Standards', *Center for Housing and Eviction Rights*, 2nd edition, 2008, 279–280, accessed 21 March 2013, www.worldwatercouncil.org/fileadmin/wwc/Programs/Right_to_Water/Pdf_doct/RWP-Legal_Res_1st_Draft_web.pdf.

138 Mekong River Commission, accessed 5 April 2013, www.mrcmekong.org/about-the-mrc/history/ and www.mrcmekong.org/about-the-mrc/vision-and-mission/.

139 Schmeier, *Governing of International Watercourses*, 140.

140 Mekong River Commission, accessed 5 April 2013, www.mrcmekong.org/about-the-mrc/upstream-partners-2/.

141 Article 20, ASEAN, 'ASEAN Agreement on Disaster Management and Emergency Response', 2005, www.asean.org/communities/asean-socio-cultural-community/item/the-asean-agreement-on-disaster-management-and-emergency-response.

Mekong Basin. With equal access to water to all citizens now being a matter of right for all individuals, the MRC role and policies assume greater significance.

6. Enforcement of the right to water during emergencies

6.1 Differing perspectives on human rights

Slight vestiges of the now-defeated 'Asian values' debate remain in South East Asian nations' approach to human rights. This has two-fold implications: Firstly, the states are hesitant and slow in adopting some of the most important treaties and protocols which relate to human rights, and secondly, humanitarian assistance efforts face multiple obstacles even during the most urgent of situations.

The importance given to sovereignty and non-interference in the South East Asian nations has traditionally been very strong.[142] As Hsien-Li notes:

> ASEAN states have for the longest time exhibited an aversion to supranationalism and intraregional criticism. They have also been hesitant in adopting regional human rights mechanism because of potential conflict with national interests vested in maintaining the status quo. While human rights are now discussed at official regional forums, there is the simultaneous declaration of the need to keep certain boundaries and steer clear of external interference in the same breath.[143]

While all ASEAN states have ratified the CEDAW and the CRC, only six out of the ten South East Asian nations (Cambodia, Indonesia, Laos, Vietnam, the Philippines and Thailand) have ratified the ICESCR and ICCPR.[144] All ASEAN states are parties to the four 1949 Geneva Conventions.[145] But only four South East Asian states, Brunei, Laos, Cambodia, and Vietnam, have ratified *Additional Protocol I*, and Brunei, Laos, Cambodia and the Philippines are parties to *Additional*

[142] Tan Hsien-Li, *The ASEAN Intergovernmental Commission on Human Rights, Institutionalising Human Rights in Southeast Asia* (New York: Cambridge University Press, 2011), 24 - 25, 141.

[143] Ibid., 141.

[144] American Bar Association, 'Experts' Note on the ASEAN Human Rights Declaration', *American Bar Association, Rule of Law Initiative*, May 2012, Table 2, 45, accessed 18 March 2013, www.americanbar.org/content/dam/aba/directories/roli/indonesia/asia_aba_roli_expert_note_asean_human_rights_declaration_05121.authcheckdam.pdf.

[145] Ibid., 2.

Protocol II.[146] In such a scenario, it will be difficult to assert a consistent right to water across the region. However, the core obligations such as the right to life and the right to an adequate standard of living are recognised in most constitutions.[147] This, along with the applicable principles of international law, could form a basis for the recognition to the right to water.

AHRD in its preamble clearly states the commitment of parties in upholding the principles under the international human rights instruments to which they are also party. Under Article 39, the states shall pursue protection and promotion of human rights by cooperating not only with each other but also with 'relevant national, regional and international institutions and organisations'.[148]

This means that the South East Asian nations are duty-bound by their own declaration to uphold the provisions embodied in the international instruments relating to water. They must also ensure that they cooperate with relevant bodies towards the realisation of this right. Hsien-Li has, however, warned that ASEAN could never become a body such as the European Union which 'supersedes the sovereignty of its member states'[149] and therefore the efficacy of the AHRD or any regional body would be directly proportional to the will of its member states and would find it tough to operate freely.

6.2 *Progressive nature of the right*

The form of recognition of the right to water signifies that this right is not a 'self-standing' right per se.[150] It is recognised as a part of existing rights such as the right to life and human dignity, health and environment. Currently, a state is obliged to ensure progressive realisation of this right. Inability to fulfil the right to water would not mean a violation of the right or a failure to uphold the right. It is only counted as a violation when the state is unwilling or negligent or discriminatory when it comes to fulfilment of the right to water.[151] Nevertheless, the burden of proof

146 Ibid., 12,13, For ASEAN member nations' commitment to international human rights treaties and international humanitarian law.

147 Ibid., 29

148 Article 39, ASEAN, 'Human Rights Declaration', 2010.

149 Tan Hsien-Li, *The ASEAN Intergovernmental Commission on Human Rights*, 141.

150 UN Office of the High Commissioner for Human Rights, 'Fact Sheet No. 35, The Right to Water', August 2010, accessed 28 March 2013, 3, www.unhcr.org/refworld/docid/4ca45fed2.html.

151 De Albuquerque, 'The Human Right to Water', 42.

lies on the state party to show that it genuinely lacked the resources to fulfil its obligations under the ICESCR.[152]

It is to be borne in mind that as per GC-15 (paragraph 37) there are nine core obligations laid down upon states, such as ensuring a safe and certain minimum amount of water to all without any discrimination especially against marginalised groups, and taking positive measures towards implementation including establishing indicators or benchmarks as well as monitoring the extent of realisation of the right. These core obligations are non-derogable.[153]

The right to water may seem to be unenforceable in practical terms during emergencies since at such a time a state can derogate from certain rights under the ICCPR, but the ICESCR offers no such derogations.[154] This brings in a stringent obligation on states to implement the right to water as provided for under ICESCR. Additionally, the *Optional Protocol to the ICESCR* will enter into force on 5 May 2013 and it will enable victims to seek justice for violations of economic, social and cultural rights. 'The entry into force of the *Optional Protocol* will also finally help place economic, social and cultural rights on an equal footing with all other human rights.'[155]

Few examples exist in relation to enforcement measures taken in cases of military conflict, such as in Iraq where a panel of Commissioners of the United Nations Compensation Commission (UNCC) in their report found Iraq liable for contamination of the Raudhatain and Umm Al-Aish aquifers in Kuwait.[156] Increased use of such measures would be a

[152] Philip Alston, *The United Nations and Human Rights: A Critical Appraisal* (Oxford: Clarendon Press, 1992), 495.

[153] GC-15 §37, 39 and 40.

[154] Sarah Joseph and Adam McBeth, *Research Handbook on International Human Rights Law* (UK: Edward Elgar Publishing, 2010), 68. See also Amrei Müller, 'Limitations to and Derogations from Economic, Social and Cultural Rights', *Human Rights Law Review* 9 (2009): 557–601, Abstract.

[155] OHCHR, 'Pillay welcomes major breakthrough enabling individual complaints on economic, social and cultural rights', *Office of the High Commissioner for Human Rights*, 6 January 2013, accessed 8 February 2013, www.ohchr.org/en/NewsEvents/Pages/DisplayNews.aspx?NewsID=12968&LangID=E. See for status of ratification of the *Optional Protocol to the International Covenant on Economic, Social and Cultural Rights*, 2008, http://treaties.un.org/Pages/ViewDetails.aspx?src=IND&mtdsg_no=IV-3-a&chapter=4&lang=en.

[156] Steven Freeland, 'Crimes Against the Environment: A role for the International Criminal Court', 352, Droit de l'environnement dans le Pacifique Problematiques et Perspectives Croisees, New Zealand Association for Comparative Law and Association de Legislation Comparee des Pays du Pacifique, 2005: www.upf.pf/IMG/pdf/16-freeland.pdf.

welcome step. But despite their utility, such measures are *post facto* and therefore of little help in an emergency. Amongst more immediate solutions, it has been contended that the current form of recognition brings the right under the paradigm of 'Responsibility to Protect' (R2P), 'to act in cases in which this right is threatened by malicious act of the governments'.[157] This obviously is a very controversial approach.

6.3 *Humanitarian agencies*

Relief agencies indeed have a vital role to play in enforcement of the right to water in humanitarian situations. The role of humanitarian agencies and actors has been recognised by GC-15.[158] It states that these entities are to cooperate with state parties in matters relating to the implementation of the right to water. They must try to promote and use this law in both policy and practice.[159] This approach would give direction to relief agencies to 'complement' and when necessary also 'supplement' the work of the government.[160] This would also help address problems like lack of sufficient data about the quality and quantity of water, its deterioration during the period of emergency, and the action taken by the government.

7. Conclusion

There is a lack of adequate focus on the effect of emergency situations on water resources in South East Asia, which is further exacerbated by climate change and developmental challenges. Considering that the problems relating to water have increased over the years and show no sign of abatement, it would be pertinent to focus on the nexus between water and emergencies, and take measures to ensure water security.

While the right to water has been recognised by the international community, it is not an independent right. It is one which is still being refined continually through domestic as well as international law and policies. Hence we see that aspects like the obligations of the state as well as the role of humanitarian agencies are still unclear, although minimum standards have been laid down.

[157] Zuanna Chociej and Zafar Adeel, 'Legal and Ethical Dimensions of a Right to Water', in *The Global water Crisis: Addressing an Urgent Security Issue*, 126.

[158] GC-15 §60. [159] Ibid., §60.

[160] The Brookings-Bern Project, 'Synthesis Report', 2.

In the South East Asian region, challenges remain in the implementation of this right as well as its use during relief operations. This is due to the region's resistance to the commonly accepted notions of human rights and its insistence on sovereignty and 'cultural relativism'. As seen above, some of the most important international instruments such as the ICCPR and ICESCR have not been ratified by certain nations in the region. Their national legislations also do not have an explicit recognition of the right to water. The enforcement mechanisms under international as well as municipal laws are still weak, which allows states to escape scrutiny for many of their actions as well as omissions.

While the ASEAN declaration gives a ray of hope, it brings with itself its own set of challenges. The will of the nations will be of paramount importance for it to have any effect. Advocacy measures that have worked thus far in the acceptance of human rights in the region will also go a long way towards ensuring that during emergencies, all persons have access to sufficient water to help them sustain themselves.

14

Indonesian compliance and its effective implementation of international norms on disaster response

HERIBERTUS JAKA TRIYANA

1. Introduction

This chapter aims to describe and critically examine Indonesia's compliance with, and its effective implementation of, an international norm on disaster response. The international norm on disaster response, which is discussed in this chapter, refers to the Association of the South East Asian Nations (ASEAN) Agreement on Disaster Management and Emergency Response (AADMER) as the only binding international norm on that matter.[1] It should be noted that AADMER reaffirms the importance of dispersing international norms in its preamble.[2] As a proactive regional framework for cooperation, coordination, technical assistance and resource mobilisation, Indonesia adopted and has effectively sought to implement AADMER since 2007.[3]

Stemming from this development and the 2004 Aceh tsunami tragedy, the Indonesian government and the House of Representatives issued Law

1 The full title of this Agreement is the 'ASEAN Agreement on Disaster Management and Emergency Response Work Programme for 2010–2015'. It was signed on 26 July 2005 in the 38th Ministerial Meetings in Vientianne, Lao and entered into force on 24 December 2009 after being ratified by all ten member states of ASEAN; www.aadmerpartnership.org/wp-content/uploads/gravity_forms/1-a9f4f059eaa51995bcd10996775a89b6/2012/09/ADMER-Agreement.pdf, accessed on 1 May 2013.

2 For example The United Nations General Assembly (UNGA) UNGA Resolution A/RES/46/182, the UNISDR 'Hyogo Framework for Action of 2005–2015 (HFA), the Active Learning Network for Accountability and Performance in Humanitarian Action (ALNAP), the Development Assistance Committee of the OECD (OECD-DAC Criteria), the Humanitarian Accountability Partnership (HAP), www.hapinternational.org, and the IDRL International Law Applicable to Disasters.

3 ASEAN, www.asean.org/resources/publications/asean-publications/item/asean-agreement-on-disaster-management-and-emergency-response-work-programme-for-2010–2015, accessed on 1 May 2013.

Number 24 of 2007 regarding disaster management (hereinafter the Law) on 26 April 2007.[4] This Law establishes *Badan Nasional Penanggulangan Bencana* (BNPB) or the National Board of Disaster Response whose main function is to strenghten regional cooperation, coordination, resource mobilisation and simplification of procedures required by AADMER[5]. In line with this function, BNPB is placed as the national focal point for disaster response as required by Article 1 (10) of AADMER[6]. Furthermore, the Law is also intended to answer some doubts arising from AADMER's implementation at domestic level, such as whether disaster risk reduction cooperation would be effective, how regional coordination could take place, and what course of action could be taken to encourage cooperation between governments, government and civil society and within societies in the ASEAN countries, particularly in Indonesia which is known as one of most disaster-prone countries in the world.[7] The aforementioned doubts are also echoed in practical and empirical reports, studies and news reports after the Law and that international norm came into force between 2008 and 2013. For example, the Mount Merapi eruption on 26 October 2010 in Central

[4] This law was issued on 26th April 2007, State Gazette No. 66 of 2007 (www.indonesia.go.id/en/). It consists of 13 chapters and 85 articles and it changes many pre-existing regulations on disaster response, e.g. Presidential Decree Number 28 of 1979 for the Formation of the Natural Disaster Management Coordinating Board, Presidential Decree Number 3 of 2001 relating to the National Coordinating Board for the Management of Disaster and Refugee, and Epidemics Law Number 4 of 1984. Due to the Aceh tsunami tragedy on 26 December 2004, the Law was relatively easy to pass between the government and the House of Representatives in response to the national and international scrutiny of the Indonesian disaster response laws and regulations. The Law was followed by the Government Regulation Number 22 of 2008 regarding the Financial Arrangement of the Disaster Management on 28 February 2008 and Government Regulation Number 23 of 2008 regarding the Role and Function of International Organisations on Disaster Management on 28 February 2008, State Gazette No. 43 and 44 of 2008.

[5] Article 10 of the Law establishes the National Board of Disaster Response whose main functions are to coordinate disaster management throughout Indonesia and to strengthen cooperation among those who have responsibility to mitigate and to rehabilitate socio-economic recovery of the affected societies guided by principles of sustainability, effectivity, socio-economic resilience and territorial sovereignty.

[6] ASEAN, AADMER, Article 1 (10), describes 'National Focal Point' as an entity designated and authorised by each party to receive and transmit information pursuant to provisions of this Agreement.

[7] www.humanitarianforum.org/pages/en/aadmer-consultation-building-the-asean-networks-disaster-risk-reduction-capacity.html, accessed on 1 May 2013; see also Angus M. Gunn, *Encyclopedia of Disaster: Environmental Catastrophes and Human Tragedies*, vol. I (London: Greenwoods Press, 2008), 98, 132 and 281.

Java, the Padang earthquake in 2010 and the Jakarta flood between January and March 2013, devastating large-scale infrastructure and countless human losses, illustrate those doubts.

To describe and critically examine Indonesia's compliance and effective implementation of AADMER, this chapter is structured into four main areas of discussion. Firstly, it will present basic legal concepts of compliance and effective implementation of a domesticated international norm. This part aims to provide background on how international law works in the Indonesian legal system. Secondly, legal aspects of cooperation, coordination, resource mobilisation and simplification of procedures in AADMER and in the Law will be analysed to reveal elements of compliance in terms of their substantance. To reach in-depth analysis, existence of national as well as local policies, programmes, actions and budgets on disaster response will be examined to find out patterns of effective implementation. In particular, without ignorance of political decentralisation policy, the discussion will be outlined to exercise primary responsibility of local goverments as the local focal point of disaster response throughout Indonesia. Thirdly, experiences of the application of the Law to several disaster events between 2008 and 2013 will be analysed. Mainly, this chapter focuses on aspects of regional cooperation, coordination, resource mobilisation and actions encouraging the participation of communities to test whether AADMER's norms had been complied with and effectively implemented. Finally, this chapter tries to conclude whether the Law truly complies and has been effectively implemented in accordance with AADMER. To this end, suggestions will also be presented to improve compliance mechanisms and effective implementation in the future.

2. Domestification process of international law in the Indonesian legal system

State compliance with international norms is determined by two mechanisms, namely domestication[8] and effective implementation.[9] Legally

[8] Markus Burgstaller, *Theories of Compliance with International Law* (Martinus Nijhoff Publishers, 2005), 85.

[9] David Otley, 'Performance Management: a Framework for Management Control System Research', *Management Accounting Research* 10 (1999), 363–382; and Eric G. Flamholtz, T. K. Das and Anne S. Tsui, 'Toward an Integrative Framework of Organisational Control, Accounting, Organisation and Society', in *Accounting, Organisations and Society* 10/1 (1985): 35–50.

speaking, domestication is defined as a national legal process giving legal effect to international law into national legal system by approval, signatory, ratification or by mutually agreed means.[10] Although its means still remain debatable,[11] it is simply understood as 'a change of state conduct or behaviour in accordance with international law in its domestic affairs'.[12] So, choices of survival, domestic values, economic position and domestic politics are acceptable reasons to make such a change.[13] For the purpose of this chapter, domestication and compliance are defined as the national legal process giving binding legal effect to a set of comprehensive rules, actions, procedures or legal determination in AADMER and how they will be implemented by Indonesia contributing to certain changes in its conduct and behaviour in disaster response.

Pursuant to Article 1 of Law Number 24 of 2007 regarding the International Treaty, once an international law (a convention, agreement or treaty), is officially declared as the law of the land by means of ratification, accession, acceptance or approval, it has a binding legal character as a law.[14] Consequently, Indonesia has consented to be bound by rights and obligations contained therein. This mechanism is well established as the most accepted theory of the domestication process explaining how international law works in municipal law in international law study.[15]

However, it is very interesting to note two distinguished legal features of this matter within the Indonesian legal system. Firstly, forms of consented declaration only fall into an act or into a presidential regulation exempting others such as provincial and regency regulations. It means that only the central government has the power to give consent to international treaty while local governments do not. As a result, the primary obligation to implement that norm is imposed on local government in their respective territories and on their societies where disaster usually takes place. Furthermore, the said forms will fall into different legal consequences since they have a different hierarchy of law consisting

[10] Malcolm N. Shaw, *International Law*, 6th Edition (Cambridge University Press, 2008), 129–133.
[11] Andrew Guzman, *How International Law Works: A Rational Choice Theory* (Oxford University Press, 2008), 22.
[12] Ibid.
[13] Anthony Wetherall, *Normative Rule Making at the IAEA: Codes of Conduct* (unpublished paper, 6 May 2005), 75.
[14] The Law was issued on 23 October 2000, official State Gazette Number 185, 2000.
[15] Shaw, *International Law*.

of a different legally binding character, pursuant to Article 7 of Law Number 12 of 2011 regarding the Creation of Regulations.[16] As commonly practised, government will use an act to ratify a treaty or a convention regulating human rights, territorial integrity, monetary, fiscal and foreign affairs to guard and keep national interests and sovereignty in a proactive way. On the other hand, presidential regulation will be used to ratify other aspects regulating less important or very technical matters without approval from the House of Representatives aiming at their immediate and prompt application.

Second, to test when a treaty is domesticated and becomes the law of the land is difficult, since a domesticated treaty has no legal binding character before the court. In fact, it cannot be used as a legal base to decide a dispute in a particular case since judges usually avoid using it and they are reluctant to give their decision based on a domesticated act or presidential regulation.[17] Due to the above-noted practice, norms in a ratified treaty are incorporated into a new act or other form of regulation as a source of law having a binding legal character. Undoubtedly, it creates a chance for a partial adoption or incorporation of certain norms and mechanisms contained in a domestic treaty.[18] Arguably, they actually lessen the binding character of a domestic treaty in a very systematic way. This phenomenon contributes to legal uncertainty in terms of widening legal gaps, legal overlap and possible conflict of norms in its implementation.[19] As a result, legal expectation arising from a domesticated treaty could be easily questioned for its compliance and its effective implementation.[20]

Indonesia approved AADMER on 5 May 2008 by Presidential Regulation Number 32 of 2008 regarding the approval of AADMER.[21] It seems

[16] Official State Gazette Number 82, 2011, entered into force on 12 August 2011.

[17] Ibrahim, 'Status Hukum Internasional dan Perjanjian Internasional di Dalam Hukum Nasional: Permasalahan Teori dan Praktek' (paper presented at the national workshop on the Indonesian Practice toward International Treaty, Surabaya, 23–25 November 2009).

[18] For example Indonesia ratified the *Convention of the Rights of the Child* 1989 by Presidential Decree Number 40 of 1990. Since the time of ratification, the Convention was inactive before the government issued numerous acts regarding children's rights, such as Act Number 20 of 2003 regarding the National Education System and Act Number 11 of 2012 regarding the Children's Tribunal System.

[19] R. Ibrahim, 'Status Hukum'.

[20] Heribertus Jaka Triyana, 'Tinjauan Yuridis Tentang Badan HAM ASEAN Dalam Sistem Hukum Nasional Indonesia', *Jurnal Mimbar Hukum* 23, No. 3 (2011): 617–619.

[21] Official State Gazette Number 73 of 2008. It only has three articles, namely statement of approval, interpretation of the agreement and entry into force of the agreement.

that a norm on disaster response is considered a less important matter compared with the aforementioned aspects. In that regulation, there are no explicit AADMER norms, revealing the difficulty of understanding its scope, area and objective. Interestingly, AADMER's norms were actually taken into account when the government created and issued the Disaster Management Law on 26 April 2007 without any acknowledgment of this regulation. The Law partially adopts AADMER's norms such as principles of disaster response,[22] coordination and regional cooperation,[23] but it affirms AADMER as the proactive regional framework for cooperation,[24] coordination,[25] technical assistance[26] and resource mobilisation in all aspects of disaster response.[27] Consequently, this adoption has inspired the issuance of Government Regulation Number 22 of 2008 regarding the Financial Supports and Management and Government Regulation Number 23 of 2008 regarding the International Organisations' Roles and Function in Disaster Response in Indonesia.[28]

[22] Article 3 regulates that disaster response shall be guided by principles of priority, prompt, effective coordination and cooperation, partnership, sustainability, empowerment and transparency which are also principles recognised in AADMER.

[23] Article 10 establishes the National Board of Disaster response whose functions are to coordinate and to maximise all efforts for disaster response; and article 28 regulates regional and international cooperation of the disaster response in Indonesia.

[24] Chapter VI of the Law prescribes the role and functions for effective cooperation between international humanitarian institutions and the government in disaster management in Articles 28 and 30. Effective coordination in mitigation, emergency and reconstruction and rehabilitation are specifically stipulated in Article 33. In Article 30, consent and appeal-based cooperation have been set to foster national and international cooperation of disaster management.

[25] Chapter IV of the Law regulates effective coordination between national, regional and local disaster management institutions whose functions are extensively set out in Articles 10 to 27. Effective coordination in mitigation, emergency and reconstruction, and rehabilitation, are specifically determined in Article 33.

[26] Chapter IX of the Law prescribes technical assistance in terms of supervision in the making of all disaster-friendly policy management in all sustainable development processes. Article 71 determines that technical assistance shall be provided in: identification of threat, potential policy-making in disasters, exploitation activities, usage of goods and services, planning in the use of land, management of natural resources, reclamation and budget-based allocation for disaster management.

[27] Chapter III of the Law regulates resource mobilisation by specifying the responsibilities and authorities among disaster-management stakeholders and beneficiaries in a very rigid attribution. For example, Articles 5 and 8 state that the central government and local government have primary responsibilities to assess and to guarantee the fulfilment of basic needs of the refugees and IDPs during the emergency phase.

[28] Government Regulation Nos. 22 and 23 of 2008 regarding the Financial Arrangement of Disaster Management on 28 February 2008 and Government Regulation Number 23 of

It can be concluded that the Law substantially complies with AADMER. However, it also gives a chance of imminent weakness for effective implementation of AADMER. Undenially, legal overlap, legal bias and legal conflicts on disaster will emerge due to partial adoption of AADMER in the Law.

3. Elements of compliance in the Indonesian disaster response law

The partial adoption of AADMER norms on coordination, cooperation and simplification of procedure are the most important aspects to be analysed in the Law. So existence of national as well as local policies, programmes, actions and budgets as required by AADMER's work programme 1 tests elements of compliance and effective implementation in three discussions as follows.

The Law has something in common firstly with Article 1 and secondly with AADMER's work programme in terms of enhancing humanitarian assistance and response coordination, providing efficient, timely and reliable response to major disasters through common implementation of operational procedures and mechanisms, and improving rapid mobilisation procedure. To achieve these tasks, BNPB is established. BNPB's ultimate mandate is to coordinate disaster management and to perform as the national focal point for national coordination at emergency, rehabilitation and reconstruction phases. As the national focal point, BNPB has succesfully drafted its strategic national action plan 2010–1014 incorporating the Hyogo Framework for Action 2005–2015 to which local disaster response refers.[29] Coordination with the Local Board of Disaster Response (*Badan Penanggulangan Bencana Daerah* (BPBD)), civil society, non-governmental organisations (NGOs) and international agencies has been improved in terms of increasing accessibility and availability of resources and information-sharing on disaster response.[30]

Secondly, the fifth component of AADMER's work programme and Article 1(3) of the AADMER Agreement initiate closer partnership

2008 regarding the Role and Function of International Organisations on Disaster Management on 28 February 2008, State Gazette Nos. 43 and 44 of 2008.

[29] UNISDR, 'International Strategy for Disaster Reduction, the Hyogo Framework of Action 2005–2015: Building the Resilience of Nations and Communities to Disaster', *ISDR* 20 and *BNPB*, 2010, Rencana Strategies Badang Nasional Penanggulangan Bencana Tahun 2010–2014, 3.

[30] *BNPB*, 4–8.

and more collaborative initiatives on disaster preparedness and response, disaster risk reduction, recovery and rehabilitation with partner organisations, international organisations, civil society, academia, the military, and United Nations specialised agencies. In fact, BNPB successfully determines its mission objective to initiate a close cooperation at tactical, operational and strategic levels among all stakeholders, especially at disaster risk reduction, until 2014.[31] This programme is well prepared in terms of gradually increasing financial support and empowerment of local capacities.[32] Regional and international partnerships with, for example, Safer Communities for Disaster Risk Reduction (SCDRR), Global Facility for Disaster Risk Reduction (GFDRR), Japan International Cooperation Agency (JICA), and the United Nations International Strategy for Disaster Reduction (UNISDR) have been strenghtened in terms of mutual cooperation, particularly in some especially remote areas prone to natural hazards: of tsunami on the west coast of Sumatra, volcanic eruptions in Java and the Sulawesi Islands, and landslides or floods in Papua and Kalimantan.[33] One of the most notable achievements is that local governments have become BNPB's partners in mitigating disaster by mapping hazards and empowering communities. For example, local coping mechanisms towards potential hazards are successfully mapped and are included in the local strategic development plan by all local governments in Indonesia.[34] Arguably, BNPB has pioneered implementation of the Community-Based Disaster Response Management (CBDRM) since 2007.[35]

Thirdly, pursuant to Article 4(c) of AADMER, simplification of procedure plays a key role in success for coordination and sustainable partnership. Prompt and just responses are placed as the most effective indicators to measure this procedure. Article 33 of the Law differentiates applicable procedures into three distinct phases of disaster response, i.e. preparedness, emergency and rehabilitation, and reconstruction

[31] Ibid., 12.

[32] 'Anggaran BNPB Tahun 2013 1 Trilyun', *Detiknews*, accessed 3 May 2013, http://news.detik.com/read/2012/09/17/184701/2022901/10/.

[33] BNPB, *Gema BNPB* 2, No. 3 (November 2011), 6–7.

[34] Indonesia has 33 provinces (*provinsi*), 500 regencies (*kabupaten*), 98 mayor (*kota*), 6,234 sub-regencies (*kecamatan*) and 70,611 villages.

[35] Heribertus Jaka Triyana, 'The Implementation of the Community-Based Natural Resources Management System Principle in the Political Decentralisation in the Natural Disaster Management Program in Indonesia: Case Studies in the Kapuk Village, Cengkareng West Jakarta Regency, the Special Province of Jakarta and in the Kalabahi Capital City of Alor Regency, the East Nusa Tenggara Province', Thesis at the Faculty of Arts, Rijks University of Groningen (2008), 25–30.

periods. As a result, different means of coordination and partnership at the tactical level (*desa* or village and *kecamatan* or sub-regency), at the operational level (*kabupaten* or regency and *provinsi* or province) and at strategic levels (*pusat* or central government), determine status of disaster into local or national concerns.[36] At the emergency and rehabilitation and recontruction periods, coordination and partnership are disticntly imposed. If disaster is determined as a local concern, local government (province and regency) led by BPBD is responsible for managing all disaster response, particularly for its effective coordination and partnership with all available local resources. On the other hand, central government led by BNPB will take full responsibility for effective supervision of local government if an event is determined to be a national concern. In order to perform their tasks, pursuant to Article 50 of the Law, BNPB and BPBD enjoy the privilege of simplifying procedures on mobilisation of resources, tools and aids, logistics supply, immigration, customs and quarantine, permits, procurement, accountability, search and rescue, and inter-departmental command and coordination. All of these standards are partially adopted from Articles 4 and 10 of AADMER.

It can be concluded that the Law absorbs and transforms important key features of AADMER, revealing certain elements of compliance. Changes of law, existence of national and local policy, programme and establishment of national and local focal points for disaster response within Indonesian contexts and perspective are evidence of this compliance. However, behaviours or actual conduct relevant to these changes needs to be analysed to measure its effective implemention, particularly with regard to disasters of local concern managed by local governments. Therefore explanation of and close attention to several disaster responses in Indonesia between 2008 and 2013 will explain this matter.

4. The implementation of AADMER and the Law between 2008 and 2013

Legal gaps always arise between normativity and empirical legal application, and so does the disaster-response norm. In Indonesia, this gap

[36] The Indonesian governance system is structured into five hierarchial structures, namely *desa* or village administrations consisting of several assemblies of autonomous societies of *dusun*, *kecamatan* or sub-regency government consisting of several village administrators, *kabupaten*, and *kota*, regency or mayor administering several sub-regency governments in one province, *provinsi* or province, administering several regencies, and mayor and central government.

mainly emerges at local rather than at national level. As such, this chapter does not intend to answer why this happens,[37] but it will seek rationales, reasons and arguments why it tends to be slightly different. Drawing on domestic politics and economic considerations will help to answer this problem. The former relates to the implementation of the decentralisation policy while the latter points to a fact that available resources shape local policy mainstreaming disaster response at the local level into two intertwining rationales.[38] Firstly, natural resources are commonly perceived as primary sources of domestic income, neglecting the fact that they are also attended by unavoidable hazards. Besides, uncontrolled exploitation of natural resources increases human vulnerability, such as in timber and sand exploitation.[39] In this regard, denial of private-sector roles in coordination and partnership places all disaster response initiatives out of the reach of BNPB and BPBD. Secondly, each local government takes primary responsibility for determining management of available natural resources, causing sectoral policies among regencies and provinces fuelled by self-interest. As a result, the 'not in my backyard' (or Nimby) syndrome justifies a pattern of ignorance of possible risks arising from management of natural resources after the implementation of the decentralisation policy.

The theory of breakdown of natural resources management proposed by Ribot helps to explain the aforementioned gap viewed from a political point of view.[40] In essence, this theory opens the view that 'decentralised natural resources management by smaller units will increase opportunity of multi-stakeholder participation, contextualise roles of civil society and open up intensive interaction among stakeholders'.[41] It means that those who have the biggest interests will have the biggest access to management and enjoyment of natural resources, and in the end this condition will strengthen their ability to cope with natural hazards

[37] Guzman, *How International Law Works, supra* note 11, 23.

[38] W. S. Adisubrata, 'Otonomi Daerah di Era Reformasi', *UPP AMP YKPN, Yogyakarta*, 2008 and R. Eman, 'Sosialisasi Peraturan Pemerintah tentang Pelaksanaan Penataan Ruang', *Workshop Paper on Dissemination of Spatial Planning*, Gadjah Mada University, 17 September 2008.

[39] Quentin Grafton et al., *The Economics of the Environment and Natural Resources* (Blackwell Publishing, 2004); and 'Decentralised Natural Resources Management and Governance System, Citanduy Watershed Management', *UNDP Report*, 2004.

[40] J. C. Ribot, 1990, 'Accountable Representation and Power Participation and Decentralized Environmental Management', *Unasylva*, vol. 50, No. 199, 1999: 18–22.

[41] Ibid.

which are extensively determined in Articles 10, 27 and 33 of the Law.[42] Furthermore, this intention is established by three following rationales, i.e. communities' involvement determines the sustainability of their level of initiatives for natural disaster risk reduction; the role of vulnerable groups and individuals is central in disaster response as it concerns their life and existence; and nobody can understand local opportunities and constraints better than themselves in the preamble of the Law.

Consequently, these are relevant in reviewing the Law's compliance with AADMER.[43] Pursuant to the Law, as the local focal point for disaster response, local governments are politically responsible for promoting participatory disaster resilience by creating a good living environment and by strengthening community action as a means for reducing human vulnerability to imminent natural hazards.[44] At the end, local capacities can be initiated and improved in terms of increasing their ability to cope with natural hazards by day-to-day coordination, partnership and simplification of procedure at the local level.[45]

Since 2008 a number of natural disasters such as tsunamis, earthquakes, floods, droughts, landslides and volcanic eruptions have occured.[46] For example, on 30 September 2009, an earthquake of 7.6 on the Richter scale devastated the West Sumatra province and killed more than 1,100 people.[47] Between 2 and 3 October 2010, floods in the Wasior district, Wondoma Bay, West Papua province, collapsed infrastructures such as roads, hospitals, churches and schools, and killed more

[42] Otley, 'Performance Management'.

[43] Triyana, 'Implementation of the Community-Based Natural Resources Management System', 25–30.

[44] Article 4 elaborates that in disaster response, the community shall be empowered to increase their protection, reduce their vulnerability, respect local customs and wisdoms, and create comprehensive communal security; Article 5 stipulates that the central and local governments must play the role of leaders in disaster response. Furthermore, Article 6 (c) states 'minimum standards for internally displaced persons shall be fulfilled in order to sustain the community's ability to cope with disaster events that disrupt their life'.

[45] Article 7(1) requires the formation of central and local policy on disaster response to be in accordance with international and regional norms upholding local needs, local culture and customs.

[46] Susanna H. Hoffman and Anthony Oliver-Smith, *Catastrophe and Culture, the Anthropology of Disaster* (Oxford, 2002), 27–29.

[47] 'Pakar Gempa: Pusat Gempa Padang Bukan di ona Subduksi', *Kompas*, accessed 19 September 2011, http:/kompas.com/read/2009/10/01/09081256/pakar.gempa.pusat.gempa.padang.bukan.di.ona.subduksi.

than 158 people.[48] On 26 October 2010, Mount Merapi erupted, killed 158 people and displaced more than 300,000 villagers including the author. Lastly, between January and March 2013, floods ruined Jakarta, the capital city of Indonesia, and killed 5 victims.[49]

From those incidents, there are five legal phenomena revealing patterns of ignorance, scepticism and denial for an effective application of AADMER in the Law at the local level of implementation. Firstly, the Law provokes deep legal gaps between its norms and its factual application in daily practice.[50] It is a general understanding that the economy-driven motive of the management of natural resources causes distinct legal splits between the application of international norms on disaster response in Indonesia.[51] Since the initiation of the political decentralisation policy in 2000,[52] local governments have exploited natural resources as their primary sources of domestic income, rather than perceiving them as potential natural hazards, increasing communities' vulnerability and risks.[53] With the purpose of increasing local capacity-building, this motive has reduced true participation of local communities as required by Article 3 of the Law.[54] As a result, the affected communities have less access to managing natural resources as part of their daily coping mechanisms.[55] In the decentralisation policy, targeting huge income has become the ultimate goal-performing development.[56] To some extent, central and local governments seem to pay less attention to true participation, accountability, sustainability, relevance, effectiveness, impact and

[48] 'Banjir Wasior: Bagaikan Tsunami Menyapu Rumah Warga', *Kompas*, accessed 6 October 2010: http://regional.kompas.com/read/2010/10/06/06583142/Bagaikan.Tsunami.Menyapu.Rumah.Warga.

[49] 'Kronologi Letusan Gunung Merapi', *Vivanews*, accessed 27 October 2010, http://nasional.news.viva.co.id/news/read/185183-ini-kronologi-letusan-gunung-merapi.

[50] Liedeke Verburg, 'Donor or Partnership: Does the Concept of A Real Partnership Represent the Relief and Rehabilitation Operations during Post Natural Disaster Situation? Case Studies: Aceh Tsunami 2004 and Yogyakarta Earthquake 2006', Thesis, Faculty of Arts Rijks University, Groningen (2007).

[51] Ribot, 'Accountable Representation'.

[52] H. Lustermann, 'Indonesia: On the Way to Federal State?', *Jurnal Mimbar Hukum* No. 42/X/2002.

[53] Bernadinus Steni, 'Desentralisasi, Koordinasi dan Partisipasi Masyarakat Dalam Pengelolaan Sumberdaya Alam Pasca Otonomi Daerah', 12, accessed 21 July 2008.

[54] Ibid., 30.

[55] Triyana, 'Implementation of the Community-Based Natural Resources Management System', 101.

[56] P. Susiloadi, 'Konsep dan Isu Desentralisasi Dalam Manajemen Pemerintahan di Indonesia', *Spirit Publik* 3, No. 2 (2007), 117–124.

transparency as the main principles of disaster response, as required by the Law and AADMER.[57]

In the Wasior flood case, the above problem has become an undeniable fact when true participation and partnership with the local community and civic society were denied in the management of the rainforests where they lived.[58] The government district of Wondama pushed its timber production to sustain its domestic income with litte attention to imminent and possible natural hazards to its local communities.[59] Arguably, limited access to information on the establishment of policies for local needs, no identification and prioritisation of the most vulnerable communities in the area of deforestation, reluctance in conducting local risk assessment, non-existence of documents on local coping mechanisms and expertise, no facilitation to the affected communities of timber production, no issuance of an Early Warning System (EWS) on massive timber production, no upgrading in disaster preparedness, and mitigation of possible forest degradation are revealed as elements of gaps in coordination and partnership.

Thus deforestation reduced the community's ability to cope with those norms, especially for effective participation and coordination. In this event, in only one day, the destruction was extensive in terms of loss of life, damage to infrastructure and environmental degradation. It is also argued that the application of AADMER's norms is weakened in terms of its normative power and factual applicability when it coincides with local development policy guided mostly by economy-driven motivation.[60] This reality could be best explained by the greediness theory in the management of natural resources proposed by Billon,[61] Porto[62] and Ballentine and Nitzschke.[63] This theory states that the inappropriate management of natural resources driven by an economic motive will cause resource scarcity and environmental degradation in a very short period of time, benefiting only the few who have the biggest access to it. In the end, it causes a systemic environmental deterioration increasing

[57] Steni, 'Desentralisasi, Koordinasi', 21. [58] Kompas, 'Pakar Gempa'. [59] Ibid.

[60] Eman, 'Sosialisasi Peraturan'.

[61] Philippe Le Billon, 'The Political Ecology of War: Natural Resources and Armed Conflicts', *Political Geography* 2 (2000): 561–84.

[62] Joao. G. Porto, 'Contemporary Conflict Analysis in Perspective', in *Scarcity and Survive: The Ecology of Africa's Conflict*, eds. J. Lind et al. (Kenya: ACTS, 1998), 1–50.

[63] Karen Ballentine and Heiko Nitschke, *Profiting from Peace: Managing Resource Dimension of Civil Wars* (Lynne Publisher, 2005).

communities' vulnerability to natural hazards and lessens their capacities and abilities to cope with them.[64]

Secondly, the Law contributes to the creation of legal bias between rights and obligations exercised by stakeholders who are responsible for disaster responses, particularly during emergency and rehabilitation phases.[65] Legal bias always ends in a protracted tension between local governments and victims.[66] In all four natural disaster events discussed in this chapter, tension has not been resolved since local governments initiated relocation and resettlement policies without proper consultation and appropriate considerations, such as economic and historical values possessed by the affected communities.[67] For the application of those policies, AADMER's norms of true, active and meaningful participation and coordination in the decision-making process, pursuant to Article 1 (5 and 6) of the Law, have been denied by advertising safety and security reasons to the victims of the affected communities.[68] In the end, linking relief and rehabilitation response has been very difficult to fit with the basic communities' needs and rights in the sense of continuing future local developments. For example, tension between the victims of the Mount Merapi eruption and those of the Yogyakarta province is still going on due to inappropriate and improper consultation.[69]

[64] Le Billon, 'The Political Ecology of War'; Porto; 'Contemporary Conflict Analysis'; and Ballentine and Nitschke, *Profiting from Peace.*

[65] 'Indonesia Law, Policies, Planning and Practices on International Disaster Response', *IFRC*, July 2005.

[66] R. A. Reed (ed.), *Technical Support for Refugees: Lessons from recent experiences*, Proceedings of the 1991 International Conference, Water, Engineering and Development Centre, Loughborough University of Technology, Loughborough, 1993; M. Sakai, 'Konflik Sekitar Devolusi Kekuasaan Ekonomi dan Politik: Suatu Pengantar', *Antropologi Indonesia* 68 (2002), iv–vii; W. P. Samadhi, 'Desentralisasi Setengah Hati: Berpindahnya "Sentralisme" ke Daerah', Demos – Center for Democracy and Human Rights Studies (2005), http://wp.demosindonesia.org/2005/11/desentralisasi-setengah-hati-berpindahnya-sentralisme-ke-daerah/.

[67] H. J. Triyana and Andi Wibowo, 'The Implementation of Article 8 of the Law Number 24 of 2007 for the Community Participation on Disaster Response to the 2010 Mount Merapi Eruption in Central Java and Yogyakarta Province. Research Report', Center for Community Services and Research, *Faculty of Law, Gadjah Mada University* (2011), 67, compared with Krisanto, 'Relokasi Korban Bencana: Legalistik v Kulturistik Historis Lereng Merapi Terhadap Rencana Relokasi,' *Kompas*, accessed 10 June 2010, http://hukum.kompasiana.com/2011/07/10/relokasi-korban-bencana-legalistik-vs-kultural-historis-kajian-penolakan-warga-lereng-merapi-terhadap-kebijakan-relokasi/.

[68] Krisanto, 'Relokasi Korban Bencana', 2.

[69] The author of this article was involved as one of the local community's legal advisors (see Triyana and Wibowo, 'The Implementation of Article 8', 88).

Article 3 of the Law redefines the government's primary functions in terms of promotion of disaster mitigation by three main rationales. Firstly, local governments would be able to give better service delivery and empowerment of people through providing better opportunities in disaster response. Second, local governments are given a significant role in formulating necessary policies, plans and legal instruments, providing financial and technical resources, coordination and linkage development, building community capacity on early warning, preparedness, relief, rescue, and shelter management. Lastly, local governments should mainstream disaster response into poverty reduction strategies as a prerequisite of the development planning process.[70] Limited access to information and participation from the affected communities contributes to their low acceptance of and adaptability for the implementation of new policies on relocation, compensation, and temporary shelter management. Based on this event, it can be concluded that elements of active, free and meaningful participation and the fair partnership as required by AADMER have been substantially less taken into consideration by local government. In this legal construction, local governments do not change their conduct and behaviour in accordance with AADMER's norms on participation and on partnership.

Thirdly, the Law tends to widen legal overlapping in terms of institutionalisation of bureaucratic coordination between central and local governments (province and district levels).[71] Simplification of procedure is required to deliver prompt and just responses. Denial of this procedure is commonly practised between central and local governments after the Law was issued, particularly on how to determine the status of natural disaster events pursuant to Article 7 (1.e).[72] In three disaster events in Padang, Wasior and the Merapi eruption, each blamed the other for the huge number of victims, large scale of destruction, and losses. Uncertainty of disaster status was caused by rigid and complex procedures to be undertaken. Fear of foreign interference which may jeopardise national integrity and sovereignty pursuant to Government Regulation

[70] R. Permana, 'Mengubah Paradigma Penanganan Bencana di Indonesia', *West Java Disaster Reduction Studies Center* (2007), 5: http://wjdrsc.files.wordpress.com/2008/03/paradigma-baru-penanganan-bencana-di-indonesia.pdf.

[71] M. Baiquni and R. Rijanta, 'Konflik Pengelolaan Lingkungan dan Sumber Daya Dalam Era Otonomi dan Transisi Masyarakat', *Bumi Lestari Journal of Environment*, vol. 7, No. 1 (2007), 1–22.

[72] It states 'authority of the determination of disaster status belongs to central and local government'.

Number 23 of 2008 Regarding the International Organisations' Roles and Function in Disaster Response in Indonesia is the most acceptable reason to implement rigid and complex procedures on foreign involvement, procurement, quarantine and customs.[73] Consequently, responses became weak and too ineffective to provide immediate basic needs.[74] Bureaucratic procedures were still of overriding importance in those events.[75]

Fourthly, the Law creates possible legal vacuums for fraud in customs and in tax for foreign aid in a simplified procedural mechanism required by AADMER.[76] In this aspect, a legal vacuum may occur as to how to show proof beyond reasonable doubt for criminal prosecutions directed at those who were allegedly responsible for loss of life due to ignorance of Article 75 of the Law. Article 75(1) determines that 'everyone is responsible for criminal prosecution and they are entitled to three years' imprisonment when they neglect disaster response norms when they are conducting their development plan initiatives'. This article is construed in a very broad legal determination imposing certain obligations on policy-makers at the local level. Consequently, the head of local government is placed as the most responsible person since he or she is the leader of regional or local development.[77] In this article, the adoption of AADMER norms such as accountability, responsibility, carefulness and good environmental governance is paramount in determining effective implementation of the Law.

In fact, in these three cases, this construction has become ineffective since the Indonesian criminal proceedings are subject to the Indonesian Criminal Procedural Code or *Kitab Undang-Undang Hukum Acara Pidana* (KUHAP). In the Code, natural disaster is legally construed as one of legal excuse to exempt individual criminal responsibility in all criminal matter either by acts of commission or omission. Consequently, the Law cannot be enforced to prosecute the alleged perpetrator in disaster events. Consequently, there is a disparity in the application of the law, causing an inevitable legal vacuum towards the implementation of the Law on disaster response. Statements that 'Indonesia has failed to bring accountability for those who are responsible for loss of life and to

[73] Triyana and Wibowo, 'The Implementation of Article 8', 57.
[74] Ibid., 58. [75] Ibid., 60.
[76] Triyana, 'The Implementation of the Community-Based Natural Resources Management System', 99.
[77] Lustermann, 'Indonesia', 16.

bring justice and/or remedy for the victims of natural disaster' are still fresh in our minds and it has become a hot issue since there has been no criminal prosecution brought before the court.[78] In simple terms, due to this situation, there will not be criminal prosecutions for those who are responsible for loss of life and material loss and collateral damages in natural disaster events in Indonesia.

Fifthly, the Law causes legal conflicts in terms of coordination in emergency, reconstruction and rehabilitation phases among government (central and local), victims, NGOs and other entities in their specific authorities and responsibilities.[79] There might be two forms of legal conflict in disaster response after the issuance of the Law, i.e. horizontal conflicts between local governments, and vertical conflicts between local governments and their communities as best illustrated by these four cases. The former is the most imminent threat for local governments when they integrate their local development policies separately from local and national development.[80] The Nimby syndrome proposed by Baiquni and Riyanta helps explain why conflicts exist between them since they hardly take into account the sustainability and interrelatedness of natural resources available in their territories.[81] Spatial and partial concepts in land-use planning have increased their looking inward for designing their own development strategies.[82] For example, in the case of the Mount Merapi eruption, the conflict between Central Java province and Yogyakarta Special Province exists in terms of financial and logistical support given by the central government.[83] This conflict also emerged between the West Sumatra and the Bengkulu provinces when the earthquake devastated the west coast of Sumatra.

The vertical conflict deals with ignorance and scepticism of communities' involvement in the disaster response. Less attention to potential natural hazards and how to cope with them, such as individual perception, knowledge of natural-disaster signs, locally safe and vulnerable

[78] Triyana and Wibowo, 'The Implementation of Article 8', 81.

[79] Y. T. Keban, 'Kerjasama Antar Pemerintah Daerah Dalam Era Otonomi', unpublished paper (2007).

[80] Triyana, 'Investasi dan Pengelolaan Ruang untuk Investasi di Daerah', Masters Thesis, Sekolah Paska Sarjana, Fakultas Hukum Universitas Gadjah Mada (2011), 6.

[81] Baiquni and Riyanta, 'Konflik Pengelola', 23.

[82] T. Notohadikusumo, 'Implikasi Etika Dalam Kebijakan Pembangunan Kawasan, Forum Perencanaan Pembangunan' (2008); and Keputusan Walikota Yogyakarta Nomor 669 Tentang Rencana Aksi Pengurangan Risiko Bencana Tahun, 2007–2011.

[83] Triyana and Wibowo, 'The Implementation of Article 8', 99.

areas from experience of past disasters, appropriate methods of survival, and social interaction as community coping strategies are the root causes of this vertical conflict.[84] Tools and techniques in terms of correct methodologies for intervention in conducting the community risk assessment, consisting of risk identification, analysis and risk evaluation conducted by local governments are not developed unless they fit with local regional development plans driven by the short-term goal of economic benefits.[85] The Mount Merapi case shows that this vertical conflict occurs when sand (as the remnant of the eruption) is being exploited by private companies in all mainstream rivers. It contributes little to the domestic compensation income, while at the same time this activity is destroying emergency routes for evacuation and making the river flow deteriorate preventing its capacity to halt possible floods of cold lava.[86] Private mining companies have earned huge profits while the affected communities have been ignored and earned nothing from such activity. Jealousy and weak mentality become the root of social conflicts such as in the Muntilan district in the Central Java province. This district suffers severely from cold lava that has displaced more than 10,000 people, while sand-mining activities have continued to operate. Undeniably, the imminent threat of vertical conflict between the community and its local government has become imminent due to environmental deterioration, jealousy, and discrimination in the accessibility of sand-mining activities.[87]

5. Concluding remarks

This chapter concludes that the Law successfully domesticates and adopts AADMER norms on coordination, partnership and simplification procedures. Thus it demonstrates Indonesian compliance. However, the effective implementation of those norms tends to be different in their application especially at the local level and with the local status of disaster events, highlighting the role and function of local governments. The absence of change of conduct of the local governments with relevance to those norms makes it hard to argue that they have been implemented effectively, even though they are so relevant in applicability to the central government and to the national disaster status.

[84] Triyana, 'Tinjauan Yuridis', 23. [85] Ibid., 11.
[86] Triyana and Wibowo, 'The Implementation of Article 8', 23. [87] Ibid., 25.

Indeed, advocacy to increase public awareness and to influence local government and BPBD to implement norms of coodination, partnership and simplified procedure on disaster response need to be raised through reviews, research, action plans and other forms of public advocacy. In particular, the involvement of the private sector, civic society and local resources should be mainstreamed in terms of coordination and partnership while simplification of procedure has to be given to the BPBD to develop its own initiatives on procurement, customs, quarantine and medical supplies at each provincial level. Giving more space to community participation and implementing a direct decision-making process at the lowest level will be a more fruitful beginning to implementing AADMER's norms effectively.

15

Enforcing aid in Myanmar: state responsibility and humanitarian aid provision

ANDREJ ZWITTER AND CHRISTOPHER K. LAMONT

1. Introduction

Whereas the norms applicable to humanitarian assistance in armed conflicts are explicit, when confronted with natural disasters humanitarian aid faces a dispersed array of legal norms. This was dramatically evident when Myanmar, reeling from the aftermath of cyclone Nargis in 2008, initially refused international humanitarian assistance. Myanmar's denial of humanitarian access raised a number of pressing questions regarding the contemporary legal practice of humanitarian aid provision. From the perspective of the body of law directly applicable to individuals, predominantly derived from international human rights law, legal norms address the rights to give and receive aid. On the other hand, state rights and obligations relate to sovereignty, territorial integrity, and non-interference. But duties among states and towards individuals also arise from treaty law, the rules of state responsibility, and from other principles of public international law. Furthermore, regional and international organisations, such as the African Union (AU), the European Union (EU) or the United Nations (UN), have *de facto* and *de lege* assumed some obligations with regard to humanitarian assistance. This chapter argues that it is only where obligations and rights overlap that an argument can be made for an effective legal aid regime in natural disasters. To illuminate this assumption this chapter will map rights and obligations in relation to individuals, states and organisations based on the case of Myanmar to come to a core body of norms governing rights and duties concerning humanitarian aid in natural disasters.

2. Cyclone Nargis and international law

Cyclone Nargis, which devastated Myanmar in 2008, provides an opportunity to illuminate contemporary international law concerning humanitarian aid in many ways. The different approaches states pursued to overcome the unwillingness of the military junta to allow access of foreign humanitarian aid in the aftermath of a cyclone that left more than 140,000 deceased and missing elucidates the workings of the international system in response to natural disasters. French Foreign Minister, Bernard Kouchner, invoked the political concept of the Responsibility to Protect (R2P) to claim that the international community of states must comply with their obligation to help the people of Myanmar and that the Security Council should issue a resolution that enforces this obligation, if necessary, based on Chapter VII of the *United Nations Charter*. This invocation of a Security Council responsibility to protect the people of Myanmar over the objections of the Myanmar government generated dissenting voices, not just from the usual dissenters to this kind of motion, China and Russia.[1] Contested reactions to the invocation of the concept of R2P illustrate the absence of consensus regarding this controversial doctrine within international society. Since the International Commission of Intervention and State Sovereignty (ICISS) presented its report on R2P, the General Assembly (A/RES/60/1, Para. 138 ff) and the Security Council (S/RES/1674) only supported the core idea of such a responsibility without expressly agreeing to be obliged by this concept beyond the normal workings of the United Nations (UN) collective security system.

What were the concrete legal issues that events in Myanmar raised? The classic Westphalian international legal system recognises the principles of sovereignty and non-interference. It is apparent that these principles have evolved substantially since the end of the cold war, the heyday of a state-centric reading of the *United Nations Charter*. The contemporary readings of the *United Nations Charter* recognise human rights and the protection of the individual as among the cornerstones of international peace and security alongside these aforementioned traditional principles. Particularly the latter principles, peace and security, are to be achieved through the cooperation of states (55, 56 *United Nations Charter*). In the case of Myanmar, where a state is unwilling or unable to deliver the aid necessary to ensure the survival of its citizens after a natural disaster, and where the situation cannot be

[1] 'France Urges UN to Force Cyclone Aid on Myanmar', *International Herald Tribune*, 7 May 2008.

qualified as an armed conflict to allow for the application of International Humanitarian Law (IHL),[2] the following questions arise:

1. What are the legal duties of that state towards its citizen?
2. What are the rights and duties of the United Nations?
3. What are the legal duties of that state towards other states?
4. What are the legal duties of other states towards that state?
5. What are the rights and enforcements of rights of other states to ensure aid?

It is beyond the scope of this chapter to respond to questions 1 and 2 in great detail. Instead, they will be addressed *en passant* in the following sections.

The rights and duties of the United Nations will be further discussed in the context of the elaboration of this chapter's core argument that the most effective legal regime to date concerning the protection of individuals in natural disasters can be found in customary law concerning state responsibility for internationally wrongful acts. However, essentially the United Nations' duty can be summarised as consisting of an obligation to ensure the facilitation of humanitarian aid provision through its specialised bodies and to protect against threats to international peace and security. In the latter case, the Security Council has the right to enforce its decisions by force through a Chapter VII resolution.

In order to adequately respond to questions 3–5 it must first be established whether the concept of R2P is even applicable and applied in current state practice and whether the current work of the International Law Commission (ILC) adds any new insights to the situation. The example of cyclone Nargis that hit Myanmar will serve as a test case for that purpose. The principal argument that this chapter makes is that human rights treaties and obligations *erga omnes* form *sui generis* of treaty obligations that contrary to other treaties do not only establish a legal relationship on the horizontal level, i.e. among states, but also a vertical and diagonal relationship between states towards the people within their own jurisdiction and states towards people in other jurisdictions. The term *relationship* is used here in place of obligation since it is not necessarily obligations that are contained within these relationships. These relationships stem from customary (state responsibility) and treaty

[2] Common Article 3 of the Geneva Conventions requires parties of an armed conflict to allow for, and if necessary provide, humanitarian aid. This obligation, however, obliges only parties to a conflict and is not applicable in purely natural disasters.

law concerning the laws of treaties. Two interpretations can be offered: firstly, a solidarist interpretation posits that states can invoke a violation of human rights on all territories and for all people if breached by another state (not only in cases of violations of *ius cogens*) and secondly, a traditionalist/pluralist interpretation that states can invoke state responsibility at least in cases of diplomatic protection for their own citizens in other countries and also for breaches of peremptory norms of international law. Juxtaposing the possible countermeasures that states have at hand in these cases with the principles of sovereignty and non-interference and the customs that have developed in state practice of how to deal with breaches of obligations of states will give a clear picture of what states can do and/or have to do. This chapter will eventually argue that the state affected by disaster has a duty to protect its own citizens and to cooperate, if necessary, with other states, but not at the expense of its territorial integrity and political independence. Furthermore, it will be argued that other states have the duty to offer aid and are permitted to use non-military sanctions to enforce aid, but that the use of force remains restricted to the authorisation by the Security Council which can only invoke Chapter VII if the seriousness and scale of the violation amounts to crimes against humanity, war crimes or genocide.

3. Brief history

Cyclone Nargis struck Myanmar's Ayeyarwady Delta on 2–3 May 2008. This tidal storm, the strongest recorded in history, killed 140,000 people and left 2.4 million people in the Delta in immediate need of humanitarian aid. Initially, the Myanmar government refused all external support for assistance, which resulted in huge frustration within the international community and led French Foreign Minister Bernard Kouchner to raise the spectre of R2P as a means of aid enforcement, after only a single Thai aircraft was permitted to enter Myanmar for the delivery of aid on 6 May.[3] On 10 May the UNHCR entered Myanmar with 22 tonnes of tents and other humanitarian supplies, and on 11 May the junta for the first time eased restrictions on foreign aid.[4] However, although United States military aircraft were allowed to land, the regime refused to

[3] Claudia Parsons, 'France Urges UN Council to Act on Myanmar Cyclone', *Reuters online*, 7 May 2008, www.reuters.com/Art./2008/05/07/idUSL07810481.

[4] 'Burma Eases Restrictions on Aid', *BBC*, 11 May 2008, section Asia-Pacific, http://news.bbc.co.uk/2/hi/asia-pacific/7394410.stm.

permit the distribution of aid by American soldiers, which prompted the United States to bypass the regime by channelling aid through private local aid groups.[5]

Eleven days later, on 22 May, United Nations Secretary-General Ban Ki-Moon visited Myanmar to facilitate unrestricted access of humanitarian workers to disaster-struck areas and on 23 May the regime declared that all aid-workers, irrespective of nationality, would be allowed to enter the country.[6] On 5 June, United States military vessels departed from the coast of Myanmar after having been denied permission to dock.[7] ASEAN was then asked to intervene to facilitate the flow of international assistance in the aftermath of the cyclone, under the Tripartite Core Group (TCG) mechanism, which also comprised the government of Myanmar and the United Nations.[8] This resulted in a mandate for ASEAN-led coordination of relief, which concluded at the end of July 2010. The coordination mechanism for further coordination after this date was handed over to the government of Myanmar.[9]

Even though alternative reports strongly emphasised that the Post-Nargis Joint Assessment Report (PONJA Report) compiled by ASEAN, the United Nations and the regime in Myanmar ignored issues of obstructions to aid, corruption and human rights abuses, none of the criticisms brought any evidence to the fore that the regime, as a policy, was misusing the control over aid.[10] This might have had to do with the immediate efforts of the United Nations, ASEAN and the international community. However, it seems that the situation was most realistically

[5] 'US Sends Aid Through Private Groups in Myanmar', *CNN.com* n.d., www.cnn.com/2008/WORLD/asiapcf/05/16/us.myanmar.

[6] 'UN Chief: Myanmar to Admit All Aid-workers', *CNN.com*, n.d., http://edition.cnn.com/2008/WORLD/asiapcf/05/23/myanmar/; 'UN Head Tours Cyclone-hit Burma', *BBC*, 22 May 2008, section Asia-Pacific, http://news.bbc.co.uk/2/hi/asia-pacific/7414015.stm.

[7] 'US Ships to Leave Cyclone-hit Myanmar After Junta Snub', *ReliefWeb*, n.d., http://reliefweb.int/node/268943.

[8] ASEAN, 'ASEANWEB – ASEAN-UN ESCAP Joint Press Release – ASEAN – UN ESCAP Convene a Post-Nargis Lessons Learning Conference, Jakarta, 27 August 2010, www.aseansec.org/25133.htm.

[9] Ibid.

[10] See: DHF, 'Post-Nargis Analysis – The Other Side of the Story', *Dag Hammarskjöld Foundation*, n.d., www.dhf.uu.se/publications/other-publications/post-nargis-analysis-%e2%80%93-the-other-side-of-the-story/; 'Discrimination over aid distribution among cyclone victims: new report', n.d., www.bnionline.net/news/miima/4558-discrimination-over-aid-distribution-among-cyclone-victims-new-report.html.

described by a senior United Nations programme director as a military junta in fear of a seaborne invasion:[11]

> The generals thought it was just another typical cyclone, where the army would hand out some rice and a few tarps and that would be it . . . The regime made some shocking mistakes early on, really horrible, when they blocked the aid. With all the international furor, they finally realised, 'This is way, way too big for us.' And after that, they did a lot. A huge national response occurred.

3. Cooperation or protection duties?

3.1 Responsibility to Protect

R2P, as a political concept, traces its origins to debates concerning the social contract between the state and its citizen.[12] It was in 1994 that the United Nations Development Programme (UNDP) in its *Human Development Report* challenged, for the first time, state-centric conceptions of security by offering the concept of human security.[13] Cohen and Deng's 'sovereignty as responsibility', for the protection of internally displaced persons (IDPs), went further and linked sovereignty and human security together.[14] Kofi Annan also challenged the international community with his 'Two Concepts of Sovereignty' to come up with a solution to the apparent tension between human- and state-centred approaches to security.[15] The ICISS issued a report entitled *Responsibility to Protect*,[16] parts of which were later adopted by the General Assembly in a political consensus that Bellamy suggests consists of three pillars:[17]

[11] 'Cyclone Nargis – Breaking Cyclone Nargis News', *The New York Times*, 30 April 2009, http://topics.nytimes.com/topics/news/international/countriesandterritories/myanmar/cyclone_nargis/index.html.

[12] David Luban, 'Just War and Human Rights', *Philosophy and Public Affairs* 9, no. 2 (1 January 1980): 160–181.

[13] United Nations Development Programme, *Human Development Report 1994* (Oxford University Press, 1994).

[14] Francis M. Deng, *Sovereignty As Responsibility: Conflict Management in Africa* (Brookings Institution Press, 1996).

[15] Kofi Annan, 'Two Concepts of Sovereignty', *The Economist*, 16 September 1999: www.economist.com/node/324795.

[16] International Commission on Intervention and State Sovereignty (ICISS), 'The Responsibility to Protect', *International Development Research Centre*, December 2001, http://responsibilitytoprotect.org/ICISS%20Report.pdf.

[17] Alex J. Bellamy, 'Should Nations Force Aid on Others?', *Natural Hazards Observer* (2010): 10–11.

1. The responsibility of the state to protect its population from genocide, war crimes, ethnic cleansing and crimes against humanity, and from their incitement;
2. The international community's duty to assist the state to fulfil its responsibility to protect;
3. The international community's responsibility to take timely and decisive action, through peaceful diplomatic and humanitarian means and, if that fails, other more forceful means, in a manner consistent with *United Nations Charter* Chapters VI (pacific measures), VII (enforcement measures), and VIII (regional arrangements). The United Nations Security Council may act in situations where states 'manifestly fail to protect their populations' from the four crimes.

In Bellamy's opinion there were three reasons why R2P should not be invoked for the case of Myanmar: firstly, it was very doubtful whether it was a case of crimes against humanity; secondly, there was no Security Council consensus; thirdly, its invocation would dilute R2P to such an extent that all the progress of the previous years to establish a political consensus about what to do in the cases of the worst crimes would be jeopardised. Whereas the second argument is not really striking as a general argument, since the Security Council could disagree that the conditions of any of the four crimes – genocide, war crimes, ethnic cleansing and crimes against humanity – were objectively met, or simply elect not to raise the question; the third argument certainly holds a political weight that must not be underestimated. However, for the purpose of this chapter it is the first argument that is most relevant and therefore will be briefly examined.

Does the junta's reaction to Nargis fall into the realm of applicability of the *Rome Statute*, specifically as a crime against humanity? Unlike crimes recognised by international criminal law, a state giving no aid or too little aid to its citizen in times of an emergency is not necessarily the result of a *mens rea* of withholding aid for the purpose of harming the population. Under these circumstances, particularly if it is unclear who within the state specifically is responsible for the delivery of aid, it is almost impossible to pinpoint the individual responsible for the commission of a crime through deliberate neglect. Intention to commit a crime against humanity is a prerequisite for conviction in terms of international criminal law. This condition must be seen as even more important when the principles of non-intervention and sovereignty are added to the equation, and if the consequence is military intervention. So if neither genocide nor war crimes are present, the question remains whether crimes against humanity were committed by the military regime so as to fulfil the requirements of R2P. This raises the question under which circumstances a state can commit crimes against humanity. Article 7.1.(k) of the *Rome Statute* defines wideseрread and systmatic crimes against humanity as follows: 'Other inhumane acts of a similar character intentionally causing great suffering, or serious injury to body or to mental or physical health.' *Litera* (k) would justify the applicability of the article. The ILC's commentary does not really shed more light on what 'other inhumane acts' could constitute other than to suggest that neglect seems not to be covered:[18]

> The Commission recognised that it was impossible to establish an exhaustive list of the inhumane acts which might constitute crimes against humanity. It should be noted that the notion of other inhumane acts is circumscribed by two requirements. Firstly, this category of acts is intended to include only additional acts that are similar in gravity to those listed in the preceding subparagraphs. Secondly, the act must in fact cause injury to a human being in terms of physical or mental integrity, health or human dignity. The subparagraph provides two examples of the types of acts that would meet these two requirements, namely, mutilation and other types of severe bodily harm.

However, if crimes against humanity are viewed in the light of case law established at the International Criminal Tribunal for the former Yugoslavia (ICTY), its applicability to the Myanmar case is even more doubtful. ICTY jurisprudence established two requirements that must be fulfilled in order for violations to constitute crimes against humanity: firstly, the presence of an international or internal armed conflict; and secondly, a close nexus between the armed conflict and the alleged offence.[19]

In this respect the trial chamber stated in *Kordić and Čerkez* 'Article 2 and 3 of the Statute set forth provisions which reflect the laws of war; plainly a pre-condition to the applicability of these Articles is the existence of an armed conflict in the territory where the crimes are alleged to have occurred.'[20] Furthermore, it established the nexus

[18] ILC, Draft Code of Crimes against the Peace and Security of Mankind with Commentaries, Report of the International Law Commission on the work of its forty-eighth session, *Yearbook of the International Law Commission* vol. II, Part Two (1996), 50, §17.

[19] HRW, 'Genocide, War Crimes, and Crimes Against Humanity: Topical Digests of the Case Law of the International Criminal Tribunal for Rwanda and the International Criminal Tribunal for the Former Yugoslavia', *Human Rights Watch* (2004): 142, 143, www.hrw.org/reports/2004/ij/digest.pdf.

[20] *Kordić and Čerkez (*Trial Chamber), 26 February 2001, §22.

between crimes against humanity and the requirements of IHL in the *Furundžija* case:[21]

> It is well established that for international humanitarian law to apply there must first be an armed conflict . . . For the purposes of Article 3 of the Statute, the nature of this armed conflict is irrelevant. [I]t does not matter whether the serious violation occurred in the context of an international or internal armed conflict, provided the following requirements are met: (i) the violation must constitute an infringement of a rule of international humanitarian law; (ii) the rule must be customary in nature or, if it belongs to treaty law, the required conditions must be met; (iii) the violation must be 'serious,' that is to say, it must constitute a breach of a rule protecting important values, and the breach must involve grave consequences for the victim; (iv) the violation of the rule must entail, under customary or conventional law, the individual criminal responsibility of the person breaching the rule.

Whereas Article 5 of the ICTY Statute explicitly narrows the scope of crimes against humanity to apply exclusively to the vicinity of armed conflict,[22] Article 3 of the *Statute of the International Criminal Tribunal for Rwanda*, and therefore the rulings of the tribunal, slightly depart from this requirement: 'The International Tribunal for Rwanda shall have the power to prosecute persons responsible for the following crimes when committed as part of a widespread or systematic attack against any civilian population on national, political, ethnic, racial or religious grounds.' Hence, the article reduces the requirement of an armed conflict to the element of a widespread or systematic attack.

Concerning the notion of attack, the trial chamber insisted in the *Semanza* case that a systematic and widespread attack must have been the trigger for the act of crime.[23] Furthermore, the 'attack may also be non-violent in nature, like imposing a system of apartheid . . . or exerting pressure on the population to act in a

[21] *Furundžija (*ICTY Trial Chamber), 10 December 1998, §258.

[22] ICTY Statute, Article 5: 'The International Tribunal shall have the power to prosecute persons responsible for the following crimes when committed in armed conflict, whether international or internal in character, and directed against any civilian population.'

[23] *Semanza (*ICTR Trial Chamber), 15 May 2003, §326: 'A crime against humanity must have been committed as part of a widespread or systematic attack against any civilian population on discriminatory grounds. Although the act need not be committed at the same time and place as the attack or share all of the features of the attack, it must, by its characteristics, aims, nature, or consequence objectively form part of the discriminatory attack.' Interestingly, the court distinguished here between the attack and the act.

particular manner'.[24] This suggests the coercive element that the tribunal relates to the elements of 'widespread' or 'systematic': 'A systematic attack means an attack carried out pursuant to a pre-conceived policy or plan'.[25] Although one might argue for a widespread consequence, the idea of criminal neglect cannot be read into the jurisdiction and the ILC commentary without having to stretch the concept of crimes against humanity to the extent that this inclusion would provide minimal legal guidance and opens the norm up to political interpretation.[26] In this line Dörmann et al. concluded from the jurisdiction of ad hoc tribunals that, concerning the interpretation of 'crimes against humanity' in the *Rome Statute* at least, wilfulness (i.e. either 'intent' or 'recklessness') has to be fulfilled and that ordinary 'negligence' is not covered. Recklessness requires that the actor must be consciously aware of the risk created.[27]

There are several arguments against the applicability of R2P. Firstly, the regime tried to provide aid itself, and the rejection of foreign aid due to a miscalculation of one's own capacity and fear of invasion does not fully fulfil the criteria of recklessness as stated above. Secondly, Myanmar did not withhold all foreign aid but rather wanted it to be channelled through governmental structures. To decide upon and regulate access of foreign humanitarian actors is the legal right of states, since it is also vested with the obligation to coordinate aid within its territory.[28] Concerning aid offered by the United States, one is certainly not surprised that Myanmar refused to allow United States armed forces personnel deployed on naval vessels near the coast of Myanmar permission to deliver aid. Myanmar, as a sovereign state, feared direct United States

[24] *Akayesu* (ICTR Trial Chamber), 2 September 1998, §581. See also *Rutaganda* (ICTR Trial Chamber), 6 December 1999, §70; *Musema* (ICTR Trial Chamber), 27 January 2000, §205; *Semanza* (ICTR Trial Chamber), 15 May 2003, §327.

[25] *Kayishema* and *Ruzindana* (ICTR Trial Chamber), 21 May 1999, §123. See also *Bagilishema* (ICTR Trial Chamber), 7 June 2001, 77.

[26] The issue of criminal neglect was however raised by US Defense Secretary Robert Gates: 'This is more akin, in my view, to criminal neglect'; 'Cyclone Nargis: One Month on, US Accuses Burma of Criminal Neglect', *World News*, guardian.co.uk, 2 June 2008, www.guardian.co.uk/world/2008/jun/02/burma.cyclonenargis.

[27] Knut Dörmann, Louise Doswald-Beck, and Robert Kolb, *Elements of War Crimes Under the Rome Statute of the International Criminal Court: Sources and Commentary* (Cambridge University Press, 2002), 43, 490.

[28] Heike Spieker, 'The Right to Give and Receive Humanitarian Assistance', in *International Law and Humanitarian Assistance*, eds. Hans-Joachim Heintze and Andrej Zwitter (Berlin, Heidelberg: Springer, 2011), 7–31.

military assistance out of a concern for espionage and attempts on the part of the United States to undermine the regime or provoke pro-democratic unrest. The situation can be best qualified as an inability of the regime to deliver the necessary aid itself as well as a lack of coordination and exacerbation of hindrance to aid delivery through fears of invasion or at least interference in internal matters. Since non-interference and political independence are amongst the highest principles international law knows, the behaviour of the military junta, even if morally abhorrent, is at least legally defensible. Indeed, it cannot be argued that there existed an intention to harm the population, and an inability of the junta to protect the population from crimes against humanity cannot be argued since there was no other perpetrator to commit such a crime. Even if such an intention can be reasonably established, the applicability of R2P still lacks the prerequisite of being a systematic attack.

For the political assessment of whether R2P is an adequate basis for arguing for a duty of states to receive aid or to give it, if necessary by force, one has to look at the broader political implications of such an approach. If R2P fails to be applicable as a tool for enforcing humanitarian aid for civilians in all cases of neglect by an unwilling or unable government, particularly in cases where no armed conflict is present, then the application of R2P, where it actually would be applicable, would be fodder for critics who claim R2P solely as being a tool to circumvent the principles of non-interference and state sovereignty. This therefore warrants taking a look at other legal and political conceptions that are applicable in both wartime and times of natural disaster to the same extent.

3.2 *The ILC and the duty to cooperate*

Since 2006, the ILC has been working on the theme of 'Protection of Persons in the Event of Disasters' to develop the concept of the duty of states to cooperate in terms of humanitarian aid. Whereas its work on state responsibility for internationally wrongful acts was for the most part a codification of statutory and customary law, its work on the duty to cooperate seems to be much more an endeavour to explore the possible dimensions of several legal norms that mention cooperation and to develop a new framework to be submitted for acknowledgement by the General Assembly and perhaps usher in a new treaty.

The current state of the workings of the ILC concerning the right to aid in natural disasters is structured around two approaches: firstly a rights-based approach, and secondly a needs-based approach.[29] The rights-based approach was considered by some committee members as a legal concept *in abstracto* taking the whole spectrum of human rights into consideration, whereas the needs-based approach would rather refer to the needs triggered by a disaster in a specific case. Agreement was seemingly found that the rights-based approach would refer to human rights of all kinds, but in particular social and economic rights.[30] Some raised doubts whether 'rights-based' would suggest that states could force aid upon other states, which is not the current state practice. 'Instead it was pointed out that the affected state is entitled to ensure proper coordination of efforts of relief, and may refuse some kinds of assistance.'[31]

The core of the legal arguments concerning the protection of persons seems to converge around two articles. Article 5 of the Draft Articles addresses the duty to cooperate, which the ILC primarily derives from Articles 55, 54 and 1 paragraph 3 *United Nations Charter*.[32] Article 9 of the Draft Articles builds the bridge to sovereignty and state responsibility, stipulating in paragraph 1 the relevance of state responsibility to ensure the protection of persons and the provision of humanitarian assistance on its territory, whereas paragraph 2 reiterates that any external assistance requires state consent.[33] The provisions on respect for and protection of human dignity and human rights (Draft Article 7 and 8) indicate that responsibilities, as introduced by the ILC, refer to the whole corpus of human rights.[34]

Now if international human rights law is the basis of duties and rights of states concerning humanitarian assistance and remedies, provided the respective human rights regimes do not prevent human rights violations, any international enforcement should follow the general rules of state responsibility (as discussed below). The question remains which conditions a potential breach has to fulfil. The ILC seems to have found agreement on the obligations affected states have to fulfil in the event of disasters:[35]

> **Article 10 – Duty of the affected State to seek assistance**
>
> To the extent that a disaster exceeds its national response capacity, the affected State has the duty to seek assistance from among other States,

[29] ILC Report, A/64/10, 2009, §155.
[30] ILC Report, A/64/10, 2009, §159–162.
[31] ILC Report, A/64/10, 2009, §162.
[32] ILC Report, A/65/10, 2010, §330, 331.
[33] ILC Report, A/67/10, 2012, §81.
[34] Ibid.
[35] Ibid.

the United Nations, other competent intergovernmental organisations and relevant non-governmental organisations, as appropriate.

Article 11 – Consent of the affected State to external assistance

1. The provision of external assistance requires the consent of the affected State.
2. Consent to external assistance shall not be withheld arbitrarily.
3. When an offer of assistance is extended in accordance with the present Draft Articles, the affected State shall, whenever possible, make its decision regarding the offer known.

Argumentum e contrario one could argue that if a state does not seek assistance, once it knows that a disaster exceeds its capacity, it has to consent to bona fide offers, provided that the offer is made in accordance with Article 9 (i.e. respecting the sovereignty of the affected state).

Initially there seems to have been a debate whether and to what extent to incorporate R2P in the Draft Articles.[36] In the light of the assessment of R2P's applicability above it has to be argued, however, that in order to ensure a politically less contested legal draft and in view of its applicability to natural disasters, reference to R2P should be refrained from. Otherwise the reference to R2P in this draft would either dissolute the legal definition of crimes against humanity and other crimes stipulated in the General Assembly and Security Council resolutions altogether,[37] or brand states unable to provide sufficient aid and with the fear of foreign influence and intervention immediately as perpetrators of crimes against humanity, or worse. A similar argument has been made by the Special Rapporteur referring to the Secretary-General, who reiterated that, until the community of states would decide otherwise, for now R2P shall only apply to the four crimes specified.[38] In any case the workings of the ILC will have to conform with the general consensus of the General Assembly that humanitarian aid 'should be provided with the consent

[36] ILC Report (A/64/10) 2009, §164.

[37] The General Assembly has affirmed R2P in the World Summit Outcome 2005 (A/RES/60/1). The Security Council has invoked R2P in S/RES/1674 (2006), reaffirming 'the provisions of §138 and 139 of the 2005 World Summit Outcome Document regarding the responsibility to protect populations from genocide, war crimes, ethnic cleansing and crimes against humanity'; S/RES/1970 (2011) and S/RES/1973 (2011) on the situation in Libya; (S/RES/1975) 2011 on the situation in Côte d'Ivoire (S/RES/1996) 2011 on the situation in South Sudan, and S/RES/2014 (2011) on the situation in Yemen.

[38] ILC Report (A/66/10) 2011; and Secretary-General Report on the Implementation of the Responsibility to Protect (A/63/677), 2008.

of the affected country and in principle on the basis of an appeal by the affected country'.[39]

Since the work of the ILC concerning the duty to cooperate is still in progress, it might be well worth a look at what can be deduced from the Articles on the Responsibility of States for Internationally Wrongful Acts (ARSIWA) in terms of enforcement of the duty to protect persons affected by disasters.

4. Human rights treaties and humanitarian aid

This section will elaborate on the nature of human rights treaties and specific norms as *erga omnes* obligations in order to prepare the ground for analysing what it means in terms of state responsibility for internationally wrongful acts. Thereby this approach follows the rights-based approach of the ILC by considering human rights, specifically the right to life, as the basis for a right to humanitarian aid and a duty to cooperate.

Human rights treaties fall within the general scope of the *Vienna Convention on the Law of Treaties* (VCLT) under Article 1.[40] That means that all parties to the *International Covenant of Civil and Political Rights* (ICCPR) and the *International Covenant of Economic, Social and Cultural Rights* (ICESCR) are bound by it due to mutual agreement.[41] Concerning human rights treaties, the novel construct they introduced was that the treaty is violated *erga omnes partes* if a state violates the rights of any individual under its jurisdiction and on its territory (Article 29 VCLT). That foreigners have an additional diplomatic protection does not affect the treaty as such, nor modify it. Furthermore, according to Article 2.1.h VCLT, third states are those that are not party to the treaty. That is quite a crucial distinction because some of the literature seems to conflate the term 'third state' with state parties to human rights conventions, which do not have citizens on the territory of another state (violated by the host state).[42] This makes a crucial difference, since state parties, as will be discussed in the section on state responsibility, can have recourse to different measures in order to sanction the violation of

[39] Strengthening of the Coordination of Humanitarian Emergency Assistance of the United Nations, GA Res. 46/182, Annex, §3, UN Doc. (A/RES/46/182), 19 December 1991.

[40] VLCT, Article 1: The present Convention applies to treaties between States.

[41] Bruno Simma, *From Bilateralism to Community Interest in International Law*, vol. 250 (Martinus Nijhoff, 1994, VI), 217, 373.

[42] See for example: Annie Bird, 'Third State Responsibility for Human Rights Violations', *European Journal of International Law* 21, no. 4 (1 November 2010): 883–900.

treaty obligations than third states, which are only entitled to measures if they concern breaches of *erga omnes* obligations.

Some authors posit that human rights treaties qualify as a self-contained regime through the provision of their own enforcement mechanisms, thereby excluding recourse to general enforcement mechanisms due to their nature of being *lex specialis.*[43] Simma rightly concludes that given the jurisprudence of the International Court of Justice (ICJ) and the logic of international law, these specialised enforcement mechanisms should rather be seen as complementary to the general norms of state responsibility, because they do not encompass all responsibilities that would derive from the general principles of state responsibility.[44] Two additional arguments against the 'self-contained system theory' can be added to Simma's assessment: firstly, the very working of the norms according to which any treaty between states (including human rights treaties) has to abide are dictated by the *ius cogens* status of the *Vienna Convention*, including the qualification of obligations *erga omnes partes*; and secondly, the fact that human rights treaties are embedded in the larger framework of the *United Nations Charter* (see Articles 1(3), 55, and 56). Thus treaty obligations are first and foremost breached by the parties to a treaty, and if the treaty provides no alternative procedure concerning the settlement of disputes with other treaty parties, general norms must be applicable. The human rights regimes require internal (and sometimes external) mechanisms in the form of legal remedies for the individual to be in place. To that extent one has to qualify Simma's general proposition that states would still have the right to use (counter-)measures for breaches of human rights law: these remedies are designed to compensate for the breach and can be said to thereby remedy such a breach. Therefore, when a state allows for procedures foreseen by human rights treaties, it can heal the breach of the obligation. If the internal remedies to address such a breach are not applied, the question remains open as to what other states can do. Simma concludes 'that states have a right to ensure that international law be respected, including a restricted right to unilateral enforcement action (countermeasures)'.[45] This leads to an understanding of human rights treaties (and other treaties that qualify individuals as objects of fulfilment of a treaty) that is quite different from other treaties. It resembles a triangle of obligations,

[43] Bruno Simma, 'Of Planets and the Universe: Self-contained Regimes in International Law', *EJIL* 17 (2006): 483–529.

[44] Ibid., 524–529.

[45] Ibid., 526.

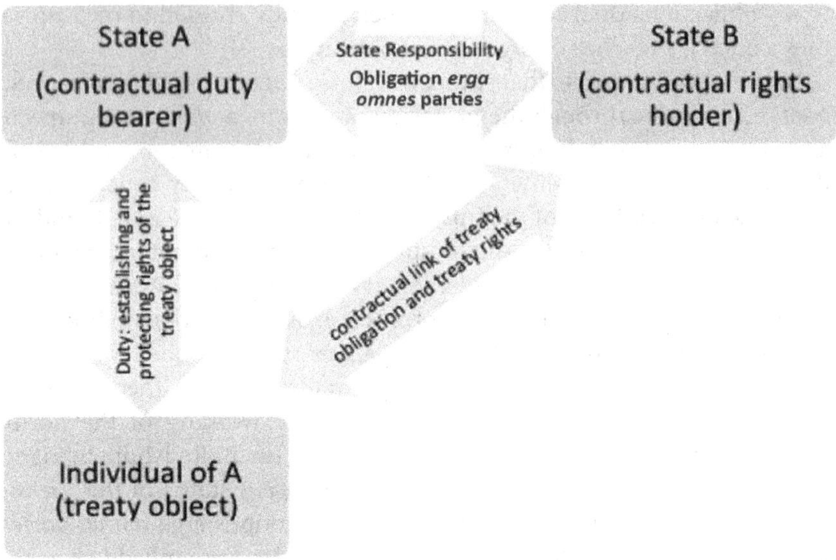

Figure 15.1: Contractual duty/rights relationship.

rights and responsibilities (see Figure 15.1). The duty-bearer is the state A. The object of fulfilment of this duty is, however, not another state B but the individuals under state A's jurisdiction. The duty is to ensure, protect and fulfil human rights for the individuals, which must not be confused with the contractual rights that stem from the treaty itself.[46] If the duty concerning the object of fulfilment (the individuals under A's jurisdiction) is not addressed, state A has breached treaty obligations with the effect that other treaty parties (state B) can claim cessation and reparation for the breach. The contractual link of treaty obligation and treaty rights (remedies) is merely established via the treaty object (independently of whether the object of fulfilment is an inanimate object or individuals). Milanovic follows a similar approach when arguing that the Genocide Convention 1948 in contractual terms of state responsibility established a 'civil' and not a 'criminal' legal relationship.[47]

[46] In other treaties between states (for example trade agreements) these treaty rights might be the same as the duties, i.e. if the rights established by the treaty are violated, the direct victim is the other state. If the object of fulfilment is different from the state, the treaty rights and obligations still concern the parties and give them recourse to remedies if the treaty object is violated in any way.

[47] Marko Milanović, 'State Responsibility for Genocide', *European Journal of International Law* 17, no. 3 (2006): 562.

Thus a violation of such treaties is not a state crime but a breach of contract.[48] Before these countermeasures can be discussed, the concept of *erga omnes* obligations in the light of human rights norms needs to be explained.

5. *Erga omnes* obligations and the right to life

States are obliged to protect human rights. This obligation derives from the ICCPR and the ICESCR as well as through the membership in the United Nations (Articles 1(3), 55, 56, *United Nations Charter*) and thereby through the applicability of the *Universal Declaration of Human Rights*, which is a defining document for wording the *United Nations Charter* with regard to human rights obligations. Furthermore, certain human rights have become *ius cogens.*

The right to humanitarian assistance is fundamentally linked to the right to life. This has been suggested by the Human Rights Committee when it opted for an interpretation that would include a duty to fulfil:[49]

> Moreover, the Committee has noted that the right to life has been too often narrowly interpreted. The expression 'inherent right to life' cannot properly be understood in a restrictive manner, and the protection of this right requires that States adopt positive measures. In this connection, the Committee considers that it would be desirable for States parties to take all possible measures to reduce infant mortality and to increase life expectancy, especially in adopting measures to eliminate malnutrition and epidemics.

Some raise the argument that the right to life would only justify a minimal right to assistance, whereas Articles 11, 12 ICESCR would provide for more space in the sense of an 'adequate standard of living' and 'the highest standard of mental and physical health'.[50] This position, however, overlooks a few problematic elements. Firstly, although Articles 11 and 12 ICESCR are not derogable in wartime, wartime imposes limitations on the ICESCR obligations of the state in accordance with

[48] Ibid., 564: 'even though the primary beneficiaries of the state obligations are individuals, these obligations still run between the state parties'.

[49] UN, Human Rights Committee, General Comment 6, Article 6 (Sixteenth session, 1982), Compilation of General Comments and General Recommendations adopted by Human Rights Treaty Bodies, UN Doc. (HRI\GEN\1\Rev.1) 1994, 6, §5.

[50] J. Benton Heath, 'Disasters, Relief, and Neglect: The Duty to Accept Humanitarian Assistance and the Work of the International Law Commission', *New York University Journal of International Law and Politics (JILP)* 43, no. 2 (2011): 439.

Article 2, which stipulates a progressive realisation of the ICESCR. Such a progressive realisation is naturally hampered in wartime. Secondly, due to their scope they rather qualify for development aid, which lacks the urgency of humanitarian aid. And thirdly, the argument for the creation of legal space is not striking as a lack of it does not prohibit states giving more aid than necessary for the fulfilment of the right to life.

The concept of *erga omnes* was recognised by the ICJ in the *Barcelona Traction* case, when it stated that:[51]

> an essential distinction should be drawn between the obligations of a State towards the international community as a whole, and those arising vis-à-vis another State in the field of diplomatic protection. By their very nature the former are the concern of all States. In view of the importance of the rights involved, all States can be held to have a legal interest in their protection; they are obligations *erga omnes.*

We have to zoom in on the terms of *ius cogens* and obligation *erga omnes*. The difference between *ius cogens* and *erga omnes* obligations is that *ius cogens* status constitutes the fundamental, peremptory character of the obligation for all states, regardless of their treaty obligations, while *erga omnes* status denotes the legal interest of all states in the protection of the relevant right.[52] Whether every state is obliged by the status of a norm itself as being non-derogable (*ius cogens*) or by the interest of every other state (*erga omnes*), the *de facto* difference might be only minimal. The ILC mentions in its commentary to Article 40 of the Articles on the Responsibility of States for Internationally Wrongful Acts[53] (henceforth: ARSIWA) that the development of the *erga omnes* concept is closely related to the system of peremptory norms of international law in the Articles 53 and 64 of

[51] ICJ, 'Barcelona Traction, Light and Power Company Limited', Second Phase, *ICJ Reports* (1970): 3, 32, §33.

[52] Law Society, Written Evidence of Joint Committee On Human Rights, the United Kingdom Parliament; see n391, 27. www.publications.parliament.uk/pa/jt200506/jtselect/jtrights/185/185we28.htm; UN Human Rights Committee, General Comment No. 31 [80], Nature of the General Legal Obligation Imposed on States Parties to the Covenant: 26/05/2004 (CCPR/C/21/Rev.1/Add.13) www.unhchr.ch/tbs/doc.nsf/(Symbol)/CCPR.C.21.Rev.1.Add.13.En?Opendocument.

[53] ILC, Draft Articles on Responsibility of States for Internationally Wrongful Acts with commentaries, *Yearbook of the International Law Commission*, vol. II Part Two 2001 (A/CN.4/SER.A/2001/Add.1 (Part 2)), Art 40. Available online at: http://untreaty.un.org/ilc/texts/instruments/english/commentaries/9_6_2001.pdf.

the *Vienna Convention of the Law of Treaties*. Article 53 VCLT especially gives us a definition of *ius cogens*, even if it is not very precise:[54]

> Article 53:
>
> A treaty is void if, at the time of its conclusion, it conflicts with a peremptory norm of general international law. For the purposes of the present Convention, a peremptory norm of general international law is a norm accepted and recognised by the international community of States as a whole as a norm from which no derogation is permitted and which can be modified only by a subsequent norm of general international law having the same character.

As the members of the ILC could not agree which norms definitely fall under the scope of application of the term 'peremptory norms of international law', the ILC decided not to give a demonstrative list.[55]

Bassiouni gives us some indicators for the identification of *ius cogens* norms. Following Bassiouni, *ius cogens* norms concerning international crimes and serious violations of human rights consist of four elements:

> (1) international pronouncements, or what can be called international *opinio juris*, reflecting the recognition that these crimes are deemed part of general customary law; (2) language in preambles or other provisions of treaties applicable to these crimes which indicates these crimes' higher status in international law; (3) the large number of states which have ratified treaties related to these crimes; and (4) the ad hoc international investigations and prosecutions of perpetrators of these crimes.[56]

In accordance with the prevailing opinion the following norms could be considered as peremptory norms of international law:[57] prohibition of aggression, slavery, genocide, elementary norms of human rights, and elementary norms of humanitarian law.

[54] VCLT, Article 53, *Vienna Convention on the Law of Treaties*, United Nations, Treaty Series, vol. 1155, 331.

[55] *Yearbook of the International Law Commission* (YBILC) 1966 II, 248, http://untreaty.un.org/ilc/publications/yearbooks/Ybkvolumes(e)/ILC_1966_v2_e.pdf.

[56] M. Cherif Bassiouni, 'Accountability for International Crime and Serious Violations of Fundamental Human Rights', *Law and Contemporary Problems* 59, No. 4 (1996): 68.

[57] See Heintschel von Heinegg, 'Die völkerrechtlichen Verträge als Hauptrechtsquellen des Völkerrechts', in *Völkerrecht*, ed. Knut Ipsen (München: Beck Juristischer Verlag; 5th edition 2008), 112–209 §15, R 59; and see Karl Zemanek, Gerhard Hafner, Stephan Wittich, 'Die völkerrechtliche Verantwortlichkeit und die Sanktionen des Völkerrechts', in *Österreichisches Handbuch des Völkerrechts*, eds. Hanspeter Neuhold, Waldemar Hummer, Christoph Schreuer (Vienna: Manz, 4th edition, 2004), vol. I, IX, 505–532, R. 2784.

Concerning the right to life, there seems to be a general agreement that it also belongs to the *ius cogens* norms.[58] Concerning Bassiouni's element of ratification, the ICCPR counts 167 state parties.[59] Article 4 paragraph 2 ICCPR meets this *sine qua non* requirement and does not permit any derogation for Article 6 ICCPR. Comparing the non-derogation clause concerning the right to life of the ICCPR with the clauses of two regional Human Rights Conventions, the ECHR[60] and the ACHR,[61] demonstrates that the *ius cogens* character of the norm as being universal seems to hold true: Article 15 paragraph 2 ECHR allows no derogation from Articles 3, 4 (paragraph 1) and 7. Article 2 – the right to life – has the same status, but deaths resulting from lawful acts of war are exempted. The *American Convention on Human Rights*[62] requires that a state must protect the right to life by law, and it likewise prohibits the derogation from it.[63]

The Inter-American Court of Human Rights argued totally in line with the prevailing opinion when it wrote in its judgment on the Street Children Case that there 'can no longer be any doubt that the fundamental right to life belongs to the domain of *ius cogens*'.[64] Murder and the forced disappearance of individuals would always be a violation of international obligations, if it is in the policy of a state.[65] Due to its universal validity, however, the right to life can be justly considered a *ius cogens* norm. It is binding on states irrespective of other conventional obligations[66] and particular agreements between states.

[58] See for example: Bertrand G. Ramcharan, *The Right to Life in International Law* (Dordrecht: Martinus Nijhoff Publishers, 1985), 186–187; Karen Parker, 'Jus Cogens: Compelling the Law of Human Rights', *Hastings International and Comparative Law Review* 12 (1989): 431–432.

[59] UN Treaty Collection, http://treaties.un.org.

[60] ECHR, *European Convention for the Protection of Human Rights and Fundamental Freedoms as amended by Protocol*, No. 11, *ECHR*, http://conventions.coe.int/Treaty/en/Treaties/Html/005.htm.

[61] ACHR, *American Convention on Human Rights*, 'Pact of San Jose, Costa Rica', www.oas.org/juridico/english/Treaties/b-32.htm.

[62] Article 4 §1 ACHR. [63] Article 27 §2 ACHR.

[64] Street Children Case (*Morales* v. *Guatemala*), Judgment of 19 November 1999, Inter-American Court of Human Rights (Ser. C) No. 63, 139, available at: www.corteidh.or.cr/seriecpdf_ing/seriec_63_ing.pdf.

[65] Wolfram Karl, 'Menschenrechtliches ius cogens – Eine Analyse von "Barcelona Traction" und nachfolgender Entwicklungen', in *Menschenrechtsschutz durch Gewohnheitsrecht*, ed. Eckhart Klein (Berlin: BWV Berliner Wissenschafts-Verlag, 2003), 122.

[66] Sara Stapleton, 'Ensuring a Fair Trial in the International Criminal Court: Statutory Interpretation and the Impermissibility of Derogation', *New York University Journal of International Law and Politics* 31 (1999): 599.

6. Enforcing humanitarian aid provision

This section deals with the consequences of violations of the right to life, as it would follow from state responsibility: in other words, what other states can do if the state affected by a disaster does not provide the necessary aid to the people in need. Therefore, it will sketch the general obligations deriving from the Articles on Responsibility of States for Internationally Wrongful Acts (ARSIWA) and analyse what distinguishes the possible measures against violations of the right to life not amounting to serious breaches of peremptory norms from measures applicable to serious violations. This will result in a systematic structure of applicable measures of enforcing humanitarian aid.

As has been established above, right to life is an *erga omnes* obligation and therefore the violation of which can be invoked by any state (Article 48.1.b ARSIWA). The invoking state may claim cessation of this act (Article 48.2.a ARSIWA) as it is the obligation of the state responsible for the internationally wrongful act (Article 30.a ARSIWA). This obligation is without prejudice of whether the wrongful act was caused by commission or omission.[67] In the case of Myanmar, the cessation of the act would have meant taking action by providing the affected population with the required aid (that Myanmar was by itself not able to fulfil its obligation will be considered below). This allows the invoking state to resort to lawful countermeasures (Article 49 ARSIWA) also in order to protect the right to life of the individuals of the state responsible (Article 54 ARSIWA).[68] Article 50.1.b ARSIWA excludes the use of force. Following the ILC '(t)he term "countermeasures" covers that part of the subject of reprisals not associated with armed conflict, and in accordance with modern practice and judicial decisions the term is used in that sense in this chapter'.[69] Adopted measures for example were:[70]

- Certain western countries [against] Poland and Soviet Union (1981). On 13 December 1981, the Polish government imposed martial law and subsequently suppressed demonstrations and interned many dissidents. The United States and other western countries took action

[67] ILC, ARSIWA Commentary to Article 2, 70, §4.

[68] ILC, ARSIWA Commentary to Article 54, 350, §1: 'By virtue of article 48 (2), such States may also demand cessation and performance in the interests of the beneficiaries of the obligation breached. Thus, with respect to the obligations referred to in Article 48, such States are recognised as having a legal interest in compliance.'

[69] ILC, ARSIWA Commentary to Part Three, Chapter II – Countermeasures, 325, §3.

[70] ILC, ARSIWA Commentary to Article 54, 351f., §3.

against both Poland and the Soviet Union. The measures included the suspension, with immediate effect, of treaties providing for landing rights of Aeroflot in the United States and LOT in the United States, Great Britain, France, the Netherlands, Switzerland and Austria. The suspension procedures provided for in the respective treaties were disregarded . . .

- Collective measures against Argentina (1982). In April 1982, when Argentina took control over part of the Falkland Islands (Malvinas), the Security Council called for an immediate withdrawal. Following a request by the United Kingdom, EC members, Australia, New Zealand and Canada adopted trade sanctions. These included a temporary prohibition on all imports of Argentine products, which ran contrary to Article XI: 1 and possibly Article III of the GATT [General Agreement on Tariffs and Trade]. It was disputed whether the measures could be justified under the national security exception provided for in Article XXI (b) (iii) of the GATT. The embargo adopted by the European countries also constituted a suspension of Argentina's rights under two sectoral agreements on trade in textiles and trade in mutton and lamb, for which security exceptions of GATT did not apply.

It was argued that the best basis for a right to humanitarian assistance would be the right to life and that this right can be considered a peremptory norm of international law. Chapter III of Part Two ARSIWA deals with serious breaches of peremptory norms, or in other words serious violations of the right to life due to a lack protection of persons in disasters.[71]

In consequence one has to render more precisely what limit has to be set to determine a violation of these peremptory norms as serious. The Article 40 paragraph 2 ARSIWA gives us a definition of a serious breach: 'A breach of such an obligation is serious if it involves a gross or systematic failure by the responsible state to fulfil the obligation'. The term 'gross' refers to the intensity of a violation – a direct assault on the values protected by the norm – while 'systematic' means that the violating act is carried out in an organised and deliberate way.[72] For *erga omnes* obligations such as the right to life, at least one of the two requirements must be fulfilled. As a systematic breach must be considered a complete denial of the value of the right to life, no matter if the denial manifests itself in law or practice (this might be equated with the term policy, as addressed above). But on account of the systematic

[71] ILC, ARSIWA Commentary to Article 40, 277.
[72] ILC, ARSIWA Commentary to Article 40, 285, §8.

nature of this act of state further violations, and in consequence a gross violation, must be expected.

All measures for non-serious breaches depicted above are also applicable to serious breaches of *ius cogens* (Chapter I and II of Part 2 ARSIWA). However, concerning serious breaches of *ius cogens norms* we talk about aggravated state responsibility. At first glance the distinction between ordinary and serious breaches causes no serious obligations for the state responsible apart from its aggravated obligation of reparation.[73] The sting of Article 41 ARSIWA on State Responsibility hits the state responsible via the obligatory measures that the community of states must take against the violator. Community, on the one hand, could mean an organised system of states such as the United Nations; on the other hand, non-institutionalised cooperation would be possible too.[74] The ILC prefers the Security Council in this role to determine an act of a state as a serious breach of peremptory norms of general international law, which is analoguous to Article 39 of the *United Nations Charter*. Following this analogy and referring to Article 41 paragraph 1 ARSIWA, the Security Council is likewise empowered to decide about any measures[75] bringing serious breaches within the meaning of Article 40 to an end.[76] These measures are first of all countermeasures as proposed by Part Three Chapter II of the ILC's ARSIWA. But Article 41 has to be read very carefully. The ILC uses the word 'measures' instead of 'countermeasures' and does not intend to specify what measures states should take.[77] A systematic-teleological interpretation makes clear that the term 'measures' includes countermeasures but goes beyond that and leaves the door open for actions of a humanitarian character, i.e. humanitarian interventions. However, the regime of the *United Nations Charter* limits cooperation of states outside of the institutional framework of the United Nations very strictly to unarmed measures,[78] which could be for example:[79]

> United States of America [against] South Africa (1986). When in 1985, the South African government declared a state of emergency in large parts

[73] Christian J. Tams, 'Do Serious Breaches Give Rise to Any Specific Obligations of the Responsible State?', *European Journal of International Law* 13 (2002): 1163.
[74] ILC, ARSIWA Commentary to Art 41, 287. [75] Chapter VII UN Charter.
[76] Article 41 §1 ARSIWA. [77] ILC, ARSIWA Commentary to Article 41, 287.
[78] See Article 2 §4 and Chapter VII of the UN Charter.
[79] ILC, ARSIWA Commentary to Article 54, 352.

> of the country; the United Nations Security Council recommended the adoption of sectoral economic boycotts and the freezing of cultural and sports relations. Subsequently, some countries introduced measures which went beyond those recommended by the Security Council. The United States Congress adopted the Comprehensive Anti-Apartheid Act which suspended landing rights of South African Airlines on US territory. This immediate suspension was contrary to the terms of the 1947 US–South African Aviation Agreement and was justified as a measure which should encourage the South African government to adopt measures leading towards the establishment of a non-racial democracy.

Such measures in the sense of Article 41 can thus go beyond counter-measures and the recommendations of the Security Council. In the case of large-scale loss of life or systematic exclusion of certain groups or areas from aid deliveries due to a malevolent government, states are therefore obliged to take measures in a cooperative effort to halt the violations.

Responsible states have the obligation to provide assurances and guarantees of non-repetition.[80] This is not specifically restricted to serious breaches[81] but meant in particular for these cases. The praxis shows us the idea that the state is responsible for the punishment of individual perpetrators of human rights is an aspect of an effective guarantee of human rights[82] as this approach arises even from treaty-based obligations such as the Geneva Conventions, the Genocide Convention, the Apartheid Convention, the *Inter-American Convention Against Forced Disappearances*, and the Torture Convention.[83] Even this duty of general international law is not only attached to widespread or systematic breaches but instead it 'is seen as a consequence of the peremptory character of a norm'.[84] An analoguous responsibility for individuals can be found in the *Rome Statute* for crimes of genocide, crimes against humanity, war crimes, and crimes of aggression.[85] This responsibility is not binding the state to jurisdiction; it binds the individual to foundations of human rights.

7. Conclusion

The reiteration that external assistance requires the consent of the state is legally fully justifiable, but it raises the question whether articulating such

[80] Tams, 'Serious Breaches', 1165. [81] Ibid., 1166. [82] Ibid., 1175.
[83] Ibid., 1174f and n. 69. [84] Ibid., 1178.
[85] Article 5, *Rome Statute of the International Criminal Court*, 1998.

a norm in the Draft Articles on the Protection of Persons in Disasters[86] might not give a reason for arguing that a state must not be coerced by the means available for ensuring state responsibility. The additional value can be seen in an affirmation of a duty to offer aid. However, such a duty of the United Nations and its members can also be deduced from the *United Nations Charter* (Articles 55 and 56) and the obligation of states to bring serious violations of the right to life to an end.

Extracting the quintessence from the work of the ILC with regards to protection of persons in the event of disasters and state responsibility for internationally wrongful acts, we can deduce two scenarios for cases of humanitarian aid enforcement:

If a disaster exceeds the response capacity of a state, it is obliged to seek assistance as appropriate (Draft Article 10) and must not arbitrarily withhold consent if aid is offered bona fide (Draft Article 11 paragraph 2). If the state fails to seek assistance or withholds its consent for a bona fide offer and the consequence is a loss of life, then:

1. In case of non-serious violations of the right to life (i.e. no gross or systematic losses of life), every state may adopt lawful countermeasures to enforce humanitarian aid provision.
2. In case of serious violations of the right to life (for example deliberate withholding of aid for certain parts of the population or large-scale loss of life), the community of state must cooperate with enforcing humanitarian aid provision.

We have demonstrated above that the case of Myanmar did not fall into the realm of the R2P as recognised by the General Assembly and the Security Council. The government of Myanmar, due to a miscalculation of its own capacity and the extent of the disaster, at first did not want foreign assistance. It later rejected the United States' offer of two military vessels and permission for United States soldiers to distribute aid with doubts about its bona fide character. It is not known whether the United States would have accepted the government of Myanmar's coordination aid delivered by American soldiers. If the junta had not given in to other foreign aid offers (such as by ASEAN), however, the 140,000 dead and missing persons with the spectre of many more people dying would most certainly have sufficed for the second scenario, where the international

[86] Protection of persons in the event of disasters: Texts and titles of draft articles 5 bis, 12, 13, 14 and 15, provisionally adopted by the Drafting Committee from 5 to 11 July 2012 (A/CN.4/L.812).

community would have been obliged to cooperate to enforce humanitarian aid. This would have allowed a large variety of (counter-)measures to halt human rights violations by omission and obstruction of international aid.

Finally we can conclude that even without R2P the protection of persons affected by disasters can be enforced, and even must be enforced by the international community in severe cases. The only difference to R2P is that, unless the humanitarian catastrophe results in a threat to international peace and security and as long as neither of the four categories of international crimes (ethnic cleansing, war crimes, genocide, crimes against humanity) are present, forceful measures by the Security Council within the parameters of Chapter VII *United Nations Charter* are very unlikely.

16

The regionalisation of humanitarian action: the role of the OAS

ABEL S. KNOTTNERUS

1. Introduction

The law and politics of humanitarian action have not been immune to regionalism. In recent years, regional institutions have become important players in the field of humanitarian action. They have assumed responsibilities in the coordination and provision of humanitarian assistance; they have strengthened the organisation of emergency prevention and preparedness; and they have also supported the more long-term process of reconstruction and recovery.[1] Other chapters in this volume explain how the European Union (EU), the African Union (AU) and the Association of South East Asian Nations (ASEAN) have affected the field of humanitarian action and examine the humanitarian obligations of states parties to regional human rights treaties. This chapter shifts the focus to the western hemisphere and explores the humanitarian role of the Organisation of American States (OAS) and the obligations of its member states under the regional human rights regime.

For a long time, the 'diplomatic culture' of intergovernmental cooperation within the Inter-American region was characterised by absolute non-intervention.[2] No exception was made for humanitarian emergencies. Every government had the unfettered right to refuse humanitarian assistance in times of armed conflict or in the aftermath of a natural disaster. Until today, Article 19 of the OAS Charter reads that 'No State or groups of States has the right to intervene, directly or indirectly, *for any reason whatever*, in the internal or external affairs of any other State'

[1] On the difference between humanitarian action and the more specific notion of humanitarian assistance, see: Heike Spieker, 'The Right to Give and Receive Humanitarian Assistance', in *International Law and Humanitarian Assistance – A Crosscut Through Legal Issues Pertaining to Humanitarianism*, ed. Hans-Joachim Heintze et al. (Heidelberg: Springer, 2011), 7–8.

[2] Monica Herz, *The Organisation of American States (OAS)* (London: Routledge, 2011), 12.

(emphasis added). In the last twenty years, however, the American states have started to reconsider the scope of non-intervention. Democracy and human rights have taken a more prominent place on the Inter-American agenda. Although, the Responsibility to Protect (R2P) is not (yet) part of its vocabulary, the OAS has also become more actively concerned with humanitarian emergencies. In 2003, the member states formally recognised as such that the regional institution should enhance the hemisphere's capability to prevent and respond to man-made and natural disasters.[3]

This chapter explores the humanitarian activities of the OAS in the following manner. Firstly, the changing role of the OAS in the sphere of regional security will be explained. After its establishment in 1948, the regional institution was not particularly involved with the prevention of and response to hemispheric security threats, and therefore also not with humanitarian emergencies. However, since the end of the cold war the outlook of the region's security agenda has altered. It is important to reflect on the reasons behind this progressive development in order to understand the current humanitarian role of the OAS (Section 2).

Secondly, the humanitarian agenda of the OAS in the context of armed conflicts (Section 3) and natural disasters (Section 4) will be addressed. The regional institution has assumed some humanitarian tasks with regard to armed conflicts and its member states have proclaimed that the OAS should support the prevention of, and humanitarian response to, natural emergencies. However, its past and scheduled humanitarian activities also demonstrate that the authority of the OAS in the field of humanitarian action is subject to some significant limitations.

Thirdly, the contributions of the Inter-American human rights system are discussed (Section 5). Although the American states have not entrusted many humanitarian responsibilities to the OAS, they no longer have the absolute right to refuse humanitarian assistance in times of armed conflict or in the aftermath of a natural disaster. By now, the regional human rights regime imposes positive obligations that require the states parties to ensure the adequate facilitation of humanitarian assistance in emergency situations. When the states parties do not fulfil this humanitarian responsibility, they might be obliged to accept humanitarian assistance from international humanitarian actors. This exemplifies, in broad terms, how the Inter-American norm of non-

[3] OAS, 'Declaration on Security in the Americas', October 28, 2003, §39, www.oas.org/documents/eng/DeclaracionSecurity_102803.asp.

intervention is being subverted in favour of human rights in the context of humanitarian action.

2. The changing role of the OAS: a brief history

The origins of inter-state cooperation in the western hemisphere can be traced back to the failed attempt of Simón Bolívar to establish a 'Union of Hispanic America' after the end of the Latin American wars of independence.[4] His Congress of Panama (1826) was the first of many Inter-American conferences that gradually created a 'diplomatic culture' of absolute non-intervention. With the establishment of the OAS in 1948, this was formalised in Articles 2, 19 and 21 of the OAS Charter. These provisions remain unamended until today. Nonetheless, the OAS and the norm of non-intervention have progressed significantly in the course of the last sixty-five years. This section takes great strides to explain how this relates to the changing role of the OAS in the field of regional security.

2.1 'Collective' security during the cold war

Following the adoption of the United Nations (UN) Charter, the OAS became the first regional security organisation under Chapter VIII. However, for over forty years the OAS rarely played its envisaged role in 'matters relating to the maintenance of international peace and security'.[5] In the cold-war environment, its actions were strictly subordinated to the 'ideational marriage between the Monroe Doctrine and the Containment of the Soviet bloc'.[6] The United States directed the OAS towards a 'collective' security regime devoted to the fight against communism. At the same time, the United States intervened in several Latin American states to realise the objectives of its containment policy without bothering much whether or not these interventions would be approved of by the OAS.

[4] On the history of Inter-American cooperation before 1948, see: Samuel Guy Inman, *Inter-American Conferences 1826–1954: History and Problems* (Washington DC: University Press of Washington, 1965).

[5] Article 52 of the UN Charter. Notable exceptions include the conflicts between Costa Rica and Nicaragua (1948–1979) and the 'Soccer War' between Honduras and El Salvador (1969).

[6] Herz, *The Organisation of American States (OAS)*, 12.

The unilateral military intervention of the United States in the Dominican Republic (1965) was probably the peak of the institution's subordination to United States foreign policy. On 25 April 1965, the United States government decided to intervene in the country to aid 'the corrupt and oppressive military oligarchic regime' and to ensure that the 'social-democratic and reformist government' of former President Juan Bosch, who had been ousted by a military coup in the fall of 1963, would not return to power.[7] Subsequently, the United States government turned to the OAS to 'legitimise the process'.[8] Although the intervention was a severe violation of the OAS Charter, the hemispheric institution did not condemn the unilateral intervention of the United States. Instead the ministers of foreign affairs made an 'urgent appeal' to all OAS member states to place trained personnel, food and medicines at the disposal of the General Secretariat of the OAS 'for the humanitarian purpose of giving succour to the population'.[9] Moreover, the OAS established the first Inter-American Peace Force (IAPF), with the objective of assisting in the restoration of peace in the Dominican Republic. By the end of June 1965, the multilateral force consisted of 1,735 troops from Latin American states and around 12,400 troops from the United States. These troops stood under Brazilian command, but more important for Washington was that they operated under the 'neutral' flag of the OAS.[10] In this way, the Johnson administration was able to transform a unilateral military intervention into a regional peace-keeping operation.

After the 'success' of the IAPF, the United States proposed to create a standing Inter-American force.[11] From a United States perspective, such a permanent multilateral force would be the perfect mechanism to contain communism in Latin America, because regional interventions would receive far less criticism than unilateral operations. However, the majority of the OAS member states proved unwilling to endorse the proposal. The 'collective' security regime was not expanded for the

[7] Howard J. Wiarda, 'The United States and the Dominican Republic: Intervention, Dependency, and Tyrannicide', *Journal of Interamerican Studies and World Affairs* 22 (1980): 247. Note that the US formally intervened to protect its nationals.

[8] Herz, *The Organisation of American States (OAS)*, 14.

[9] OAS, 'Tenth Meeting of Consultation of Ministers of Foreign Affairs – Second Plenary Session', 4 May 1965, www.oas.org/council/MEETINGS%20OF%20CONSULTATION/Actas/Acta%2010.pdf.

[10] OAS, 'Tenth Meeting'. G. Pope Atkins, *Encyclopedia of the Inter-American System* (Westport: Greenwood Publishing Group, 1997), 267.

[11] Ibid., 267–268.

simple reason that many Latin American countries feared that this would only bring about more unilateral interventions in the western hemisphere. As such, United States interventionism strengthened the regional norm of non-intervention.

In the 1970s and the 1980s, the chasm between the United States and Latin America deepened, and the influence of the OAS on matters of regional security declined. The hemispheric institution did not establish a second peacekeeping force and was sidelined in many of the region's inter- and intra-state conflicts. The institution did not play an important role in the early years of the Central American crisis (1980–1990) or in the Malvinas/Falklands War (1982). Moreover, the OAS failed to respond to the unilateral interventions of the United States in Grenada (1983) and Panama (1989). 'Collective' security resulted in collective inaction during the course of the cold war.

2.2 *Cooperative security during the 1990s*

Since the implosion of the Soviet empire, the 'traditional concept of regional security', which focused on the non-hemispheric threat of communism, has eroded.[12] In the course of the 1990s, regional cooperation was reinvented and the OAS increasingly began to address hemispheric threats to regional security. For example, the OAS became more concerned with terrorism, the arms trade, drugs trafficking, anti-democratic forces, migration, refugees and natural disasters. In order to enhance the region's security efforts, several new regional bodies were established like the Committee on Hemispheric Security, the Inter-American Committee against Terrorism and the Inter-American Drug Abuse Control Committee. Furthermore, the OAS amplified its contributions to the peaceful resolution of armed conflicts, supported the initiation of confidence and security-building measures between its member states, and actively promoted the progressive development of democracy and human rights in its policy statements.

How can this transition from 'collective' security to what has been labelled 'cooperative security' be explained?[13] For one thing, during the

[12] Carolyn M. Shaw, *Cooperation, Conflict and Consensus in the Organisation of American States* (New York: Palgrave Macmillan, 2004), 153.

[13] Many commentators have used these terms to compare the regional security agenda of the OAS before and after the end of the cold war. See for example: Brigitte Weiffen, 'Persistence and Change in Regional Security Institutions: Does the OAS Still Have a

1990s non-hemispheric threats were effectively non-existent. With the collapse of the Soviet Union, communism crumbled and was no longer perceived as the main threat to regional security. This links up to the second and probably most important reason why the OAS could expand its agenda, namely that intergovernmental decision-making in the western hemisphere was no longer strictly subordinated to United States foreign policy. During the cold war, United States interventionism strengthened the regional norm of non-intervention. In contrast, in the beginning of the 1990s the Clinton administration encouraged a process of 'networked multilateralism', which supported regional cooperation.[14]

According to Carolyn Shaw the developments in the 1990s did not mark a 'distinct break from the past', because the decision-making process in the OAS continued to be based on consensus-building.[15] From a strictly procedural point of view she is right; as of today, majority decision-making remains rare within the OAS. However, the importance of the complete transformation of the socio-political context should not be underestimated. While the norm of non-intervention remains strong, human rights and democracy have started to curtail its scope.

2.3 *The 2003 Declaration on Security in the Americas*

The gradual expansion of the hemispheric security agenda also resulted in a formal redefinition of the region's security concerns. During the 2003 Special Security Conference in Mexico, the member states adopted the 'Declaration on Security in the Americas'. This document recognised that the security threats of the American States have a 'multidimensional nature', and that the traditional concept of security 'should be expanded to encompass new and non-traditional threats, which include political, economic, social, health and environmental aspects'.[16] Moreover the

Project?', *Contemporary Security Policy* 33 (2012): 370. Herz, *The Organisation of American States (OAS)*, 41.

[14] Andrew Cooper and Thomas Legler, *Intervention Without Intervening? The OAS Defense and Promotion of Democracy in the Americas* (New York: Palgrave Macmillan, 2007), 19–22. Within the study of international relations, scholars have explained the new role of the OAS in the post-cold-war world very differently. For a short overview of the different theoretical propositions, see: Betty Horwit, *Transformation of the Organisation of American States: A Multilateral Framework for Regional Governance* (London: Anthem Press, 2010), 4–8.

[15] Herz, *The Organisation of American States (OAS)*, 152.

[16] OAS, 'Declaration on Security in the Americas', §39.

member states affirmed that the 'protection of human beings' is the 'basis and purpose of security'.[17]

It was in light of this broadened definition of hemispheric security that the American states also programmed a more active role for the OAS in the field of humanitarian action. In the Declaration, they voiced their concern 'over natural and man-made disasters that afflict states of the Hemisphere' and pledged 'to strengthen the existing Inter-American mechanisms and develop new cooperation mechanisms to improve and broaden the region's response capability in preventing and mitigating the effects of these disasters'.[18] Furthermore, the member states emphasised that the protection of refugees and internally displaced persons (IDPs) should be enhanced, and expressed their support for the humanitarian demining programmes and disarmament efforts of the OAS.[19]

However, the member states did not include any references to humanitarian intervention or to the responsibility to protect in the Declaration.[20] As of today, the OAS has not agreed on any regional law for humanitarian intervention like, for example, the African Union has done.[21] While the 'traditional core OAS principles of sovereignty and non-intervention are being subverted in favour of increased support of democracy and human rights', this has not (yet) lead to a 'paradigm shift' with regard to the presumed responsibilities of the American states.[22] Although its scope is not the same as sixty-five years ago, non-intervention continues to be the guiding norm of hemispheric cooperation. As the following sections will show, this regional norm also thwarts the humanitarian agenda of the OAS.

3. Humanitarian action and armed conflicts

Since the end of the cold war, the western hemisphere has been the second most peaceful region in the world according to the Uppsala

[17] Ibid., §E. [18] Ibid., §39 [19] Ibid., §34, 20.

[20] For a discussion of the Latin American perspective on humanitarian intervention, see for example: Hernan Vales, 'The Latin American View on the Doctrine of Humanitarian Intervention', *The Journal of Humanitarian Assistance* (2001), accessed 29 March 2013, http://sites.tufts.edu/jha/archives/1491.

[21] AU, Article 4(h) of the AU Constitutive Act. For a more extensive discussion on the AU and humanitarian intervention, see: Tom Kabau, 'The Responsibility to Protect and the Role of Regional Organisations: an Appraisal of the African Union's Interventions', *Goettingen Journal of International Law* 4 (2012): 49–92.

[22] Hugo Caminos, 'The Role of the OAS in the Promotion and Protection of Democratic Governance', *Recueil Des Courses* 273 (1998): 195.

Conflict Data Programme.[23] In particular, the number of inter-state conflicts has dropped drastically. Partly due to the diplomatic efforts of the OAS, there has been only one inter-state war in the Americas since 1989.[24] However, the low number of inter-state conflicts does not foretell that the region has been relieved from the humanitarian consequences of armed conflicts.[25] For one thing, internal armed conflicts have taken place in nineteen of the thirty-five OAS member states, which in some cases have also led to severe humanitarian emergencies.[26] Furthermore, the physical and psychological damage of earlier inter- and intra-state conflicts still requires humanitarian action.

This section draws a bird's eye-view of the humanitarian responsibilities that the OAS has assumed during and after armed conflicts. For this purpose a distinction will be made between the humanitarian activities that have been arranged in the course of its peace missions and the structural humanitarian programmes of the OAS. After having introduced these various humanitarian efforts, this section will briefly reflect on the strengths and weaknesses of this first facet of the humanitarian agenda of the OAS.

3.1 *The humanitarian actions of peace missions*

After the IAPF left the Dominican Republic, it took almost 25 years before the OAS decided to set up a second Inter-American peace mission.[27] In August 1989, when a political solution for the Central American crisis was within reach, the Secretary-Generals of the OAS and the United Nations agreed to establish the International Commission for Support and Verification (ICSV).[28] Within this joint mission a strict division of tasks was arranged between the United Nations and the

[23] Uppsala Conflict Data Programame (2013/04/01) UCDP Conflict Encyclopedia: www.ucdp.uu.se/database, Uppsala University Department of Peace and Conflict Research www.ucdp.uu.se/gpdatabase/gpregions.php?regionSelect=5-Southern%20Americas.

[24] The 'Cenepa War' between Ecuador and Peru (1995).

[25] The Uppsala Conflict Data Programme defines 'armed conflict' as 'a contested incompatibility that concerns government and/or territory where the use of armed force between two parties, of which at least one is the government of a state, results in at least 25 battle-related deaths in one calendar year'.

[26] Uppsala Conflict Data Programme.

[27] For an overview of all 'OAS peace missions', see: 'OAS Peace Missions', accessed 29 March 2013, www.oas.org/sap/peacefund/PeaceMissions/.

[28] For a more extensive discussion on the ICSV, see: Jennie K. Lincoln and César Sereseres, 'Resettling the Contras: The OAS Verification Commission in Nicaragua', in

OAS. The United Nations facilitated the reintegration of combatants in Honduras and Costa Rica, while the OAS assumed complete responsibility over the demobilisation of Nicaraguan combatants and the broader transitional process in the country. During the course of the mission (1990–1997) the OAS fulfilled many humanitarian tasks, including the distribution of food and clothing to approximately 120,000 people in Nicaragua.[29] Moreover, the OAS became actively involved with humanitarian demining operations.

In the early 1990s, the OAS and the United Nations also established a joint peace mission in Haiti. The OAS/United Nations International Civilian Mission in Haiti (ICMH), with a size of around two hundred officials, operated next to a United Nations peacekeeping mission and was responsible for a wide range of tasks. For example, the ICMH had to monitor, promote and protect human rights; reinforce democracy; accelerate economic development; and support the professionalisation of national institutions.[30] Furthermore, the mission had to facilitate humanitarian relief by organising legal and medical assistance programmes for victims. In contrast to the ICSV, where the OAS and the United Nations agreed on a strict division of tasks, the ICMH became the first and, until now, last 'fully integrated' mission of the two organisations.[31] Although the OAS officials were mostly involved in electoral monitoring and human rights observation, they cooperated closely with the United Nations officials on all aspects of the mission's mandate.

In addition to its joint operations in Nicaragua and Haiti, the OAS has also set up peace missions without United Nations involvement, including the OAS Special Mission to Suriname (1992–2000) and most recently the OAS Mission to Support the Peace Process in Colombia (2004–today). The first mission focused on the promotion of democracy, but also coordinated the disarmament of illegal armed groups, supported

Peacekeeping and Democratisation, ed. Tommie Sue Montgomery (Miami: North-South Center Press, 2000), 17–36.

[29] OAS, 'OAS Peace Missions', accessed 29 March 2013, www.oas.org/sap/peacefund/PeaceMissions/.

[30] For more information on the objectives and results of the ICMH, see: Taylor Wentges, 'Electoral Monitoring and the OAS/UN International Civil Mission to Haiti', *Peacekeeping and International Relations* 25 (1996): 43–56. UN, 'OAS Peace-Building Experiences: Progress Achieved, Lessons Learned, and Future Possibilities', OAS/UN International Civilian Mission, accessed 29 March 2013: www.un.org/rights/micivih/rapports/peacebu.htm.

[31] Joaquín Tacsan, 'Searching for OAS/UN Task-Sharing Opportunities in Central America and Haiti', *Third World Quarterly* 18 (1997): 505.

humanitarian demining operations and contributed to the reintegration of former combatants into Suriname's society.[32] The second OAS peace mission is still active and intends, in broad terms, to remove participants from the ongoing violence and to seek better conditions for victim communities.[33] Both these two missions have fulfilled humanitarian tasks. However, their humanitarian role has not been as expansive as the humanitarian efforts of the joint OAS–UN operations in Nicaragua and Haiti, which could count on more financial and geopolitical support.

3.2 *Humanitarian programmes*

In addition to the humanitarian actions of its peace missions, the OAS has also established humanitarian programmes to deal with some of the causes and consequences of armed conflicts in a more structural manner. Let us consider three prominent examples.[34] The first and perhaps most stirring one is the programme for 'Comprehensive Action against Anti-personnel Mines' (CAAM), which was set up after the success of the humanitarian demining activities in Nicaragua. This programme has an 'eminently humanitarian nature' and intends 'to re-establish safe and secure living conditions for mine-affected populations, reduce the risks and dangers of unexploded ordnance (UXO) and antipersonnel mines, and return previously mined land to productive use'.[35] At this moment, CAAM supports demining activities in Nicaragua, Columbia, Ecuador and Peru by offering, inter alia, technical support, mine-risk education for affected communities and humanitarian assistance to victims.[36]

32 On the OAS Special Mission to Suriname, see: OAS, 'Special Mission to Suriname (1992–2000)', accessed 29 March 2013, www.oas.org/sap/peacefund/forumevents/IAPF2010/REISAE-SPECIALMISSIONTOSURINAME-PresentationSep2010.pdf.

33 For a more extensive discussion of the peace process in Colombia, see Chapter 17. For a recent update on the OAS Peace Mission in Colombia, see OAS, 'Sixteenth Quarterly Report of the Secretary General to the Permanent Council on the Mission to Support the Peace Process in Colombia', 15 March 2012, www.oas.org/consejo/Documents%20DOC2012.asp.

34 Note that the three examples discussed under this heading are not exhaustive. Other programmes of the OAS could have been considered as well, including: activities related to the promotion of international humanitarian law; the Inter-American programmes on persons who have disappeared and the provision of assistance to members of their families; and the OAS resolutions on the right to the truth.

35 OAS, 'Comprehensive Action against Antipersonnel Mines (AICMA)', accessed 29 March 2013: www.oas.org/dsp/english/cpo_desminado.asp.

36 For a more extensive discussion of CAAM, see: Carl E. Case, 'A Mine-free Central America: How Can We Improve on Success?', *Journal of ERW and Mine Action* 14

Secondly, the OAS has initiated programmes on disarmament. Limiting the availability of arms is an important humanitarian objective for conflict prevention and reduction, but also for improving the humanitarian situation in the aftermath of armed conflicts.[37] One of the most remarkable achievements of the OAS in this regard is the *Inter-American Convention against Illicit Manufacturing of and Trafficking in Firearms, Ammunition, Explosives, and Other Related Materials* (CIFTA, 2001), which has been ratified by all OAS member states except for Canada, Jamaica and the United States.[38] CIFTA is the first legally binding regional instrument in the world on the illicit trafficking of small arms and light weapons (SALW). It attempts to diminish the humanitarian consequences of SALW by obliging states, inter alia, to criminalise their illicit manufacturing and trade; to develop licensing systems for the export, import, and transit of SALW; and to maintain records of weapon transactions. Unfortunately, many Latin American states fail to comply with these requirements in the absence of an enforcement mechanism. Yet CIFTA and the other disarmament programmes of the OAS are no paper tigers. Above all, they have established a normative benchmark for (gradual) disarmament within the western hemisphere.[39]

Thirdly, the OAS has been concerned with the protection of refugees and IDPs. According to its website, the OAS has 'taken concrete actions to tackle' this issue, for it is 'one of the dark challenges facing the region'.[40] Nevertheless, apart from its contributions in specific conflicts like Nicaragua and Colombia, the OAS has not been very much involved with the more structural protection of persons who are forced to leave their homes due to armed conflicts. The regional institution has not

(2010): 6–10, accessed 29 March 2013, http://maic.jmu.edu/journal/journal%20pdfs/142.pdf.

[37] Martin Griffiths, 'Small Arms Proliferation: A Humanitarian Concern', in *Disarmament as Humanitarian Action: A discussion on the occasion of the 20th anniversary of the United Nations Institute for Disarmament Research (UNIDIR)* (Geneva: United Nations Publication, 2001), 5. (Griffiths argues that 'if it is at least a humanitarian concern and possibly a humanitarian objective to reduce or prevent conflict, then the issue of arms transfers, and arms control and disarmament, becomes central to the humanitarian world'.)

[38] OAS, 'Signatories and Ratifications', accessed 29 March 2013, www.oas.org/juridico/english/sigs/a-63.html.

[39] For a more extensive discussion of CIFTA, see: Kierstan Lee Carlson, 'Fighting Firearms with Fire in the OAS: A Critical Evaluation of the Inter-American Convention against the Manufacturing of and Trafficking in Firearms, Ammunition and other Related Materials', *The American University International Law Review* 25 (2010): 611–648.

[40] OAS, 'Refugees', accessed 29 March 2013: www.oas.org/en/topics/refugees.asp.

adopted a convention or created a humanitarian body for this purpose. In contrast to the first two examples, the humanitarian 'programme' of the OAS on the protection of refugees and IDPs only consists of non-binding resolutions in which the member states are encouraged to implement existing international (legal) instruments.[41] In other words, the OAS has not set up a comprehensive humanitarian programme for refugees and IDPs, but has only stimulated its member states to ensure their adequate protection.[42]

3.3 The humanitarian agenda of the OAS before, during and after armed conflicts

Although the importance of these various humanitarian activities is not to be questioned, one cannot help but notice some significant limitations to the humanitarian agenda of the OAS before, during and after armed conflicts. Most importantly, there have been many conflicts within the region in which the OAS has hardly played any humanitarian role at all. In fact, in the majority of the internal armed conflicts that took place since 1989, the concerned states did not allow any external interference by the OAS.

Furthermore, in the few countries where the OAS did become involved, its peace missions were subject to serious political and material constraints. In the first place, all activities had to be approved by the government of the respective state. The mandate of each mission resulted from intensive negotiations between the government and the OAS. This has made the OAS peace missions subject to the critique that they only advance the interests of the incumbent government. The one-sided focus build into the mandate of the peace missions could be especially problematic in internal armed conflicts where the political legitimacy of the governmental authority is disputed by some of the parties or when the

[41] General Assembly of the OAS (GA), Resolution 2232, 'Protection of Asylum Seekers, Refugees, and Returnees in the Americas', 6 June 2006, www.oas.org/dil/AG-RES_2232_XXXVI-O-06_eng.pdf; General Assembly of the OAS (GA), Resolution 2229, 'Internally Displaced Persons', 6 June 2006, www.oas.org/cji/DIL/AG-RES_2229_XXXVI-O-06_eng.pdf.

[42] Note, however, the role of the Inter-American human rights regime in protecting refugees and IDPs. For a more extensive discussion, see: Clara Sandoval, 'A Critical View of the Protection of Refugees and IDPs by the Inter-American System of Human Rights: Re-assessing its Powers and Examining the Challenges for the Future', *International Journal of Refugee Law* 43 (2005): 43–65.

government has not acted in accordance with international humanitarian law and/or human rights law during the course of the conflict.[43] Secondly, all peace missions were faced with very deficient financial and human resources. This also explains why the humanitarian tasks of the OAS peace missions have been less expansive in Suriname and Colombia than in Nicaragua and Haiti, because for the last two peace missions the United Nations took care of most of the costs. Apart from its support to humanitarian demining operations and disarmament efforts, the OAS has not been able to afford much in terms of humanitarian assistance.

Finally, the scope of the humanitarian programmes has also been quite limited. For sure, these programmes do not allow the OAS to coordinate the facilitation of international humanitarian assistance or to oblige member states to accept humanitarian aid. The authority of the OAS in the context of armed conflicts has been far more confined. Firstly, the regional organisation has been allowed to support specific humanitarian activities, like humanitarian demining, but only to the extent that the respective state desires its involvement and only when there are sufficient resources available. Second, the OAS has developed progressive programmes on disarmament, but the OAS has not been authorised to effectively verify and enforce their implementation. Third, the OAS has set up humanitarian programmes on other issues like the protection of refugees and IDPs, but these programmes tend to consist only of non-binding resolutions that encourage the OAS member states to take certain humanitarian actions.

In short, there is no doubt that armed conflicts are on the humanitarian agenda of the OAS. However, during and after armed conflicts this agenda will often have an ad hoc character in the sense that the projected humanitarian activities of the OAS are strongly dependent on the specific interests of the concerned states. In general, the authority of the OAS to independently exercise humanitarian responsibilities in the context of armed conflicts is very narrow.

[43] See for example the previous criticism of Human Rights Watch (HRW) about the OAS Mission in Colombia. HRW, 'Smoke and Mirrors – Colombia's demobilisation of paramilitary groups', August 2005, www.hrw.org/reports/2005/colombia0805/index.htm. ('In practice, however, the OAS Mission has played a highly questionable role, serving primarily as a rubber stamp for the actions taken by the Colombian government. Throughout, the OAS Mission has been silent about the problems with the process, and as a result, has helped to give the process a veneer of international legitimacy'.)

4. Humanitarian action and natural disasters

The Americas have been confronted not only with armed conflicts, but also with the devastation 'caused by diverse natural disasters, including floods and droughts caused by El Niño, earthquakes, volcanic eruptions, tsunamis, and hurricanes'.[44] Most recently, the destructive earthquakes in Haiti and Chili, which hit the western hemisphere within the first two months of 2010, have brutally reminded the OAS countries of their vulnerability to natural disasters. Moreoever, these last two sudden-onset natural disasters have fostered a debate on the contributions that the OAS could make in the prevention of and the humanitarian response to natural disasters. In June 2012, this debate showed its first actual result with the adoption of the so-called 'Inter-American Plan for Disaster Prevention and Response and the Coordination of Humanitarian Assistance' (IAP), which the OAS Secretary-General José Miguel Insulza heralded as a 'a great step forward'.[45]

This plan was composed by a Joint Working Group of the Permanent Council and the Permanent Executive Committee of the Inter-American Council for Integral Development. During its preparatory sessions the Working Group consulted the officials of members states, but also invited experts from international humanitarian organisations like the IFRC and (sub-)regional organisations such as the Andean Committee for Disaster Prevention and Response.[46] Based on its own research and on the recommendations of the officials and experts, the Working Group and later the General Assembly of the OAS (GA) decided that the regional institution should pursue four general objectives with regard to natural disasters: firstly, supporting risk reduction, secondly, promoting national

[44] OAS General Assembly, 'Existing Mechanisms for Disaster Prevention and Response and Humanitarian Assistance among the Member States', Resolution 2750, 4 June 2012, www.oas.org/en/sla/docs/AG05796E04.pdf.

[45] Ibid. OAS Permanent Executive Committee of the Inter-American Council for Integral Development, 'General Framework for the "Inter-American Plan for Disaster Prevention and Response and the Coordination of Humanitarian Assistance"', 10 May 2012, www.oas.org/en/cidi/cepcidi_documentos_docs12.asp (hereafter: IAP); OAS, Secretary-General of the OAS, 'Inauguration of the Forty-Second Regular Session of the OAS General Assembly', 3 June 2012, www.oas.org/en/about/speech_secretary_general.asp?sCodigo=12-0033.

[46] OAS, 'Report of the Substantive Meetings of the Joint Working Group of the Permanent Council and CEPCIDI on Existing Mechanisms for Disaster Prevention and Response and Humanitarian Assistance (Report prepared by the Chair)', 4 March 2011, 1–5, www.oas.org/en/cidi/cepcidi_grupos_trabajo_DESASTRES_docs.asp (hereafter: Report of the Working Group).

preparedness and response systems, thirdly, encouraging member states to ensure the effective facilitation of international humanitarian assistance and fourthly, strengthening the coordination among existing international humanitarian assistance mechanisms.[47] A closer look at these four objectives gives some insight on the range of humanitarian activities that the OAS has instituted and intends to undertake in preventing and responding to natural disasters.[48] Subsequently, this section will briefly reflect on the strengths and weaknesses of this second facet of the humanitarian agenda of the OAS.

4.1 Risk reduction

Firstly, the OAS is supporting risk-reduction mechanisms in accordance with the Hyogo Framework of Action, which is the ten-year plan of the United Nations Office for Disaster Risk Reduction.[49] In order to realise the goals set by the Hyogo Framework, the IAP plans that the OAS will continue to promote the coordination and exchange of knowledge through existing hemispheric mechanisms like Inter-American Committee on Natural Disaster Reduction and the Inter-American Network for Disaster Mitigation. Furthermore, the OAS will have to support the efforts of its member states to strengthen local and community disaster risk management by, again, promoting the coordination and the exchange of knowledge, but also by developing training workshops on, inter alia, disaster risk management and awareness-raising. Overall, the OAS's role in risk reduction is mainly directed in the IAP to the provision of knowledge to the member states, who will decide for themselves how to decrease the risks posed by natural disasters.

4.2 National preparedness and response systems

Second, the IAP foresees that the OAS will contribute to the strengthening of national preparedness and response systems. For this purpose, the OAS will have to promote the improvement of early

[47] Note that the IAP only lists three general objectives. For the purpose of clarification, this chapter addresses national preparedness and the facilitation of international humanitarian assistance as separate general objectives.

[48] The discussion of the four objectives is based on the IAP and the report of the Working Group.

[49] UNISDR, 'Hyogo Framework for Action (HFA)', *The United Nations Office for Disaster Risk Reduction,* accessed 29 March 2013, www.unisdr.org/we/coordinate/hfa.

warning systems and the conclusion of international agreements when required by the threats of the respective weather or telluric phenomena. Concerning the contemplated actions of the OAS, these are restricted to the promotion of information-sharing on the national preparedness and response systems. In due time, a procedural handbook for emergency, disaster and early warning situations might also be compiled, but the member states will remain to decide for themselves how they want to prepare for the future response to natural disasters.

4.3 *Facilitation of international humanitarian assistance*

Third, the OAS is going to encourage member states to ensure the effective facilitation of international humanitarian assistance. More than the first two objectives, this issue was subject to considerable debate during the sessions of the Working Group. In particular the non-state experts stressed the ongoing problems with the entry of humanitarian assistance personnel and supplies to emergency areas in the Americas. The debated difficulties included the provision of visas, custom proced ures, access and transit routes, restricted areas, tax questions, national coordination and immunities.

Some of these issues were previously addressed in the context of the *Inter-American Convention to Facilitate Disaster Assistance* (ACFDA), which was approved by consensus in 1991. More than twenty years later, this Convention remains the only legally binding regional instrument on humanitarian assistance within the western hemisphere and it covers, inter alia, the requirement to request and accept humanitarian assistance (Article II), the designation of a national coordinating authority to oversee the assistance (Article III) and the free transit of duly identified supplies and personnel (Articles V and VII).[50] The problem with the ACFDA, however, is that it has only entered into force for the three states that have ratified it (Nicaragua, Panama and Peru) and for the two states who have acceded to it at a later moment (the Dominican Republic and Uruguay).[51] The other thirty member states of the OAS are not a party to this Convention. Moreover, many of the expressed difficulties with regard to the facilitation of humanitarian assistance are not subject to

[50] OAS, *Inter-American Convention to Facilitate Disaster Assistance*, 6 July 1991, www.oas.org/juridico/english/treaties/a-54.html.

[51] OAS, 'Signatories and Ratifications', accessed 29 March 2013, www.oas.org/juridico/english/sigs/a-54.html.

this Convention, including, for example, the role of specialised sub-regional organisations and non-state actors.

During the preparatory sessions of the Working Group, many officials and experts argued that all this shows the need to develop 'a suitable, updated tool that is accepted by the countries of the Hemisphere' and that can create 'harmonisation of the various existing initiatives in an overall framework'.[52] In their opinion, the obvious way forward would be to reopen and update ACFDA. However, while this recommendation was incorporated in the first report of the Working Group, it was not included in the final IAP.[53] Instead, the OAS is now envisaged to encourage the member states to incorporate international humanitarian assistance standards and guidelines (the 'Guidelines on Facilitation and National Regulation of the International Operations of Rescue in Disasters and Assistance for Initial Recovery' of the IFRC) into their own response regulations. The OAS will have to realise this objective, again, through the exchange of information which might result in a National Procedural Handbook on how to adhere to international humanitarian assistance standards.

Clearly, the majority of the member states did not agree with the recommendation to reopen and update ACFDA. Although the Guidelines of the IFRC cover many of the expressed concerns about the facilitation of humanitarian assistance, their implementation is left to the discretion of the member states. They found it inappropriate to regulate the facilitation of humanitarian assistance in a legally binding document.

4.4 Coordination of international humanitarian assistance

The fourth and final objective of the IAP is that the OAS will have to improve the coordination among existing international humanitarian assistance mechanisms. This is where the 'key comparative advantage' of the OAS, which is its installed capacity in most of the member states through its country offices, would have the most significant impact.[54] Therefore, the IAP plans that the OAS will play a prominent and perhaps even leading role in encouraging increased levels of regional and sub-regional coordination. For this purpose, the OAS will, inter alia, have to support the development of sub-regional emergency plans,

[52] OAS, 'Report of the Joint Working Group', 20, 22. [53] Ibid., 26–27. [54] Ibid., 6.

promote the utilisation of coordinating tools for humanitarian supplies, realise a systematised document of national contributions in terms of country facilities for humanitarian response, and improve the dialogue between the OAS and other relevant actors. Although these intended activities do not seem very impressive in terms of humanitarian boots on the ground, the experiences of previous disaster responses show their importance. The lack of coordination among the existing humanitarian assistance mechanisms in response to, for example, the earthquake in Haiti has raised serious concerns.[55] Potentially, the OAS could make a difference in these kinds of situations where hundreds of humanitarian actors are involved.[56]

4.5 The humanitarian agenda of the OAS before, during and after natural disasters

Taken together, the four objectives of the IAP visualise two different trajectories for regional cooperation on natural disasters. On the one hand, the scheduled activities of the OAS show the significant constraints of its humanitarian agenda. On most objectives the member states will decide for themselves how to proceed. On the other hand, the IAP programmes a prominent role for the OAS in supporting domestic efforts through the exchange of knowledge, but in particular through enhancing the coordination of international humanitarian assistance.

However, to what extent the OAS will be able to institute the activities of the IAP will strongly depend on the particular interests of its thirty-five member states. The resolution adopted by the General Assembly in June 2012, which endorsed the IAP, emphasised that the recommendations of the Working Group are to be implemented 'on a voluntary basis by the member states'.[57] Moreover, the envisaged activities 'shall be subject to the availability of financial resources from voluntary and/or other external financing, and in no case will be charged against the

[55] See Chapter 18.

[56] Elizabeth Ferris, 'Megatrends and the Future of Humanitarian Action', *International Review of the Red Cross* 93 (2011): 935–936. ('The proliferation of actors in humanitarian action, particularly in high-profile emergencies, will make issues of co-ordination more difficult and complex ... The experience with clusters in Haiti illustrates this dilemma: the health cluster, for example, had over 500 participants in its regular co-ordination meetings.')

[57] OAS GA, 'Existing Mechanisms for Disaster Prevention'.

Regular Fund of the OAS Program Budget'.[58] This leaves us with the unsatisfying conclusion that it is too early to determine whether the IAP is really 'a great step forward'.[59] As of today, however, none of the projected activities have been realised.

5. Humanitarian assistance and the Inter-American human rights system

The previous sections illustrated that the regional norm of non-intervention continues to guide Inter-American cooperation on humanitarian action. However, despite the fact that the American states have not authorised the OAS to play a leading humanitarian role, these states no longer have the absolute right to refuse humanitarian assistance in times of armed conflict, or in the aftermath of a natural disaster either. They have to adhere to certain standards of humanitarian assistance under regional human rights law. When American states do not fulfil this humanitarian responsibility in an appropriate manner, they might be obliged to accept humanitarian assistance from international humanitarian actors. This exemplifies how the regional norm of non-intervention is subverted in favour of human rights in the context of humanitarian action. After having introduced the human rights provisions which are relevant for the facilitation of humanitarian assistance in armed conflicts and natural disasters, this section concludes by briefly reflecting on the contributions of the Inter-American human rights system to the law of humanitarian action.

5.1 Humanitarian assistance and armed conflicts

In the context of international and non-international armed conflicts, the first legal regime to consider is international humanitarian law (IHL). The Geneva Conventions and Additional Protocols include binding obligations for states with regard to humanitarian assistance (the provision of physical services like food and shelter) and humanitarian protection (the provision of legal immunity from armed attack).[60] In addition

[58] Ibid.

[59] OAS, Secretary-General, 'Inauguration of the Forty-Second Regular Session'.

[60] For an overview of the relevant IHL provisions on humanitarian assistance, see: Spieker, 'The Right to Give and Receive Humanitarian Assistance', 18. On the distinction between humanitarian assistance and humanitarian protection, see: Marie-José Domestici-Met,

to IHL, it is firmly established, most notably by the International Court of Justice in the 2004 Wall Opinion that human rights law continues to apply in armed conflicts. This is the case, unless the respective state has lawfully derogated from its human rights obligations.[61]

What requires our attention here is that some provisions of the *American Convention on Human Rights* (ACHR) are relevant for the facilitation of humanitarian assistance in armed conflicts.[62] In particular, the right to life should be considered (Article 4). Article 27 lists this right as non-derogable, which means that it continues to apply in armed conflicts just as in any other humanitarian emergency. Moreover, both the Human Rights Committee and the Inter-American Court have stated that the right to life requires the adoption of positive measures.[63] Under certain circumstances, this positive duty could also oblige states to ensure the adequate facilitation of humanitarian assistance.

'Humanitarian Action – A Scope for the Responsibility to Protect? Part I: Humanitarian Assistance Looking for a Legal Regime Allowing its Delivery to Those in Need under any Circumstances', *Goettingen Journal of International Law* 3 (2009): 398–402. Note that this section limits itself to humanitarian assistance and does not discuss legal obligations to offer adequate humanitarian protection.

61 ICJ, 'Legal Consequences of the Construction of a Wall in the Occupied Palestinian Territory', *International Court of Justice*, 9 July 2004, §106, www.icj-cij.org/docket/files/131/1671.pdf.

On the applicability of Inter-American human rights law in the context of armed conflicts and, more specifically, on the derogation provisions of the ACHR, see: Héctor Faúnde Ledesma, *The Inter-American System for the Protection of Human Rights* (San José: Inter-American Human Rights Institute, 2007): 91–131.

62 Much has been written on the intricate relationship between IHL and international human rights law. Some authors have discussed the possible implementation of IHL by regional human rights courts. This has been a hotly debated topic in relation to some of the early jurisprudence of the Inter-American Commission, which directly applied to IHL. On the application of IHL by the Commission and subsequently the Court, see: Lindsay Moir, 'Law and the Inter-American Human Rights System', *Human Rights Quarterly* 25 (2003): 181–212; Emiliano J. Buis, 'The Implementation of International Humanitarian Law by Human Rights Courts: The Example of the Inter-American Human Rights System', in *International Humanitarian Law and Human Rights Law,* ed. Roberta Arnold et al. (Leiden: Koninklijke Brill, 2008), 269–293. It goes beyond the scope of this chapter to discuss whether and to what extent the Inter-American Commission and Court can apply the IHL provisions on humanitarian assistance and protection.

63 Human Rights Committee, General Comment 6 (Article 6) (Sixteenth session, 1982), Compilation of General Comments and General Recommendations Adopted by Human Rights Treaty Bodies, UN Doc. HRI/GEN/1/Rev.6 at 127 (2003); Inter-American Court of Human Rights, 'Case of the *Ituango Massacres* v. *Colombia*', 1 July 2006, §130–131, www.corteidh.or.cr/docs/casos/articulos/seriec_148_ing.pdf.

In fact, the American Commission on Human Rights has adopted precautionary measures in previous proceedings that called for the provision of adequate humanitarian assistance.[64] These measures were based on the responsibility of the parties to take the necessary actions in guaranteeing the life of the involved people. Other rights have been invoked for the purpose of the provision of humanitarian support as well, including the right to humane treatment (Article 5), the right to personal liberty and security (Article 7), the rights of the family (Article 17) and the rights of the child (Article 19).[65] As of today, the Commission has not (yet) been asked to issue precautionary measures on the facilitation of humanitarian assistance in the context of an international or non-international armed conflict; that is to say in a situation where IHL would apply as well. However, in light of the existing jurisprudence of the American Court of Human Rights there is no reason to assume that the positive duty under regional human rights law to ensure the adequate provision of humanitarian assistance does not apply in these kind of situations.[66] This means that the relevant provisions of the ACHR and in particular the right to life contain affirmative obligations for American states to ensure the adequate access to humanitarian assistance in armed conflicts. As such, the Inter-American human rights regime can complement IHL.

5.2 Humanitarian assistance and natural disasters

As in armed conflicts, the relevant provisions of the ACHR also continue to apply in the aftermath of a natural disaster. So much has also been confirmed in the precautionary measures that the Commission has adopted on the facilitation of humanitarian assistance in the context of at least one natural disaster. In February 2010, only one month after the earthquake devastated large parts of Haiti, the Commission issued a press statement, stressing the duty of the Haitian government and all other humanitarian actors on the ground to respect human rights obligations

[64] For a discussion of the relevant cases, see: Eva Rieter, *Preventing Irreparable Harm – Provisional Measures in International Human Rights Adjudication* (Antwerp: Intersentia, 2010), 528–530.

[65] Ibid. For a broader discussion on the relevance of human rights for the facilitation of humanitarian assistance, see: Rebecca Barber, 'Facilitating humanitarian assistance in international humanitarian and human rights law', *International Review of the Red Cross* 91 (2009): 371–392.

[66] See n. 61 and n. 62.

during the emergency situation.[67] Later that year, in November 2010, the Commission granted precautionary measures for the residents of five camps for IDPs in response to a petition which claimed that forced evictions were carried out in their emergency encampments.[68] The Commission asked the Haitian government, inter alia, 'to adopt a moratorium on the expulsions for the camps'; 'to ensure that those who have been illegally expelled ... are transferred to places with minimum sanitary and security conditions'; and 'to ensure that international cooperation agencies have access to the camps for internally displaced persons'.[69]

In particular, this last recommendation is very remarkable. Apparently, the positive duty to ensure the adequate access to humanitarian assistance refers not only to the maximum of the state's available resources, but also to 'those available from the international community through international co-operation and assistance'.[70] This means that the government of Haiti would be obliged to accept the offer of humanitarian assistance, when failing to ensure minimum sanitary and security conditions. Although the Haitian government failed to implement the precautionary measures, the significance of this decision should not be questioned.[71] The Commission showed that the regional human rights regime offers substantive protection for the provision of humanitarian assistance in the aftermath of natural disasters. Of course, the decision is only the first of its kind, but it definitely illustrates that the American states have to adhere to certain standards for the facilitation of

[67] OAS, Inter-American Commission on Human Rights, Press Release No. 11/10, 'IAHCR stress duty to respect human rights during the emergency in Haiti', 2 February 2010, www.cidh.oas.org/Comunicados/English/2010/11-10eng.htm.

[68] OAS, Inter-American Commission on Human Rights, PM 367-10, 'Forced Evictions from Five Camps for Displaced Persons, Haiti', *OAS*, 15 November 2010, www.oas.org/en/iachr/decisions/ precautionary.asp.

[69] Ibid.

[70] CESCR (Committee on Economic, Social and Cultural Rights), 'General Comment No. 3: The Nature of States Parties Obligations Article 2(1) of the Covenant', *UNHCHR*, 14 December 1990, §13, www.unhchr.ch/tbs/doc.nsf/0/94bdbaf59b43a424c12563ed0052b664.

[71] On the enforcement of these specific precautionary measures, see: Nicole Philips, Kathleen Bergin, Jennifer Goldsmith and Laura Carr, 'Enforcing Remedies from the Inter-American Commission on Human Rights: Forced Evictions and Post-Earthquake Haiti', *Human Rights Brief* 19 (2011): 13–18. Inter-American Commission on Human Rights, 'Follow-up Report on the Situation of Human Rights in Haiti', 2010, http://lib.ohchr.org/HRBodies/UPR/Documents/session12/HT/OAS-OrganisationAmericanStates-AnnualReportInterAmericanCommissionHumanRights2010-eng.pdf.

humanitarian assistance under regional human rights law. When looking at the bigger picture, such positive obligations exemplify how the regional norm of non-intervention is being subverted in favour of human rights in the context of humanitarian action.

5.3 The Inter-American human rights system and the law of humanitarian action

For a long time, regional human rights law could not play such a role. In May 1948, seven months prior to the conclusion of the *Universal Declaration of Human Rights*, the countries of the western hemisphere adopted the 'American Declaration of the Rights and Duties of Man'.[72] This was a document full of noble intentions, but not binding upon its signatories and without a mechanism to promote and protect the envisaged civil–political and social–economic rights. In those days, regional human rights law was just a paper tiger. Today, the Inter-American human rights system does have a binding human rights treaty (i.e. the ACHR since 1979) and a significant institutional structure (i.e. the Commission and the Court). The impact of the regional human rights regime on the American states has increased up to a point that its jurisprudence certainly curtails the regional norm of non-intervention.

The development of the Inter-American human rights system also affects the law of humanitarian action. First of all, it is clear that regional human rights law applies before, during and after natural disasters. Although there is not yet anything close to a full 'cycle of protection' in the Americas, some 'progress' can be noted.[73] So far, the Commission has issued two precautionary measures on the facilitation of humanitarian assistance in natural disasters[74] and convened two special hearings on

[72] For a more extensive introduction on the history and institutional contours of the Inter-American human rights system, see: Robert K. Goldman, 'History and Action: The Inter-American Human Rights System and the Role of the Inter-American Commission on Human Rights', *Human Rights Quarterly* 31 (2009): 856–887. Note that not all OAS member states have ratified the ACHR (including the US, Canada, Guyana and several small island states).

[73] Cf. Chapter 9.

[74] OAS, Inter-American Commission on Human Rights, PM 367–10. Inter-American Commission on Human Rights, PM 340–10, 'Women and Girls Residing in 22 Camps for Internally Displaced Persons in Port-au-Prince, Haiti', 22 December 2010, www.oas.org/en/iachr/decisions/precautionary.asp.

'human rights and disasters'.[75] Second of all, it has been firmly established (and debated) that regional human rights law continues to apply during and certainly also after armed conflicts. In fact, the jurisprudence of the Commission and the Court on regional human rights obligations with regard to armed conflicts has been far more elaborate than that on natural disasters.[76] Unfortunately, it goes beyond the scope of this chapter to introduce this jurisprudence and to explain how it relates to the constitutionalisation and/or fragmentation of humanitarian norms. That will have to be done elsewhere. What matters here is that the Inter-American Commission and Court are in the process of specifying the regional human rights obligations before, during and after humanitarian emergencies. In the years ahead, this will likely result in a further regionalisation of the law of humanitarian action.

6. Concluding remarks

The landscape of humanitarian action is changing rapidly. The international humanitarian system is adapting to the new dynamics of armed conflicts and natural disasters, while at the same time it is trying to digest the ongoing proliferation of humanitarian actors.[77] Another game-changer is the regionalisation of humanitarian action. In recent years, regional institutions have become important humanitarian players and regional human rights bodies have started to determine the human rights obligations before, during and after humanitarian emergencies.

In light of this regionalisation of the law and politics of humanitarian action, this chapter has explored the humanitarian role of the OAS. For a long time, this hemispheric organisation did not fulfil any significant humanitarian responsibilities. Its member states simply did not authorise the OAS to do so. The regional norm of non-intervention made no exception for humanitarian emergencies. In the last twenty years, however, American states have started to reconsider the scope of

[75] OAS, Inter-American Commission on Human Rights, 'Protection of Human Rights in Natural Disasters', 3 March 2006, www.oas.org/es/cidh/audiencias/Hearings.aspx?Lang=en&Session=19. Commission on Human Rights, 'Human Rights Situation during the Natural Disaster in Venezuela', *OAS*, 3 March 2000, www.oas.org/es/cidh/audiencias/Hearings.aspx?Lang=en&Session=43.

[76] See n. 42, 61 and 62.

[77] On these 'megatrends' for humanitarian action, see: Ferris, 'Megatrends and the future of humanitarian action', 915–938.

non-intervention. This has resulted, inter alia, in a more ambitious humanitarian agenda for the OAS.

In 2003, the OAS member states formally recognised that regional cooperation on humanitarian action is required to enhance the capability of the Americas to prevent and respond to man-made and natural disasters. Although the sincerity of the Declaration is not to be doubted, the past and scheduled humanitarian activities of the OAS demonstrate that its authority in the field of humanitarian action remains subject to major limitations. As it turns out, the regional norm of non-intervention continues to thwart the humanitarian agenda of the OAS. The regional institution has not really been able to play a leading role before, during and after humanitarian emergencies. The OAS has fulfilled a number of humanitarian tasks in the context of armed conflicts and natural disasters, but these are generally subordinate to the perceived interests of the national governments.

For sure, this is not the whole story. The times are gone that American states had a 'carte blanche' in humanitarian emergencies. The regional norm of non-intervention is subverted in favour of human rights in the context of humanitarian action. Trails of this ongoing development can be seen in the IAP of 2012, which programmes a prominent role for the OAS in enhancing the coordination of international humanitarian assistance, but perhaps even more in the progressing jurisprudence of the Inter-American human rights system.

To conclude, the OAS is contributing to the regionalisation of humanitarian action. Although its humanitarian role might be seen as less 'impressive' than those from the other regional institutions that are discussed in this volume, the study of the law and politics of humanitarian action will have to keep a close eye on developments in the western hemisphere. Inter-American cooperation is moving forward and humanitarian responsibilities are definitely on its agenda. The responsibility to protect may not be part of this, but the member states are beginning to share some of their other humanitarian responsibilities with the OAS.

17

Providing relief in times of war: the role of the ICRC in the Colombian conflict during the Uribe administration (2002–2010)

SANDRA BORDA

1. Introduction

Civil conflicts are one of the most challenging scenarios for humanitarian organisations. The dynamics of those conflicts not only affect the ability of these organisations to provide relief and assistance, but also force them to define in clear terms the nature of their missions and their priorities in countries that suffer from this type of confrontation. In other words, the intensification of military hostilities, the presence or absence of peace dialogues, temporal agreements to cease hostilities, among many other changes in the nature of the relationship between warring parties, do have an effect on the strategies humanitarian organisations adopt and implement. In this chapter, I observe how the intensification of the military confrontation in Colombia during the Uribe administration affected or shaped the role of the ICRC (International Committee of the Red Cross) in that country. I argue that the renewal of hostilities that took place in Colombia since the end of peace dialogues in 2002 had a twofold effect: On one hand, it made the ICRC's choice of prioritising gaining access to victims over denouncing abuses by parties to the conflict even starker.[1] To be sure, it made it more difficult for the organisation to find an area of overlap or intersection between these two goals. On the other hand, given the nature of that choice, it forced the organisation to be more vocal and public about the scope and limits of its activities under these new circumstances.

[1] I assume here that the difference between human rights and humanitarian organisations lacks clarity. Most organisations combine their duty to denounce violations to human rights with their commitment to provide relief, although under different formulas. I thank an anonymous evaluator of this chapter for pushing me to clarify this point.

I develop this argument first by explaining how this change in the dynamics of the Colombian conflict unfolded. Second, I explain how this new situation led to a more difficult scenario for humanitarian action by the ICRC. Third, I explain the role of the ICRC in kidnap cases and in the debate about the nature of the Colombian conflict to illustrate how the organisation opted for gaining access over denouncing government and guerrilla abuses, and how it communicated the nature and dimensions of its role. Here, I show how the virtual impossibility of peace negotiations made the hostage situations even more uncertain and this pushed the ICRC to make extra efforts to provide them with basic care, to create conditions for their release, and also to set up and communicate the limits and scope of their activities in the context of various negotiations to release different groups of hostages. This process affected deeply but in diverse ways this organisation's principles of neutrality and independence and it forced it to declare publicly its inability to act as anything different than a facilitator and, at most, a mediator. On a more conceptual level, I also highlight in this section how the ICRC confronted the state on the definition of the Colombian conflict. While the government insisted on the definition of insurgent groups as a terrorist threat and on denying the existence of a civil conflict, this organisation kept supporting the use of *civil* or *internal conflict* to define the Colombian war. This last activity is probably the one in which the ICRC was more vocal although it managed to avoid a polarised scenario with the government, like the one human rights advocacy organisations were immersed in. This is probably the only field in which the ICRC acted more publicly, and it is not hard to understand why: by their very own definition, humanitarian organisations would not be able to assist victims of the Colombian confrontation if that confrontation was not defined as an internal or civil conflict, as the Additional Protocols of 1977 to the Geneva Conventions stipulate. An acceptance of the Colombian situation as one of 'a terrorist threat against a legitimate and democratic state', in the words of President Uribe, would singlehandedly eliminate the humanitarian space in that country. I examine this debate and the ICRC contribution in Section 4. In the final section of this chapter, I suggest some future lines of questioning to advance further research on the impact of changes in civil confrontations on the role of humanitarian organisations.

I analyse the ICRC because even though it is an organisation that has privileged the task of providing relief to victims over public denunciation, it had a very dynamic relationship with the government during this particular period: it was part of every single process that led to the release of hostages, it had permanent access to both parties to the conflict and acted as an honest broker in moments of crisis, it was the only organisation formally and officially allowed by the government to talk to insurgent groups, and it was one of the most salient voices that promoted the respect for humanitarian law throughout the conflict. Additionally, the ICRC has strengthened its presence in Colombia since the beginning of its work in this country in 1969:[2] Colombia is the scene of the largest ICRC operation in the Americas (in 2010 its expenditure in Colombia was 36,284 Swiss francs) and its work involves protecting civilians, helping displaced persons and conflict-affected communities, visiting detainees, promoting international humanitarian law, and helping people affected by weapons contamination. Its activities through the years have allowed the ICRC to gain respect and acceptance by all parties to the Colombian conflict. More generally, this organisation has been one of the first 'and no doubt the most persistent in trying to expand humanitarian protection from international to internal wars [and it] has played a major part in broadening the scope of humanitarian concern from international to internal war'.[3] Therefore, the ICRC provides a crucial case to evaluate the impact of changes in the dynamics of military conflict on the behaviour of humanitarian organisations.

2. The intensification of Colombia's war

After numerous failed attempts to find a peaceful and negotiated solution to the Colombian conflict, the most recent from 1998 to 2002,[4] Colombians elected (on the first round in a two-rounds system and with 53 per cent of the popular vote)[5] the candidate who offered an 'iron fist'

[2] In 1969 the government permitted delegates to visit people detained in relation to the conflict. 'As the conflict intensified and humanitarian needs increased, a Headquarters Agreement was signed in May 1980 between the government and the ICRC, allowing the agency to implement the full range of activities in support of victims of the conflict.' See Maurizio Geremia, 'Neutrality, Impartiality and Independence in Colombia: an ICRC Perspective', *Humanitarian Exchange Magazine* 45 (2010), accessed 19 October 2011, www.odihpn.org/report.asp?id=3040.

[3] David P. Forsythe, 'The ICRC: a Unique Humanitarian Protagonist', *International Review of the Red Cross* 89, No. 865 (2007): 66.

[4] 'Hardliner elected Colombian president', *BBC News*, 27 May 2002, http://news.bbc.co.uk/2/hi/americas/2008674.stm.

[5] It is also interesting to note that since his election in 2002, Uribe has maintained some of the highest approval ratings of any Latin American president, usually around 70–80 per cent. In

approach for dealing with guerrilla groups. Alvaro Uribe personified the frustration most Colombians felt with what appeared to be the insurgency's lack of commitment with peace.[6] Hence his political campaign insisted on the inadequacy of a political solution to the conflict. Uribe's argument was simple and clear: insurgent groups did not have a political agenda, they were threatening democratic institutions and did not have popular support. On the contrary, they constantly attacked civilians in their war against a democratic and legitimate state. Consequently, a military response was the only possible way to end what he labeled 'a terrorist threat'[7].

Additionally, the Uribe administration had at its disposal unprecedented resources to wage war against the insurgency, since the United States involvement in the war against illegal drugs gradually, but increasingly, overlapped with Colombia's civil confrontation. In December 1998, under the presidency of Andrés Pastrana (1998–2002), the United States and Colombia '[laid] the groundwork for the expansion of (bilateral) military cooperation . . . The proposed new aid would intensify all (anti-narcotics) efforts, with the largest set of initiatives – categorised as "the push into Southern Colombia coca-growing areas" – designed to prepare the US-created army battalions to operate in 'a known guerrilla stronghold'.[8] By March 1999, the United States government issued new guidelines that, according to Isaacson, allowed for the sharing of intelligence about guerrilla activity in Colombia's southern drug-producing region, even if the information was not directly linked to any sort of anti-narcotics operation. Hence, 'Plan Colombia' – as this very institutionalised

2008, his approval rating hit an impressive 81 per cent, one of the highest levels of his entire presidency. In June 2008, after *Operation Jaque*, Uribe's approval rate rose to an unprecedented 91.47 per cent. Sandra Borda, 'The Internationalization of Domestic Conflicts: A Comparative Study of Colombia, El Salvador And Guatemala'. Dissertation for the Faculty of the Graduate School of the University of Minnesota, May 2009, p. 113.

[6] In fact, this lack of commitment was finally revealed by Fidel Castro when he wrote in his extensive memoir that the FARC-EP's (Revolutionary Armed Forces of Colombia – Popular Army, the biggest insurgent organisation in Colombia) General Secretariat, months before starting peace dialogues with the government in 1998, told the Cuban diplomatic mission in Colombia about their intention to sustain negotiations for a couple of years, to gain a good image and, more importantly, to gain some time to be able to reorganise militarily. Fidel Castro, *La Paz en Colombia* (Editora Política, 2008), 105–106 and 120–124.

[7] Borda, 'Internalization of Domestic Conflicts', 113.

[8] Adam Isacson, 'Getting In Deeper. The United States' Growing Involvement in Colombia's Conflict', *CIP International Policy Report* (2000).

form of cooperation between the United States and Colombia was called – consolidated an already existing trend of adding counterinsurgency goals to the pre-existing war against illegal drugs in Colombia. President Pastrana himself later acknowledged that 'Plan Colombia' was a mechanism designed to debilitate the guerrillas and prevent them from leaving the negotiating table.[9]

By the end of Pastrana's administration, and right after peace talks with the insurgents officially ended in February 2002, the audience in the United States could not have been more receptive to an approach that finally and formally recognised the link between guerrillas, narcotics and terrorism; a link that the Colombian government had been promoting for a long period of time. The 9/11 attacks marked the emergence of new parameters in United States foreign policy that were strikingly compatible with the Colombian government's new militaristic approach to its domestic struggle.[10] The first step had already been taken since FARC-EP (Revolutionary Armed Forces of Colombia – Popular Army),[11] the ELN (National Liberation Army)[12] and paramilitary groups had been included in the United States list of international terrorist organisations early in October 2001. Subsequently, by May 2002 and just months before President Uribe took office, Colombia's ambassador in Washington articulated the connection between the global war against terrorism and Colombia's civil confrontation in an even clearer way:

> While the United States' attention is fixed on fighting terrorism in Afghanistan, the Middle East and Asia, a grave threat lurks in the Americas. Colombia is the leading theater of operations for terrorists in the Western Hemisphere. Under the false pretense of a civil war, Colombian guerrilla groups have ravaged the nation with violence financed by cocaine consumers in the United States. The Bush administration,

[9] Andrés Pastrana, *La Palabra Bajo Fuego* (Editorial Planeta, 2005).

[10] See Sandra Borda, *La Internacionalización de la paz y de la guerra en Colombia durante los gobiernos de Andrés Pastrana y Alvaro Uribe. Busqueda de legitimidad politica y capacidad militar* (Ediciones Uniandes, 2013).

[11] FARC-EP is mainly a peasant organisation, proclaiming itself to be a revolutionary agrarian, anti-imperialist Marxist-Leninist group of Bolivarian inspiration. It was created during the '50s and '60s and according to former Colombian Armed Forces Commander Admiral Édgar Cely, it had a total of 18,000 members in 2010.

[12] The ELN is a revolutionary, avowedly Marxist guerrilla group that has been operating in several regions of Colombia since 1964. Their membership is estimated at around 5,000 guerrillas as of 2010.

> appropriately, is pushing in Congress to have anti-narcotics aid expanded to strengthen Colombia's ability to defeat terrorists.

And to reinforce the construction of the already recognised association between insurgency and illegal drugs, he asserted:

> Drugs are the root of almost all violence in Colombia. It is simple: everywhere there are poppies or coca in Colombia, there are guerrillas and paramilitaries. The Pastrana administration has moved aggressively to sever ties between the armed forces and the paramilitary group called the United Self-Defense Forces of Colombia (AUC), which is itself involved in the drug trade; in 2001 government forces, including police, captured 992 paramilitaries and killed 116. Where there are guerrillas and paramilitaries, there are terror and violence against civilians. While they may hide behind a Marxist ideology, Colombia's leftist guerrillas have ceased to be a political insurgency. They have traded their ideals for drug profits.[13]

Given the atmosphere of fear created by the newborn war against terrorism, the Colombian government was successful in including Colombia as part of the United States's international war on terrorism. As a result, Pastrana attempted to include an emergency supplemental operation to change the destination of United States military aid. The Colombian government asked the United States Congress to approve a specific bill that would explicitly authorise the use of military assistance to combat both drug trafficking and illegal armed groups. Already in March the Bush administration declared through Secretary of State Colin Powell that it was willing to openly support Colombia's counter-insurgent efforts:

> It could be necessary for us to give Colombia additional support, out of the anti-narcotics basket, to face this threat to its survival as a nation ... even though so far policy has been framed by the Andean Regional Initiative and that Plan Colombia has remained, as it was approved by Congress, 90 per cent focused on fighting illegal drugs, reality has changed and this implies we need to review our policy.[14]

On 21 March 2002, the Bush administration issued a request to the House of Representatives and by 24 May, it had approved versions of an 'emergency supplemental appropriation' – a bill that would approve

[13] Luis A. Moreno, 'Aiding Colombia's War on Terrorism', *The New York Times*, 3 May 2002.

[14] '¿Un Nuevo Plan Colombia?', *Revista Semana*, 1036 (2002).

the use of about 28 billion dollars in new funding for 2002 to address counter-terror priorities. This bill, as was expected, included several provisions relevant to Colombia. A House–Senate Conference Committee finished reconciling differences in mid-July between both houses' versions of the bill.[15] The bill stated that in fiscal year 2002, funds available to the Department of State for assistance to the government of Colombia shall be available to support 'a unified campaign against narcotics trafficking, against activities by organisations designated as terrorist organisations such as the Revolutionary Armed Forces of Colombia (FARC), the National Liberation Army (ELN), and the United Self-Defense Forces of Colombia (AUC), and to take actions to protect human health and welfare in emergency circumstances, including undertaking rescue operations'. It also stipulated that the newly elected President of Colombia (Uribe) had 'committed, in writing, to establish comprehensive policies to combat illicit drug cultivation, manufacturing, and trafficking (particularly with respect to providing economic opportunities that offer viable alternatives to illicit crops) and to restore government authority and respect for human rights in areas under the effective control of paramilitary and guerrilla organisations'.[16]

Hence, President Uribe continued building a stronger than ever military alliance between Washington and Bogota, an alliance that would contribute not only to Colombia's war against drugs, but more importantly, would support the state's military efforts against insurgent groups (see Figure 17.1).

As a result, the internal war intensified during this period (2000–2010) and the human rights and humanitarian situation in Colombia seriously deteriorated. The intensification of military hostilities and the absence of a solid and credible peace proposal by any of the warring parties constituted a profound change in the dynamics of the conflict. This change, in turn, made the tension between humanitarian groups' objective of gaining access to victims and their goal of denouncing human rights abuses even stronger. In other words, under these new circumstances it was more difficult to find a middle ground between their necessity to

[15] Sergio Gómez, 'Recursos Antidrogas, Ahora Contra La Guerrilla', *El Tiempo* (July 20th, 2002).

[16] USCIS, 107th Congress of the United States of America, 2002. Pub. L. 107–206 Making Supplemental Appropriations For Further Recovery From And Response To Terrorist Attacks On The United States For The Fiscal Year Ending 30 September 2002, and For Other Purposes, 2 August 2002, accessed 22 November 2011, www.uscis.gov/ilink/docView/PUBLAW/HTML/PUBLAW/0-0-0-25343.html.

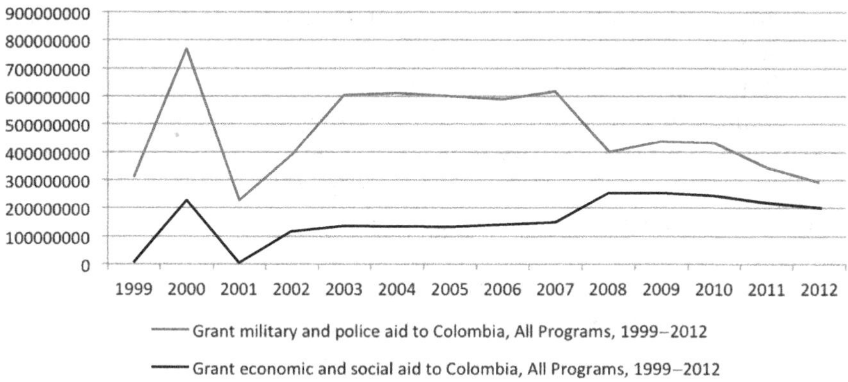

Figure 17.1: Military, police, economic and social US aid to Colombia, 1999–2012.

negotiate with parties to the conflict in order to gain access to victims and their commitment to denounce these same parties' violations of international humanitarian law. Humanitarian organisations were pushed more systematically towards one or the other extreme of this continuum. Consequently, groups such as Amnesty International and Human Rights Watch, which have privileged the politics of shame and very vocal denunciation of abuses, became louder and harsher critics of governmental practices, getting further away from obtaining access to victims of Colombia's war; and groups which had privileged access over denunciation, such as the ICRC, were pushed further away from denunciation, even under very extreme conditions. As a consequence and under duress, the ICRC was pushed to send public messages about gaining access to victims as their main goal, about being willing to practise discretion in order to gain this access and, more generally, about the scope and limits of their own activities. In sum, the intensification of the war not only made humanitarian work more difficult, it also pushed human rights and humanitarian organisations to make hard choices and to reaffirm publicly their identity and principles and to be more vocal about their role in the context of widespread military aggression.

3. Gaining access to victims in an adverse environment

As soon as the peace process between FARC-EP and the government collapsed at the end of the Pastrana administration, the military conflict intensified and providing humanitarian assistance became more challenging. This was due to two main factors. Firstly, the escalation of military hostilities that resulted from the implementation of the 'democratic security' policy ended up undermining the civilian population's security and deepening and broadening the humanitarian crisis in Colombia. This government initiative aimed at consolidating state control throughout Colombia, denying sanctuary to insurgents and perpetrators of violence, protecting the population through the increase of state presence and a reduction in violence, paradoxically produced more insecurity. Furthermore, the 'democratic security' policy led to a gradual disappearance of the distinction between civilians and combatants. In areas of high military activity, for instance, civilians were constantly asked for information about the guerrillas in exchange for governmental rewards, putting communities in a dangerous situation.[17] The government also promoted the creation and expansion of a more institutionalised network of civilian informants (*Red de Cooperantes*) and of 'Hometown Soldiers' (*Soldados Campesinos*) using emergency powers President Uribe invoked soon after taking office in 2002: by the end of 2004, more than 20,000 civilians had been recruited into Uribe's new programmes to provide security in more than 500 rural municipalities. The initiatives were similar to the controversial Convivir militias he had created and supported as governor of Antioquia (north-east department), some of which turned into nothing more than fronts for paramilitary death squads. In addition, some of those informant networks had incorporated former members of illegal paramilitary drug gangs and were secretly authorised by the government to work with paramilitary blocs in order to obtain information about insurgent groups.[18] This situation created further distrust among parties to the conflict and exacerbated their suspicions vis-à-vis any third party, such as civilians or humanitarian organisations. For the ICRC, it forced them to implement additional efforts to demonstrate their compliance with the principles of neutrality and impartiality.

Secondly, the Uribe administration constantly tried to co-opt organisations in charge of providing relief, especially to displaced communities,[19] endangering their activities in the field. By creating the CCAI

[17] Samir Elhawary, 'Protegiendo civiles y mejorando la seguridad en Colombia: ¿Cuál es la diferencia?', *Humanitarian Exchange Magazine* 45 (2010), accessed 19 October 2011, www.odihpn.org/report.asp?id=3063.

[18] 'Exparas en las redes de cooperantes', *El Espectador* (4 March 2011).

[19] IDMC (Internal Displacement Monitoring Centre) and NRC (Norwegian Refugee Council): 'a reliable Colombian NGO [*Consultoría para los Derechos Humanos y el Desplazamiento*, or CODHES] has reported that 280,000 people were newly displaced in 2010, adding to previous displacement to create a total number of 5.2 million internally

(Center for Integral Action Coordination), an institution under the presidential agency Acción Social – AS (Social Action and International Cooperation), the government attempted to address the needs of civilians affected by the armed conflict and to channel and coordinate most forms of international cooperation through this institution. For some, this agency has used humanitarian action to achieve non-humanitarian goals and, consequently, aid has been perceived as politicised and partial, even by its own recipients. This has been a long-lasting debate in Colombia: on one side, some organisations argue that focusing the majority of their efforts on supporting government institutions such as AS rather than increasing their direct engagement with communities of displaced people, in an environment of insecurity, fear and impunity, is not enough. This argument suggests that criticism directed at the government and higher levels of independence from it are necessary. On the other side, resource constraints, others argue, do not always make it feasible for these organisations to fully engage in providing direct assistance.[20] This situation is aggravated by the fact that 'it does not seem that the current situation will change, with most donor governments reducing support to Colombia on the basis that it is a democratic middle-income country and is therefore not a key priority'.[21] Hence, according to this last argument, the only possible scenario is providing relief through government agencies.

Even though the ICRC is one of the few agencies that prioritises direct involvement with communities instead of allying with the government, this close association between most humanitarian organisations and the government made them look, in the eyes of FARC-EP, like groups working with and for the government, which made their access to remote areas of the country under total or partial insurgent control even more difficult. In various instances, FARC-EP sent communiqués to these

displaced people (IDPs). The government, however, registered only 109,000 people as IDPs during the year. The total, cumulative figure also varies significantly, as the government had registered a total of 3.6 million IDPs by December 2010. In the first quarter of 2011, the government has registered 16,000 IDPs, which would signal a decline of displacement in 2011. As before, the problem of under-registration in the government registry remains significant', in 'Colombia, Property restitution in sight but integration still distant', 5 September 2001, accessed 22 November 2011: www.internal-displacement.org/8025708F004BE3B1/(httpInfoFiles)/BD3251F80AB23B61C12579020047223A/$file/Colombia-Overview-Sept2011.pdf.

[20] Samir Elhawary, 'Between War and Peace: Land and Humanitarian Action in Colombia', HPG – *Humanitarian Policy Group*, ODI (Working paper, 2007): 19.

[21] Elhawary, 'Between War and Peace'.

humanitarian organisations to let them know that they were considered military targets.[22] Even though the ICRC was the only organisation formally allowed by the government to communicate with the guerrillas and even though its neutrality was partially recognised by warring parties, its access to victims was seriously undermined during the years of the Uribe administration.

As I show in section 3, for the ICRC to demonstrate its neutrality was an elusive objective also due to additional factors such as the government's abuse of the ICRC emblem. All these situations hindered the organisation's ability to persuade FARC-EP of their impartiality and achieve their goal of simply providing relief to the victims of the confrontation. As Geremia argues, 'neutrality is not a given: no one is neutral by essence or by merely declaring themselves so. Neutrality is a quality that must be recognised by the parties themselves, as they perceive it through the ICRC's actions and communications.'[23] These actions and communications turned into a more challenging goal for the ICRC during Uribe's years.

By October 2002, the head of the ICRC delegation in Colombia had declared that the humanitarian situation in Colombia had deteriorated significantly and that the intensification of military hostilities had had very visible humanitarian consequences provoking summary executions, disappearances, internal displacement and aggression against medical missions.[24] Only two months after this declaration, the ICRC had to suspend its humanitarian aid to the village of La Gabarra (municipality of Tibú, Norte de Santander near the border with Venezuela) after FARC-EP stole one of their cars and burned two other ones; these cars were transporting humanitarian aid to internally displaced people in the area of Norte de Santander.[25] In April 2004, the ICRC had to abandon the municipality of Saravena, Arauca, also close to the border between Venezuela and Colombia, due to the lack of guarantees of protection for their activities.[26]

By 2004, the situation had not improved. In September, the ICRC announced it would reduce the size of its office in Villavicencio (capital

[22] Francisco Rey, 'La participación militar en la acción humanitaria: reflexiones sobre el caso colombiano', *Humanitarian Exchange Magazine*, 45 (2010), accessed 19 October 2011, www.odihpn.org/report.asp?id=3061.

[23] Geremia, 'Neutrality, Impartiality and Independence'.

[24] 'Se criollizó el DIH', *El Tiempo*, 6 October 2002.

[25] 'Cruz Roja Internacional indignada con las FARC', *El Tiempo*, 16 April 2003.

[26] 'Salió CICR de Saravena', *El Tiempo*, 3 April 2004.

city of the department of Meta, east of Bogotá) and that they would close their office in San José del Guaviare (eastern Colombia, capital of the department of Guaviare) for two months. According to Schaerer, the head of the ICRC delegation in Colombia at that time, the organisation was facing many problems in this region and they were having less and less access to victims; none of the parties to the conflict were providing enough security guarantees for them to enter these areas. Normally the dominant party provides these guarantees but due to the profound changes the conflict was experiencing at that point, ICRC's contacts were not available any more, communication was harder and they had lost the ability to enter these remote locations safely.[27] The organisation stated that it would take some time to adapt to this new form the conflict had adopted, and only then would they be able to continue providing relief to victims.[28] This trend was later confirmed by the publication of the ICRC 2004 report in which the organisation declared that it could only transmit one message to one of the hostages and that during that year, only 13 hostages were released. The ICRC also reported 46 infractions against medical missions and 43 victims.[29]

These events continued during most of the Uribe administration. In 2009, the ICRC reported that armed clashes in rural areas were putting local communities in constant danger and exposing them to violations of international humanitarian law such as 'murder of and/or attacks on persons protected by international humanitarian law; forced disappearances; sexual violence; hostage-taking; forced recruitment; physical and/or psychological abuse; and forced displacement'.[30] By 2010, the ICRC registered 65 infractions against their medical mission and reported cases in which medical delegates were not allowed access to victims of combats and doctors were threatened and attacked.[31] In this scenario, each opportunity the ICRC had to consolidate and demonstrate its neutrality was crucial in order to gain trust by the parties to the conflict and, consequently, to gain access to victims. In the next section, I argue that the ICRC's role as mediator in kidnap cases provided them with these

27 'CICR reestructura su organización en los Llanos', *El Tiempo*, 24 September 2004.

28 'Cambios en el Comité Internacional de la Cruz Roja', *El Tiempo*, 27 January 2005.

29 'En el 2004, la Cruz Roja solo logró transmitir mensaje a un secuestrado', *El Tiempo*, 6 May 2005.

30 ICRC, 'Annual Report, Colombia', *International Committee of the Red Cross* (ICRC), Delegation in Colombia, 2009, 11–12.

31 AFP, 'Cruz Roja preocupada por ataques a misiones médicas en Colombia', *El Tiempo*, 14 April 2011.

crucial opportunities. During hostage release operations, the ICRC was forced to reaffirm its neutrality in order to be able to provide assistance and it also needed to manage high levels of discretion vis-à-vis the conflicting parties in order to facilitate the liberation of hostages. Kidnap cases demonstrated the ICRC′s stronger commitment to providing direct relief and its detachment from denunciation techniques and practices.

4. The ICRC as mediator in kidnap cases

In Colombia, insurgent groups have been responsible for around 60 per cent of perpetrated kidnap cases. This is a practice that criminal organisations and guerrilla and paramilitary groups use in order to demand ransoms and increase their financial resources, to intimidate politicians, to terrorise or coerce activists, and to increase their leverage vis-à-vis the government. As Figure 17.2 shows, since 2000, the number of kidnap cases has decreased dramatically, to an important extent due to governmental security policies in place. However, the accumulated number of kidnapped people has remained high and this situation gave significant leverage to insurgent organisations.

After peace dialogues collapsed in February 2002, both the government and the families of kidnap victims contacted the United Nations and the ICRC to ask the organisation to put pressure on FARC-EP leaders to release their hostages. The insurgent group insisted that they would only release the police and military members they held captive

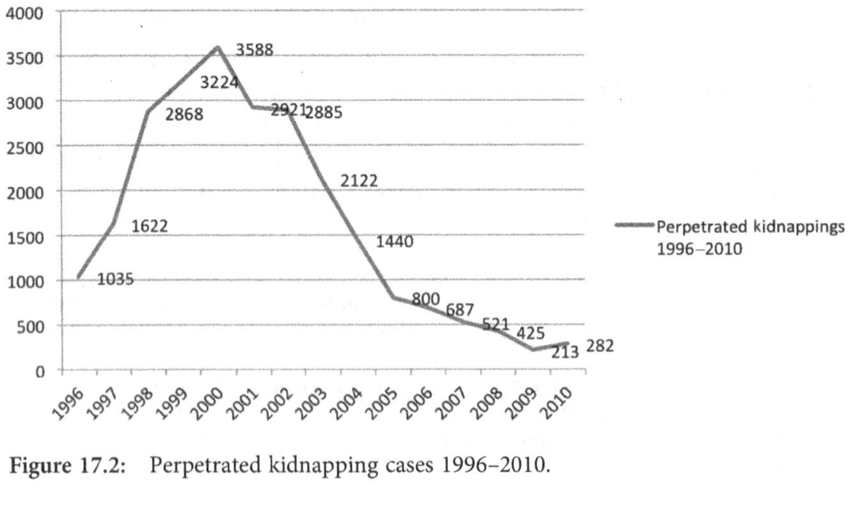

Figure 17.2: Perpetrated kidnapping cases 1996–2010.

(whom they consider to be prisoners of war) through exchanges with the government for imprisoned FARC-EP members. The insurgents demanded a demilitarised zone including two towns (Florida and Pradera, in southern Colombia) in the strategic region of Valle del Cauca, where much of the current military action against them was taking place. The goal was to set up a neutral space in order to advance what became known in Colombia as the 'Humanitarian Exchange'. The request was rejected by the Uribe government. However, both government and the victims' families continued asking the ICRC to act as facilitator of this exchange. Faced with this scenario, the ICRC decided to clarify the nature of their organisation and of their activities in Colombia by asserting that they could only be in charge of logistic matters once the parties had reached an agreement about the release of guerrilla members and hostages, but they could not participate in any sort of negotiation or as mediators.[32]

The range of activities the ICRC could pursue in a situation like this was very limited. Kidnap is clearly a violation of international law and that fact prevented the ICRC from negotiating with those who were implementing this practice. The head of the ICRC in Colombia at that point, Juan Pedro Schaerer, stated that an agreement to release the hostages would be political and not humanitarian, and that strict compliance with international humanitarian law would require not an exchange but the immediate and unconditional release of all the hostages by FARC-EP.[33] Hence, the ICRC could not be part of such a political solution. They could strive to ensure that some of the fundamental rights of kidnapped victims were respected: they could hold talks with the persons abducted in order to provide psychological support (although FARC-EP rarely allowed for this to happen), they could receive messages from victims and send them to their families (this was a normal practice during the release of small groups of hostages), and they could be involved in the release, bringing the abducted person safely out of the danger area and taking him/her back home.[34]

In fact, the ICRC participated in the release of various groups of hostages during 2008 and 2009. However, the role the organisation

[32] 'Cruz Roja dice que no es mediadora', *El Tiempo*, 31 December 2002.
[33] 'CICR dice que prestará apoyo a las liberaciones', *El Tiempo*, 18 February 2004.
[34] 'El CICR no estará en negociación', *El Tiempo*, 28 April 2003 and Thomas Jenatsch, 'The ICRC as a Humanitarian Mediator in the Colombian Conflict: Possibilities and Limits', *International Review of the Red Cross*, 323 (1998).

played suffered various changes due to the inclusion of the Venezuelan government in the process of liberation and also due to the military operations the Colombian government advanced in order to release hostages by force. The role of the Venezuelan government was very noticeable for the first time during the process that led to the release of the first group of congressmen and women in February 2008. On that occasion, the ICRC acted as facilitator. FARC-EP asked for the participation of the Venezuelan government and changed its original plan to give, confidentially, the location for the release operation to the ICRC. Instead, they decided to give it to the Chávez government. In previous operations, FARC-EP had always given the list of geographic coordinates defining the area where hostages would be released to the ICRC. This information had to be handled under very strict confidentiality since, if the government knew the location, it could attempt a military rescue and the capture of the guerrilla group in charge of the release. On this occasion though, the Venezuelan government refused to share the coordinates with the ICRC and only gave this information to the Venezuelan delegates, who in turn gave it to the helicopter pilot in charge of the rescue team transportation.[35] Even though both helicopters were flying with a Red Cross emblem, the members of this organisation did not have any information about the operation and could not have reacted in case of emergency.[36] Yves Heller, ICRC's spokesperson in Colombia, later declared that it was a challenge for the organisation to jointly be part of release operations with the Venezuelan government and that it required a complex coordination effort with the ICRC delegation in Venezuela and the government, since the latter had not been part of an operation like this before.[37] However, in order to serve as a facilitator of this operation and to have access and provide medical assistance to the released hostages, the ICRC had to play under these new rules imposed by the insurgency.

Another scenario in which the ICRC had to privilege its interest in access and relief over denunciation and confrontation with the government took place during the highly publicised release of Ingrid Betancourt, three American military contractors and eleven members of the

[35] 'Gobierno de Colombia autorió a Venezuela misión humanitaria de liberación de secuestrados', *El Tiempo*, 25 February 2008.

[36] '2 horas tendrán guerrilleros para la retirada', *El Tiempo*, 27 February 2008.

[37] 'CICR no tiene solicitudes de las FARC para liberar más secuestrados', *El Tiempo*, 6 June 2008.

Colombian military and police. This was a military operation that took place in July 2008 in which, according to the government, FARC rebels were tricked into handing over the hostages to actual Colombian security forces posing as members of a fictitious non-governmental organisation that supposedly would fly the captives to a camp to meet rebel leader Alfonso Cano. Various aspects of the operation were apparently designed to imitate the previous hostage liberation described above, including the actual composition of the group and the type and markings of the helicopters used. Later, and due to video footage collected during the mission, it became clear that the Colombian military intelligence misused an official International Red Cross emblem during this rescue operation.

This motivated a debate in Colombia. The government insisted that, compared to the effect and the benefits of the operation, the use of the emblem was a small detail, and public opinion and opposition leaders were overreacting. Later, President Uribe announced that an internal investigation had found that one of the officers who participated in the operation had individually decided to make unauthorised use of the Red Cross emblem, claiming that he was nervous and feared the presence of armed guerrillas. At the end, the government publicly apologised to the ICRC. The striking factor in this episode was the slow and very moderate reaction of the ICRC. Firstly, it took the organisation a week to publicly declare that it had not been part of *Operación Jaque* (this is the name the government assigned to this release operation) and then the ICRC reacted in a written communiqué in which they argued that the emblem was recognised by the Geneva Conventions and its Additional Protocols, and that it had to be respected under all circumstances and should never been used by anyone. The ICRC reminded everyone that respect for this emblem allows ICRC's representatives to have access to victims of the civil conflict and to protect them.[38] In a radio interview, an ICRC representative declared that the organisation accepted the government's apologies and that it would not initiate legal action against the Colombian government.

The ICRC reaction was criticised by many for being too soft with the government.[39] The organisation never stated, for instance, that the

[38] 'Emblema de la Cruz Roja tiene que ser respetado en todas las circunstancias, recordó la entidad', *El Tiempo*, 16 July 2008.

[39] Yaned Ramírez, 'Engaño en "Jaque" podría haberse hecho sin usar el emblema, dice representante de CICR en Colombia', *El Tiempo*, 15 August 2008.

misuse of the emblem constituted a war crime according to the Geneva Conventions and that it could endanger the work of official humanitarian workers in the future. The ICRC insisted that they preferred private exchanges with the parties to the conflict and in this non-denunciatory spirit they did not want to be part of the public debate which was taking place.[40] In fact, the incident was over when, in Geneva, Red Cross spokesman Florian Westphal declared that 'it was important for us that this clarification was made by the Colombian authorities at the highest level' and said that the international organisation accepted the Colombian government's explanation.[41] The ICRC strategy on this occasion was to avoid further confrontation with the government, at least publicly, in order to keep working with governmental authorities in its effort to provide relief to the victims of kidnappings.

At the beginning of 2006, the ICRC and the Colombian government had another confrontation during the release of another group of hostages. On this occasion, the government seriously threatened the liberation of hostages when it broke the agreement with the ICRC and allowed the overflight of military aeroplanes in the area where a humanitarian commission was supposed to meet the guerrilla group assigned to release the hostages.[42] This information was given to the press by members of this humanitarian commission and the ICRC only when the final release of the hostages was over. They stated that, indeed, the military overflights were a source of tension. The written communiqué ends by stating that 'the ICRC insists that it was the excellent collaboration between the parties and the people involved in this process that permitted the release of these hostages'.[43] The government continued supporting ICRC's activities that would facilitate the hostages' return to their homes and it made public its trust towards this organisation and its humanitarian activities.[44] As Forsythe suggests, this is due to the fact that 'authorities often cooperate with the ICRC because they know that the organisation will not interfere with, or have important impact on, the

[40] Ramírez, 'Engaño en "Jaque"'.

[41] 'Colombian Soldier Wore Red Cross Logo in Hostage Rescue', *The New York Times*, 17 July 2008.

[42] 'Se permitieron sobrevuelos comerciales, no militares, responde la Cruz Roja a Juan Manuel Santos', *El Tiempo*, 6 February 2009.

[43] 'Se permitieron sobrevuelos comerciales'.

[44] L. G. Forero, 'Cita de Uribe con jefe de la Cruz Roja Internacional', *El Tiempo*, 28 January 2010.

major issues at stake in the conflict concerned'.[45] Additionally, for a government that was accused internationally of being openly hostile to these humanitarian organisations, being able to say they were co-operating with the ICRC was always an asset. Not publicly challenging the behaviour of the government was, in turn, the price the organisation had to pay in order to advance more discreet tactics that allowed them access to the victims of this war.

Even though some analyses of the role of humanitarian organisations advocate total independence from states,[46] the ICRC has adopted in Colombia a pragmatic approach in which they discretely negotiate with both parties to the conflict (state and insurgency) in order to provide safeguards for the humanitarian space without losing independence, and this has produced a mutually beneficial relationship.[47]

It is important to highlight that these understandings between the government and the ICRC were exceptional during the Uribe administration. This government implemented a policy of containment against international criticism of its own record in terms of human rights violations that led it to have a very hostile and contentious relationship with humanitarian organisations and human rights advocacy groups.[48] As part of this containment strategy, the government constantly accused human rights and humanitarian organisations of being the political arm of insurgent groups. In 2002, the government expelled three human rights activists from the country;[49] in 2003, the Minister of Defence announced the beginning of an investigation that attempted to determine the 'real' identity of human rights NGOs and their links with so-called terrorist organisations; by 2008, Uribe himself accused human rights organisations of being 'human rights traffickers', organisations with a political façade that would only hide their cowardice – he called them 'politicians serving terrorism's interests'.[50] It is indeed very noteworthy that the ICRC never had an episode of open confrontation with the

[45] Forsythe, 'The ICRC: a unique humanitarian protagonist', 76.

[46] David Rieff, *A Bed for the Night: Humanitarianism in Crisis* (Simon and Shuster, 2003).

[47] Michael Barnett, 'Review Essay: What is the Future of Humanitarianism?', *Global Governance* 9 (2003): 401–416.

[48] Sandra Borda, 'Política exterior y derechos humanos en Colombia: un manual para la contención de la presión internacional', in *Derechos humanos en la política exterior. Seis casos latinoamericanos*, eds. Natalia Saltalamacchia and Ana Covarrubias (Mexico: ITAM/Miguel Angel Porrúa, 2011), 123–60.

[49] 'Deportan y Expulsan a Tres Españoles', *El Tiempo*, 18 September 2002.

[50] 'La Ira presidencial', *Revista Semana* 1115, 15 September 2003.

government when most of the other organisations working in Colombia did. Forsythe explains this difference in a very eloquent way:

> Pierre Boissier wrote that the organisation (the ICRC) was conscious of its need for cooperation from public authorities and therefore was careful not to proceed beyond the realm of their consent. Yet victims of war and of power politics are victimised precisely because of the policies of these same public authorities. It is precisely these governments that have killed millions in the past decades. That is why advocacy groups like Amnesty International and Human Rights Watch, that also do not run service programmes inside states, believe in a more adversarial relationship with states that features attempted public pressure – the naming and shaming game. They believe in the necessity of uncomfortable conflict, while the ICRC's neutral protection is based on hope for quiet co-operation.[51]

In spite of this, in the following section I explore the only instance of direct and open confrontation between the ICRC and the government, a public discussion about the nature of the Colombian conflict that put at risk the very presence and activities of this and other humanitarian organisations in the country.

5. Conflict or terrorism? The struggle on the definition of the Colombian confrontation

As was discussed at the beginning of this chapter, part of the strategy that the Colombian government implemented in order to obtain additional military resources from the United States to fight its war against insurgent groups was to frame[52] the Colombian conflict in terms of the global

[51] Forsythe, 'The ICRC: a Unique Humanitarian Protagonist', 72.

[52] According to Goffmann, frames are employed as attempts to strategically construct some parts of one's own experience in a way that is compatible with the counterpart's world-view, mainly in order to obtain what is desired from it. The party then presents itself to its counterpart in a planned and calculated manner by using frames or, as Goffmann conceptualises them, definitions of situations built in accordance with principles of organisation which govern events – at least social ones – and our subjective involvement in them. Erving Goffman, *Strategic Interaction* (Philadelphia: University of Pennsylvania Press, 1969), 155.

For instance, states tend to engage in framing with powerful states in order to obtain military and logistic support from them. State parties to conflicts assess the powerful state, read its intentions, unveil its priorities and then attempt to present themselves, through the interaction, in a way that allows them to coordinate their actions with the actions and preferences of the powerful state. By framing its own motivations and actions in a way that resonates with the powerful state's own motivations and actions, state parties to the conflict construct a world-view they share with other international actors;

war against terror. By defining the insurgent organisations as terrorist groups the government attempted to undermine their status as political actors and also to obtain resources from a hegemony, the United States, that would find a terrorist discourse much closer to its own interests (especially after 9/11) than a civil-war approach with no international connotations. However, even though the 'terrorisation' of the Colombian conflict shortened the distance between Colombia and the United States and facilitated an unprecedented flow of resources, it provoked an almost immediate clash between the government and humanitarian and human rights organisations. For these organisations, the definition of the Colombian struggle as a civil war was of fundamental importance in order to force the parties to the conflict to comply with international humanitarian law. *Additional Protocol II* of the Geneva Conventions clearly states in Part I, Article 1, that its scope is the protection of victims of armed conflicts that take place in 'the territory of a High Contracting Party between its armed forces and dissident armed forces or other organised armed groups which, under responsible command, exercise such control over a part of its territory as to enable them to carry out sustained and concerted military operations and to implement this Protocol'.[53] If the Colombian situation was accepted as one in which only terrorist groups operate against the state, these organisations would lose a strong and precise legal framework such as Protocol II, that regularly provides the set of criteria they could use to monitor and evaluate the parties' behaviour during war. Without this legal framework, there would be no standards by which to observe and judge the behaviour of both actors, insurgency and government, in times of war. Humanitarian and human rights organisations would lose their leverage.

This debate over the definition and nature of the Colombian conflict lasted for most of the Uribe administration. In June 2003, the United Nations Human Rights High Commission office in Colombia revealed a document entitled 'On the Importance of the Humanitarian Principle that Distinguishes an Internal Armed Conflict'. In it, the office asserted that there was an internal armed conflict in Colombia and not just

and by doing this, they obtain the expected payoff or, to be more precise, political, military and logistic support to fight the insurgency in their countries. This is the case of the Colombian government and its framing of the domestic conflict as part of the global war on terror post 9/11. Borda, *La Internacionalización de la paz y de la guerra.*

53 *Additional Protocol to the Geneva Conventions of 12 August 1949, and Relating to the Protection of Victims of Non-International Armed Conflicts (Protocol II)*, 1125 UNTS 609, Article 1.

organisations using terrorist tactics. Moreover, it concluded that this distinction was crucial to distinguish combatants from non-combatants, to protect the civilian population, and to hold illegal armed groups and state armed forces accountable in terms of international humanitarian law. This document was a clear response to President Uribe who, weeks before, had declared 'we do not call this violence a conflict. We do not recognise the actors with the title of combatants. They are terrorists.'[54] In February 2005, President Uribe reiterated that it was not valid to define terrorists (guerrilla groups) as equal opponents when there is a legitimate democracy and a state that obeys the rule of law. By May 2005, the ICRC entered the controversy and, from Geneva, the organisation responded to the president by stating that there was an internal conflict in Colombia and that, consequently, all the parties to this conflict were obliged to respect international humanitarian law instead of treating this set of norms as a political instrument.[55] In the middle of this debate, some media outlets even stated that one of the direct implications of not recognising the Colombian confrontation as a civil or internal conflict was that humanitarian organisations such as the ICRC would be expelled from the country.[56]

Later in 2005, the government went even further in defining the 'rules of the game' for international actors present in Colombia at that time in its effort to define the Colombian confrontation as terrorism and not internal conflict. It distributed to all diplomatic corps by e-mail a memo entitled 'Guidelines for the Approach of International Cooperation Projects Developed in Colombia'. In it, the government tried to deter the use of diplomatic language that did not agree with the official position. Explicitly, it stipulated that diplomatic missions in Colombia should not use the term 'armed conflict' or 'non-state actors', 'armed actors', or 'actors in conflict' since, according to the government, the use of this terminology would place these illicit groups in the same position as public legal forces. Terms such as 'civil protection', 'communities of peace', 'peace territory', 'humanitarian regions or fields', and 'observatory of humanitarian situation' were defined as ambiguous and, according to the memo, they should not be used by the international community when setting the standards for international cooperation.[57] Roberto

[54] 'Guerrilla si es combatiente', *El Tiempo*, 1 July 2003.

[55] 'Sí hay conflicto: Cruz Roja Internacional', *El Tiempo*, 5 May 2005.

[56] 'Orinoquía: en guerra o amenazada', *El Tiempo*, 17 May 2005.

[57] Bibiana Mercado, 'Gobierno busca alinear lenguaje diplomático', *El Tiempo*, 13 June 2005.

Meier, UNHCR's delegate in Colombia, responded by saying publicly that the agency would leave the country if it received this same set of instructions through traditional diplomatic channels (i.e. the Minister of Foreign Affairs). He also revealed that the document was not signed and it was not legally binding.[58]

In spite of the government's position, international and humanitarian organisations – including the ICRC – insisted on the necessity of recognising the Colombian confrontation as an internal conflict and continued advocating compliance with international humanitarian law. With the arrival of a new government in 2010, this debate has practically vanished. New president Juan Manuel Santos has publicly accepted the definition of Colombia's confrontation as a civil war and has committed himself to comply with human rights and international humanitarian law.

6. Conclusions

In this chapter I propose a two-step conceptual argument. Firstly, I have argued that the intensification of the war and the absence of a solid and credible peace proposal by any of the parties to a conflict pushes humanitarian organisations to reaffirm publicly their identity and principles, and to be more vocal about their role in the context of widespread military hostilities. Second, I have stated that, under these circumstances, the tension between humanitarian groups' objective of gaining access to victims and their goal of denouncing human rights abuses becomes even stronger due to the intensification of the military and political confrontation. To be sure, it is more difficult to find a middle ground or an overlapping area between the necessity to negotiate with parties to the conflict in order to gain access to victims, and their commitment to denounce these same parties' violations of international humanitarian law. Hence, humanitarian organisations are pushed more systematically towards one or the other extreme of this continuum. A combination of these two arguments suggests that humanitarian and human rights organisations, under a situation of acute military confrontations and no prospects for peace, would tend to be more vocal and to state publicly their own choice in terms of prioritising either direct provision of aid or public denunciation of abuses.

[58] 'Circular del Comisionado podría causar la salida de Acnur del país', *El Tiempo*, 17 July 2005.

I have selected the ICRC to show how, during the Uribe administration, this organisation was pushed further away from denunciation and made great efforts to send public messages about having access to victims as their main goal and about being willing to practise discretion in order to gain this access. I did this by illustrating how increasing military hostilities made it even more difficult for the ICRC to gain access to victims, by showing how the hostage situation constituted a scenario for this organisation to publicly state the limits and scope of its activities and its interest in access over denunciation and, finally, by referring to the only instance of confrontation between the ICRC and the government on the definition and nature of the civil conflict.

However, in order to further prove this point, it would be necessary to observe how human rights organisations interested more in denunciation than in the direct provision of assistance also followed the same path of publicly defining and refining their own identity as human rights advocacy groups. Following the idea that identity construction is always a relational and a social process, then it is possible to state that a change in the nature of the relationship between these organisations and the government would necessarily produce new forms of presenting these organisations' selves, as Goffman puts it. If the ICRC went through the process of presenting itself in the context of the Colombian conflict as an organisation that prioritises access over denunciation and constantly chose the former over the latter, then it is expected that organisations which prioritise denunciation over access would engage in the same sort of public presentation of themselves.[59]

In addition, it would also be crucial to observe how these organisations construct their own identities and how they present themselves in contexts of peace processes accompanied by cessation of military hostilities, or peace processes amidst military aggression. Further comparative research about the relationship between these organisations in Colombia and in other contexts is necessary in order to grasp more effectively the impact of the dynamics of conflicts over human rights and humanitarian organisations' behaviour.

59 Borda, 'Política exterior y derechos humanos en Colombia'.

18

Humanitarian assistance and failed states: still an issue of sovereignty? The case study of Haiti

HANS-JOACHIM HEINTZE

1. Introduction

The Republic of Haiti, which came into being as an independent state in 1804, is a country of grinding poverty in the Caribbean. It shares the island of Hispaniola with the Dominican Republic, which gained independence from Haiti in 1844. With a total area of 27,750 square km, Haiti is roughly the size of Belgium. It has a population of 9.7 million, with a substantial proportion – 2.5 million people – concentrated in the Port-au-Prince metropolitan area. Haiti's gross domestic product (GDP) of approximately 6.69 billion US dollars is low compared with that of its neighbour, the Dominican Republic, which, with roughly the same population size as Haiti, is achieving an annual GDP of around 45.72 billion US dollars.

Some four million Haitians live abroad, mainly in the United States. This is one of the reasons why the country's fate has generated such interest worldwide. Haiti's severe poverty and decades of political instability are other factors which have prompted the international community to focus attention on Haiti. Frequent natural disasters have worsened conditions in Haiti, but none had such devastating effects as the earthquake in January 2010.

On 12 January 2010, Haiti was hit by an earthquake measuring 7.0 on the Richter scale. The earthquake's epicentre was located close to the densely populated capital, Port-au-Prince. Most of the city was destroyed. The country's already poor infrastructure collapsed, making it extremely difficult to deliver aid to the victims. According to figures published by the Haitian government at the end of March 222,570 people died as a result of the natural disaster and 300,572 were injured.[1] In other words, despite having occurred in such a small area, the earthquake caused

[1] See: www.haitispecialenvoy.org/key_statistics.

almost as many deaths as the tsunami in the Indian Ocean in late 2004, which affected an entire world region and claimed some 226,000 lives. The number of casualties in the Haiti earthquake will never be determined precisely, however.

The earthquake also destroyed or badly damaged around 60 per cent of the buildings in the capital. According to the United Nations (UN), three-quarters of the one million people made homeless by the disaster have received emergency shelter from international aid organisations.

The disaster which befell Haiti on 12 January was caused by one of the natural events which are by no means uncommon in this world region. However, its appalling impacts were exacerbated by Haiti's status as what the literature commonly terms a 'failed state'. Throughout its history, Haiti has been beset by political instability, with frequent interventions by the United States, which exercised de facto control over Haiti from 1915 to 1934. The United States' role was then taken over by various oppressive Haitian leaders, who ruthlessly exploited the country.[2] After a series of coups, the first free elections in Haiti took place in 1990, and were won by President Jean-Bertrand Aristide. He assumed office in February 1991 but was overthrown by a military coup in September the same year. This was followed by human rights violations on a massive scale, prompting the Organisation of American States (OAS) to condemn the actions of the military.

The United Nations General Assembly also stressed the illegality of the coup and consequently refused to recognise the new regime. However, a Security Council response to the situation was blocked by China and India, which – along with various Latin American states – viewed the situation as an internal matter for Haiti. It was only when the grave human rights violations created a large-scale exodus of Haitian refugees to the United States that the Security Council finally took action, also in response to a request from Haiti's own Permanent Representative. Invoking Chapter VII of the *United Nations Charter*, the Security Council finally imposed an oil and arms embargo on Haiti. This brought the ruling generals to heel and forced them to agree to negotiations with the United States. The outcome was the Governors Island Agreement, which included a commitment that President Aristide would be restored to power.[3]

[2] Julia Leininger, 'Haiti, Conflict', in Online *Max Planck Encyclopedia of Public International Law*, www.mpepil.com.

[3] Hans-Joachim Heintze, 'Völkerrecht und demokratische Staatsordnung, Anmerkungen anlässlich des internationalen Engagements zur Wiederherstellung der Demokratie in Haiti', *Verfassung und Recht in Übersee*, 1 (1996), 6.

However, the military regime reneged on the agreement, so the Security Council adopted Resolution 940 (1994) authorising military intervention by a multinational force.[4] The United States-led force entered Haiti unopposed, forcing the departure of the military regime shortly before any actual fighting began. Aristide was reinstated, but Haiti remained a fragile state, suffering unprecedented levels of corruption, mismanagement and crime under Aristide's presidency.

After Aristide rigged the vote in the 2000 elections, fighting broke out and the situation in Haiti steadily deteriorated. By 2004, almost half the country was under rebel control, and Aristide was forced into exile.

In order to support Haiti's reconstruction, the United Nations Security Council voted to deploy various (military) missions. The United Nations Stabilisation Mission in Haiti (MINUSTAH), established by Security Council Resolution 1542 on 30 April 2004, should be mentioned in particular.[5] MINUSTAH was deployed after Aristide's departure, because the Security Council deemed the situation in Haiti to be a threat to peace and security in the region. It was also responding to an official request from acting President Boniface Alexandre asking for a multinational peacekeeping force for Haiti. MINUSTAH's mandate was to restore a secure and stable environment, to promote the political process (democratic elections, decentralisation), and to monitor the human rights situation. At operational level, all the activities of the various United Nations agencies were coordinated by MINUSTAH.[6] In the early days, this innovative mission faced great difficulties in stabilising the situation.

It was only after coercive measures were taken to create a secure and stable environment that improvements were achieved. Nonetheless, the security situation remained fragile, and attempts to disarm the militias and criminal gangs were unsuccessful. Measures to set up a functioning police force and establish the rule of law also faltered.[7]

The Security Council has regularly extended MINUSTAH's mandate, most recently with the adoption of Resolution 2012 on

[4] See Simon Chesterman, Thomas M. Franck, David M. Malone, *Law and Practice of the United Nations* (New York: United Nations, 2008), 360.

[5] Security Council (S/RES/1542), 'The Question Concerning Haiti', 30 April 2004.

[6] Cf. Harvey Langholtz, Boris Kondoch and Alan Wells, *International Peacekeeping, The Yearbook of International Peace Operations*, vol. II (Leiden: Martinus Nijhoff Publishers, 2007), 404 *et seq*.

[7] Julia Leininger, 'Democracy and UN Peace-Keeping – Conflict Resolution Through State-Building and Democracy Promotion in Haiti', in *Max Planck Yearbook of United Nations Law 10*, eds. Armin von Bogdandy and Rüdiger Wolfrum (2006), 517.

14 October 2011.[8] While welcoming the fact that some progress has been achieved after the earthquake, the Security Council has determined on each occasion that the situation in Haiti still constitutes a threat to international peace, and it therefore continues to act under Chapter VII of the *United Nations Charter*.

2. International attempts of state-building

In general political theory, states are defined as political and legal associations with effective sovereignty over a geographic area and populations which comply with the following three qualifications: a defined territory; a permanent population; and government. They are bound by the provisions of international law in their relations with other states, and they regulate their internal affairs in accordance with the principles of self-government. There is currently no legal definition of what constitutes a failed state, but various attempts have been made to describe it.[9]

Such entities lack 'functioning statehood'. Their internal governance structures are collapsing or have never been fully established. The state's monopoly on the use of force – a fundamental achievement of humankind – no longer exists, or never existed at all. A 'failed state' lacks government institutions with the capacity not only to take but also to enforce decisions. The vacuum created by the absence of effective governance is filled by chaos and anarchy, interspersed with despotic excesses resulting from intermittent attempts to restore order. Notionally, however, the failed state continues to exist, for it retains its legitimacy in the eyes of the international community despite its inability to govern at home.[10]

This legitimacy is guaranteed by the international community, not least because – especially in light of the large number of 'quasi-states' – the regulatory concept of a community of sovereign states would otherwise be called into question. The countries frequently mentioned in this context, besides Haiti, are Somalia and Afghanistan. These are states whose existence in law will continue until their peoples, invoking the right of self-determination, establish a new state. With a view to maintaining international stability, the international community has an interest in functioning statehood and supports it in a variety of ways.

[8] Security Council (S/RES/2012), 'The Question Concerning Haiti', 14 October 2011.

[9] Malcolm N. Shaw, *International Law*, 6th ed. (Cambridge University Press, 2008), 196.

[10] Daniel Thürer, 'Failing States', in Online *Max Planck Encyclopedia of Public International Law*, www.mpepil.com.

Therefore the Security Council underlines in its Statement of the President S/PRST/2011/7 of 6 April 2011:

> The Security Council reaffirms its strong commitment to the sovereignty, independence, territorial integrity and unity of Haiti, and emphasises that the Government and people of Haiti bear the primary responsibility for the attainment of peace and stability, and for the recovery efforts in Haiti. The Council acknowledges the contribution the international community is making to support the stabilisation process in Haiti, including the strengthening of its legislative, judicial and executive institutions.[11]

This statement reflects the importance of a long-term approach. The cutback of the international involvement is in many cases premature. In the literature, such state-building is defined as a catalogue of measures which aim to stabilise a system of government, without necessarily being based on western ideas of democracy.[12] Nation-building, on the other hand, is intended to create a consciousness – in the sense of a national identity – which supports the consolidation of a state and also includes democracy-building and economic development.[13]

However, creating a properly functioning state is a complex task, even with massive political, military and economic support from the international community. An effective state-building strategy must be based on a deep understanding of the country in question, its history, society, and culture. In the initial stages of international involvement, knowledge of Haiti was quite poor among the international actors.

However, Haiti is no exception, as the example of Afghanistan vividly demonstrates. During the cold war, the superpowers were unable to resist the temptation to exploit the political conflicts in Afghanistan for their global power games. The Soviet Union committed massive military resources in a ten-year effort to shore up what it saw as an ideologically acceptable regime in Afghanistan, while the United States supported the opposing forces which later evolved into the Taliban. These forces, in turn, emerged as the victors in the civil war which followed the Soviet withdrawal and turned against the United States and its allies.

[11] Security Council (S/PRST/2011/7), 'Statement by the President of the Security Council on the Question Concerning Haiti', 6 April 2011.

[12] Simon Chesterman et al., *Making States Work: From State Failure to State-Building*, 16. United Nations University, International Peace Institute Policy Papers, July 15, 2004: www.ipinst.org/publication/policy-papers/detail/140-making-states-work-from-state-failure-to-state-building.html.

[13] Amitai Etzioni, 'A Self-restrained Approach to Nation-building by Foreign Powers', *International Affairs* 80 (2004): 7.

This history of intervention is part and parcel, as well as an expression, of state failure in Afghanistan. The threat that Afghanistan, as a failed state, poses to its own people, its neighbourhood and indeed to global stability is now obvious. In Somalia, too, the failure of the state has become an international threat, as is evident, not least, from the problem of piracy in the Gulf of Aden and far beyond. Yet again, it is becoming apparent that failed states can pose a threat to regional and even to international peace and security. As the examples show, the failure of a state can have various consequences under international law; international or national responses must comply with the principle of proportionality. In Afghanistan, for example, the Taliban regime was overthrown in a military intervention by the United States, prompted by the Taliban's involvement in international terrorism, and was replaced by a new government, whereas the international community has responded to state failure in Somalia by deploying naval units to safeguard the freedom of movement and security of shipping from pirate attacks. However, this is merely a response to the international manifestations of state failure in Somalia. Since the unsuccessful intervention in Somalia in 1992/1993, the international community has shown little desire to help re-establish a functioning state in Somalia or commit any resources for this purpose.

In Haiti, on the other hand, the failure of the state was manifested at other levels, in the form of mismanagement, corruption, violence and a lack of respect for human dignity. Key functions of the state were not performed. The first priority here, then, was to protect the population from the effects of their country's fragile statehood, although the state's inability or its leaders' unwillingness to provide security for their own population had international implications as well. The exodus of refugees and soaring levels of crime began to pose a threat to peace in the region, prompting the international community to intervene on several occasions.

3. Failed states as a threat to peace

Failed states pose a threat to domestic and often external security, and require intensive efforts by the international community to restore a functioning state. Despite the high costs associated with these endeavours, the international community must provide continuous support for this purpose. The objectives and means by which this is achieved must be proportionate and may vary from case to case. The example of Haiti shows that in failed states, the costs of reconstruction, not only after conflicts but also after natural disasters, are far higher than those associated with the provision of consistent support to establish effective systems of governance.

The large-scale exodus of refugees triggered by the massive human rights violations after the military coup in 1991 prompted the United Nations Security Council to adopt Resolution 940 (1994) authorising humanitarian intervention in Haiti,[14] led by the United States. The stated aims were to reinstate the democratically elected President, Jean-Bertrand Aristide, and to end the human rights violations. At first glance, it might seem that the Security Council was intent on enforcing the Haitian people's right to a democratic form of government. However, such an impression is misleading.[15]

Failed states are a highly unsuitable field for experimenting with western-style democratisation. In failed states, the main priority is to establish institutions which enable the populace to live in conditions compatible with human dignity, with the problems of democratic state-building being addressed only as the next step.[16] In Haiti, it became apparent that in 1994, the expectations of what Aristide's democratically elected government could or would achieve were too high. The international community and particularly the United States were relying on rapid democratisation taking place in a country which, in practice, was still characterised by colonial structures. Due to mismanagement by Aristide's government, valuable time that could have been spent on building institutions of governance was wasted.

Numerous United Nations missions – starting in 1996 with Resolution 1063 and including efforts to safeguard Haiti's elections and the establishment of a United Nations Civilian Police Mission in Haiti (MIPONUH) under Resolution 1141 (1997), later extended by Resolution 1277 (1999)[17] – were also unable to provide any real guarantee that the

[14] Security Council (S/RES/940), 'Authorisation to Form a Multinational Force under Unified Command and Control to Restore the Legitimately Elected President and Authorities of the Government of Haiti and Extension of the Mandate of the UN Mission in Haiti', 31 July 1994.

[15] Daniel Erikson, 'The Haiti Dilemma', *Brown Journal of World Affairs* 10 (2004): 285 *et seq.*

[16] Marina Ottaway, 'Rebuilding State Institutions in Collapsed States', *Development and Change* 33 (2002): 1001 *et seq.*

[17] Security Council (S/RES/1063), 'The Situation in Haiti, 28 June 1996'; Security Council (S/RES/1141), 'The Situation in Haiti', 28 November 1997; Security Council (S/RES/1277), 'The Situation in Haiti', 30 November 1999.

Haitian government would perform the state's functions effectively. Finally, following the outbreak of violence in 2004, Resolution 1542 authorised the establishment of MINUSTAH under Chapter VII of the *United Nations Charter*.[18]

The mission has been extended on a year-by-year basis ever since. Under MINUSTAH's mandate, the United Nations' objective, with this mission, is to pursue an ambitious exercise in nation-building. Hence in the preamble to Resolution 1892 (2009), the Security Council underlines the contribution to political stability and consolidation of democracy in Haiti.[19] The list of tasks to be performed by this United Nations mission reads like a nation-building textbook, for it makes reference to promoting democratic dialogue between key stakeholders in the country, achieving significant progress on the rule of law, public safety and public order, institutional reform and development. Other objectives include security sector reform, the establishment of a judicial reform programme to strengthen the administration of justice, and measures to tackle crime, human trafficking and the threats along Haiti's land and sea borders. To monitor implementation of this broad mandate, the Security Council appointed former United States President Bill Clinton as Special Envoy for Haiti.[20]

To what extent these objectives have been fulfilled is a matter for debate. The fact that after the earthquake, the United Nations Secretary-General, speaking on 29 March 2010, said that renewal, not restoration of the status quo ante, should be the goal for Haiti, is telling.[21] MINUSTAH has faced a similar problem to all the United Nations' missions: the expectations of what it could achieve were too ambitious, and the available resources were inadequate. Nonetheless, the list of objectives certainly points in the right direction to overcome the collapse of governance in Haiti and restore a functioning state.

The rudimentary nation-building process was savagely interrupted by the earthquake. This disaster befell a state which was already barely functioning. In particular, it had never been in a position to fulfil its obligation to guarantee the protection and security of its citizens or

[18] Security Council (S/RES/1542), 'The Question concerning Haiti', 30 April 2004; Jochen A. Frowein, Nico Krisch, 'Article 39', in *The Charter of the United Nations*, 2nd ed., ed. Bruno Simma (Oxford University Press, 2002), 723 *et seq*.

[19] Security Council (S/RES/1892), 'The Question concerning Haiti', 13 October 2009.

[20] UN Doc. (S/2009/439), §86.

[21] Ban Ki-moon, 'Renewal, not Restoration, Should be the Goal for Haiti', *Washington Post* 29 (March 2010).

enforce the rule of law. In consequence, the impacts of the natural disaster were bound to be more devastating here than in countries with a properly functioning system of governance. Sadly, nature itself supplied evidence to support this hypothesis in March 2010, when another major earthquake occurred on the same continent, this time in Chile. Chile's functioning system of governance and institutions meant that the relief effort could be organised swiftly, limiting the extent of the human suffering. By contrast, the people of Haiti were helplessly exposed to the appalling aftermath of the earthquake. The international dimension of this natural event as a threat to peace also cannot be ignored. Inevitably, many Haitians were attempting to leave the country.

4. Obligations concerning humanitarian aid

Natural and man-made disasters can endanger or claim human lives and do not stop at national borders. A theoretical and practical distinction is often made between the provision of emergency relief in response to natural disasters, and humanitarian assistance in the context of wars and conflicts.[22] In Haiti's case, however, this distinction does not apply. Here, both forms of assistance are required, for the natural disaster has simply exacerbated – albeit dramatically – the existing conflicts. In such a situation, the humanitarian dimension must, as a matter of principle, be the priority. This raises the question of the obligations of the affected country and the international community under international law.[23] Doubtless there is a general duty to cooperate in cases of disaster relief and Article 5 of the ILC constitutes such an obligation.[24] However, the exact extent of the obligation is still under discussion.

4.1. Obligation to provide information

The affected country has an obligation, under customary international law, to notify other states of the event and its effects.[25] This obligation

[22] Budislav Vukas, 'Humanitarian Assistance in Cases of Emergency', Online *Max Planck Encyclopedia of Public International Law*, www.mpepil.com.

[23] Karel Wellens, 'Revisiting Solidarity as a (Re-)Emerging Constitutional Principle: Some Further Reflections', in *Solidarity: A Structural Principle of International Law*, eds. Rüdiger Wolfrum, Chie Kojima (Heidelberg: 2010), 17.

[24] UN Doc. (A/CN.4/652), §17.

[25] Andreas von Arnauld, 'Völkerrechtliche Informationspflichten bei Naturkatastrophen', *Archiv des Völkerrechts* 43 (2005): 279 *et seq.*

arises from each state's responsibility to protect the lives and physical integrity of the people living on its territory and, where relevant, elsewhere, if the event also endangers people outside the affected state's own jurisdiction. The threat to human life is the truly dramatic aspect of natural disasters. However, the obligation to notify other states depends, in turn, on the affected state having functioning institutions, for the data that form the basis of risk assessment and mitigation can only be collected and analysed if sovereign powers are being exercised effectively throughout the affected state's territory. By definition, a failed state affected by a natural disaster will require assistance from the international community, especially from the highly developed countries. In Haiti's case, this obligation fell primarily on the United States, which, since the overthrow of President Aristide in 1991 and the ensuing mass exodus in the direction of the United States, has scaled up its use of satellite-based intelligence systems in order to remain fully informed about developments in this western-hemisphere country. During a disaster, this kind of intelligence can be crucially important for the organisation of relief operations, and may even be helpful in detecting signs of an impending disaster, thereby supporting mitigation of its impacts. Against this background one has to claim that the highly developed countries should utilise all the scientific, technical and technological options at their disposal to provide failed states affected by disasters and humanitarian organisations with the information required for relief operations; this should take place as swiftly as possible and no charges should be imposed. The same applies to early warning and disaster prevention systems.

The obligation to provide information can also be seen as an outflow of the duty to cooperate, which is mentioned in Article 17 of the final ILC Draft Articles on the Law of the Transboundary Aquifers: 'States shall provide scientific, technical, logistical and other cooperation to other States experiencing an emergency. Cooperation may include coordination of international emergencies actions and communications, making available emergency response personnel, emergency response equipment and supplies, scientific and technical expertise and humanitarian assistance'.[26] The *Tampere Convention* constitutes a duty to prompt telecommunication assistance to mitigate the impact of a disaster.[27]

[26] UN Doc. (A/63/10) §53. [27] See UN Doc. (A/CN.4/652) §90.

4.2. Obligation to provide humanitarian aid

In accordance with the principle of humanity, the international community is obliged to provide assistance to the victims of disasters. The Geneva Conventions (Articles 23 and 55 in particular) and Article 70 of the *Additional Protocol I* impose a fundamental obligation on states to ensure and allow the passage of humanitarian aid. The Geneva Conventions apply in situations of armed conflict. The regulations concerning humanitarian assistance in cases of natural disasters are not that developed. The United Nations argues that the positive law remains unclear and the doctrine is clearly divided.[28] Even Eduardo Valencia-Ospina, the Special Rapporteur on the Protection of Persons in the Event of Disasters comes, against the background of many legally non-binding resolutions, to the conclusion that concerning the entitlement to humanitarian assistance 'it could be said to be implicit in international human rights law'.[29]

However, the provision of humanitarian aid must comply with the principles of impartiality, independence and neutrality which means that, in general, it should not be undertaken by states themselves. States must, however, assist humanitarian operations. The principle of humanity not only provides the moral and legal basis for the provision of aid; it also prohibits discrimination in such provision.[30]

It is immaterial which group or faction the victims belong to: aid must be provided on an impartial basis. It must also comply with the principle of proportionality; in other words, based on identified needs, the weakest and most vulnerable must be assisted first.[31] In order to fulfil these requirements, humanitarian organisations must be independent and must not be subject to states' control or supervision. They must also uphold the principle of neutrality, which means that they must not take a position in a conflict.[32] This is particularly important in the case of armed conflicts, but also applies to natural disasters.[33]

[28] UN Doc. (A/CN.4/590), 11 December 2007, §251.

[29] UN Doc. (A/CN.4/598), 5 May 2008, §54.

[30] Peter Macalister-Smith, *International Humanitarian Assistance: Disaster Relief Actions in International Law and Organisation* (Dordrecht: Martinus Nijhoff Publishers, 1985), 52 *et seq*.

[31] Robin Coupland, 'Humanity: What is it and How Does it Influence International Law?', *International Review of the Red Cross* 844 (2001): 969 *et seq*.

[32] Heike Spieker, 'Humanitarian Assistance, Access in Armed Conflict and Occupation', Online *Max Planck Encyclopedia of Public International Law*, www.mpepil.com.

[33] UN Doc. (A/46/182), 19 December 1991.

Aid is not divorced from politics, however. After all, besides the humanitarian organisations, a range of other actors such as government representatives, United Nations organisations or multinational forces are also involved in the provision of aid, all of whom pursue political interests.

A key factor in the politicisation of humanitarian aid is that when major disasters such as the Haiti earthquake occur, cooperation between the aid agencies and assisting countries' armed forces is unavoidable. In such cases, the mandate governing the military operation, which is decided at political level, invariably clashes with the principles of independence, impartiality and neutrality which govern the work of humanitarian non-governmental organisations.

Furthermore, the mass media also have a politicising effect, since politicians and non-governmental organisations are keen to show themselves in a good light.[34] Aid agencies are heavily dependent on donations to carry out their relief operations and rely on the media to broadcast their appeals and reach their target audience. Indeed, humanitarian assistance is popular with the general public in countries that provide relief, and the public offers generous emotional and financial support for 'humanitarian' operations. When it comes to securing a share of the available funds, however, there are no holds barred: all the humanitarian agencies attempt to exert influence and compete to raise their profile via the mass media. This makes it almost impossible to present a more detailed, critical and nuanced picture. Natural disasters in failed states or military dictatorships should not be seen as an opportunity to voice criticism of conditions in these countries.

The cyclone which caused devastation in Myanmar (Burma) on 2 May 2008, for example, became a vehicle for a political campaign against the country's leaders, who had brutally crushed opposition to the regime the previous year. After the cyclone, the country's military leaders refused to allow international aid organisations to operate freely in the country. This prompted sharp criticism from the western countries, with French Foreign Minister Bernard Kouchner even calling for the 'Responsibility to Protect' (R2P) to be invoked as the basis for the delivery of humanitarian aid, if necessary against the will of the military government.[35] As a

[34] Adam Roberts, 'The Role of Humanitarian Issues in International Politics in the 1990s', *International Review of the Red Cross* 833 (1999): 19 *et seq.*

[35] Alpaslan Özerdem, 'The "Responsibility to Protect" in the Context of Natural Disasters: Another Excuse for Interventionism?', unpublished conference paper presented at the

consequence of this campaign, the real issue, namely the relief operation itself, largely faded from view. In fact, the humanitarian organisations were able to deliver their aid as far as the – albeit completely over-stretched – airport in Rangoon. From there, it was transported into the affected areas by local staff, with whom the aid agencies had been cooperating very effectively for many years. The politically motivated campaign against Burma's leaders tended to disrupt the provision of aid. The fact that the country's leaders used the relief operation to gain the goodwill of the people and therefore concealed the actual origin of the goods by re-labelling them did not alter the fact that aid did arrive in the country and that it was inappropriate to use the crisis as an opportunity to voice criticism of its leaders. The outcome of the political campaign against the military leaders was a regrettable decline in the willingness to donate on the part of the public in the donor states, who had gained the impression that the aid was not reaching the victims.

Therefore politicians must resist the temptation to link humanitarian aid for victims of a natural disaster with political demands for regime change or improvements in the human rights situation. Access to the media must be used solely to draw attention to the humanitarian crisis and thus encourage the general public to give the requisite support to the relief operation.

5. Humanitarian assistance, state-building and human rights

The term 'humanitarian' is in vogue in modern international law. Undoubtedly, this is associated with the emergence of human rights as a new branch of international law over the past sixty years. In reality, these rights impose drastic conditionality on state sovereignty. Respecting human rights is now one of the fundamental obligations of every state, and includes the duty to protect the rights of all persons under its jurisdiction. In light of this obligation, which must be fulfilled unconditionally, the question which arises is, what happens if a state is unwilling or unable to comply with this obligation.[36] In failed states, the latter, at least, is often the case. As recent state practice shows, in such cases the

World Conference of Humanitarian Studies, Groningen (2009), 14 *et seq*. For a discussion of Myanmar see Zwitter and Lamont's contribution to this volume.

[36] Peter-Tobias Stoll, 'Responsibility, Sovereignty and Cooperation – Reflections on the Responsibility to Protect', in *International Law Today: New Challenges and the Need for Reform?*, eds. Doris König et al. (Berlin: Springer, 2008), 12.

international community may consider that it has no option but to intervene using all necessary means – including military means – in accordance with the provisions of the *United Nations Charter*, even though Article 2, paragraph 7 and Article 2, paragraph 4 of the *United Nations Charter* prohibit intervention in matters which are essentially within the domestic jurisdiction of any state, as well as the unilateral use of force in international relations.

A key feature of modern international law is that its enforcement is centred on a system of collective security within the United Nations framework. In this system, a legal relationship is established between the individual members, i.e. all the states currently in existence. The members pledge that they will uphold the norms enshrined in the *United Nations Charter*. In the event of these norms being violated, law-abiding countries can seek to influence the behaviour of the law-breaker via the organs of the system of collective security, in accordance with the principle of proportionality. The most stringent sanctions are envisaged in cases when international peace is violated or threatened; in such cases, the relevant body representing the international community, namely the United Nations Security Council, can compel – by military or non-military means – the state concerned to revert to law-abiding behaviour.[37]

In 'classic' international law, only inter-state conflicts were regarded as a threat to peace, with aggression by one state against another being viewed as a breach of the peace. This changed after the end of the cold war: from then on, the full potential of the *United Nations Charter* could be used to protect human rights. The implications of this development were revealed with particular clarity in the case of Somalia, where the dictator Mohamed Siad Barre had been overthrown in 1991, leading to a complete collapse of law and order. The capital Mogadishu was destroyed in the ensuing inter-clan fighting, which lasted for some time. The war and drought caused famine, but anarchy and violence prevented international aid from getting through. When the United Nations Secretary-General was informed about the conditions in the country, he put the issue on the Security Council agenda. A number of states refused to address the issue of Somalia on the grounds that the United Nations was prohibited from intervening in member states' internal affairs. This objection lost its impact, however, when Somalia's own chargé d'affaires

[37] Kurt Mills, *Human Rights in the Emerging Global Order: A New Sovereignty*? (Houndmills: Palgrave Macmillan, 1998), 166 *et seq*.

at the United Nations ultimately requested the Security Council to turn its attention to the human tragedy unfolding in his country. As this sequence of events shows, the majority of countries continue to respect others' sovereignty, including that of failed states. Finally, with the adoption of Resolution 794 on 3 December 1992, the Security Council authorised member states to deploy a military intervention force to enable the delivery.[38]

This was an historic decision: for the first time, a government's inability to fulfil its responsibility to protect the people under its jurisdiction was regarded as a threat to regional peace. In 1992, the Security Council authorised the United States to assume command of the military operation, known as 'Restore Hope'. Differences of opinion arose over its mandate, however, and although the mission was successful in that the Somali people were supplied with aid, it was unsuccessful to the extent that it failed to rebuild a functioning state in Somalia. This failure was due to the fact that the military was not given a clear mandate on how to deal with the warlords and clan chiefs. Furthermore, no effort had been made to analyse the causes of the conflict or Somalia's social structures; instead, one of the clan leaders, quite arbitrarily, was held responsible for the conflict.

The deployment of the military had tragic consequences for the further provision of humanitarian aid once the acute crisis had abated. Due to the military's role in enforcing the delivery of aid, the traditional and well-functioning contacts between regional warlords/clan chiefs and the humanitarian organisations which had been operating in the country for years were interrupted. After the abrupt withdrawal of the troops – which was viewed by the warring factions as a victory and by the United States as a defeat – it proved impossible to re-establish these relationships, which were based on mutual recognition, to their former extent. This had a detrimental effect on the provision of humanitarian aid.[39]

Thus policy-makers must ensure that the opportunities afforded by the *United Nations Charter* to safeguard human rights in accordance with R2P are utilised. As the first step, this means that grave human rights

[38] Christiane Philipp, 'Somalia – a Very Special Case', in *Max Planck Yearbook of United Nations Law 9*, eds. Armin von Bogdandy and Rüdiger Wolfrum (Berlin, Heidelberg: Springer, 2005), 517 *et seq.*

[39] Adam Roberts, 'The United Nations and Humanitarian Intervention', in *Humanitarian Intervention and International Relations*, ed. Jennifer I. Welsh (Oxford University Press, 2006), 71 *et seq.*

violations must be defined as a threat to peace. Adequate resources must then be deployed to safeguard human rights, possibly including the use of military force under a United Nations mandate. Military interventions must be subject to clear and precise rules of engagement.

6. Sovereignty of failed states in crisis situations

A key issue to be addressed is to what extent the sovereignty of a failed state poses an obstacle to international engagement: 'By its very nature, cooperation is likely to appear in conflict with the sovereign prerogatives in the recipient State'.[40] Therefore Article 9 of the ILC Draft Article on the Protection of Persons in the Event of Disasters places the affected state by virtue of its sovereignty at the forefront of all assistance, and limits other actors to a complementary role.

In the case of Haiti, for example, President René Garcia Préval expressed frustration that the Haitian government had been bypassed in the coordination of the relief effort, while Ecuador's President Rafael Correa lambasted what he saw as 'imperialism among the donors'.[41] A particular criticism was that most of the money donated goes back to the donor countries. This criticism raises further questions: to what extent can and should the government of a failed state be involved in humanitarian relief operations? And where should the goods distributed as part of the relief effort come from? Legally, even failed states are sovereign states. Thus the United Nations Security Council, in the preamble to its Resolution 1892 (2009) states explicitly that it reaffirms 'its strong commitment to the sovereignty, independence, territorial integrity and unity of Haiti'.

This implies that the aid must be coordinated, as a matter of principle, with the (national) government of the failed state concerned. However, this responsibility is likely to overwhelm the government, since it does not exert effective control over the entire national territory. Furthermore, the country's rudimentary government institutions are invariably discredited in the eyes of the populace due to mismanagement, corruption and criminal associations. Therefore the strengthening of the institutions was one of the most urgent claims of the international community.[42]

[40] UN Doc. (A/CN.4/652) §21.

[41] 'Haitis Präsident fühlt sich übergangen', *Die Zeit*, 30 January 2010, www.zeit.de/gesellschaft/zeitgeschehen/2010-01/haiti-gewalt-beziehungen-schule.

[42] 'Haiti: The Stakes of the Post-Quake Elections', *International Crisis Group*, Report No. 35 (Washington, 2010), 18.

A further factor undermining the state's capacities to deal with the aftermath of the earthquake was that large numbers of Haiti's local police were victims of the disaster. One of the most serious problems affecting the relief effort, besides the collapse of Haiti's infrastructure, therefore proved to be the total absence of public security and law and order. As a consequence, it was impossible to guarantee the systematic provision of aid to those in need.

Thus the problems in Haiti reaffirmed the increase in demand for international humanitarian assistance. The impact of natural disasters has dramatically increased.[43] To that extent, the immediate acceptance of the United States' offer to deploy 11,000 troops in Haiti is understandable. A further 4,000 troops followed at the end of January. The troops' mandate was clearly defined: to maintain order and support the distribution of emergency supplies. The troops were present on the streets and distributed food, although this was not coordinated with the humanitarian organisations and fell short of professional standards, in that aid was not distributed to those in need in a planned manner but was handed out indiscriminately.

This in turn caused such scenes of chaos that the humanitarian organisations were forced to temporarily suspend their systematic, needs-based distribution of food aid, which was based on ID cards as proof of entitlement. The question, then, is why the armed forces' role was not restricted to maintaining order but also included involvement in the distribution of humanitarian aid. This can only be explained in terms of the general chaos prevailing in Haiti and the United States' attempt – for domestic policy reasons – to demonstrate that it was actively assisting its neighbour. A further factor may have been the desire to increase the local population's acceptance of the presence of foreign troops by having them play a role in the relief operation, thus reducing the risk of food riots and clashes between aid-workers and people desperate for help. The criticism voiced by Venezuela and Bolivia, which described the deployment of United States troops as an occupation, is unfounded: as the operation was approved by the Haitian government, this view lacks any legal basis. Haiti's sovereignty was respected, despite the deployment of foreign troops in the country. It may be necessary to deploy armed forces to help mitigate the impacts of disasters. This must be based, as a matter of principle, on a United Nations Security Council mandate and must

[43] Randolph Kent et al., *The Future of Humanitarian Assistance: The Role of the United Nations* (New York: United Nations, 2004), 6.

respect the sovereignty of the state concerned. The troops' mandate must be clearly defined and coordinated with the humanitarian organisations. The priority is to create a secure and stable environment in order to ensure that aid genuinely reaches those in need and does not contribute to the emergence of a 'crisis economy'.

7. Humanitarian aid and state failure in Haiti

The earthquake reversed efforts to establish functioning state structures in Haiti and created chaotic conditions, which persisted for some time. Due to the lack of a functioning state, many people have had no option but to remain in the devastated downtown area of the capital, Port-au-Prince. They were forced to personally defend their legal claims to the plots of land where their homes once stood. As the land registers no longer existed and Haiti had no administration, they simply waited around in the ruins of their homes, in appalling and unhygienic conditions. With the hurricane season just around the corner, the outbreak of epidemics was almost inevitable. Nonetheless, people were unwilling to move to the refugee camps being set up outside the city, for by doing so, they are likely to lose what is left of their property. It would also put them at even greater risk of falling victim to crime. In the capital, due to the lack of a police presence, they had formed private neighbourhood militias to provide at least a modicum of security.

The conditions in Haiti showed that the humanitarian operation, on its own, was not able to assist the victims of the disaster in accordance with its own principles. Under these conditions, it was not always those in greatest need who got priority access to aid, as there was no system of local governance to provide a guiding hand. The international relief effort began immediately after the disaster, and its coordination swiftly passed to the United Nations Office for the Coordination of Humanitarian Affairs (OCHA).

Although the United Nations' own team in Haiti was very badly affected by the earthquake, the tasks of assessing needs and coordinating the relief effort very soon began. Difficulties inevitably arose, however, because the government of Haiti was unable to play a joint role with the United Nations in coordinating the relief effort.

The relief operation was intended to supply the victims of the earthquake with basic essentials as quickly as possible. In this particular case, key priorities were search and rescue, the provision of accommodation, security, food and clean water. Mainly due to the lack of a police presence, these tasks could only be implemented to a partial extent. Normally, the reconstruction phase would begin around ten weeks after a disaster. After a major disaster on the scale of the Haiti earthquake, the reconstruction process will last for many years and will require close cooperation with the country's government. The participation of local politicians and functionaries at every stage of the planning and decision-making process will also support the establishment of a functioning state, especially as components and objectives of the subsequent development process must be integrated into the reconstruction phase. As part of the process, capacity-building by local experts and institution-building are essential in order to reduce vulnerability to future disasters. The psychological effects of the disaster, too, can be overcome most effectively by involving local people in the reconstruction process. This concept, which combines emergency relief, reconstruction and development in a process known as the continuum, obviously makes sense. When it works, it can genuinely contribute to building better governance and a functioning state. To date, however, very little practical experience has been gained with this concept.[44] Emergency relief in Haiti could only make a contribution to building a functioning state because it was linked with reconstruction and development support. Policy-makers had to ensure that the international community and humanitarian organisations remain engaged in Haiti for a longer period of time and are adequately resourced. In order to mitigate the impacts of the earthquake and state failure, local partners were needed who were accepted by the populace and had a measure of authority. Efforts to build better governance and the functioning of the state were therefore accompanied by measures to support the development of a civil society.

8. Consequences of the R2P for Haiti-like crises?

The concept of the international community's R2P has emerged over the past decade. It is derived from the general obligation of all states to protect every individual within their jurisdiction. If a state is unwilling or unable to protect its populations from genocide, crimes against

[44] Verband Entwicklungspolitik deutscher Nichtregierungs-organisationen e.V. (VENRO), 'Linking Relief, Rehabilitation and Development – Ansätze und Förderinstrumente zur Verbesserung des Übergangs von Nothilfe, Wiederaufbau und Entwicklungszusammenarbeit', VENRO-Arbeitspapier 17, February 2006, 3: www.venro.org/fileadmin/Publikationen/arbeitspapiere/arbeitspapier_17.pdf.

humanity, ethnic cleansing or war crimes, the responsibility to protect passes to the international community. In justifying this concept the International Commission on Intervention and State Sovereignty (ICISS) deals with the long history of humanitarian interventions and appreciates its usefulness because it clearly underlines the goal to assist human beings at risk. However, ICISS avoids using the term 'humanitarian intervention', as humanitarian organisations consider this term as an expression of an increasing militarisation.[45]

In the text endorsing the R2P concept, which the United Nations General Assembly voted on in 2005, the international community is represented by the Security Council. The concept developed by ICISS, which formed the starting point for the United Nations resolution, envisaged that following the failure of the Security Council to act, a military intervention may be undertaken by a coalition of law-abiding states as a last resort, with due regard for the principle of proportionality and with the prospect of success. This remains a contentious issue.

What is certain, however, is that the resolution adopted by the General Assembly establishes an obligation for the international community to intervene in cases of grave human rights violations.[46] In Haiti's case, it is beyond doubt that the government does not or cannot guarantee human rights, starting with the security of its citizens and respect for their human dignity. To date, the Security Council has taken action in respect of Haiti by invoking its obligation to maintain international peace.

However, the recognition of R2P offers the opportunity to take action without resorting to this device. It could thus be invoked to justify measures which go far beyond maintaining international peace and security and aim to safeguard human security in the country concerned. In the past, international policy in fragile states like Haiti has been criticised for being too normative and sovereignty-oriented.[47] In accordance with the principle of R2P, the international community should in future start from the premise that failed states' sovereignty is no obstacle to international efforts to establish functioning statehood, if the states concerned cannot fulfil their fundamental obligation to protect their own populations, which is a constituent element of sovereignty. The legal

[45] Kithure Kindiki, 'International Law on Trial: The Darfur Crisis and the Responsibility to Protect Civilians', *International Community Law Review* 9 (2007): 450.

[46] UN Doc. (A/63/677), §50 *et seq.*

[47] Ian Christoplos, Dorothea Hilhorst, *Human Security and Capacity in Fragile States.* Disaster Studies Occasional Paper 01 (Wageningen University Press: 2009), 17.

consequences, however, are quite unclear. Therefore some scholars consider the concept too ambiguous.[48]

Even before the earthquake, the Haitian government was unable to prevent state failure in Haiti. The deployment of MINUSTAH brought about some improvements but did not, in practice, establish a functioning state. The Security Council responded to the natural disaster by adopting Resolution 1908 (2010), which increased the number of troops deployed in Haiti to 8,940 and the police component to 3,711, compared with 6,940 and 2,211 respectively in 2009.[49] It is probably obvious that this was an inadequate response to the chaotic conditions in Haiti.

Against this background the traditional United Nations approach of cooperation with the Haitian government and donor conferences did not meet the challenges. It was estimated that the country needs around 11.5 billion US dollars in aid for comprehensive reconstruction and development over the next ten years. The donor conference in March 2010 secured pledges of around 9.9 billion US dollars, far surpassing expectations. The European Union is the largest donor to Haiti and intends to contribute 1.6 billion US dollars. Motivated by a desire to exert political influence, countries such as Venezuela have pledged substantial sums as well. However, pledges are all very well, but the actual provision of funds is quite another matter. Furthermore, the willingness to donate invariably wanes once the disaster and its tragic individual fates have vanished from the headlines. This happens in all natural disasters once the initial shock has abated, and in Haiti's case is reinforced by the public's mistrust of the government agencies supposedly responsible for reconstruction. In that sense, even the financing of emergency relief could pose problems in Haiti. A further concern is that some potential donors will argue that the Haitian government is not a partner who can be trusted to make appropriate use of donated funds.

The international community's emergency relief operation in Haiti moved into the reconstruction phase in 2010, which required close cooperation with the government and other local agencies. In view of the massive extent of human suffering, there was no time available to test whether this cooperation worked. Therefore one of the lessons of the Haiti disaster is that other forms of international assistance must be considered.

[48] Carlo Focarelli, 'The Responsibility to Protect and Humanitarian Intervention: Too Many Ambiguities for a Working Doctrine', *Journal of Conflict and Security Law* 13 (2008): 192.

[49] Security Council (S/RES/1908), 'The Question Concerning Haiti', 19 January 2010.

There are various possible options. Haiti faced a crisis comparable to the situation in East Timor in 1999. The United Nations had established a mission in East Timor in June 1999 whose mandate was to organise and monitor a referendum on the future of this former Portuguese colony, which was occupied by Indonesia. When the referendum produced a clear majority in favour of independence, pro-Indonesian militias embarked on a campaign of violence and terror, murdering and displacing the people of East Timor. The East Timorese elite in particular fell victim to the massacres.

There was a complete collapse of law and order, and the infrastructure was destroyed. The United Nations mission was also attacked, forcing staff to flee. The Indonesian armed forces, which the government was now powerless to control, not only tolerated the situation, which was in effect a civil war; it was apparent that they were implicated from the start. Finally, after lengthy prevarication, the Indonesian government agreed to the deployment of an international peacekeeping force for East Timor in September 1999.

One persistent criticism levelled at the United Nations was that this deployment came far too late, as the violence perpetrated by the Indonesian militias had been predicted well in advance. After Indonesia renounced all its claims to East Timor in October 1999, its officials were withdrawn, leaving the country without any civil administration. The United Nations Security Council then adopted Resolution 1272 (1999), establishing a United Nations Transitional Administration in East Timor (UNTAET). It was endowed with overall responsibility for the administration of East Timor and was empowered to exercise all legislative and executive authority.

It was mandated to provide security and maintain law and order, to establish an effective administration, to assist in the development of civil and social services, and to ensure the coordination and delivery of humanitarian assistance, rehabilitation and development assistance. The mission was headed by a Special Representative, who was empowered to amend and repeal laws. The original sixteen-month mandate was extended twice. Thus for the first time, a new state was born under the United Nations' administration. Without the United Nations to act as 'midwife', this state-building process would have been impossible. Some authors evaluated the role of the United Nations as an agent for a *sui generis* legal person of the self-determination unit of East Timor.[50]

[50] Ralph Wilde, *International Territorial Administration: How Trusteeship and the Civilizing Mission Never Went Away* (Oxford University Press: 2008), 188.

The question is whether this example could provide some useful ideas to help consolidate the situation in Haiti as well. The scale of the complex emergency in Haiti is such that it exceeded the Haitian government's capacities. Already a failed state prior to the disaster, Haiti needed intensive support from the international community in order to stabilise the situation. In particular, after such a crisis in a failed state, security and protection must be provided for the local population and international aid-workers. The economy must also be rebuilt. With a view to facilitating the requisite coordination and to establish the administration on a secure footing, it would be helpful to consider whether, with the consent of the Haitian government, a temporary international administration for such a fragile state as Haiti should be put in place. Thus one can argue that an international administration should act as the United Nations in East Timor: as the self-determination unit of the people of Haiti. This would be an expression of international solidarity.[51]

9. Conclusions

The funds pledged at the donor conference in March 2010 are intended to help Haiti to move towards a better future after a devastating natural disaster. In this way, the international community is not only fulfilling its humanitarian obligations; by supporting the establishment of a functioning state and good governance, its aim is also to mitigate the threat to peace emanating from Haiti. The massive sums of money pledged are not an a priori guarantee of a successful outcome, i.e. that the people of Haiti will be able to live in peace and dignity in future. Some of these funds must therefore be used to establish a functioning state in Haiti. Humanitarian aid can make a contribution to this process if it forms part of the continuum with reconstruction and development. As a prerequisite, the international community must acknowledge its continued responsibility for Haiti once the initial media interest has waned. It must also strictly monitor the use of funds and work closely with local partners. It goes without saying that the government of Haiti has a key role to play, and that Haiti's sovereignty must be respected. According to

[51] Laurence Boisson de Chaournes, 'Responsibility To Protect: Reflecting Solidarity?', in *Solidarity: A Structural Principle of International Law*, eds. Rüdiger Wolfrum and Chie Kojima (Berlin: Springer, 2010), 109.

the current definition, sovereignty also entails a state's obligation to respect human rights and protect its citizens from natural and man-made disasters. From this, we can derive a right and a duty for the international community to demand and support the establishment of a functioning state also by restricting the sovereignty of a failed state, being a victim of natural disaster. That is the lesson learned from the Haiti earthquake.

19

Principles of neutrality and impartiality of humanitarian action in the aftermath of the 2011 Libyan conflict

KUBO MAČÁK

1. Introduction

Have the principles of neutrality and impartiality of humanitarian action become a myth, a dead concept emptied of its contents due to the reality of modern asymmetrical armed conflicts? This chapter considers the events of the Libyan civil war of 2011 against the legal backdrop of international humanitarian law (IHL) to argue that although these two principles have been placed under severe strain in Libya, any reports of their death would nonetheless be greatly exaggerated. Although the trend of their weakening that has been observed in the wars in Iraq and Afghanistan has in some ways continued, they still constitute, in law and in practice, the guiding principles of humanitarian action.

Neutrality and impartiality of humanitarian action[1] are not strict legal obligations incumbent upon every humanitarian agent acting in situations of extreme human need and suffering. They are, however, generally considered to be 'fundamental principles' or 'pillars' of humanitarian action.[2] They have acquired legal relevance due to their repeated affirmation in numerous international legal documents of both binding and non-binding

I would like to thank Ana Beduschi, Max Forte, Slávka Mačáková, Mona Sadek, Mike Sanderson and Noam Zamir for their time and advice, which they have generously shared with me during the preparation of this paper.

1 In this chapter, 'humanitarian action' is understood narrowly as action aimed to protect the victims of armed conflicts by providing them with food, water, sanitation, shelter, health services and other forms of emergency assistance as well as by ensuring that violations are monitored and addressed, but excluding measures whose implementation carries a political charge such as post-conflict development and social work.

2 See, e.g., Kenneth Anderson, 'Humanitarian Inviolability in Crisis: The Meaning of Impartiality and Neutrality for UN and NGO Agencies Following the 2003–2004 Afghanistan and Iraq Conflicts', *Harvard Human Rights Journal* 17 (2004): 41.

nature. Actors that have thus committed themselves to adhere to these principles include various states,[3] the United Nations (both through its General Assembly[4] and the Security Council[5]), the European Union,[6] the International Committee of the Red Cross (ICRC),[7] and a plethora of humanitarian non-governmental organisations (NGOs).[8] As 'fundamental principles of the Red Cross', they have been given further recognition in the Geneva Conventions and their *Additional Protocol I*.[9]

Due to a lack of a generally accepted definition, the content of these principles as understood by the relevant actors may slightly differ. As used in general language, the two terms might even appear synonymous.[10] However, for the purposes of this chapter, we may attempt to delimit their core as follows. The principle of neutrality requires the humanitarian actors to remain ideologically free and to not favour any of the conflict parties.[11] The principle of impartiality requires these actors

[3] See e.g., SFDFA, 'Humanitarian Access in Situations of Armed Conflict: Field Manual – Version 1.0', Swiss Federal Department of Foreign Affairs, 2011, www.cdint.org/documents/PAIV_111118_Humanitarian_Access_FieldManual_mit_Inhalt.pdf., section 3.2; 'Saving Lives, Preventing Suffering and Building Resilience: The UK Government's Humanitarian Policy', UK Department for International Development, 2011, www.dfid.gov.uk/Documents/publications1/1/The UK Government's Humanitarian Policy September 2011_Final.pdf, 6.

[4] A/RES/46/182, 1991, Annex, §2. These principles were frequently reaffirmed by the General Assembly in the following years. See e.g., A/RES/51/194, 1996, preambular §12; A/RES/58/114, 2003, preambular §4; A/RES/60/124, 2005, preambular §4; A/RES/61/134, 2006, preambular §4; A/RES/62/94, 2007, preambular §3; A/RES/63/139, 2008, preambular §3; A/RES/66/119, 2011, preambular §3.

[5] UN SC PRSt 1997/34, 19 June 1997, 2; S/RES/1296, 2000, preambular §11; UN SC PrSt 2004/46, 14 December 2004, 2; S/RES/1674, 2006, §21.

[6] *Treaty on the Functioning of the European Union*, Article 214(2) (hereinafter 'TFEU').

[7] XXth International Conference of the Red Cross, 'Proclamation of the Fundamental Principles of the Red Cross', *IRRC* 56 (1965): 573–4.

[8] See e.g., 'MSF Charter', *MSF*, 3 January 2011, www.msf.org/msf/articles/2011/03/the-medecins-sans-frontieres-charter.cfm; 'IOM Migration Crisis Operational Framework', IOM, Res. 1243 (CI), 27 November 2012; 'Organisation Report', International Rescue Committee, June 2011, http://rootcause.org/documents/DR-IRC.pdf.

[9] *Geneva Convention I*, Article 44(2); *Geneva Convention IV*, Article 63(1)(a); *Additional Protocol I*, Article 81(2)-(3) (hereinafter 'GC' and 'AP', respectively).

[10] See, e.g., 'Neutral', Thesaurus.com, http://thesaurus.com/browse/neutral ('Definition: *impartial*, noncommital') (emphasis added).

[11] Marion Harroff-Tavel, 'Neutrality and Impartiality – The Importance of These Principles for the International Red Cross and Red Crescent Movement and the Difficulties Involved in Applying Them', *IRRC* 873 (1989): 537; Anderson, 'Humanitarian Inviolability', 56; Council of the European Union, Joint Statement by the Council and the Representatives of the Governments of the member states meeting within the Council, the European Parliament and the European Commission: The European Consensus on

to provide aid only on the basis of, and in proportion to, the need of the victims.[12] The two principles are thus complementary[13] and are aimed to ensure the distribution of assistance irrespective of the prevailing political or military balance or perceived military necessity[14] and, correspondingly, to protect the safety of humanitarian actors by maintaining their perception as being concerned solely with the needs of the victims.[15]

The importance of humanitarian principles thus cannot be overstated. However, in recent discourse, commentators have mourned their demise, arguing that they are no longer followed by the relevant state and non-state actors. For example, Kurt Mills complained in 2005: 'The traditional ideals of neutrality, impartiality, and independence have become myth. Rather than being at the margins of conflict, humanitarianism is now embedded within contemporary conflict. States use humanitarian norms and actors for their own ends.'[16] The two defining large-scale wars of the first decade of the twenty-first century, Iraq and Afghanistan, have occasioned a wave of criticism decrying the abandonment of impartiality and neutrality in those conflicts. Critics have highlighted as problematic the instrumentalisation of humanitarian action by western militaries,[17] conflation of humanitarian and development roles of humanitarian agents,[18] and the general blurring of lines between political, military, and humanitarian agendas.[19]

Humanitarian Aid, OJ 2008 C 25/1, C 25/2, §12 (hereinafter 'The European Consensus on Humanitarian Aid').

12 Harroff-Tavel, 'Neutrality and Impartiality', 538; Anderson, 'Humanitarian Inviolability', 56; The European Consensus on Humanitarian Aid, §13.

13 Due to their complementarity, this chapter generally considers the two principles together, except where expressly stated otherwise.

14 Anderson, 'Humanitarian Inviolability', 56.

15 Alice Gadler, 'Armed Forces as Carrying Both the Stick and the Carrot? Humanitarian Aid in US Counterinsurgency Operations in Afghanistan and Iraq', *Goettingen Journal of International Law* 3-1 (2011): 227.

16 Kurt Mills, 'Neo-Humanitarianism: The Role of International Humanitarian Norms and Organisations in Contemporary Conflict', *Global Governance* 11-2 (2005): 161.

17 Vincent Bernard, 'Editorial: The Future of Humanitarian Action', *IRRC* 884 (2011): 892; Fiona Terry, 'The International Committee of the Red Cross in Afghanistan: Reasserting the Neutrality of Humanitarian Action', *IRRC* 881 (2011): 175; Mills, 'Neo-Humanitarianism', 177–9.

18 Antonio Donini, 'Between a Rock and a Hard Place: Integration or Independence of Humanitarian Action?', *IRRC* 881 (2011), 152; Anderson, 'Humanitarian Inviolability', 42–3.

19 Claudia McGoldrick, 'The Future of Humanitarian Action: An ICRC Perspective', *IRRC* 884 (2011): 966; Anderson, 'Humanitarian Inviolability', 64; Gadler, 'Armed Forces', 231.

This is the background of the analysis provided in this chapter, which is divided into three main sections. Section 2 provides the legal framework applicable to the provision of humanitarian action during the Libyan conflict from the perspective of IHL. Section 3 analyses how principles of neutrality and impartiality of humanitarian action have been respected by the quantitative and qualitative nature of aid provided in Libya by external actors. Section 4 analyses to what extent the conflict posed a challenge to neutrality and impartiality with respect to agents of humanitarian action, contrasting the different problems faced by humanitarian agencies on the one hand and multi-purpose actors on the other. The conclusion draws lessons to be learned from the analysis presented and supports as its basis the central claim of this chapter: that the two principles, even if badly battered during the war, are still alive and kicking.

2. Legal framework

Norms of IHL apply only in situations of armed conflict. In order to analyse humanitarian action provided in the scope of the Libyan war of 2011 through the lens of IHL, we thus first need to determine which phases of violence since its outbreak in February of that year met the legal criteria for one of the two main types of armed conflict.[20] It is argued here that the situation in Libya became a non-international armed conflict (NIAC) towards the end of February. The NIAC between the government and the rebel forces was then complemented by an international armed conflict (IAC) between the state of Libya and the foreign intervening forces. It is as of now factually unclear whether the growing collusion between the intervening states and the Benghazi-based insurgents surpassed the level required to transform the latter into another party of the IAC. In any event, norms of NIAC and IAC both applied to the events in Libya at various times.[21]

The NIAC in Libya commenced when the fighting reached a level of intensity and when the rebels achieved a level of organisation required by

[20] On classification of armed conflicts, see generally Dapo Akande, 'Classification of Armed Conflicts: Relevant Legal Concepts', in *International Law and the Classification of Conflicts*, ed. Elisabeth Wilmshurst (Oxford University Press, 2012), 32–79.

[21] The analysis in this section is based on a recent article on the qualification of the Libyan conflict, co-written by the present author. See Kubo Mačák and Noam Zamir, 'The Applicability of International Humanitarian Law to the Conflict in Libya', *International Community Law Review* 14–4 (2012): 403.

law and international jurisprudence.[22] The intensity requirement was met when non-violent protests in several Libyan cities grew into armed confrontations in late February 2011, with heavy armed forces deployed by the government[23] and with the insurgents forcefully taking over garrisons and towns all across Libya.[24] The organisation requirement was met when the resistance fighters formed geographically rooted militias (*kataeb*) led by military commanders and capable of enforcing compliance with IHL within their ranks.[25] In addition, opposition armed forces established themselves in the eastern city of Benghazi and by late February they were controlling several other cities including Shahat, Tobruk, and Misrata.[26] The key requirement of partial territorial control, triggering the applicability of *Additional Protocol II*, was thus also met by that point of time in Libya.[27]

According to the International Criminal Tribunal for the former Yugoslavia (ICTY)'s interpretation of the terms of Common Article 2 to the Geneva Conventions, an IAC begins when there is 'a resort to armed force between States'.[28] In the Libyan conflict, this situation materially came about on 19 March, when the United States, the United Kingdom,

[22] *Tadić* (Jurisdiction Appeal) IT-94-1-AR72 (2 October 1995), §70 ('[A non-international] armed conflict exists whenever there is . . . *protracted* armed violence between governmental authorities and *organised* armed groups or between such groups within a State'; emphases added).

[23] See e.g., 'Libya Unrest: Scores Killed in Benghazi "Massacre"', BBC, 20 February 2011, www.bbc.co.uk/news/world-africa-12517327; 'Report: Libya Air Force Bombs Protesters Heading For Army Base', *Haaretz*, 21 February 2011, www.haaretz.com/news/world/report-libya-air-force-bombs-protesters-heading-for-army-base-1.344775; STRATFOR, 'Unrest and the Libyan Military', *STRATFOR*, 21 February 2011, www.stratfor.com/analysis/20110220-unrest-libyan-military.

[24] Arab Organisation for Human Rights, 'Report of the Independent Civil Society Fact-Finding Mission to Libya' (January 2012), §48; UN Human Rights Council, 'Report of the International Commission of Inquiry to Investigate All Alleged Violations of International Human Rights Law in the Libyan Arab Jamahiriya', UN Doc. (A/HRC/17/44) 12 January 2012, §28, 55.

[25] UN Human Rights Council, 'Report of the International Commission of Inquiry on Libya', UN Doc. (A/HRC/19/68), 2 March 2012, Annex I, §61–63 (hereinafter 'International Commission of Inquiry March 2012 Report').

[26] Alexander Diados, 'Benghazi, Cradle of Revolt, Condemns Gaddafi', *The Star*, 23 February 2011, http://thestar.com.my/news/story.asp?file=/2011/2/24/worldupdates/2011-02-23T222628_01_NOOTR_RTRMDNC_0_-550982-4&sec=Worldupdates (confirming the establishment of control over Benghazi); International Commission of Inquiry March 2012 Report, §55 (regarding Shahat, Tobruk and Misrata).

[27] AP II, Article 1(1).

[28] *Tadić* (Jurisdiction Appeal), §70; see also Jean Pictet, *Geneva Convention Relative to the Protection of Civilian Persons in Time of War: Commentary* (Geneva: ICRC, 1958), 20.

and France used its naval and airborne forces to attack targets in Libya.[29] The fact that the North Atlantic Treaty Organisation (NATO) assumed formal and operational control of all international forces on 31 March did not change the qualification of the conflict; it only made NATO a party to the conflict, equally bound by the rules of IHL.[30] For now, it remains an open question whether this parallel IAC merged at some point with the NIAC described in the previous paragraph. A plausible argument to that effect could be made if it were proven that the rebels forfeited their operational autonomy and accepted a degree of control by NATO.[31] However, the reports of the establishment in Benghazi of a 'joint operations centre', allegedly tasked with the co-ordination of NATO and rebels' operations against Gaddafi, have not been authoritatively confirmed to this day.[32]

On this basis, this chapter considers the situation in Libya as featuring two parallel conflicts, a NIAC between the government and the rebels, and an IAC between the government and the intervening forces. The IHL obligations of this triangle of conflict parties, including the duties pertaining to the provision of humanitarian assistance, thus differed depending on the conflict pair that formed the factual background for the relevant events. The main difference relevant for our purposes, besides the generally more robust and detailed regulation of IACs, is the requirement of state consent to humanitarian assistance provided in its territory in the scope of a NIAC.[33]

[29] See, e.g., 'Allied Strikes Sweep Libya as West Intervenes in Conflict', *The Guardian*, 20 March 2011, www.guardian.co.uk/world/2011/mar/19/libya-air-strikes-gaddafi-france; 'Libya: US, UK and France Attack Gaddafi Forces', *BBC News*, 20 March 2011, www.bbc.co.uk/news/world-africa-12796972.

[30] For detailed analysis, see Mačák and Zamir, 'The Applicability', 416–8.

[31] The cooperation between NATO and the rebels would thus meet the 'overall control' test propounded by the jurisprudence of ICTY, which requires (1) the provision of financial and training assistance, military equipment and/or operational support to the non-state party and (2) the participation in the organisation, coordination or planning of military operations by the intervening state. See *Tadić* (Appeal Judgement) IT-94-1-A (15 July 1999), §131, 145, 162.

[32] See Bruno Waterfield, 'Libya: British Military Advisers Set up "Joint Operations Centre" in Benghazi', *The Telegraph*, 18 May 2011, www.telegraph.co.uk/news/worldnews/africaandindianocean/libya/8521977/Libya-British-military-advisers-set-up-joint-operations-centre-in-Benghazi.html (confirmation by the UK); Maher Chmaytelli and Peter S. Green, 'Libya Rebels, NATO Don't Have Joint Operations, Official Says', *Bloomberg*, 16 April 2011, www.bloomberg.com/news/2011-04-16/libya-rebels-nato-don-t-have-joint-operations-official-says.html (confirmation by the rebels and denial by NATO).

[33] See subsection 4.1 below.

3. Nature of humanitarian action

The Libyan conflict affected virtually the entire territory of the state of Libya. Civilians living in almost all areas of the country were exposed to the dangers of armed violence and to shortages of basic supplies and services including, among many other things, food, water, fuel and medical attention. Both sides of the conflict in official statements repeatedly acknowledged the dire nature of the situation and requested outside humanitarian assistance. For example, Lynn Pascoe, the United Nations Under-Secretary-General for Political Affairs, reported in May 2011 to the United Nations Security Council that the Libyan government demanded from the United Nations to arrange for the resumption of the supply of fuel to 'ensure the continuation of basic services' and that the rebel-led National Transitional Council complained that it had 'only 40 per cent of the funds needed to cover its budget for April and May'.[34] Both sides continued to report severe shortages and requested later that the Libyan state assets that had been frozen under the terms of the United Nations Security Council resolution 1973 (2011)[35] be released and used 'to meet humanitarian needs'.[36]

Although it is beyond the scope of this chapter to provide a definitive assessment of the humanitarian aid provided to the individual belligerents in Libya, a number of indications cast a shadow on the purported neutrality and impartiality of the assistance provided in two different but intertwined ways. These relate to the qualitative and quantitative nature of aid provided during the conflict.

3.1 Quantitative assessment

The first problematic quantitative aspect is that the majority of aid designated for Libya originated in those countries that participated in the multinational military intervention that ended up supporting the insurgents. Out of ten European countries that contributed the most,[37] only two did not take part in the NATO-led military operations: Germany and Finland,[38] of which the latter has long been committed

[34] UN Doc. (S/PV.6541), 31 May 2011, 2. [35] See n. 111 below.

[36] UN Doc. (S/PV.6595), 28 July 2011, 2.

[37] 'Humanitarian Aid in Libya: How Much Has Each Country Donated?', *The Guardian*, 22 August 2011, www.guardian.co.uk/news/datablog/2011/aug/22/libya-humanitarian-aid-by-country.

[38] 'Nato Operations in Libya: Data Journalism Breaks Down Which Country Does What', *The Guardian*, 22 May 2011, www.guardian.co.uk/news/datablog/2011/may/22/nato-libya-data-journalism-operations-country.

to a policy of military neutrality and non-alignment.[39] It could plausibly be objected that countries that intervened militarily only happened to be those that ordinarily provide humanitarian aid, in line with the general trend according to which it is the global west that provides the majority of aid.[40] This objection, however, only brings us to the second problematic aspect, namely that the rebels and areas under their control profited disproportionately more from international aid than the government and government-controlled areas.

In large part, this disproportion arose from the actions of an informal 'contact group' established in late March 2011[41] and comprised of about forty nations that made no secret of their dislike of Gaddafi.[42] At its meeting in June 2011, the members of the contact group pledged more than 1 billion dollars in support for the Libyan opposition.[43] In addition, at the behest of this group,[44] the rebels were allowed to benefit from about 1.5 billion dollars of Libyan assets that were unfrozen by the Sanctions Committee of the United Nations Security Council in August 2011.[45]

It also appears from early reports from the conflict that virtually all outside assistance was intended for the eastern, rebel-controlled part of Libya[46] and that as the conflict was underway, areas controlled by the

39 Marco Wyss, 'Military Transformation in Europe's Neutral and Non-Neutral Allies', *The RUSI Journal* 156–2 (2011): 46–7. The Finnish foreign minister expressed the support of his country for the UN Security Council Resolution 1973, 2011 but stated that this support 'would take the form of humanitarian aid, including help with the evacuation of refugees'. Hans Lödén, 'Reaching a Vanishing Point? Reflections on the Future of Neutrality Norms in Sweden and Finland', *Cooperation and Conflict* 47–2 (2012): 275–6.

40 Cf. Bernard, 'Editorial', 891 (noting that the headquarters of all main humanitarian agencies are in the western world).

41 UN Doc. (S/PV.6509), 2.

42 'Libya: Gaddafi Must Step Down, Says "Contact Group"', *BBC News*, 14 April 2011, www.bbc.co.uk/news/world-africa-13058694.

43 '$1 Billion Is Pledged to Support Libya Rebels', *The New York Times*, 9 June 2011, www.nytimes.com/2011/06/10/world/africa/10diplo.html?_r=0.

44 'US Seeks to Aid Libyan Rebels With Seized Assets', *The New York Times*, 5 May 2011, www.nytimes.com/2011/05/06/world/africa/06diplo.html?_r=0; 'Diplomats In Rome Discuss Aid To Libyan Rebels', *National Public Radio*, 5 May 2011, www.npr.org/2011/05/05/136011941/diplomats-discuss-aid-to-libyan-rebels.

45 See UN Doc. (S/PV.6606), 30 August 2011, 3 (UN Secretary-General's confirmation of the unfreezing).

46 See, e.g., 'French Aid Bolsters Libyan Revolt', *The New York Times*, 28 February 2011, www.nytimes.com/2011/03/01/world/europe/01france.html; 'Opposition in Libya Struggles to Form a United Front', *The New York Times*, 8 March 2011, www.nytimes.com/2011/03/09/world/africa/09rebels.html.

government suffered from worse shortages than their better-supplied rebel-held counterparts.[47] These facts in combination therefore indicate that the aid designated to alleviate the hardships of the Libyan conflict originated disproportionately in the countries intervening in support of one side of the conflict and that it benefited disproportionately persons associated with that side.

3.2 Qualitative assessment

Qualitatively, some of the aid disbursed to the rebels, but not to the government forces, exceeded what can legitimately be considered humanitarian assistance and constituted assistance of the kind that could significantly affect the insurgents' war effort. According to the International Court of Justice (ICJ)'s ruling in *Nicaragua* v. *United States of America*, provision of assistance going beyond 'food, clothing, medicine and other humanitarian assistance', and especially of 'weapons, weapons systems, ammunition, or other equipment, vehicles, or material which can be used to inflict serious bodily harm or death' cannot be considered as humanitarian aid.[48] Their provision to the rebels would thus amount to unlawful interference with the internal affairs of Libya and to a violation of the principles of impartiality and neutrality.

But perhaps such assistance could be justified on the basis of the Security Council authorisation contained in Resolution 1973. The arguments that the international coalition overstepped the mandate to protect civilians and civilian-populated areas given to it by the Security Council in order to effectuate regime change in Libya will be discussed below.[49] However, is it correct to argue that the enabling resolution, understood as limited to the civilian-protection aim, allowed for the transfer of military supplies *in furtherance of this mandate*? If such aid was permitted by the terms of the resolution, this permission would prevail over the requirements arising from the principles of neutrality and impartiality by virtue of Article 103 of the United Nations Charter.[50]

[47] UN Doc. (S/PV.6595), 28 July 2011, 3.

[48] Military and Paramilitary Activities in and against Nicaragua (*Nicaragua* v. *United States* of America), Merits, Judgment, *ICJ Reports 1986*, §97 and 242.

[49] See section 4.2.1 below.

[50] UN Charter, Article 103; see also Lockerbie case (*Libya* v. *United Kingdom*) (Request for the Indication of Provisional Measures), *ICJ Reports 1992*, 15, §39 (obligations imposed by the Security Council acting under Chapter VII of the UN Charter trump any conflicting international law obligations).

It should be recalled that the predecessor Resolution 1970 expressly established an arms embargo in its operative paragraph 9. Under its terms, any 'direct or indirect supply, sale or transfer' or arms and related materiel to Libya was prohibited, irrespective of who (if anyone) would benefit from such a transaction.[51] It is true that Resolution 1973 authorised United Nations member states to take all necessary measures 'notwithstanding paragraph 9 of resolution 1970 (2011)'.[52] However, as a resolution permitting the use of force in international relations, Resolution 1973 represents an exception from the general prohibition on the use of force[53] and thus its terms should be interpreted restrictively, in line with the general principle of law that exceptions from a rule are to be construed narrowly.[54] The most likely motive for the inclusion of the quoted phrase in the newer resolution was to allow the coalition to transport *their own* military matériel to Libya.[55] Moreover, the resolution does allow the implementing states to act either 'nationally' or 'through regional organisations or arrangements', but it does not, notably, allow for action in collusion with other (sub-state) entities.[56] The narrow interpretation advocated here thus precludes the transfer of military equipment to one of the parties even under the terms of Resolution 1973.[57] It is also in line with the unequivocal statement of the NATO Secretary-General from March 2011 that the resolution did not allow the arming of the rebels, although, admittedly, his view was not shared by all NATO member states.[58]

51 S/RES/1970, 2011, §9. 52 S/RES/1973, 2011, §4.

53 See, e.g., Malcolm N. Shaw, *International Law*, 6th ed. (Cambridge: CUP, 2008), 1123–4.

54 Cf. Roman law principles of *Exceptiones sunt strictae interpretationis* or *Singularia non sunt extendenda.* See also Dan Sarooshi, *United Nations and the Development of Collective Security: the Delegation by the UN Security Council of its Chapter VII Powers* (Oxford University Press, 1999), 44–6 (the requirement of narrow construction of powers delegated by the Security Council is a consequence of the application of the *delegatus non potest delegare* doctrine to the Council); Ben Saul, 'The Legality of the Use of Force against Iraq in 2003: Did the Coalition Defend or Defy the United Nations?', *UCLA J. Int'l L. & Foreign Aff.* 8 (2003): 315 (resolutions authorising the use of force must be construed narrowly to protect the Council's control over its own process).

55 Christian Pippan, 'The 2011 Libyan Uprising, Foreign Military Intervention, and International Law', *Juridikum: Zeitschrift für Kritik-Recht-Gesellschaft* 2 (2011): 167.

56 Cf. S/RES/1973, 2011, §4 and 8.

57 Contra Dapo Akande, 'Does SC Resolution 1973 Permit Coalition Military Support for the Libyan Rebels?', *EJIL: Talk!*, 31 March 2011, www.ejiltalk.org/does-sc-resolution-1973-permit-coalition-military-support-for-the-libyan-rebels/; Pippan, 'The 2011 Libyan Uprising', 167–8.

58 'Confusion Reigns Over Arming Libyan Rebels', *Sky News*, 31 March 2011, http://news.sky.com/story/844958/confusion-reigns-over-arming-libyan-rebels.

There have been a number of reports that outside states provided military assistance to the insurgents in Libya. Few countries expressly admitted doing so. Qatar did in April 2011, seemingly on the basis of its earlier recognition of the National Transitional Council (NTC) as the legitimate government of Libya.[59] It was rightly pointed out, however, that prior to consolidation of control over territory by the rebels, such recognition would have been premature and thus unlawful under international law.[60]

France acknowledged its military aid and attempted to justify it under the humanitarian rationale of protecting the civilians from the government troops.[61] Once the weapons are distributed, however, the donor country has, even if genuine in its aims, very little leverage over how they would eventually be used. What is more, according to journalistic reports and counter to the official proclamations, France had at least contemplated that French arms would be used by the rebels in their efforts to topple the regime in power.[62]

Other countries may have been providing arms and military training to the rebels more covertly. Even prior to the military intervention, the United States, United Kingdom and France were reported to have sent several hundred 'defence advisors' to train and support the insurgent forces in eastern Libya.[63] Additional covert deployments of special forces by Egypt, France, Italy, Qatar, the UAE and the United Kingdom were reported during and after the conflict, usually accompanied by denials from the authorities.[64] Finally, the rebels themselves confirmed having received military assistance from countries 'that supported their uprising', without specifying the exact sources of that support.[65]

[59] 'Libyan Rebels Say They're Being Sent Weapons', *The New York Times*, 16 April 2011, www.nytimes.com/2011/04/17/world/africa/17libya.html.

[60] Stefan Talmon, 'Recognition of the Libyan National Transitional Council', *ASIL Insight*, 16 June 2011, www.asil.org/insights110616.cfm.

[61] 'French Military Air-Dropped Arms to Libya Rebels', *France 24*, 29 June 2011, www.france24.com/en/20110629-french-military-confirms-airdropping-arms-libya-kadhafi-rebel#.

[62] Ibid.

[63] 'US, UK, French Forces Land in Libya', *Pakistan Observer*, 26 February 2011, http://pakobserver.net/detailnews.asp?id=78009.

[64] Paul D. Williams and Alex J. Bellamy, 'Principles, Politics, and Prudence: Libya, the Responsibility to Protect, and the Use of Military Force', *Global Governance* 18 (2012): 291; 'Libyan Rebels "Receive Foreign Training"', Al Jazeera, 3 April 2011, www.aljazeera.com/news/africa/2011/04/201142172443133798.html.

[65] 'Libyan Rebels Say They're Being Sent Weapons', *The New York Times*, 16 April 2011, www.nytimes.com/2011/04/17/world/africa/17libya.html.

It will be a task for historians and perhaps criminal investigators to confirm or deny authoritatively these reports of military assistance to the rebels. For the purposes of this chapter, it is sufficient to say that to the extent that aid to the rebels exceeded the range of permissible humanitarian assistance outlined in *Nicaragua*, it could not be considered justified under general international law or under the terms of Resolution 1973. In addition, as its provision was not mirrored in principle nor in extent by any commensurate aid provided to the governmental side, it cannot be seen as consistent with the principles of neutrality and impartiality, either.

4. Agents of humanitarian action

The conflict posed a further challenge to impartiality and neutrality of humanitarian action with respect to agents of humanitarian action. The two principal types of agents active in Libya were humanitarian agencies, with the ICRC at the forefront, and multi-purpose actors, such as outside states and especially international organisations, featuring prominently the United Nations, NATO, and the European Union. Each of these two types faced somewhat different difficulties relevant to our scrutiny.

4.1 Humanitarian agencies

First of all, humanitarian agencies struggled primarily for equal access to the conflict victims. This section describes some of the problems of access during the conflict and places them within the framework of IHL. The discussion is unavoidably sketchy. On the one hand, the present analysis can correct some of the earlier generalisations such as that the ICRC was able to conduct its operations for the whole duration of air operations in the entire territory of Libya;[66] in fact, the ICRC itself complained several times of difficulties of access.[67] On the other hand, this chapter has no ambition to paint an exhaustive picture of the humanitarian situation in

[66] Bruno Pommier, 'The Use of Force to Protect Civilians and Humanitarian Action: The Case of Libya and Beyond', *IRRC* 884 (2011): 1081.

[67] See, e.g., ICRC, 'Libya: ICRC Makes Urgent Call for Access to Wounded', 24 March 2011, www.icrc.org/eng/resources/documents/update/2011/libya-update-2011-03-24.htm (with respect to most areas affected by conflict in March); ICRC, 'Libya: First Access to the Remote Area of Sabha', 3 June 2011, www.icrc.org/eng/resources/documents/update/2011/libya-update-2011-06-03.htm (with respect to the southern city of Sabha, which the ICRC got to only in June); ICRC, 'Libya: Safe Access Needed to Sirte and Bani Walid',

Libya and examples chosen may be representative, but due to the scope of this chapter they have to remain anecdotal.

Unquestionably, the primary responsibility for the provision of humanitarian aid to the victims of wars lies with the territorial state.[68] This is simply a reflection of the state's sovereignty which entails the responsibility for those living within its territory.[69] In the territory in which the state has lost control to a non-state armed group, such as the NTC-led rebels in the Libyan conflict, this primary responsibility is complemented by a corresponding duty that arises for the non-state actor in question. This can be inferred from 'the dependence of the population on the humanitarian aid offered to it and . . . the principles of humanity and inviolability binding on all parties'.[70] In the Libyan context, the responsibility of both conflict parties to ensure the protection of civilians was underscored by Resolution 1973.[71] In any event, practical impossibility, difficulty or even unwillingness may prevent the conflict parties from fulfilling their primary duties towards the civilian population. In that case, the subsidiary role of relief societies, both domestic and foreign, comes to the fore.[72]

Although the conflict parties are prohibited from using starvation of civilians, broadly understood,[73] as a method of combat,[74] whether or not they are obliged to enable free passage of all humanitarian assistance to all civilians depends on the conflict qualification. In IACs, conflict parties must only grant free passage to medications intended for all civilians, whereas other forms of humanitarian assistance such as foodstuffs and clothing are to be obligatorily granted passage only to specified vulnerable groups of children under fifteen, expectant mothers, and maternity

23 September 2011, www.icrc.org/eng/resources/documents/news-release/2011/libya-news-2011-09-23.htm (with regard to Sirte and Bani Walid in September).

[68] Yves Sandoz, Christophe Swinarski, and Bruno Zimmermann, *Commentary on the Additional Protocols of 8 June 1977 to the Geneva Conventions of 12 August 1949* (Geneva: ICRC, 1987), 1477, §4871 (hereinafter 'APs Commentary').

[69] See, inter alia, A/RES/46/182, Annex, §4.

[70] Ruth Abril Stoffels, 'Legal Regulation of Humanitarian Assistance in Armed Conflict: Achievements and Gaps', *IRRC* 855 (2004): 520.

[71] S/RES/1973, 2011, preambular §4.

[72] GC IV, Article 23; AP I, Article 70(1); GCs, Common Article 3; AP II, Article 18.

[73] The prohibition does not only cover food, but also 'objects indispensable to the survival of the civilian population', including agricultural areas, drinking water installations, and irrigation works.

[74] AP I, Article 54; AP II, Article 14.

cases.[75] All other relief action is 'subject to the agreement of the Parties concerned' in such actions, which naturally includes the belligerent parties.[76] It is debated whether, if the aid offered meets the requisite conditions,[77] the agreement may be withheld only if the aid amounted to a threat to the sovereignty of the target state[78] or for any reason, as long as it is not arbitrary or capricious.[79] In contrast, in NIACs, any and all relief action is always contingent on the consent of the territorial state.[80] Interestingly, there is no corresponding written legal requirement of consent given by the non-state party in control of a part of the territory, although in practice, its consent is clearly indispensable, as well.[81] In any event, by demanding unconditionally that 'the Libyan authorities' ensure the rapid and unimpeded passage of humanitarian assistance,[82] the Security Council has significantly weakened the possibility of the conflict parties claiming a right to deny their consent to offers of relief action.

Perhaps at least partially aware of these considerations, neither of the conflict parties attempted to justify any significant instance of prevention of access by legal arguments going to the necessity *vel non* of consent or agreement given by such a party. It can thus be assumed that neither the government nor the rebels were aware of any justifiable reason for such denials and these measures should accordingly be considered as *prima facie* indications of violations of the rules on humanitarian access.

It should not be denied that relief action may be prevented by objectively existing security-related constraints, especially while hostilities are ongoing. Humanitarian agencies reported the existence of such situations on numerous occasions. For example, the NGO *Médecins Sans Frontières (MSF)* complained that insecurity made it impossible to bring

[75] GC IV, Article 23(1). [76] AP I, Article 70(1);

[77] AP I, Article 70(1) (the civilian population is not adequately provided with fundamental supplies and the aid is 'humanitarian and impartial in character and conducted without any adverse distinction').

[78] APs Commentary, 819, §2805 (basing this interpretation on the *travaux préparatoires* of AP I).

[79] Yoram Dinstein, *The Conduct of Hostilities under the Law of International Armed Conflict*, 2nd ed. (Cambridge University Press, 2010), 227.

[80] AP II, Article 18(2).

[81] Michael Bothe, 'Relief Actions', in *Encyclopedia of Public International Law*, vol. 4, ed. Rudolf Bernhardt (Amsterdam: Elsevier, 1992), 171, cited in Heike Spieker, 'Humanitarian Assistance, Access in Armed Conflict and Occupation', in *The Max Planck Encyclopedia of Public International Law*, ed. Rüdiger Wolfrum (Oxford University Press, 2008, online edition, www.mpepil.com), §29.

[82] S/RES/1973, 2011, §3.

humanitarian aid to Tripoli in February 2011[83] and Misrata and Ras Lanuf in March 2011.[84] Provided that these conditions are not deliberately brought about in order to hamper the provision of aid, they do not result in accountability under IHL and must be accepted as an unfortunate fact of war.[85]

However, certain incidents left no doubt that the parties did not fully respect their access obligations. We will look at three situations in more detail: the beginning of the conflict in February and March, the siege of Misrata by Gaddafi's forces between March and May, and the siege of Sirte by the NTC in September and October.

Firstly, in the first phase of the conflict prior to the international intervention, the Libyan government put on a resolute face towards mounting international pressure, including calls for enabling humanitarian access. It refused to permit the humanitarian convoys to enter those cities, such as Misrata and Ajdabiya, which it was attempting to recapture.[86] Moreover, according to media reports and NGO statements, Gaddafi's forces were preventing medical teams from reaching the wounded in the places of hostilities.[87] These reports would indicate a violation of the rules on humanitarian access by the government at the time.

Following the international intervention in March 2011, the Libyan government agreed to negotiate to allow foreign aid inside the country. The crowning achievement of this effort was an agreement signed with the United Nations on 17 April according to which Libya allowed international humanitarian access to all areas affected by the conflict.[88]

[83] MSF, 'MSF Team in Libya Trying to Reach Areas Affected by Violence', 24 February 2011, www.doctorswithoutborders.org/news/article.cfm?id=5053&cat=field-news.

[84] MSF, 'Libya: Aid Access to Violence-Affected Areas Blocked', 2 March 2011, www.doctorswithoutborders.org/press/release.cfm?id=5076&cat=press-release; 'Libya: MSF Seeking More Ways to Assist Wounded', *MSF*, 8 March 2011, www.doctorswithoutborders.org/news/article.cfm?id=5085&cat=field-news.

[85] Cf. ICRC, 'International Humanitarian Law and the Challenges of Contemporary Armed Conflicts', October 2011, www.icrc.org/eng/assets/files/red-cross-crescent-movement/31st-international-conference/31-int-conference-ihl-challenges-report-11-5-1-2-en.pdf, 24 (observing that security-related constraints are among the main reasons limiting humanitarian access in practice).

[86] Williams and Bellamy, 'Principles, Politics and Prudence', 278.

[87] MSF, 'Libya: Urgent Priority Must Be Given to Doctors and Medical Materials', 25 February 2011, www.doctorswithoutborders.org/press/release.cfm?id=5063&cat=press-release; 'Gaddafi loyalists launch offensive', Al Jazeera, 11 March 2011, www.aljazeera.com/news/africa/2011/03/201131041228856242.html.

[88] UN Doc. (S/PV.6527) 3 May 2011, 3; see also 'Libyan Government Promises Aid-workers Access, UN Says', *BBC*, 19 April 2011, www.bbc.co.uk/news/world-africa-13125616.

In the official government proclamations, Libya insisted that it was acting consistently with this agreement.[89]

Secondly, between the months of March and May, some of the most protracted fighting of the conflict unfolded in the city of Misrata situated on the Mediterranean coast in north-western Libya.[90] Gaddafi's forces placed the city under siege and very early on, a Libyan army general reportedly gave an order not to allow any 'supply cars, fuel and other services to enter the city of Misrata from all gates and checkpoints'.[91] It appears, however, that both sides of the conflict contributed to inflicting hardship on the inhabitants of Misrata. For the most part of the siege, the rebels controlled the access to the city by sea and the government forces were in control of the land access.[92] The United Nations humanitarian chief Valerie Amos complained in April that 'the opposition' was preventing humanitarian access via the city's port.[93] The complaints against the government's conduct during the siege were even more severe. Gaddafi's forces continued to block access to Misrata by road despite the humanitarian agreement with the United Nations, thus occasioning serious shortages among the civilian population.[94] After the rebels allowed the usage of the Misrata port for humanitarian purposes, it became 'the only lifeline for humanitarian aid and an evacuation route for the war-wounded'.[95] This did not, however, stop the government forces from attempting to destroy the port by numerous attacks[96] and from launching land-mines on it.[97]

[89] See, e.g., UN Doc. (S/PV.6541), 31 May 2011, 4.

[90] International Commission of Inquiry March 2012 Report, §73.

[91] 'Gaddafi Files Show Evidence of Murderous Intent', *The Guardian*, 18 June 2011, www.guardian.co.uk/world/2011/jun/18/gaddafi-misrata-war-crime-documents.

[92] See e.g., 'Libya Rebels Ask Nato for Help as Gaddafi Forces Bombard Misrata', *The Guardian*, 2 May 2011, www.guardian.co.uk/world/2011/may/02/libya-rebels-gaddafi-bombard-misrata.

[93] 'The Risk for Aid-workers in Libya', *The World*, 19 April 2011, www.theworld.org/2011/04/the-risk-for-aid-workers-in-libya/.

[94] Amnesty International: 'The Battle for Libya', 34; International Commission of Inquiry March 2012 Report, §554; 'Misratah – Under Siege and Under Fire', *Amnesty International* (2011), 6.

[95] International Commission of Inquiry March 2012 Report, §87; see also Amnesty International, 'The Battle for Libya', 8.

[96] Amnesty International, 'The Battle for Libya', 34; International Commission of Inquiry March 2012 Report, §73.

[97] 'Land Mines Descend on Misrata's Port, Endangering Libyan City's Supply Route', *The New York Times*, 6 May 2011, www.nytimes.com/2011/05/07/world/africa/07libya.html?_r=0; International Commission of Inquiry March 2012 Report, §73; Amnesty International, 'The Battle for Libya', 54.

In summary, these actions prevented humanitarian aid from accessing war-torn Misrata and delayed the evacuation of the victims of the war.

There is little to add from the legal standpoint. Siege warfare is not prohibited as such in NIACs.[98] It must not, however, bring about the starvation of civilians.[99] The means used by the government and, to a lesser extent, the rebel forces as well as the indications of intent found in the proclamations by the government, indicate that violations of the relevant rules of IHL had been committed in relation to Misrata.

Finally, we turn to the closing phase of the conflict in September and October when, following the fall of Tripoli, the remnants of Gaddafi's forces retreated to the last remaining loyalist outposts in Sirte and Bani Walid. The tables had turned and now the insurgents encircled these cities and mounted military pressure against them. As the siege began, the rebels threatened to cut off essential supplies and did not hide their intention to starve the inhabitants to induce surrender.[100] They reportedly prevented humanitarian aid-workers from entering Sirte, exacerbating the existing shortages of basic necessities, medical supplies, electricity and water.[101] At the same time, civilians were not allowed to leave the city and were subjected to prolonged controls at checkpoints by the NTC forces.[102] Again, the situation was further aggravated by the other side: Gaddafi loyalists reportedly robbed food stores, leaving unaligned civilians with even fewer resources available.[103] It took at least two weeks until the ICRC finally managed to negotiate access to Sirte and provide the first humanitarian aid to the

[98] Cf. APs Commentary, 1457, §4796–7. [99] AP II, Article 14.

[100] 'UN Warns Libya Is Short of Water, Fuel, Medicine', *Fox News*, 2 September 2011, www.foxnews.com/world/2011/09/02/un-warns-libya-is-short-water-fuel-medicine/; 'Libya Crisis: Rebel Leaders Hoping to Starve Gaddafi Stronghold of Sirte into Submission', *The Telegraph*, 28 August 2011, www.telegraph.co.uk/news/worldnews/africaandindianocean/libya/8728752/Libya-crisis-Rebel-leaders-hoping-to-starve-Gaddafi-stronghold-of-Sirte-into-submission.html.

[101] International Commission of Inquiry March 2012 Report, §576; 'United Nations Team Arrives in Libya', *CNN*, 2 September 2011, http://articles.cnn.com/2011-09-02/world/libya.war_1_water-shortages-bottled-water-moammar-gadhafi/3?_s=PM:WORLD; 'UN Says Cannot Get Supplies into Libya Stronghold', *Reuters*, 26 September 2011, www.reuters.com/article/2011/09/26/libya-aid-idAFL5E7KQ2MM20110926>.

[102] Maximilian Forte, *Slouching Towards Sirte: NATO's War on Libya and Africa* (Montreal: Baraka, 2012), 95–97.

[103] 'NTC Claims Humanitarian Disaster in Gadhafi Stronghold', *CNN*, 19 September 2011, http://articles.cnn.com/2011-09-19/africa/world_africa_libya-war_1_gadhafi-forces-gadhafi-loyalists-moammar-gadhafi?_s=PM:AFRICA.

inhabitants.[104] All of this conduct of the conflict parties, if factually true, constituted a violation of humanitarian access obligations.

What impact does the described pattern of conduct have on the principles of neutrality and impartiality of humanitarian action? Both parties nominally acknowledged the application of the rules on humanitarian access to the situation in Libya.[105] By preventing the outside aid from reaching the civilians whose allegiance lay with the enemy or even those who only happened to find themselves in the territory controlled by the other side, the conflict parties certainly hindered fully impartial disbursement of aid. They did not, however, attempt to justify their conduct by any legal reasons; in fact, when justification was given, it was claimed that access was prevented due to 'security reasons'.[106] The attempts to deny the existence of alleged violations only strengthen the principles which would thus have been violated.[107] The deplorable events described in this section thus deserve to be referred to post-conflict accountability processes,[108] but they have not undermined the analysed principles.

4.2 Multi-purpose actors

The second type of humanitarian agents acting inside Libya were the multi-purpose actors like states and intergovernmental organisations including the United Nations, NATO, and the European Union. The label 'multi-purpose' denotes the fact that these actors were pursuing their political and military goals simultaneously with their humanitarian aims. In other recent conflicts, most notably Iraq and Afghanistan,

[104] Amnesty International, 'Warring Libyan Forces Must Allow Humanitarian Aid Reach Sirte', *Amnesty International*, 3 October 2011, www.amnesty.org/en/news-and-updates/warring-libyan-forces-must-allow-humanitarian-aid-reach-sirte-2011-10-03.

[105] See n. 88 above (re Libyan government's humanitarian agreement with the UN); NTC Press Statement, August 2011, http://ntclibyaus.files.wordpress.com/2011/08/ntc-ps-laws2.pdf (re NTC's acknowledgement of applicability of Common Article 3 and AP II to the situation in Libya).

[106] See, e.g., 'UN Says Cannot Get Supplies into Libya Stronghold', *Reuters*, 26 September 2011, www.reuters.com/article/2011/09/26/libya-aid-idAFL5E7KQ2MM20110926.

[107] Cf. *Nicaragua* v. *United States of America*, §186 (a state that resorts to justifications contained within a rule, which it is alleged to have violated, confirms rather than weakens the rule in question).

[108] Denial of humanitarian assistance may constitute one of several possible international crimes. See generally Christa Rottensteiner, 'The Denial of Humanitarian Assistance as a Crime under International Law', *IRRC* 835 (1999): 555–582.

principles of impartiality and neutrality were seen as most endangered precisely by the 'blurring of lines' between the variously defined tasks of such multi-purpose actors. In this section, we focus on two main issues facing these actors: the question of overstepping the mandate given to the implementing states by the Security Council in Resolution 1973 and the question of separation of humanitarian and other activities in the conduct of intergovernmental organisations.

4.2.1 Security Council mandate

Did the execution of the mandate given to the states by the Security Council in March 2011 overstep its legal boundaries? It is uncontested that the international coalition's use of military force targeted exclusively forces belonging to one side of the conflict. We can thus hardly speak of 'neutrality' with respect to the military action undertaken by the allied states. However, since the intervention in Libya was conducted for humanitarian purposes, it would ordinarily have had to follow the principle of neutrality, and avoid assisting one or the other side's military efforts. The interpretation of the legal mandate in Resolution 1973 thus acquires critical importance. It has long been understood that obligations imposed by the Security Council acting under Chapter VII of the *United Nations Charter* trump any conflicting international law obligations.[109] Therefore, the authorisation of the Security Council would override any commitment to the principle of neutrality the intervening states would otherwise have under international law, provided, of course, that it would allow them to associate with a party to the conflict.

It would be incorrect to describe the resolution as entirely neutral vis-à-vis the conflict parties. It expressly condemned acts of violence perpetrated by the government forces and remained silent with respect to the conduct of the insurgents.[110] It strengthened and extended the asset freeze of persons closely associated with the regime imposed by the preceding Resolution 1970.[111] It further extended the travel ban, again imposed by Resolution 1970, to additional representatives of the regime.[112] None of these restrictions were applicable to persons associated with the other conflict party.

[109] Lockerbie case (*Libya* v. *United Kingdom*), 15, §39.
[110] Cf. S/RES/1973, 2011, preambular §6.
[111] S/RES/1973, 2011, §19 and 22, and Annex I; see also S/RES/1970, 2011, §17 and Annex II.
[112] S/RES/1973, 2011, §22 and Annex I; see also S/RES/1970, 2011, §15 and Annex I.

Nevertheless, the resolution did not authorise the use of force to assist the insurgents in their armed struggle or even to remove Gaddafi's regime altogether.[113] An express authorisation of this sort was given by the Security Council during the Haiti crisis in the early 1990s when it authorised member states 'to form a multinational force' and 'to use all necessary means to facilitate the departure from Haiti of the military leadership [and] the prompt return of the legitimately elected President'.[114] In contrast, Resolution 1973 was much more restrictive in its terms:

> [Security Council a]uthorises Member States that have notified the Secretary-General, acting nationally or through regional organisations or arrangements, and acting in cooperation with the Secretary-General, to take all necessary measures, notwithstanding paragraph 9 of resolution 1970 (2011), *to protect civilians and civilian populated areas under threat of attack in the Libyan Arab Jamahiriya, including Benghazi*, while excluding a foreign occupation force of any form on any part of Libyan territory[.][115]

The mandate to protect civilians, without siding with one of the conflict parties, is in line with most of the recent practice of the Security Council.[116] Still, several abstaining members expressed their concern that the resolution left unclear the extent to which enforcement measures could be used permissibly under the resolution.[117] For the same reasons as above, it is submitted here that any ambiguity left by the wording of a Security Council resolution should be construed restrictively against a broad use of force, in order to allow only the minimum force necessary to achieve the goals stated in the resolution.[118]

In the first weeks of the intervention, it appeared that this approach was also adopted by the intervening states. In early April NATO warned the rebels not to target civilians and threatened them that such attacks

[113] See section 3.2 above for the assessment of the qualitative nature of aid permitted by Resolution 1973.

[114] S/RES/940, 1994, §4. [115] S/RES/1973, 2011, §4 (emphasis added).

[116] See e.g., S/RES/1270, 1999, §14 and S/RES/1289, 2000, §10 (regarding the situation in Sierra Leone); S/RES/1706, 2006, §12 (regarding the situation in Darfur); S/RES/1861, 2009, §7 (regarding the situation in Chad and the Central African Republic); but cf. S/RES/1975, 2011, §3 and 6 (authorising the use of force to protect civilians in Côte d'Ivoire while urging President Laurent Gbagbo to step aside).

[117] See, especially, UN Doc. (S/PV.6498), 17 March 2011, 6 (statements of the representatives of India and Brazil), 8 (statement of the representative of Russia), 10 (statement of the representative of China).

[118] See notes 53, 54 above.

would be followed with retaliatory strikes.[119] In the same period, the rebels reported feeling 'disappointed' by NATO for not heeding their requests to strike against particular government targets.[120] In the early phases of the conflict it thus appeared plausible that as soon as the situation would be stabilised and the civilians put out of immediate danger, outside use of force would cease.

Although there had been some earlier calls for Gaddafi to step down,[121] the position of the intervening states began to shift following the publication in mid-April of an influential open letter signed by the American and French presidents and the British prime minister.[122] In it, they pledged to maintain military pressure on Gaddafi's government until a transition process would take place in Libya, emphasising expressly that in order for that transition to succeed, 'Gaddafi must go, and go for good'.[123] The informal Libya contact group – which counted among its members all of the intervening states – appropriated this position soon after and continued to openly call for the end of Gaddafi's regime.[124]

These proclamations were accompanied by corresponding action on the ground. Abandoning their initial hesitation, international forces provided the insurgents with unyielding aerial support in their struggle to defeat Gaddafi. According to some reports, a joint operations centre was established in Benghazi with the aim to 'coordinate and make more effective the processing of military and tactical information back to NATO'.[125] During the battle of Tripoli, NATO destroyed the building of the Libyan state television, poignantly described by *The New York Times* as 'a purely political tool that only directly threatened civilians

[119] 'NATO Warns Rebels Against Attacking Civilians', *The New York Times*, 1 April 2011, www.nytimes.com/2011/04/01/world/africa/01civilians.html?_r=1&src=twrhp&pagewanted=all.

[120] 'Libyan Rebels "Disappointed" by NATO', *Al Jazeera*, 6 April 2011, www.aljazeera.com/news/africa/2011/04/201145191641347449.html.

[121] See e.g., European Council, EUCO 7/1/11 REV 1, 11 March 2011, §7 ('Colonel Kadhafi Must Relinquish Power Immediately').

[122] Barack Obama, David Cameron, and Nicolas Sarkozy, 'Libya's Pathway to Peace', *The New York Times*, 14 April 2011, www.nytimes.com/2011/04/15/opinion/15iht-edlibya15.html.

[123] Ibid. [124] Pommier, 'The Use of Force', 1068.

[125] Bruno Waterfield, 'Libya: British Military Advisers Set up "Joint Operations Centre" in Benghazi', *The Telegraph*, 18 May 2011, www.telegraph.co.uk/news/worldnews/africaandindianocean/libya/8521977/Libya-British-military-advisers-set-up-joint-operations-centre-in-Benghazi.html. See notes 31, 32 above for the relevance of this centre's existence for conflict qualification.

perhaps by boring them'.[126] Finally, the air strikes continued even after the fall of the capital and after the loyalists retreated into the cities of Sirte and Bani Walid, at a time when any claims of Gaddafi posing a threat to the civilians became very difficult to justify.

One of the states that voted in favour of Resolution 1973, South Africa, made a strong proclamation in June 2011 emphasising that its intention at the time of the vote had been 'to ensure the protection of civilians as well as unhindered access to humanitarian aid' but 'never regime change'.[127] Similar complaints that the mandate had been overstepped came from states that had initially abstained.[128] Although, according to Russia, NATO was requested to submit a report on its compliance with the mandate, this had not been done.[129] It thus appears fairly safe to conclude that the Security Council mandate had not been respected during the Libyan conflict[130] and that instead, a *coup d'état humanitaire* took place there.[131]

Correspondingly, the non-neutral implementation of the mandate contributed to the weakening of the principle of neutrality of humanitarian action. In addition, the prospects of Security Council-authorised humanitarian action in similar situations in the future have probably diminished because countries known for their more conservative approach to United Nations-mandated use of force such as China and Russia have grown even more wary of the risk that the agreed mandate would be stretched beyond expectation.[132]

[126] 'NATO Strikes at Libyan State TV', *The New York Times*, 30 July 2011, www.nytimes.com/2011/07/31/world/africa/31tripoli.html.

[127] UN Doc. (S/PV.6566), 27 June 2011, 4.

[128] See e.g., UN Doc. (S/PV.6531), 10 May 2011, 20 (statement of the Chinese representative); UN Doc. (S/PV.6620), 16 September 2011, 2 (statement of the Russian representative).

[129] Statement of the Russian representative to the Security Council at a press conference on 2 December 2011, www.unmultimedia.org/tv/webcast/2011/12/press-conference-ambassador-vitaly-churkin-president-of-the-security-council.html.

[130] Contra Mehrdad Payandeh, 'The United Nations, Military Intervention, and Regime Change in Libya', *Virginia Journal of International Law* 52 (2012): 387–91 (arguing that regime change might have been a legitimate *means* to pursue the *goal* of protection of civilians established by the Security Council).

[131] The term is Rony Brauman's. See Pierre Haski, 'Rony Brauman: "De quel droit demander à Kadhafi de partir?"', *Rue89*, 15 April 2011, www.rue89.com/2011/04/15/rony-brauman-de-quel-droit-demander-a-kadhafi-de-partir-200152.

[132] See also Letter from the Permanent Representative of the Russian Federation to the United Nations addressed to the Secretary-General, UN Doc. (A/66/594–S/2011/758), 7 December 2011 (calling on behalf of the BRICS countries for strict implementation of

4.2.2 Blurring the lines

Traditionally, there was a clear dividing line between the categories of actors who were involved in a conflict and those responding to it. This division safeguarded the neutrality and impartiality of humanitarian aid as the agents of response did not share the political motivations of the agents involved in the conflict. As intergovernmental organisations gradually took on both of these roles in modern conflicts, they came under fire for blurring the traditional lines. In this subsection, we look at the extent to which three key intergovernmental players – NATO, the United Nations and the European Union – succeeded in maintaining the separation of their various roles in Libya.

Leaving aside the question of the use of force discussed above, as for humanitarian aid narrowly understood, NATO was a relatively straightforward case. Consistent with its predominantly military character, it portrayed its role as enabling humanitarian assistance, but not as direct provision of aid to the conflict parties. Even before the intervention, NATO announced that it was moving additional ships into the region to support humanitarian assistance efforts.[133] NATO's own statistics speak of over 2,500 air, ground and maritime movements of humanitarian character being 'de-conflicted' (or provided with safe passage) by the Alliance.[134] Although arguments have been made to the effect that NATO's role was not limited to maritime and aerial operations under the Security Council mandate, NATO never brought ground troops into Libya to protect humanitarian convoys on land.[135] Notably, such deployment was also opposed by the Libyan government, even after it

Security Council decisions and noting that these countries considered it inadmissible to forcibly impose political solutions on the states in the Middle East and North Africa); Letter from the Permanent Representative of Brazil to the United Nations addressed to the Secretary-General, UN Doc. (A/66/551-S/2011/701), 9 November 2011, §10 (warning against the misuse of the R2P concept for 'purposes other than protecting civilians, such as regime change').

[133] Williams and Bellamy, 'Principles, Politics and Prudence', 277–78; see further NATO, 'NATO Ready to Support International Efforts on Libya', 10 March 2011, www.nato.int/cps/en/natolive/news_71446.htm.

[134] NATO, 'Operation UNIFIED PROTECTOR Final Mission Stats', 2 November 2011, www.nato.int/nato_static/assets/pdf/pdf_2011_11/20111108_111107-factsheet_up_factsfigures_en.pdf.

[135] See, e.g., Payandeh, 'The United Nations', 385–86; Michael N. Schmitt, 'Wings over Libya: The No-Fly Zone in Legal Perspective', *Yale Journal of International Law Online* 36 (2011): 46.

concluded the April humanitarian agreement allowing unimpeded access for humanitarian aid into Libya.[136]

There have been some indications that on several occasions NATO prioritised its military objectives over the humanitarian needs of the civilian population. The most prominent of these was the case of the 'left-to-die boat' with seventy-two people on board who had been drifting at sea for over two weeks in March and April without fuel, food, or drinking water, before washing up on the Libyan shores with only nine survivors. The harrowing fate of the escapees attracted media attention and resulted in an extensive report by the Parliamentary Assembly of the Council of Europe.[137] The report shows that although the drifting rubber boat had been in the vicinity of at least two NATO military vessels, the Alliance failed to react to the distress calls and left the passengers to their own devices.[138] According to the report, this failure was a consequence of the general lack of preparations for the foreseeable exodus of people fleeing the conflict.[139] If the factual assessment in the report is correct, NATO's conduct would amount to a violation of its law of the sea obligations to search and rescue persons in distress.[140] However, it appears to confirm that NATO did not see its role as a direct humanitarian actor in the Libyan conflict and consequently did not significantly contribute to the blurring of the lines analysed in this subsection.

The United Nations found itself in a more precarious situation. It had to reconcile its role as, on the one hand, the organisation providing the mandate to use force inside Libya, including against the government forces and installations, and, on the other hand, the organisation tasked to provide humanitarian relief to the conflict victims on both sides. At a meeting of relief agencies in Cairo in June 2011, Panos Moumtzis, the United Nations humanitarian coordinator for Libya, acknowledged this challenge and noted that 'the humanitarian team carries the same United Nations flag as the Security Council'.[141]

[136] 'Libya "No" to Foreign Troops with UN Aid', *Mumbai Mirror*, 20 April 2011, www.mumbaimirror.com/news/world/Libya-no-to-foreign-troops-with-UN-aid/articleshow/.

[137] Council of Europe, 'Lives Lost in the Mediterranean Sea: Who is Responsible?', *CoE*, 29 March 2012, http://assembly.coe.int/CommitteeDocs/2012/20120329_mig_RPT.EN.pdf> (hereinafter 'CoE report').

[138] Ibid., §8. [139] Ibid., §11. [140] UNCLOS, Article 98(1).

[141] Humanitarian Partnership Forum 'Sharaka', 'Final Report Humanitarian Partnership Forum "Sharaka"', Semiramis Intercontinental, Cairo, 6 June 2011, available at

Nevertheless, the United Nations confirmed on several occasions its commitment to the principles of impartiality and neutrality of humanitarian action with respect to the Libyan conflict.[142] United Nations representatives maintained constant contact with both sides[143] and succeeded in convincing the conflict parties to permit access for humanitarian agencies to all areas of Libya.[144]

Conversely, the perception of the United Nations as a strictly neutral humanitarian actor was put in doubt by its simultaneous preparation for a post-Gaddafi era. In April 2011, the United Nations established the position of Special Adviser to the Secretary-General on Post-Conflict Planning for Libya and appointed Ian Martin to fill it. He then seamlessly became the head of the United Nations Support Mission for Libya (UNSMIL) when it was created by the Security Council in September 2011 at the behest of the new Libyan authorities.[145] Through Mr Martin and later UNSMIL, the United Nations focused on development goals and political stabilisation, thus going beyond strict neutrality, considering that such aims inevitably favoured the eventually victorious side in the civil war.

This degree of two-facedness probably contributed towards some of the domestic backlash against the organisation. In a notable incident that followed the death of the son of Muammar Gaddafi, Saif al-Arab, in a NATO bombing in April 2011, the United Nations office in Tripoli was ransacked by angry local mobs, leading to the temporary withdrawal of all international staff.[146] We may thus conclude that the United Nations struggled to maintain a clear-cut and understandable separation of its strictly humanitarian and other broader roles during the Libyan conflict.

Finally, the activity of the European Union can be given somewhat better marks from the perspective of role separation. Since the adoption of the Lisbon Treaty, the European Union benefits from a clear legal basis outlining the principles underlying its humanitarian action and separating the humanitarian objectives from other foreign policy goals of the

www.humanitarianforum.org/data/files/29_final_report_humanitarian_partnership_forum_29_june_2011.pdf, 15.

142 UN, 'Strengthening of the Coordination of Emergency Humanitarian Assistance of the United Nations', 16 May 2011, UN Doc. (A/66/81–E/2011/117) www.un.org/en/ecosoc/julyhls/pdf11/sg_report_on_strengthening_coordination_a-66-81_e-2011-117.pdf, §71, 74 and 80(a).

143 See, e.g., UN Doc. (S/PV.6509), 4. 144 See n. 88 above. 145 S/RES/2009, 2011.

146 'UN Staff Leave Tripoli after Mob Attack', *Al Jazeera*, 2 May 2011, www.aljazeera.com/news/africa/2011/05/201151225143642809.html.

European Union.[147] It has thus introduced an explicit European Union competence in the field of humanitarian aid relating to the provision of 'ad hoc assistance and relief and protection for people in third countries who are victims of natural or man-made disasters'.[148] Such operations by the European Union must 'be conducted in compliance with the principles of international law and with the principles of impartiality, neutrality and non-discrimination'.[149]

In Libya, the need for this separation was acutely felt. The European Union participated through its foreign policy arm, the External Action Service, in the anti-Gaddafi contact group, and it consistently maintained an anti-Gaddafi position in the public proclamations of its representatives.[150] These actions clearly overstep the boundaries of the principle of neutrality. However, the European Union's humanitarian arm, the Directorate-General for Humanitarian Aid and Civil Protection of the European Commission (known under the acronym of its predecessor as ECHO[151]), maintained that it operated independently from the External Action Service and that it was 'blind to political, religious, or any other considerations'.[152] ECHO disbursed assistance totalling over 80 million euros in the form of emergency aid and repatriation operations.[153] It did so mainly through partner organisations whose dedication to neutrality and impartiality has long been established, including the ICRC, the International Organisation for Migration (IOM), and the United Nations High Commission for Refugees (UNHCR).[154] The ICRC President Jakob Kellenberger himself accepted that the funding priorities of ECHO were 'one of the best proofs' of its attachment to the principles of humanitarian action.[155] Legal and operational separation of humanitarian aid from

[147] Before the Lisbon Treaty entered into force, humanitarian aid was based on Article 179 of the EC Treaty, which dealt with development policy.

[148] TFEU, Article 214(1). [149] TFEU, Article 214(2).

[150] See, e.g., European Council, EUCO 7/1/11 REV 1, 11 March 2011, §7; Statement by Catherine Ashton, 22 August 2011, http://reliefweb.int/sites/reliefweb.int/files/resources/F_R_253.pdf.

[151] ECHO stood for 'European Community Humanitarian Office' and it was established in 1992 by Regulation (CE) No. 1257/96. It transformed into a Directorate-General in 2004.

[152] ICRC, 'Discussion: What are the Future Challenges for Humanitarian Action?', 908 (statement by Commissioner Kristalina Georgieva).

[153] ECHO, 'Timeline of the Libyan Crisis', 17 February 2012, http://ec.europa.eu/echo/media/photos/picture_stories/libya06_en.htm.

[154] ECHO, 'Libyan Crisis: Humanitarian Partners', 18 August 2011, http://ec.europa.eu/echo/files/aid/countries/libya_partners_funding_en.pdf.

[155] ICRC, 'Discussion: What are the Future Challenges for Humanitarian Action?', *IRRC* 884 (2011): 909 (statement by ICRC president Jakob Kellenberger).

other foreign policy priorities thus seemed to have dispelled concerns over impartiality and neutrality of European Union humanitarian action in the Libyan conflict.[156]

5. Conclusion

There is no doubt that humanitarian principles of impartiality and neutrality carry great importance even in the aftermath of the Libyan conflict. Both sides of the conflict certainly bear their share of responsibility for preventing humanitarian access to the victims on the ground. However, without the general understanding that humanitarian agents do not, or at least should not, have any other loyalty except to the persons in need, even the limited observance of the law would become illusory. We must therefore learn from the lessons of Libya to protect these principles for the future.

For the states that are not directly affected by the conflict as it is not taking place in their territory, these lessons may be drawn on two levels. Firstly, the aid they decide to provide to a conflict-stricken country should not quantitatively favour one of the conflict sides, nor should it exceed what can qualitatively be considered legitimate humanitarian aid. Secondly, if there is a Security Council mandate allowing outside states to intervene to protect the civilians affected by the conflict, its implementation should be based on a restrictive interpretation of its terms. To do otherwise means to risk that the Security Council will be unwilling to permit similar action in future crises, as has been demonstrated by the unfortunate Syrian situation so soon after Libya.

It is a sad role of the academic to point to the violations committed by the conflict parties while being fully aware that future conflicts will hardly be much different. However, even this cloud has a silver lining. Both conflict parties in Libya have formally acknowledged their acceptance of

[156] This conclusion might have had to be modified if the EU's offer to deploy a military force to protect humanitarian agencies in Libya had been accepted and activated by the UN. The EU decided to create the European Union Force-Libya (EUFOR Libya) in April 2011; its deployment had been, however, contingent on a request being made by the OCHA. Since the UN Under-Secretary-General for Humanitarian Affairs and Emergency Relief Coordinator, Valerie Amos, considered this military operation unnecessary and useful only as a last resort, the request was never made. Had the EUFOR been deployed, its military nature and its support of humanitarian operations would very likely have further contributed to the blurring of lines described in this section. See further Pommier, 'The Use of Force', 1069–70.

IHL obligations relating to humanitarian access, and neither of them has attempted to claim that these duties would be unfair or unfeasible for reasons of military necessity. Similarly, they have not claimed a right only to allow aid to 'their own' civilian population; on the contrary, if the alleged violations were reacted upon in any way by the belligerents, it was to deny that anything like that had happened. The principles and the rules relating to humanitarian action thus survive intact and even reaffirmed by this conduct, as it is rather their implementation that was found wanting.

Finally, some good practice can be identified in the conduct of the international organisations involved in the Libyan conflict. 'Dunantist' agencies such as the ICRC and MSF have again shown that it is principally possible to act in an impartial and neutral way, although their efforts were certainly hampered in many ways by other actors on the ground. The European Union has served as a positive example of a multipurpose actor capable of satisfactory legal and operational separation of its humanitarian and non-humanitarian roles. Conversely, NATO and United Nations involvement in the conflict rather put the principles of impartiality and neutrality under further strain on account of the far-reaching interpretation of the Security Council mandate by NATO, and the United Nations' blurring of lines between its various roles.

Humanitarian principles of impartiality and neutrality have certainly not died in Libya. Commitment to them, as to fundamental principles of humanitarian action, has been confirmed by virtually all key actors in that conflict. Likewise, the conduct of many of them has indeed been guided by these principles. At the same time, it is undeniable that the Libyan events have put these principles under considerable strain. It was the aim of this chapter to highlight the most notable of those instances and thus contribute in a modest way to the strengthening of these principles in the future.

Conclusion

ANDREJ ZWITTER, CHRISTOPHER K. LAMONT,
HANS-JOACHIM HEINTZE, JOOST HERMAN

Laws, norms, politics and practices surrounding humanitarian action show, as the chapters in this book demonstrate, that constitutionalisation and fragmentation occur at the same time. Finding a clear-cut answer, however, to whether either fragmentation or constitutionalisation is advantageous or detrimental to the development of international law of humanitarian action, is much harder. This task becomes complex because the role and value of constitutionalisation and fragmentation of international law in the field of humanitarian action always necessitates an inquiry also as to whether either of the two trends leads to an improvement or a deterioration in the humanitarian situation of beneficiaries.

The introduction presented several criteria that would serve to gain a better understanding what the actual, observable processes are. The following sub-section will, therefore, take a retrospective look at the previous chapters through the lens of these criteria and thereby will try to add to the constitutionalisation/fragmentation debate by taking the chapters as quasi-empirical evidence. To that end the criteria have been assigned to two sections: 'From the local to the global' will elaborate on criteria and corresponding chapters that indicate a strong bottom-up trend of norm fertilisation, i.e. where the individual, local and national concerns give rise to norm development in the international sphere. 'From the global to the local' traces the top-down norm influence. By reordering the concepts encompassed by the constitutionalisation/fragmentation debate this concluding chapter will thus demonstrate that the actual complexity of legal reality by far extends beyond the Manichean delineations that this debate tends to draw. Acknowledging that many readers (including some of the editors of this book) read academic books based on topical interest and sometimes from back to front, each sub-chapter will conclude with a list of chapters that those ready might want to revisit in the light of the criteria of the constitutionalisation/fragmentation debate.

1. From the local to the global

1.1 Shift of decision-making power away from the national order

One of the main indicators for a constitutionalisation tendency of international law is claimed to be the trend of eroding sovereignty through diverting decision-making power away from the national to the regional and international levels. Looking back at the constitutive chapters of this book, particularly Montag's evaluation of the growing powers and obligations of the United Nations Security Council, seems to testify to such a trend. At the same time a counter-example can be found in Dabiru Patnaik's elaboration of the ILC's Draft Articles which empower the state's capability of decision-making at least *de lege* if not necessarily in political terms. The case of Myanmar and the abstention of the international community from enforcing aid through force (Zwitter and Lamont) somehow stands juxtaposed with the case study of Haiti (Heintze), a state that, due to a complete lack of decision-making power during the onset of the crisis, also lacked sovereignty.

- Chapter 5: Issues of state consent and international humanitarian assistance in disasters: the work of the International Law Commission, *Dabiru Sridhar Patnaik*
- Chapter 6: United Nations involvement in humanitarian assistance: competences of the Security Council to face today's obstructions, *Heike Montag*
- Chapter 15: Enforcing aid in Myanmar: state responsibility and humanitarian aid provision, *Andrej Zwitter and Christopher K. Lamont*
- Chapter 18: Humanitarian assistance and failed states: still an issue of sovereignty? The case study of Haiti, *Hans-Joachim Heintze*

1.2 Complementarity of national, regional and international (sectoral – i.e. humanitarian) normative orders

This criterion describes a complementation of different normative orders by sector-specific and problem-derived norms which lead to a fragmentation of international law by establishing thematic pools of norms such as humanitarian action-related international law. This trend can signify either side of the constitutionalisation/fragmentation debate. One particular element is that norms emerge out of local or national problems and make it the way to regional and/or international levels where they manifest in laws and guidelines or vice versa. Of particular interest to this criteria are the chapters of Kocken, describing the legal theoretical normative pluralist conundrum, and Spieker, engaging in how international sectoral norms or regional frameworks define the options for domestic disaster response. Correspondingly, Philip takes a closer look at the Asian debate on the right to water. Borda approaches this phenomenon from a process-oriented viewpoint with regard to the ICRC's role in Colombia.

- Chapter 7: International norms informing domestic disaster response schemes, *Heike Spieker*
- Chapter 10: Assessing the complex normative pluralism in humanitarian crises: do local norms matter? *Joris Kocken*
- Chapter 13: Humanitarian assistance and the right to water: an ASEAN region perspective, *Diana Philip*
- Chapter 17: Providing relief in times of war: the role of the ICRC in the Colombian conflict during the Uribe administration (2002–2010), *Sandra Borda*

1.3 Political fragmentation of sectors of international law and cross-fertilisation of sectoral norms with the humanitarian sector

Sectoralisation is at the core of this criterion. It describes the issue-related inception of international norms such as norms that emerge around humanitarian action. At the same time it describes a trend where agents make use of norms in other sectors (such as human rights) to fill the open spaces and legal gaps created by a responsive norm creation. Jansen-Wilhelm's reinterpretation of the human rights basis of the duty of states to accept humanitarian action is a clear example of this cross-fertilisation, as is the blurring of the lines between military and humanitarian aid (Mačák). Broberg's chapter looks at norm-interaction from an issue-related perspective with regard to the problem of corruption and misappropriation of aid.

- Chapter 8: A duty to accept humanitarian assistance under the ICESCR, *Stefanie Jansen-Wilhelm*
- Chapter 11: Thou shall not ... misappropriate humanitarian aid – on European Union humanitarian aid and the fight against corruption, *Morten Broberg*
- Chapter 19: Principles of neutrality and impartiality of humanitarian action in the aftermath of the 2011 Libyan conflict, *Kubo Mačák*

2. From the global to the local

2.1 Proliferation of international norms of humanitarian action to lower levels of normative orders

International law, analogous to constitutional norms, can give guidance to regional and national legislation. For example, the international norms and guidelines of the Hyogo Framework For Action 2005–2015 informed very concretely how disaster risk reduction laws in Indonesia were designed (Triyana). Even soft law and standards like the IDRL Guidelines inform law-making in African countries (Boswijk). This can lead to the effect that below the national level, local norms can become more and more marginalised as a result (Kocken).

- Chapter 1: International law and humanitarian space in the twenty-first century: challenged relationships, *Joost Herman*
- Chapter 10: Assessing the complex normative pluralism in humanitarian crises: do local norms matter? *Joris Kocken*
- Chapter 12: Developments in African disaster response law and the African Union: a view from the field, *Sanne Boswijk*
- Chapter 14: The Indonesian compliance and its effective implementation to international norms on disaster response, *Heribertus Jaka Triyana*

2.2 De-Internationalisation (regionalisation/localisation) of institutions and norms concerning humanitarian action

Regionalisation is a particular trend of fragmentation driven not so much by the specificity of the issue. As the chapters indicate, the more probable drivers are the desire to take regional ownership in certain processes or the belief that a localised approach would either be a duty imposed by international norms or a superior approach to a certain issue. Whereas Giladi's exploration of the ICRC's legal mandate ambiguity is a show-case to the contrary, i.e. a de-regionalisation, Hesselman's treatment of regional human rights regimes and their governance of humanitarian action demonstrate exactly this regionalisation. This is also explored by Knottnerus in his chapter about the OAS. Likewise, localisation can be observed in Triyana's report about Indonesia's efforts of implementing international guidelines, as well as the development of African disaster response mechanisms described by Boswijk.

- Chapter 4: The utility and limits of legal mandate: humanitarian assistance, the International Committee of the Red Cross, and mandate ambiguity, *Rotem Giladi*
- Chapter 9: Regional human rights regimes and humanitarian obligations of states in the event of disaster, *Marlies Hesselman*
- Chapter 12: Developments in African disaster response law and the African Union: a view from the field, *Sanne Boswijk*
- Chapter 14: The Indonesian compliance and its effective implementation to international norms on disaster response, *Heribertus Jaka Triyana*
- Chapter 16: The regionalisation of humanitarian action: the role of the OAS, *Abel S. Knottnerus*

2.3 Emancipation of the individual as subject of international law in the field of humanitarian action

The individual moving into the centre of attention of international law is a trend that we can observe particularly strongly since the 1970s and in an accelerated way after the end of the cold war. By many this trend was referred to as human security. On the one hand, the emancipation of the individual in international law has an eroding effect on international law as it challenges the principles of sovereignty and non-interference. On the other hand, the strengthening of the individual as international legal subject also prioritises international human rights law over less beneficial national or local norms. Salomons argues that only a rights-based approach is conducive to an effective protection of individuals, and prepares the ground for linking relief, rehabilitation and development. This is also indicated by the fact that a rights/obligations distinction is not supported by the current humanitarian and human rights regime (Kuijt). Regional human rights regimes that start to develop their own obligatory standards for humanitarian assistance testify to that as well (Hesselman).

- Chapter 1: International law and humanitarian space in the twenty-first century: challenged relationships, *Joost Herman*
- Chapter 2: The perils of Dunantism: the need for a rights-based approach to humanitarianism, *Dirk Salomons*
- Chapter 3: A humanitarian crisis: reframing the legal framework on humanitarian assistance, *Emilie E. Kuijt*
- Chapter 9: Regional human rights regimes and humanitarian obligations of states in the event of disaster, *Marlies Hesselman*

2.4 *Specialisation of international/regional/local regulations on humanitarian action and crises*

As discussed in the introduction, specialisation is an element of fragmentation. This trend describes the process of norm-development in very specific areas of state conduct. Specifically with regard to soft law, norm-development relates more and more to non-state agents as well. Humanitarian action is one of these areas of specialisation. In the area of soft law we can, for example, find the Guiding Principles on Internal Displacement, the so-called 'Pinheiro Principles', or the IASC Operational Guidelines on the Protection of Persons in Situations of Natural Disasters (Spieker). Boswijk recounts several examples of this specialisation on the regional level of the African Union (for example the AU's draft African Humanitarian Policy Framework) and on state level (for example Namibia's Disaster Risk Management Act 2012).

- Chapter 7: International norms informing domestic disaster response schemes, *Heike Spieker*
- Chapter 12: Developments in African disaster response law and the African Union: a view from the field, *Sanne Boswijk*

3. Fragmentation and constitutionalisation in a time of globalisation

International law of humanitarian action demonstrates how fragmentation and constitutionalisation go hand in hand. The effects of globalisation of state engagement have led to humanitarian relief provided and financed by states for other states. This has taken such dimensions that the ILC saw it as necessary to codify principles of 'Protection of Persons in the Event of Disasters'. NGOs, regional and international organisations develop guidelines in order to regulate how to provide relief aid. As mentioned above, eventually the question of the benefits and downsides of constitutionalisation or fragmentation in the area of humanitarian action always has to be answered in the light of the effect on beneficiaries. It is thus also a moral question. The purpose of all these endeavours definitively is to improve a still-dysfunctional interaction between different levels of norms, which can cause negative effects for beneficiaries (for example by delaying the import of foodstuffs in the event of famine). As has been shown in the previous chapters, different regions are currently at different stages of mainstreaming their disaster response laws. It is clear that no region in the world has yet succeeded in mainstreaming their norms to ensure smooth disaster response. However, that these processes are important remains beyond question; both fragmentation and constitutionalisation are observable at the same time, both were set in motion on purpose, and the purpose is to improve the conditions of beneficiaries in the event of disasters.

BIBLIOGRAPHY

'¿Un Nuevo Plan Colombia?' *Revista Semana*, 1036, 2002.

'$1 Billion Is Pledged to Support Libya Rebels'. *The New York Times*, 9 June 2011. www.nytimes.com/2011/06/10/world/africa/10diplo.html?_r=0.

'2 horas tendrán guerrilleros para la retirada'. *El Tiempo*, 27 February 2008.

'Allied Strikes Sweep Libya as West Intervenes in Conflict'. *The Guardian*, 20 March 2011. www.guardian.co.uk/world/2011/mar/19/libya-air-strikes-gaddafi-france.

'Anggaran BNPB Tahun 2013 1 Trilyun'. *Detiknews*. Accessed 3 May 2013. http://news.detik.com/read/2012/09/17/184701/2022901/10/.

'Banjir Wasior: Bagaikan Tsunami Menyapu Rumah Warga'. *Kompas*. Accessed 6 October 2010. http://regional.kompas.com/read/2010/10/06/06583142/Bagaikan.Tsunami.Menyapu.Rumah.Warga.

'Bloody Clashes in Indonesia's Maluku Claim Another Life'. *Jakarta Globe*, 8 March 2012. Accessed 7 April 2013. www.thejakartaglobe.com/news/bloody-clashes-in-indonesias-maluku-claim-another-life/503346.

'Burma Eases Restrictions on Aid'. *BBC News*, 11 May 2008. http://news.bbc.co.uk/2/hi/asia-pacific/7394410.stm.

'Cambios en el Comité Internacional de la Cruz Roja'. *El Tiempo*, 27 January 2005.

'CICR dice que prestará apoyo a las liberaciones'. *El Tiempo*, 18 February 2004.

'CICR no tiene solicitudes de las FARC para liberar más secuestrados'. *El Tiempo*, 6 June 2008.

'CICR reestructura su organización en los Llanos'. *El Tiempo*, 24 September 2004.

'Circular del Comisionado podría causar la salida de Acnur del país'. *El Tiempo*, 17 July 2005.

'Colombian Soldier Wore Red Cross Logo in Hostage Rescue'. *The New York Times*, 17 July 2008.

'Compilation: General Recommendations and Concluding Observations Relevant to the Rights of Indigenous Women'. *Forest Peoples Programmes*, September 2012. Accessed 23 June 2013. www.forestpeoples.org/sites/fpp/files/news/2011/06/Compilation%20CEDAW%20%20ENG%20(Update%20September%202012).pdf.

'Confusion Reigns Over Arming Libyan Rebels'. *Sky News*, 31 March 2011. http://news.sky.com/story/844958/confusion-reigns-over-arming-libyan-rebels.

'Cruz Roja dice que no es mediadora'. *El Tiempo*, 31 December 2002.

'Cruz Roja Internacional indignada con las FARC'. *El Tiempo*, 16 April 2003.

'Cruz Roja preocupada por ataques a misiones médicas en Colombia'. *El Tiempo*, 14 April 2011.

'Cyclone Nargis – Breaking Cyclone Nargis News'. *The New York Times*, 30 April 2009. http://topics.nytimes.com/topics/news/international/countriesandterritories/myanmar/cyclone_nargis/index.html

'Cyclone Nargis: One Month on, US Accuses Burma of Criminal Neglect'. *The Guardian*, 2 June 2008. www.guardian.co.uk/world/2008/jun/02/burma.cyclonenargis.

'Deportan y Expulsan a Tres Españoles'. *El Tiempo*, 18 September 2002.

'Diplomats In Rome Discuss Aid To Libyan Rebels'. *National Public Radio*, 5 May 2011. www.npr.org/2011/05/05/136011941/diplomats-discuss-aid-to-libyan-rebels.

'Egypt "Lifts" Travel Ban on US NGO Workers'. *BBC News*. Last updated on 1 March 2012. www.bbc.co.uk/news/world-us-canada-17210327.

'El CICR no estará en negociación'. *El Tiempo*, 28 April 2003.

'Emblema de la Cruz Roja tiene que ser respetado en todas las circunstancias, recordó la entidad'. *El Tiempo*, 16 July 2008.

'En el 2004, la Cruz Roja solo logró transmitir mensaje a un secuestrado'. *El Tiempo*, 6 May 2005.

'Exparas en las redes de cooperantes'. *El Espectador*, 4 March 2011.

'Fact File: Dambusters Raid'. 17 *BBC*, May 1943. Accessed 30 March 2013. www.bbc.co.uk/history/ww2peopleswar/timeline/factfiles/nonflash/a1057402.shtml.

'Famine-hit Zambia Rejects GM Food Aid'. *BBC News*. Last modified on 29 October 2002. http://news.bbc.co.uk/2/hi/africa/2371675.stm.

'Foreign Rescue Team Delayed By Japanese Bureaucracy'. *ABC News*. Accessed on 1 April 2013. http://abcnews.go.com/International/japanese-bureaucracy-delays-foreign-search-rescueteams/story?id=13126904#.UWg2Sb9pu2w.

'France Urges UN to Force Cyclone Aid on Myanmar'. *International Herald Tribune*, 7 May 2008.

'French Aid Bolsters Libyan Revolt'. *The New York Times*, 28 February 2011. www.nytimes.com/2011/03/01/world/europe/01france.html.

'French Military Air-Dropped Arms to Libya Rebels'. *France 24*, 29 June 2011. www.france24.com/en/20110629-french-military-confirms-airdropping-arms-libya-kadhafi-rebel#.

'Gaddafi Files Show Evidence of Murderous Intent'. *The Guardian*, 18 June 2011. www.guardian.co.uk/world/2011/jun/18/gaddafi-misrata-war-crime-documents.

'Gaddafi Loyalists Launch Offensive'. *Al Jazeera*, 11 March 2011. www.aljazeera.com/news/africa/2011/03/201131041228856242.html.

'Gobierno de Colombia autorió a Venezuela misión humanitaria de liberación de secuestrados'. *El Tiempo*, 25 February 2008.

'Guerrilla si es combatiente'. *El Tiempo*, 1 July 2003.

'Haitis Präsident fühlt sich übergangen', *Die Zeit*, 30 January 2010, www.zeit.de/gesellschaft/zeitgeschehen/2010-01/haiti-gewalt-beziehungen-schule.

'Hardliner elected Colombian president', *BBC News*, 27 May 2002, http://news.bbc.co.uk/2/hi/americas/2008674.stm.

'Humanitarian Aid in Libya: How Much Has Each Country Donated?'. *The Guardian*, 22 August 2011. www.guardian.co.uk/news/datablog/2011/aug/22/libya-humanitarian-aid-by-country.

'Indonesia's Clean Drinking Water Crisis Worst in Southeast Asia: Expert'. *Jakarta Globe*, 5 July 2012. Accessed 22 February 2013.www.thejakartaglobe.com/health/indonesias-clean-drinking-water-crisis-worst-in-southeast-asia-expert/528758.

'Kronologi Letusan Gunung Merapi'. *Vivanews*. Accessed 27 October 2010. http://nasional.news.viva.co.id/news/read/185183-ini-kronologi-letusan-gunung-merapi.

'La Ira presidencial'. *Revista Semana* 1115, 15 September 2003.

'Land Mines Descend on Misurata's Port, Endangering Libyan City's Supply Route'. *The New York Times*, 6 May 2011. www.nytimes.com/2011/05/07/world/africa/07libya.html?_r=0.

'Libya Crisis: Rebel Leaders Hoping to Starve Gaddafi Stronghold of Sirte into Submission'. *The Telegraph*, 28 August 2011. www.telegraph.co.uk/news/worldnews/africaandindianocean/libya/8728752/Libya-crisis-Rebel-leaders-hoping-to-starve-Gaddafi-stronghold-of-Sirte-into-submission.html.

'Libya: Gaddafi Must Step Down, Says "Contact Group"'. *BBC News*, 14 April 2011. www.bbc.co.uk/news/world-africa-13058694.

'Libya "No" to Foreign Troops with UN Aid'. *Mumbai Mirror*, 20 April 2011. www.mumbaimirror.com/news/world/Libya-no-to-foreign-troops-with-UN-aid/articleshow/.

'Libya Rebels Ask Nato for Help as Gaddafi Forces Bombard Misrata'. *The Guardian*, 2 May 2011. www.guardian.co.uk/world/2011/may/02/libya-rebels-gaddafi-bombard-misrata.

'Libya Unrest: Scores Killed in Benghazi "Massacre"'. *BBC News*, 20 February 2011. www.bbc.co.uk/news/world-africa-12517327.

'Libya: US, UK and France Attack Gaddafi Forces'. *BBC News*, 20 March 2011. www.bbc.co.uk/news/world-africa-12796972.

'Libyan Government Promises Aid-workers Access, UN Says'. *BBC News*, 19 April 2011. www.bbc.co.uk/news/world-africa-13125616.

'Libyan Rebels "Disappointed" by NATO'. *Al Jazeera*, 6 April 2011. www.aljazeera.com/news/africa/2011/04/201145191641347449.html.

'Libyan Rebels "Receive Foreign Training"'. *Al Jazeera*, 3 April 2011. www.aljazeera.com/news/africa/2011/04/201142172443133798.html.

'Libyan Rebels Say They're Being Sent Weapons'. *The New York Times*, 16 April 2011. www.nytimes.com/2011/04/17/world/africa/17libya.html.

'Libya's Pathway to Peace'. *The New York Times*, 14 April 2011. www.nytimes.com/2011/04/15/opinion/15iht-edlibya15.html.

'NATO Operations in Libya: Data Journalism Breaks Down Which Country Does What'. *The Guardian*, 22 May 2011. www.guardian.co.uk/news/datablog/2011/may/22/nato-libya-data-journalism-operations-country.

'NATO Strikes at Libyan State TV'. *The New York Times*, 30 July 2011. www.nytimes.com/2011/07/31/world/africa/31tripoli.html.

'NATO Warns Rebels Against Attacking Civilians'. *The New York Times*, 1 April 2011. www.nytimes.com/2011/04/01/world/africa/01civilians.html?_r=1&src=twrhp&pagewanted=all.

'NTC Claims Humanitarian Disaster in Gadhafi Stronghold'. *CNN*, 19 September 2011. http://articles.cnn.com/2011-09-19/africa/world_africa_libya-war_1_gadhafi-forces-gadhafi-loyalists-moammar-gadhafi?_s=PM:AFRICA.africa_libya-war_1_gadhafi-forces-gadhafi-loyalists-moammar-gadhafi?_s=PM:AFRICA.

'Opposition in Libya Struggles to Form a United Front'. *The New York Times*, 8 March 2011. www.nytimes.com/2011/03/09/world/africa/09rebels.html.

'Orinoquía: en guerra o amenazada'. *El Tiempo*, 17, May 2005.

'Pakar Gempa: Pusat Gempa Padang Bukan di ona Subduksi'. *Kompas*. Accessed 19 September 2011. http://kompas.com/read/2009/10/01/09081256/pakar.gempa.pusat.gempa.padang.bukan.di.ona.subduksi.

'Red Tape Delays Africa Aid Airlift'. *Al Jazeera*. Last modified on 27 July 2011. www.aljazeera.com/news/africa/2011/07/201172771619757561.html.

'Rehabilitation and Development'. *Venro-Arbeitspapier* 16 (2006): 3.

'Report: Libya Air Force Bombs Protesters Heading For Army Base'. *Haaretz*, 21 February 2011. www.haaretz.com/news/world/report-libya-air-force-bombs-protesters-heading-for-army-base-1.344775.

'The Risk for Aid-workers in Libya'. *The World*, 19 April 2011. www.theworld.org/2011/04/the-risk-for-aid-workers-in-libya/.

'Salió CICR de Saravena'. *El Tiempo*, 3 April 2004.

'Se criollizó el DIH'. *El Tiempo*, 6 October 2002.

'Se permitieron sobrevuelos comerciales, no militares, responde la Cruz Roja a Juan Manuel Santos'. *El Tiempo*, 6 February 2009.

'Sí hay conflicto: Cruz Roja Internacional'. *El Tiempo*, 5 May 2005.

'Top Five Worst Natural Disasters of 2011'. 31 December 2011. Accessed 25 March 2013. www.globalpost.com/dispatch/news/regions/asia-pacific/japan/111229/worst-natural-disasters-2011.

'UN Chief: Myanmar to Admit all Aid-workers'. *CNN*, n.d., http://edition.cnn.com/2008/WORLD/asiapcf/05/23/myanmar/.

'UN Head Tours Cyclone-hit Burma'. *BBC News*, 22 May 2008. http://news.bbc.co.uk/2/hi/asia-pacific/7414015.stm.

'United Nations Team Arrives in Libya'. *CNN*, 2 September 2011, http://articles.cnn.com/2011-09-02/world/libya.war_1_water-shortages-bottled-water-moammar-gadhafi/3?_s=PM:WORLD.

'Uno-Generalsekretär ornig über schleppende Hilfe'. *Spiegel Online*, 12 May 2008. www.spiegel.de/panorama/0,1518,552830,00.html.

'UN Warns Libya Is Short of Water, Fuel, Medicine'. *Fox News*, 2 September 2011. www.foxnews.com/world/2011/09/02/un-warns-libya-is-short-water-fuel-medicine/.

'UN Says Cannot Get Supplies into Libya Stronghold'. *Reuters*, 26 September 2011. www.reuters.com/article/2011/09/26/libya-aid-idAFL5E7KQ2MM20110926>.

'UN Staff Leave Tripoli after Mob Attack'. *Al Jazeera*, 2 May 2011. www.aljazeera.com/news/africa/2011/05/201151225143642809.html.

'US Seeks to Aid Libyan Rebels With Seied Assets'. *The New York Times*, 5 May 2011. www.nytimes.com/2011/05/06/world/africa/06diplo.html?_r=0.

'US Sends Aid Through Private Groups in Myanmar'. *CNN.com* n.d., www.cnn.com/2008/WORLD/asiapcf/05/16/us.myanmar.

'US, UK, French Forces Land in Libya'. *Pakistan Observer*, 26 February 2011. http://pakobserver.net/detailnews.asp?id=78009.

'Vietnam Warns of Water Conflicts'. *AFP*, 7 September 2012. www.google.com/hostednews/afp/article/ALeqM5grQeVwutLgCMASLtuccOtxjKGO9A?docId=CNG.ed18aee1f8d766ca66096e5c8b6c1e1a.b41.

Abrisketa, Joana. 'The Right to Humanitarian Aid: Basis and Limitations'. In *Reflections on Humanitarian Action: Principles, Ethics and Contradictions*, ed. Humanitarian Studies Unit, 55. London/Stirling: Pluto Press, 2001.

ACHPR. *The African Charter on Human and Peoples' Rights* (ACHPR). 1981. www.achpr.org/files/instruments/achpr/banjul_charter.pdf.

'Initial and Combined Report of the Republic of Côte D'Ivoire to the African Commission on Human Rights and Peoples' Rights'. Accessed 1 April 2013. www.achpr.org/files/sessions/52nd/state-reports/1-1994-2012/initial_combined_periodic_report_194_2012_eng.pdf.

Nairobi Principles. 'Principles and Guidelines on the Implementation of Economic, Social and Cultural Rights in the *African Charter on Human and Peoples' Rights*'. www.achpr.org/files/instruments/economic-social-cultural/achpr_instr_guide_draft_esc_rights_eng.pdf.

ACHPR and ACtHRP. www.achpr.org/communications/ and www.african-court.org/en/index.php/2012-03-04-06-06-00/list-cases.

Active Learning Network for Accountability and Performance in Humanitarian Action (ALNAP). *The State of the Humanitarian System*. London: ODI, 2012.

Adisubrata, W. S. 'Otonomi Daerah di Era Reformasi'. *UPP AMP YKPN, Yogyakarta*, 2008.

AICHR. 'Five-year Work Plan of the ASEAN Intergovernmental Commission on Human Rights'. 2010–2015. Accessed 1 April 2013. http://aichr.org/documents/.

'Terms of Reference'. *ASEAN Intergovernmental Commission on Human Rights*, 2009. http://aichr.org/about/.

Akande, Dapo. 'Classification of Armed Conflicts: Relevant Legal Concepts'. In *International Law and the Classification of Conflicts*, ed. Elisabeth Wilmshurst. Oxford University Press, 2012.

Akso, Tim Studi. *Partnership for Governance Reform in Indonesia*. Bogor: UNDP, 2004. http://lbprastdp.staff.ipb.ac.id/files/2010/12/WP-1-Arya-untuk-EGPS-Citanduy-2004-Final.pdf

Albright, Madeleine and Herbert De Soto. Commission on Legal Empowerment of the Poor, *Making the Law work for Everyone*, vol. I. New York, Commission on Legal Empowerment of the Poor and United Nations Development Programme 2008. www.unrol.org/files/Making_the_Law_Work_for_Everyone.pdf.

Alston, Philip. *The United Nations and Human Rights: A Critical Appraisal*. Oxford: Clarendon Press, 1992.

Alston, Philip and G. Quinn. 'The Nature and Scope of State Parties' Obligations under the International Covenant on Economic, Social and Cultural Rights'. *Human Rights Quarterly* 9 (1987): 156–229.

American Bar Association. 'Experts' Note on the ASEAN Human Rights Declaration'. *American Bar Association, Rule of Law Initiative*, May 2012. Accessed 18 March 2013. www.americanbar.org/content/dam/aba/directories/roli/indonesia/asia_aba_roli_expert_note_asean_human_rights_declaration_05121.authcheckdam.pdf.

American Convention on Human Rights. 'Pact of San Jose, Costa Rica'. ACHR. www.oas.org/juridico/english/Treaties/b-32.htm.

Amnesty International. 'The Battle for Libya'. *Amnesty International*, 2011.

'Iraq: UN Security Council Considers the Humanitarian Panel's Report on Sanctions'. AI INDEX: MDE 14 June 1999.

'Misratah – Under Siege and Under Fire'. Amnesty International, 2011.

'Sudan Darfur: "Too Many People Killed for No Reason"'. *Amnesty International*, 3 February 2004. Accessed 25 March 2013. www.amnesty.org/en/library/asset/AFR54/008/2004/en/452c12ed-d640-11dd-ab95-a13b602c0642/afr540082004en.html.

'Warring Libyan Forces Must Allow Humanitarian Aid to Reach Sirte'. *Amnesty International*, 3 October 2011, www.amnesty.org/en/news-and-updates/warring-libyan-forces-must-allow-humanitarian-aid-reach-sirte-2011-10-03.

Anand, R. P. *Studies in International Law and History: Asian Perspective*. New Dehli: Martinus Nijhoff, The Hague and Lancer Books, 2004.

'Universality of International Law: An Asian Perspective'. Accessed 15 May 2012. www.profrpanand.org/sites/default/files/articles/UniversalityofIL.pdf.

Anderson, Kenneth. 'Humanitarian Inviolability in Crisis: The Meaning of Impartiality and Neutrality for UN and NGO Agencies Following the 2003–2004 Afghanistan and Iraq Conflicts'. *Harvard Human Rights Journal* 17 (2004): 41–74

Annan, Kofi. 'Two Concepts of Sovereignty'. *The Economist*, 16 September 1999. www.economist.com/node/324795.

Arab Human Rights Committee. Arab Charter on Human Rights. *International Human Rights Reports* 893 (2005). Accessed 1 April 2013. www1.umn.edu/humanrts/instree/loas2005.html.

Arab Organisation for Human Rights. 'Report of the Independent Civil Society Fact-Finding Mission to Libya'. January 2012.

Armstrong, J. D. 'The International Red Cross Committee and Political Prisoners'. *International Organisation* 39 (1985): 615–642.

Arnison, Nancy D. 'International Law and Non-Intervention: When do Humanitarian Concerns Supersede Sovereignity?' *Fletcher Forum of World Affairs* 17 (1993): 199–211.

Arnison, Nancy D. ASEAN (Association of South East Asian Nations). 'Agreement on Disaster Management and Emergency Response'. Vientiane, 26 July 2005. www.asean.org/communities/asean-socio-cultural-community/item/the-asean-agreement-on-disaster-management-and-emergency-response.

ASEAN Agreement on Disaster Management and Emergency Response Work Programme for 2010–2015. Accessed on 1 May 2013. www.asean.org/resources/publications/asean-publications/item/asean-agreement-on-disaster-management-and-emergency-response-work-programme-for-2010-2015.

ASEAN Charter; Terms of Reference of the ASEAN Intergovernmental Commission on Human Rights. ASEAN Human Rights Declaration. 21st ASEAN Summit in Phnom Phen, Cambodia on 18 November 2012. http://aichr.org/documents/.

'ASEAN Declaration on the Protection and Promotion of the Rights of Migrant Workers'. Accessed 1 April 2013. www.asean.org/communities/asean-political-security-community/item/asean-declaration-on-the-protection-and-promotion-of-the-rights-of-migrant-workers-3.

'ASEAN-UN ESCAP Joint Press Release – ASEAN – UN ESCAP Convene a Post-Nargis Lessons Learning Conference', Jakarta, 27 August 2010'. n.d. www.aseansec.org/25133.htm.

'*Charter of the Association of Southeast Asian Nations*'. 13th ASEAN Summit, Singapore, 2007. www.asean.org/archive/publications/ASEAN-Charter.pdf.

ASEAN Human Rights Declaration. Association of South East Asian Nations (ASEAN), 19 November 2012. Accessed 15 February 2013. www.unhcr.org/refworld/docid/50c9fea82.html.

'Selected Basic ASEAN Indicators as of 14 January 2013'. *ASEAN Stats*. Accessed 1 April 2013. www.asean.org/images/2013/resources/statistics/Selected%20Key%20Indicators_/SummaryTable.pdf.

'Women and Girls: The Visible Force of Resilience Children and Women of ASEAN, Step Up for Disaster Risk Reduction!' 12 October 2012. Accessed 1 April 2013. www.asean.org/news/asean-secretariat-news/item/women-and-girls-the-visible-force-of-resilience-children-and-women-of-asean-step-up-for-disaster-risk-reduction-a-joint-commemoration-of-the-asean-day-for-disaster-management-and-the-international-day-for-disaster-reduction?category_id=27.

Asian Development Bank. 'Asian Water Development Outlook 2013: Measuring Water Security in Asia and the Pacific'. Asia Pacific Water Forum, 2013. www.adb.org/sites/default/files/pub/2013/asian-water-development-outlook-2013.pdf.

Asian Research Center for Migration. 'Children Caught in Conflicts: The Impact of Armed Conflict on Children in South East Asia'. *Asian Research Center for Migration, Institute of Asian Studies*, Chulalongkorn University, 2007. www.crin.org/docs/CIDA_Caught_Conflict.pdf.

Atkins, G. P. *Encyclopedia of the Inter-American System*. Westport: Greenwood Publishing Group, 1997.

AU (African Union). *African Charter on the Rights and Welfare of the Child*, 1990. www.au.int/en/sites/default/files/Charter_En_African_Charter_on_the_Rights_and_Wlefare_of_the_Child_AddisAbaba_July1990.pdf.

'Constitutive Act of the African Union'. *Adopted by the 36th Ordinary Session of the Assembly of Heads of State and Government*, 11 July 2000. Lome, Togo. Accessed 1 April 2013. http://au.int/en/sites/default/files/Constitutive_Act_en_0.htm.

African Union Convention for the Protection and Assistance of Internally Displaced Persons. Adopted by the Special Summit of the Union held in Kampala, Uganda. 23 October 2009. http://au.int/en/content/african-union-convention-protection-and-assistance-internally-displaced-persons-africa.

Tunis Reporting Guidelines. 'State Party Reporting Guidelines for Economic, Social and Cultural Rights in the African Charter on Human and Peoples' Rights'. www.achpr.org/files/instruments/economic-social-cultural-guidelines/achpr_instr_tunis_reporting_guidelines_esc_rights_2012_eng.pdf.

Auden, W. H. 'First Things First'. 1956. Accessed 7 April 2013. www.poets.org/viewmedia.php/prmMID/19467.

Babel, Mukand S. and Shahriar M. Wahid. 'Fresh Water Under Threat: South East Asia Vulnerability Assessment of Fresh Water Resources to Environmental Change, Mekong River'. UNEP, 2009. Accessed 31 March 2013. www.unep.org/pdf/SEA_Water_report.pdf.

Bailey, Sydney and Sam Saws. *The Procedure of the UN Security Council.* Oxford: Clarendon Press, 1998, 3rd ed.

Baiquni M. and R. Rijanta. 'Konflik Pengelolaan Lingkungan dan Sumber Daya Dalam Era Otonomi dan Transisi Masyarakat'. *Bumi Lestari Journal of Environment*, vol. 7, No. 1 (2007), 1–22.

Ballentine, Karen and Heiko Nitschke. *Profiting from Peace: Managing Resource Dimension of Civil Wars.* Boulder: Lynne Rienner Publishers, 2005.

Barber, Rebecca. 'Facilitating Humanitarian Assistance in International Humanitarian and Human Rights Law'. *International Review of the Red Cross* 91, No. 874 (2009): 371–392. www.icrc.org/eng/assets/files/other/irrc-874-barber.pdf.

'Protecting the Right to Housing in the Aftermath of Natural Disasters: Standards in International Human Rights Law'. *International Journal of Refugee Law* 20 (2008): 432–68.

Barnett, Michael. 'Review Essay: What is the Future of Humanitarianism?'. *Global Governance* 9 (2003): 401–416.

Barnett, Michael and Thomas G. Weiss. 'Humanitarianism: A Brief History of the Present'. In Barnett and Weiss, *Humanitarianism in Question: Politics, Power, Ethics*, 15–24.

Humanitarianism in Question: Politics, Power, Ethics. Ithaca: Cornell University Press, 2008.

Bartholomeus, Lance. 'The Legal Framework of Humanitarian Assistance in the UN System'. 7th AIDA IHL Forum, Al-Ram, 10 May 2006. www.diakonia.se/documents/public/ihl/ihlfoum/th7/lance_legal_framework_of_humanitarian_assistance_in_the_un_system_final.pdf.

Barutciski, M. 'A Critical View on UNHCR's Mandate Dilemmas'. *Int'l J. of Refugees L.* 14 (2002): 365–381.

Bassiouni, M. Cherif. 'Accountability for International Crime and Serious Violations of Fundamental Human Rights'. *Law and Contemporary Problems* 59, No. 4 (1996): 63–74.

Bekker, Gina. 'The African Committee of Experts on the Rights and Welfare of the Child'. In *The African Regional Human Rights System: 30 Years after the African Charter on Human and Peoples' Rights*, ed. Manisuli Ssenyonjo. Leiden: Martinus Nijhoff Publishers, 2012, 249–264.

Bell Daniel A. and Joseph H. Carens. 'The Ethical Dilemmas of International Human Rights and Humanitarian NGOs: Reflections on a Dialogue

Between Practitioners and Theorists'. *Human Rights Quarterly* 26, No. 2 (2004): 303–329.

Bellamy, Alex J. 'Should Nations Force Aid on Others?'. *Natural Hazards Observer* (2010): 422–28.

Benton Heath, J. 'Disasters, Relief, and Neglect: The Duty to Accept Humanitarian Assistance and the Work of the International Law Commission'. *New York University Journal of International Law and Politics (JILP)* 43, No. 2 (2011): 419–477.

Berdal, Mats R. and David M. Malone. *Greed and Grievance: Economic Agendas in Civil Wars*. Boulder: Lynne Rienner Publishers, 2000.

Bernard, Vincent. 'Editorial: The Future of Humanitarian Action'. *IRRC* 884 (2011): 891–989.

Best, Geoffrey. *War and Law Since 1945*. Oxford University Press, 1994.

Binder, Andrea and Claudia Meier. 'Opportunity Knocks: Why Non-Western Donors Enter Humanitarianism and How to Make the Best of it'. *International Review of the Red Cross* 93 (2011): 1135–1149.

Bird, Annie. 'Third State Responsibility for Human Rights Violations'. *European Journal of International Law* 21, No. 4 (1 November 2010): 883–900.

Bird, Jeremy, Wouter Lincklaen Arriens and Dennis Von Custodio. 'Water Rights and Water Allocation: Issues and Challenges for Asia'. Water for All Series 17. *Asian Development Bank*, 2009. www.adb.org/sites/default/files/pub/2009/Water-Rights.pdf.

Blondel, J.-L. 'Getting Access to the Victims: Role and Activities of the ICRC'. *Journal of Peace Research* 24 (1987): 307–314.

BNI Online. 'Discrimination Over Aid Distribution Among Cyclone Victims: new report'. n.d. www.bnionline.net/news/miima/4558-discrimination-over-aid-distribution-among-cyclone-victims-new-report.html.

BNPB (*Badan Nasional Penanggulangan Bencana*) Indonesian National Board of Disaster Response, *Gema BNPB* 2, No. 3 (November) 2011.

Boissier, Pierre. *History of the ICRC: From Solferino to Tsushima*. Geneva: Henry Dunant Institute, 1985.

Boisson de Chaournes, Laurence. 'Responsibility To Protect: Reflecting Solidarity?'. In *Solidarity: A Structural Principle of International Law*, ed. Rüdiger Wolfrum and Chie Kojima, 109. Berlin: Springer, 2010, 93–110.

Bolaños Enrique, Tania. *Anwendung des humanitären Völkerrechts auf militärische Interventionen der Vereinten Nationen in internen bewaffneten Konflikten unter besonderer Beachtung der bewaffneten Konflikte in Afrika*. Konstanz: Hartung-Gorre Verlag, 2011.

Bond for International Development. 'Anti-Bribery Principles and Guidance for NGOs – June 2011'. www.mango.org.uk/Pool/NGO-Anti-bribery-Principles-and-Guidance-Final.pdf.

Borda, Sandra. 'Política exterior y derechos humanos en Colombia: un manual para la contención de la presión internacional'. In *Derechos humanos en la política exterior. Seis casos latinoamericanos*, ed. Natalia Saltalamacchia and Ana Covarrubias. Mexico: ITAM/Miguel Angel Porrúa, 2011, 123–60.

La Internacionalización de la paz y de la guerra en Colombia durante los gobiernos de Andres Pastrana y Alvaro Uribe. Busqueda de legitimidad politica y capacidad military. Universidad de los Andes: Ediciones Uniandes, 2013.

The Internationalization of Domestic Conflicts: A Comparative Study of Colombia, El Salvador And Guatemala, Dissertation for the Faculty of the Graduate School of the University of Minnesota, May 2009. wwwprof.uniandes.edu.co/~sborda/publicaciones/2009%20-%20The%20internationalization%20of%20domestic%20conflicts.%;20A%20comparative%20study%20of%20Colombia,%20El%20Salvador%20and%20Guatemala.pdf.

Boswijk, Sanne. 'SADC Members Convene to Enhance Legal Preparedness in the Region'. *Disaster Law Newsletter*, October 2012. Accessed on 13 April 2013. www.ifrc.org/en/what-we-do/idrl/latest-news/disaster-law-newsletter-october-2012/sadc-60169/.

Bothe, Michael. 'Friedenssicherung und Kriegsrecht'. In *Völkerrecht*, ed. Wolfgang Graf Vitzthum. Berlin, New York: Walter de Gruyter, 2010, 5th edn., 589–667.

'Relief Actions'. In *Encyclopedia of Public International Law*, vol. 4, ed. Rudolf Bernhardt, 171. Amsterdam: Elsevier, 1992, 168–171.

Botswana. Employment of Non-Citizens Act Chapter 47, 02, as amended by Act 19, 1992. www.ilo.org/wcmsp5/groups/public/—ed_protect/—protrav/—ilo_aids/documents/legaldocument/wcms_125672.pdf

Boutros-Ghali, Boutros. *An Agenda for Development*. New York: United Nations, 1995.

Boyd, David R. 'Right to Water: Moving from International Action to National Recognition'. In *The Global Water Crisis: Addressing an Urgent Security Issue*, eds. Harriet Bigas, Tim Morris, Bob Sandford and Safar Adeel, 132. Thomas S. Axworthy, 2011–2012. www.inweh.unu.edu/WaterSecurity/documents/WaterSecurity_FINAL_Aug2012.pdf.

Brauman, Rony and Joelle Tanguy. 'The MSF Experience'. *MSF*, 1998. Accessed on 31 March 2013. www.doctorswithoutborders.org/work/field/msfexperience.cfm.

Bridgman, Raymond L. *The First Book of World Law: A Compilation of the International Conventions to Which the Principal Nations Are Signatory, with a Survey of Their Significance*. Boston: Ginn and Company Publishers, 1911. www.archive.org/details/firstbookworldl01foungoog.

Brookings-Bern Project on Internal Displacement. 'Synthesis Report of Regional Workshop on Protecting and Promoting Rights in Natural Disasters in South East Asia: Prevention and Response'. May 14–15, 2010. Accessed

1 April 2013. www.brookings.edu/~/media/events/2010/5/14%20idp%20indonesia%20workshop/0514_idp_indonesia_workshop.pdf.

Buchanan-Smith, Margaret. *How the Sphere Project Came Into Being: A Case Study of Policy Making in the Humanitarian Aid Sector and the Relative Influence of Research*. London: Overseas Development Institute, 2003, Working Paper 215.

Bueno de Mesquita, Judith, Paul Hunt and Rajat Khosla. 'The Human Rights Responsibility of International Assistance and Cooperation in Health'. In *Universal Human Rights and Extraterritorial Obligations*, ed. Mark Gibney and Sigrun I. Skogly. Philadelphia: University of Pennsylvania Press, 2010, 104–129.

Buergenthal, Thomas. 'Human Rights'. *The Max Planck Encyclopedia of Public International Law*. www.mpeil.de.

Buffard, Isabelle and Karl Zemanek. 'The "Object and Purpose" of a Treaty: An Enigma?'. *Austrian Review of International and European Law* 3 (1998): 311–345.

Bugnion, Francois. *The International Committee of the Red Cross and the Protection of War Victims*. Oxford: Macmillan, 2003.

Buis, Emiliano. J. 'The Implementation of International Humanitarian Law by Human Rights Courts: The Example of the Inter-American Human Rights System'. In *International Humanitarian Law and Human Rights Law*, ed. Roberta Arnold et al. Leiden: Koninklijke Brill, 2008, 269–293.

Bundesregierung. 'Merkel: UN-Sicherheitsrat mit Myanmar befassen'. *Bundesregierung*, 9 May 2008. www.bundesregierung.de/Content/DE/Archiv16/Artikel/2008/05/2008-05-09-bk-birma.html.

Burgstaller, Markus. *Theories of Compliance with International Law*. Martinus Nijhoff Publishers, 2005.

Buruma, Ian and Avishai Margalit. *Occidentalism: The West in the Eyes of Its Enemies*. New York: Penguin Press, 2004.

Buttlar, Stein von. *Völkerrecht*. Köln, München: Carl Heymanns Verlag, 2009.

Caminos, Hugo. 'The Role of the OAS in the Promotion and Protection of Democratic Governance'. *Recueil Des Courses* 273 (1998): 107–237.

CARE International. 'CARE International Annual Report 2011'. Accessed 13 April 2013. www.care-international.org/Annual-Report/annual-report.html.

Carlson, Kierstan Lee. 'Fighting Firearms with Fire in the OAS: A Critical Evaluation of the Inter-American Convention against the Manufacturing of and Trafficking in Firearms, Ammunition and other Related Materials'. *The American University International Law Review* 25 (2010): 611–648.

Caron, David D. 'Addressing Catastrophes: Conflicting Images of Solidarity and Self-interest'. In *The international Aspects of Natural and Industrial Catastrophes*, ed. David D. Caron and Charles Leben. Martinus Nijhoff, Hague Academy of International Law, 2001, 3–29.

Carribean Disaster Emergency Management Agency. 'Agreement Establishing the Caribbean Disaster Emergency Management Agency'. Accessed 4 June 2013. www.caricom.org/jsp/secretariat/legal_instruments/agreement_cdema.pdf.

Case, Carl E. 'A Mine-free Central America: How Can We Improve on Success?'. *Journal of ERW and Mine Action* 14 (2010): 6–10. Accessed 29 March 2013. http://maic.jmu.edu/journal/journal%20pdfs/142.pdf.

Castro, Fidel. *La Paz en Colombia*. Editora Política, 2008.

CDC (Centers for Disease Control). 'Assessing Access to Water and Sanitation'. *Centers for Disease Control and Prevention*, 31 October 2012. Accessed 23 June 2013. www.cdc.gov/healthywater/global/assessing.html.

CESCR (Committee on Economic, Social and Cultural Rights). 'Consideration of Reports Submitted by States Parties under Articles 16 and 17 of the Covenant – Concluding Observations' (E/C.12/1/Add.57, 21 May 2001.

General Comment 3: 'The Nature of States Parties Obligations' (Fifth session, 1990), UN Doc. E/1991/23, annex III at 86 (1991), reprinted in Compilation of General Comments and General Recommendations Adopted by Human Rights Treaty Bodies, UN Doc. HRI/GEN/1/Rev.6 at 14 (2003). www.unhchr.ch/tbs/doc.nsf/0/94bdbaf59b43a424c12563ed0052b664.

General Comment 4, 'The Right to Adequate Housing' (Sixth session, 1991), UN Doc. E/1992/23, annex III at 114 (1991), reprinted in Compilation of General Comments and General Recommendations Adopted by Human Rights Treaty Bodies, UN Doc. HRI/GEN/1/Rev.6 at 18 (2003)

General Comment 12, 'The Right to Adequate Food' (Twentieth session, 1999), UN Doc. E/C.12/1999/5 (1999), reprinted in Compilation of General Comments and General Recommendations Adopted by Human Rights Treaty Bodies, UN Doc. HRI/GEN/1/Rev.6 at 62 (2003).

General Comment 13, 'The Right to Education' (Twenty-first session, 1999), UN Doc. E/C.12/1999/10 (1999), reprinted in Compilation of General Comments and General Recommendations Adopted by Human Rights Treaty Bodies, UN Doc. HRI/GEN/1/Rev.6 at 70 (2003).

General Comment 14, 'The Right to the Highest Attainable Standard of Health' (Twenty-second session, 2000), UN Doc. E/C.12/2000/4 (2000), reprinted in Compilation of General Comments and General Recommendations Adopted by Human Rights Treaty Bodies, UN Doc. HRI/GEN/1/Rev.6 at 85 (2003).

General Comment 15, 'The Right to Water' (Twenty-ninth session, 2003), UN Doc. E/C.12/2002/11 (2003), reprinted in Compilation of General Comments and General Recommendations Adopted by Human Rights Treaty Bodies, UN Doc. HRI/GEN/1/Rev.6 at 105 (2003).

General Comment 17, 'The Right of Everyone to Benefit from the Protection of the Moral and Material Interests Resulting from any Scientific, Literary or

Artistic Production of which He or She is the Author' (Article 15, paragraph 1 (c), of the Covenant), UN Doc. E/C.12/GC/17 (2006).

General Comment 18, 'The Equal Right of Men and Women to the Enjoyment of all Economic, Social and Cultural Rights' (Article 6), (Thirty-fifth session, 2006), UN Doc. E/C.12/GC/18 (2006).

General Comment 19, 'The Right to Social Security' (Article 9), (Thirty-ninth session, 2007), UN Doc. E/C.12/GC/19 (2008).

General Comment No. 21,'The Right of Everyone to Take Part in Cultural Life' (Article 15, Paragraph 1 (a)), UN Doc. E/C.12/GC/21 (2009).

Chandler, David. 'The Road to Military Humanitarianism: How the Human Rights NGO's shaped a new Humanitarian Agenda'. *Human Rights Quarterly* 23 (2001): 678–700.

Chapman, Audrey and Sage Russell. *Core Obligations: Building a Framework for Economic, Social and Cultural Rights*. Antwerp: Intersentia, 2002.

Chellaney, Brahma. *Water: Asia's New Battleground*. India: Harper Collins, 2011.

Chesterman, Simon, Michael Ignatieff and Ramesh Chandra Thakur. *Making States Work: From State Failure to State-Building*. United Nations University, International Peace Institute Policy Papers, 15 July 2004: www.ipinst.org/publication/policy-papers/detail/140-making-states-work-from-state-failure-to-state-building.html.

Chesterman, Simon, Thomas M. Franck and David M. Malone. *Law and Practice of the United Nations*. New York: Oxford University Press, 2008.

Chmaytelli, Maher and Peter S. Green. 'Libya Rebels, NATO Don't Have Joint Operations, Official Says'. *Bloomberg*, 16 April 2011. www.bloomberg.com/news/2011-04-16/libya-rebels-nato-don-t-have-joint-operations-official-says.html.

Chociej, Zuanna and Zafar Adeel. 'Legal and Ethical Dimensions of a Right to Water'. In *The Global Water Crisis: Addressing an Urgent Security Issue*, 122–127.

Christoplos, Ian and Dorothea Hilhorst. *Human Security and Capacity in Fragile States*. Disaster Studies Occasional Paper 01, Wageningen University, 2009.

Claude, Richard P. and Burns H. Weston. *Human Rights in the World Community: Issues And Action*. Philadelphia: University of Pennsylvania Press, 2006.

Cockayne, James and David Malone. 'The Security Council and the 1991 and 2003 Wars in Iraq'. In *The United Nations Security Council and War – The Evolution of Thought and Practice since 1945*, ed. Vaughan Lowe, Adam Roberts, Jennifer Welsh, Dominik Zaum. Oxford University Press, 2008, 384–405.

Collier, Paul. *The Bottom Billion*. New York: Oxford University Press, 2007.

Collinson, Sarah and Samir Elhawary. 'Humanitarian Space: a Review of Trends and Issues'. *HPG Report* 32 (2012): 1–26. Committee on the Elimination of Discrimination Against Women, 'Concluding Observations: Ecuador', UN

Doc. (A/49/38) §499–545 (1994), §509, www1.umn.edu/humanrts/cedaw/cedaw-Ecuador.htm.

Committee on the Rights of the Child, 'General Comment No. 4, Adolescent Health and Development in the Context of the Convention on the Rights of the Child' (Thirty-third session, 2003), UN Doc. CRC/GC/2003/4 (2003).

Concannon, Brian and Beatrice Lindstrom. 'Cheaper, Better, Longer Lasting: a Right-Based Approach to Disaster Response in Haiti'. *Emory International Law Review* 25 (2011): 1145–1191.

Coomans, Fons. 'Application of the International Covenant on Economic Social and Cultural Rights in the Framework of International Organisations'. *Max Planck Yearbook of United Nations Law* 11 (2007): 359–390.

'The Extraterritorial Scope of the International Covenant on Economic, Social and Cultural Rights in the Work of the United Nations Committee on Economic, Social and Cultural Rights'. *Human Rights Law Review* 11 (2011): 1–35.

Cooper, Andrew and Thomas Legler. *Intervention Without Intervening? The OAS Defense and Promotion of Democracy in the Americas*. New York: Palgrave Macmillan, 2007.

Council of Europe. 'Lives Lost in the Mediterranean Sea: Who is Responsible?'. *CoE*, 29 March 2012. http://assembly.coe.int/CommitteeDocs/2012/20120329_mig_RPT.EN.pdf>.

Council of the European Union. Council Regulation (EC) No. 1257/96 of 20 June 1996 concerning humanitarian aid, OJ L163/1

Joint Statement by the Council and Representatives of the Governments of the Member States meeting within the Council, the European Parliament and the European Commission (2008/C25/01), 'The European Consensus on Humanitarian Aid', *Official Journal of the European Union*, 30.1.2008, C25/1–C25/12.

Council for Research on the Epidemiology of Disasters. 'The EM-DAT Glossary'. Accessed 12 March 2013. www.emdat.be/glossary/9#term81.

Coupland, Robin. 'Humanity: What is it and How Does it Influence International Law?' *International Review of the Red Cross*, 844 (2001): 969–989.

Craswell, Eric T. 'Water and Poverty in Southeast Asia – The Research Agenda from a Global Perspective'. Accessed 19 March 2013. www.gwsp.org/fileadmin/downloads/Asian_Ag_Prod_Journal.pdf.

Craven, Matthew C. R. *The International Covenant on Economic, Social and Cultural Rights: A Perspective on its Development*. Oxford: Clarendon Press, 1998.

D'Aspremont, Jean. 'Contemporary International Rule-making and the Public Character of International Law'. *International Law and Justice Working Paper*, December 2006. Accessed 27 December 2010. www.iilj.org.

Dag Hammarskjöld Foundation. 'Post-Nargis Analysis – The Other Side of the Story'. DHF, n.d. www.dhf.uu.se/publications/other-publications/post-nargis-analysis-%e2%80%93-the-other-side-of-the-story/.

Dan-Harry, Rachel Ordu. 'UN Human Rights Council Affirms Safe Drinking Water and Sanitation as a Human Right'. *Unitarian Universalist Service Committee*, 15 October 2010. Accessed 25 March 2013. www.uusc.org/blog/entry/2404/un_human_rights_council_affirms_safe_drinking_water_and_sanitation_human_right.

DanChurchAid. 'Anti-Corruption Policy'. www.danchurchaid.org/content/download/77278/642671/version/1/file/AntCorruptPol_Eng_Final_WEB.pdf.

DANIDA, *Joint Evaluation of Emergency Assistance to Rwanda* (JEEAR). Accessed 8 November 2011. www.um.dk/danida/evalueringsrapporter/1997-=_rwanda.

Danish Broadcasting Corporation. 'Dansk FN-chef i Somalia: Vi bestikker de mange militser for at få maden frem: 25.000 kr. pr. Lastbil'. *U-landsnyt*, 10 February 2009. www.u-landsnyt.dk/nyhed/10-02-09/dansk-fn-chef-i-somalia-vi-bestikker-de-mange-mili.

Dapo Akande, C. 'Does SC Resolution 1973 Permit Coalition Military Support for the Libyan Rebels?'. *EJIL: Talk!*, 31 March 2011. www.ejiltalk.org/does-sc-resolution-1973-permit-coalition-military-support-for-the-libyan-rebels/.

Darcy, James and Charles-Antoine Hoffmann. 'According to Need? Needs Assessment and Decision-making in the Humanitarian Sector'. *HPG Report* 15 (2003): 1–71.

De Albuquerque, Catarina. *The Human Right to Water and Sanitation, The Legal Framework and a Guide to Advocacy, for Field Review*. France: ACF, 2009. www.worldwatercouncil.org/fileadmin/wwc/Right_to_Water/Project_8_HRTWS_in_Emergencies_Handbook.pdf.

De Mello, Sergio Vieira. 'UN USG for Humanitarian Affairs,' OCHA. Accessed 5 June 2013. www.internal-displacement.org/8025708F004CFA06/(httpKeyDocumentsByCategory)/37BEFA013DA18845802570A000467AA1/$file/GPsEnglish.pdf.

De Montesquieu, Charles. *The Spirit of Laws*. Complete text available at: www.constitution.org/cm/sol-02.htm.

De Wet, Erika. 'The International Constitutional Order'. *International and Comparative Law Quarterly* 55 (2006): 51–76.

Deng, Francis M. *Guiding Principles on Internal Displacement*. UN Doc. E/CN.4/1998/53/Add.2, 11 February, New York, 1998.

Sovereignty As Responsibility: Conflict Management in Africa. Washington: Brookings Institution Press, 1996.

Denne, Sarah. 'Re-thinking Humanitarian Aid in the Post-Gulf War Era: the International Committee of the Red Cross Takes the Lead'. *Case W. Res. J. Int'l L.* 39 (2007–8): 867–895.

Dennis, Michael J. 'Application of Human Rights Treaties Extraterritorially in Times of Armed Conflict and Military Occupation'. *American Journal of International Law* 99 (2005): 119–141.

Department for International Development. 'Saving lives, preventing suffering and building resilience: The UK Government's Humanitarian Policy'.

UK Department for International Development, 2011. www.dfid.gov.uk/Documents/publications1/1/TheUKGovernment'sHumanitarianPolicySeptember2011Final.pdf.

Diados, Alexander. 'Benghazi, Cradle of Revolt, Condemns Gaddafi'. *The Star*, 23 February 2011. http://thestar.com.my/news/story.asp?file=/2011/2/24/worldupdates/2011-02-23T222628_01_NOOTR_RTRMDNC_0_-550982-4&sec=Worldupdates.

Dijkzeul, Dennis. 'Inleiding: Internationaal management van menslievendheid' (Introduction: International Management of Humanity). In *Humanitaire Ruimte: Tussen onpartijdigheid en politiek* (Humanitarian Space: In between Impartiality and Politics), ed. Dennis Dijkzeul, and Joost Herman. Gent: Academia Press, 2009/2010, 7–12.

Dijkzeul, Dennis and Dirk Salomons. 'De politieke economie van humanitaire ruimte' (The Political Economy of Humanitarian Space). In *Humanitaire Ruimte: Tussen onpartijdigheid en politiek* (Humanitarian Space: In between Impartiality and Politics), ed. Dennis Dijkzeul, and Joost Herman. Gent: Academia Press, 2009/2010, 29–64.

Dijkzeul, Dennis and Joost Herman. 'Hooggestemde beginselen en het kleinste kwaad' (Lofty Principles and the Smallest Evil). In *Humanitaire Ruimte: Tussen onpartijdigheid en politiek* (Humanitarian Space: In between Impartiality and Politics), ed. Dennis Dijkzeul, and Joost Herman. Gent: Academia Press, 2009/2010, 328–330.

Dinstein, Yoram. *The Conduct of Hostilities under the Law of International Armed Conflict*. Cambridge University Press, 2010, 2nd ed.

'The Right to Humanitarian Assistance'. *Naval War College Review* 4 (2000): 77–91.

Domestici-Met, Marie-José. 'Humanitarian Action – A Scope for the Responsibility to Protect? Part I: Humanitarian Assistance Looking for a Legal Regime Allowing its Delivery to Those in Need under any Circumstances'. *Goettingen Journal of International Law* 3 (2009): 397–416.

Donati, Federica and Margret Vidar. 'International Legal Dimensions of the Right to Food'. In *Global Obligations for the Right to Food*, ed. George Kent. Lanham: Rowman & Littlefield Publishers Inc., 2008, 47–88.

Donini, Antonio. 'Between a Rock and a Hard Place: Integration or Independence of Humanitarian Action?'. *IRRC* (2011): 141–157.

'Beyond Neutrality: On the Compatibility of Military Intervention and Humanitarian Assistance'. *Fletcher Forum of World Affairs* 19 (1995): 31–45.

Donini, Antonio and Ian Smillie. *The Golden Fleece*. Boulder: Kumarian Press, 2012.

Donnelly, Kristina, M-L. Ha, H. Cooley and J. Morrison. 'Water as a Casualty of Conflict: Threats to Business and Society in High-Risk Areas'. June 2012. Accessed 18 March 2013. http://unglobalcompact.org/docs/issues_doc/Environment/Water_as_a_casuality.pdf.

Dorf, Yvonne. *Völkerrecht*. Munich: C. H. Beck, 2011.

Dörmann, Knut, Louise Doswald-Beck and Robert Kolb. *Elements of War Crimes under the Rome Statute of the International Criminal Court: sources and commentary*. Cambridge University Press, 2002.

Drews, Christian. *Post-Conflict Peace-Building*. Baden-Baden: Nomos, 2001.

Dula, Peter. 'Constantine, Colonialism and the NGOs'. *Mennonite Central Committee*, 2007. Accessed 8 November 2011. www.gordon.edu/ccs/usaspeakers/peterdula.

Dulles, Cardinal Avery, SJ. 'Christianity and Humanitarian Action'. In *Traditions, Values and Humanitarian Action*, ed. Kevin M. Cahill, MD. New York: Fordham University Press, 2003, 5–20.

Dunant, Henri. *A Memory of Solferino*. Geneva : ICRC, 1986.

Dungel, Joakim. '*Humanitarian Use of Force?: The Right to Afford Humanitarian Assistance in Internal Armed Conflicts*'. MA thesis, University of Gothenburg, 2004. http://gupea.ub.gu.se/bitstream/2077/2013/1/200422.pdf.

'A Right to Humanitarian Assistance in Internal Armed Conflicts Respecting Sovereignty, Neutrality and Legitimacy: Practical Proposals to Practical Problems'. *Journal of Humanitarian Assistance* (2004). Accessed 31 May 2013. http://sites.tufts.edu/jha/archives/838.

Ebersole, Jon M. 'The Mohonk Criteria for Humanitarian Assistance in Complex Emergencies: Task Force on Ethical and Legal Issues in Humanitarian Assistance'. *Human Rights Quarterly* 17 (1995): 192–208.

ECHR. *The European Convention for the Protection of Human Rights and Fundamental Freedoms* (ECHR). 1950. http://conventions.coe.int/Treaty/en/Treaties/Html/005.htm.

Eckstein, Gabriel. 'Water Scarcity, Conflict and Security in a Climate Change World: Challenges and Opportunities for International Law and Policy'. *Texas Wesleyan University School of Law*, 9 December 2009. http://papers.ssrn.com/sol3/papers.cfm?abstract_id=1425796.

ECOSOC (UN Economic and Social Council). 'Guiding Principles on Internal Displacement' (E/CN.4/1998/53/Add.2), 11 February 1998.

'Strengthening of the Coordination of Emergency Humanitarian Assistance of the United Nations'. Resolution (E/2012/L.11), 11 July 2012.

ECOWAS (Economic Community of West African States). 'ECOWAS Code of Conduct on Humanitarian Action in the Pipeline'. *ECOWAS Press Release* No. 257, 2012. Accessed on 30 March 2013. http://news.ecowas.int/presseshow.php?nb=257&lang=en&annee=2012.

ECSR (European Committee on Social Rights). 'Conclusions Former Yugoslav Republic of Macedonia', 2009. Accessed 1 April 2013. www.coe.int/t/dghl/monitoring/socialcharter/Conclusions/State/MKDXIX2_en.pdf.

'Conclusions Greece', 1998. Accessed 1 April 2013. www.coe.int/t/dghl/monitoring/socialcharter/Conclusions/Year/XIV1Vol1_en.pdf.

'Conclusions Moldova', 2009. Accessed 1 April 2013. www.coe.int/t/dghl/monitoring/socialcharter/Conclusions/State/Moldova2009_en.pdf.

'Conclusions Turkey', 2003. Accessed 1 April 2013. www.coe.int/t/dghl/monitoring/socialcharter/Conclusions/State/TurkeyXVI2_en.pdf.

ECtHR (European Court of Human Rights). 'Annual Report 2012'. Accessed 1 April 2013. www.echr.coe.int/NR/rdonlyres/9A8CE219-E94F-47AE-983C-B4F6E4FCE03C/0/2012_Rapport_Annuel_EN.pdf.

Elhawary, Samir. 'Between War and Peace: Land and Humanitarian Action in Colombia'. *HPG – Humanitarian Policy Group*, ODI (Working paper, 2007).

'Protegiendo civiles y mejorando la seguridad en Colombia: ¿Cuál es la diferencia?'. *Humanitarian Exchange Magazine* 45 (2010). Accessed 19 October 2011. www.odihpn.org/report.asp?id=3063.

Eman, R., 'Sosialisasi Peraturan Pemerintah tentang Pelaksanaan Penataan Ruang'. *Workshop Paper on Dissemination of Spatial Planning*, Gadjah Mada University, 17 September 2008.

Erikson, Daniel. 'The Haiti Dilemma'. *Brown Journal of World Affairs* 10 (2004): 285–297.

Etzioni, Amitai. 'A Self-restrained Approach to Nation-building by Foreign Powers'. *International Affairs* 80 (2004): 1–17.

European Commission, Report from the Commission to the European Parliament and the Council – Annual Report on the European Union's Humanitarian Aid and Civil Protection Policies and their Implementation in 2011, COM (2012).

European Commission – ECHO (EU Humanitarian Aid and Civil Protection) Commission Paper. 'Control Mechanism Applicable to Partners'. http://ec.europa.eu/echo/files/partners/humanitarian_aid/fpa/A_or_P_assessment_en.pdf.

'Disaster Preparedness Regional Initiatives in SE Asia', *ECHO*, 2007. http://ec.europa.eu/echo/files/policies/dipecho/presentations/se_asia_11_07_en.pdf.

'ECHO Fact Sheet: East and South East Asia, and the Pacific'. *European Commission*, 2012. Accessed 9 March 2013. http://ec.europa.eu/echo/files/aid/countries/factsheets/esea_en.pdf.

'ECHO's Finances'. http://ec.europa.eu/echo/funding/finances_en.htm.

Framework Partnership Agreement with Humanitarian Organisations (2008–2012). http://ec.europa.eu/echo/partners/humanitarian_aid/fpa_en.htm.

'Humanitarian Aid: Frequently Asked Questions'. MEMO/07/238, Brussels 13 June 2007. http://europa.eu/rapid/press-release_MEMO-07-238_en.htm.

'Libyan Crisis: Humanitarian Partners'. *ECHO*, 18 August 2011. http://ec.europa.eu/echo/files/aid/countries/libya_partners_funding_en.pdf.

'Timeline of the Libyan Crisis'. *ECHO*, 17 February 2012. http://ec.europa.eu/echo/media/photos/picture_stories/libya06_en.htm.

Ewins, Pete, Paul Harvey, Kevin Savage and Alex Jacobs. 'Mapping the Risks of Corruption in Humanitarian Action'. *Overseas Development Institute* (July 2006). www.odi.org.uk/resources/download/607.pdf.

Federal Political Dept. *Final Record of the Diplomatic Conference of Geneva 1949.* Berne, 1951. www.loc.gov/rr/frd/Military_Law/pdf/.

Feinäugle, Clemens. *Hoheitsgewalt im Völkerrecht: Das 1267-Sanktionsregime der UN und seine rechtliche Fassung.* Heidelberg: Springer, 2011.

Ferris, Elizabeth. 'Megatrends and the future of humanitarian action'. *International Review of the Red Cross* 93 (2011): 915–938.

Financial and Administrative Framework Agreement (FAFA). http://ec.europa.eu/echo/partners/humanitarian_aid/fafa_en.htm.

Fischer, Horst. 'International Disaster Response Law Treaties: Trends, Patterns and Lacunae'. *International Disaster Response Laws, Principles and Practice: Reflections, Prospects and Challenges.* Geneva: IFRC, 2003: 24–46.

'Kollektive Sicherheit und Verteidigungsbündnisse'. In *Völkerrecht*, ed. Knut Ipsen. Munich: Verlag C. H. Beck, 2004, 5th ed., 1107–1131.

Fisher, David. 'Fast Food: Regulating Emergency Food Aid in Sudden-Impact Disasters'. *Vanderbilt Journal of Transnational Law* 40 (2007): 1127–52.

'Overview of Current Legal Frameworks Applicable to International Disaster Response Law'. In IFRC, *Law and Legal Issues in International Disaster Response Law: a Desk Study*, 33–82. Geneva: IFRC, 2007.

Flamholtz, Eric G., T. K. Das, and Anne S. Tsui. 'Toward an Integrative Framework of Organisational Control, Accounting, Organisation and Society'. *Accounting, Organisations and Society* (1985): 35–50.

Focarelli, Carlo. 'Duty to Protect in Cases of Natural Disasters'. *The Max Planck Encyclopedia of Public International Law*, 2010. www.mpepil.com.

'The Responsibility To Protect and Humanitarian Intervention: Too many Ambiguities for a Working Doctrine'. *Journal of Conflict & Security Law* 13 (2008): 191–213.

Forero, L. G. 'Cita de Uribe con jefe de la Cruz Roja Internacional'. *El Tiempo*, 28, January 2010.

Forsythe, David P. *The Humanitarians: The International Committee of the Red Cross.* Cambridge University Press, 2005.

'The ICRC: a Unique Humanitarian Protagonist'. *International Review of the Red Cross* 89, No. 865 (2007): 63–96.

'UNHCR's Mandate: The Politics of Being Non-Political'. *New Issues in Refugee Research Series, Working Paper* 33 (2001): 1–34.

Forte, Maximilian. *Slouching Towards Sirte: NATO's War on Libya and Africa* (Montreal: Baraka, 2012).

Freeland, Steven. 'Crimes Against the Environment – A role for the International Criminal Court'. Droit de l'environnement dans le Pacifique Problematiques et Perspectives Croisees, New Zealand Association for Comparative Law and Association de Legislation Comparee des Pays du Pacifique, 2005. www.upf.pf/IMG/pdf/16-freeland.pdf.

Frowein, J. A. and Nico Krisch. 'Article 39'. In *The Charter of the United Nations*, ed. Bruno Simma, vol. I, Oxford University Press, 2002: 717–729 .

Fuller, Lon L. *The Morality of Law*. New Haven: Yale University Press, 1969, revised edition.

Gadler, Alice. 'Armed Forces as Carrying Both the Stick and the Carrot? Humanitarian Aid in US Counterinsurgency Operations in Afghanistan and Iraq'. *Goettingen Journal of International Law* 3–1 (2011): 217–250.

Gardiner, Richard K. *Treaty Interpretation*. Oxford University Press, 2008.

Gasser, Hans-Peter and Nils Melzer. *Humanitäres Völkerrecht: Eine Einführung*. Urich, Basel, Geneva: Nomos, Schulthess, 2012, 2nd ed.

Gazzini, Tarcisio. 'A Unique Non-State Actor: the International Committee of the Red Cross'. *Human Rights and International Legal Discourse* 4 (2010): 32–46.

Geiss, Robin. 'Humanitarian Safeguards in Economic Sanctions Regimes: A Call for Automatic Suspension Clauses, Periodic Monitoring, and Follow-Up Assessments of Long-Term Effects'. *Harvard Human Rights Journal* 18 (2005): 167–199.

Gennet, Terry. 'Civil War in South East Asia and the Pacific: Conflict Resolution and the Problem of Recurrence'. In *Unravelling Internal Conflicts in East Asia and the Pacific: incidence, consequences and resolution*, ed. Jacob Berkovitch and Karl DeReuben Jr, 96. Maryland: LexingtonBooks, 2011. Accessed 30 March 2013.

Gerber, Paul. 'ASEAN Human Rights Declaration: a Step Forward or a Slide Backwards?'. *MONASH University*, 21 November 2012. Accessed 23 June 2013. http://theconversation.com/asean-human-rights-declaration-a-step-forward-or-a-slide-backwards-10895.

Geremia, Maurizio. 'Neutrality, Impartiality and Independence in Colombia: an ICRC Perspective'. *Humanitarian Exchange Magazine* 45 (2010). Accessed 19 October 2011. www.odihpn.org/report.asp?id=3040.

Giladi, Rotem. 'An Ambiguous Mandate: The Making of the ICRC Conventional Relief Mandate, 1946–1960' (forthcoming).

Ginbar, Yuval. 'Human Rights in ASEAN – Setting Sail or Treading Water'. *Human Rights Law Review* 10 (2010): 508–518.

Gleick, Peter H. 'Water and Conflict: Fresh Water Resources and International Security'. *International Security* 18, No. 1 (Summer, 1993): 79–112. www.pacinst.org/reports/international_security_gleick_1993.pdf.

'Water and Terrorism'. *Water Policy* 8 (2006): 481–503. Accessed on 6 April 2013. www.pacinst.org/reports/water_terrorism.pdf.

Global Humanitarian Assistance. 'Public Support for Humanitarian Crises Through NGOs'. *Development Initiatives*, 2009. www.globalhumanitarianassistance.org/wp-content/uploads/2010/07/2009-Focus-report-Public-support-for-humanitarian-crises-through-NGOs.pdf.

Gnaediger, Angelo. *Humanitarian Principles – The Importance of their Preservation during Humanitarian Crises.* Speech at Lisbon Conference 'Humanitarian Aid', October 2007.

Goffman, Erving. *Strategic Interaction.* Philadelphia: University of Pennsylvania Press, 1969.

Goldman, Robert K. 'History and Action: The Inter-American Human Rights System and the Role of the Inter-American Commission on Human Rights'. *Human Rights Quarterly* 31 (2009): 856–887.

Gómez, Sergio. 'Recursos Antidrogas, Ahora Contra La Guerrilla'. *El Tiempo*, 20 July 2002.

Gould, Charles W. 'The Right to Housing Recovery After Natural Disasters'. *Harvard Human Rights Journal* 22 (2009): 169–204.

Grafton, Quentin, Wiktor Adamowicz, Diane Dupont, Harry Nelson, Steven Renzetti, Robert J. Hill. *The Economics of the Environment and Natural Resources.* Oxford: Blackwell Publishing, 2004.

Griffiths, Martin. 'Small Arms Proliferation: A Humanitarian Concern'. In *Disarmament as Humanitarian Action: A discussion on the occasion of the 20th Anniversary of the United Nations Institute for Disarmament Research (UNIDIR).* Geneva: United Nations Publications, 2001: 5–7.

Grombach Wagner, Johanna. 'An IHL/ICRC Perspective on Humanitarian Space'. *Humanitarian Exchange Magazine* 23 (2005). www.odihpn.org/humanitarian-exchange-magazine/issue-32/an-ihl/icrc-perspective-on-humanitarian-space.

Guzman, Andrew. *How International Law Works: A Rational Choice Theory.* Oxford University Press, 2008.

Gunn, Angus M. *Encyclopedia of Disaster: Environmental Catastrophes and Human Tragedies.* London: Greenwood Press, 2008, vol. I.

Hadiprayitno, Irene I. 'The Institutionalisation of Human Rights in ASEAN'. In *Defending Human Rights: Tools for Social Justice*, ed. Lintel I., A. Buyse and B. McGonigle Leyh, Volume in Honour of Fried van Hoof at the Occasion of his Valedictory Lecture and the 30th Anniversary of the Netherlands Institute of Human Rights. Cambridge: Intersentia, 2012, 49–70.

Hafner, Gerhard. 'Pros and Cons Ensuing from Fragmentation of International Law'. *Michigan Journal of International Law* 25 (2003–2004): 849–863.

Hardcastle, Rohan and Adrian Chua. 'Victims of Natural Disasters: The Right to Receive Humanitarian Assistance'. *The International Journal of Human Rights* 4 (1997): 35–49.

Harper, Erica. 'International Law and Standards Applicable in Natural Disaster Situations'. *Report for International Development Law Organisation*. Rome: (2009). http://sheltercentre.org/sites/default/files/Natural%20Disasters%20Manual%20%28IDLO%202009%29_1.pdf.

Harroff-Tavel, Marion. 'Neutrality and Impartiality – The Importance of These Principles for the International Red Cross and Red Crescent Movement and the Difficulties Involved in Applying Them'. *IRRC* 873 (1989): 536–552.

Hart, Herbert L. A. *The Concept of Law*. Oxford: Clarendon Press, 1961.

Haski, Pierre. 'Rony Brauman: "De quel droit demander à Kadhafi de partir?"'. *Rue 89*, 15 April 2011. www.rue89.com/2011/04/15/rony-brauman-de-quel-droit-demander-a-kadhafi-de-partir-200152.

Hauslohner, Abigail. 'Egypt's NGO Crisis: How Will US Aid Play in the Controversy?'. *Time*. Last modified on 9 February 2012. www.time.com/time/world/article/0,8599,2106420,00.html.

Heinegg, Heintschel von. 'Die völkerrechtlichen Verträge als Hauptrechtsquellen des Völkerrechts'. In *Völkerrecht*, ed. Knut Ipsen. München: Beck Juristischer Verlag, 5th edition, 2008: 112–209.

Heintze, Hans-Joachim. 'Convergence Between Human Rights Law and International Humanitarian Law'. In Heintze and Zwitter, *International Law and Humanitarian Assistance*, 83–102.

'Völkerrecht und demokratische Staatsordnung, Anmerkungen anlässlich des internationalen Engagements zur Wiederherstellung der Demokratie in Haiti', *Verfassung und Recht in Übersee*, 1 (1996): 6–30.

Heintze, Hans-Joachim and Andrej Zwitter. *International Law and Humanitarian Assistance. Legal Issues Pertaining to Humanitarianism*. Berlin: Springer, 2011.

Henckaerts, Jean-Marie. 'Study on Customary International Humanitarian Law: A Contribution to the Understanding and Respect for the Rule of Law in Armed Conflict'. *International Review of the Red Cross* 87, No. 857 (2005): 175–212.

Henckaerts Jean-Marie and Louise Doswald-Beck. *Customary International Humanitarian Law*, vol. I: *Rules*. New York: Cambridge University Press, 2005.

Herman, Joost. 'Humanitaire bewegingsruimte in de 21e eeuw: de rol van het recht' (Humanitarian Space for Manoeuvre in the 21st century: the Role of Law). In *Humanitaire Ruimte: Tussen onpartijdigheid en politiek* (Humanitarian Space: In between Impartiality and Politics), ed. Dennis Dijkzeul and Joost Herman. Gent: Academia Press, 2009/2010, 65–90.

Herman, Joost and Dennis Dijkzeul. 'Current Challenges to Humanitarianism'. *The Broker*, 24 (2010): 65–90.

Herz, Monica. *The Organisation of American States (OAS)*. London: Routledge, 2011.

Hesselman, Marlies. 'Establishing a Full "Cycle of Protection" for Disaster Victims: Preparedness, Response and Recovery according to Regional and International Supervisory Bodies'. *Tilburg Law Review* 18, No. 2 (2013), 106–132.

Hilhorst, Dorothea. *Saving Lives or Saving Societies? Realities of Relief and Reconstruction*. Wageningen University Press, 2007.

Hilhorst, Dorothea and B. J. Jansen. 'Constructing Rights and Wrongs in Humanitarian Action: Contributions from a Sociology of Praxis'. *Sociology: The Journal of the British Sociological Association* 46 (2012): 891–905.

Hilhorst, Dorothea and B. J. Jansen. 'Humanitaire ruimte als arena: een perspectief op de alledaags praktijk' (Humanitarian Space as Arena: a Perspective on Everyday Practice). In *Humanitaire Ruimte: Tussen onpartijdigheid en politiek* (Humanitarian Space: In between Impartiality and Politics), ed. Dennis Dijkzeul and Joost Herman. Gent: Academia Press, 2009/2010, 124–156.

Hilhorst, Dorothea and Nadja Schmiemann. 'Humanitarian Principles and Organisational Culture: Everyday Practice in MSF-Holland'. *Development in Practice* 12 (2002): 490–500.

Hobe, Stephan. *Einführung in das Völkerrecht*. Tübingen: Narr Francke Attempto Verlag, 2008, 9th ed.

Hoffman, Peter J. and Thomas. G. Weiss. *Sword and Salve: Confronting New Wars and Humanitarian Crises*. Lanham: Rowman and Littlefield, 2006.

Hoffman, Susanna H. and Anthony Oliver-Smith. *Catastrophe and Culture, the Anthropology of Disaster*. Oxford: James Currey, 2002.

Holtzendorff, Franz von. *Handbuch des Völkerrechts*. Berlin: C. Habel, 1887.

Homan, Kess. 'Civiel-militaire relaties in complexe noodsituaties' (Civil-Military Relations in Complex Emergencies). In *Humanitaire Ruimte: Tussen onpartijdigheid en politiek* (Humanitarian Space: In between Impartiality and Politics), ed. Dennis Dijkzeul, and Joost Herman. Gent: Academia Press, 2009/2010, 257–279.

Homer-Dixon Thomas F. 'Environmental Scarcities and Violent Conflict: Evidence from Cases'. *International Security* 19, No. 1 (Summer, 1994): 5–40. http://graduateinstitute.ch/webdav/site/iheid/shared/summer/IA2009_readings/MD1.pdf.

Horwit, Betty. *Transformation of the Organisation of American States: A Multilateral Framework for Regional Governance*. London: Anthem Press, 2010.

HPN (Humanitarian Policy Network). 'ASEAN's Role in the Cyclone Nargis Response: Implications, Lessons and Opportunities'. Accessed 8 November 2011. www.odihpn.org/humanitarian-exchange-magazine/issue-41/aseans-role-in-the-cyclone-nargis-response-implications-lessons-and-opportunities.

HRW (Human Rights Watch). 'Civil Society Denounces Adoption of Flawed ASEAN Human Rights Declaration: AHRD falls far below international standards'. *Human Rights Watch*, 19 November 2012. Accessed 25 March 2013. www.hrw.org/news/2012/11/19/civil-society-denounces-adoption-flawed-asean-human-rights-declaration.

'Genocide, War Crimes, and Crimes Against Humanity: Topical Digests of the Case Law of the International Criminal Tribunal for Rwanda and the International Criminal Tribunal for the Former Yugoslavia'. *Human Rights Watch* (2004): 142, 143, www.hrw.org/reports/2004/ij/digest.pdf.

'Smoke and Mirrors – Colombia's Demobilisation of Paramilitary Groups'. August 2005. www.hrw.org/reports/2005/colombia0805/index.htm.

Hsien-Li, Tan. *The ASEAN Intergovernmental Commission on Human Rights, Institutionalising Human Rights in Southeast Asia*. New York: Cambridge University Press, 2011.

Human Rights Investigations. 'NATO Bombs the Great Man-Made River'. *Human Rights Investigations*, 27 July 2011. http://humanrightsinvestigations.org/2011/07/27/great-man-made-river-nato-bombs/.

Humanitarian Partnership Forum 'Sharaka', 'Final Report Humanitarian Partnership Forum "Sharaka"', Semiramis Intercontinental, Cairo 6 June, 2011, available at www.humanitarianforum.org/data/files/29_final_report_humanitarian_partnership_forum_29_june_2011.pdf, 15.

Humanitarian Practice Network. 'Operational Security Management in Violent Environments'. *Good Practice Review* 8 (Revised Edition). London, 2010.

Humanitarian Response Index 2010. Madrid: DARA, 2010.

IAEA. 'Convention on Assistance in the Case of a Nuclear Accident or Radiological Emergency'. 26 February 1987. Accessed 6 June 2013. www.iaea.org/Publications/Documents/Infcircs/Others/infcirc336.shtml.

Ibrahim, R. '*Status Hukum Internasional dan Perjanjian Internasional di Dalam Hukum Nasional: Permasalahan Teori dan Praktek*'. Paper presented at the National Workshop on the Indonesian Practice Toward International Treaty, Surabaya, 23–25 November 2009.

ICDO (International Civil Defence Organisation). 'Framework Convention on Civil Defence Assistance'. 22 May 2000. Accessed 6 June 2013. www.icdo.org/files/framework-convention.pdf.

ICG. 'Haiti: The Stakes of the Post-Quake Elections'. *International Crisis Group*, Report No. 35 (Washington, 2010).

ICJ (International Court of Justice). 'Barcelona Traction, Light and Power Company'. *ICJ Reports* (1970): 3, 32.

'ICJ condemns fatally flawed ASEAN Human Rights Declaration'. *International Commission of Jurists*, 19 November 2012. Accessed 25 March 2013. www.icj.org/icj-condemns-fatally-flawed-asean-human-rights-declaration/.

'Legal Consequences of the Construction of a Wall in the Occupied Palestinian Territory'. *International Court of Justice*, 9 July 2004. www.icj-cij.org/docket/files/131/1671.pdf.

ICJ (Advisory Opinion). 'Conditions of Admission of a State to Membership in the United Nations (Article 4 of the Charter). 28 May 1948.

(Advisory Opinion). 'Legality of the Threat or Use of Nuclear Weapons'. *ICJ Reports* (1971): 66–85.

(Advisory Opinion). Legal Consequences for States of the Continued Presence of South Africa in Namibia (South West Africa) Notwithstanding Security Council Resolution 276 (1970). *ICJ Reports* (1971): 16–66.

ICNL (The International Center for Not-for-profit Law). 'NGO Law Monitor: Ethiopia'. *ICNL.* Last modified on 20 February 2013. www.icnl.org/research/monitor/ethiopia.html.

ICRC (International Committee of the Red Cross). '17th International Red Cross Conference: Stockholm, August 1948: Report'. 1948. www.loc.gov/rr/frd/Military_Law/pdf/RC_XVIIth-RC-Conference.pdf.

Annual Report 2011. Geneva: ICRC, 2012.

'Annual Report, Colombia'. International Committee of the Red Cross *(ICRC)*, Delegation in Colombia, 2009.

Assembly of the ICRC. 'Assistance Policy'. *IRRC* 855 (2004): 677–693.

'Assistance: General Introduction'. *ICRC*, 2000. Accessed on 31 March 2013. www.icrc.org/eng/assets/files/other/assistance-general-report-intro-2000.pdf.

'Civilians in war'. *ICRC*, 1 October 1995. Accessed 1 March 2013, www.icrc.org/eng/resources/documents/misc/57jmk.htm#a6.

'Code of Conduct for the International Red Cross and Red Crescent Movement and NGOs in Disaster Relief'. 31 December 1994. www.ifrc.org/Global/Publications/disasters/code-of-conduct/codeconduct_signatories.pdf.

'*Convention for the Amelioration of the Condition of the Wounded in Armies in the Field.* Accessed 8 November 2011. www.icrc.org/eng/resources/documents/misc/57jnvr.htm.

'Course of Five Lessons on the Geneva Conventions'. Geneva: ICRC, 1962.

'Discussion: What are the Future Challenges for Humanitarian Action?'. *IRRC* 884 (2011): 1–15.

'Draft Additional Protocols to the Geneva Conventions of August 12 1949' (1973), www.loc.gov/rr/frd/Military_Law/pdf/RC-Draft-additional-protocols.pdf

Draft Revised or New Conventions for the Protection of War Victims Established by the International Committee of the Red Cross with the Assistance of Government Experts, National Red Cross Societies and Other Humanitarian Associations–XVIIth International Red Cross Conference. Stockholm, August 1948.

Geneva Convention III Relative to Treatment of Prisoners of War, 1946. www.icrc.org/ihl.nsf/FULL/375.

Geneva Convention IV Relative to the Protection of Civilian Persons in Time of War, 12 August 1949. www.icrc.org/ihl.nsf/full/380.

'*The ICRC's Mission Statement*'. ICRC, 19 June 2008. Accessed on 31 March 2013. www.icrc.org/eng/resources/documents/misc/icrc-mission-190608.htm.

'The International Committee of the Red Cross: Its Missions and Work'. *IRRC* 874 (2009): 399, 401–2.

International Humanitarian Law: Answers to Your Questions. Geneva: ICRC, 2002.

International Humanitarian Law and the Challenges of Contemporary Armed Conflicts'. *ICRC*, October 2011. www.icrc.org/eng/assets/files/red-cross-crescent-movement/31st-international-conference/31-int-conference-ihl-challenges-report-11-5-1-2-en.pdf.

'International Red Cross and Red Crescent Movement'. www.icrc.org/eng/who-we-are/movement/index.jsp.

'Libya: First Access to the Remote Area of Sabha'. *ICRC*, 3 June 2011. www.icrc.org/eng/resources/documents/update/2011/libya-update-2011-06-03.htm.

'Libya: ICRC Makes Urgent Call for Access to Wounded'. *ICRC*, 24 March 2011. www.icrc.org/eng/resources/documents/update/2011/libya-update-2011-03-24.htm.

'Libya: Safe Access Needed to Sirte and Bani Walid'. *ICRC*, 23 September 2011. www.icrc.org/eng/resources/documents/news-release/2011/libya-news-2011-09-23.htm.

'Myanmar: Clean Water Reaches Isolated Residents in Dedaye'. *ICRC*, 28 May 2008. www.icrc.org/eng/resources/documents/feature/2008/myanmar-feature-280508.htm.

'The Neutral Intermediary Role of the ICRC: at the Heart of Humanitarian Action'. Accessed 25 May 2013. www.icrc.org/eng/resources/documents/interview/neutral-intermediary-interview-070708.htm.

'Philippines: Red Cross Delivers Vital Aid'. ICRC Resource Centre, 23 December 2011. Accessed 6 April 2013. www.icrc.org/eng/resources/documents/update/2011/philippines-update-2011-12-23.htm.

'Protection Policy'. *IRRC* 871 (2008): 751.

Report on the Preliminary Conference of National Red Cross Societies for the Study of the Conventions and of Various Problems Relative to the Red Cross, Geneva, 26 July to 3 August 1946: Documents Furnished by the ICRC, vol. IV: Specific Red Cross Problems.

'*Report on the Work of the Conference of Government Experts for the Study of the Conventions for the Protection of War Victims*'. Geneva, 14–26 April 1947.

Statutes of the International Committee of the Red Cross, 21 June 1973, revised on 20 July 1998 and 8 May 2003 (entry into force 3 October 2103), accessed 8 November 2011. www.icrc.org/eng/resources/documents/misc/icrc-statutes-080503.htm.

Statutes of the International Red Cross and Red Crescent Movement. ICRC, 1986. Accessed on 31 March 2013. www.icrc.org/eng/assets/files/other/statutes-en-a5.pdf.

'Syria: ICRC Helps Provide Clean Water for 10 Million People'. ICRC, 17 December 2012. Accessed 1 March 2013. www.icrc.org/eng/resources/documents/update/2012/12-17-syria-water.htm.

IDI (Institut de Doit International). 'History'. www.idi-iil.org/idiE/navig_history.html.

'Humanitarian Assistance'. *Bruges Session*, 2 February 2003.

IDMC (Internal Displacement Monitoring Centre) and NRC (Norwegian Refugee Council). 'Colombia, Property Restitution in Sight but Integration still Distant'. 5 September 2001. Accessed 22 November 2011. www.internal-displacement.org/8025708F004BE3B1/(httpInfoFiles)/BD3251F80AB23B61C12579020047223A/$file/Colombia-Overview-Sept2011.pdf.

'Internal Displacement in South and South East Asia'. *Internal Displacement Monitoring Center* (IDMC), 2011. www.internal-displacement.org/8025708F004BE3B1/(httpInfoFiles)/0E27234251BE6E48C12579E400369AA9/$file/global-overview-asia-2011.pdf.

IFRC (International Federation of Red Cross and Red Crescent Societies). Accessed on 5 June 2013: www.ifrc.org/en/what-we-do/idrl/meetings-and-events/past-events/workshop-on-disaster-law-and-the-drought-relief-operations-in-the-horn-of-africa-17-19-april-2012/

'Annotations to the Draft Guidelines for the Domestic Facilitation and Regulation of International Disaster Relief and Initial Recovery Assistance', October 2007: www.ifrc.org/PageFiles/125652/annotations.pdf.

'Disasters in Africa: the Case for Legal Preparedness'. IFRC, 2011.

'Complex/Man-made Hazards: Complex Emergencies'. Accessed 12 March 2013. www.ifrc.org/en/what-we-do/disaster-management/about-disasters/definition-of-haard/complex-emergencies/.

'Guidelines for the Domestic Facilitation and Regulation of International Disaster Relief and Initial Recovery Assistance'. IFRC, 30 November 2007.

IDRL in Sierra Leone: 'Legal Preparedness Study for Strengthening the Legal and Policy Framework for Foreign Disaster Response'. *IFRC*, 2011, 34.

'IDRL Programme: Plan 2010–2011'. Geneva: IFRC, 2010.

'Indonesia Law, Policies, Planning and Practices on International Disaster Response'. IFRC, July 2005.

'International Disaster Response Laws, Rules and Principles (IDRL) Programme: Plan 2010–2011', accessed 5 June 2013. www.ifrc.org/PageFiles/53419/MAA000041 0p.pdf

Law and Legal Issues in International Disaster Response: A Desk Study. International Federation of the Red Cross and Red Crescent Societies (IFRC). Geneva, 2007.

'Model Act for the Facilitation and Regulation of International Disaster Relief and Initial Recovery Assistance'. IFRC, March 2013. Accessed on 12 April 2013. www.ifrc.org/en/what-we-do/idrl/model-act-on-idrl/.

'Strengthening Legal Preparedness for International Disaster Assistance in Namibia'. IFRC/Namibia Red Cross Society, draft of December 2012.

'Types of Disasters: Definitions of Hazards'. Accessed 21 October 2011. www.ifrc.org/en/what-we-do/disaster-management/about-disasters/definition-of-hazard/.

'What is a Disaster?' Accessed 12 March 2013. www.ifrc.org/en/what-we-do/disaster-management/about-disasters/what-is-a-disaster/.

ILC (International Law Commission). Articles on Responsibility of States for Internationally Wrongful Acts (ARSIWA) with ommentaries, *Yearbook of the International Law Commission*, vol. II, Part 2, 2001 (A/CN.4/SER.A/2001/Add. 1 (Part 2)), Art 40. Available online at: http://untreaty.un.org/ilc/texts/instruments/english/commentaries/9_6_2001.pdf.

Report of the International Law Commission on the Work of its Forty-eighth Session. *Yearbook of the International Law Commission* vol. II, Part Two, 1996.

Yearbook of the International Law Commission (YBILC), 1966, II. http://untreaty.un.org/ilc/publications/yearbooks/Ybkvolumes(e)/ILC_1966_v2_e.pdf.

Yearbook of the International Law Commission, vol. II, Part 2, 2001 (A/CN.4/SER.A/2001/Add.1 (Part 2)). http://untreaty.un.org/ilc/texts/instruments/english/commentaries/9_6_2001.pdf.

Inaumi, Mitsue. 'Towards the Establishment of a Regional Human Rights Mechanism in Asia'. In *Defending Human Rights: Tools for Social Justice*, ed. Ida Lintel, Antoine Buyse and Brianne McGonigle Leyh. Volume in Honour of Fried van Hoof at the Occasion of his Valedictory Lecture and the 30th Anniversary of the Netherlands Institute of Human Rights. Cambridge: Intersentia, 2012, 71–84.

Inman, Samuel Guy. *Inter-American Conferences 1826–1954: History and Problems*. Washington DC: University Press of Washington, 1965.

Institute of International Law, Sixteenth Commission, Resolution. 'Humanitarian Assistance'. Bruges Session, 2 September 2003.

Inter-Agency Standing Committee, 'Inter-Agency Contingency Planning Guidelines for Humanitarian Assistance', IASC, www.who.int/hac/network/interagency/news/contingency_guidelines/en/.

'Products'. Accessed 14 April 2013. www.humanitarianinfo.org/iasc/pageloader.aspx?page=content-products-default.

Intergovernmental Conference on Emergency Telecommunications. *Tampere Convention on the Provision of Telecommunication Resources for Disaster*

Mitigation and Relief Operations. 18 June 1998. Accessed 13 April 2013. www.itu.int/ITU-D/emergencytelecoms/tampere.html.

International Atomic Energy Agency. 'Convention on Assistance in the Case of a Nuclear Accident or Radiological Emergency'. 18 November 1986. Accessed 1 April 2013. www.iaea.org/Publications/Documents/Infcircs/Others/infcirc336.shtml.

International Commission on Intervention and State Sovereignty (ICISS). 'The Responsibility to Protect'. International Development Research Centre, December 2001. http://responsibilitytoprotect.org/ICISS%20Report.pdf.

International Crisis Group. *The Rule of Law in Independent Kosovo*. Europe Report No. 204, 2010.

International Human Rights Law Clinic, Boalt Hall School of Law. 'When Disaster Strikes: A Human Rights Analysis of the 2005 Gulf Coast Hurricanes'. The Inter-American Commission of Human Rights General Situation Hearing on Natural Disaster and Human Rights, 3 March 2006. Accessed 1 April 2013. www.law.berkeley.edu/files/IHRLC/Briefing_Paper_Report_When_Disaster_Strikes_2_Mar_06.pdf.

International Institute of Humanitarian Law in San Remo, 'Guiding Principles on the Right to Humanitarian Assistance, April 1993', www.peacepalacelibrary.nl/ebooks/files/IIHL4_en.pdf

International Law Commission (ILC) Discussions. Accessed 17 June 2013. http://untreaty.un.org/ilc/guide/6_3.htm.

International Review of the Red Cross (*IRRC*), vol. 33, No. 297 (1993): 519-525.

Institite of International Law, 'Humanitarian Assistance', Sixteenth Commission, Resolution, Bruges Session 2, September 2003

IOM (International Organisation for Migration). 'IOM Migration Crisis Operational Framework'. Res. 1243 (CI), 27 November 2012.

IRC (International Rescue Committee). 'Financial information and Annual Report', accessed 13 April 2013, www.rescue.org/about/financial-information.

'Organisation Report'. International Rescue Committee, June 2011. http://rootcause.org/documents/DR-IRC.pdf.

IRIN (International Regional Information Networks). 'IDPs: African IDP Convention Comes into Force'. *IRIN*, 6 December 2012. Accessed 31 May 2013. www.irinnews.org.

'Unregistered IDPs in Myanmar's Rakhine Without Aid'. *IRIN*, 25 March 2013. Accessed 25 March 2013. www.irinnews.org/Report/97729/Unregistered-IDPs-in-Myanmar-s-Rakhine-without-aid.

'WASH Woes for Myanmar's Rakhine IDPs'. *IRIN*, 18 January 2013. Accessed 20 March 2013. www.irinnews.org/Report/97279/WASH-woes-for-Myanmar-s-Rakhine-IDPs.

IRRC (International Review of the Red Cross). XXth International Conference of the Red Cross. 'Proclamation of the Fundamental Principles of the Red Cross', *IRRC* 56 (1965): 573–4.

Isacson, Adam. 'Getting In Deeper. The United States' Growing Involvement in Colombia's Conflict'. CIP International Policy Report (2000).

ISDR. 'International Strategy for Disaster Reduction, the Hygo Framework of Action 2005–2015: Building the Resilience of Nations and Communities to Disaster'. *ISDR* 20 and *BNPB*, 2010. www.unisdr.org/we/inform/publications/1037.

ITU (International Telecommunication Union). 'Provision of Telecommunication Resources for Disaster Mitigation and Relief Operations'. 18 June 1998. Accessed 13 April 2013. www.itu.int/ITU-D/emergencytelecoms/tampere.html.

IWMI (International Water Management Institute). 'IWMI research in South East Asia'. Accessed 9 March 2013. http://sea.iwmi.org/Data/Sites/14/Documents/pdfs/iwmi_south_east_asia_brochure.pdf.

Jacob, Jijo. 'Factbox – Key Facts About Cyclone Nargis'. *Reuters* (US edn.). Accessed 6 April 2013. www.reuters.com/article/2009/04/30/idUSSP420097.

Jansen-Wilhelm, Stefanie. *A Duty to Accept Aid in the Aftermath of a Disaster*. Forthcoming, 2014.

Jenatsch, Thomas. 'The ICRC as a Humanitarian Mediator in the Colombian Conflict: Possibilities and Limits'. *International Review of the Red Cross* 323 (1998). www.icrc.org/eng/resources/documents/article/other/57jpch.htm.

JICA (Japan International Cooperation Agency). 'Water Problems at Angkor Wat'. March 2009. Accessed 6 April 2013. www.jica.go.jp/english/news/focus_on/water/water_1.html.

Johnson, Constance. 'ASEAN: Leaders Adopt Human Rights Declaration'. *Global Legal Monitor*, The Library of Congress, 21 November 2012. Accessed 23 June 2013. www.loc.gov/lawweb/servlet/lloc_news?disp3_l205403405_text.

Joseph, Sarah and Adam McBeth. *Research Handbook on International Human Rights Law*. Cheltenham: Edward Elgar Publishing, 2010.

Junod, Dominique. *The Imperiled Red Cross and the Palestine Eret-Yisrael Conflict 1945–1952*. London: Kegan Paul, 1996.

Kabasakal Arat, Zehra F. *Human Rights Worldwide: A Reference Handbook*. Santa Barbara: ABC Contemporary World Issues Series, 2006.

Kabau, Tom. 'The Responsibility to Protect and the Role of Regional Organisations: an Appraisal of the African Union's Interventions'. *Goettingen Journal of International Law* 4 (2012): 49–92.

Kälin, Walter. 'Report of the Representative of the Secretary-General on the Human Rights of Internally Displaced Persons'. UN Doc. (A/HRC/10/13/Add.1) 2009.

Karl, Wolfram. 'Menschenrechtliches ius cogens – Eine Analyse von "Barcelona Traction" und nachfolgender Entwicklungen'. In *Menschenrechtsschutz durch Gewohnheitsrecht*, ed. Eckhart Klein Berlin: BWV Berliner Wissenschafts-Verlag, 2003, 102–22.

Keban, Y. T. 'Kerjasama Antar Pemerintah Daerah Dalam Era Otonomi'. Unpublished paper (2007).

Kellenberger, Jakob. 'Speaking out or Remaining Silent in Humanitarian Work'. *IRRC* 855 (2004): 593.

Striving to Improve Respect for International Humanitarian Law. San Remo: Keynote Speech XXVIIIth Round Table, 2004.

Kelsen, Hans. *Reine Rechtslehre*. Wien: Deuticke, 2nd ed., 1960.

Kent, Randolh, Mark Dalton, Karin von Hippel and Ralf Maurer. *The Future of Humanitarian Assistance: the Role of the United Nations*. New York: United Nations (2004).

Ki-moon, Ban. 'Renewal, not Restoration, Should be the Goal for Haiti'. *Washington Post* 29 (March 2010).

Kiderlen, Hans F. *Von Triest nach Osttimor: Der völkerrechtliche Rahmen für die Verwaltung von Krisengebieten durch die Vereinten Nationen*. Berlin, Heidelberg: Springer, 2008.

Killander, Magnus. 'The African Commission on Human and Peoples' Rights'. In *The African Regional Human Rights System: 30 Years after the African Charter on Human and Peoples' Rights*, ed. M. Ssenyonjo. Leiden: Martinus Nijhoff Publishers, 2012: 235–248.

Kindane, Won. 'Managing Forced Displacement by Law in Africa: The Role of the New African Union IDPs Convention'. *Vanderbilt Journal of Transnational Law* 44 (2011): 1–85.

Kindiki, Kithure. 'International Law on Trial: The Darfur Crisis and the Responsibility to Protect Civilians'. *International Community Law Review* 9 (2007): 445–473.

Kinver, Mark. 'Asian Nations "Face Greatest Natural Disaster Risk"'. *BBC News*, 15 August 2012. Accessed 30 March 2013. www.bbc.co.uk/news/science-environment-19254685.

Kirkpatrick, David D. 'In Parts of Syria, Lack of Assistance "Is a Catastrophe"'. *New York Times*, 8 March 2013.

Klein, Eckart and Stefanie Schmahl. 'Die Internationalen und die Supranationalen Organisationen'. In *Völkerrecht*, ed. W. Graf Vitzthum. Berlin, New York: Walter de Gruyter, 2010, 5th edn., 263–388.

Klitgaard, R. *Controlling Corruption*. Berkeley, Los Angeles, London: University of California Press, 1988.

Kolstad, Ivar, Verena Frit, and Tam O'Neil. 'Corruption, Anti-corruption Efforts and Aid: Do Donors Have the Right Approach?'. *Working Paper* 3 (January 2008). www.odi.org.uk/resources/download/1525.pdf.

Koskenniemi, Martti. *From Apology to Utopia: The Structure of International Legal Argument*. Cambridge University Press, 2005.

Kouchner, Bernard. 'Burma'. *Le Monde*, 20 May 2008.

Krähenbühl, Pierre. 'The ICRC's Approach to Contemporary Security Challenges: A Future for Independent and Neutral Humanitarian Action'. *IRRC* 855 (2004): 505–513.

Kreidler, Corinna. 'Corruption as an Internal Problem for Emergency Operations'. *The Journal of Humanitarian Assistance* (July 2006). http://sites.tufts.edu/jha/files/2011/04/a190.pdf.

'Risking Embezzlement'. *D+C – Magazine for Development and Cooperation*, December 2006. www.gi.de/E+/content/archive-eng/12-2006/tribune_art2.html.

Krieger, Heike. 'A Conflict of Norms: The Relationship Between Humanitarian Law and Human Rights Law in the ICRC Customary Law Study'. *Journal of Conflict and Security Law* 11 (2006): 265–291.

Krisanto. 'Relokasi Korban Bencana: Legalistik v Kulturistik Historis Lereng Merapi Terhadap Rencana Relokasi'. *Kompas*. Accessed 10 June 2010. http://hukum.kompasiana.com/2011/07/10/relokasi-korban-bencana-legalistik-vs-kultural-historis-kajian-penolakan-warga-lereng-merapi-terhadap-kebijakan-relokasi/.

Lailach, Martin. *Die Wahrung des Weltfriedens und der internationalen Sicherheit als Aufgabe des Sicherheitsrates der Vereinten Nationen*. Berlin: Duncker und Humblot, 1998.

Langholtz, Harvey, Boris Kondoch and Alan Wells. *International Peacekeeping, The Yearbook of International Peace Operations*. Leiden: Martinus Nijhoff Publishers, 2007, vol. II.

Larson, Kjetil M., Camilla G. Cooper and Gro Nystuen. *Searching for a 'Principle of Humanity' in International Humanitarian Law*. Cambridge University Press, 2013.

Lavoyer, Jean.-Philippe and Louise Maresca. 'The Role of the ICRC in the Development of International Humanitarian Law'. *International Negotiation* 4 (1999): 501, 503–527.

Law Society. Written Evidence of Joint Committee On Human Rights, the United Kingdom Parliament. www.publications.parliament.uk/pa/jt200506/jtselect/jtrights/185/185we28.htm.

Le Billon, Philippe. 'The Political Ecology of War: Natural Resources and Armed Conflicts'. *Political Geography* 2 (2000): 561–84.

'The Political Economy of War: What Relief Agencies Need to Know'. *HPN Network Paper* 33 (2000). www.odihpn.org/documents/networkpaper033.pdf.

Ledesma, Héctor F. *The Inter-American System for the Protection of Human Rights*. San José: Inter-American Human Rights Institute, 2007.

Leininger, Julia. 'Democracy and UN Peace-Keeping – Conflict Resolution Through State-Building and Democracy Promotion in Haiti'. In *Max Planck Yearbook of United Nations Law* 10, ed. Armin von Bogdandy and Rüdiger Wolfrum (2006): 465–530.

'Haiti, Conflict'. In Online *Max Planck Encyclopedia of Public International Law*, www.mpepil.com.

Lincoln, Jennie K. and César Sereseres. 'Resettling the Contras: The OAS Verification Commission in Nicaragua'. In *Peacekeeping and Democratisation*, ed. Tommie Sue Montgomery. Miami: North-South Center Press, 2000, 17–36.

Lödén, Hans. 'Reaching a Vanishing Point? Reflections on the Future of Neutrality Norms in Sweden and Finland'. *Cooperation and Conflict* 47-2 (2012): 271–284.

Loescher, Gil. *The UNHCR and World Politics: A Perilous Path*. Oxford University Press, 2001.

Lorenz, Frederic M. 'The Protection of Water Facilities under International Law'. UNESCO and World Water Assessment Programme, Norway, 2003. Accessed 6 April 2013. http://unesdoc.unesco.org/images/0013/001324/132464e.pdf.

Luban, David. 'Just War and Human Rights'. *Philosophy and Public Affairs* 9, no. 2 (1 January 1980): 160–181.

Lubell, Noam. 'Challenges in Applying Human Rights Law to Armed Conflict'. *International Review of the Red Cross* 87 (2005): 740.

Luhmann, N. 'Humanitäre Hilfe in Burma: Das Geheimnis des Deltas'. *Jungle World*, June 5, 2008. http://jungle-world.com/artikel/2008/23/21929.html.

Lustermann, H. 'Indonesia: On the Way to Federal State?'. *Jurnal Mimbar Hukum* 42/X (2002): 5–17.

'Maastricht Principles on Extra-Territorial Obligations (ETOs) of States in the Area of Economic, Social and Cultural Rights', 28 September 2011 (final version adopted 29 February 2012). www.fian.org/fileadmin/media/publications/2012.02.29_-_Maastricht_Principles_on_Extraterritorial_Obligations.pdf

Mačák, Kubo and Noam Zamir. 'The Applicability of International Humanitarian Law to the Conflict in Libya'. *International Community Law Review* 14–4 (2012): 403.

Macalister-Smith, Peter. *International Humanitarian Assistance: Disaster Relief Actions in International Law and Organisation*. Dordrecht: Martinus Nijhoff Publishers, 1985.

Macharia-Mokobi, Elisabeth. 'International Disaster Response Law (IDRL) in Botswana: An Audit on Legal Preparedness for Facilitating and Regulating International Disaster Assistance'. *Botswana Red Cross Society*, draft of March 2013, 82–84.

Magone, Claire, Michael Neuman and Fabrice Weissman. *Humanitarian Negotiations Revealed: The MSF Experience.* New York: Columbia University Press, 2011.

Martin, Michael F. 'Vietnamese Victims of Agent Orange and US-Vietnam Relations'. *Congressional Research Service,* 29 August 2012. Accessed 5 March 2013. www.fas.org/sgp/crs/row/RL34761.pdf.

Maus, Sylvia. 'Human Rights in UN Peacekeeping Missions: A Framework for Humanitarian Obligations?'. In Heintze and Zwitter, *International Law and Humanitarian Assistance* 103–128.

Maxwell, D., P. Walker, C. Church, P. Harvey, K. Savage, S. Bailey, R. Hees, and M.-L. Ahlendorf. 'Preventing Corruption in Humanitarian Assistance – Final Research Report'. *Transparency International.* Berlin 2008. http://transparency.dk/wp-content/uploads/2011/06/Preventing_Corruption_in_Humanitarian_Assistance_Report_July_2008.pdf.

Mbazira, Christopher. 'Enforcing the economic, social and cultural rights in the African charter on Human and Peoples' Rights: Twenty Years of Redundancy, Progression and Significant Strides', *African Human Rights Law Journal,* 6/2 (2006), 358–381.

McGoldrick, Claudia. 'The Future of Humanitarian Action: An ICRC Perspective'. *IRRC* 884 (2011): 965–991.

Mehrdad Payandeh, Contra. 'The United Nations, Military Intervention, and Regime Change in Libya'. *Virginia Journal of International Law* 52 (2012): 387–91.

Mekong River Commission. Accessed 5 April 2013. www.mrcmekong.org/about-the-mrc/history/ and www.mrcmekong.org/about-the-mrc/vision-and-mission/.

Accessed 5 April 2013. www.mrcmekong.org/about-the-mrc/upstream-partners-2/.

Mercado, Bibiana. 'Gobierno busca alinear lenguaje diplomático'. *El Tiempo,* 13, June 2005.

Merry, Sally E. 'Legal Pluralism'. *Law & Society Review* 22 (1988): 869–896.

Michel, Louise *Post-tsunami Relief Effort: the Commission's Humanitarian Response and the Need for Sound Aid Management.* Speech/05/177, Brussels, 15 March 2005. http://reliefweb.int/node/168620.

Milanović, Marko. 'State Responsibility for Genocide'. *European Journal of International Law* 17, No. 3 (2006): 553–604.

Mills, Kurt. *Human Rights in the Emerging Global Order: A New Sovereignty?* Houndmills: Palgrave Macmillan, 1998.

'Neo-Humanitarianism: The Role of International Humanitarian Norms and Organisations in Contemporary Conflict'. *Global Governance* 11–2 (2005): 161–183.

Minear, Larry. *The Humanitarian Enterprise: Dilemmas and Discoveries*. Bloomfield: Kumarian Press, 2002.

'The Theory and Practice of Neutrality: Some Thoughts on the Tensions'. *IRRC* 81 (1999): 63–71.

Minear, Larry. David Cortwright, Julia Wagler, George A. Lopes and Thomas G Weiss. 'Toward More Humane and Effective Sanctions Management: Enhancing the Capacity of the United Nations System'. *Occasional Paper* 31, Providence, RI: Brown University (1998).

Moir, Lindsay. 'Law and the Inter-American Human Rights System'. *Human Rights Quarterly* 25 (2003): 181–212.

Molier, Gelijn. *De (on)rechtmatigheid van humanitaire interventie (The (Il)legality of Humanitarian Intervention)*. Boom: Meppel, 2003.

Moore, Jonathan. *Hard Choices: Moral Dilemmas in Humanitarian Intervention*. Lanham: Rowman and Littlefield, 1998.

Moreno, Luis A. 'Aiding Colombia's War on Terrorism'. *The New York Times*, 3 May 2002.

MSF (Médecins Sans Frontieres). 'Libya: Aid Access to Violence-Affected Areas Blocked'. *MSF*, 2 March 2011. www.doctorswithoutborders.org/press/release.cfm?id=5076&cat=press-release.

'Libya: MSF Seeking More Ways to Assist Wounded'. *MSF*, 8 March 2011. www.doctorswithoutborders.org/news/article.cfm?id=5085&cat=field-news.

'Libya: Urgent Priority Must Be Given to Doctors and Medical Materials'. *MSF*, 25 February 2011. www.doctorswithoutborders.org/press/release.cfm?id=5063&cat=press-release.

'MSF Charter and Principles'. Accessed 25 May 2013. www.msf.org/msf-charter-and-principles.

'MSF Team in Libya Trying to Reach Areas Affected by Violence'. *MSF*, 24 February 2011. www.doctorswithoutborders.org/news/article.cfm?id=5053&cat=field-news.

Muigai, Githu. 'From the African Court of Human and Peoples' Rights to the African Court of Justice and Human Rights'. In *The African Regional Human Rights System: 30 Years after the African Charter on Human and Peoples' Rights*, ed. M. Ssenyonjo. Leiden: Martinus Nijhoff Publishers, 2012: 265–282.

Müller, Amrei. 'Limitations to and Derogations from Economic, Social and Cultural Rights'. *Human Rights Law Review* 9 (2009): 557–601.

Namibia. Disaster Risk Management Act, Act No. 10, 2012, http://www.preventionweb.net/files/28778 _namibiadisasterriskmanagementact1.pdf.

Namibia's Disaster Risk Management Authorities, November 2011. Accessed 5 June 2013. www.ifrc.org/en/what-we-do/idrl/latest-news/idrl-newsletter-december-2011/windhoek-workshop-explores-namibias-legal-preparedness-for-disasters/.

Nan, Madalina E. 'New Humanitarianism with Old Problems: the Forgotten Lessons of Rwanda'. *The Journal of Humanitarian Assistance* (2010). http://sites.tufts.edu/jha/archives/780

Narine, Shaun. 'Human Rights Norms and the Evolution of ASEAN: Moving Without Moving in a Changing Regional Environment'. *Contemporary Southeast Asia* 34 (2012): 365–388

NATO (North Atlantic Treaty Organisation). 'Joint Press Briefing on Events Concerning Libya'. *NATO*, 12 April 2011. www.nato.int/cps/en/natolive/opinions_72290.htm?selectedLocale=en.

'NATO and Libya'. www.nato.int/cps/en/natolive/topics_71652.htm.

'NATO Ready to Support International Efforts on Libya'. *NATO*, 10 March 2011. www.nato.int/cps/en/natolive/news_71446.htm.

'Operation Unified Protector. Final Mission Stats'. *NATO*, 2 November 2011. www.nato.int/nato_static/assets/pdf/pdf_2011_11/20111108_111107-factsheet_up_factsfigures_en.pdf.

'Press Briefing on Libya'. *NATO*, 5 April 2011. www.nato.int/cps/en/natolive/opinions_72027.htm?selectedLocale=en.

'Unified Protector'. NATO Operation, Ministry of Defence Republic of Latvia, www.mod.gov.lv/en/Par_aisardibas_noari/Politikas_istenosana/Latvijas_%20daliba_starpt_oper/NATO_operac/Libija_Unified_Protector.aspx.

Natural Disaster Data Book 2011. Asian Disaster Reduction Center, 2011. www.adrc.asia/publications/databook/ORG/databook_2011/pdf/DataBook2011_e.pdf.

Notohadikusumo, T. 'Implikasi Etika Dalam Kebijakan Pembangunan Kawasan, Forum Perencanaan Pembangunan'. *PSPR UGM* (2008).

Nuland, Victoria. 'ASEAN Declaration on Human Rights'. Press Statement, US Department of State, Washington DC, 20 November 2012. Accessed 31 March 2013. www.state.gov/r/pa/prs/ps/2012/11/200915.htm.

OAS (Organisation of American States). *Additional Protocol to the American Convention on Human Rights in the Area of Economic, Social and Cultural Rights*. San Salvador Protocol, The Eighteenth Regular Session of the General Assembly of OAS, 17 November 1988. Accessed 1 April 2013. www.oas.org/juridico/english/treaties/a-52.html.

The American Convention on Human Rights (ACHR). 1969. www.oas.org/dil/treaties_B-32_American_Convention_on_Human_Rights.pdf.

American Convention on Human Rights. The Inter-American Specialised Conference on Human Rights, San José, Costa Rica, 22 November 1969. www.oas.org/en/iachr/mandate/Basics/3.AMERICAN%20CONVENTION.pdf.

American Declaration of the Rights and Duties of Man. *The Ninth International Conference of American States*, Bogotá, Colombia, 1948. www.oas.org/en/iachr/mandate/Basics/2.AMERICAN%20DECLARATION.pdf.

'Comprehensive Action Against Antipersonnel Mines (AICMA)'. *OAS*. Accessed 29 March 2013. www.oas.org/dsp/english/cpo_desminado.asp.

'Declaration on Security in the Americas'. *OAS*, October 28, 2003. www.oas.org/documents/eng/DeclaracionSecurity_102803.asp.

'Economic and Social Rights in Haiti Following the Earthquake'. 138th Period of Sessions, 28 March 2010. www.oas.org/es/cidh/audiencias/Hearings.aspx?Lang=en&Session=118.

'Evaluation of Human Rights in the Americas During IACHR Regular Sessions'. *IACHR Press Release* No. 07/06, 17 March 2006. Accessed 1 April 2013. www.cidh.oas.org/Comunicados/English/2006/7.06eng.htm.

'Human Rights Situation During the Natural Disaster in Venezuela'. 106th Period of Sessions, 3 March 2000, *AICHR*. www.oas.org/es/cidh/audiencias/Hearings.aspx?Lang=en&Session=43.

Inter-American Convention to Facilitate Disaster Assistance. *OAS*, 6 July 1991. www.oas.org/juridico/english/treaties/a-54.html.

'OAS Peace Missions'. Accessed 29 March 2013. www.oas.org/sap/peacefund/PeaceMissions/.

'Protection of Human Rights in Natural Disasters'. 124th Period of Sessions, 3 March 2006, *AICHR*. www.oas.org/es/cidh/audiencias/Hearings.aspx?Lang=en&Session=19.

'Refugees', *OAS*. Accessed 29 March 2013. www.oas.org/en/topics/refugees.asp.

'Report of the Substantive Meetings of the Joint Working Group of the Permanent Council and CEPCIDI on Existing Mechanisms for Disaster Prevention and Response and Humanitarian Assistance (Report prepared by the Chair)'. *OAS*, 4 March 2011. www.oas.org/en/cidi/cepcidi_grupos_trabajo_DESASTRES_docs.asp.

'Signatories and Ratifications'. *OAS*. Accessed 29 March 2013. www.oas.org/juridico/english/sigs/a-63.html.

'Sixteenth Quarterly Report of the Secretary-General to the Permanent Council on the Mission to Support the Peace Process in Colombia'. 15 March 2012. www.oas.org/consejo/Documents%20DOC2012.asp.

'Special Mission to Suriname (1992–2000)'. *OAS*. Accessed 29 March 2013. www.oas.org/sap/peacefund/forumevents/IAPF2010/REISAE-SPECIAL-MISSIONTOSURINAME-PresentationSep2010.pdf.

'Tenth Meeting of Consultation of Ministers of Foreign Affairs – Second Plenary Session'. *OAS*, 4 May 1965. www.oas.org/council/MEETINGS%20OF%20CONSULTATION/Actas/Acta%2010.pdf.

OAS General Assembly. 'Existing Mechanisms for Disaster Prevention and Response and Humanitarian Assistance among the Member States'. Resolution 2750, 4 June 2012. www.oas.org/en/sla/docs/AG05796E04.pdf.

'Internally Displaced Persons'. Resolution 2229. 6 June 2006. www.oas.org/cji/DIL/AG-RES_2229_XXXVI-O-06_eng.pdf.

'Protection of Asylum Seekers, Refugees, and Returnees in the Americas', Resolution 2232, 6 June 2006. www.oas.org/dil/AG-RES_2232_XXXVI-O-06_eng.pdf.

OAS Inter-American Commission on Human Rights. 'Chapter V of the Annual Report of the Inter-American Commission on Human Rights'. 2010. Accessed 1 April 2013. www.cidh.org/annualrep/2010eng/Chap.V.HAITI.doc.

'Follow-up Report on the Situation of Human Rights in Haiti'. 2010. http://lib.ohchr.org/HRBodies/UPR/Documents/session12/HT/OAS-OrganisationAmericanStates-AnnualReportInterAmericanCommissionHumanRights2010-eng.pdf.

'Forced Evictions from Five Camps for Displaced Persons, Haiti'. PM 367–10, 15 November 2010. www.oas.org/en/iachr/decisions/ precautionary.asp.

'Human Rights Situation during the Natural Disaster in Venezuela'. Hearing, 106th Period of Sessions, 3 March 2000. www.oas.org/es/cidh/audiencias/Hearings.aspx?Lang=en&Session=43.

'Inhabitants of the Community of Omoa', Honduras, PM 17/10, November 8, 2011, http://www.oas.org/en/iachr/decisions/precautionary.asp.

Press Release No. 11/10. 'IAHCR Stress Duty to Respect Human Rights During the Emergency in Haiti'. 2 February 2010. www.cidh.oas.org/Comunicados/English/2010/11-10eng.htm.

'Protection of Human Rights in Natural Disasters', Hearing, 124th Period of Sessions, 3 March 2006. http://www.oas.org/es/cidh/audiencias/Hearings.aspx?Lang=en&Session=19

'Women and Girls Residing in 22 Camps for Internally Displaced Persons in Port-au-Prince, Haiti'. PM 340/10 (2010), 22 December 2010. www.oas.org/en/iachr/decisions/precautionary.asp.

OAS Permanent Executive Committee of the Inter-American Council for Integral Development. 'General Framework for the "Inter-American Plan for Disaster Prevention and Response and the Coordination of Humanitarian Assistance"'. 10 May 2012. www.oas.org/en/cidi/cepcidi_documentos_docs12.asp.

Secretary-General of the OAS. 'Guidance on Integrated Missions'. 9 February 2006.

'Inauguration of the Forty-Second Regular Session of the OAS General Assembly'. *OAS*, 3 June 2012. www.oas.org/en/about/speech_secretary_general.asp?sCodigo=12-0033.

OCHA (Office for the Coordination of Humanitarian Affairs). 'A Brief History of OCHA'. Office for the Coordination of Humanitarian Affairs (OCHA). http://ochaonline.un.org/AboutUs/tabid/3939/language/en-US/Default.aspx.

'Consolidated Appeal Process', accessed 8 November 2011. www.unocha.org/cap/about-the-cap/faqs.

'Draft Syria Humanitarian Assistance Plan'. Accessed 1 March 2013. www.unocha.org/cap/appeals/draft-syria-humanitarian-assistance-response-plan-2012.

Fact-sheet No. 13, 'International Humanitarian Law and Human Rights'. www.ohchr.org/Documents/Publications/FactSheet13en.pdf.

Financial Tracking Service, Consolidated and Flash Appeals 2012. Accessed 13 April 2013. http://fts.unocha.org.

'Glossary of Humanitarian Terms in Relation to the Protection of Civilians in Armed Conflict'. 2004. http://un-interpreters.org/glossaries/ocha%20glossary.pdf.

'Guidelines on Internal Displacement'. *OCHA*, 2001. www.unocha.org/top-stories/all-stories/humanitarian-chief-highlights-disaster-management-south-east-asia.

'Humanitarian Chief Highlights Disaster Management in South East Asia'. *OCHA*, 23 March 2012. Accessed 3 April 2013. www.unocha.org/top-stories/all-stories/humanitarian-chief-highlights-disaster-management-south-east-asia.

'IASC Operational Guidelines On The Protection Of Persons In Situations Of Natural Disasters', the Brookings–Bern Project on Internal Displacement, January 2011. Accessed 3 June 2013. http://ochanet.unocha.org/p/Documents/Operational%20Guidelines.pdf.

'OCHA on Message: Humanitarian Principles'. Accessed 13 June 2013, http://ochanet.unocha.org/p/Documents/OOM-humanitarianprinciples_eng_June12.pdf.

'Water Scarcity and Humanitarian Action, Key Emerging Trends and Challenges'. OCHA Occasional Briefing Series 4, September 2010. Accessed 19 March 2013. http://ochanet.unocha.org/p/Documents/OCHA%20OPB%20Water%20%2011Nov10%20fnl.pdf.

Odinkalu, Anselm Chidi, 'Analysis of Paralysis or Paralysis by Analysis? Implementing Economic, Social, and Cultural Rights Under the African Charter on Human and Peoples' Rights', *Human Rights Quarterly*, 23/2, (2001), 327–369.

OECD (Organisation for Economic Cooperation and Development. The Development Assistance Committee of the OECD (OECD-DAC Criteria), www.oecd.org/dac/.

OHCHR (Office of the High Commissioner for Human Rights). 'Handbook on Housing and Property Restitution for Refugees and Displaced Persons: Implementing the "Pinheiro Principles"'. March 2007. Accessed 6 June 2013. www.ohchr.org/Documents/Publications/pinheiro_principles.pdf.

'A Landmark Decision to Make the Right to Water and Sanitation Legally Binding'. 6 October 2010. Accessed 30 March 2013. www.ohchr.org/EN/NewsEvents/Pages/RightToWaterAndSanitation.aspx.

Convention on the Rights of the Child, 1989. www2.ohchr.org/english/law/pdf/crc.pdf.

'Fact Sheet No. 35, The Right to Water'. August 2010. Accessed 28 March 2013. www.unhcr.org/refworld/docid/4ca45fed2.html.

International Covenant on Economic, Social and Cultural Rights. Accessed 1 June 2013. www.ohchr.org/EN/ProfessionalInterest/Pages/CESCR.aspx.

International Legal Protection of Human Rights in Armed Conflict. New York, Geneva: United Nations, 2011.

'Pillay Welcomes Major Breakthrough Enabling Individual Complaints on Economic, Social and Cultural Rights'. Office of the High Commissioner for Human Rights, 6 January 2013. Accessed 8 February 2013. www.ohchr.org/en/NewsEvents/Pages/DisplayNews.aspx?NewsID=12968&LangID=E.

'UN Rights Chief Welcomes Focus on Human Rights and Democracy, calls for Review of ASEAN Draft Human Rights Declaration'. *Office of the High Commissioner for Human Rights*, 8 November 2012. www.ohchr.org/en/NewsEvents/Pages/DisplayNews.aspx?NewsID=12753&LangID=E.

OIC (Organisation of Islamic Cooperation). 'Cairo Declaration on Human Rights in Islam'. Accessed 1 April 2013. www.oic-oci.org/english/article/human.htm.

Covenant of the Rights of the Child in Islam, OIC Doc. (OIC/9-IGGE/HRI/2004/Rep.Final). Accessed 1 April 2013. www.oic-oci.org/english/convenion/Rights of the Child In Islam E.pdf (*sic*).

Resolution (2/38-LEG). '*On the Establishment of the OIC Independent Permanent Human Rights Commission*'. Council of Foreign Ministers, Astana, Republic of Kaakhstan, 28–30 June 2011.

Statute of the OIC Independent Permanent Human Rights Commission, OIC Doc. (OIC/IPCHR/2010/STATUTE). Accessed 1 April 2013. http://oic-info.org/sites/default/files/user_upload/RessolutiononOICIPHRCandStatute.pdf.

Onuma, Yasuaki. *A Transcivilisational Perspective on International Law*. Martinus Nijhoff, 2010.

Oraá, Jaime. *Human Rights in States of Emergency in International Law*. Oxford: Clarendon Press, 1992.

'The Protection of Human Rights in Emergency Situations under Customary International Law'. In *The Reality of International Law: Essays in Honour of Ian Brownlie*, ed. Guy S. Goodwin-Gill and Stefan Talmon, 423. Oxford: Clarendon Press, 1999: 413–437.

Otley, David. 'Performance Management: a Framework for Management Control System Research'. *Management Accounting Research* (1999): 363–382.

Ottaway, Marina. 'Rebuilding State Institutions in Collapsed States'. *Development and Change* 33 (2002): 1001–1003.

Ouguergouz, F. 'African Charter on Human and Peoples' Rights'. *The Max Planck Encyclopedia of Public International Law*, 1981. www.mpepil.com.

Özerdem, Alpasan. 'The "Responsibility to Protect" in the Context of Natural Disasters: Another Excuse for Interventionism?'. Unpublished conference paper presented at the *World Conference of Humanitarian Studies*, Groningen (2009).

Pacific Institute. 'Water Conflict Chronology List'. *Pacific Institute*. Accessed 5 April 2013. www.worldwater.org/conflict/list/.

'Water Conflict Chronology Timeline'. *Pacific Institute*. Accessed 28 March 2013. www.worldwater.org/conflict/timeline/.

Parker, Karen and Lyn Beth Neylon. 'Jus Cogens: Compelling the Law of Human Rights'. *Hastings International and Comparative Law Review* 12 (1989): 411–463.

Parsons, Claudia. 'France Urges UN Council to Act on Myanmar Cyclone'. *Reuters online*, 7 May 2008. www.reuters.com/Art./2008/05/07/idUSL07810481.

Pastrana, Andrés. *La Palabra Bajo Fuego*. Editorial Planeta, 2005.

Patnaik, Dabiru Sridhar. 'International Law and Responsibility to Protect: South Asian Perspective'. *Journal of Global Studies, An Occasional Supplement* (2013): 173–189.

'Towards an International Legal Framework for the Protection of Individuals in the Event of Disasters: An Initial Inquiry'. In Heintze and Zwitter, *International Law and Humanitarian Assistance*, 129–141.

Paust, Jordan. 'The Libya Conflict'. www.law.uh.edu/news/faculty-news/summer2011/0630Paust.pdf.

Payandeh, Mehrdad. 'The United Nations, Military Intervention, and Regime Change in Libya'. *Virginia Journal of International Law* 52 (2012): 355–403.

Permana, R. 'Mengubah Paradigma Penanganan Bencana di Indonesia'. *West Java Disaster Reduction Studies Center* (2007). http://wjdrsc.files.wordpress.com/2008/03/paradigma-baru-penanganan-bencana-di-indonesia.pdf.

Philipp, Christiane. 'Somalia – a Very Special Case'. In *Max Planck Yearbook of United Nations Law* 9, ed. Armin von Bogdandy and Rüdiger Wolfrum, 517 *et seq*. Berlin, Heidelberg: Springer, 2005, 517–554.

Philips, Nicole, Kathleen Bergin, Jennifer Goldsmith and Laura Carr. 'Enforcing Remedies from the Inter-American Commission on Human Rights: Forced Evictions and Post-Earthquake Haiti'. *Human Rights Brief* 19 (2011): 13–18.

Pickrell, John. 'The Worst Natural Disasters in Recent History'. *ABC Environment*. Last modified 2 May 2011. www.abc.net.au/environment/articles/2011/04/27/3197103.htm.

Pictet, Jean S. *Commentary: The Geneva Convention Relative to the Treatment of Prisoners of War*. Geneva: ICRC, 1960.

'Commentary on the Geneva Conventions of 12 August 1949, Convention IV Relative to the Protection of Civilian Persons in Time of War'. International Committee of the Red Cross (Article 10) Geneva (1948): 98–99.

The Fundamental Principles of the Red Cross: Commentary. Geneva: Henry-Dunant Institute, 1979.

Geneva Convention Relative to the Protection of Civilian Persons in Time of War: Commentary. Geneva: ICRC, 1958.

Pilar, Ulrike von. *Humanitarian Space under Siege*. Bad Neuenahr: Background Paper Symposium Europe and Humanitarian Aid, 1999.

Pippan, Christian. 'The 2011 Libyan Uprising, Foreign Military Intervention, and International Law'. *Juridikum: Zeitschrift für Kritik-Recht-Gesellschaft* 2 (2011): 159–169.

Pommier, Bruno. 'The Use of Force to Protect Civilians and Humanitarian Action: The Case of Libya and Beyond'. *IRRC* 884: (2011): 1063–1083.

Porto, Joao G. 'Contemporary Conflict Analysis in Perspective'. In *Scarcity and Survive: The Ecology of Africa's Conflict*, eds. J. Lind et al.. Kenya: ACTS, 1998, 1–50.

Quénevet, Noëlle. 'The History of the Relationship Between International Humanitarian Law and Human Rights Law'. In *International Humanitarian Law and Human Rights Law: Towards a New Merger in International Law*, ed. Roberta Arnold and Noëlle Quénevet, 8–10. The Netherlands: Martinus Nijhoff Publishers, 2008.

Radtke, Richard K. 'Bomben auf Rangun?: Maynmar und die "Responsibility to Protect"'. *Welthungerhilfe, Brennpunkt* 3 (2008): 4.

Ramcharan, Bertrand G. *The Right to Life in International Law*. Dordrecht: Martinus Nijhoff Publishers, 1985.

Ramírez, Yaned. 'Engaño en "Jaque" podría haberse hecho sin usar el emblema, dice representante de CICR en Colombia'. *El Tiempo*, 15 August 2008.

Ratner, Steven R. 'Law Promotion Beyond Law Talk: The Red Cross, Persuasion, and the Laws of War'. *EJIL* 22 (2011): 459–5063.

Ratner, Steven R. and Rotem Giladi. 'The Role of the ICRC'. In *The Geneva Conventions of 1949 – Commentary*, ed. Andrew Clapham, Marco Sassòli and Paola Gaeta. OUP, forthcoming.

Rausch, Anne. *Responsibility to Protect: Eine juristische Betrachtung*. Frankfurt/M: Peter Lang Verlag, 2011.

Reed, R. A. (ed.), *Technical Support for Refugees: Lessons from Recent Experiences*, Proceedings of the 1991 International Conference, Water, Engineering and Development Centre, Loughborough University of Technology, Loughborough, 1993.

Rehman, Javaid. *International Human Rights Law*. London: Longman, 2010.

ReliefWeb. 'Glossary for Humanitarian Terms of 2008'. Project, August 2008. http://reliefweb.int/sites/reliefweb.int/files/resources/4F99A3C28EC37D0E-C12574A4002E89B4-reliefweb_aug2008.pdf.

ReliefWeb. 'US Ships to Leave Cyclone-hit Myanmar After Junta Snub'. *ReliefWeb*, n.d. http://reliefweb.int/node/268943.

Revised European Social Charter, adopted by the Council of Europe Organisation, Strasbourg, 3.V.1996. Accessed 1 April 2013. http://conventions.coe.int/Treaty/en/Treaties/Html/163.htm.

Rey, Francisco. 'La participación military en la acción humanitaria: reflexiones sobre el caso colombiano'. *Humanitarian Exchange Magazine*, 45 (2010). Accessed 19 October 2011. www.odihpn.org/report.asp?id=3061.

Ribot, J. C. 'Accountable Representation and Power Participation and Decentralized Environmental Management', *Unasylva*, vol. 50, No. 199, 1999: 18-22.

Richardson, Michael. 'Dams in China Turn the Mekong Into a River of Discord'. *Yale Global Online*, 16 July 2009. Accessed 29 March 2013. http://yaleglobal.yale.edu/content/dams-china-turn-mekong-river-discord.

Rieff, David. *A Bed for the Night: Humanitarianism in Crisis*. New York: Simon and Schuster, 2002.

Rieter, Eva. *Preventing Irreparable Harm: Provisional Measures in International Human Rights Adjudication*. Antwerp: Intersentia, 2010.

Rishmawi, Mervat. 'The Arab Charter on Human Rights and the League of Arab States: An Update'. *Human Rights Law Review* 10 (2010): 170–72.

'The League of Arab States; Recent Developments on Human Rights and Social Justice'. In *Defending Human Rights: Tools for Social Justice*, ed. Ida Lintel, Antoine Buyse and Brianne McGonigle Leyh, 45. Volume in Honour of Fried van Hoof at the Occasion of his Valedictory Lecture and the 30th Anniversary of the Netherlands Institute of Human Rights. Cambridge: Intersentia, 2012, 41–48.

Roberts, Adam. 'The Role of Humanitarian Issues in International Politics in the 1990s'. *International Review of the Red Cross* 833 (1999): 19–43.

'The United Nations and Humanitarian Intervention'. In *Humanitarian Intervention and International Relations*, ed. Jennifer I. Welsh, 71 *et seq*. Oxford University Press, 2006, 71–97.

Roht-Arriaza, Naomi and Sara C. Aminadeh. 'Solidarity Rights: Development, Peace, Environment, Humanitarian Assistance'. In *Max Planck Encyclopedia of Public International Law*, ed. Rüdiger Wolfrum, §19. Oxford Publication International Law, 2007. http://opil.ouplaw.com/view/10.1093/law:epil/9780199231690/law-9780199231690-e1470?rskey=7mnqKb&result=7&prd=EPIL

Rottensteiner, Christa. 'The Denial of Humanitarian Assistance as a Crime under International Law'. *IRRC* 835 (1999): 555–582.

Rousseau, Charles. *Droit International Public*. Paris: Sirey, 1970, vol. I.

Sakai, M. 'Konflik Sekitar Devolusi Kekuasaan Ekonomi dan Politik: Suatu Pengantar'. *Antropologi Indonesia* 68 (2002): iv–vii.

Salzberg, Aaron. 'Foreign Policy and International Water Development'. Accessed 25 March 2013. www.youtube.com/watch?v=s_CUt4wq4Xg.

Salman, M. A. and Siobhán McInerney-Lankford. 'Human Right to Water: Legal and Policy Dimensions'. *World Bank*, 2004. Accessed 23 June 2013. www-wds.worldbank.org/external/default/WDSContentServer/WDSP/IB/2004/

10/18/000090341_20041018135134/Rendered/PDF/302290PAPER0Human0right0to0H20.pdf.

Samadhi, W. P. 'Desentralisasi Setengah Hati: Berpindahnya "Sentralisme" ke Daerah'., (2005) Demos –Center for Democracy and Human Rights Studies. http://wp.demosindonesia.org/2005/11/desentralisasi-setengah-hati-berpindahnya-sentralisme-ke-daerah/.

Sandoz, Yves. 'Article 69'. In *Commentary on the Additional Protocols of 8 June 1977 to the Geneva Conventions of 12 August 1949*, ed. Yves Sandoz, Christophe Swinarski and Bruno Zimmerman. Geneva: ICRC, 1987: 811–814.

'Le droit d'initiative du Comité international de la Croix-Rouge'. *German Yearbook of International Law* 22 (1979): 352–373.

'The International Committee of the Red Cross as Guardian of International Humanitarian Law'. *ICRC*, 1998. Accessed on 31 March 2013. www.icrc.org/eng/resources/documents/misc/about-the-icrc-311298.htm.

Sandoz, Yves, Christophe Swinarski, and Bruno Zimmermann. *Commentary on the Additional Protocols of 8 June 1977 to the Geneva Conventions of 12 August 1949*. Geneva: ICRC, 1987.

Sandoval, Clara. 'A Critical View of the Protection of Refugees and IDPs by the Inter-American System of Human Rights: Re-assessing its Powers and Examining the Challenges for the Future', *International Journal of Refugee Law* 43 (2005): 43–65.

Sarooshi, Dan. *United Nations and the Development of Collective Security: the Delegation by the UN Security Council of its Chapter VII Powers*. Oxford University Press, 1999.

Sassòli, Marco A., Antoin Bouvier and Anne Quintin. *How Does Law Protect in War?* Cambridge University Press, 3rd ed., 2011.

Sassòli, Marco and Laura M. Olson. 'The Relationship Between International Humanitarian and Human Rights Law Where it Matters: Admissible Killing and Internment of Fighters in Non-International Armed Conflicts'. *IRRC* 90 (2008): 599–627.

Saul, Ben. 'The Legality of the Use of Force against Iraq in 2003: Did the Coalition Defend or Defy the United Nations?' *UCLA J. Int'l L. & Foreign Aff.* 8 (2003): 267–329.

Savage, Kevin, Mulbah S. Jackollie, D. Maxim Kumeh and Edwin Dorbor. 'Corruption Perceptions and Risks in Humanitarian Assistance: a Liberia Case Study'. *HPG Background Paper* (2007): 11. www.odi.org.uk/resources/download/287.pdf.

Save the Children. 'A Chance for Every Child: our Trustees' Report and Financial Statementes 2011'. Accessed 13 April 2013. www.savethechildren.org.uk/resources/online-library/chance-every-child-our-trustees-report-and-financial-statements-2011.

Schmeier, Suzanne. *Governing of International Watercourses: The Contribution of River Basin Organisations to the Effective Governance of Internationally Shared Rivers and Lakes*. London: Routledge, 2013.

Schmitt, Michael. N. 'Wings Over Libya: The No-Fly Zone in Legal Perspective'. *Yale Journal of International Law Online* 36 (2011): 45–58.

Schneider-Enk, Michaela. *Der völkerrechtliche Schutz humanitärer Helfer in bewaffneten Konflikten: Die Sicherheit des Hilfspersonals und die 'neuen' Konflikte*. Hamburg: Verlag Dr. Kovac, 2008.

Schulte, Maren. 'Profile in Disaster Law Advocacy: Captain Jean Damascène Kayitana'. *Disaster Law Newsletter*, February 2013. Accessed on 14 April 2013. www.ifrc.org/fr/introduction/-droit-des-catastrophes/dernieres-nouvelles-et-derniers-rapports-sur-le-droit-des-catastrophes/disaster-law-newsletter-february-2013/profile-in-disaster-law-advocacy-captain-jean-damascene-kayitana-60800/.

Schütze, Julia-Pia. *Die Zurechenbarkeit von Völkerrechtsverstößen im Rahmen mandatierter Friedensmissionen der Vereinten Nationen*. Berlin: Duncker & Humblot, 2011.

Sepúlveda, Magdalena. *The Nature of the Obligations under the International Covenant on Economic, Social and Cultural Rights*. Antwerp: Intersentia, 2003.

Severino, Rodolfo C. 'ASEAN's declaration advances human rights in Asia'. *ASEAN Studies Centre*, 8 February 2013. Accessed 18 June 2013. www.eastasiaforum.org/2013/02/08/aseans-declaration-advances-human-rights-in-asia/.

SFDFA (Swiss Federal Department of Foreign Affairs). 'Humanitarian Access in Situations of Armed Conflict: Field Manual – Version 1.0'. *Swiss Federal Department of Foreign Affairs*, 2011. www.cdint.org/documents/PAIV_111118_Humanitarian_Access_FieldManual_mit_Inhalt.pdf.

'Humanitarian Access in Situations of Armed Conflict: Handbook on the Normative Framework'. *The Swiss Federal Department of Foreign Affairs* 1 (2011): 44–56.

SFG. 'Cost of Conflict in the Middle East'. 2009. http://www.strategicforesight.com/publication_pdf/39166Cost%20of%20Conflict%20in%20the%20Middle%20East.pdf.

Shaw, Carolyn M. *Cooperation, Conflict and Consensus in the Organisation of American States*. New York: Palgrave Macmillan, 2004.

Shaw, Malcolm. N. *International Law*. Cambridge University Press, 2008, 6th ed.

Simma, Bruno. 'Article 2 (V)'. In *The Charter of the United Nations: A Commentary*, ed. Bruno Simma. Munich: C. H. Beck, 2002, 2nd edn., vol. I, 136–139.

'Fragmentation in a Positive Light'. *Michigan Journal of International Law* 25 (2003–2004): 845–848.

'Of Planets and the Universe: Self-contained Regimes in International Law'. *EJIL* 17 (2006): 483–529.

From Bilateralism to Community Interest in International Law. Leiden: Martinus Nijhoff, 1994, VI, vol. 250.

Simon, Annette. *UN-Schutzzonen – Ein Schutzinstrument für verfolgte Personen?: Eine Analyse anhand der internationalen Schutzzone im Irak, in Ruanda und Bosnien-Herzegowina mit besonderem Blick auf die schweren Menschenrechtsverletzungen in der safe area Srebrenica*. Berlin, Heidelberg, New York: Springer, 2005.

Slaughter, Anne-Marie. 'Intervention, Libya, and the Future of Sovereignty'. *The Atlantic*, 4 September 2011. www.theatlantic.com/international/archive/2011/09/intervention-libya-and-the-future-of-sovereignty/244537/.

South Africa. Disaster Management Act, Act No. 57, 2002, http://www.saflii.org/za/legis/consol_act/dma2002191/

Southwick, Katherine G. 'Bumpy Road to the ASEAN Human Rights Declaration'. *Asia Pacific Bulletin* 197 (22 January 2012). Accessed March 27, 2013. www.eastwestcenter.org/sites/default/files/private/apb197_1.pdf.

Sphere Handbook. 'Water Supply Standard 1: Access and Water Quantity'. *The Sphere Handbook: Humanitarian Charter and Minimum Standards in Humanitarian Response*. Accessed 30 March 2013. www.spherehandbook.org/en/water-supply-standard-1-access-and-water-quantity/.

Sphere Project. 'Humanitarian Charter and Minimum Standards in Humanitarian Response'. *The Sphere Project*. Accessed at 30 March 2013. www.spherehandbook.org.

Spieker, Heike. 'Humanitarian Assistance, Access in Armed Conflict and Occupation'. In *The Max Planck Encyclopedia of Public International Law*, ed. Rüdiger Wolfrum. Oxford University Press, 2008–, online edition, www.mpepil.com.

Spieker, Heike. 'The Right to Give and Receive Humanitarian Assistance'. In Heintze and Zwitter, *International Law and Humanitarian Assistance*, 7–32.

Ssenyonjo, Manisuli. 'Economic, Social and Cultural Rights in the African Charter'. In *The African Regional Human Rights System: 30 Years after the African Charter on Human and Peoples' Rights*, ed. Manisuli Ssenyonjo. Leiden: Martinus Nijhoff Publishers, 2012, 55–100.

'An Introduction to the Development of the African Regional Human Rights System'. In *The African Regional Human Rights System: 30 Years after the African Charter on Human and Peoples' Rights*, ed. Manisuli Ssenyonjo. Leiden: Martinus Nijhoff Publishers, 2012, 3–26.

Stapleton, Sara. 'Ensuring a Fair Trial in the International Criminal Court: Statutory Interpretation and the Impermissibility of Derogation'. *New York University Journal of International Law and Politics* 31 (1999): 535–610.

Steni, Bernadinus. 'Desentralisasi, Koordinasi dan Partisipasi Masyarakat Dalam Pengelolaan Sumberdaya Alam Pasca Otonomi Daerah'. Accessed 21 July 2008.

Stoddard, Abby. 'Humanitarian NGOs: Challenges and Trends'. *HPG Policy Briefs* 12 (2003): 1–4.

Stoddard, Abby, Adele Harmer, and Katherine Haver. 'Providing Aid in Insecure Environments: Trends in Policy and Operations'. *HPG Briefing Paper* 24 (2006): 1–4.

Stoffels, Ruth A. 'Legal Regulation of Humanitarian Assistance in Armed Conflict: Achievements and Gaps'. *International Review of the Red Cross* 86 (2004): 515–545.

Stoll, Peter-Tobias. 'Responsibility, Sovereignty and Cooperation – Reflections on the Responsibility to Protect'. In *International Law Today: New Challenges and the Need for Reform?*, ed. Doris König, Peter-Tobias Stoll, Volker Röben and Nele Matz-Luck. Berlin: Springer, 2008, 1–16.

STRATFOR (Strategic Forecasting, Inc.). 'Unrest and the Libyan Military'. 21 February 2011. www.stratfor.com/analysis/20110220-unrest-libyan-military.

Sturcke, James. 'South Korea Demands North Korea Apology for Flash Flood that Killed Six'. *The Guardian*, 8 September 2009. Accessed 30 March 2013. www.guardian.co.uk/world/2009/sep/08/south-korea-flood-kills-campers.

Susiloadi, P. 'Konsep dan Isu Desentralisasi Dalam Manajemen Pemerintahan di Indonesia'. *Spirit Publik* 3, No. 2 (2007) : 117–124.

Tacsan, Joaquin. 'Searching for OAS/UN Task-Sharing Opportunities in Central America and Haiti'. *Third World Quarterly* 18 (1997): 489–508.

Talmon, Stefan. 'Recognition of the Libyan National Transitional Council'. *ASIL Insight*, 16 June 2011. www.asil.org/insights110616.cfm.

Tamanaha, Brian Z. 'The Folly of the Societal Scientific Concept of Legal Pluralism'. *The Journal of Law and Society* 20 (1993): 192–217.

Tams, Christian J. 'Do Serious Breaches Give Rise to Any Specific Obligations of the Responsible State?'. *European Journal of International Law* 13 (2002): 1161–1180.

Terry, Fiona. *Condemned to Repeat? The Paradox of Humanitarian Action*. Ithaca: Cornell University Press, 2002

'The International Committee of the Red Cross in Afghanistan: Reasserting the Neutrality of Humanitarian Action'. *IRRC* 881 (2011): 173–188.

'Myanmar: Golfing with the Generals', in Magone, Neuman and Weissman, *Humanitarian Negotiations Revealed: The MSF Experience*, 123–146.

Thompson, Larry. '*Humanitarian Emergencies: Why Does Kosovo Get More Aid Than the Congo?*'. Paper for the International Council of Voluntary Agencies Conference on NGOs in a Changing World Order, Geneva, 14–15 February 2003.

Thürer, Daniel. 'Dunant's Pyramid: Thoughts on Humanitarian Space'. *International Review of the Red Cross* 89 (2007): 47–61.

'Failing States'. In Online *Max Planck Encyclopedia of Public International Law*. www.mpepil.com.

Transparency International. 'Handbook of Good Practices: Preventing Corruption in Humanitarian Operations', 31 January 2010. http://www.transparency.org/whatwedo/pub/handbook_of_good_practices_preventing_corruption_in_humanitarian_operations.

'Resist – Resisting Extortion and Solicitation in International Transactions'. International Chamber of Commerce, United Nations Global Compact. *World Economic Forum*, 2011. www.transparency.org/content/download/43250/690884/file/RESIST_09-05-09.pdf.

'In the Wake of Disaster: Preventing Corruption in Tsunami Relief and Reconstruction'. *In Focus* 2005. http://archive.transparency.org/news_room/in_focus/2005/tsunami.

Triyana, Heribertus Jaka. 'The Implementation of the Community-Based Natural Resources Management System Principle in the Political Decentralisation in the Natural Disaster Management Program in Indonesia: Case Studies in the Kapuk Village, Cengkareng West Jakarta Regency, the Special Province of Jakarta and in the Kalabahi Capital City of Alor Regency, the East Nusa Tenggara Province'. Thesis at the Faculty of Arts, Rijks University of Groningen (2008), 25–30.

'Investasi dan Pengelolaan Ruang untuk Investasi di Daerah'. Masters Thesis, Sekolah Paska Sarjana, Fakultas Hukum Universitas Gadjah Mada (2011).

'Tinjauan Yuridis Tentang Badan HAM ASEAN Dalam Sistem Hukum Nasional Indonesia'. *Jurnal Mimbar Hukum* 23, No. 3 (2011): 611–628.

Triyana, Heribertus Jaka and Andi Wibowo. 'The Implementation of Article 8 of the Law Number 24 of 2007 for the Community Participation on Disaster Response to the 2010 Mount Merapi Eruption in Central Java and Yogyakarta Province, Research Report'. Center for Community Services and Research, Faculty of Law, Gadjah Mada University (2011).

Tsui, Edward, 'Analysis of Normative Development in Humanitarian Resolutions since the Adoption of 46/182', *Independent Review to OCHA* (2009): 1–32.

Tyagi, Yogesh. 'The Concept of Humanitarian Intervention Revisited'. *Michigan Journal of International Law* 16 (1995): 901, 883–910.

United Nations (UN) Charter (1UNTS XVI), signed on 26 June 1945, San Francisco, entry into force on 24 October 1945. UN. Convention for the Elimination of all forms of Discrimination against Women (CEDAW) 1979. www.un.org/womenwatch/daw/cedaw/text/econvention.htm#article14.

'General Assembly Adopts Resolution Recognising Access to Clean Water, Sanitation as Human Right by Recorded Vote of 122 in Favour, None

Against and 41 Abstentions'. 28 July 2010. Accessed 1 March 2013. www.un.org/News/Press/docs/2010/ga10967.doc.htm.

'General Comment No. 7: Implementing Child Rights in Early Childhood'. *Committee on the Rights of the Child.* UN Doc. (CRC/C/GC/7/Rev.1) 2006. Accessed 23 June 2013. www1.umn.edu/humanrts/crc/comment7.html.

International Convention on the Rights of Persons with Disabilities, 1999. www.un.org/disabilities/convention/conventionfull.shtml.

'MONUC Background'. www.un.org/en/peacekeeping/missions/monuc/background.shtml.

'OAS Peace-Building Experiences: Progress Achieved, Lessons Learned, and Future Possibilities'. OAS/UN International Civilian Mission. Accessed 29 March 2013. www.un.org/rights/micivih/rapports/peace-bu.htm

Rome Statute of the International Criminal Court. UN Doc. (A/CONF.183/9). http://untreaty.un.org/cod/icc/statute/romefra.htm. 'UNAMID Background'. www.un.org/en/peacekeeping/missions/unamid/background.shtml.

'UNMIS Background', www.un.org/en/peacekeeping/missions/unmis/background.shtml.

'UNMISET'. www.un.org/en/peacekeeping/missions/past/unmiset/index.html.

UN Department of Public Information. 'Somalia – UNOSOM I'. www.un.org/Depts/DPKO/Missions/unosomi.htm.

UN Doc. (A/34/180) 18 December 1979. *Convention on the Elimination of All Forms of Discrimination against Women,* 1981. General Assembly, Resolution 34/180.

UN Doc. (A/39/46) 10 December 1984. *Convention against Torture and Other Cruel, Inhuman or Degrading Treatment or Punishment,* 1987. General Assembly, Resolution 39/46.

UN Doc. (A/44/25) 20 November 1989. *Convention on the Rights of the Child,* 1990. General Assembly Resolution 44/25.

UN Doc. (CCPR/C/USA/CO/3/Rev.1).UN Human Rights Committee. Concluding Observations on the United States, 2006.

UN Doc. (CEDAW/C/IDN/CO/5) CEDAW. Concluding Observations on Indonesia, 2007.

UN Doc. (CERD/C/USA/CO/6). UN Committee on the Elimination of all Forms of Racial Discrimination, Concluding Observations on the United States of America, 2008.

UN Doc. (E/C.12/1/Add.90). Committee on Economic, Social and Cultural Rights. 'Concluding observations of the Committee on Economic, Social and Cultural Rights – Israel'. 23 May 2003.

UN ESC. 'General Comment No. 15: The Right to Water'. United Nations Economic Social and Cultural Council, 2002 (E/C.12/2002/11). Accessed 1 March 2013. www.unhchr.ch/tbs/doc.nsf/0/a5458d1d1bbd713fc1256cc400389e94/$FILE/G0340229.pdfUN ESCAP (United Nations Economic and

Social Commission for Asia and the Pacific). 'Preview Green Growth Resources and Resilience Environmental Sustainability in Asia and Pacific'. United Nations Publication (ST/ESCAP/2582) 2010. www.unescap.org/esd/environment/flagpubs/ggrap/documents/Green%20Growth-16Sept%20(Final).pdf.

UN ESC. 'Statistical Yearbook for Asia and Pacific 2011'. Accessed 30 March 2013. www.unescap.org/stat/data/syb2011/ii-environment/water-availability-and-use.asp.

UN ESC. 'Statistical Yearbook for Asia and Pacific 2012' UN ESCAP, 6 November 2012. www.unescap.org/stat/data/syb2012/index.asp.

UN General Assembly (GA), Resolution (A/67/L.39). 'Strengthening of the Coordination of Humanitarian and Disaster Relief Assistance of the United Nations, Including Special Economic Assistance: Strengthening of the Coordination of Emergency Humanitarian Assistance of the United Nations'. 7 December 2012.

Resolution (A/RES/46/182). 'Strengthening of the Coordination of Humanitarian Emergency Assistance of the United Nations'. December 1991. Accessed on 30 March 2013. www.un.org/documents/ga/res/46/a46r182.htm.

UN Human Rights Committee. 'General Comment 6' (Article 6) (Sixteenth session, 1982). Compilation of General Comments and General Recommendations Adopted by Human Rights Treaty Bodies, UN Doc. HRI/GEN/1/Rev.6 at 127 (2003). Human Rights Committee, General Comment 29, States of Emergency (Article 4), UN Doc. CCPR/C/21/Rev.1/Add.11 (2001), reprinted in Compilation of General Comments and General Recommendations Adopted by Human Rights Treaty Bodies, UN Doc. HRI/GEN/1/Rev.6 at 186 (2003).

General Comment 31, Nature of the General Legal Obligation on States Parties to the Covenant, UN Doc. CCPR/C/21/Rev.1/Add.13 (2004).

UN Human Rights Council. 'Report of the International Commission of Inquiry to Investigate All Alleged Violations of International Human Rights Law in the Libyan Arab Jamahiriya'. UN Doc. (A/HRC/17/44) 12 January 2012.

'Report of the International Commission of Inquiry on Libya'. UN Doc. (A/HRC/19/68) 2 March 2012.

UN News Centre. 'Myanmar: UN Aid Reaches People in Conflict-affected Kachin Area'. *UN News Centre*. Accessed 4 April 2013. www.un.org/apps/news/story.asp?NewsID=44257#.UUhsHjf7yQ.

'UN Official Welcomes ASEAN Commitment to Human Rights, But Concerned Over Declaration Wording'. *UN News Centre*, 19 November 2012. Accessed 1 April 2013. www.un.org/apps/news/story.asp?NewsID=43536#.UUNOvay1LSg.

UN Security Council Sanctions Committees. www.un.org/Security Council/committees/.

UN Treaty. Accessed on 13 April 2013. http://untreaty.un.org/ilc/guide/6_3.htm.

UNHCR (United Nations High Commissioner for Refugees. *Convention and Protocol Relating to the Status of Refugees*, 1951 and 1967. www.unhcr.org/3b66c2aa10.html.

'Myanmar'. *UNICEF* Humanitarian Action for Children, 2011. Accessed 19 March 2013. www.unicef.org/hac2011/files/HAC2011_4pager_Myanmar.pdf.

'Myanmar 2013 UNHCR Country Operations Profile'. Accessed 18 March 2013. www.unhcr.org/pages/49e4877d6.html.

Statute of the Office of the United Nations High Commissioner for Refugees. www.unhcr.org/3b66c39e1.html. Accessed 13 August 2013.

UNICEF. 'Guiding Principles: International Law and Principles that Guide UNICEF's Action in Emergencies'. www.unicef.org/emerg/index_32032.html. Accessed 13 August 2013.

UNISDR (United Nations Office for Disaster Risk Reduction). 'Hyogo Framework for Action (HFA)'. Accessed 29 March 2013. www.unisdr.org/we/coordinate/hfa.

United Nations Development Programme. *Human Development Report 1994.* New York: Oxford University Press, 1994.

United Nations Water Conference, 14-25 March 1977, Mar del Plata. Report of the United Nations Water Conference, UN Doc. (E/CONF.70/29). www.ielrc.org/content/e7701.pdf.

UNOPS (United Nations Office for Project Services). 'Water Treatment'. UNOPS. www.unops.org/english/whatwedo/services/physical-infrastructure/experience-capacity/Pages/water-treatment.aspx.

UN Secretary-General. 'Guidance on Integrated Missions'. 9 February 2006.

UN Secretary-General of the OAS. 'Inauguration of the Forty-Second Regular Session of the OAS General Assembly'. *OAS*, 3 June 2012. www.oas.org/en/about/speech_secretary_general.asp?sCodigo=12-0033.

Unson, John. 'Moro Rebs to Poison Sources of Water?'. *PhilStar*, 26 March 2003. www.philstar.com/nation/200342/moro-rebs-poison-sources-water.

UNTS (United Nations Treaty Series). *Additional Protocol to the Geneva Conventions of 12 August 1949, and Relating to the Protection of Victims of International Armed Conflicts (Protocol I).* 1125 UNTS 3.

Additional Protocol to the Geneva Conventions of 12 August 1949, and Relating to the Protection of Victims of Non-International Armed Conflicts (Protocol II), 1125 UNTS 609.

Convention Relative to the Treatment of Prisoners of War. 12 August 1949. 75 UNTS 135 (1950).

Uppsala Conflict Data Program (2013/04/01): *UCDP Conflict Encyclopedia*: www.ucdp.uu.se/database.

Uppsala Conflict Data Program (2013/04/01): 'Thailand'. *UCPD Conflict Encyclopaedia.* Accessed 30 March 2013. www.ucdp.uu.se/gpdatabase/gpcountry.php?id=154&regionSelect=7-Eastern_Asia.

Uppsala University Department of Peace and Conflict Research. www.ucdp.uu.se/gpdatabase/gpregions.php?regionSelect=5-Southern%20Americas.

US Citizenship and Immigration Services. 107th Congress of the United States of America, 2002. Accessed 22 November 2011. www.uscis.gov/ilink/docView/PUBLAW/HTML/PUBLAW/0-0-0-25343.html.

US Department of State. 'Global Water Security, Intelligence Community Assessment'. February 2012. www.dni.gov/files/documents/Special%20Report_ICA%20Global%20Water%20Security.pdf.

Valencia-Ospina, Eduardo (Special Rapporteur of the International Law Commission). 'Fifth Report on the Protection of Persons in the Event of Disasters', UN Doc. (A/CN.4/652) 9 April 2012.

'Fourth Report on the Protection of Persons in the Event of Disasters'. UN Doc. (A/CN.4/643), 11 May 2011.

'Preliminary Report on the Protection of Persons in the Event of Disasters'. 5 May 2008, UN Doc. (A/CN.4/598).

'Protection of Persons in the Event of Disaster'. In 'Second Report on the Protection of Persons in the Event of Disasters'. United Nations' International Law Commission and its Special Rapporteur, 7 May 2009.

Vales, Hernan. 'The Latin American View on the Doctrine of Humanitarian Intervention'. *The Journal of Humanitarian Assistance* (2001). Accessed 29 March 2013. http://sites.tufts.edu/jha/archives/1491.

Van Baarda, Th. A. 'Moral Ambiguities Underlying the Laws of Armed Conflict'. *Yearbook of International Humanitarian Law* 11 (2010): 3–49.

Van Steenberghe, Raphael. 'Non-State Actors from the Perspective of the International Committee of the Red Cross'. In *Participants in the International Legal System*, edited Jean D'Aspremont. Oxford: Routledge, 2011, 204–232.

Vasciannie, Stephen. 'International Law and Disasters'. *Jamaica Observer*, 27 June 2010. Accessed 3 May 2011. www.jamaicaobserver.com/columns/International-law-and-disasters_7744354.

Vaurs-Chaumette, Anne-Laure. 'Peoples and Minorities'. In *The Law of International Responsibility*, ed. James Crawford, Allen Pellet and Simon Olleson. Oxford University Press, 2010, 993–1004.

Verband Entwicklungspolitik deutscher Nichtregierungs-organisationen e.V. (VENRO), 'Linking Relief, Rehabilitation and Development-Ansätze und Förderinstrumente zur Ver-besserung des Übergangs von Nothilfe, Wiederaufbau und Entwicklungszusammenarbeit', VENRO-Arbeitspapier nr. 17, February 2006. www.venro.org/fileadmin/Publikationen/arbeitspapiere/arbeitspapier_17.pdf.

Verburg, Liedeke. 'Donor or Partnership, Does the Concept of A Real Partnership Represent the Relief and Rehabilitation Operations during Post Natural Disaster Situation, Case Studies: Aceh Tsunami 2004 and Yogyakarta Earthquake 2006'. Thesis, Faculty of Arts, Rijks University, Groningen (2007).

Verdirame, Guglielmo and Barbara Harrell-Bond. *Rights in Exile – Janus-faced Humanitarianism*. New York: Berghahn Books, 2005.

Verdross, Alfred. *Die Verfassung der Völkerrechtsgemeinschaft*. Wien: J. Springer, 1926.

Vermillion, Douglas L. 'Finding Solutions to Asia's Water Challenges through Integrated Water-Resources Management'. Background Note Issued Prior to the Meeting, accessed 31 March 2013. http://publications.iwmi.org/pdf/h032971.pdf.

Viljoen, Frans. 'The African Human Rights System and its Potential For Delivering, or at Least Contributing to, Social Justice'. In *Defending Human Rights: Tools for Social Justice*, ed. Ida Lintel, Antoine Buyse and Brianne McGonigle Leyh. Cambridge: Intersentia, 2012, Volume in Honour of Fried van Hoof at the Occasion of his Valedictory Lecture and the 30th Anniversary of the Netherlands Institute of Human Rights.

International Human Rights Law in Africa. Oxford University Press, 2011, Second Edition.

Virally, Michel. 'Review Essay: Good Faith in Public International Law'. *American Journal of International Law* 77 (1983): 130.

Von Arnauld, Andreas. 'Völkerrechtliche Informationspflichten bei Naturkatastrophen'. *Archiv des Völkerrechts* 43 (2005): 279–311.

Vukas, Budislav. 'Humanitarian Assistance in Cases of Emergency'. Online *Max Planck Encyclopedia of Public International Law*. www.mpepil.com.

Wainwright, Elsina. 'Conflict Prevention in Southeast Asia and the South Pacific'. April 2010. www.humansecuritygateway.com/documents/CIC_ConflictPreventionInSoutheastAsiaAndTheSouthPacific.pdf.

Waititu, Ernest. 'Diminishing Water Resources Threaten Peace'. 26 May 2009. Accessed 30 March 2013. http://pulitercenter.org/articles/diminishing-water-resources-threaten-peace.

Waldron, Jeremy. 'Is the Rule of Law an Essentially Contested Concept (in Florida)?'. *Law and Philosophy* 21 (2002): 137–164.

Waterfield, Bruno. 'Libya: British Military Advisers Set up "Joint Operations Centre" in Benghazi'. *The Telegraph*, 18 May 2011. www.telegraph.co.uk/news/worldnews/africaandindianocean/libya/8521977/Libya-British-military-advisers-set-up-joint-operations-centre-in-Benghazi.html.

WaterLex. Cambodia. Accessed 5 April 2013. http://faolex.fao.org/cgi-bin/waterlex.exe?rec_id=000060&database=waterlex&search_type=link&lang=eng&format_name=ERALL&table=wtl.

Indonesia. Accessed 5 April 2013. http://faolex.fao.org/cgi-bin/waterlex.exe?rec_id=000040&database=waterlex&search_type=link&lang=eng&format_name=ERALL&table=wtl.

Laos. Accessed 5 April 2013. http://faolex.fao.org/cgi-bin/waterlex.exe?rec_id=000043&database=waterlex&search_type=link&lang=eng&format_name=ERALL&table=wtl.

Thailand. Accessed 5 April 2013. http://faolex.fao.org/cgi-bin/waterlex.exe?rec_id=000032&database=waterlex&search_type=link&lang=eng&format_name=ERALL&table=wtl.

Vietnam. Accessed 5 April 2013. http://faolex.fao.org/cgi-bin/waterlex.exe?rec_id=000050&database=waterlex&search_type=link&lang=eng&format_name=ERALL&table=wtl].

Weckel, Philippe. *La Concurrence des Traités Internationaux*. Thèse Strasbourg III, 1986.

Weiffen, Brigitte. 'Persistence and Change in Regional Security Institutions: Does the OAS Still Have a Project?'. *Contemporary Security Policy* 33 (2012): 360–383.

Wellens, Karel. 'Revisiting Solidarity as a (Re-)Emerging Constitutional Principle: Some Further Reflections'. In *Solidarity: A Structural Principle of International Law*, eds. R. Wolfrum, C. Kojima, Heidelberg: Springer, 2010: 3–38.

Wentges, Taylor. 'Electoral Monitoring and the OAS/UN International Civil Mission to Haiti'. *Peacekeeping and International Relations* 25 (1996): 43–56.

Wetherall, Anthony. *Normative Rule Making at the IAEA: Codes of Conduct.* Unpublished paper, 6 May 2005.

WHO. 'Definitions: Emergency'. Accessed 21 October 2011. www.who.int/hac/about/definitions/en/index.html.

'Guidelines for Medicine Donations'. *World Health Organisation*, 2010.

'Inter-agency contingency planning guidelines for humanitarian assistance'. *IASC*. www.who.int/hac/network/interagency/news/contingency_guidelines/en/.

'Technical Notes on Drinking Water, Sanitation and Hygiene during Emergencies'. *World Health Organisation*, 2011. Accessed 30 March 2013. www.who.int/water_sanitation_health/publications/2011/tn9_how_much_water_en.pdf.

Wiarda, Howard J. 'The United States and the Dominican Republic: Intervention, Dependency, and Tyrannicide'. *Journal of Inter-American Studies and World Affairs* 22 (1980): 247–260.

Wilde, Ralph. *International Territorial Administration: How Trusteeship and the Civilizing Mission Never Went Away.* Oxford University Press: 2008.

Williams, Paul D. and Alex J. Bellamy. 'Principles, Politics, and Prudence: Libya, the Responsibility to Protect, and the Use of Military Force'. *Global Governance* 18 (2012): 273–297.

Wolf, Aaron. T. '"Water Wars" and Water Reality: Conflict and Cooperation Along International Waterways'. In *Environmental Change, Adaptation and Security*, ed. Steve C. Lonergan. Netherlands: Kluwer Academic Publishers, 1997: 251–265.

Wolfrum, Rüdiger. 'Article 1' and 'Article 55 (a) and (b)'. In *The Charter of the United Nations: A Commentary*, ed. B. Simma, Munich: C. H. Beck, 2002, vol. II: 897–917.

'Solidarity amongst States: An Emerging Structural Principle of International Law'. *Indian Journal of International Law* 49 (2009): 1–19.

Wolfrum, Rüdiger and Dieter Fleck, 'Enforcement of International Humanitarian Law'. In *Handbook of International Humanitarian Law*, edited by Dieter Fleck, 675, 713–4. Oxford University Press, 2008: 675–722.

Wood, Michael. 'United Nations, Security Council'. In *MPEPIL online*, edited by Rüdiger Wolfrum, §23. www.mpepil.com/.

World Vision. 'Financial Accountability'. Accessed 13 April 2013, www.worldvision.org/content.nsf/about/why-donate.

World Water Council. 'Legal Resources for the Right to Water and Sanitation International and National Standards'. *Center for Housing and Eviction Rights*, 2nd edn, 2008. Accessed 21 March 2013. www.worldwatercouncil.org/fileadmin/wwc/Programs/Right_to_Water/Pdf_doct/RWP-Legal_Res_1st_Draft_web.pdf.

Wyss, Marco. 'Military Transformation in Europe's Neutral and Non-Neutral Allies'. *The RUSI Journal* 156–2 (2011): 44–51.

Yun, Joseph. 'Challenges to Water and Security in Southeast Asia'. 23 September 2010. Accessed 18 March 2013. www.state.gov/p/eap/rls/rm/2010/09/147674.htm.

Zemanek, Karl, Gerhard Hafner and Stephan Wittich. 'Die völkerrechtliche Verantwortlichkeit und die Sanktionen des Völkerrechts'. In *Österreichisches Handbuch des Völkerrechts*, ed. Hanspeter Neuhold, Waldemar Hummer and Christoph Schreuer. Vienna: Manz, 4th edn, 2004, vol. I, IX, 505–532.

Zwanenburg, Marten. 'United Nations and International Humanitarian Law'. In *MPEPIL online*, edited by Rüdiger Wolfrum, §48 *et seq*. www.mpepil.com/.

Zwitter, Andrej. 'United Nations' Legal Framework of Humanitarian Assistance'. In Heintze and Zwitter, *International Law and Humanitarian Assistance*, 51–70.

INDEX